HARM TO SELF

The MORAL LIMITS

VOLUME THREE

NEW YORK OXFORD

of the CRIMINAL LAW

Harm to Self

JOEL FEINBERG

OXFORD UNIVERSITY PRESS

Oxford University Press

Oxford New York Toronto
Delhi Bombay Calcutta Madras Karachi
Petaling Jaya Singapore Hong Kong Tokyo
Nairobi Dar es Salaam Cape Town
Melbourne Auckland

and associated companies in
Berlin Ibadan

Copyright © 1986 by Oxford University Press, Inc.

First published in 1986 by Oxford University Press, Inc.,
200 Madison Avenue, New York, New York 10016

First issued as an Oxford University Press paperback, 1989

Oxford is a registered trademark of Oxford University Press

Library of Congress Cataloging in Publication Data

Feinberg, Joel, 1926–
The moral limits of the criminal law.

Includes index.
Contents: v. 1 Harm to others—v. 2. Offense to others—
v. 3. Harm to self.
1. Criminal law—Philosophy. 2. Criminal law—
Moral and religious aspects. I. Title.
ISBN 0-19-503746-4
ISBN 0-19-505923-9 (PBK)

2 4 6 8 10 9 7 5 3

Printed in the United States of America

For Betty yet again

About the Longer Work

Harm to Self is the third volume in a four-volume work, *The Moral Limits of the Criminal Law*. The volumes have been published separately at short intervals, each with a brief synopsis of the earlier volumes. Volume one, *Harm to Others*, discusses the concept of harm, its relation to interests, wants, hurts, offenses, rights, and consent; hard cases for the application of the concept of harm, like "moral harm," "vicarious harm," and "posthumous harm"; the status of failures to prevent harm; and problems involved in assessing, comparing, and imputing harms. Volume two, *Offense to Others*, discusses the modes and meanings of "offense" as a state distinct from harm; offensive nuisances; profoundly offensive conduct (like mistreatment of dead bodies, desecration of sacred symbols, and the public brandishing of odious political emblems like swastikas and K.K.K. garments); pornography, obscenity, and "dirty words." Volume four, *Harmless Wrongdoing*, will discuss the various positions often called "legal moralism," including the claims that criminal prohibitions can be justified by their role in strengthening community ties and preserving a way of life, enforcing true morality, preventing wrongful gain from exploitation even when it has no proper "victim," elevating taste, and perfecting character.

Synopsis of Volumes
One and Two

The basic question of the longer work that volume one introduces is a deceptively simple one: What sorts of conduct may the state rightly make criminal? Philosophers have attempted to answer this question by proposing what I call "liberty-limiting principles" (or equivalently, "coercion-legitimizing principles") which state that a given type of consideration is always a morally relevant reason in support of penal legislation even if other reasons may in the circumstances outweigh it. Each volume of *The Moral Limits of the Criminal Law* corresponds to a leading liberty-limiting principle (but see the longer list, with definitions, of ten such principles at the end of this synopsis). The principle that the need to prevent harm to persons other than the actor is always a morally relevant reason in support of proposed state coercion I call *the harm to others principle* ("the harm principle" for short). At least in that vague formulation it is accepted as valid by nearly all writers. Controversy arises when we consider whether it is the *only* valid liberty-limiting principle, as John Stuart Mill declared.

Three other coercion-legitimizing principles, in particular, have won widespread support. It has been held (but not always by the same person) that it is always a good and relevant reason in support of penal legislation that (1) it is necessary to prevent hurt or offense (as opposed to injury or harm) to others (*the offense principle*); (2) it is necessary to prevent harm to the very person it prohibits from acting, as opposed to "others" (*legal paternalism*); (3) it is necessary to prevent inherently immoral conduct whether or not such conduct is harmful or offensive to anyone (*legal moralism*). I defined "liberalism" in respect to the subject matter of this book as the view that the harm and offense principles, duly clarified and qualified, between them exhaust the class of morally relevant reasons for criminal prohibitions. ("Extreme liberalism" rejects the offense principle too, holding that only the harm principle states an acceptable reason.) I then candidly expressed my own liberal predilections.

The liberal program of this work is twofold. Volumes one and two propose interpretations and qualifications of the liberal liberty-limiting principles that are necessary if those two principles are to warrant our endorsement (assuming from the start that they do warrant endorsement). Assuming that the harm and offense principles are correct, we ask, how must those principles be understood? What are we to mean by the key terms "harm" and "offense," and how are these vague principles to be applied to the complex problems that actually arise in legislatures? Volumes one and two attempt to define, interpret, qualify, and buttress liberalism in such ways that in the end we can say that the refined product is what liberalism must be to have its strongest claim to plausibility, and to do this without departing *drastically* from the traditional usage of the liberal label or from the motivating spirit of past liberal writers, notably John Stuart Mill. The second part of the liberal program, to which Volumes three and four are devoted, is to argue against the non-liberal principles (especially paternalism and moralism) that many writers claim must supplement the liberal principles in any adequate theory.

Volume one then proceeds to ask what is the sense of "harm" in the harm principle as we shall understand it in this work. I distinguish at the outset a non-normative sense of "harm" as setback to interest, and a normative sense of "harm" as a *wrong*, that is a violation of a person's rights. Examples are given of rare "non-harmful wrongs," that is wrongs that do not set back the wronged party's interests, and more common "non-wrongful harms," that is setbacks to interest, like those to which the "harmed party" consented, that do not violate his rights. Neither of these will count as "harms" in the sense of the harm principle. Rather, that sense will represent the overlap of the other two senses, and apply only to setbacks of interests that are also wrongs, and only to wrongs that are also setbacks to interests. Chapters 1 and 2 are devoted to problems about harm that stem from its character as a setback to interest, while Chapter 3 discusses in more detail the features of harmful acts that stem from their character as violations of rights.

Chapter 2 discusses hard cases for the application of the concept of harm: Does it make sense to speak of "moral harm," "vicarious harm," "posthumous harm," or "prenatal harm"? First, can we harm a person by making him a worse person than he was before? Plato insisted that "moral harm" *is* harm (and severe harm) even when it does not set back interests. But our analysis of harm denies Platonism. A person does not necessarily become "worse off" when he becomes "worse"; he is "morally harmed" only if he had an antecedent interest in having a good character. Second, can we harm one person by harming another? This question I answer in the affirmative. *A* causes "vicarious harm" to *B* when *B* has an interest in *C*'s welfare or in *C*'s character, and *A* then directly harms or corrupts *C*. Third, can a person be harmed by his own death or by events that occur after his death? These questions raise extremely subtle problems that defy brief summary. My conclusion, however, is that death can be a harm to the person who dies, in virtue of the interests he had ante-mortem that are totally and irrevocably defeated by his death. Posthumous harm too can occur, when a "surviving interest" of the deceased is thwarted after his death. The subject of a surviving interest, and of the harm or benefit that can accrue to it after a person's death, is the living person ante-mortem whose interest it was. Events after death do not retroactively produce effects at an earlier time (as this account may at first suggest), but their occurrence can lead us to revise our estimates of an earlier person's well-being, and correct the record before closing the book on his life.

As for prenatal harms, I argue that fetuses (even if they are not yet persons) can be harmed in the womb, but only on the assumption that they will eventually be born to suffer the harmful consequences of their prenatal injuries. People can also be harmed by wrongful actions that occurred before they were even conceived, when the wrongdoer deliberately or negligently initiated a causal sequence that he might have known would injure a real person months or years later. I even conceded that in certain unusual circumstances a person might be harmed by the act of being given birth when that was avoidable. I denied, however, that a person can be harmed by the very act of sexual congress that brings him into existence unless he is doomed thereby to be born in a handicapped condition so severe that he would be "better off dead." If a child was wrongfully conceived by parents who knew or ought to have known that he would be born in a handicapped condition less severe than *that*, then he cannot later complain that he was wronged, for the only alternative to the wrongful conception was for him never to have come into existence at all, and he would not have preferred that. If parents are to be legally punished for wrongfully bringing other persons into existence in an initially handicapped condition, but one that is preferable to nonexistence, it will have to be under the principle of legal moralism. The harm principle won't stretch that far.

Another difficult analytic question, discussed in Chapter 4, is whether the harm principle will stretch to cover blamable failures to prevent harm. I consider the standard arguments in the common law tradition against so-called "bad samaritan statutes" that require persons to undertake "easy rescues" under threat of legal punishment for failure to do so. I reject all of these arguments on the grounds either that they systematically confuse active aid with gratuitous benefit, or that they take far too seriously the problem of drawing a non-arbitrary line between reasonably easy and unreasonably difficult rescues. (Similar line-drawing problems exist throughout the law, and most have been found manageable.) I conclude then that requiring people to help prevent harms is sometimes as reasonable a legal policy as preventing people, by threat of punishment, from actively causing harms. The more difficult question is whether this conclusion marks a departure from the harm principle as previously defined. I argued that it does not, partly on the ground that omissions, under some circumstances, can themselves be the cause of harms. To defend *that* contention, I must rebut powerful arguments on the other side, and in the final section of Chapter 4 I attempt to do so.

The final two chapters (5 and 6) of Volume one attempt to formulate "mediating maxims" to guide the legislature in applying the harm principle to certain especially complicated kinds of factual situations. Its formulation, up to that point, is so vague that without further guidance there may be no way in principle to determine how it applies to merely minor harms, moderately probable harms, harms to some interests preventable only at the cost of harms to other interests irreconcilable with them, structured competitive harms, imitative harms, aggregative harms, accumulative harms, and so on. I argue for various supplementary criteria to govern the application of the harm principle to these difficult problems, thus giving its bare bones some normative flesh and blood. These supplementary guides take a variety of forms. Some are themselves independent moral principles or rules of fairness. Others apply rules of probability or risk assessment. Others are common-sense maxims such as the legal *de minimis* rule for minor harms. Others distinguish dimensions of interests to be used in comparing the relative "importance" of conflicting harms in interest-balancing, or for putting the "interest in liberty" itself on the scales. Others are practical rules of institutional regulation to avoid the extremes of blanket permission and blanket prohibition in the case of aggregative and accumulative harms. As a consequence of these and other mediating maxims, the harm principle begins to lose its character as a merely vacuous ideal, but it also loses all semblance of factual simplicity and normative neutrality.

Volume two opens with a discussion of the meaning of "offense." Like the word "harm," "offense" has both a general and a specifically normative sense, the former including in its reference any or all of a miscellany of disliked mental states, and the latter referring to those states only when caused by the wrongful (right-violating) conduct of others. Only the latter sense—wrongful offense—is intended in the offense principle. The question raised by Chapter 7 is whether there are any human experiences that are harmless in themselves yet so unpleasant that we can rightly demand legal protection from them even at a cost to other persons' liberties. The affirmative answer to this question, though not subject to proof, is supported by hypothetical examples ("A ride on the bus") of offensive conduct to which the reader is asked to imagine himself an unwilling witness.

Chapter 8 uses the model of nuisance law, borrowed mainly from the law of torts, to suggest how the offense principle should be mediated in its application to repugnant but harmless conduct. Inevitably, balancing tests must be devised for weighing the seriousness of the inconvenience caused to the offended party against the reasonableness of the offending party's conduct. The seriousness of the offensiveness must be determined by (1) the intensity and durability of the repugnance produced, and the extent to which repugnance could be anticipated to be the general reaction to the conduct that produced it; (2) the ease with which unwilling witnesses can avoid the offensive display; and (3) whether or not the witnesses have assumed the risk themselves of being offended. These factors must be weighed as a group against the reasonableness of the offending party's conduct as determined by (1) its personal importance to the actor himself and its social value generally; (2) the availability of alternative times and places where the conduct would cause less offense; and (3) the extent, if any, to which the offense is caused by spiteful motives. There is no simple formula for reading the balance when the reasonableness of conduct, as so measured, is weighed against the seriousness of the offense in its various dimensions. There are some easy cases that fall clearly under one or another standard in such a way as to leave no doubt how they must be decided. One cannot be *wrongly* offended by that to which one fully consents, for example, so the *Volenti* standard ("one cannot be wronged by that to which one consents") preempts all the rest when it clearly applies. In some cases, even though no one standard is preemptive, all the applicable standards pull together toward one inevitable decision. In genuinely hard cases, however, when standards conflict and none apply in a preemptive way, when for example a given kind of conduct is offensive to a moderate degree and only moderately unreasonable, there will be no automatic way of coming to a clearly correct decision, and no substitute for judgment.

Chapter 9 begins by acknowledging that nuisance law is an inadequate model for understanding what it calls "profound offenses." These mental states have a different felt "tone" from mere nuisances, best approximated by saying that they are deep, profound, shattering, or serious, and even when one does not perceive the offending conduct directly, one can be offended at the very idea of that sort of thing happening even in private. Moreover, profound offense offends because the conduct that occasions it is believed to be wrong; that conduct is not believed to be wrong simply and entirely because it offends someone. Profound offenses are usually experienced, therefore, as entirely impersonal. The offended party does not think of *him-*

self as the victim in unwitnessed flag defacings, corpse mutilations, or religious icon desecrations, and he does not therefore feel aggrieved (wronged) on his own behalf. Chapter 9 then continues by raising the famous "bare knowledge problem" for liberalism. Can liberal principles support a criminal prohibition of private (unwitnessed) and harmless conduct on the ground that some persons need protection from the profound offense attendant on the bare knowledge that such conduct is, or might be for all we know, occuring somewhere behind drawn blinds? I concede that the offense principle mediated by the balancing tests does not give the liberal all the reassurance he needs. I observe, however, that in the case of profound offense from unwitnessed acts it is not the offended party himself who needs "protection." His grievance is not a personal one made in his own behalf. He feels outraged at what he takes to be wrongful behavior, but is not himself wronged by it. (This is part of what is meant by classifying his offense as "profound.") The offensive conduct is wrongful *and* it is a cause of a severely offended mental state. But that is not yet sufficient for it to be a "wrongful offense" in the sense intended in a truly liberal offense principle. The offense-causing action must be more than wrong; it must be *a wrong* to the offended party, in short a violation of *his* rights. If his impersonal moral outrage is to be the ground for legal coercion and punishment of the offending party, it must be by virtue of the principle of legal moralism to which the liberal is adamantly opposed. It is likely then that there is no argument open to a liberal that legitimizes punishing private harmless behavior in order to prevent bare-knowledge offense.

Chapter 10 turns to the concept to the obscene, a form of acute offensiveness which, unlike "profound offensiveness," is inseparable from direct perception. The chapter is devoted to the "judgmental sense" of "obscene," that in which the word serves to express an adverse judgment on that to which it is applied. Discussion of the two other primary senses of "obscene" is undertaken in the following chapters. (These two nonjudgmental senses of "obscene" are that in which it is simply a synonym of "pornographic," as in prevailing American legal usage, and that in which it is a conventional label for a certain class of impolite words.) To call something obscene in the standard judgmental uses of that term is to condemn that thing as shockingly vulgar or blatantly disgusting, for the word "obscene," like the word "funny," is used to claim that a given response (in this case repugnance, in the other amusement) is likely to be the general one and/or to endorse that response as appropriate. The term "pornographic," on the other hand, is a purely descriptive word referring to sexually explicit writing and pictures designed entirely and plausibly to induce sexual excitement in the reader or observer. To use the terms "obscene" and "pornographic" interchangeably then, as if they necessarily referred to precisely the same things, is to beg the essentially controversial question of whether any or all (or only) pornographic materials really are obscene.

Chapter 11, "Obscenity as Pornography," contrasts pornographic writing with literary and dramatic art, grudgingly acknowledges the possibility of pornographic pictorial art, poetry, and (with difficulty) program music, explains why sex (of all things) can be obscene, and then concludes in an extended examination of "the feminist case" against pornograpy. Unlike more traditional arguments against pornography, especially those enshrined in law, which tacitly appeal to legal moralism and moralistic paternalism, recent feminist arguments either make a plausible appeal to empirical data in applying the harm principle, or else invoke the offense principle, not in order to prevent mere "nuisances," but to prevent profound offense analogous to that caused to the Jews of Skokie by the American Nazis, or to the blacks in a town where the K.K.K. rallies. The two traditional legal categories involved in the harm-principle arguments are defamation and incitement (to rape). I find the defamation argument ("Pornography degrades women") defective. I treat the incitement argument with respect, leaving the door open to criminal prohibitions of pornography legitimized on liberal (harm principle) grounds should better empirical evidence accumulate, while expressing skepticism over simple causal explanations of male sexual violence. The argument from profound offense is the more interesting, and the closest to acceptability even on present evidence, but in the end I decline to endorse it because of subtle but telling differences between pornography and other models of profound offense relied upon in the argument. I conclude that "wherever a line is drawn between permission and prohibition, there will be cases close to the line on both sides of it."

Chapter 12 returns to more traditional ways of discussing the moral and legal status of pornography from the period before people thought of treating its more egregious forms primarily under the headings of affront and danger to women. In particular, a leading alternative to the liberal way of treating the problem is considered in detail, namely that which has prevailed in the American courts in so-called obscenity cases. After a thorough criticism of decisions from *Hicklin* to *Roth*, and from *Roth* to *Paris Adult Theatre*, the chapter concludes: "Where pornography is not a nuisance, and (we must now add) not a threat to the safety of women, it can be none of the state's proper business."

The final four chapters (13 to 16) deal with obscene language—the so-called "dirty words." The primary function of these words, I suggested, is simply to offend, but by virtue of that basic function, obscene words have a number of highly useful derivative functions that would make their disappearance from the language regrettable. These words have an immediate offensive impact almost entirely because they violate taboos against uttering certain sounds or writing certain marks. In defying the taboos against the very utterance of the proscribed sounds, we underline, emphasize, call attention to ourselves and what we are doing or saying, express disrespectful attitudes either toward the norms themselves, or toward our listeners or the subject of our discourse. That in turn enables us, depending on other contextual features, to achieve such derivative purposes as deep expression, counter-evocation, suppression of pain and conquest of fear, the disowning of assumed pieties, effective badinage, emphatic insult, challenge, provocation, and even the triggering of waggish or ribald laughter. The "paradox of obscenity" grows out of this assertion that the primary and immediate job of obscenities is to violate the general taboos against their own use. Looked at in a utilitarian light, it is as if the main point of having the taboos in the first place is to make their violation possible so that certain "derivative" purposes can be achieved. What seems paradoxical is that if we all understood the rationale of the rules in this way, then none of us would take them very seriously as independently grounded norms and their "magic" would disappear; they could no longer achieve their useful derivative purposes. In Chapter 15, "Obscene Words and Social Policy," I try to resolve, or at least soften, this paradox, in the course of arguing against those who would attempt to rid the language of obscene words either through encouraging the use of euphemism or through deliberate overuse. In Chapter 16, "Obscene Words and the Law," I distinguish among "bare utterance and instant offense," offensive nuisance, and harassment. Applying the standards of earlier chapters, I conclude that the offense principle, properly mediated, cannot justify the criminal prohibition of the bare utterance of obscenities in public places even when they are used intentionally to cause offense. Offensive nuisance through the constant bombardment of obscenities can properly be prohibited, but only when the words are used in such a way as to constitute harassment. This chapter concludes by endorsing a liberal case against the regulation of indecent language on radio and television, rejecting the majority arguments in *F.C.C. v. Pacifica Foundation*.

The main purposes of Volume two are to endorse the offense principle, to show why it is plausible to affirm that the prevention of harmless offenses is among the legitimate purposes of the criminal law, and to propose a set of mediating maxims and balancing tests for applying the offense principle to difficult social problems, while minimizing the possibility of its abuse.

Definitions of Liberty-limiting Principles

1. *The Harm Principle:* It is always a good reason in support of penal legislation that it would be effective in preventing (eliminating, reducing) harm to persons other than the actor (the one prohibited from acting) *and* there

is no other means that is equally effective at no greater cost to other values.*

2. *The Offense Principle:* It is always a good reason in support of a proposed criminal prohibition that it is necessary to prevent serious offense to persons other than the actor and would be an effective means to that end if enacted.†

3. *The Liberal Position* (on the moral limits of the criminal law): The harm and offense principles, duly clarified and qualified, between them exhaust the class of good reasons for criminal prohibitions. ("The extreme liberal position" is that only the harm principle states a good reason . . .)

4. *Legal Paternalism* (a view excluded by the liberal position): It is always a good reason in support of a prohibition that it is necessary to prevent harm (physical, psychological, or economic) to the actor himself.

5. *Legal Moralism* (in the usual narrow sense): It can be morally legitimate to prohibit conduct on the ground that it is inherently immoral, even though it causes neither harm nor offense to the actor or to others.

6. *Moralistic Legal Paternalism* (where paternalism and moralism overlap *via* the dubious notion of a "moral harm"): It is always a good reason in support of a proposed prohibition that it is necessary to prevent *moral harm* (as opposed to physical, psychological, or economic harm) to the actor himself. (Moral harm is "harm to one's character," "becoming a worse person," as opposed to harm to one's body, psyche, or purse.)

7. *Legal Moralism* (in the broad sense): It can be morally legitimate for the state to prohibit certain types of action that cause neither harm nor offense to anyone, on the grounds that such actions constitute or cause evils of other ("free-floating") kinds.

8. *The Benefit-to-Others Principle:* It is always a morally relevant reason in support of a proposed prohibition that it is necessary for the production of some *benefit* for persons other than the person who is prohibited.

9. *Benefit-Conferring Legal Paternalism:* It is always a morally relevant reason in support of a criminal prohibition that it is necessary to *benefit* the very person who is prohibited.

10. *Perfectionism* (Moral Benefit Theories): It is always a good reason in support of a proposed prohibition that it is necessary for the improvement (elevation, perfection) of the character—

---

*The clause following "and" is abbreviated in the subsequent definitions as "it is necessary for . . . ," or "the need to . . ." Note also that part of a conjunctive reason ("effective *and* necessary") is itself a "reason," that is, itself has some relevance in support of the legislation.

†The clause following "and" goes without saying in the subsequent definitions, but it is understood. All the definitions have a common form: X is necessary to achieve Y (as spelled out in definition 1) and is an effective means for producing Y (as stated explicitly in definitions 1 and 2).

    a. of citizens generally, or certain citizens other than the person whose liberty is limited (*The Moralistic Benefit-to-Others Principle*), or

    b. of the very person whose liberty is limited (*Moralistic Benefit-Conferring Legal Paternalism*).

Principles 8, 9, and 10b are the strong analogues of the harm principle, legal paternalism, and moralistic legal paternalism, respectively, that result when "production of benefit" is substituted for "prevention of harm."

Acknowledgments

Various parts of this volume, from small passages to the major sections of whole chapters, have already been published in independent articles. I am grateful to the publishers for permission to republish these copyrighted materials here. Although my essay "Legal Paternalism," *Canadian Journal of Philosophy*, vol. 1, no. 1 (1971), has been entirely recast, several paragraphs of the original version survive intact in Chapters 17, 19, and 20. The final paragraphs of Chapter 18 and the bulk of Chapter 19 were part of the annual Civil Liberties Lectures at the University of Notre Dame Law School, which I delivered in 1982. The lectures were published under the title "Autonomy, Sovereignty, and Privacy: Moral Ideals in the Constitution?" in *The Notre Dame Law Review*, vol. 58 (1983). Section 7 of Chapter 25 was published originally as "Victims' Excuses: The Case of Fraudulently Procured Consent," in *Ethics*, vol. 6 (1986).

In the summer of 1984 I was fortunate to receive a grant from the National Endowment for the Humanities to conduct a Summer Seminar for College Teachers. Twelve gifted philosophers discussed this manuscript thoroughly and critically. I am grateful to every one of them for helpful suggestions, but I would like to acknowledge especially the assistance of Joan Callahan, Alan Fuchs, and Eugene Schlossberger, all of whom (alas) remain in disagreement with various parts of the book. In the autumn of 1984 the manuscript was further debated by an unusually talented group of graduate students in a seminar at the University of Arizona. Every one of them helped me too, but I am especially grateful to David Schmitz, Robert Schopp, and Rod Wiltshire. On this particular volume I received no help from Josiah S. Carberry. For that too I am grateful.

Contents

HARM TO SELF

17

Legal Paternalism

1. Diverse meanings of "paternalism"

My aim thus far has been to formulate the most plausible liberty-limiting principles that might yet be called, with historical and linguistic propriety, "liberal." Liberalism, as I have understood it, is the view that the harm and offense principles, *and only these*, state good and relevant reasons for state coercion by means of the criminal law. We have seen that these principles, until they are interpreted, qualified, and mediated by various standards, are largely vacuous. Accordingly, we have concentrated thus far on fleshing them out with normative substance in a way that makes them more useful, without departing from the moral attitudes that provide them with their initial appeal. Now it is time to consider the negative part of the traditional liberal thesis, that *no other* proposed liberty-limiting (or coercion-legitimizing) principles can have moral propriety. Historically it has been this negative contention that has been dearest to the liberal's heart and most likely to meet determined opposition from his opponents. John Stuart Mill was especially emphatic in excluding from the class of tenable legitimizing principles that which allows the prevention of harm to the actor himself to be a justification for invading his liberty:

> His own good, either physical or moral is not a sufficient warrant. He cannot be rightfully compelled to do or forbear because it will be better for him to do so, because it will make him happier, because in the opinion of others, to do so would be wise . . . These are good reasons for remonstrating with him, or reasoning with him, or persuading him, or entreating him, but not for compelling him or visiting him with any evil in case he do otherwise.[1]

3

The illiberal principle so emphatically rejected by Mill can be stated somewhat more exactly as follows: *It is always a good and relevant (though not necessarily decisive) reason in support of a criminal prohibition that it will prevent harm (physical, psychological, or economic) to the actor himself.* In recent years this principle has most often borne the not altogether felicitious name of "legal paternalism."[2] I will continue that usage here since it has now become standard, but the term "paternalism," nonetheless, is unfortunate in at least two ways. In the first place, the word is derogatory and thus tends to be tendentious and question-begging in its bare application. Paternalism is something we often *accuse* people of. It suggests the view that the state stands to its citizens as a parent (or perhaps a male parent!) stands to his children, and that normal adults might properly be treated as if they were children. This sounds so outrageous that we would expect hardly anyone to confess to even paternalistic tendencies, much less boldly affirm the paternalistic principle and wave the paternalistic banner. Yet the view that the state has a right to protect persons from their own folly seems to provide the rationale for many criminal statutes that few would wish to repeal. Many illustrious thinkers in the past have endorsed it (usually by another name), and even so liberal a thinker as H. L. A. Hart seems to grant it his reluctant assent.[3] The pejorative term then hardly seems fair to those whose views it caricatures. "Paternalism" is a label that might have been invented by paternalism's enemies.[4]

Another reason why "paternalism" is an unfortunate term for our present purposes is that it lends itself to confusion with other things that may also be called "paternalistic." First of all, the quite respectable proposed legitimizing principle of that name, which does after all purport to be solicitous of the interests of the persons it would protect, can easily be confused with attitudes, practices, and rules that are not even remotely benevolent. Suppose for example that the management of a factory or a store treats its employees as if they were school children, not for "their own good"—the management couldn't care less about their own good—but for the sake of greater efficiency and, ultimately, greater profits. Suppose that workers must have the permission of their supervisors to leave the work area to go to the toilet, or that only letters from a doctor can excuse absences.[5] Such rules express a lack of trust and respect for the workers, who are not allowed to freely exercise their own initiative. Self-respecting adult laborers will respond with indignation and *accuse* their employer of "paternalism." Hardly anyone in a more or less liberal democracy could argue, without embarrassment, for the right of the state to be "paternalistic" in the same sense, though many will complain that various bureaucratic governmental restrictions on initiative are in fact paternalistic in this degrading and altogether unbenevolent way.

Still another kind of practice is sometimes called "paternalistic" even though it is highly benevolent, and not at all demeaning. Insofar as the term "paternalism" is derogatory it is especially inappropriate for this class of cases, yet it does cite an analogy to a particular aspect of parental relations with children, one that is hardly objectionable even when it is part of a government's relations with (some) adults. I refer to parental restrictions that are meant to protect the child not from himself but rather from harm caused by others. When a parent rushes to save a child from a pummeling inflicted by an older and larger child, he is being zealously "paternalistic" in this sense. The state is similarly "paternalistic" when it creates special crimes against "child abuse," and enforces, with a special zeal, legislation protective of children. Most of us would agree that such practices, while analogous in certain ways to parental behavior, nevertheless do not deserve the derogation that seems to be expressed by the word "paternalism."

The following distinction between two families of senses of the word "paternalism" then suggests itself:

1. *Presumptively blamable paternalism*, which consists in treating adults as if they were children, or older children as if they were younger children, by forcing them to act or forbear in certain ways, either—
   a. (*benevolent paternalism*) "for their own good," whatever their wishes in the matter (this may or may not be blamable in the last analysis; that is the question at issue), or—
   b. (*nonbenevolent paternalism*) for the good of other parties (e.g. teachers or factory managers), whatever their own wishes in the matter. (This is generally thought to be blamable.)
2. *Presumptively nonblamable paternalism*, which consists of defending relatively helpless or vulnerable people from external dangers, including harm from *other* people when the protected parties have not voluntarily consented to the risk, and doing this in a manner analogous in its motivation and vigilance to that in which parents protect their children.

Type 1b, the kind of paternalism that is most clearly objectionable, is not very precisely defined because of the vagueness of the phrase "treat adults as if they were children." Not every case, of course, of the "nonbenevolent" treatment of adults by authorities for the authorities' own good is properly called paternalistic in any sense. The rules of prisons, I should imagine, treat adults not as if they were children but rather as prisoners; military rules treat soldiers not as children but as soldiers; the training regimens of athletic teams treat adults not as children but as athletes. What makes nonbenevolent authoritative governance paternalistic is a certain (vague) kind of demeaning spirit implicitly suggested by the phrase "as if children." The treatment must seem arbitrary and unnecessary, and expressive of a lack of the trust that is normally due to adults.

Perhaps the best example of presumptively nonblamable paternalism is that expressed in the ancient but still vital principle of the Anglo-American law, the doctrine of *parens patriae*.[6] American courts, following English precedents, have long held that the state has a "sovereign power of guardianship" over minors and other legally incompetent persons, which confers upon it the right, or perhaps even the duty, to look after the interests of those who are incapable of protecting themselves. This power presumably includes the protection of incompetents from themselves, though that is not the way it is most characteristically exercised. More typically the state invokes the doctrine of *parens patriae* to protect helpless persons from harm at the hands of *other persons* and from other external dangers. Children, for example, sometimes need protection from *their own parents*, and the state as a kind of "parent of last resort" is ultimately the sole source of such protection. Similarly, mentally disordered adults who are so deranged they are unable to seek treatment for themselves are entitled by the doctrine of *parens patriae* to psychiatric care under the auspices of the state, and other classes of helpless adults, those in their dotage and the physically handicapped poor, are also entitled to care and protection. Lightning, in its diverse forms, can strike any of us, so if state protection of the uniquely helpless is "paternalism," let us make the most of it.

It is all too easy however to confuse the "nonblamable paternalism" of government protection of the helpless, those who either freely choose to receive the proferred help or else are no longer capable of freely choosing anything, from the presumptively blamable imposition of government "help" on unwilling persons who are still quite capable of deciding for themselves. The confusion is especially common in respect to so-called "mentally ill" persons. Many persons who are properly called "mentally ill" or "disturbed" are subject to upsetting emotions and distortion of affect, but are not so cognitively deranged as to be legally incompetent. Indeed many of them keep their intellectual capacities altogether unimpaired throughout their "illness," and some do not wish to be confined and treated in mental hospitals.[7] The forcible incarceration of such persons cannot be justified under the doctrine of *parens patriae*, for that legal principle in its forcible application extends only to those unfortunates who are rendered literally incapable of deciding whether to seek medical treatment themselves, and even in those cases, the doctrine grants power to the state only to "decide for a man as we assume he would decide for himself if he were of sound mind."[8]

For the remainder of this discussion we shall consider *only* paternalism in sense (1a), and distinguish it sharply from both blamably nonbenevolent "paternalism" (1b) and presumptively nonblamable government action in accordance with the *parens patriae* principle. We shall consider paternalism only in the sense in which it is a proposed principle for the moral legitimization of criminal legislation. (For that specific proposition we can reserve the name "legal paternalism.") It is regrettable that the word "paternalism" tends to be pejorative and that it is also the name for other governmental practices, both clearly malign (1b) and clearly benign (2), but if we disavow the derogation in advance (at least until we have established its appropriateness by argument), and dismiss the rival senses as beyond our present concern, we need not be misled.

Other ambiguities can be disposed of quickly. Like any other "ism" word, "paternalism" can refer either to a practice or a theory. If a private person or a legislator acts or votes paternalistically, one might describe his action as "an instance of paternalism," that is an instance of paternalistic practice, perhaps without wishing to imply that the paternalistic person holds a paternalistic theory, or indeed any other theory. On the other hand, a philosopher might be properly described as an adherent of paternalism simply because he holds the view that paternalistic behavior is (sometimes) justified, even though his own practice is not paternalistic. He may never even have the occasion, much less the desire, to act paternalistically. Our present discussion is concerned with evaluating a paternalistic *theory* (namely, a liberty-limiting principle) of that name.[9]

We must also distinguish, as many writers do, between paternalistic behavior generally and paternalistic rules that are coercive interferences with liberty. A paternalistic act, as Bernard Gert and Charles Culver have conclusively shown,[10] need not be coercive or interfere with anyone's liberty of action. The medical context, in which Gert and Culver are primarily interested, offers many examples of noncoercive paternalism, from prescribing placebos for anxious but healthy patients to withholding the truth from deathbed patients.

> Consider the case where a doctor lies to a mother on her deathbed when she asks about her son. He tells her that her son is doing well, even though he knows that the son has just been killed trying to escape from prison after having been indicted [a fact unknown to his mother] for multiple rape and murder.[11]

Perhaps the only thing such acts have in common with penal statutes and bills of legislation with which this discussion is concerned, and in virtue of which they are both called "paternalistic," is that the treatment (deception in the one case, coercion in the other) given certain persons is justified in terms of their own good, whatever they themselves may think of the matter. And as Gert and Culver point out, the behavior (or rule) is of a kind—lying, coercively threatening—that normally *requires* justification.

The distinctions between coercive and noncoercive paternalism, and between private behavior and public laws, cut across one another. Some paternalistic legislation is noncoercive, for example welfare programs of "aid in kind" in which vouchers or food stamps earmarked for specific purposes are awarded instead of cash, and statutes that render certain kinds of contracts null and void. In both of these examples the justification appeals to the good of the affected parties, but does not take the form of prohibitive pronouncements backed up by criminal sanctions. Again, it is the latter with which we are primarily, though not exclusively, concerned here.

2. Types of paternalistic coercive laws

If *legal* paternalism is the theory or principle that recognizes the need to prevent self-inflicted harm as a legitimizing reason for coercive legislation, what then are the various sorts of legislation it supports? Here we can use the word "paternalistic" as an adjective describing neither actions nor justificatory theories, but rather types of laws and proposed laws which the justificatory theory supports. Then we can rephrase our question as follows: What are the various types of paternalistic coercive laws?

Some paternalistic coercive laws *require*, while others *forbid* certain kinds of behavior. Kleinig labels these categories respectively "active" and "passive" paternalism, apparently because the former requires action and the latter requires refraining from action. In the active category are laws that require motorists to wear seat belts while driving, motorcyclists to wear helmets, hunters to wear red caps or shirts, and sailors to wear life preservers. In the passive category are laws that prohibit swimming at dangerous or unguarded beaches, the use of narcotic drugs, the private use of fireworks, suicide, and private consensual transactions deemed dangerous to one of the contracting parties.

Another distinction is between *mixed* and *unmixed* paternalistic laws. (Kleinig refers to these as "pure" and "impure" paternalism.) The mixed kind of restrictive law is justified partly by the aim of preventing people from suffering harm at their own hands, or with their own consent at the hands of others, and partly for other reasons, for example the desire to protect still other persons, or the general public. Unmixed paternalistic laws have no motive or reason other than preventing self-harm or consented-to harm from others.

A third distinction is between coercive laws justified by an appeal to the need to protect people from self-caused *harms* and those whose justification rests on the desire that people act in a way that will be to their own positive *benefit*. The principle invoked in the former case (which Kleinig calls "negative paternalism") is the principle of legal paternalism proper, or "harm-preventing paternalism," as we shall sometimes call it. The principle involved in the latter case (Kleinig's "positive paternalism") might better be labeled "extreme paternalism,"[12] or (better still) "benefit-promoting paternalism."[13] We shall postpone discussion of it until Chapter 33.

A fourth distinction, and one we will make much of in subsequent chapters, is that between paternalistic laws applied to the single-party case (e.g., laws prohibiting suicide, self-mutilation, and drug use) and paternalistic laws applied to the two-party case (e.g., laws prohibiting euthanasia, dueling, and drug sales). The two-party cases are paternalistic when one party's request for (or consent to) the action of a second party does not give the second party license to do what the first party wants (or is willing) to have done. If the second party nevertheless carries out his agreement then *he* has violated the law and will be punished. The law prevents the first party from having what he wishes done and in that way interferes with *his* liberty on the grounds that it knows best what is for his own good. For that reason the law is paternalistic toward the first party even when the crime it defines is committed by the second party. Thus, for example, if *B* desperately needs immediate capital for an investment scheme, which he can get only by borrowing from *A* at 50% interest in violation of a usury law, then *A* is punished for violating the statute, which forbids *lending* (not borrowing) at excessive rates of interest. But even though the law's sanctions are not applied directly to *B*, his liberty too is restricted by the law, and his choices are frustrated. Since the avowed purpose of the law is to protect *B* (rather than *A*), whatever his own wishes in the matter, the law is paternalistic in respect to *B*. (In some two-party cases, both parties are made subject to the sanctions even though the law is meant to protect only one, the solicitor or purchaser. Prostitution statutes that punish the "John" as well as the prostitute satisfy this description.)

In his groundbreaking and influential 1970 article on paternalism, Gerald Dworkin applies the labels "pure" and "impure" paternalism to the one- and two-party cases.[14] These terms are unfortunate, I think, insofar as they suggest that the two-party cases are paternalistic in a less genuine, watered-down sort of way. I suggest, therefore that the terms "direct" and "indirect" paternalism are more fitting. In the direct cases,

> the class of persons whose freedom is restricted by the threat of punishment is identical with the class of persons whose benefit is intended to be promoted by such restrictions. Examples: the making of suicide a crime, requiring passengers to wear seat belts, requiring a Christian Scientist to receive a blood transfusion. In the case of "impure" [indirect] paternalism, in trying to protect the welfare of a class of persons we find that the only way to do so will involve restricting the freedom of other persons besides those who are benefitted.[15]

In practice, almost all directly paternalistic laws are single-party cases, but in principle, Dworkin's definition leaves logical room for directly paternalistic restrictions in two-party cases. It is conceivable, for example, that laws might prohibit certain kinds of consensual transactions and apply sanctions only to the initiator, requester, or purchaser, even though the point of the prohibition is to protect *him*, not the responder or seller. In that case, the law is directly paternalistic in that "the class of persons whose freedom is restricted is identical with the class of persons whose benefit is intended to be promoted, and yet two parties must be mentioned in the definition of the crime. Alternatively, *both* parties might be made criminally liable in which case the statute is both directly and indirectly paternalistic if it is meant to protect only one of the parties from the other. In the typical instance, however, in most actual legal systems, two-party cases are treated in the indirectly paternalistic fashion, so that for them, Dworkin's distinction between direct and indirect (or "pure" and "impure" as he put it) corresponds with our distinction between single-party and two-party cases. In principle, however, the two distinctions overlap but do not coincide.

It is important to point out, before leaving this preliminary topic, that legal paternalism is two quite different principles depending on how we interpret the word "harm." Most of the examples we have discussed in this section seem to suggest that the concept of harm that is presupposed is simple damage to a person's interest, whether consented to or not. In that case, "harm" as it occurs in the principle of legal paternalism bears a different sense from that it bears in the harm to others principle, in which it refers to wrongful (unconsented to) infliction of damage only. If the reason for prohibiting B from purchasing the marijuana he desires from A is that we must protect B from the lung and nervous system damage that might be caused by using that drug, then the fact that B consented to the transaction, even requested it, is quite irrelevant. Only the objective danger to his lungs and nervous system counts. On the other hand, if the reason for the prohibition is to protect B only from *wrongfully* inflicted harms and dangers, then the fact that he consented is all important, and the prohibition will not apply to him except insofar as his "consent" is ungenuine. But in the latter case, the law preventing A from selling the forbidden drug to B is justified by the harm to others principle rather than "indirect paternalism," for that principle prevents A from inflicting damage or the risk of damage on B without B's genuine consent. The difference between the harm to others principle and indirect paternalism then reduces to this. The harm to others principle forbids A from imposing a harmful drug on B without B's genuine consent, but permits A to give or sell a dangerous drug to B with B's genuine consent; whereas indirect paternalism forbids A from delivering a dangerous drug to B whether or not B genuinely consents. In overriding B's consent, the paternalistic law overrules his judgment and restricts his liberty "for his own good."

If we are to avoid hopeless terminological confusion between the harm principle, as interpreted in Volume One, and legal paternalism, as it applies "indirectly" in two-party cases, we had better stipulate one crucial definitional difference between them. Whereas the harm principle is understood to employ the word "harm" in the sense of "wrongful injury" (so that "to harm" means in part "to wrong"), legal paternalism, as defined in section 1 of this chapter, employs the word "harm" in the sense of simple setback to interest whether "wrongful" or not. It follows that the harm principle is mediated in its application by the *Volenti* maxim* whereas legal paternalism is not. *B*'s consent to *A*'s action, even though that action is harmful or dangerous to *B*'s interests, exempts *A* from criminal liability under the harm principle, but does not exempt him under indirect legal paternalism.

Consider how these distinctions work out in practice. Suppose that *A* and *B* have agreed that *A*, either as a gift or for a price, will do something that seems to endanger *B*'s interests. The danger of harm to *B* is treated in significantly different ways by rules derived from the harm principle alone and rules derived from legal paternalism.

1. The harm principle says in effect to *A*, "You may not do anything that will probably harm *B*," and then adds, "except (of course) with *B*'s consent." The exceptive clause indicates that "harm" is used partly in the sense of "wrong," and that the harm principle is mediated by *Volenti*, which decrees that for the purpose of the principle, consented-to harm is not to count as harm.
2. Indirect legal paternalism says in effect to *B*, "*A* may not do what you wish him to do (or are willing to have him do) if it will probably harm you," and then adds, "whether you consent or not." "In order to protect you from your own bad judgment (in consenting) and from *A*'s harmful act, the law may threaten *A* with criminal liability if he does what you, in your foolishness, wish (or are willing for) him to do." The denial of exonerating effect to *B*'s consent indicates that this principle employs the word "harm" in the sense of simple damage to interests, and is not mediated by *Volenti*.

If (1) did not have its exceptive clause recognizing the exempting effect of consent, then in the case where *B* does consent, the harm principle would be equivalent in its consequences to indirect legal paternalism, and the distinction between the two would be effectively erased. Similarly, if (2) *did* have an exceptive clause ("except when you consent") then, in the case in which *B* consents, the results would be the same as under the harm principle, and the distinction would collapse from the other direction. Clarity requires that the two principles be plainly distinguishable. Therefore, "to harm" will mean "*wrongly* to set back interests" in the formulation of the harm principle, and simply to inflict damage in the principle of legal paternalism.

**Volenti non fit injuria.* A person is not wronged by that to which he consents.

3. Hard and soft paternalism

The principle of legal paternalism as here defined is what many writers have come to call "hard paternalism" in contrast to a more compromising version of the principle, now standardly called "soft paternalism."[16] The distinction, which is of the first importance, has to do with the weight attached to the voluntariness of a person's action in the one-party case and the voluntariness of his consent in the two-party case. Hard paternalism will accept as a reason for criminal legislation that it is necessary to protect competent adults, against their will, from the harmful consequences even of their fully voluntary choices and undertakings. As we have just seen, the principle justifies overruling free and informed consent in the two-party case, and it overrules fully voluntary individual choices in the single-party case. Since it imposes its own values and judgments on people "for their own good," it seems well named by the label "paternalism."

It is not as clear that "soft paternalism" is "paternalistic" at all, in any clear sense. Certainly its motivating spirit seems closer to the liberalism of Mill than to the protectiveness of hard paternalism. Soft paternalism holds that the state has the right to prevent self-regarding harmful conduct (so far it *looks* "paternalistic") *when but only when* that conduct is substantially nonvoluntary, or when temporary intervention is necessary to establish whether it is voluntary or not. In the two-party case, soft paternalism would permit B to agree to an arrangement with A that is dangerous or harmful to B's interests, *if but only if* B's consent to it is voluntary. To the extent that B's consent is not fully voluntary, the law is justified in intervening "for his sake." The phrase "for his sake" sounds paternalistic, but the soft paternalist points out that the law's concern should not be with the wisdom, prudence, or dangerousness of B's choice, but rather with whether or not the choice is truly his. Its concern should be to help implement B's real choice, not to protect B from harm as such. After all, to whatever extent B's apparent choice stems from ignorance, coercion, derangement, drugs, or other voluntariness-vitiating factors, there are grounds for suspecting that it does not come from his own will, and might be as alien to him as the choices of someone else. The harm to others principle permits us to protect a person from the choices of other people; soft paternalism would permit us to protect him from "nonvoluntary choices," which, being the genuine choices of no one at all, are no less foreign to him.

Given this account of the soft paternalist's motives, questions naturally arise over the status of the soft paternalist principle. Is it an independent liberty-limiting principle at all? If it is, should it be considered a *kind* of paternalism or, less misleadingly given its liberal motivation, an anti-paternalistic principle? Alternatively, perhaps it should be classified with the

harm to others principle as a "version" of *it*, since it authorizes restraint of
conduct that threatens a person with harm not from another person but from
a source that is equally "other" from himself.

The latter course was once recommended by Tom L. Beauchamp who
concluded his early discussion of the matter by claiming that "weak paternalism is not paternalism in any interesting sense since it is not a liberty-limiting
principle independent of the harm to others principle."[17] When a person
unknowingly or unwillingly endangers himself and we intervene to protect
him, Beauchamp rightly noted, then we are not protecting him from himself
(that is, his own will or purposes) but from some factor external to his will:

> It is not a question of protecting a man *against himself* or of interfering with his
> liberty of action. He is not *acting* at all in regard to this danger. He needs
> protection from something which is precisely *not himself*, not his intended action,
> not in any remote sense of his own making.[18]

So far, so good, but it does not follow that soft paternalism is reducible to the
harm to others principle. In the single-party case of nonvoluntary self-harming conduct it is *as if* the actor needs protection from another person, but of
course it is not literally true that there is some other person in a comparable
state of ignorance, retardation, or intoxication who must be restrained from
"harming others." Surely in single-party cases, there is no second party who
can be interfered with, arrested, tried, and convicted of some crime corresponding to the harm involuntarily caused to himself by the single party. On
the other hand, in two-party cases in which the first party's consent is not
free and informed, the second party's conduct can be interfered with to
prevent him from harming (wronging) the first party under rules certified by
the harm principle. Here Beauchamp's point does apply.

Consider then only two-party cases and the identical way in which the
harm and soft-paternalistic principles apply to them. Suppose that *B* is ill-
informed and drunk when he "consents" to *A*'s proposal, and that the act
proposed by *A* will be very dangerous to *B*'s interests. The harm to others
principle justifies interfering with *A* in this case to protect *B* from possible
personal harm to which he has not voluntarily consented. To prevent *A*'s
action would be to prevent him from wronging *B*. Soft paternalism yields the
same result. Since *B*'s self-threatening act of "consent" was substantially less
than fully voluntary, he (*B*) can be interfered with (the interference, of
course, incidentally restricts *A* too) to protect him from a choice that was not
fully his own. At the very least we have grounds in this case for suspecting
that *B*'s fully informed and sober choice might not correspond with his
uninformed drunken one, and that justifies us, under soft paternalism, in
preventing the transaction until it can be determined what *B*'s real choice is.
Let us suppose then that the next morning, after being fully informed and

while cold sober, *B* consents all over again to the same dangerous proposition. The harm to others principle no longer provides a reason for preventing *A*'s action and the consequent implementation of *B*'s will. *B* may in fact be harmed, but he has assumed the risk of harm with his eyes wide open while fully informed and uncoerced, so *A*'s act, even with the worst of the anticipated outcomes, will not have wronged him. Again, soft paternalism concurs. It permitted interferene if but *only if B*'s choice were less than voluntary, or to allow time to put the matter to the test. Now there are no further grounds that it can recognize for continuing the restraint. If we still believe that interference is warranted to protect *B*, it can only be on hard paternalistic grounds, that is the ground of legal paternalism proper.

Even in respect to single-party cases, however, when soft paternalism cannot be reduced to the harm principle, it is severely misleading to think of it as any kind of paternalism. Beauchamp must be given credit for seeing this. Since we are committed to using the label "soft paternalism," because of its current widespread usage, we should think of it as a principle in accord with the animating spirit of liberalism, and one the liberal could endorse in addition to the harm principle, even though it is not technically absorbable into the harm principle except by a kind of absurd fiction (that such factors as ignorance are themselves "other persons" who can be targets of legal threats). Rather than tamper with the standard definitions of hard and soft paternalism, then, we can enlarge our definition of "liberalism" so that it now is the view that the harm principle, the offense principle, *and* "soft paternalism" are the only morally valid liberty-limiting principles.

Surely, John Stuart Mill would qualify as a liberal in this sense. Anyone with his basic attitudes might argue as follows. If a person wishes to end his own life (say) and the interests of no other persons will be directly affected for the worse thereby, he is entitled to do so, and the law may not interfere. It is *his* life, after all, and no one else's, and his choice alone should determine its fate. But if we see a normally calm person who we know has been experimenting with hard drugs go into a sudden frenzy and seize a butcher knife with the clear intention of cutting his own throat, then we do have the right to interfere. In so doing we will not be interfering with his real self or blocking his real will. That we may not do. But his drug-deluded self is *not* his "real self," and his frenzied desire is *not* his "real choice," so we may defend him against these threats to his autonomous self, which is quite another thing than throttling that autonomous self with external coercion. Interference on this ground is no more illiberal than interference to prevent him from harming or offending an unwilling second party.

The difficulty with this solution to the terminological question is that soft paternalism is not exactly a liberty-limiting principle, in the sense of this book, of any kind. It does not purport to guide the legislator to the kinds of reasons that can support proposed *criminal* legislation. In fact it legitimizes certain private and public interferences with liberty so that they may *not* be prevented by the criminal law. Thus in effect it has the form of a negative principle for the legislator. It tells him that a certain class of alleged justifying reasons are *not* valid. It is *not* an acceptable reason in support of proposed criminal legislation that it is necessary to prevent the sorts of interferences soft paternalism permits. Interfering with an apparently demented suicide attempt, for example, should *not* be a crime.

The need to prevent persons from harming themselves nonvoluntarily, of course, is a good reason for much non-punitive state interference with liberty: denying applications, invalidating contracts, issuing temporary restraining orders, imposing civil commitment, and so on. The point I am endeavoring to make here is simply that it is never a morally valid reason for statutes threatening the nonvoluntary self-endangerer himself with criminal punishment. But then, in modern times no one has ever said that it is.

Soft paternalism can also be understood, in part, as a *denial* of the liberty-limiting principle I have called "legal paternalism"—that principle which legitimizes interfering with the fully voluntary, self-regarding choices of competent adult persons. We could then adopt as our favored terminology that which identifies "paternalism" with what we have called "hard paternalism," and attaches the label *"soft anti-paternalism"* to what we have called "soft paternalism," the latter view being, after all, one which contradicts (hard) paternalism, but one which, like the harm principle, permits interference only in the absence of voluntariness or genuine consent. Then as "soft anti-paternalists," we would never speak, as many writers do, of "justified paternalism," since we would identify "paternalism" with hard paternalism, and hold that paternalistic interferences, so understood, are *never* justified. Calling our position "soft anti-paternalism," of course, would imply that there must be a contrasting position called "hard anti-paternalism". Such a contrasting view is indeed possible. A theory could be called "hard anti-paternalistic" insofar as it declined to legitimate interferences even with some choices known to be involuntary; or declined to interfere with dangerous self-regarding choices of unknown degree of voluntariness even for the purpose of determining how voluntary they are; or declined ever to impose compulsory education about risks, or state-administered testing to assess the understanding of risks, or to require licensing for self-regarding dangerous behavior; or generally used laxer standards of voluntariness than the typical soft paternalist.

I would prefer to use the novel terminology of the preceding paragraph, but I fear that so great a departure from the conventional terms of discussion would, on the whole, be more confusing than clarifying. I shall reluctantly continue, therefore, to use the standard terminology of "hard and soft parternalism," while muttering, from time to time, in *sotto voce*, that soft paternalism is really no kind of paternalism at all.

4. What makes a restriction paternalistic?

Both coercive statutes threatening punishment, on the one hand, and noncriminal statutes and policies that levy taxes, invalidate and nullify contracts, impose legal disabilities and civil liabilities, withhold recognition of certain defenses in civil cases, or compel lifesaving medication, surgery, or indefinite hospitalization, on the other hand, are sometimes called "paternalistic." What is it that all these legal mechanisms, criminal and noncriminal, have in common? They all restrict the liberties or powers of persons, in the case of criminal laws by direct threat of punishment, in the noncriminal examples by other means, sometimes including punishment as a "back-up sanction," and purport to do this for "the good" of, or more commonly to prevent harm to, the very persons whose liberties are restricted.

But when is the paternalistic reason the "real reason" for the rule in question? There are two kinds of reasons why this question can sometimes be difficult. The first is that most paternalistic rules are "mixed paternalistic laws." They are supported by reasons of a number of kinds, including the need to protect the directly restricted party himself, but also to protect third parties from indirect harm, and even the general public from a kind of diffuse harm. When these reasons seem plausible in a given case they reenforce one another, creating a kind of multiple rationale which is only partly paternalistic. We shall consider some of the problems raised by mixed rationales in §5 below.

Another difficult problem is raised by rationales that are understood to be alternative rather than conjunctive. Sometimes a legislature passes a law for one kind of reason and decades later it is justified by a quite different sort of reason. One of these reasons may seem to pass muster and the other may seem illegitimate. In that case how do we tell what the "real reason" is?

Here we must distinguish among "conscious reasons," "deep motivations," "implicit rationales," and "true justifications." A legislator might honestly cite one factor as "his reason" for voting for a bill, when unknown to him there may be a better reason that in fact supports the bill. Alternatively, he may know about the better reason, but reject it as a poor reason. "*The* reason" for the law, the reason that in fact supports it, may not then be the reason that impelled a legislator to vote for it. And even among the majority of legislators who vote the bill into law, there may be a large number of operative reasons, so that no one of them is the conscious reason of the legislative majority, much less the whole legislature, for creating the law. There may, in short, be a reason for a law which was not the legislature's reason for making it law. The conscious rationale of a legislator then might not be the rationale that truly justifies his vote. It might not even be the reason which accurately explains his vote, for the factors that motivated him on a deep level to vote for the bill might be different reasons still. His true motivation, in that case, does not coincide with his cited reason.

What then is "the true reason" for the law? Sometimes we can construct an implicit rationale for the law that need not necessarily coincide with anyone's actual reasons or deep motives for supporting it, but that nevertheless provides it with a plausibly coherent rational reconstruction. "This is how the law actually functions in our society; this is the job it is tacitly understood to be doing; this is what people assume it is for." Whether or not the implicit rationale of the law coincides with the factors that truly legitimize or justify it is an open question, depending on the law. If we are liberals we may find the implicit rationale to be paternalistic and therefore unacceptable. On the other hand, the implicit rationale may appear at first sight to be paternalistic, but closer examination may disclose other functions of the law that lend it coherence and truly justify it. Indeed the paternalistic rationale may collapse as a realistic account of how the law is enforced and defended in practice.

Consider some examples of laws with alternative rationales. Gerald Dworkin lists sixteen examples of "paternalistic interferences" but at least three of them, as they actually function in most legal systems, are more plausibly subject to nonpaternalistic interpretations. The first of these are: "Laws regulating certain kinds of sexual conduct, for example homosexuality among consenting adults in private."[19] In this country, at least (and I suspect in most Western nations), those who wish to use the law to harass and punish adult homosexuals have no benevolent concern whatever for "the good" of the parties themselves. They find the bare thought of the "crime against nature" so repugnant and/or threatening that they take that to be reason enough for making even private, consensual, deviant conduct criminal (the offense principle). Or they hold on biblical or other grounds that homosexuality is inherently sinful regardless of its circumstances or consequences, and that its wickedness alone is sufficient warrant for its criminal prohibition (pure legal moralism). Surely J. F. Stephen was not being "paternalistic" when, speaking of homosexuality, he ranted that "there are acts of wickedness so gross and outrageous that they must be prevented at any cost to the offender . . ."[20]

Neither were those American state legislatures paternalistic who made homosexual "sodomy" a capital offense! In fact whenever the criminal penalty for violating a statute is far more severe than the harm to self risked by the offender, it is difficult to explain the law as an expression of protective solicitude toward prospective violators. When the penalty for smoking one marijuana cigarette is up to thirty years in prison,[21] clearly the law is more plausibly interpreted as an expression of moral abhorrence or of fear of catastrophic public harm, than of "parental" concern for the health or safety of vulnerable youths. One would expect *unmixed* paternalistic laws to have more gentle penalties than laws with different rationales. Parents, after all, do not imprison or hang their children for their own good, for the harms thus inflicted are greater than the harms meant to be prevented, rendering the protective rationale senseless.

The second dubious example from Dworkin are "laws compelling people to spend a specified fraction of their incomes on the purchase of retirement annuities (Social Security)."[22] Here there *is* a possible paternalistic rationale. Purchase of the annuities is both prudent and compulsory. I suspect that the assumption behind the legislation, however, was that few citizens would be compelled to save against their will, so that the law functions less to compel the unwilling than to *enable* the vast majority to do what they desperately want to do (make their old age and that of their parents and loved ones secure), and cannot otherwise do efficiently. The economic assumptions behind social security programs, on this interpretation, were that profit-making private companies are unable to achieve an adequate level of benefit for an adequately low level of cost, and that without compulsory participation the government could not do it either. The loss to the great majority would be a harm to their interest in security, and the compulsion of the others is meant to protect the majority from this harm. That is not paternalistic treatment of anyone. The unwilling are told in effect: "You must participate even if you think it is not in *your* interest to do so, because it is manifestly in the interests of all the others, and the public interest too, that you do so. The compulsion is for their sakes, not yours."[23]

A final example from Dworkin is still more difficult: "Laws against dueling."[24] If we think of the historical setting for this prohibition in a certain way, the laws will surely seem paternalistic. Think of duelists as a specifically delineated cult of sportsmen and adventurers, much on the model, say, of motorcycle racers and mountain climbers. Imagine the legislator speaking to the prospective duelist in this way: "What you propose to do is extremely hazardous to your health. Therefore, for the sake of your own safety, you may not do it." Violation of the law would carry a severe penalty of its own, and if the opposing duelist is maimed or killed, his prior consent, or assumption of the risk, would not be accepted as a defense to criminal charges of mayhem or homicide.

That model, however, does not fit the facts. Nearly all of us are happy that the practice of dueling has been stamped out, as were our ancestors, no doubt, when the original prohibitions came into force. Even many of the tiny minority of dissenters must have been secretly relieved. We don't have perfect unanimity, of course, on this or any other social issue, but we are close enough to that state to bring another, quite nonpaternalistic, model so close to the facts that it can serve as an "implicit rationale" for the prohibition. I refer to that proposed by Richard Arneson in a recent helpful article:

> Consider . . . restrictions on dueling. Suppose every person in a society prefers most of all not to be confronted with dueling situations, and second prefers to preserve his honor by making the conventionally appropriate response to dueling situations when they arise. Assume that a legal ban on dueling prevents any dueling situations from arising. On these assumptions, and assuming further that persons have no other desires that are relevant to the issue of dueling regulations, a legal ban against dueling would be nonpaternalistic, since nobody's freedom is being restricted against his will. Of course, in any actual society not everybody will have this pattern of desires, but if it is this pattern of desires that generates reasons for forbidding dueling, then the antidueling law (even if it is unfair or unjust) is nonpaternalistic.[25]

Again, the proper analysis is not that a vanishing minority of persons desiring to challenge and/or respond in defense of their "honor" are denied the right to do so out of concern for their own safety, but rather that almost all of us wish to be protected against potential harassment of a peculiar kind, even those who would otherwise respond in the traditional way. The implicit rationale seems to invoke the harm to others principle.

Most of Dworkin's dubious examples (I exclude the sex-crime one), and many others like them, are instances of good reasonable laws that most of us would be loath to change. If, therefore, they are taken to rest exclusively or mainly on a paternalistic basis, then the liberal argument against paternalism is undermined. So it is useful to look for an "implicit rationale" that is not paternalistic, so that the contest between the liberal and the hard paternalist, at least at this early stage, is still open. Later we shall look at some other *prima facie* "paternalistic statutes" that are reasonable, and continue the argument. At this stage it is sufficient to note that many examples presented by defenders of hard paternalism as instances of "justified paternalism" may be clearly justified, but not clearly paternalism.

Arneson's general strategy in the face of examples of "justified paternalism" contains two interconnected elements. First, his definition of "paternalism" makes it a necessary condition that the coercive rule be applied *against the will* of those subject to it. Second, in determining whether a given statute is paternalistic, he asserts that we must look at the actual motives and purposes of those who legislate, interpret, and enforce it.

His definition of a paternalistic rule or policy (note that it is not the definition of a "liberty-limiting principle", although one can easily be derived from it) is lucid and precise—"Paternalistic policies are restrictions on a person's liberty which are justified exclusively by consideration for that person's own good or welfare, and which are carried out either against his present will (when his present will is not explicitly overridden by his own prior commitment) or against his prior commitment (when his present will is explicitly overriden by his prior commitment.)"²⁶ Our earlier definition covers the case in which the person subject to the rule has it carried out against his will, in virtue of the clause "whatever he may think of the matter" and the proviso that consent has no effect. To the paternalistic legislator, it is a matter of indifference whether a subject's will is in harmony with, or in opposition to, the law. In virtue of the law's generality it applies to both classes alike. Thus, if ninety-nine percent of the citizens share the negative attitudes toward dueling described so well by Arneson, then the law against dueling (on his definition) is not paternalistic as applied to them. But it is paternalistic if applied "against their will" to the dissenting one percent. This, it seems to me, is an unnecessary relativizing of the concept of "paternalism", at least as it applies to *general* coercive rules and policies. But Arneson's ingenious arguments against classifying as "paternalistic" certain obviously reasonable statutes is sufficiently supported by the second element of his approach, the appeal to actual motives, or as I would prefer to understand it, to actual "implicit rationales."

When most of the people subject to a coercive rule approve of the rule, and it is legislated (interpreted, applied by courts, defended in argument, understood to function) *for their sakes*, and not for the purpose of imposing safety or prudence on the unwilling minority ("against their will"), then the rationale of the rule is *not* paternalistic. In that case we can attribute to it as its "purpose" the *enablement* of the majority to achieve a collective good, and not, except incidentally as an unintended byproduct, the enforcement of prudence on the minority. Depending on the collective good involved, the costs and benefits, and the comparative sizes of the majority and minority, the statute may be fair or unfair, wise or unwise, but in either case, it will not be "paternalistic."

Arneson has no difficulty showing how on his definition the *act* of taking an unconscious injured person to the hospital, and the *act* of shoving out of harm's way a man who is unknowingly in the path of a runaway truck, are *not* paternalistic.²⁷ We presume in both cases what is overwhelmingly probable, namely that what we are doing is in accord with, not against, the man's will, though we don't have a chance in the circumstances to find out for sure. But now consider a pair of *rules* requiring persons to take unconscious injured persons to the hospital and to shove unaware persons out of the path of runaway vehicles. Because of their generality these rules apply both to the over ninety-nine percent of unconscious injured parties and unaware potential accident victims whose will is to live, and to the tiny minority of those who would have preferred the alternative fate. Rather than say that the rule is nonpaternalistic for the majority but paternalistic when applied "against their wills" to the minority, as Arneson's definition seems to imply, we can say that the rule is nonpaternalistic *tout court*, because its rationale is to enable people to do what they want, not to impose safety on those who would voluntarily commit suicide.

This revised Arneson approach also helps us to explain why consumer protection laws are *not* paternalistic.[28] To be sure, the "Truth in Advertising" act, for example, which requires clear labeling of ingredients, quantities, and terms of sale, protects unwary customers who could protect themselves if they were attentive or demanding enough, and departs from the rugged individualism of *Caveat emptor*. It clearly *is* a case of paternalism of the benevolent, "presumptively nonblamable" kind distinguished in section 1 of this chapter, and economic individualists are fond of applying the term "paternalism" to it, borrowing that label's derogation so well earned in other contexts. The Pure Food and Drug Laws empower government agencies to require food producers, under pain of criminal penalty, to satisfy set standards of sanitation and purity, and to forego using ingredients declared to be dangerous to health, like Red Dye No. 2. These laws are general and they are coercive, but are they paternalistic in the present sense? I think not. The coercion is directed against one class of persons, the food processors, in order to protect a second class of persons, namely the vast majority of food buyers. It appears that the legitimizing principle supporting the legislation is the harm to others principle, not legal paternalism. But what about the tiny minority that would prefer to assume the announced risk of cancer to get a more life-like color in their frozen strawberries? What about the tiny group that would happily purchase substantially impure foods for substantially lower prices if given the option? Isn't the Pure Food Law paternalistic in respect to them? Not if the implicit rationale of the law—the account of its role, function, and motivation that most coheres with the known facts—is to enable the majority to secure its goals, not to enforce prudence on the unwilling minority. It may be, of course, that the law in question has both purposes, in which case it has a mixed rationale. On the other hand, it could be that interference with the voluntary risk-taking of the minority is an indifferent or unwelcome byproduct of protecting the good of the majority, preferred to more flexible arrangements that would respect the wishes of majority and minority groups alike only because of their heavy administrative and economic costs. Where alternative arrangements that would satisfy both groups at tolerable cost are obviously available, then the interpretation of the "implicit rationale" as paternalistic gains plausiblity.

5. Legal paternalism, the harm principle, and "garrison thresholds"

There are many cases, as we have seen, of criminal prohibitions that can be defended, at least initially, on two distinct grounds, both the need to protect individuals from the harmful consequences of their own acts *and* the need to prevent social harm generally. Sometimes the public interest is so clearly at stake that the paternalistic rationale is quite redundant and an opponent of paternalism can defend the prohibition in question entirely on liberal grounds. Indeed, the public interest is always involved, at least to some small extent, when persons harm themselves. Society is deprived of the services of the injured party, and must also bear the more direct social costs of cleaning up, rescuing, retrieving, or repairing. If fifty thousand persons kill themselves every year by their own choice or through reckless disregard of their own safety, then millions of dollars of tax money are not paid to the treasury, millions of dollars are paid out in social security and death benefits, millions more are spent on police teams, ambulances, and hospitals. Even the sanitation workers who sweep the debris and wash the blood off the roads are paid from public funds. Self-caused deaths and injuries, in the aggregate, are a considerable public inconvenience, at the very least.

It must be a presupposition of the present discussion, however, that there is no necessity that public harm be caused in sufficient degree to implicate the harm principle whenever an individual deliberately injures himself or assumes a high risk of so doing.[29] In modern Western societies, at least, the presupposition seems safe enough. There are persons whose suicides, for example, would harm no one directly, and even benefit their survivors and obviate the great expense of their continued maintenance. And in other examples where the public interest *is* necessarily affected, the degree of harm to it seems altogether too trivial to justify, by itself, imposing burdensome constraints. We can assume, therefore, that in some societies, at least, and at some times, a line can be drawn (as Mill claimed it could in Victorian England) between other-regarding behavior and conduct that is primarily and directly self-regarding and only indirectly and remotely, therefore trivially, other-regarding.[30] If this assumption is false, then there is no interesting problem concerning legal paternalism, and certainly no practical legislative problem, since all "paternalistic" restrictions, in that case, could be defended as necessary to protect persons other than those restricted, and hence would not be (wholly) paternalistic.

One can imagine societies, however, in which our presupposition would not hold. To take a simple model, imagine a beleaguered garrison of settlers under attack from warlike Indians. Everyone is working furiously to repel the assault. The men are all firing at the mounted marauders while the women load the muskets, and children pour water on fires started by flaming arrows. At the peak of the excitement, John Wayne becomes so bored and depressed, that he withdraws with the announced intention of killing himself. "After all," he says, "my life is my own and what I do with it is my own business." Of course, he could not be more wrong. What he does is *everybody* else's business since the issue is so close that the withdrawal of one party threatens to tip the balance. There is no distinction in these circumstances between self-regarding and other-regarding, or between not helping and positively harming. Anyone who does not help inflicts serious harm on all the others. Insofar as any larger, more complex, society resembles the garrison situation, the debate over legal paternalism is otiose.

One way in which a society can approach the garrison model is through a steady accumulation of individual withdrawals, though each may seem in its own terms primarily self-regarding. A nonproductive life devoted entirely to lotus-eating, opium smoking, or heroin shooting, in which all of one's waking moments are spent cultivating or enjoying dreamy euphoric states, may be "no one else's business" when one, or a hundred, or ten thousand self-supporting persons do it of their own free choice. But when ten percent of the whole population choose to live that way, they become parasitical, and the situation approaches the threshold of serious public harm. When fifty percent choose to live that way it may become impossible for the remainder to maintain a community at all. The closer any society is to what we might call "the garrison threshold," the more the harm principle comes into play, until at a given point, any further withdrawals pose a clear and present danger, and can be emphatically prohibited by the harm principle without any help from the principle of legal paternalism.

6. Presumptive cases for and against legal paternalism

I said in section 1 that legal paternalism is "presumptively blamable." Why should that be? Why should the coercion-legitimizing principle itself, even when stripped of its derogatory label and its misleading associations, tend spontaneously to evoke repugnance? Part of the answer, I think, is that when it is applied by another party to oneself it seems arrogant and demeaning. It says in effect that there are sharp limits to my right to govern myself even within the wholly self-regarding sphere, that others may intervene even against my protests to "correct" my choices and then (worst of all) justify their interference on the ground (how patronizing!) that they know my own good better than I know it myself. It is that "justification" that is most unpleasantly analogous to parental behavior. Parents can be expected to justify their interference in the lives of their children, telling them for example what they must eat and when they must sleep, on the ground that "Daddy knows best." Legal paternalism seems to imply that since the state often can know the interests of individual citizens better than the citizens know them themselves, it stands *in loco parentis* as a permanent guardian of those interests even against the free choices of the persons whose interests they are. Put in this way, paternalism seems a preposterous doctrine. If adults are treated (*in this fashion*) "as children," they will in time come to be like children. Deprived of the right to choose for themselves, they will soon lose the power of rational judgment and decision. Even children, after a certain point, had better not be "treated as children," else they will never acquire the outlook and capability of responsible adults.

Yet if we reject hard paternalism entirely, and deny that a person's own good is ever a valid ground for coercing him, we seem to fly in the face of both common sense and our long-established customs and laws. In the criminal law, for example, a prospective victim's freely granted consent is no defense to the charge of mayhem or homicide. The state simply refuses to permit anyone to agree to his own disablement or killing. The law of contracts, similarly, refuses to recognize as valid, contracts to sell oneself into slavery, or to become a mistress, or a second spouse. Any ordinary citizen is legally justified in using reasonable force to prevent another from mutilating himself or committing suicide. No one is allowed to purchase certain drugs even for therapeutic purposes without a physician's prescription (Doctor knows best). The use of other drugs, such as heroin, for pleasure merely, is permitted under no circumstances whatever. It is hard to find any plausible rationale for all such restrictions apart from the argument that beatings, mutilations, and death, concubinage, slavery, and bigamy are always bad for a person whether he or she knows it or not, and that antibiotics are too dangerous for any nonexpert, and heroin for anyone at all, to take on his own initiative.

The trick is stopping short once we undertake this path, unless we wish to ban whiskey, cigarettes, and fried foods, which tend to be bad for people too, whether they know it or not. One writer backs up his charge that legal (hard) paternalism justifies too much, by contending that in principle it would "justify the imposition of a Spartan-like regimen requiring rigorous physical exercise and abstention from smoking, drinking, and hazardous pastimes.[31] Tom Beauchamp, who quotes this passage with approval, adds an additional complaint of his own that legal paternalism might impose either direct or indirect criminal sanctions against medical experimenters and/or volunteer subjects, or at the very least warrant forceful interferences for "the good" of the subject, overruling his voluntary choice:

> Suppose, for example, that a man risks his life for the advance of medicine by submitting to an unreasonably risky experiment, an act which most would think not in his own interest. Are we to commend him or coercively restrain him? Paternalism strongly suggests that it would be permissible to coercively restrain such a person. Yet if that is so, then the state is permitted to restrain coercively its morally heroic citizens, not to mention its martyrs, if they act—as such people frequently do—in a manner "harmful" to themselves. I do not see how paternalism can be patched up by adding further conditions about the actions of heroes and martyrs . . .[32]

The cases for and against legal paternalism then can be summed up as follows. In favor of the principle is the fact that there are many laws now on the books that *seem* to have hard paternalism as an essential part of their implicit rationales, and that some of these at least, seem to most of us to be sensible and legitimate restrictions.[33] It is also a consideration in favor of paternalism that preventable personal harm (set-back interest) is universally thought to be a great evil, and that such harm is no less harmful when self-caused than when caused by others. If society can substantially diminish the net amount of harm to interests caused from *all* sources, that would be a great social gain. If that prospect provides the moral basis underlying the harm to others principle, why should it not have application as well to self-caused harm and thus support equally the principle of legal paternalism?

On the other side, it is argued that a consistent application of legal paternalism would lead to the creation of new crimes that would be odious and offensive to common sense, leading to the general punishment of risk-takers, the enforcement of prudence, and interference with saints and heroes. Moreover, hard paternalistic justification of any restriction of personal liberty is especially offensive morally, because it invades the realm of personal autonomy where each competent, responsible, adult human being should reign supreme.

However it is approached, the problem of paternalism is a problem requiring reconciliation of apparently conflicting considerations. On the one hand, we are challenged to reconcile our general repugnance for paternalism with the seeming reasonableness of some apparently paternalistic regulations. On the other hand, we are challenged to reconcile, somehow, our legitimate concern with diminishing over-all harm with the threatened proliferation of criminal prohibitions enforcing a "Spartan-like regime" of imposed prudence.

Two broad strategies suggest themselves. We can first of all remind ourselves that legal paternalism, like all of the other coercion-legitimizing principles, is defined not in terms of necessary and sufficient conditions for justified interferences with political liberty, but rather in terms of "good and relevant reasons." (See Vol. 1, Chap. 1, §3.) To say that the need to protect people from their own foolishness is always *a* "good and relevant reason" for coercive legislation, is not to say that it is in any given case a decisive reason. Rather, it leaves open the possibility that in that case reasons of a quite different kind weigh on the other side, and that those other reasons (including respect for personal autonomy) may in the circumstances have still greater weight. Thus, it is possible to defend legal paternalism, as we have defined it, while arguing against paternalistic legislation in particular cases. We can call this approach "the balancing strategy." The anti-paternalist has a heavier argumentative load to carry. He must not only argue against particular legislation with apparently paternalistic rationales; he must argue that paternalistic reasons never have *any* weight on the scales at all. In his eyes they are morally illegitimate or invalid reasons by their very natures, since they conflict head on with defensible conceptions of personal autonomy.[34]

The most promising strategy for the anti-paternalist is to construct a convincing conception of personal autonomy that can explain how that notion is a moral trump card, not to be merely balanced with considerations of harm diminution in cases of conflict, but always and necessarily taking moral precedence over those considerations. Then he must consider the most impressive examples of apparently reasonable paternalistic legislation, and argue, case by case, either that they are not reasonable, or that they are not (hard) paternalistic. The latter project will almost certainly lead him to defend "soft paternalism" as an alternative, essentially liberal, rationale for most of what seems reasonable in paternalistic restrictions. For that reason, we can call this approach "the soft-paternalist strategy."

Since part of the purpose of this book is to determine what is salvageable in the traditional liberal doctrine, the following chapters will be devoted to explicating personal autonomy, considering alternative autonomy-respecting rationales, and in particular, elaborating a soft-paternalistic theory of how forcible implementation of a person's will can accord with his personal autonomy.

18

Autonomy

1. Conceptions of personal autonomy

Those who have experienced, or can experience hypothetically in their imaginations, irksome constraints justified wholly on paternalistic grounds, will testify that their resentment is not mere frustration or antipathy. Rather it has the full flavor of moral indignation and outrage. Their grievance is not simply that they have been unnecessarily inconvenienced or "irked," but rather that in some way they have been violated, invaded, belittled. They have experienced something analogous to the invasion of their property or the violation of their privacy. They want to protest in such terms as "*I'm* in charge *here*," "No one can tell me what I must do with *my own* time," and "What I do with *my own* life is no one else's business." The indignant feelings, in short, are those provoked by a sense of one's rightful prerogatives having been usurped. Moreover, the paternalistic "justifications" for the invasions rub salt in the wound by denying the very existence of the privacy, independence, and prerogatives asserted in the protests, and thereby are also belittling, degrading, or demeaning.

Philosophers have long had an expression to label the realm of inviolable sanctuary most of us sense in our own beings. That term is *personal autonomy*. The word "autonomy" is obviously derived from the Greek stems for "self" and "law" or "rule", and means literally "the having or making of one's own laws." Its sense therefore can be rendered at least approximately by such terms as "self-rule," "self-determination," "self-government," and "independence." These phrases are all familiar to us from their more frequent, and often more exact, application to states and institutions. Indeed it is plausible that the original applications and denials of these notions were to states and that their attribution to individuals is derivative, in which case "personal autonomy" is a political metaphor.[1]

When applied to individuals the word "autonomy" has four closely related meanings. It can refer either to the *capacity* to govern oneself, which of course is a matter of degree; or to the *actual condition* of self-government and its associated virtues; or to an *ideal of character* derived from that conception; or (on the analogy to a political state) to the *sovereign authority* to govern oneself, which is absolute within one's own moral boundaries (one's "territory," "realm," "sphere," or "domain"). Note that corresponding to these senses of "autonomous" there are parallel senses of the term "independent": The *capacity* to support oneself, direct one's own life, and be finally responsible for one's own decisions; the *de facto condition* of self-sufficiency which consists in the exercise of the appropriate capacities when the circumstances permit; the ideal of self-sufficiency; and the sense, applied mainly to political states, of *de jure sovereignty* and the right of self-determination.[2]

2. *Autonomy as capacity*

It is possible in theory, I suppose, to possess both the capacity and the condition without the right of self-government. It is clearly possible to possess the right and the capacity while falling short of the condition. But it does not seem possible either to achieve the condition or to possess the right while lacking (totally lacking) the capacity. Thus all those who have argued for a natural sovereign autonomy have agreed that persons have the right of self-government if and only if they have the capacity for self-government. That capacity in turn is determined by the ability to make rational choices, a qualification usually so interpreted as to exclude infants, insane persons, the severely retarded, the senile, and the comatose, and to include virtually everyone else. It is commonly said of those who qualify that they and only they are *competent* to govern themselves. As it is used in the law, the word "competence," referring to the possession of legal powers, expresses an all or nothing concept.[3] A being is "competent" (legally capable) of committing a crime, for example, only if it is a human being, of a certain age and mental condition. Unlike primitive systems, our law refuses to recognize that animals, plants, and inanimate objects, or human infants or lunatics can commit delicts, "no matter how hard they might try."

As Kelsen points out, the concept of "jurisdiction" is "nothing but the general concept of competence as applied to a special case. Jurisdiction properly so called is the competence of courts."[4] Similarly, one might add that "standing" is the competence to be a plaintiff or petitioner in certain forms of litigation. These concepts are also accurately rendered by the word "qualification." Not only is legal qualification all or nothing (not a matter of degree); it is relativized to contexts, applying or not applying to given persons depending on which legal role is at issue. Jones, a legislator, is competent to (help) make laws but lacks the legal power to make people married. The Reverend Mr. Smith is competent to conduct weddings but incompetent to legislate. Jones is neither more nor less competent than any other unqualified person to change people's marital status. In this sense of the word, "competence" is not a matter of degree permitting such comparisons; you are either competent or not, all or nothing. But some people exercise more kinds of legal competence than others. Judges are competent to create or alter more kinds of legal relationships than clergymen. Karen Quinlan, in her incurable coma, was no longer competent to produce any legal changes whatever—not competent to consent, not even "competent" to commit a crime.

Daniel Wikler, in an important article,[5] has pointed out how these legal and legal-like concepts of competence differ from a more familiar commonsense notion of competence as natural ability. Wikler calls this ordinary notion "the relativist conception" to indicate that it applies to capabilities that people have in various degrees. Scales of intelligence, for example, employ such a notion, extending from the profoundly retarded, to the mildly retarded, the average, the bright, and the gifted. Those at the one end of the scale are less "competent" (capable) intellectually than those in the middle and at the other end. We also distinguish those who are intellectually competent in various degrees, on the one hand, from those who are simply incompetent, on the other, but where we draw that line is in part relative to the requirements of the tasks we are assigning. When we make the distinction in a general way with no specific tasks in mind, we do it in an unavoidably arbitrary fashion. "We draw it somewhere between the levels of capacity of normal adults and of the mildly retarded, but relative to the gifted, normal adults are impaired or incompetent [in this sense]."[6] In contrast, Wikler's second notion of competence, which although it does not refer to the "power" to create status or alter legal relations, nevertheless resembles in one respect the legal conceptions described above, is a "threshold conception." Like Wikler's first sense, it refers to natural abilities rather than legal powers, but above a certain minimum (say of intelligence or age) competence in this sense is possessed in equal degree by all who have it, no matter how much they differ in degree of competence in the other sense; and below the threshold, everyone is equally incompetent despite other differences among them. In this "threshold sense of natural competence," the following remark of Wikler's is quite unexceptionable: "Though a person may have more intelligence than another, he will be no more *competent* at performing certain tasks; his added power is simply an unused surplus. Those lacking enough intelligence for the task will be incompetent to perform it; while those having sufficient intelligence will be equally competent however great the difference in their intellectual levels."[7]

It is the threshold conception of natural competence—minimal relevant capability for a task—that is used in stipulations of necessary and sufficient conditions for the sovereign right of self-government ascribed to individuals. Some competent persons are no doubt more richly endowed with intelligence, judgment, and other relevant capabilities than others, but above the appropriate threshold they are deemed no more competent (qualified) than the others at the "task" of living their own lives according to their own values as they choose. In respect to qualification for rightful self-government, their greater resources are "simply an unused surplus."

The actual condition of self-government, however, is differently related to competence. The person whose relevant capacities are just above the bare threshold of competence that qualifies him for *de jure* self-government may rightfully rule himself, but in fact he may rule himself badly, unwisely, only partially. He may in fact have relatively little personal autonomy in the sense of *de facto* condition, but like a badly governed nation, he may retain his sovereign independence nevertheless. A genuinely incompetent being, below the threshold, is incapable of making even foolish, unwise, reckless, or perverse choices. Jellyfish,[8] magnolia trees, rocks, newborn infants, lunatics, and irrevocably comatose former "persons," if granted the right to make their own decisions, would be incapable of making even "stupid" choices. Being stupid, no less than being wise, is the sole prerogative of the threshold-competent.

In summary, capacities relevant to self-government do differ in the degree to which they are possessed by various competent persons. Therefore, above a minimal threshold, the autonomy that is defined in terms of those capacities is also a property admitting of "more" and "less." The actual condition of self-government (and its associated virtues), which defines "autonomy" in the second sense, also is subject to differences in degree. Some people are "more in control of themselves" than others, have more prudence, sagacity, self-reliance, authenticity, or integrity than others. The explanation of these differences may in some cases be that the better governed (or more self-governed) people have more of the capacities that define autonomy in the first sense. But that is not the only possible explanation. Dispositions of character, feeling, or sensibility, and differences in life circumstances too, may be contributing factors. In any case, the fourth sense of autonomy—*de jure* independence—is not a matter of more or less. It belongs equally to the wise and the foolish, and is determined only by that competence which is itself not a matter of degree.

In the next section we shall examine the second family of senses of "autonomy", all derived from conceptions of the condition of self-government. That will be followed by a discussion, in section 4, of the ways in which that conception requires modification if it is to serve as an attractive ideal for human character. Then throughout the remainder of this and subsequent chapters, when we speak of "autonomous persons," we shall refer, unless otherwise indicated, to persons who are autonomous in a quite different sense, those who have a right to self-determination analogous in certain ways to the right of nations to be politically independent, and it will be tacitly understood that the persons so designated are, of course, autonomous in the capacity sense as well. But it would take us too far afield to say more about the presupposed capacities here.[9]

3. Autonomy as condition

A person with both the capacity for, and right to, self-government may in fact be an unwilling slave to another, with no opportunity to exercise his rights and capacities. Such a person falls short of autonomy in the sense that he does not actually govern himself, whatever his rights and capacities. What is it then to be in the actual condition of self-government? Whatever else we mean by autonomy in this sense, it must be a good and admirable thing to have, not only in itself but for its fruits—responsibility, self-esteem, and personal dignity. Autonomy so conceived is not merely a "condition," but a condition to which we aspire as an ideal.

We must mention first of all, however, that *de facto* self-government pre-supposes *luck*.[10] If a person's luck is bad, circumstances beyond his control can destroy his opportunities. I do not govern myself if you overpower me by brute force and wrongfully impose your will on mine, or if illness throws me into a febrile stupor, delirium, or coma, or if poverty reduces me to abject dependence on the assistance of others. (Similarly a nation may not be able to govern itself in time of famine, or when stripped of its natural resources.) So a certain amount of good luck, no less than capability, is a requisite condition of *de facto* autonomy. Sometimes, however, unlucky circumstances can actually contribute to autonomy, as when a person is so situated than he can depend only on himself. He stands alone with no one else to help; hence he is "thrown on his own resources," and develops firm habits of self-reliance.

For the most part when we think of a person as possessing or lacking *de facto* autonomy we think of him as neither enviable for his material good fortune nor pitiable for his bad luck (though these may be presupposed) as much as admirable for his excellence of character or blamable for his deficiencies. In normal circumstances, opportunity is more or less available for most people; the autonomous person is the one who makes the most of it. Autonomy, so understood, refers to a congeries of virtues all of which derive from a conception of self-determination, though sometimes by considerable extension of that idea. These virtues, in fact, are a remarkably miscellaneous lot, united only by a family resemblance, and a connection, however far removed, to the generating idea of self-government. The virtues, moreover, are causally and conceptually interconnected, and corresponding to each is a distinctive way of falling short of the composite ideal. Let us consider some of the chief items in this blend.

Self-possession. The autonomous person, as the saying goes, is "his own man" or "her own woman." He/she doesn't "belong" to anyone else, either as property or as possession. Anyone who would deal in her affairs must come to terms with *her*, or her agent. It will not do to negotiate only with her parents or her boss, and she has no "keeper."

Distinct self-identity (individuality). The autonomous person is no mere reflection of another who doesn't have a sense of his own identity. He is not exhaustively defined by his relations to any particular other. For example, he may protest that he is not content to be known and described merely as the former husband of some movie star, as the newspapers might have it.

Authenticity; self-selection. To the degree to which a person is autonomous he is not merely the mouthpiece of other persons or forces. Rather his tastes, opinions, ideals, goals, values, and preferences are all authentically *his*. (His moral principles are too, it goes without saying, but these will be considered below as a special case.) One way of being inauthentic, so understood, is to be an habitual and uncritical conformist who receives his signals from some group whose good opinion he needs, or from unknown tastemakers in the advertising agencies and public relations firms. The inauthentic person of this type is essentially the manipulated consumer. He has no taste in music or clothes except for what is fashionable this season. If blue flatters his complexion while green makes him appear sallow and sickly, yet green is "in," he will buy all green shirts, aesthetic considerations be damned. And if his temperament inclines him to a life style that is currently out of favor with his peers, he will adopt a different life style instead, even if it ill-fits and ill-becomes his temperament. Even his opinions and "convictions" will be chosen in the way he chooses his clothes, for their conformity to the public "image" he wishes to present for the approval of his peers. He can construct no rationale for his beliefs other than that they are the beliefs held by those to whom he responds (if he even knows who *they* are), and can give no reason for thinking that *their* beliefs (like those of some reasonably selected authority) might be correct.[11]

There is an equal and opposite way of failing to be authentic which was more common a century or two ago in the era of "rugged individualists." What David Riesman called "inner directedness" is no more a form of authenticity than the "other-directedness" (conformism) more common today. On the old pattern of inauthenticity, a set of "generalized but nonetheless inescapably destined goals"[12] and standards are implanted in the child by his parents, their authoritative source internalized, so that they become his forever more. He is no more capable of subjecting these governing ideals to rational criticism and then modifying them where necessary than the other-directed person is, for he has within him a kind of "psychological gyroscope" that keeps him steadily on his course on pain of powerful guilt feelings. This mechanism allows him "to appear far more independent than he really is: he is no less a conformist than the other-directed person, but the voices to which he listens are more distant, of an older generation, their cues internalized in his childhood."[13]

A person is authentic to the extent that, unlike both the inner-directed and the other-directed person, he can and does subject his opinions and tastes to rational scrutiny. He is authentic to the extent that he can and does alter his convictions for reasons of his own, and does this without guilt or anxiety. The authentic person will buy his clothes in part to match his purse, his physical characteristics, and his functions; he will select his life style to match his temperament, and his political attitudes to fit his ideals and interests. He cannot be loftily indifferent to the reactions of others, but he is willing to be moved by other considerations too.

Self-creation (self-determination). The autonomous person is often thought of as a "self-made man." He cannot, of course, be literally and wholly self-made without contradiction. Even his character as authentic cannot be entirely the product of his own doing. To suppose otherwise is to conceive of authenticity in such an exalted way that its criteria can never be satisfied, or else to promote the ideal of authenticity in a self-defeating way. To reflect rationally, in the manner of the autonomous-authentic person, is to apply some already accepted principles, in accordance with the rules of rational procedure, to the test of more tentative principles or candidates for principles, judgments, or decisions. Rational reflection thus presupposes some relatively settled convictions to reason from and with. If we take authenticity to require that *all* principles (beliefs, preferences, etc.) are together to be examined afresh in the light of reason on each occasion for decision, then nothing resembling rational reflection can ever get started.

The point is a modest one, but commonly overlooked by those whose conception of autonomy is unrealistically inflated. It is simply that a person must already possess at least a rudimentary character before he can hope to *choose* a new one. The other side of that point is that if a child needs to "learn to be authentic," it must be the case the he is not already authentic when he starts. There can be no magical *ex nihilo* creation of the habit of rational reflection.[14] Some principles, and especially the commitment to reasonable self-criticism itself, must be "implanted" in a child if she is to have a reasonable opportunity of playing a part in the direction of her own growth.

Yet we do speak of "self-made persons" and find warrant for such talk in philosophers as different as Aristotle[15] and Sartre.[16] What can we mean by it if we want both to make conceptual sense and to describe a plausible model of personal autonomy? A common-sense account of self-creation (the term "self-determination" has a less grating and paradoxical sound) can be given, provided we avoid the mistake of thinking that there can be no self-determination unless the self that does the determining is already fully formed. In the continuous development of the relative-adult out of the relative-child there is no point before which the child himself has no part in his own shaping, and after which he is the sole responsible maker of his own character and life plan. Such a radical discontinuity is simply not part of anyone's personal history. The extent of the child's role in his own shaping is, instead, a process of continuous growth already begun at birth. From the very beginning that process is given its own distinctive slant by the influences of heredity and early environment. At a time so early that the questions of how to socialize and educate the child have not even arisen yet, the twig will be bent in a certain definite direction. From then on, the parents in promoting the child's eventual autonomy will have to respect that initial bias. From the very beginning, then, the child must—inevitably *will*—have some input in his own shaping, the extent of which will grow continuously even as the child's character itself does. After that, the child can contribute towards the making of his own self and circumstances in ever increasing degree. These contributions are significant even though the child is in large part (especially in the earliest years) the product of external influences over which he has no control, and his original motivational structure is something he just finds himself with, not something he consciously creates. Always the self that contributes to the making of the newer self is the product both of outside influences *and* an earlier self that was not quite as fully formed. That earlier self, in turn, was the product both of outside influences and a still earlier self that was still less fully formed and fixed, and so on, all the way back to infancy. At every subsequent stage the immature child plays a greater role in the creation of his own life, until at the arbitrarily fixed point of full maturity, he is at last fully in charge of himself, his more or less finished character the product of a complicated interaction of external influences and ever-increasing contributions from his own earlier self. At least that is how growth proceeds when parents and other authorities raise a child with maximal regard for the autonomy of the adult he will one day be. That is the most sense that we can make of the ideal of the "self-made person," but it is an intelligible idea, I think, with no paradox in it.

Perhaps we are all self-made in the way just described, except those who have been severely manipulated, indoctrinated, or coerced throughout childhood. But the self we have created in this way for ourselves will not be an authentic self unless the habit of critical self-revision was implanted in us early by parents, educators, or peers, and strengthened by our own constant exercise of it. Self-creation in the authentic person must be a process of self-*re*-creation, rationally accommodating new experiences and old policies to make greater coherence and flexibility. Self-creation is possible but not *ex nihilo.* At the dawn of rational self-awareness, as Gerald Dworkin points out,

> We simply find ourselves motivated in certain ways, and the notion of choosing, from ground zero, makes no sense. Sooner or later we find ourselves, as in Neurath's metaphor of the ship in mid-ocean, being reconstructed while sailing, in mid-history. But [insofar as we are autonomous] we always retain the possibility of stepping back and judging where we are and where we want to be.[17]

Self-legislation. No one took the ideal of autonomy in its literal sense, *auto* (self) *nomos* (law), more seriously than Immanuel Kant. His third formulation of the categorical imperative requires that we act so that our will "can regard itself at the same time as making universal law through its maxim."[18] The moral law exerts a compelling force on us, but only because our rational will is the very author (legislator) of the law to which it is subject. It is this state of being at once author and subject of the law that Kant calls "autonomy" and praises in his most glittering terms. Kant makes it abundantly clear that the authority of the moral law, the source of its binding obligation, is our own rational will. If we did not legislate the law ourselves through our own free wills it would not be binding on us.[19] "A man is only bound to act in conformity with his own will," he maintains, though he goes on to add immediately, "a will, however, which is designed by nature to give universal laws."[20] This qualification seems *prima facie* to be a giving with one hand and a taking away with the other, much as if Kant were to strike a blow for autonomy by maintaining that a person is bound by the laws of mathematics only insofar as he freely embraces them by an act of his rational will, and then add that our rational will, of course, is "designed by nature" to be attuned to mathematical truths, and the only source of those truths. The freedom to govern oneself in the realm of mathematical belief, in that case, is rather strained.

Nevertheless, there is a natural anarchistic interpretation of Kant which accords with one loose strand, at least, of our ordinary notions of autonomy, according to which the autonomous individual "lays down his own law" or even is "a law unto himself". Robert Paul Wolff, for example, draws from

the Kantian premise the conclusion that an autonomous person cannot become "subject to the will of another. He may do what another tells him, but
not because he has been told to do it . . . For the autonomous man, there is
no such thing, strictly speaking, as a command."²¹ If laws bind only because
they have been self-imposed, then no person is subject to the authority of
any other person, and no one *must* ever do anything against his own will.

While Kant's anarchistic hand seems to grant Wolff this license, his rationalistic other hand seems quickly to take it away. At places in his book, *A
Theory of Justice*, John Rawls seems to represent this second strand in the
Kantian conception. The emphasis in Rawls's conception of autonomy is not
so much on one's *free* will as on one's *rational* will. There are objectively
correct moral principles to which all persons are subject whatever their actual
choices, and these are the foundation principles that *would* be chosen by a
group of hypothetical rational and impartial persons in a position of equality.
"Thus acting autonomously is acting from principles that we would consent
to as free and equal rational beings, and that we are to understand in this
way."²² No matter that a person does not in fact consent to the rational
principles; what is required is that hypothetical persons in certain circumstances *would* consent to them, and presumably he would too if only he were
more rational. A rebellious outlaw or a conniving egoist might live by quite
different principles, but on Rawls's view he would not be acting autonomously when he lies and cheats and steals. Autonomous persons, apparently,
unlike autonomous nation-states, cannot at the same time be wicked, dishonorable, or selfish. For us to hold that an evil person does not truly govern
himself, we must identify his "true self" with impersonal reason, rather than
with his actual values and commitments.

One strand of Kantian autonomy (emphasizing "legislation") then seems to
support anarchism in politics and unattractive moral isolation as a character
trait ("*I* make *my own* laws"), while the other strand (emphasizing moral
objectivity) supports moral rectitude at the expense of genuine independence.
A conception of moral autonomy which avoids these extremes would be
preferred.

Moral authenticity. Intertwined with the notions of self-legislation and hypothetical rational consent in the Kantian philosophy, and perhaps underlying
them, is a more familiar (and less confused) conception of moral autonomy
which is but a special case of the concept of authenticity. The autonomous
person is not only he whose tastes and opinions are authentically his own; he
is also one whose moral convictions and principles (if he has any) are genuinely his own, rooted in his own character, and not merely inherited. It is
possible in principle for an (otherwise) autonomous person—a person who
genuinely governs himself—to have no moral convictions at all, and to base

his conduct not on principle but only on prudential policies. But insofar as the autonomous person's life is shaped by moral beliefs, they are derived neither by mindless conformism nor unthinking obedience to authority, but rather from a committed process of continually reconstructing the value system he inherited.

Kant was surely right in attributing a compelling personal dignity to the man or woman who is morally authentic. No tenable conception of autonomy as an ideal would acknowledge the attainment of that ideal by a human parrot or automaton. The person whose moral beliefs are not rooted in her own system of reasons is an object of the contempt of bullies and demagogues. Her "convictions" are so shallow they can be lightly "washed" from her brain by seduction, indoctrination, or suggestion. The morally autonomous person, provided she is free of coercion, will change her convictions only in response to argument; and she will not abandon her foundation beliefs (even if she is forced to act against them) even under intimidation.

Kant is misleading, however, when he makes legal statutes the model for moral convictions, even for our more general moral principles. Consider the great diversity of moral controversies that require us to take moral stands, however tentatively. What is our judgment about abortion?, mercy killing?, preferential treatment for the unjustly disadvantaged?, sexual equality?, contraception?, "free love?", public school prayer sessions?, capital punishment for murderers?, redistribution of wealth through steeply graduated income taxes?, painful experimentation on animals? Even the most thoroughly autonomous person will be constantly balancing and juggling his judgments on these questions, attempting to make them fit with his governing principles and cohere with one another, with no awkward tensions or disharmonies among them. If he simply borrows his views from an alleged moral authority whose word is "law" for him, not attempting to fit his reasons into a coherent scheme, or if he drifts along with the opinions characteristic of his class or station, he fails to be morally authentic. The rough untidy data of morality do not fit the statutory model very snugly, unless we think of "moral statutes" as containing voluminous complexes of exceptive clauses, qualifications, exemptions, and defenses. If we think of them as imposing clear duties of action and omission, directly apprehensible by all those who are subject to them, then we are left, in the difficult cases, with sizable blocs of "subjects" who interpret the duties differently or reject them altogether, and no "moral judiciary" to give authoritative guidance. In any event, the morally authentic person doesn't simply lay down his law; rather he reflects, and balances, and compromises.

A thorough treatment of moral authenticity would distinguish between relatively singular moral judgments and relatively general moral principles. A person's principles, in turn, can be divided into those that underlie and support his judgments (about such matters as equality, taxation, abortion, etc.), on the one hand, and those by which he tries to live his own life and regulate his own conduct, on the other. The latter, which can be called "personal moral principles," are at first sight more like the bills of legislation that were before Kant's mind. If a person *decides*, for reasons of his or her own, to forego all sex outside of marriage, he makes, as it were, a vow of chastity, and assumes a duty whose binding force (as he will see it) derives from his own will. He has bound himself, which is to say that he is subject to a "law" of his own making. There is a surprisingly small range, however, over which this model seems to have any plausible application. Again, when conflicts loom between self-imposed duties, the morally autonomous person must do more than lay down another law to himself. Now he must be his own moral court; he must weigh and balance interests, reconcile and distinguish cases, reason and decide, on his own.

Typically, the occasions for moral choice and decision are precisely when these duties conflict. At the more general level where principles are adopted (or discovered), there is relatively little choice even for the morally authentic person. Could the autonomous person, living in a social world with well-defined social practices and customs, genuinely adopt a principle that he should participate in such practices while breaking all the rules? Can he "decide," or "legislate for himself" that he should make and accept promises but violate his own? Can he adopt as his "principle" (in the United States) that he will always drive on the left side of the road? Where there are settled practices, defined by well-understood conventions, can the autonomous person invent his own alternative rules for playing the public game, and then adopt those rules as his "principles"? Gerald Dworkin hardly exaggerates when he writes: "It makes no more sense to suppose we invent the moral law for ourselves than to suppose that we invent the language we speak for ourselves."[23]

The morally authentic person, then, is severely limited in his choice of moral principles, and in respect to general rules that derive from social practices, it seems fair to say that he has scarcely any choice at all. Choosing and deciding come in at lower levels of generality when principles conflict. But we hardly ever select among rival moral principles at a general level. That is not to say that there cannot be autonomous persons who are wicked, cruel and mean (see *infra*, §4), or even self-governed persons whose lives are regulated by evil policies. Immoral authenticity is as real as its moral counterpart. In theory we all have a choice between the moral life and its amoral and immoral alternatives. But if we opt to govern our lives by *moral* principle, then insofar as our subsequent moral convictions are authentically our own, certain life policies will no longer be eligible for our choice. We cannot even consider, for example, the Satanic life-principle that we should inflict as much pain as we can, or the principle that we should promote our interests at all costs to those who might get in our way. Persons who opt otherwise, to repeat, may be thoroughly self-governing (autonomous), but in order for moral principles to be authentically their own, they must have moral principles in the first place. Those who most conspicuously fall short of *de facto* autonomy are not those who are wicked, but rather those whose "morality" is a mindless reflex. To summarize: the morally authentic person *has* moral principles, and they are *his own* principles, but that does not imply that his will is their source or ground, or necessary for their objective validation.

Moral independence. Wendell Wilkie, speaking of nation-states, once wrote that "sovereignty is something to be used, not hoarded." Much the same could be said of personal moral autonomy. Social rules define ongoing practices, many as old as human society, that were here when we were born and will long survive us. Many of these rules enable us to commit ourselves to others and/or be the recipients of others' commitments. In many cases we inherit our moral commitments, and in still others we have no control over the process. We are committed to the support of our parents, for example, even though we did not ask to be born, and war and famine, whose causes were altogether beyond our influence, or the chance discovery of an injured person, impose their own duties whether we like it or not. But with luck, if we so desire, we can minimize our commitments and thus achieve a greater amount of *de facto* moral independence. We may, if we wish, go through life unmarried, or forego having children, or near neighbors. We may make as few promises as possible to others, incur no debts, join no partnerships. The picture that emerges from all of this is that of an uncommitted person, maximally independent[24] of the demands of others. Yet it is hard to imagine such a person with the moral virtues that thrive on involvement—compassion, loyalty, cooperativeness, engagement, trust. If we think of autonomy as *de facto* independence simply, then the uncommitted person is an autonomy-hoarder, who scores high on our scale. But if we think of autonomy as the name of a condition which is itself admirable, a kind of ideal condition, then the uncommitted person is subject to demerits on his score. He is clearly no paragon.

In fact, we should conceive of *de facto* autonomy in such a way that it is not diminished by voluntary commitments, at least below a reasonable threshold. The person who is harrassed and dominated by a thousand peremptory moral creditors may be admirable, but he has bargained away much of the control of his own affairs. He too must get low marks for *de facto* independence. No matter how admirable he may be, he has not been lucky, and thus fails, perhaps through no fault of his own, to achieve autonomy (control over his own life). But short of such extremes, there should be no conflict between moral autonomy conceived as an ideal, and moral commitment. Consider the analogous case of nations. The United States is committed to the defense of Western Europe from attack, to the honoring of its trade agreements and formal treaties, to the care of its own helpless, and so on, but that hardly tempts anyone to speak of its degree of independent self-government as thereby diminished.

Integrity (self-fidelity). A person of integrity is faithful to his own principles. Integrity therefore presupposes moral authenticity, but the opposite is not true. One must *have* moral principles of one's own in order to act in fidelity to them, but one might very well fail to act as one's authentic principles dictate on a given occasion when one is "morally weak" in the presence of temptation or distracting passions. One would expect (with Plato and Aristotle) that the more authentic one's principles, and the more firmly and rationally they are held, the less likely one is to betray them. That may be true, but even complete moral authenticity is no guarantee of unfailing integrity. One reason for this (perhaps the only reason) is that other dispositions of character may sometimes have a greater motivating power than moral principle. (It would be obfuscatory to insist "by definition" that moral motivation is necessarily the most powerful kind.) When the motive that leads one away from one's principles is self-gain (as in bribery) or passionate pleasure (as in seduction) we are severely critical of the offender. A true person of integrity ("rock-like integrity" as we say) cannot be bought. Even a substantial amount of intimidation, if directed at the person of integrity, should be of no avail, since this virtue should be almost as resistant to fear as to the prospect of pleasure. When the motive that proves more powerful than principle is neither a self-regarding nor a malevolent one, when pity, mercy, sympathy, benevolence, or compassion erodes one's resolution, judgment is not as harsh. True integrity will not be displaced by tender feelings either, but that is not always to its credit.[25] Integrity is a virtue very intimately tied to our conception of autonomy, but even autonomy is not the whole of virtue, and may be made to look bad if it keeps bad company. (Imagine an inflexibly conscientious Robbespierre.)

Self-control (self-discipline). In the case of nation states there are positive and negative aspects of self-government, and insofar as we take the analogy seriously, we should expect to find their counterparts in individual self-government. A person governs himself when he is *not* governed "from the outside" by someone else, and when he *does* govern from the inside—when he is "in control of himself."[26] It is possible, of course, both politically and personally, for one to be independent of outside control and yet to fall short of self-government because *no one* is in control. In politics this state is called anarchy, a condition which is neither heteronomy (government by another), nor autonomy (government by self), but no government at all.

Plato is the philosopher who has taken the positive aspect of the metaphor of self-government most seriously.[27] In his view, there is an "office" in the human mind that is properly occupied by that part of the soul that is meant to rule. When that office stands empty or is usurped by an alien or rebellious element, then the whole human organism is out of kilter, just as if the function of the heart or liver were left unfulfilled or hampered by disease. This political model of the human mind requires the conception of a larger and a narrower self. The inner core self is the "ruling part" with which we most intimately identify. The self outside the inner core is "internal" relative to the outside world, but external relative to the ruling part. This is the self "meant by nature" to be ruled. It includes the body, the passions, and particular desires, appetites, and emotions. The inner core is usually identified with "Reason," but if reason is to have any opportunity to do its job then (taking liberties with Plato) we must also attribute to it the materials it works with—one's most deeply entrenched first principles, ideals, goals, and values. Practical regulation by reason presupposes some relatively settled convictions to reason from and with, though as we have seen in the discussion of authenticity, even these convictions are subject to revision as internal coherence may require. The whole human economy of elements works smoothly when each does it proper job and does not usurp the function of another, and the one element that "plainly bears upon it the marks of authority over all the rest,"[28] that element whose job it is to rule, is the inner-core self, also called "reason" or "conscience," with its basic normative tools (principles, ideals, etc.).

If we democratize this picture somewhat we can reinterpret legitimate self-government as a constitutional monarchy, ruled by King Reason under the terms of a basic charter of values, the two together—king and charter—forming that inner-core self which is the "real person." The model becomes even more democratic if we adopt David Hume's conception of reason as "the slave of the passions."[29] If Hume had spoken of a servant instead of a slave and endorsed a democratic conception of authorities as "public servants," his metaphor might not have been far from the mark, for then it would have permitted us to derive the authority of practical reason from the desires it regulates. So conceived, reason is like a traffic cop directing cars to stop and go in an orderly fashion so that they might get to their diverse destinations all the more efficiently, without traffic jams and collisions. The person whose desires obey no internal regulator will be torn this way and that, and fragmented hopelessly. Such a person fails to be autonomous not because of outside government but because of his failure to govern himself. He will also fail to be free from constraint insofar as his constituent desires thwart one another in internal jams and collisions. At its worst, where self-control has collapsed, such a condition approaches that which Emile Durkheim found to be a leading cause of suicide, for which he originally coined the term "anomie."[30]

Self-reliance. In one respect this traditional virtue is the reverse side of moral independence. The morally independent person does not bind himself to others any more than he can help. The self-reliant person does not rely on the commitments of others to him. In certain areas of his life, at least, he doesn't need others, and dispensable needs he doesn't want. Schemes of cooperation imposing two-way commitments he will skirt warily. So construed, however, "the traditional virtue" is not much of a virtue at all. Perhaps more admirable is the trait of being *able* to rely on oneself if or when others fail. It is indeed a virtue, and not merely a self-regarding one, to have inner resources—strength, courage, ingenuity, toughness, resilience. Intellectual and moral resourcefulness are virtues of mind and character, but having economic and material resources is in large part a matter of luck; so like other elements in the oddly mixed ideal of autonomy, self-reliance is as much an ideal of circumstance as a virtue or ideal of character. Extreme moral resourcefulness, on the other hand, may be enough to permit a person to get along with hardly any physical resources at all, but it will not cure him of disease or prevent him from dying if hit by lightning. There are limits even to stoic self-reliance.

Ralph Waldo Emerson, in his celebrated essay on self-reliance, praises under that name authenticity, moral independence, integrity, and most of the other components of complex autonomy.[31] When he comes to speak of self-reliance proper, however, he makes a different and better case for it. In certain areas of life—the very most important ones—self-reliance consists not merely in having a self that one *can* rely on; it consists rather in having a self that one *must* rely on. A person's highest good in life is self-fulfillment, and by its very nature, fulfillment is not something that can be achieved for the self by someone else. Others can help and provide necessary means, but no one can simply make a gift to a person of his self-fulfillment. No one can make a gift of personal excellence. Insofar as these goods are produced by others for us, they are bogus goods made of plastic. "Nothing can bring you peace," Emerson writes, "but yourself. Nothing can bring you peace but the triumph of principles."[32] And even these, one might add, may not be sufficient if your luck is bad enough.

Initiative (self-generation). Not only are the autonomous person's tastes, opinions, and principles authentically his own; so are his projects and enterprises, designs and strategies. Autonomous persons might differ in their activity or passivity as collaborators, without being more or less autonomous as a result, and the responder to a proposal is as responsible for his reaction to it as the proposer is for his initiative.[33] But if a person, through his fixed habits, hardly ever initiates any undertakings on his own, if his activities fall into patterns determined by others' proposals, if his time between projects is spent "sitting by the telephone" waiting for someone to suggest something, then we should think him somewhat deficient, at the very least, in autonomy, even if his lifetime of responsive activity is full and meaningful, and such that he could take responsibility for. Such a person is not "governed" by those to whom he responds, but he is far more dependent on them than an authentic and self-reliant person would wish to be.

Responsibility for self. "The root idea in autonomy," says Richard Arneson, "is that in making a voluntary choice a person takes on responsibility for all the foreseeable consequences to himself that flow from this voluntary choice."[34] At first sight it would seem that responsibility is derivative from *de facto* autonomy rather than its "basic idea." Those judgments of responsibility that are made after the fact (as opposed to those made prospectively in warnings and assignments) are a diverse lot, but most of them ascribe to their subjects past agency (identify them as the doer of some deed), causation of some state of affairs, credit or blame, answerability, accountability, liability to reward, punishment or some other responsive treatment, or simply liability to the judgment, if only "for the record," that certain propositions are true of them.[35] That is a lot of work for the one word "responsible" to do. If a person acts autonomously then he qualifies for many such retrospective responsibility judgments about what he did. He is properly subject to the judgment that he did the act, that its consequences are to be charged to him, perhaps that he gets credit or blame for the result, or that the costs of repairing the damage are to be charged to his account, or that he is the one who should be required to "answer," or to give an accounting of what happened. On the other hand, insofar as a person's act was not autonomous (or that the actor was not an autonomous person) the retrospective responsibility judgments must be revised or withdrawn. If, for example, he was out of control when he "acted," then it is not even true, without severe qualification, that he acted at all. If he was governed by another in what he did (acting as a mere agent, servant, or pawn), then the consequences may not be chargeable to his account, but rather to that of his master. If his opinions and tastes are not authentically his own but simply reflect those of his manipulators or peer group, then he is not even subject, without severe qualification, to the judgment that they truly represent or belong to him.[36] *De facto* autonomy, it would seem, is a conceptually presupposed condition of most judgments of responsibility.

The connection between autonomy and responsibility, however, also works in the other direction: responsibility is a contributing cause of the development of autonomy. How does one promote in a child the development of self-possession, distinct identity, authenticity, self-discipline, self-reliance, and the other components of the autonomous ideal? Surely part of the required technique is to *assign* (prospectively) responsibilities, that is tasks that require initiative, judgment, and persistence, and after which the assignee must answer for his successes and failures. A corollary of prospective assignments, of course, are retrospective judgments of credit, blame, and the like.

"Responsibility" is itself the name of a specific set of virtues. We speak not only of people being responsible *for* actions and consequences, and responsible *to* others; we also speak of them as being responsible *tout court*. A responsible person is a fit subject of responsibility assignments, and a qualified subject of restrospective ascriptions, in virtue of his possession of the appropriate traits for the exercise of responsibility. The responsible person is contrasted both with irresponsible and nonresponsible (incompetent) persons. Unlike the irresponsible person, he is steady, trustworthy, and reliable; he has the virtues of good judgment, initiative, and self-reliance that make for the effective use of discretion in problem-solving; he can do things on his own. Insofar as this list of virtues overlaps the list that defines autonomy, then obviously, assumptions of responsibilities, practice at discharging them, and willingness to answer afterwards, are effective means of developing ever greater *de facto* autonomy. But the two lists only overlap; they do not coincide. Independent judgment, self-reliance, and initiative are on both lists, but trustworthiness, dependability, steadiness (as opposed to recklessness) and especially the willingness to take on new commitments are more firmly on the responsibility list than they are on the autonomy list, just as moral independence and self-legislation, sometimes assigned to the autonomy list, have no necessary place in the account of responsibility.

4. Autonomy as ideal

The challenge to the philosopher who would characterize autonomy as an ideal complex of character traits is to fashion a conception sufficiently similar to that of the actual condition of self-government that the word "autonomy" remains a suitable designation for it, and yet which describes a character type genuinely worthy of admiration and emulation in the modern world. As we have seen, our conception of autonomy as actual condition is sufficiently vague and uncertain to allow us considerable flexibility. Not all of its components are equally central, and the pedigrees of some are so far removed from original models of political governance as to be stretched and dubious. So we can treat the twelve-part sketch in section 3 as a faithfully vague account of a concept, but one which must now be whittled down and reshaped if it is to make an attractive ideal.

It is important to emphasize at the outset that even a refined conception of autonomy will be at best only a partial ideal, for since it is consistent with some important failings it is insufficient for full moral excellence. No further analysis can be expected to rule out as impossible a selfish but autonomous person, a cold, mean, unloving but autonomous person, or a ruthless, or cruel autonomous person. After all, a self-governing person is no less self-governed if he governs himself badly, no less authentic for having evil principles, no less autonomous if he uses his autonomy to commit aggression against another autonomous person. The aggressor is morally deficient, but what he is deficient in is not necessarily autonomy. He may have more than enough of that.

We can only hope to refine a conception of ideal autonomy according to which *other things being equal*, it is better to be autonomous than not. If we are successful, it will follow that *insofar* as a person is autonomous, he is to that extent admirable. Indeed "autonomy," if we construct the ideal carefully, might even designate a necessary element in any full ideal of human character. But since it can coexist so comfortably with striking moral flaws, it cannot be the whole ideal.

As it stands, the ramshackle conception of actual autonomy set forth in Section 3 will not do, without severe restriction, even as a partial ideal of character. Some of its components are doubtful virtues to begin with; others are virtues only within limits that are narrower than those customarily drawn; still others seem to be confused in their very conception. The Kantian notion of self-legislation, long associated with the concept of autonomy, seems to present us *either* with the picture of a proud anarchist who accepts no commitments he has not himself made, who can commit or uncommit himself at will to anyone or anything, and is in principle capable of "inventing" his own moral principles, *or*, if with Rawls we follow Kant's rationalistic and objectivist bent, a concept of a person who can act autonomously even when he acts against his will, if his compelled behavior would have been chosen by some hypothetical persons more "rational" than he. Moral independence is a less confusing concept, but no more attractive as an ideal. It is one thing to avoid the state of moral overcommitment which, like literal indebtedness, can lead to its own kind of bankruptcy, but quite another to arrange one's life deliberately to minimize involvement with, and therefore commitment to, other persons on the grounds that commitment *per se* diminishes autonomy. It would take a misanthrope or egoist (though perhaps a principled one) even to aim at such an ideal.

Even integrity, when it is so rock-ribbed that it constricts spontaneous human feeling, can be overrated as a virtue, though when it begins to appear objectionable we probably would deny it its laudatory title, and call it "moral fanaticism." When it is a trait of an autonomous person self-governed by narrow or cruel principles, it is a "virtue" that makes him all the more rigid and repellant. Self-reliance, when extreme and "principled," can become not only an unsocial virtue but an anti-social one, inhibiting cooperative participation in group projects. When touched even lightly with pride or self-righteousness it inhibits helpfulness and charity. Self-control, to be rational and worthy of admiration, requires delicate accommodation among diverse elements within the self. It must be clear to the Humean traffic cop what the right-of-way rules are among conflicting desires and values, and he must apply those rules with gentle but firm consistency in the interest of inner harmony. When the self in control is a ruthless autocrat (King Reason) imposing order with an iron hand, then inner conflict is squelched only at great cost to elements of the self, and the presentation of rigid narrowness to the outside world. Self-control can be totalitarian repression, and self-discipline can become self-tyranny. The inner peace so secured is won only by driving dissident elements underground to plot subversion. Self-reliance, independence, and self-control can indeed be virtues, but they are not the sorts of virtues which are such that the more one has the better. They are virtues only when their elements exist in just the right degree, neither too little nor too much.

There is a danger in discussing, in the abstract, the ideal qualities of a human being. Our very way of posing the question can lead us to forget the most significant truth about ourselves, that we are social animals. No individual person selects "autonomously" his own genetic inheritance or early upbringing. No individual person selects his country, his language, his social community and traditions. No individual invents afresh his tools, his technology, his public institutions and procedures. And yet to *be* a human being is to be a part of a community, to speak a language, to take one's place in an already functioning group way of life. We come into awareness of ourselves as part of ongoing social processes. Their fruits and instruments, precedents and records, wisdom and follies accumulate through the centuries and leave indelible marks on all the individuals who are a part of them. And all individuals *are* a part of these social histories. We can no more select our historical epoch than we can select the country of our birth and our native tongue.

How do these truisms affect our thinking about personal autonomy? Very clearly they place *limits* on what the constituent virtues of autonomy can be. The human world does not and cannot consist of millions of separate sovereign "islands" each exercising his own autonomous choice about what, where, how, and when he shall be, each capable of surviving and flourishing, if he so chooses, in total independence of all the others, each free of any *need* for the others. The danger for the philosopher who forgets for a moment these truisms is to overreact to the human flaws we call inauthenticity, conformism, other-determination, lack of integrity, lack of self-control, over-reliance on others, passive responsiveness, and the like, and assume that excellence consists in the states furthest from them on a common scale of measurement.

It is impossible to think of human beings except as part of ongoing communities, defined by reciprocal bonds of obligation, common traditions, and institutions. Any conception of ideal human virtue must be consistent with this presupposition. What liberals have always rightly deplored has been the effects on individual character of social manipulation, the condition in which individuality is swallowed up by the collective mass, and persons are interchangeable parts in an great organic machine. But philosophers are not forced to choose between totalitarian collectivism and atomic individualism. If that were so there would be no alternative to despair. Whatever their other ideological affinities, all social philosophers should attempt to describe the same ideal, that in which persons are integrated into communities rather than assimilated to social organisms or isolated in atomic units. The ideal of the autonomous person is that of an authentic individual whose self-determination is as complete as is consistent with the requirement that he is, of course, a member of a community.

5. Autonomy as right

The final sense of "autonomy," and the one to which we shall devote the whole of Chapter 19, is suggested by the language of international law in which autonomous nation-states are said to have the sovereign right of self-determination. It has become common in recent years, however, for "autonomy" and "sovereignty" to be distinguished in political discourse. Great Britain is a sovereign nation which under certain circumstances may be willing to grant more "local autonomy," but never full sovereignty, to its constituent parts, Wales and Scotland. Similarly, Egyptians and Israelis negotiate greater "autonomy" (or home rule) for the West Bank Palestinians. Sometimes the word used for the granting of limited "autonomy" is "devolution" in the sense of "the delegation of portions or details of duties to subordinate [local] officers or committees."[37] In any case, whatever the word used, the concept is sharply contrasted with that of full national sovereignty. If Scotland were to win sovereignty, it would become an entirely separate and independent nation.

Sovereignty and (mere) political autonomy seem to differ in at least two respects. First, autonomy is partial and limited, while sovereignty is whole and undivided. The autonomous region governs itself in some respects but not in others, whereas the sovereign state does not relinquish its right to govern entirely when it delegates autonomy. When the state grants home rule to a regional section, its own ultimate authority is not diminished, since in devolution sovereignty is not something given away in divisible parcels. (On the other hand, if the state intends to give away some of its sovereignty it has a sovereign right to do *that* too, as the United Kingdom did when it recognized the independence of India.)

A more important difference is that the authority of the sovereign state is a right, whereas the authority of the autonomous region is a revocable privilege. The sovereign grants autonomy freely at his pleasure and withdraws it at his will. Local autonomy is delegated; sovereignty is basic and underivative. Sovereignty is, in a sense, an ultimate source of authority.

If there is such a thing as "personal sovereignty," then presumably it belongs to all competent adults and to no newborn infants, but before the point of qualification for full sovereignty, children must be understood to have various degrees of "local autonomy." The analogy may be forced somewhat, though it does rest on some moral similarities. It becomes difficult, however, to think of the near-adult teenager as deriving *all* of his autonomy by parental delegation. A certain minimum, at least, he has by natural right, even if his privileges to use the family car, to stay out past midnight, and the like, are delegated and revocable. Because of the special sense assigned to the word "autonomy" in political discourse, I prefer to borrow the stronger term "sovereignty" for the fourth sense of "moral autonomy"; but where I do use the word "autonomy" in what follows I intend it simply to mean "personal sovereignty," not something analogous to the weaker kind of "local autonomy." Now we can proceed to examine carefully the analogy between sovereign nations and "sovereign persons."

Most theories of sovereignty are about the concept of sovereignty *in* the state rather than our concern, the sovereignty *of* the state. According to the theory deriving from Bodin and Hobbes and developed by Blackstone, Austin, and Dicey, there is (on some versions) or ought to be (on others) a determinate source of ultimate authority and/or power in every state—a monarch, council, legislature, or electorate. This sovereign person, or body of persons, is the "uncommanded commander" of society. It has become more and more difficult to apply this theory to modern states with their constitutional checks and balances, their universal electorates, and counterpoised social classes. But while the concept of the determinate internal sovereign has fallen out of favor, the concept of national sovereignty *vis a vis* external powers continues to be applied routinely in international forums. Sovereignty in this sense is what one nation "recognizes" in another when it acknowledges that the other is an independent nation, as opposed to an empty territory, or land occupied only by roving tribes without stable political institutions, or a regional segment or colony of another country.

Empty territory is not a state, but a political state is territory and more. The additional element is best expressed by the term "jurisdiction". A sovereign state is territory under a kind of unconditional and absolute jurisdiction. The assertion that "the state is sovereign," according to Bernard Crick, is "usually a tautology, just as the expression 'sovereign state' can be a pleonasm. For the concept of 'the state' came into use at about the same time as the concept of sovereignty, and it served the same purpose and had substantially the same meaning."[38] The state is the juridical entity that maintains sovereignty over a territory, no matter how its own internal lines of authority are organized, and sovereignty is the form of legal control a state exercises over its territory. Thus we mention "sovereignty" in the very definition of a state, and we mention "state" in the very definition of sovereignty.

Perhaps the concept of a "nation" can take us further toward an understanding of the conceptual complex "sovereign-state." Here we must proceed with caution for the word "nation" is treacherously vague. Sometimes it is still used interchangeably with "state"; "France" is the name of both a nation and a state. That is probably its original usage,[39] but it can now also be used to refer to the entity that can acquire its own state, and can be said to deserve to be a state even before it actually is one. We can refer to that second, and still obscure sense of "nation" as the "prepolitical" sense. In this sense a "nation" may exist before it acquires its own state, or after it loses it, or it may exist in numerous states, as talk of "the Arab nation" testifies. On the other hand, people of distinct ethnic, linguistic, and religious backgrounds can co-exist as citizens of the same nation because they use still other criteria to identify their fellow nationals. Such criteria include a common national self-image as the shared focus of their sentiment and loyalty, or an extended history of faithful support and collaboration.[40] Thus, "French, German, and Italian-speaking Swiss are simply three sorts of Swiss: their national image transcends or embraces linguistic differences, and it would be odd to make distinctions of nationality where they make none themselves."[41]

Where does a sovereign right of political independence come from: dispensations?, contracts?, conquests? There is no single obviously correct answer for a question this general. Suffice it to say, for our purposes, that apart from philosophical skeptics, nobody in practice seriously questions that Peru, for example, is a sovereign nation with the exclusive prerogative of governing its own territory, and the same is true of all the other established national states. That is just what a nation naturally is: a collection of individuals given a high degree of unity by common cultural elements who in fact occupy a territory over which they have established a system of law or authority. Nations need to become states if they are to survive and flourish as nations. And the phrase "sovereign state" is a redundancy.

If there is an analogous kind of personal sovereignty, where does *it* come from? one way of looking at individuals is to regard them, in a parallel way, as just naturally persons, so that the phrase "sovereign person" would also be a redundancy. In fact the word "person" has an ambiguity directly parallel to that of the word "nation." "Nation" can refer, as we have seen, either to a juridical entity, the state, or to a collection of individuals united by various kinds of cultural bonds into a cohesive group. Similarly, "person" can refer to the entity that is a proper subject of such moral predicates as "right" and "duty,"[42] or it can refer to the unity of a collection of diverse psychic elements—memories, loyalties, preferences, opinions—which puts on them all the stamp of a single self.[43] "One self" is the analogue of "one people"; it provides the sense of "person" analogous to the pre-political "nation." Indeed, most normal people have achieved a degree of personal integration far stronger than the social integration that unifies national groups. If anything, one would expect the case for a "natural" personal sovereignty to be even stronger than that for its political counterpart. The other sense of person ("an appropriate locus of rights and duties") is essentially juridical. It refers to a moral agent and possessor of rights, as "naturally sovereign" over itself as the state is over its territory; and just as some have argued that pre-political nations need to be (sovereign) states, so one might argue, do integrated individual selves *need* to be (juridical) persons. Whether the analogy can be fruitfully pursued further is the question to which we must now turn.

A word of caution, however, is required at this point. The system of nation-states has not always served the world well, as its sorry record of wars attests. The walls of national sovereignty may weaken and crumble as a sense of world community grows, nourished by increasing cultural homogeneity and spurred by a common dread of nuclear holocaust. The case for individual sovereignty conceived on the national model, however, as we have seen, may well be stronger than the partial analogy between persons and nations suggests, for where that analogy fails, the differences tend to strengthen rather than weaken the attribution of individual sovereignty. There are cases, and not merely hypothetical ones, in which a sovereign state chooses to exterminate a part of its own population, just as a sovereign person might choose to have one of his own limbs or organs removed. But the morally crucial difference between these cases is obvious. The "parts" of persons are themselves nonpersons: desires, values, purposes, organs, limbs. The "parts" of nations, however, are themselves persons with their own sovereign rights. A state may intervene in a neighboring state's internal affairs to protect the lives of sovereign persons threatened with extermination, but a second party may not interfere, in a parallel way, in a sovereign person's "internal affairs" to protect the "rights" of desires, organs, and the like, for the latter, being nonpersons, have no rights of their own. This is another example of a difference between nations and persons that strengthens the concept of personal sovereignty even as it weakens the concept of national sovereignty that served as its model. What I have been proposing here simply is that the individual be thought of in the terms in which *for better or worse* we have thought of nations in the past, even if we cease thinking of nations in that way in the future.[44]

19

Personal Sovereignty and its Boundaries

1. Domain boundaries

It must remain a matter for debate whether a concept of personal sovereignty like that sketched in the previous chapters has any proper application to individuals in the real world. I can only hope to show that the concept makes sense, that it stands ready for use as a tool of our moral judgments if we want it. I shall now attempt to render it more explicit while still preserving its fit with a familiar segment of our moral discourse in which something implicitly like it seems to be presupposed. In so doing, I shall be sketching as coherent a doctrine as I can of sovereign self-rule applied to individuals. Obviously, argumentative uses of the doctrine both in law and morals will be effective only to the degree that the doctrine itself is persuasive. Demonstration of the doctrine is not possible, but the reader may find that it resonates with something in his most fundamental moral attitudes—particularly some of the attitudes he holds toward himself.

Consider then once more our basic political analogy. In what ways might the autonomous individual be analogous to the autonomous state? The politically independent state is said to be sovereign over its own territory. Personal autonomy similarly involves the idea of having a domain or territory in which the self is sovereign. But whereas international conventions and treaties have long since defined the idea of "national territory" with some precision, the "boundaries" of the personal domain are entirely obscure and controversial. To be sure, even the territorial boundaries of nations are subject to some dispute and uncertainty, for example over how far up into the atmosphere they extend,[1] and how far offshore. But the concepts of political "sovereignty" and "territory" are clear enough to permit international lawyers and diplomats to work on such problems in nonarbitrary ways with every hope of success. In the case of personal autonomy, no attempt to adjudicate "boundary disputes" can even be made until agreement is reached on the conceptual question of what a "personal domain" is.

The easiest answer is the one that takes the territorial metaphor most seriously. A sovereign nation's territory is a geographical entity measured in miles or kilometers, and coordinates on maps. Perhaps the personal domain is also defined by its spatial dimensions. Perhaps it consists simply of a person's body. We do speak of an inviolate right which is infringed whenever another person inflicts a harmful or offensive contact on one's body without one's consent—an unwanted caress, a slap, a punch in the nose, a surgical operation, or even a threatening move that provokes the reasonable apprehension of such contacts. That must be part of what we mean by personal autonomy. After all, we speak of "bodily autonomy," and acknowledge its violation in cases of assault, battery, rape, and so on. But surely our total autonomy includes more than simply our bodily "territory," and even in respect to it, more is involved than simple immunity to uninvited contacts and invasions. Not only is my bodily autonomy violated by a surgical operation ("invasion") imposed on me against my will; it is also violated in some circumstances by the withholding of the physical treatment I request (when due allowance has been made for the personal autonomy of the parties of whom the request is made). For to say that I am sovereign over my bodily territory is to say that I, and I alone, decide (so long as I am capable of deciding) what goes on there. My authority is a discretionary competence, an authority to choose and make decisions.

If a man or woman voluntarily chooses to have a surgical operation that will render him or her infertile and a physician is perfectly willing to perform it, then the person's "bodily autonomy" is infringed if the state forbids it on some such ground as wickedness or imprudence. If no other interests are directly involved, the decision is the person's own and "nobody else's business," as we say, or "a matter between the person and his/her doctor only." To say that one's body is included in one's sovereign domain then, is to say more than that it cannot be treated in certain ways without one's consent. It is to say that one's consent is both necessary and sufficient for its rightful treatment in those ways. The concept of a discretionary competence implies both negative rights (e.g., the right *not* to have surgery imposed on oneself against one's will) and positive rights (e.g., the right to have surgery performed on oneself if one voluntarily chooses—and the surgeon is willing).

Still taking the territorial model seriously, we might enlarge our conception of the personal domain to include not only one's body (that is, one's right to decide by one's own choice insofar as that is possible what happens in and to one's body), but also a certain amount of "breathing space" around one's body, analogous perhaps to offshore fishing rights in the national model. You can violate my autonomy without actually touching my body, by entering and remaining, uninvited, in my personal space, or by transmitting into that space unwanted spectacles, sounds, or odors. My right to determine by my own choice what enters my field of experience is one of the various things meant by the "right of privacy," and so interpreted, that right is one of the elements of my personal autonomy. My personal space, however, diminishes to the vanishing point when I enter the public world. I cannot complain that my rights are violated by the hurlyburly, noise, and confusion of the busy public streets; I can always retrace my steps if the tumultuous crowds are too much for me. One difference, then, between personal and national "territory" is that the former but not the latter shrinks and expands with differing circumstances. After all, national territories are not in constant movement across the surface of the earth (except for the snail's pace of continental drift which hardly affects the point). Where one has one's domicile, however, and where one owns land, there one has space that is entirely one's own, where uninvited intruders (with certain necessary and well-understood exceptions) may not enter. Thus contractual possession and land ownership are also defined by discretionary rights and form a part, but by no means the whole, of our personal autonomy. On my land, apart from emergencies that bring the public interest sharply into play, and comparable rights of my landowning neighbors, I and I alone am the one who decides what is to happen.

Even discretionary control of body, privacy, and landed property together do not exhaust a plausible conception of personal autonomy. The kernel of the idea of autonomy is the right to make choices and decisions—what to put into my body, what contacts with my body to permit, where and how to move my body through public space, how to use my chattels and physical property, what personal information to disclose to others, what information to conceal, and more. Some of these rights are more basic and more plausibly treated as indispensable than others. Put compendiously, the most basic autonomy-right is the right to decide how one is to live one's life, in particular how to make the critical life-decisions—what courses of study to take, what skills and virtues to cultivate, what career to enter, whom or whether to marry, which church if any to join, whether to have children, and so on.

The first difficulty for a conception of a sovereign personal domain is the question of whether the imposing concept of "sovereignty" applies to the myriad options of lesser significance, the choice of whether or not to fasten a seat belt, for example, or whether to wear a red or green shirt while hunting. If we take the model of national sovereignty seriously, we cannot make certain kinds of compromises with paternalism. We cannot say for, example, that interference with the relatively trivial self-regarding choices involves only "minor forfeitures" of sovereignty whereas interference with the basic life-choices involves the virtual abandonment of sovereignty, for sovereignty is an all or nothing concept; one is entitled to absolute control of whatever is within one's domain however trivial it may be. In the political model, a nation's sovereignty is equally infringed by a single foreign fishing boat in its territorial waters as by a squadron of jet fighters flying over its capital city. Both are equally violations of sovereign rights, though the one, of course, is a more serious or important infringement than the other. If the offending nation respects the sovereignty of the other nation, it respects all of it, and will not think of *justifying* its infringement on the ground that the invasion of sovereignty was relatively trivial and counterbalanced by considerations of convenience or efficiency. Only a nation's own sovereignty (in the guise, say, of "self-defense") may ever be placed on the scales and weighed against another nation's acknowledged sovereignty, for sovereignty decisively out-weighs every other kind of reason for intervention.

If the liberal wishes to abandon his quarrels with the paternalist over statutes requiring seat belts, red shirts, and other trivial things, and build his wall against paternalism on more serious issues, he is well advised then not to say that the relatively trivial statutes are only minor invasions of autonomy, and that autonomy-infraction is a matter of degree suitable for the weighing scales. It would make better sense conceptually to draw the boundaries of personal sovereignty differently in the first place, so that they confer their absolute protection only on the critical life-decisions.

My personal domain then consists of my body, privacy, landed and chattel property, and at least the *vital* life-decisions, perhaps among other things, but where exactly are its "territorial boundaries" drawn? Each of our candidate liberty-limiting principles and their various combinations, when linked to a theory of personal autonomy, can provide its own account of domain boundaries. Actually, however, some of these candidate principles of coercion-legitimation seem implausible as accounts of domain boundaries simply because they draw the boundaries so tight that a person has very little "self-rule" at all. If, for example, the boundaries of my legitimate self-rule are determined by the combination of the principles of moralism and paternalism, rigorously interpreted, then I may make no life-decision that is objectively harmful to me or improper, as determined by standards which are independent of my own will, and which are interpreted and enforced independently of my own judgment. On this view, the criterion of what I may rightfully choose is what is independently right, not what I wish to do. Except for the realm of the prudentially and morally indifferent, then, I have no real choice at all, and if the standards of self-endangerment and moral propriety are strict, hardly any decision will be a matter of indifference.

The unsupplemented harm and offense principles suggest a natural starting place for the attempt to draw domain boundaries. According to those principles, we may locate within the personal domain all those decisions that are "self-regarding," that is which primarily and directly affect only the interests of the decision-maker. Outside the personal domain are all those decisions that are also other-regarding, that is which directly and in the first instance affect the interests or sensibilities of other persons. Clear examples of other-regarding choices are those that decide N.A.T.O.'s defense policies, or fix the public tax rate, or determine whom some *other* person shall marry, or choose whether to steal money from a careless merchant's till. Clear examples of wholly self-regarding decisions are less easy to come by because "No man is an island," and every decision is bound to have some "ripple-effect" on the interests of others. As John Stuart Mill pointed out,[2] however, a rough and serviceable distinction, at least, can be drawn between decisions that are plainly other-regarding (like the examples cited above) and those that are "directly," "chiefly," or "primarily" self-regarding. There will be a twilight area of cases that are difficult to classify, but that is true of many other workable distinctions, including that between night and day.

In an earlier work I commented favorably on Mill's contention that no one should be punished simply for being drunk but that a policeman should be punished for being drunk on duty. In contrast to Mill's policeman (or for that matter a drunken driver), I considered

> a hard working bachelor who habitually spends his evening hours drinking himself into a stupor, which he then sleeps off, rising fresh in the morning to put in another hard day's work. His drinking does not *directly* affect others in any of the ways of the drunk policeman's conduct. He has no family; he drinks alone and sets no direct example; he is not prevented from discharging any of his public duties; he creates no substantial risk of harm to the interests of other individuals. Although even his private conduct will have some effects on the interests of others, these are precisely the sorts of effects Mill would call "indirect" and "remote." First, in spending his evenings the way he does, our solitary tippler is *not* doing any number of other things that might be of greater utility to others. In not earning and spending more money, he is failing to stimulate the economy (except for the liquor industry) as much as he might. Second, he fails to spend his evening time improving his talents and making himself a better person . . . Third, he may make those of his colleagues who like him sad on his behalf. Finally, to those who know of his habits he is a "bad example."[3]

All of these indirect effects together are insufficient to warrant our locating the solitary tippling of the bachelor outside the boundaries of his sovereign domain. (Note how preposterous it would be for one nation to intervene forcibly in the internal affairs of another on the grounds that it is not sufficiently stimulating the world economy; it is not sufficiently improving its own culture; it makes other nations sad on its behalf; and it sets a bad example for "emergent nations"!)

What plausible alternative is there to using the distinction between self- and other-regarding decisions, such as it is, as a guide to mapping the boundaries of personal autonomy? Perhaps there is none, in which case we shall have to say that legal paternalists have no conception of their own of personal autonomy, rather than that they have a rival conception. In that case, insofar as we are committed to *some* intuitive notion of personal autonomy we must reject legal paternalism, or at least hold it under grave suspicion ("presumptively false"). If, on the other hand, legal paternalism has its own notion of personal autonomy, its associated domain-boundaries must be defined not by a person's primarily self-regarding choices, but rather by his own true interests or real good.

2. One's right versus one's good

Perhaps the fairest way of putting the presumptive case against legal paternalism is to say that even when conjoined with other principles, it has at best a very limited conception of personal autonomy. Even though it is consistent with the recognition of a person's right of self-determination, it subordinates that *right* to the person's own *good*.

The concept of a person's "own good" is analytically linked to the concept of his personal interest, but interests may vary considerably among persons so that there is no one conception of a personal good that applies to everyone. Nevertheless, most philosophers have been sympathetic to the idea of "natural interests" that grow out of our inherited constitutions as human beings, and which can be characterized sufficiently abstractly to accommodate individual differences. A majority view, associated with the writings of Plato, Aristotle, Rousseau, Hegel, and Mill, among others, identifies a person's good ultimately with his *self-fulfillment*—a notion that is certainly not identical with that of autonomy or the right of self-determination. Self-fulfillment is variously interpreted, but it is usually understood to require the development of one's chief aptitudes into genuine talents in a life that gives them scope, the unfolding of all basic tendencies and inclinations, both those that are common to the species and those that are peculiar to the individual, and the active realization of the universal human propensities to plan, design, and make order. Self-fulfillment, so construed, is not the same as achievement and not to be confused with pleasure or contentment, though achievement is often highly fulfilling, and fulfillment is usually highly gratifying. Other conceptions of a person's own good identify it with achievement, or contentment, or happiness (in the sense of predominant pleasantness or conscious satisfaction). On all these accounts one's good is conceptually distinct from one's right of self-government.[4]

No one would deny, however (not even the convinced legal paternalist), that a person's good and the exercise of his autonomous right are closely related, at least instrumentally. If one holds that the good is self-fulfillment and, like Mill, that development of the basic human faculties of choice and reasoned decision are components of self-fulfillment, then one must embrace the conclusion that the right to the unhampered exercise of choice is an indispensable *means* to one's own good.[5] Moreover, if one holds, also like Mill, that in the majority of cases an individual knows better than any outsider can what is good for him,[6] then it follows that allowing individuals, whenever possible, to choose for themselves, even to choose risky courses, is the policy most likely to promote their personal fulfillment, even though in some cases individuals may predictably exercise their autonomous choice unwisely.

There are only four standard ways of treating the relation between personal autonomy and personal good. The first of these is especially attractive to the paternalist, namely to derive the right of self-determination *entirely* from its conducibility to a person's own good (usually conceived as self-fulfillment). That right then is not a *sovereign* right, not ultimate, basic, or "natural," but entirely derivative and instrumental. On this view we may exercise a right to self-determination only because, and only insofar as, it promotes our good to do so. Nevertheless, an instrumental conception of the right of self-government, if strong enough, will differ only in rare instances, when applied to particular cases, from a conception of that right as basic and sovereign. John Stuart Mill's *On Liberty* is an instructive case in point. Mill made such a strong case for the instrumental utility of self-determination that he was able to fool both himself and his critics into thinking that he was an unremitting foe of legal paternalism. (See the discussion in §5 below of Mill's rejection of slavery contracts.) Mill insists that a given normal adult is much more likely to know his own interest, talents, and natural dispositions (in the fulfillment of which consists his good) than is any other party, and is much more capable therefore of directing his own affairs to the end of his own good than is a government official or a legislator. The individual's advantages in this regard seem so great that for most practical purposes we could hold that recognition and enforcement of the right of self-determination is a causally necessary condition for the achievement of the individual's own good. Thus, Mill argued in *On Liberty* that the attempt even of a genuinely benevolent state to impose upon an adult an external conception of his own good is almost certain to be self-defeating, and that an adult's own good is "best provided for by allowing him to take his own means of pursuing it."[7]

It is logically open to Mill to argue (as he sometimes seems ready to) that the relation between a person's right of self-determination and his good of self-fulfillment is not merely a strong instrumental connection but an invariant correspondence. On this second view, whatever harm a person might do to "his own good" by foolishly exercising his free choice would in every case necessarily be outweighed by the greater harm done by outside interference and direction. This is the position that would enable Mill to maintain his utilitarian commitment to the reduction of harms and his exceptionless opposition to paternalism *both*, so it must have had some appeal to him. Moreover, he has shown impressively that there is always and necessarily a cost to a person whenever outside judgment is forcibly substituted for his own choice, and that in an overwhelming preponderance of cases the intervention will be self-defeating, but he has not and could not show that necessarily in *every* case the cost will be greater than the harm prevented and that the intervention will defeat its own purpose. For the most part, therefore, Mill seems prepared to acknowledge that the correspondence between self-direction and self-fulfillment is contingent and subject to infrequent exceptions (the first view). In those rare cases where we can *know* that free exercise of a person's autonomy will be against his own interest, as for example when he freely negotiates his own slavery in exchange for some other good, there, Mill concedes, we are justified in interfering with his liberty in order to protect him from extreme harm. At that point, Mill is finally ready to admit paternalistic reasons into his (otherwise) liberal scheme of justification.

A third standard interpretation of the right of self-determination holds that it is entirely *underivative*, as morally basic as the good of self-fulfillment itself. There is no necessity, on this view, that free exercise of a person's autonomy will promote his own good, and even where self-determination is likely, on objective evidence, to lead to the person's own harm, others do not have a right to intervene coercively "for his own good." By and large, a person will be better able to achieve his own good by making his own decisions, but even when the opposite is true, others may not intervene, for autonomy is even more important than personal well-being. The life that a person threatens by his own rashness is after all *his* life; it *belongs* to him and to no one else. For that reason alone, he must be the one to decide—for better or worse—what is to be done with it in that private realm where the interests of others are not directly involved.[8] This is the interpretation that follows from a pure conception of individual sovereign autonomy, and anyone who holds such a conception, tacitly or explicitly, can find no appeal in—indeed is logically precluded from embracing—legal paternalism.

A fourth way of regarding the adult's right of autonomy proposes a compromise. It thinks of autonomy as neither derivative from nor more basic than its possessor's own good (self-fulfillment), but rather as coordinate with it. In the more plausible versions of this view,[9] a person's own good in the vast majority of cases will be most reliably furthered if he is allowed to make his own choices in self-regarding matters, but when self-interest and self-determination do not coincide, one must simply do one's best to balance autonomy against personal well-being, and decide between them intuitively, since neither has automatic priority over the other. This compromise, of course, will not satisfy the liberal adherent of personal sovereignty since it restricts individual authority to some degree even in the wholly self-regarding domain; but it is consistent with a kind of legal paternalism as we have defined it, for its proponent can concede that paternalistic considerations, where they apply, are always relevant as reasons of some weight, even when they conflict with reasons of other kinds and may not be decisive. This modestly paternalistic theory allows room for personal autonomy but does not conceive of it on the model of territorial sovereignty, since it permits it to be balanced against other considerations, and thereby deprives it of its trumping effect.

In summary, once one has distinguished the personal right of self-determination from "one's personal good" (self-fulfillment or other), one might hold them to be related in any of the following ways:

1. They always and necessarily correspond, so that the best way to promote a person's own good is to permit him the unhampered exercise of his "moral muscles" in purely self-regarding matters, and thereby also exploit his presumably much greater reliability in judging his own interest. If "necessity" is too strong a conception of the correspondence, one might weaken this account and render it more plausible by contending that the correspondence, while contingent and subject in principle to exceptions, is in fact so close to being invariant, that it would be good public policy to conclusively presume it to be so. In that manner errors of judgment about other people's "true self-interest" would be minimized if not eliminated. (This is a mode of argument open to Mill to which he sometimes seems tempted.) Thus, even though there is no underivative sovereign right of self-determination, practically speaking it is just as if there were. The right to the exclusive government of oneself in the self-regarding realm is derived from its conducibility to one's own good, but even though this instrumental connection is merely empirical, it should be treated as exceptionless, and therefore, in its practical effects, no different from a sovereign right.

2. They usually correspond, but in those rare cases when they do not, a person's good has priority even over his right of self-determination. That right therefore is neither "sovereign" nor exceptionless. It is entirely derived from its general conducibility to its possessor's own good, so in cases where it conflicts with that good, clearly it has no force. A person does not have a right to "go to hell on his own" if others can prevent it. Mill

also seems to argue in *this* way in places (notably in his discussion of voluntary slavery), but probably the best interpretation of his considered view is one of the more consistently anti-paternalistic ones [(1) or (3) below].[10]

3. They usually correspond, but in those rare cases when they do not, a person's right of self-determination, being sovereign, takes precedence even over his own good. Interference in these cases is justified only when necessary to determine whether his choice is voluntary, hence truly his, or to protect him from choices that are not truly his; but interference with his informed and genuine choices is not justified to protect him from unwisely incurred or risked harms. He has a sovereign right to choose in a manner we think, plausibly enough, to be foolish, provided only that the choices are truly voluntary. We have called this approach "the soft paternalist strategy."[11]

4. They usually correspond, but in those rare cases when they do not, we must balance the person's right against his good and weigh them intuitively. This is hard enough to do in individual cases; it may raise even more difficult problems for the legislator who must reason intuitively about whole classes of cases. If the legislator must decide, for example, whether to vote for a bill requiring drivers to buckle their seat belts on pain of penalty, he must balance against one another such considerations as the magnitude of harm prevented, on the one hand, and the degree to which the motorist's liberty is restricted, on the other, and generalize over the whole diverse class of motorists. (We have called this "the balancing strategy."[12]) Strictly speaking, this is a form of hard legal paternalism, since it accepts as a relevant reason for a criminal prohibition the defense of persons from their own voluntary choices, but unlike the still harder paternalism presupposed in (2) above, it does not make that reason decisive in *every* conflict with a person's self-determination. Still, neither this view nor (2) has a place for a genuinely sovereign right of self-government in the self-regarding realm.

Of the four positions, (1) and (3) are opposed to (hard) legal paternalism, whereas (2) and (4) support that principle, (2) more strongly than (4). As between the anti-paternalist positions (1) and (3), only (3) is consistent with an underivative sovereign right of self-determination, which I count, somewhat sanguinely, as an advantage. Moreover, in its strongest version (the necessary correspondence thesis) (1) is empirically implausible, and in its weaker version, in which the presumption of correspondence is justified on practical grounds, there may be problems of justice when the presumption fails to hold in fact. I cannot conceal my own preference for position (3). As the only view consistent with a conception of personal sovereignty, it accords uniquely with a self-conception deeply imbedded in the moral attitudes of most people and apparently presupposed in many of our moral idioms, especially when used self-defensively ("my life to live as I please," "no one else's business," etc.)

When the exercise of a person's sovereign right conflicts with what is truly good for him (those "rare cases"), (3) defends the choice nevertheless. If that seems an absurd result, the reader should put himself in the position of the person interfered with. Presumably, if he genuinely chose the alternative that is in fact bad for him, he did not choose it because *he* believed it was bad for him. That would be so irrational that it would put the voluntariness of his choice in doubt, and as we shall see, the soft-paternalistic strategy might then be used to justify interference on liberal grounds. If he chose that alternative because *he* believed it good (or at least not bad) for himself, then either the difference between him and his would-be constrainers is over some matter of fact about which he is simply mistaken, in which case he would welcome being set right, or it is about the nature of his self-interest, or the reasonableness, given his values, of the risks he wishes to assume. In that case, the disagreement would be more intractable, and the reader would not welcome having his own judgment overruled, or the "better values" of others substituted for his own.

There is still another possibility. The person may have chosen to act as he did *despite* believing the consequences would be bad for his self-interest. Perhaps he wishes to sacrifice "his own good," or some part of it, for the sake of others, or for some treasured cause; or perhaps he deliberately values short-term good over his future good in the long run. Identifying with the person in one of those cases, does the reader genuinely prefer "suppression for his own good" over facilitation of his own fully informed choice? If not, how then can he have a different preference for others? Even in the cases where the person subsequently regrets his choice, he may not regret that he had not been forcibly prevented from making it. There must be a right to err, to be mistaken, to decide foolishly, to take big risks, if there is to be any meaningful self-rule; without it, the whole idea of *de jure* autonomy begins to unravel.

3. Autonomy contrasted with liberty and de facto freedom

A particularly perplexing form of the conflict between one's sovereign right and one's own good is that which arises when a person exercises his sovereignty to alienate some of his own liberty at some future time. Does one's future liberty lie beyond the boundaries of one's sovereignty so that others may interfere with present choices for its protection? Discussions of this question from Mill to the present have been marred by a failure to distinguish with consistent clarity between *de jure* autonomy (or sovereignty) and *de facto* liberty (freedom). For that reason, we shall linger over that conceptual distinction before applying it to the substantive question about domain boundaries.

Both "liberty" and "autonomy" have *de jure* as well as *de facto* senses. The *de jure* sense of "liberty" is the juridical notion of a "permission," "license," or "privilege" allowed by some rule or authority. It corresponds to one of the senses of a "right," that in which "a right to do X" is equivalent in meaning to "the absence of a duty not to do X." The word "liberty," even though largely interchangeable in legal contexts with forms of the word "freedom" ("a liberty" equals "a freedom," though we do not speak of "having a freedom," and "at liberty to" equals "free to," though we do not speak of "at freedom to"), seems more at home in those contexts, where it has long been a technical term linked in various ways to terms like "right" and "duty," than does the word "freedom." Outside of rule-governed contexts, however, "liberty" and "freedom" are *not* interchangeable, for "freedom" refers to the *de facto* absence of effective constraints to actual or possible choices, whereas "liberty" more typically refers only to the absense of rule-imposed (or authority-imposed) duties. When the rules imposing duties are not effectively enforced, for example, one might enjoy *de facto* freedom to act in the forbidden ways, in which case one is free (*de facto*) to do that which one is not at liberty (*de jure*) to do. Conversely we may be at liberty (*de jure*) to do what we are not free (*de facto*) to do when circumstances other than enforced rules prevent us from doing what we are legally permitted to do, as when A and B are both at liberty to possess an unclaimed ten dollar bill they see on the street, but B, being better situated and quicker of foot, gets to it first, thus preventing A from doing what he was at liberty to do. Thus there are circumstances both in which one *can* do what one *may not* do, and in which one *may* do what one *cannot* do.

When the direct or indirect sources of the inability to act are the acts or policies of other people, as opposed to such impersonal factors as disease, ignorance, lack of physical strength, laws of nature, acts of God, and the like, we speak of one's lack of *freedom* to do what one cannot do.[13] A special case then of the lack of *de facto* freedom is that in which the law leaves one not at liberty to do something, and the "other people" who effectively prevent one from doing the forbidden thing are legislators, policemen, and public officials. We could coin the term "*de facto* liberty" for the freedom that is restricted by such legal arrangements, as opposed to the "*de facto* freedom" that is nullified by other sorts of people and other sorts of constraints. Then we can treat "*de facto* liberty" as one kind of *de facto* freedom, namely that which Isaiah Berlin calls "political freedom."[14] Since the language of freedom is more comprehensive than that of "*de facto* liberty," in that it includes the latter as a special case, an adequate analysis of freedom will apply to it too, with appropriate modifications.

I have already sketched such an analysis in Vol. 1, Chap. 5, §7. We can now make that analysis perfectly general by distinguishing freedom of action (including *de facto* liberty, or political freedom) from freedom of choice (or free will), and adding a brief analysis of the latter to supplement the analysis already given of the former. The extent of our freedom of action is determined not by any of our own characteristics or powers. Rather it is entirely a function of the circumstances we find ourselves in. Insofar as those circumstances contain open options (unlocked switches in our railroad metaphor), just to that extent do we have freedom of action. A person has an "open option" in respect to some possible action, *X*, when nothing in his objective circumstances prevents him from doing *X* if he should choose, and nothing in his objective circumstances requires him to do *X* if he should choose not to. What he wants to do, what he actually chooses to do, what he believes his options to be, how aware he is of his circumstances, are all quite irrelevant to the question of what options he actually has, just as they are irrelevant to the question of what the temperature of the surrounding air is. What options are open to him is entirely a function of the existence and location of external barriers and obstacles. (And if it is specifically *political* freedom we are talking about, it is wholly a matter of the existence and location of specifically political or legal barriers.) Freedom of action then is understood the way the "unsophisticated person" in Schopenhauer's account understands it: "I can do what I will. If I will to go to the left, I go to the left; if I will to go to the right, I go to the right. This depends entirely on my will; therefore, I am free."[15]

Schopenhauer, however, quickly raises another question: I can (sometimes) do what I will, but when if ever am I free to will otherwise? What does it mean to be free of interference to *choose* as I wish? The alcoholic, for example, may have an intense desire to choose not to have another drink, but when his host returns with the bottle, he finds himself, to his despair, choosing contrary to his own wishes. Such a person may have freedom of action (for whatever that is worth), including political liberty (the law neither required nor prohibited another drink), but he lacked freedom of choice (free will).[16] He was free to act as he chose, but not free to choose as he wished. He suffered from no lack of opportunity to abstain, but he succumbed anyway, because of impaired psychological capacities.[17] His option to choose was closed even though his option to act was open. It is as if there were a network of railroad tracks within each person's psyche with switches open to some possible choices and locked closed to others. Our freedom of choice on balance is a function of the number and fecundity of such options left open, including options we would never wish to exercise (Diagram 19-1).

De facto autonomy:	The actual condition of self-government
De jure autonomy:	The sovereign right of self-government
De jure liberty:	The juridical notion of a privilege allowed by some rule or authority. The absence of rule-imposed (or authority-imposed) duties.
De facto freedom of action:	The absence of effective constraints from any external personal source to actual or possible choices to act. (The presence of open act-options.)
De facto freedom of choice:	The absence of effective constraints from any internal source to actual or possible desires to choose to act. (The presence of open choice-options.)
De facto political freedom ("*De facto* liberty"):	One subcategory of *de facto* freedom of action, namely the absence of effective constraints from political authorities enforcing legal rules or commands.

Diagram 19-1. *De facto* and *de jure* senses of autonomy, liberty, and freedom.

So construed, freedom is an important good in human life. We have seen (Vol. 1, Chap. 5, §7) that most people have a welfare interest in maintaining an essential minimum of freedom, and a security interest in having more open options still, and that some people even have a kind of "accumulative interest" in enjoying as much freedom as possible, "well beyond necessity or security." Minimal liberty is an essential good for most of us, much like economic sufficiency or health.[18] Greater amounts of freedom are for many of us goods to be treasured like art objects, natural beauty, adventure, achievement, power, or love. But it is very important to recognize that freedom is one kind of good among many, that people have been known to get along well with very little of it, that rational persons are often willing to "trade" large amounts of it for goods of other kinds, including simple contentment, that philosophers have proclaimed the "dreadfulness" of the burden of too much of it, and that sometimes the "price" of an increment of freedom, as measured in other goods, is a bad bargain. The *de jure* autonomous person will surely reserve the right to "trade off" his *de facto* freedoms for goods of other kinds, as measured on his own scale of values and determined by his own judgment.

There is no paradox then when a morally autonomous person exercises his sovereign right of self-government to diminish his own *de facto* freedom of action. Provided only that his consent be free and informed, he might even submit to manipulative treatments designed to close some of his options to *choose*. It will be instructive to examine how those treatments, often called "behavior control," sometimes are, and sometimes are not, consistent with *de jure* autonomy. These manipulative techniques can be employed either to close or to open a person's options to choose, either with or without his consent. Each of the four combinations has its own effect on freedom, and its own reflection on *de jure* autonomy.[19]

When manipulation is used to open a person's options with his voluntary consent, there is an enlargement of freedom and no violation of autonomy; hence, this is the least troublesome category. For example, suppose a person so suffers from claustrophobia that he cannot bring himself to enter any small confined place, not even the closet where his guests have left their coats. Suppose a therapist proposes a series of treatments designed gradually to increase his tolerance through conditioning and hypnosis. The patient consents to the treatments, fully understanding the theories on which they are based and the risks they might involve. As a consequence his phobia is destroyed and he now has one kind of option he did not have before, namely to choose to enter or not to enter confined places as he pleases. Indirectly, many other options are also opened up. It is now open to him, for example, to enter elevators, to work in photographic darkrooms, or to become a cloakroom attendant.

Another patient might consent in a fully voluntary way to manipulative behavior control designed to close one of his options and thereby open up many others. An alcoholic, for example, may voluntarily take a drug that will make him violently ill if he ingests as little as a half ounce of alcohol in a two-week period, thus effectively shutting off his option to accept drinks. As a consequence, many other options far more valuable to him are now opened, and he can function in the world once more. He was "manipulated into his freedom," to be sure, but his own consent to the treatment made him a party to it, so that it became a form of self-manipulation as morally innocuous as setting an alarm clock before retiring and the many other "tricks" free persons play on themselves.

In other cases, persons freely consent to manipulative treatment designed to close some of their options when there is either a certainty or a high risk that this loss of freedom will *not* be compensated by a greater gain in freedom on balance. A person who suffers from uncontrollable rages or chronic suicidal depression may elect to undergo psychosurgery knowing full well that the technique is inexact and may not have its intended effects, and also that there is a substantial risk that the treatment will restore him to tranquillity at the cost of his becoming a docile vegetable, unable to initiate any projects or enterprises of his own. The risks may seem reasonable to him and unreasonable to those with authority over him, or he might actually have a considered preference for vegetative docility over his present intolerable condition, a preference that seems reasonable to him but unreasonable to those who have authority over him. The question these cases pose for social policy is a troublesome one: should such persons be permitted to consent to treatment that is likely to diminish their freedom by restricting their future options irrevocably, for the sake of a good that they have come to value more than their freedom? On the assumption that consent can be fully voluntary in such circumstances, it would be to respect an individual's own choice to permit him his dangerous manipulative treatment, and it would violate his autonomy to deny it for what we take to be his "own good." An autonomous being has the right to make even unreasonable decisions determining his own lot in life, provided only that his decisions are genuinely voluntary (hence truly his own), and do not injure or limit the freedom of others.

The most odious kind of case is the manipulation of a person without his consent (even without his knowledge) in order to close many of his options to choose as he pleases in the future. Patients or prisoners (the two are easily confused in totalitarian countries) can be drugged, put under total anesthesia, and then made to undergo lobotomies or other kinds of surgical manipulation or mutilation of the brain. Psychotropic drugs used in small quantities and electric stimulation of the brain for short periods have less severe effects and are revocable, but when imposed on a person without his consent or, worse, without his knowledge, they are hardly distinguishable on moral grounds from assault and battery. The moral status of the situation is not affected by the motives of the controller. Whether he be kindly and benevolent or malicious and cynical, the effect of his actions is drastically to diminish freedom of choice *and* to violate personal autonomy. The case is complicated morally, however, when the patient, having lost his competence to govern himself and his capacity, therefore, to grant his voluntary consent, has no autonomy left to violate. In such cases, a person can be made no worse in respect to freedom and autonomy than he already is, and behavior control may reduce his pain and anxiety and promote the convenience of those who must govern him. Respect for personal autonomy, however, requires that the benefit of every doubt be given to the patient, that every effort be made to improve his lot without irrevocably destroying his capacity to govern himself.

The final kind of case is perhaps the most troublesome. That is when manipulative techniques are used to open a person's options and thus increase his freedom on balance, but without his consent. Here indeed a person is "manipulated into freedom," not with his own connivance, but without his knowledge, and perhaps even against his will. Being involuntarily suffered, such treatment is necessarily a violation of a person's right to be his own master and to make the choices himself that vitally affect his future. It therefore abridges his autonomy while expanding his freedom (by opening options). When interests of third parties are not involved, every person's moral right to govern himself surely outweighs the "right" of benevolent intermeddlers to manipulate him for his own advantage, whether that advantage be health, wealth, contentment, or freedom. If there is such a thing as personal sovereignty, even the subsequent increase in a person's freedom is no reason for invading his domain without his consent. One's own freedom or liberty cannot, any more than any other good of one's own, override *de jure* autonomy.

4. Autonomous forfeitures of liberty and autonomy itself

Given the contrast between *de facto* freedom and *de jure* autonomy (personal sovereignty), it is not incoherent to speak of an autonomous forfeiture either of the good of freedom or the right of self-government itself. Not only can such forfeitures occur; they are beyond the legitimate powers of others to prevent, provided that they are voluntary, and that personal sovereignty covers a domain whose boundaries are drawn in accordance with the self-and-other-regarding criterion. If we assume with John Stuart Mill (excluding his occasional lapses) and the grand liberal tradition that the domain of the sovereign individual consists of all his activities that do not seriously impinge on the important interests of other people, then we can say that *respect for a person's autonomy is respect for his unfettered voluntary choice as the sole rightful determinant of his actions except where the interests of others need protection from him.* Whenever a person is compelled to act or not to act on the grounds that he must be protected from his own bad judgment even though no one else is endangered, then his autonomy is infringed. From the moral point of view, this is just as if one sovereign state invaded the air space or offshore fishing waters of another, or sent armies to occupy a part of its land, or otherwise violated its sovereignty. Whether an autonomous person's liberty is interfered with in the name of his own good or welfare, his health, his wealth, or even *his future open options*—which are themselves constituents of his well-being—it is still a violation of his personal sovereignty. After all, sovereign political states do not claim the right to impose their benevolent interventions on other sovereign states; how then can autonomous individuals coerce other autonomous individuals into conduct deemed conducive to their own long-range good?

The point applies just as much to coercion of another that is intended to increase his *de facto* freedom (open options) as it does to compulsions and prohibitions intended to promote any other element of a person's will-being. It is of course the right and the duty of a parent forcibly to prevent a small child from harming his own future interests, even without the child's consent. It is a duty of parents to keep as many as possible of a child's central life-options open until the child becomes an autonomous adult himself, and can decide on his own how to exercise them.[20] But it is paternalism in an objectionable sense forcibly to prevent an autonomous adult from voluntarily trading some of his own "open options" for preferred benefits of another kind. A rational adult could have very good reasons for giving away all of his worldly goods, or even terminating his own life, or in the most extreme hypothetical case, even for selling himself into slavery, and thus perhaps irrevocably closing his most fecund options. And even if we do not think much of his reasons, we may have to concede that he is making a perfectly genuine voluntary choice of his own, albeit an unreasonable one by our standards. Though such a choice might seem unreasonable to us, or might be one that we could never make, it need not be an insane or nonresponsible choice. In some cases we might better think of it as saintly, heroic, courageous, adventurous, romantic, or just plain odd. In any case, if the chooser is an autonomous adult deciding voluntarily, the choice must be his to make and not ours, and the responsibility too is his to take. That is what follows from our description of him as an autonomous person with sovereign control over his own domain. A perfectly autonomous person would have in Mill's words the *"power of voluntarily disposing of his own lot in life,"*[21] even if that involved forfeiting his *de facto* freedom in the future.

The point applies equally to voluntary refusals to increase one's own freedom. If we hold fast to our distinction between one's balance of *de facto* freedom construed in terms of the number and fecundity of the options actually open to a person, on the one hand, and personal autonomy interpreted as the sovereign right to decide within one's own proper domain, on the other, we can make sense out of Rousseau's infamous phrase "forced to be free" (though probably not the sense Rousseau intended).[22] But though that notion be intelligible and coherent, no advocate of personal sovereignty can rest content with efforts to justify invasions of autonomy by citing the increase in *de facto* freedom thereby brought about. It *is* possible to have the area of one's freedom to act enlarged by force, and when this happens, some of one's options are closed by a violent or coercive act that at the same time causes many more options, or options of greater fecundity, to open. Thus a person might be dragged struggling and kicking over the border from a cruel police state into a liberal democracy. He may have resisted out of mere habit, or family loyalty, or because he genuinely preferred tyranny to freedom. Not everyone appreciates having open options and the difficult burden of having always to choose for oneself what one shall do. But whatever a person's motives for resisting the expansion of his options, the condition so described is one of greater freedom of action. It is important to note, however—and this has been my primary thesis thus far—that benign as our motives might be, insofar as we force a person against his will into a condition he did not choose, we undermine his status as a person in rightful control of his own life. We may be right when we tell him that greater freedom of action is for his own good in the long run, but we nevertheless violate his autonomy if we force our better conception of his own good upon him.

Does a person act within the proper boundaries of his personal sovereignty when he voluntarily forfeits *de jure* autonomy itself? As we have seen, (*supra* Chap. 18,§5) there is neither conceptual nor (necessarily) moral difficulty when a political state renounces some part of its sovereignty. Imperial powers forfeit their right to rule over colonies, and federal states grant full independence to locally autonomous regions. It is very difficult to think of an analogous way in which a person could renounce "a part" of his sovereignty, unless we think perhaps of a master relinquishing his claim to "rule" over a slave through an act of manumission, or in a more farfetched example still, an organ-donor forfeiting his "sovereignty over" a kidney, or another "region-ally autonomous part." It is easier to think of individuals renouncing *total* sovereignty, and simply "going out of business" as independent persons, much as a state might decide through some legitimate parliamentary body to dissolve itself.

Consider then the hypothetical example of a sovereign national state volun-tarily relinquishing its own autonomy. If the Canadian Parliament, following its own constitutional rules, voted unanimously to accept an American invita-tion to become the fifty-first state, but was then prevented from doing so by threats of military intervention by the Soviet Union, boycott by the British Commonwealth, and condemnation by the United Nations, Canada might well claim that its autonomy had been violated by the coercion that pre-vented it from implementing its own sovereign will. It might charge that coercion had prevented it from "voluntarily disposing of its own lot in the future," no less an infringement of present sovereignty for being a protection of future independence. Such a claim, I think, would be both coherent, and in this political case at least, well-founded.

What this example shows is that the idea of sovereign renunciation of sovereignty is a coherent one in the political arena where the concept of sovereignty has its original home. It is neither unstable, contradictory, nor paradoxical. If we transfer the whole concept of sovereignty from the nation to the person, then we should expect the same implications for the personal forfeiture of autonomy. Of course, it is open to one to deny that the idea of sovereignty applies to persons in the first place, but if one is friendly to that notion, one must face up to its implications.

5. Total and irrevocable forfeiture: the riddle of voluntary slavery

What would a total and irrevocable forfeiture of freedom or autonomy look like? The example that has most frequently come to the minds of philosophers is a rather extreme form of the institution of chattel slavery in which slaveholders "own" their slaves in the way they own tables and chairs, cows and horses. The owners have exclusive and permanent proprietary rights over the slaves, who in turn have no enforcible rights against their masters.[23] The point of the practice is to provide inexpensive labor for the owner; the slave has the dubious advantage of assured (but not contracted) sustenance and the "security" of life tenure. The latter advantages have almost always been insufficient to induce people to become slaves voluntarily. Rather slaves are captured in war, or forcibly abducted, or treacherously lured from their prior condition of freedom, and kept in their servitude by stern and, if necessary, violent measures. If nevertheless, untypically, two persons signed an agreement whereby one would become the permanent slave of the other, that compact, as Mill reminds us, "in this and most other civilized countries . . . would be null and void, neither enforced by law nor by opinion."[24] The question raised by this bizarre example is on what grounds this universal nullification rests. If the only reasons that seem always available are those provided by legal paternalism, then the liberal must either allow, at least in this one extreme case, that paternalistic reasons may be morally valid grounds for legal policies, or else he must deny that the firm policy against "voluntary slavery" is morally well-founded.

There is, of course, a strange artificiality in the example. In the first place, it is not an example of a direct criminal prohibition. Entering into a slavery contract is not in this and other civilized countries the name of a *crime*. The state simply refuses to offer, as a kind of service, a mechanism for creating legal obligations of the appropriate kind, just as it refuses to provide the legal mechanism for producing homosexual or bigamous marriages. Homosexual couples and bigamous trios might complain that their *liberty* is infringed thereby, but such a complaint would not be convincing. A legal disability consequent on the state's failure to produce a service (or confer a "legal power") is not the same as a legal duty to desist enforced by the threat of punishment for disobedience. How can one "disobey" the nonpossession of a legal power? Furthermore, as John Hodson points out, "the law's refusal to enforce slavery contracts does not prevent anyone from living in *de facto* slavery,"[25] just as, I might add, the law's failure to provide legal devices that enable two people of the same sex, or two people of one sex and one of the other, to be legal spouses, does not prevent people in these combinations from cohabiting on intimate terms. If the parties to these *de facto* arrangements wish, in addition, to bind themselves morally to one another, there is no force to stop them.

The law's refusal to recognize slavery contracts does have indirect consequences, however, for the criminal law. If a third party "liberates" the slave by abducting him, that would be a crime against the slaveholder's property analogous to theft. Moreover, if the owner has the slave's legally effective consent, in advance, to anything he might do—a kind of irrevocable blank check, so to speak—then the owner has a legal privilege to mistreat the slave in ways that would otherwise be crimes. By not recognizing the slavery contract as valid, the law thereby undermines the slaveholder's defense to charges of false imprisonment (if he should lock the slave in his quarters), assault and battery (if he should use corporal punishment on the slave), or murder (if he should destroy his "property"). On the other hand, if the slavery arrangements were merely *de facto*, then there would be legally enforcible limits on what the owner could do to the slave with or without the slave's prior blanket consent. That would constitute a limit on the slaveholder's liberty, but not an *additional* restriction, so he has not been deprived of a liberty he formerly had.

Would the refusal to legally recognize the contract interfere with the *slave's* liberty? Hodson says no, on the ground that the slave may still subject himself to the will of his master "in all the ways associated with slavery; he may act only on the command or with the permission of another and his life may be devoted to doing the bidding of this other person,"[26] even though the arrangement is only *de facto*. Only those actions of the master that are crimes are actions the slave is not free to submit to (in the sense that the master is not at liberty to perform them). But then the master would have no reason to punish, incarcerate, or destroy the other person if the other is his wholly willing slave in any case. The only point in ever doing these things would be to exercise sheer wanton cruelty—sadism, if you will, so it would seem that in failing to recognize the slavery contract, the state restricts only the sadomasochistic options of the would-be slave. But these were options closed to the person before he even entered *de facto* slavery, so the state has not deprived him of liberties he once had. The only new liberty *contractual* slavery would confer on him would be the liberty to be locked up, beaten or killed, pointlessly and wantonly, when or if his master so chooses. His own "choice" in advance to submit to those kinds of treatment would be of suspect voluntariness, unless of course he "genuinely loved Big Brother" and wanted nothing more than faithful prostration before his omnipotent will.

Mill took the problem to be one of protecting the would-be slave, rather than the would-be owner, from the consequences of his own voluntary agreements, and insofar as his solution would justify a legal policy (of non-validation) on those terms, it is paternalistic in spirit. Let us focus on the possible motives of this hypothetical odd duck, the voluntary would-be slave. Why would anyone in his right mind ever want to enter into such a relationship with another? (Insofar as someone is *not* in his right mind, just so far does his agreement fall short of the voluntariness required for valid consent, in which case the state can refuse to enforce it without infringing his autonomy.) Possible motivations can be divided into two categories. Either the would-be slave finds the prospect of slavery intrinsically appealing or he is willing to endure it for the sake of other benefits to be conferred by the owner as contractual "consideration." If the former, he may have a powerful psychological need of atonement for some sin, or for the achievement of perfect self-discipline through a kind of self-abasement, or he may feel a philosophical imperative to lose his sense of self-centeredness altogether through devoted service and unconditional commitment to another, or a religious need to achieve genuine humility through the lowliest status he can acquire. Some of these motives will be of doubtful genuineness, and should no doubt be checked carefully for voluntariness before the contract is validated, but it would be dogmatic to insist that necessarily and in each case, all motives in this category must fail the test of voluntariness. Voluntary self-enslavement for some of these reasons seems no crazier than the solitary forms of holy asceticism, like choosing the life of an anchorite in the desert, wearing sackcloth and ashes, and mortifying the flesh.

If the would-be slave's motives fall into the first category, then there is hardly any reason why he needs a legal contract from a willing would-be owner. If he wants *de facto* slavery there is no legal barrier to his goal. If he wishes irrevocability, he is free to make his own binding commitment both to himself and to the other, just as unmarried lovers might vow lifelong unmarried fidelity to one another without benefit of legal enforcement. So, with the exception of the protection against otherwise criminal mistreatment which would be waived in a legally recognized slavery contract of the extreme kind, there is really no point or need, from the point of view of the would-be slave, in having such a contract. And there are additional reasons which he might or might not share with the state, for not having such a contract. In the unlikely future event that the *slave* changes his mind and wants to leave the arrangement, then in the absence of an irrevocable contract, he may do so, and that would be to his advantage. If, in the more likely event that he never changes his mind (and the master remains willing) he may continue in the arrangement without benefit of contract. At the most, he would need a contract to protect him from the master's change of mind, but if his motive is instant and total obedience to his master's will in all things, it would not be likely that he would wish to impose himself on the master *against* the master's will.

What protection would a legal contract offer the slaveholder, still assuming the slave's motives are of the first category, and no additional consideration has been contributed by the master? In the first place, it would be a very odd contract indeed if it enforced only promises from the slave to the owner and imposed no reciprocal obligation on the owner. But even assuming the legal coherence of such a supposition, the legal guarantees enforced by the state would be utterly otiose, for by hypothesis, the owner has made no invest-ment in the arrangement to be "protected." He has contributed no *quid pro quo* and made no reciprocal promises. Enforcing a promise to him when he has made none in return—and an irrevocable promise at that—would not be to "protect" him, so much as to dump a huge gratuitous advantage on him. One does not have to be a legal paternalist to find reasons against such an absurd policy, especially when the alternative does not, in any usual sense, infringe anyone's liberty.

The more plausible category of possible motives of the would-be slave is the second one. He is willing to take his chances with inescapable servitude to this particular master, not because of its intrinsic appeal, or his philosophi-cal or religious imperatives, but because of some *offer* the would-be owner makes him as an inducement. If we are still speaking of the most extreme form of chattel-slavery, in which the slave loses *all* his rights, then the consideration presumably is to be paid in advance while the would-be slave is still a free negotiator. If it were a promise of future wages or minimal working conditions, on the other hand, then once the slave had lost his rights, the promise could be broken with impunity. Very likely the consid-eration would be paid in advance to a third-party, who would maintain his own right to the benefit after the would-be slave had become an actual slave, and lost all his own rights. We can imagine any number of intelligible (though not attractive) motives in this category for entering irrevocable right-less slavery. A person might agree to become a slave in exchange for ten million dollars to be delivered in advance to a loved one or to a worthy cause, or in payment for the prior enjoyment of some supreme benefit, as in the Faust legend. (It is more difficult but not impossible to imagine correspond-ing motives of the purchaser.) We are imagining now a would-be slave who is no pathological masochist, not neurotic, not obsessed with guilt, not even eccentric in his values, but rather (say) a genuinely benevolent person who wants to provide for a sickly widow's children, or do what he takes to be the maximal good with his life by contributing an immense sum to medical research, or to a favored political cause. He has no independent desire for self-sacrifice, but he is willing to assume a dangerous risk of future damage to his self-interest for the sake of the contribution he can make now. Is that example, in its bare description, any stranger than risking one's life and limb to race motorcycles or climb mountains?

When payment has been made in advance, the purchaser *can* then in theory be protected by a legal contract. Otherwise, if his slave runs away, he has lost his ten million and the slave too. Enforcement in this case would, therefore, have the point (its sole point, I think) of protecting the owner at the expense of his slave in that special contingency when the slave has a change of mind. But it takes little imagination to think of countervailing reasons for nonenforcement. What would enforcement consist in? Forcible return of the escapee in irons; civil suits against all who may have assisted him; organized manhunts, either by private parties with legal permission and cooperation, or by the police; prosecution of diverse third parties for such crimes against property as incitement to escape, aiding and abetting escape, withholding information about escapees, and so on. Such activities would be a demoralizing public spectacle, analogous to tolerating the starvation on the public streets of poor wretches who had gambled unwisely with their lives in other ways. And they would trample grossly on the interests of many third parties. These are but some of the many possible nonpaternalistic reasons for refusing to recognize slavery contracts.

What were Mill's reasons for refusing to validate slavery agreements? Virtually his entire argument is expressed, with admirable succinctness, in the following oft-quoted passage:

> The ground for thus limiting his [the would-be slave's] power of voluntarily disposing of his own lot in life is apparent, and is very clearly seen in this extreme case. The reason [in general] for not interfering, unless for the sake of others, with a person's voluntary acts is consideration for his liberty. His voluntary choice is evidence that what he so chooses is desirable, or at least endurable, to him, and his good is on the whole best provided for by allowing him to take his own means of pursuing it. But by selling himself for a slave, he abdicates his liberty; he foregoes any future use of it beyond that single act. He therefore defeats, in his own case, the very purpose which is the justification of allowing him to dispose of himself. He is no longer free, but is thenceforth in a position which has no longer the presumption in its favor that would be afforded by his voluntarily remaining in it. The principle of freedom cannot require that he should be free not to be free.[27]

The first and most natural interpretation of this argument is as an appeal not to a sovereign *right* to "dispose of one's own lot in life" but to a person's own *good* in the long run, or more precisely to one element of his good, his overall freedom. On this interpretation Mill is faithful to his own promise in Chapter 1 to forego appeal to natural rights and restrict his arguments to utilitarian considerations.[28] The appeal in this case is to each *individual's* own good and not necessarily to the public good (social utility), but it is at least consistent with an overarching utilitarian scheme of justification, as appeal to an underivative sovereign right would not be. *De facto* freedom, on this interpretation, is one good or benefit—indeed, a supremely important one— among many, and its loss, one evil—indeed, an extremely serious one—

among many types of harm. The aim of the law being to maximize beneficial goods and (especially) to prevent harms of all kinds and from all sources, the law must take a negative attitude, in general, toward forfeitures of, as well as interference with, freedom. Still, by and large, and in all but the most extreme cases, Mill is saying, legal paternalism is an unacceptable policy because in attempting to impose upon a person an external conception of his own good, it is very likely to be self-defeating. The key to this interpretation is Mill's language in this crucial passage: "His voluntary choice is *evidence* that what he so chooses is desirable, or at least endurable to him, and his good is *on the whole* best provided for by allowing him to take his own means of pursuing it." "Evidence" is not necessity, and "on the whole" means "in most but not all possible cases." Contrast this cautious instrumental approach with Mill's more absolutistic language in other places where he decrees that protection of others is "the sole end" warranting legal coercion, and its "only rightful purpose," and that in self-regarding matters, the individual's "independence is of right absolute," and over himself "the individual is sovereign."[29] If he had consistently followed the approach suggested by the absolutistic language, Mill's opposition to hard paternalism would have conceded *no* exceptions. If he had committed himself to (instead of merely flirting with) the principle of unqualified respect for a person's voluntary choice *as such*, even when it is the choice of a loss of freedom, he could have remained adamantly opposed to paternalism even in the most extreme cases of self-harm, for he would then be committed to the view that there is something more important (even) than the avoidance of self-harm. The principle that shuts and locks the door leading to legal paternalism is that every person has a human right to "voluntarily dispose of his own lot in life" whatever the effect on his own net balance of benefits (including "freedom") and harms.

Mill's ultimate explicit appeal in the slavery argument, on the other hand, appears to be what is called in the current jargon "freedom maximization." Some recent writers have followed him in this regard.[30] If these writers mean "*de facto* freedom" as opposed to *de jure* liberty, they are referring to a good that could in some cases be *increased* by entering into slavery. Where a slave-owner is humane and benevolent he may in fact permit the slave to enjoy even more freedoms than he had before, but these freedoms would be revocable privileges, since slaves *ex hypothesi* have no rights. Under the legal system of the nation the slave, simply in virtue of being a slave, has no *liberty* (against his owner) enforced by law. Mill seems to be speaking of *de facto* freedom in the passage quoted, but the example of the privileged slave might have been sufficient to persuade him to shift to jural liberty as the governing value. If that is what he meant, we have a second interpretation of his argument. But liberty too is a means to a person's good which a sovereign chooser might voluntarily decide to trade off for some other value, so the second interpretation is no more favorable to *de jure* autonomy, and no firmer a bar to hard paternalism, than the first.

If hard paternalism is justified only as a means to the maximization of personal freedom *cum* political liberty, then it is justified in far more than the "one extreme case" of slavery. A person's freedom is extinguished by his death, so all suicide and euthanasia would have to be banned for the sake of maintaining the future freedom of those who would prefer to die. Cigarettes and fried foods, as Arneson points out,[31] by reducing the life spans of those who use them, reduce the net balance of freedom over the long run. By way of this slippery slope we may end up with a "liberal" (Millian) justification for a "Spartan regime" of enforced health and hygiene. Moreover, all voluntary agreements that commit the parties to any significant narrowing of their options for the sake of any other kind of expected good could be forbidden, on the ground that no other "good" is as good for one as one's freedom. Mill would have been better advised to oppose hard paternalism on absolutist grounds and to base his opposition to permitting slavery contracts on the various good reasons that are autonomy-respecting. If one is not in principle "free not to be free" then one does not enjoy *de jure* autonomy.

On a third interpretation of Mill, he did not really intend to base his whole case for liberty on freedom-maximization (despite his language in the quoted passage) but rather on the maximization of personal and/or social utility, interpreted in turn as a maximal fulfillment of desires and reduction of frustrations. Arneson shows how easily freedom-maximization folds into the preference–satisfaction criterion. Speaking of the slippery slope argument that would commit Mill to the banning of cigarettes and fried foods, he writes: "Perhaps one could avert this repressive consequence by stipulating that various freedoms must be weighted by their importance to the agent, so that a man who loves fried food may lose more by the denial of the freedom to enjoying a greasy diet than he would gain by the freedom to enjoy a longer, fat-free existence. But this gambit threatens to collapse freedom-maximization into utility-maximization."[32] The criterion subtly shifts from "open options" to "preferred options" to "personal preference as such." A person could then be prevented from doing what he prefers to do at a given time on the ground that his present preference will lead to a greater balance of frustrated preferences later in his life. This interpretation destroys the central role of *de facto* freedom in the argument, which Mill presumably would not consider an advantage, and further it would be another appeal to one's good over one's sovereign right, another argument for enforced prudence, another ineffective barrier to creeping paternalism. In effect it justifies telling a presumably autonomous adult that he may not do what he wishes to do now on the sole ground that "he will be sorry later."

78   HARM TO SELF

A final interpretation of the quoted passage takes it to be a simple deviation from the main drift of Mill's argument in *On Liberty* which, as is indicated in Mill's frequent use of political metaphors like "sovereign," "dominion," "reign supreme," and so on, is profoundly respectful of *de jure* autonomy. There are other places in the same chapter where Mill reveals his familiarity with, and firm grasp of, the distinction between *de jure* autonomy and *de facto* freedom, although he nowhere used the *word* "autonomy." Richard Arneson calls our attention to Mill's discussion of Mormon polygamy,[33] where he expresses a surprisingly permissive attitude. Arneson points out that

> Mill characterizes polygamous marriages as "a riveting of the chains of one half of the community." Much like a benighted person who voluntarily contracts himself into slavery, except on a smaller scale, the Mormon wife relinquishes her freedom over the long run. Mill explicitly traces his "disapprobation" of Mormon polygamy to his understanding that this institution constitutes a "direct infraction" of the principle of liberty. But while a Mormon wife does not live freely, she does live autonomously, if *she is living out a fate she has chosen for herself without compulsion or coercion.* Of Mormon marriage, Mill says, "It must be remembered that this relation is as much voluntary on the part of the women concerned in it, and who may be deemed the sufferers by it, as is the case with any other form of the marriage institution." Mill's hesitation in this quotation must stem from a doubt as to how voluntary can be any person's choice to marry when the only alternatives society tolerates are one form of marriage or spinsterhood.[34]

My only quibble with Arneson in this passage is over the phrase "live autonomously." In some hypothetical examples (whether true of polygamy or not) one can autonomously choose a life in which all further *de jure* autonomy is forfeited. It would be misleading to describe the career consequent upon that choice as one of "living autonomously," but it would be an autonomously chosen life in any case, and to interfere with its choice would be to infringe the chooser's autonomy at the time he makes the choice, that is to treat him in a manner precluded by respect for him as an autonomous agent. I suspect that Arneson would agree.

If one's very autonomy can be alienated (effectively renounced), is there nothing then that an autonomous agent may not alienate? The answer to this question, I think, is that even an autonomous person cannot effectively alienate certain duties, and the responsibility for what he does. Suppose that *A*, the slaveholder, commands *B*, his voluntary slave, to murder *C*, an innocent third party. To obey the command, *B* would have to violate his own duty to *C* (not to kill him), which is logically correlated with *C*'s right against him (not to be killed). For *B* to alienate that duty would be for him to alienate one of *C*'s rights, which is absurd. Even an autonomous being cannot give up what was not his in the first place. If after the murder, *B* pleads in his own defense that he was a mere instrument in *A*'s hands with no will of his own, and that "instruments don't kill people, only people kill people," the excuse is unacceptable for the same reason that obedience to a higher authority cannot excuse atrocities. No man can make himself into a *mere* instrument of another's will. Even an autonomous agent cannot alienate his ultimate accountability.[35]

6. Alternative rationales for not enforcing slavery agreements

It remains here only to sketch some additional grounds for withholding legal recognition of slavery contracts, some of which *are* autonomy-respecting. One kind of argument is based on the extreme unlikelihood that the agreement to become another's slave can satisfy the requisite high standards of voluntariness. (See Chap. 20, §§7 and 8.) Since the renunciation of rights is both total and irrevocable in this kind of transaction, the standards of voluntariness employed must be higher than for any other kind of agreement (except perhaps suicide pacts and voluntary euthanasia requests). The risks are so great that the possibility of mistake must be reduced to a minimum. It is by no means impossible for a given slavery agreement to be voluntary, but the grounds for suspicion are so powerful that the testing would have to be thorough, time-consuming, and expensive. The legal machinery for testing voluntariness would be so cumbersome and expensive as to be impractical. Such procedures, after all, would have to be paid for out of tax revenues, the payment of which is mandatory for taxpayers. (And psychiatric consultant fees, among other things, are very high.) It would be a mistake, however, to attach much significance to financial costs as a practical reason for not recognizing slavery contracts. We can assume that the total number of such contracts would be very small, so that even if *per capita* testing costs were high, the net expense would not be. Moreover, the prospective slaveholder could be required to pay the costs of checking voluntariness, taking the burden entirely off the general public.[36] The more important point is that even expensive legal machinery might be so highly fallible that there could be no sure way of determining voluntariness, so that some mentally ill people, for example, might become enslaved. Given the uncertain quality of evidence on these matters, and the strong general presumption of nonvoluntariness, the state might be justified simply in presuming nonvoluntariness conclusively in every case as the least risky course. Some rational bargain-makers might be unfairly restrained under this policy, but on the alternative policy, even more people, perhaps, would become unjustly (mistakenly) enslaved, so that the evil prevented by the absolute prohibition would be greater than the occasional evil permitted. The principles involved in this argument are of the following two kinds: (1) It is better (say) that one hundred people be wrongly denied permission to be enslaved than that one be wrongly permitted, and (2) if we allow the institution of "voluntary slavery" at all, then no matter how stringent our tests of voluntariness are, it is likely that a good many persons will be wrongly permitted.

One general ground for placing voluntariness under suspicion is suggested by Arneson. He likens slavery contracts to usurious loans in that both generally result from negotiations in which the parties are in an unequal bargaining position. When one bargainer has so much stronger an initial advantage than the other, there is a "coercive effect" (see Chap. 24) on the weaker party's agreement that renders it less than fully voluntary. If there is a famine in which B is nearing starvation, and A is willing to sell him a loaf of bread for some exorbitant price, then B has hardly any choice but to pay that cost. If the state intervenes by posting a legal limit to the price that may be charged for bread, it does not overrule B's considered will for the sake of some hypothetical "rational will" better attuned to its own good; rather it implements his actual will which is to avoid both starvation and exhaustion of his savings, and protects him from another party who would use superior strength to harm his interests. "My own feeling," writes Arneson, "is that nonpaternalistic reasoning of this sort is sufficiently realistic to justify any anti-slavery or anti-usury laws that are in fact justifiable."[37] I am not so sure. If would-be slaves are typically people who are so pressured by desperate circumstances that they would pay any price, even permanent slavery, for some desired good, like (say) a loaf of bread, then anti-slavery laws are simply the limiting case of anti-usury laws, and anti-extortion laws. There could even be nonpaternalistic justification for *criminal* statutes making it punishable to offer goods as inducements for slavery commitments, for example by publicly advertising slavery positions or privately soliciting among desperate persons. But the most persuasive examples I could dream up of rational consent to slavery were instances of extremely benevolent or idealistic persons, not desperate ones, and offers in the millions of dollars, not merely loaves of bread. People more typically are "forced" to agree to servitude in times of total anarchy, when they need the protection of the powerful lords who would enslave them. (That is how some of the institutions of feudalism arose from the chaos following the collapse of the Roman Empire.) So, very likely, Arneson's reconstruction of a nonpaternalistic rationale for nonrecognition of slavery contacts is not "realistic" for this country in this age.

There are at least two other possible rationales for anti-slavery laws, one of which invokes the (public) harm principle with some special minor premises, and the other a relatively palatable version of legal moralism. The former is available to a follower of Mill, while the latter of course is not. The reasoning Mill might have accepted is a variant of the "public charge" argument commonly used in the nineteenth century against permitting even those without dependents to assume the risk of penury, illness, and starvation. We could let people gamble recklessly with their own lives, and then adopt inflexibly unsympathetic attitudes toward the losers. "They made their beds," we might say in the manner of some proper Victorians, "now let them sleep in them." But this would be to render the whole national character cold and hard. It would encourage insensitivity generally and impose an unfair economic penalty on those who possess the socially useful virtue of benevolence. Realistically, we just can't let people wither and die right in front of our eyes; and if we intervene to help, as we inevitably must, it will cost us a lot of money. There are certain risks then of an apparently self-regarding kind that persons cannot be permitted to run, if only for the sake of others who must either pay the bill or turn their backs on intolerable misery. This kind of argument, which can be applied equally well to the slavery case, especially in the instance where the slave changes his mind, is an indirect application of the harm to others principle.

The moralistic argument against slavery contracts may not in the end withstand scrutiny (see Chaps. 28 through 30), but it is worth mentioning here because it has at least the merit of being nonpaternalistic. One might argue that what is odious in "harsh and unconscionable" contracts, even when they are voluntary on both sides, is not that a person should suffer the harm he freely risked, but rather that another party should "exploit" or take advantage of him. What is to be prevented, according to this line of argument, is one person exploiting the weakness, or foolishness, or recklessness of another. if a weak, foolish, or reckless person freely chooses to harm or risk harm to himself, that is all right, but that is no reason why another should be a party to it, or be permitted to benefit himself at the other's expense. (This principle, however, can only apply to extreme cases, else it will ban all competition.) Applied to voluntary slavery, the principle of nonexploitation might say that it is not aimed at preventing one person from being a slave so much as preventing the other from being a slave-owner. The basic principle of argument here is a form of legal moralism. To own another human being, as one might own a table or a horse, is to be in a relation to him that is inherently immoral, and therefore properly forbidden by law. The antiexploitation principle is not congenial to the liberal, though it may provide (as we shall see in Chap. 32) the implicit rationale, and a nonpaternalistic one, for a group of crimes now on the books as diverse as ticket scalping, prostitution, and blackmail.

7. Deciding for one's future self: commitment and revocability

Slavery contracts are theoretically interesting constructs with which to test theories, but otherwise are of very little practical interest. There are more familiar examples, however, of irrevocable commitments that purport to bind one's own future self as well as other parties. These purported commitments are irrevocable, but unlike slavery, they are neither total nor necessarily permanent, since the committed performances or forebearances are often dated for a specific future time. They can result from contractual agreements, as when the seller of a business agrees not to open a competing business in the same city as the buyer, or from extracted promises, as when A gets B to promise to enforce A's current resolution, if necessary, against A's own future self.

These cases provide important tests for a theory of autonomy, since they show how an adequate conception of personal sovereignty must not only mark the "spatial" and topical boundaries of the personal domain, but must also provide for the shifting "temporal boundaries" as well. Individuals often knowingly exercise their autonomy at a particular time, in a way intended to diminish their freedom at some future time, and sometimes when that future time comes, the same sovereign self has second thoughts and demands his freedom back. In some cases the earlier forfeitures were understood all along to be tentative and revocable, but in other cases the earlier self had either bound himself contractually not to revoke, or else issued explicit instructions to an agreeable party to disregard any contrary instructions from one's future self. Does my sovereignty at the present time reign over my future selves? Can I cancel now their right to a change of mind? Or is their freedom in this respect the one thing I cannot be free to alienate, as Mill claimed?

We can make a start toward separating the easy from the difficult cases by asking which request, that of the early self to bind the later, or that of the later self for a release, is closer to being a genuinely voluntary one, or one that reflects the settled disposition of the chooser as an enduring self over time. The problem will be relatively easy when either the future self's choice or the present self's is substantially less than voluntary. There are various homey examples of later choices that are defective in this way. Suppose, for example, that I ask a friend to wake me at five in the morning and urge him to pay no heed to my future self's protests at that hour. When five o'clock comes along, and wakened from a sound sleep I announce a change of mind, the friend is entitled to give greater weight to the clearheaded, deliberate resolution of the earlier self, than to the incoherent, sleepy mumblings of the later one. Similarly, if I have a drinking problem, and I urge my host not to pour me more than two drinks at next week's party "no matter what I say at the time," and he promises to do so at my request, then when my compulsive, excited, abandoned future self renounces my earlier request, the party host should think of the earlier request as the controlling one.

Similarly, a second party can sometimes confidently support the earlier self when its will conflicts with that of the later self, on the grounds that the later self's contrary "choice" is the result of coercion or fraud, and hence is not wholly voluntary. Those reasons were certainly the ground of the decision of Odysseus' sailors not to unbind him, despite his urgent requests, when he was under the influence of the Sirens.[38] Odysseus was warned by Circe, before his ship departed from her island, that he was headed on a dangerous course, first to the the place of the Sirens, whose beautiful singing literally enchants all those who hear it, and leads them to their deaths. Following Circe's advice, Odysseus has his sailors plug their ears so that they won't be enchanted, but he himself wants to hear the beautiful music without being trapped, so he tells his sailors to bind him to the mast, and orders them not to release him until safely out of harm's way, even if he should command them to do so. Under the alluring influences of the Sirens, Odysseus does "change his mind," but his sailors wisely keep the promise they made to his earlier self, rightly inferring that the earlier self was the real Odysseus.

On the other hand, there are occasions on which one might judge retrospectively that the instructions of the earlier self were less voluntary than the contrary preferences of the later self. Perhaps the earlier self had been "beside himself" with rage or some other judgment-clouding emotion, whereas his later self is calm and convincingly reasonable. Or an earlier self, in a deep but temporary depression induced by a shocking event, or perhaps even by a drug, extracts a promise from a friend not only to do something at a future time but to treat the request as irrevocable, and then the later self, having recovered his calm and thought the matter over, asks to revoke the earlier request. Once more, to honor the later request over the earlier would not be to violate the autonomy of the whole person over time.

The hardest case is that in which the conflicting decisions of earlier and later selves appear to be equally voluntary. Which takes precedence then? The answer to which we are committed by our discussion so far seems to favor the earlier self in that case, but we shall have to retest that answer against intuitively difficult examples. First, however, I shall restate the position toward which a theory of personal sovereignty seems to incline us. When the earlier self in a fully voluntary way renounces his right to revoke in the future (or during some specified future interval), or explicitly instructs another, as in the Odyssean example, not to accept contrary instructions from the future self, then the earlier choice, being the genuine choice of a sovereign being, free to dispose of his own lot in the future, must continue to govern. After all, the earlier self and the later are the same self, not morally distinct persons, but rather one person at different times. Talk of "the earlier self" and "the later self" is only a useful *façon de parler*. If it is taken literally as referring to two distinct beings, it can only generate confusion, for then we shall have no way of explaining how one fully autonomous person can bind another fully autonomous person without the latter's consent. All of our ordinary notions of responsibility, as well as such basic moral practices as promise-making, presuppose a continuity of personal identity between earlier and later stages of the same self. Without that presupposition, very little of the idea of personal autonomy can be salvaged either. If I am not free to forfeit future liberties for present benefits, my lifelong "supply" of liberties may thus be maximized (against my present will), but since I am not permitted to decide *now* on how liberties and other benefits are to be distributed over the future course of my life, the domain of my self-government has been diminished severely in its temporal dimensions, and the *de facto* "freedom" left to my future selves may seem small compensation (especially since I shall pass on to them my present frustrations and resentments).

We could leave the matter at that and proceed to our next business, but caution dictates that we pause first, and examine the case for the other side. What does the contrary argument look like?[39] It employs, in the first place, a quite different conception of personal identity. On its terms, when an earlier self voluntarily agrees or resolves that his later self do something and that the agreement be irrevocable, and his later self, equally voluntarily, wishes to revoke the earlier agreement, the case is not always to be treated as one sovereign person "changing his mind" later, but at least sometimes as a close conflict between two equally sovereign persons. Not every "later self," of course, simply in virtue of being later than an earlier one, is therefore distinct in identity from that earlier one, but only a later self who has undergone a thorough sea-change of basic values. The seller who, after an interval of a year, comes to think that her earlier irrevocable agreement not to reopen a business in competition with the purchaser was unwise is not on that ground alone a "different person" from the woman who made the original agreement. A convicted murderer, however, who after seven years on Death Row has acquired an education, achieved genuine repentance, and reconstructed his personality and character, might well be described seriously (and not just as a *façon de parler*) as "not the same person" as the vicious criminal who committed the murder seven years earlier.

The second part of the case against irrevocability when earlier and later selves conflict would be to invent or discover convincing examples for which the "two distinct sovereign selves" interpretation seems plausible. Donald Regan proposes several examples of distinct personal identities that seem unconvincing to me if only because the "changes of mind" involved do not seem sufficiently thorough. He suggests that in restraining a would-be smoker we protect *another* person, namely, his later self, who having contracted lung cancer, may have renounced his earlier habit and become thereby, for moral purposes, "a different man." Again—

> What about the [motor]cyclist who rides without a helmet? What makes her a different person after her accident? The answer, I think, is that the cyclist is a different person, in the relevant respect, if she is no longer the sort of person

who would ignore her future well-being for the sake of small increments of personal utility. Of course it is not certain that having the accident will produce any such change in the cyclist. But it seems likely to. In many cases, I should think, the cyclist will not merely wish she had behaved differently in the past. She will have a new appreciation of the virtue of prudence and will alter her attitude toward risk in the future. If the cyclist changes in this way, then she is a different person, who deserves protection against the foolish behavior of her earlier self.[40]

Of course, the cyclist is not literally a different person after her accident. Even Regan would admit that she does not get a new name, a new license, a new police record, that her marriage is not annulled, and her debts are not cancelled. She is a different person, Regan suggests, in "some respects" or "for some purposes" but not for others. But this seems mere word play if it means no more than "she used to be reckless but now that she has been hurt she sees the point of being more careful and has become more careful." In every other way, including deep and important ways, she is still the same old Mary Jones. It is one thing to tell the earlier Mary Jones that she must be forced to do what she doesn't want to in order to protect a second party, but quite another to justify the interference in those terms while meaning only that if or when she becomes more prudent she will not or would not regret the interference. The more overtly paternalistic language seems much less contrived and more honest.

Even the example of the reformed murderer, in whom deep and pervasive character changes have occurred, fails to be convincing, and for still another reason. Certain important descriptions of the gentle sensitive person in Death Row presuppose for their intelligibility an *identity* with the savage beast who earlier committed a murder, and a continuity of development of the same self. If he is "reformed," for example, he has *changed himself* in centrally important ways from what he used to be, and that is quite another thing than dying and being reborn. Genuine repentance, as well as such states as contrition, remorse, the feeling of guilt, and the desire for atonement, all require some sense of continuity with the past and self-identity with an earlier wrongdoer. The essence of these states is the deliberate taking of *responsibility* for an earlier doing. To deny one's identity with the wrongdoer is to evade or deny responsibility for his crimes, quite another thing from repentance. When multiple murderer Paul Crump's death sentence was commuted to life imprisonment without possibility of parole, Illinois Governor Kerner wrote, "The embittered, distorted man who committed a vicious murder no longer exists . . . Under these circumstances it would serve no useful purpose to take this man's life . . . " I take that to be a rhetorical way of saying that since Paul Crump is no longer embittered and distorted, there is no good reason to take his life.[41]

The closest thing to a persuasive example of changed personal identity is also the most ingenious one, that invented by Derek Parfit in his much discussed paper "Later Selves and Moral Principles."[42] Parfit's example is also directly relevant to our present purposes since it involves an irrevocable commitment binding on an unwilling later self:

> Let us take a nineteenth century Russian who, in several years, should inherit vast estates. Because he has socialist ideals, he intends, now, to give the land to the peasants. But he knows that in time his ideals may fade. To guard against this possibility, he does two things. He first signs a legal document, which will automatically give away the land, and which can only be revoked with his wife's consent. He then says to his wife, "If I ever change my mind, and ask you to revoke the document, promise me that you will not consent."[43]

We can imagine then that "Boris" (the name provided by Donald Regan) does undergo a change as he grows older, and eventually abandons his socialist ideals for more conservative (and self-serving) principles, just as his earlier self had feared. When he finally inherits the estates, he implores his bewildered wife to consent to a revocation of the earlier agreement. If she stands firm she will be honoring her solemn promise to the earlier Boris; if she gives in, she will retroactively restrict the earlier Boris's power to determine his own lot in life. The early Boris, when he made his agreement with her, was in deadly earnest, acting on his principles, freely, with his eyes wide open to the possible consequences. "The root idea of autonomy," says Arneson, "is that in making a voluntary choice a person takes on responsibility for all the foreseeable consequences to himself that flow from this voluntary choice."[44] If Mrs. Boris reneges she will be releasing Boris from responsibility for his fully voluntary and autonomous commitment. His request too is a genuine reflection of his governing principles. Why should he, an autonomous person, be governed, he asks, by the dead hand of an earlier self who no longer exists? What then should Mrs. Boris do?[45]

Mrs. Boris put herself under a solemn obligation when she freely made the promise while well aware of the risks. Boris waived his right at that time to release her, so his subsequent change of mind cannot nullify her duty. Even on Regan's theory of personal identity, the duty stands, for even if the early Boris is now dead, the promise once made to him is still in force. Obviously, promises can remain in force after the death of the promisee, otherwise how can we account for the moral incumbency of wills and insurance policies? But Boris is not dead; he is simply different—very, very different, to be sure, but different in precisely the ways the young Boris foresaw as a danger when he resigned his right ever to release the promisor. The contingency that provided the whole reason for the irrevocability clause in the first place can hardly be invoked after the fact as the reason for revoking. The commitment then remains binding, and Mrs. Boris' duty is plain.

Perhaps, nevertheless, Mrs. Boris ought to relent, and deliberately decline to do her duty, out of pity, or from simple humanity. Renouncing an obligation is a morally serious thing, not to be done routinely whenever performance would lead to hardship. In extreme cases, however, after giving due weight to honor, the sanctity of agreements, and the necessity of trust, it may be true that a person, albeit with grave misgivings and deep reluctance, ought to renounce a genuine obligation. In these cases, it does not follow that the rightly renounced obligation could not have been a true obligation in the first place.[46] It much better serves the cause of moral clarity to call a spade a spade. To invent a theory of personal identity that permits one to say that the later self is not the same self as that to whom the promise was made, is to evade responsibility for what one is doing. Candor requires that one confess that one has broken faith with a promisee because in the circumstances other factors seemed to have even more weight than fidelity. There is more to morality than the legalistic realm of rights and duties, central as that realm is. If Mrs. Boris' refusal to consent to revocation would plunge Boris into permanent and severe misery, then that fact is a reason for relenting, though it will be very difficult for Mrs. Boris to determine whether it is a decisive reason. Hers is a hard decision, but the problem is better described as a conflict between her plain obligation and other types of moral reasons rather than as a conflict between obligations.

8. Personal sovereignty compared with constitutional "privacy"

The United States Supreme Court in recent years appears to have discovered a basic constitutional right suggestive of our "sovereign personal right of self-determination," and has given it the highly misleading name of "the right to privacy." Descriptions of the right vary from case to case, but one common element it seems to share with "personal sovereignty" is the notion that there is a domain in which the individual's own choice must reign supreme.[47] On the boundaries of this "zone" is a "wall" against state interference: in respect to protected choices, "the state shall make no law . . . " The first criminal statute to be invalidated by the Court on the ground that it penetrated the protected zone was a Connecticut statute prohibiting the use "by any person" of contraceptives, and permitting any doctor who counsels their use to be prosecuted and punished as if he were the principal offender. In the famous case of *Griswold v. Connecticut*,[48] in which Dr. Griswold and another physician associated with the Planned Parenthood League of Connecticut appealed their convictions for counseling birth control, all the justices agreed with Justice Stewart that this statute was (at the least) "an uncommonly silly law," but there was some hesitation about striking it down since there is no explicitly named right in the Constitution that it could plausibly be said to contravene. Justices Stewart and Black found "uncommon silliness" to be an insufficient ground for unconstitutionality and dissented from the majority who found the right of privacy implied, though not explicitly named or defined, by various constitutional guarantees.

Justice Douglas offered an explanation of how the unnamed right was "implied" by the explicit ones. As I interpret him, the explanation has two parts. In the first place, the implied right is a necessary condition for the fulfillment of the explicit right; and secondly, the unnamed right is presupposed by the only coherent rationale that can be provided for the explicit right. Thus, we could have no effective right of free speech, unless in addition to the right to utter or to print (that is, the explicit core right), we also had "the right to distribute, the right to receive, the right to read and freedom of inquiry, freedom of thought, and freedom to teach . . . "[49] These implied rights are a long way from the strict letter of the law, but without them constitutional rights would not be such powerful guarantees and the shrunken core rights themselves, like "free speech," would be insecure. Without the peripheral rights, moreover, the core right would stand stripped of coherent rationale or explanation. Justice Douglas then pointed to other examples of rights not named in the Bill of Rights but without which the explicit rights would lack meaning or point. In a metaphor that is now famous he referred to the "penumbra" (shadowy area) surrounding each explicit right in which implied rights may (or must) be inferred.

In Justice Douglas's usage, the Constitution contains various "zones" (note the plural) of privacy, each implied by a primary right as part of its "penumbra." Justice Douglas's examples indicate that he means by "zone of privacy" simply zone of individual discretion. The individual's right of association creates a zone in which he and only he may decide with whom he shall associate or affiliate; his fourth amendment right against unreasonable searches and seizures implies his exclusive right to live as he pleases within his own home. At other places Justice Douglas speaks as if there were *one* zone of privacy, perhaps that formed by the complicated intersection of the various enumerated discretionary rights. In any case, the right of married couples to their own sex lives and procreational decisions "lies within the zone of privacy created by several fundamental constitutional guarantees."[50] Presumably free speech, free association, and the security of the home, among others, would make less sense, and be less secure, without it.

Justice Douglas then turns to another line of argument that not only seems to undercut the first but shows why the penumbral right established by the first is not well named "the right of privacy." He points out that the Connecticut statute is *overbroad* in any case. He seems to concede implicitly, as the remainder of his colleagues grant explicitly, that "safeguarding marital fidelity" is a proper state purpose, and that *arguendo*, there is some "rational," that is, plausibly inferred, connection between that purpose and the statute in question. But even granted all that, Justice Douglas writes that "a governmental purpose to control or prevent activities constitutionally subject to state regulation may not be achieved by means which sweep unnecessarily broadly and thereby invade the area of protected freedoms."[51] Douglas questioned whether "we [would] allow the police to search the sacred precincts of marital bedrooms for telltale signs of the use of contraceptives."[52] Certainly that *would* be a violation of *privacy* in the familiar everyday sense of the word! But Justice Douglas implies that this constitutional deficiency would be avoided by a statute that did not forbid the *use* of contraceptives, but only regulated their manufacture or sale.[53] That alternative statute could be enforced without any peeking into private chambers. As the least intrusive way of implementing a "legitimate" state purpose, Justice Douglas may be implying, such a statute would not violate marital privacy.

In effectively preventing married couples from using contraceptive devices, however, even the less intrusive legislation would infringe the autonomy of married couples, and diminish their capacity to decide for themselves in what would otherwise be a zone of discretion, that of choices related to marital sexual intimacies and reproductive decisions. That zone of sovereignty has nothing to do with privacy in the ordinary sense (a liberty to enjoy one's solitude unwitnessed, unintruded upon, even unknown about in certain ways); but it is central to the constitutional doctrine of privacy-as-autonomy that Justice Douglas had seemed to be working out in his first line of argument. If he had continued on his first path, he would have declared even the less intrusive hypothetical legislation to be a violation of marital autonomy, and he would have taken a much more skeptical look at the allegedly "proper state purpose" it would so economically subserve. Justice Goldberg, in his concurring opinion, emphasizes the argument from unnecessary intrusion and even concedes that "[the] State of Connecticut does have statutes, the constitutionality of which is beyond doubt, which prohibit adultery and fornication. These statutes," he adds, "demonstrate that means for achieving the basic purpose of protecting marital fidelity are available to Connecticut without the need to 'invade the area of protected freedoms'."[54] The logic of this passage implies that the constitutional right of marital privacy, for Justice Goldberg, covers only the right to be unintruded upon, unwitnessed, and undisclosed in one's solitude, that is, privacy in the familiar pre-technical sense. The deeper right to discretionary control, so reminiscent of *de jure* autonomy, which was suggested at the beginning of Justice Douglas's opinion, by that route goes down the drain. I suspect that if the word "autonomy" had been used in the first place, instead of "privacy," the dangers of equivocation would have been obviated, and these confusions avoided.

If there is truly a doctrine of personal *autonomy* in recent Supreme Court decisions under the label of "privacy," what are the boundaries of the posited autonomous domain? For a time, the line of decisions following *Griswold* and extending its right of privacy to new areas encouraged many liberal observers to suspect that the "privacy" protected by the Court was really personal autonomy, and its domain boundaries those determined by the self-and-other-regarding distinction, just as John Stuart Mill might have wished. The right to marital privacy bestowed in *Griswold* was extended in *Eisenstadt v. Baird*[55] from married to unmarried couples. In *Loving v. Virginia*[56] it was used to strike down the miscegenation statutes used by southern states since the Civil War to restrict the right to marry whomever one wishes, regardless of race. In *Stanley v. Georgia*,[57] the right to privacy discovered in *Griswold* was held to support the sanctity of the home, including the right to witness pornographic movies in one's own bedroom. In *Moore v. East Cleveland*,[58] the Court struck down zoning restrictions on the rights of extended families to live together in a single dwelling. In *Roe v. Wade*[59] the Court granted to all pregnant women the discretionary right, derived from the right of privacy, to decide whether to continue or to terminate their own pregnancies, free from repressive criminal legislation, at least in the first two trimesters.

The decisions take a zig-zag path, but they do exhibit a pattern. The zone of privacy is extended from the essential intimacies of the marital relation, to heterosexual intimacies generally, to decisions about whom to marry, to decisions about "family planning," childrearing, modes of family living, and finally to decisions about the termination of pregnancy. One feature these various rights seem to have in common is that they are concerned with areas of individual and collective (family) conduct that are essentially self-regarding in Mill's sense.[60] "From the first, the Court's development of a right to privacy has suggested to philosophically minded commentators the possible elevation to constitutional status of Mill's principle of liberty," wrote one philosophically minded commentator;[61] but as it turned out his enthusiasm was premature, for the Court then did a turnabout, and in a series of illiberal decisions, ruled that privacy does *not* extend to couples living in "open adultery," or to certain self-regarding but idiosyncratic life-styles, or to the use and cultivation of marijuana even in the "sanctity" of one's own home, or to the consensual viewing of pornographic films in places of public accomodation, or to the length and style of policemen's hair, or to homosexual intercourse between consenting adults in private. Now liberal critics, stripped of their earlier hopes, charged that the Court was arbitrary and erratic in its mapping of domain boundaries and that "once it began to protect the rights of 'consenting adults' in *Griswold*, it could not without gross and apparent inconsistency stop short of reading into the Constitution some version of Mill's principle."[62]

A closer reading of the opinions even in the earlier favorable cases, however, would not have encouraged the hope that a doctrine of personal sovereignty with Millian domain boundaries was being read into the United States Constitution. It is true that the right of privacy discovered in the penumbra of primary constitutional rights is meant to be a personal autonomy and not merely "privacy" in the more accustomed sense of rightful solitude or anonymity. But the interpretations of the right by the judges who discovered it would have disappointed Mill in at least two ways: their notion of what is a "proper state purpose," and their definitions of domain boundaries. The Court at the time of *Griswold* had long since endorsed a formula for balancing restrictive legislation against individual rights. The personal liberties involved are either relatively unimportant or else "fundamental." Unquestioned constitutional guarantees like free speech and free exercise of religion are clearly fundamental.) If the encroachment by the statute on personal liberties is relatively insignificant, or the liberty itself not fundamental, then the offending statute will pass constitutional muster provided only that (1) it is meant to effect some legitimate state purpose, and (2) it has some "rational relationship" to the achievement of that purpose, that is, that there is some minimally plausible, even if unproven and unlikely, instrumental connection with that purpose. The test is much stricter, however, when the liberty restricted is a fundamental one (as the constitutional right to privacy may be presumed to be). In that case the state interest must be more than "proper"; it must be *compelling*. And the statute's relationship to that purpose must be more than "rational"; it must be *necessary*. The Connecticut anti-contraceptive statute clearly was not necessary for achieving its avowed purpose, but that purpose, the discouragement of adultery, Justice Douglas implies, and Justice Goldberg states (in an opinion joined by Chief Justice Warren and Justice Brennan), is a legitimate state policy.[63] (Goldberg does not say that the state interest in marital fidelity is "compelling," and implies that it is not, but nevertheless he finds the constitutionality of criminal statutes prohibiting adultery and fornication "beyond doubt.")[64]

In an earlier Connecticut birth control case, *Poe v. Ullman*,[65] Justice Harlan, in a manner that would please Lord Devlin more than Mill, also concedes in a dissenting opinion the legitimacy of a state interest in the "moral welfare of its citizenry," and speaks with cautious tolerance of Connecticut's view that the morality of its citizens may be protected "both directly, in that it considers the practice of contraception immoral in itself, and instrumentally, in that the availability of contraceptive materials tends to minimize 'the disastrous consequences of dissolute [adulterous] action' "[66] (presumably venereal disease and unwanted pregnancy). He makes it plain that even the right of privacy may be restricted where necessary to promote a legitimate state interest. "Thus, I would not suggest that adultery, homosexuality, fornication, and incest are immune from criminal enquiry, however privately practiced . . . "[67] What is the difference between these regulations and those that are barred by the right of privacy? Harlan answers thus:

> It is one thing when the State exerts its power either to forbid extramarital sexuality altogether, or to say who may marry, but it is quite another when, having acknowledged a marriage and the intimacies inherent in it, it undertakes to regulate by means of the criminal law the details of that intimacy.[68]

Justice Harlan then, and most of his colleagues and successors, recognized the very anti-Millian interest in "enforcing the requirements of decency" as a constitutionally legitimate one so long as it is not pressed unnecessarily beyond the proper boundaries of privacy. Other justices on the Court have drawn those boundaries rather more widely than Justice Harlan. But I have found none who has boldly employed the Millian formula. It is not simply in virtue of being primarily self-regarding that decisions involving marital sex and family planning fall within the zone of constitutional privacy. If that were all, then decisions whether to wear protective helmets, seat belts, and life preservers would be similarly protected. Rather, the Court, in its various ways, has circumscribed as "private" those decisions that involve the most *basic* of the self-regarding decisions. Chief Justice Burger summarized the earlier decisions accurately in 1973 when he stated that privacy envelops "only personal rights that can be deemed 'fundamental' or 'implicit in the concept of ordered liberty.' This privacy right encompasses and protects the personal intimacies of the home, the family, marriage, motherhood, procreation, and childrearing . . . "[69] It encompasses use of pornography in one's home, but not drug taking, even in one's home (a difficult distinction), and not voluntarily watching "obscene movies in places of public accommodation."[70] The boundary line, in short, tends to follow, however erratically, the line of those liberties which are most fecund, those exercised in the pivotally central life decisions and thereby underlying and supporting all the others.

As we have seen, one could similarly draw more narrowly the boundaries of the domain of personal sovereignty. There could well be some advantages in such a conception over the "self-and-other regarding" test of more orthodox liberalism. The liberal could then abandon his quarrel with the paternalist over relatively trivial safety restrictions such as requirements that seat belts or life preservers be worn in the appropriately dangerous circumstances. But instead of arguing like Gerald Dworkin that "in the final analysis . . . we are justified in making sailors take along life preservers because this minimizes the risk of harm to them at the cost of a trivial interference with their freedom,"[71] the liberal could argue that such interference is no infringement whatever of personal sovereignty since domain boundaries are not drawn around all primarily self-regarding choices but only those self-regarding critical life-choices that "determine one's lot in life." In that way the liberal can take his stand on such issues as marriage and career choices, experimental life styles, food and drug use, sexual freedom, dangerous sports that are a central part of some people's lives (e.g., mountain climbing), suicide, and euthanasia. He can argue for an inviolable personal sovereignty that is not affected by minor safety regulations, because he has drawn the boundaries of the sovereign domain more narrowly so as to protect only the life choices that matter, those which reflect the person in some essential and fundamental way. This move would be analogous to drawing the offshore limits of national sovereignty at three miles instead of twelve or fifteen. An international fishing treaty by which all signatories accept a three-mile limit would not be a violation of national sovereignty, not even a "small" or "insignificant" one. Sovereignty would still be sacrosanct and unviolated unless (say) a given small country is forced by a powerful fishing nation to agree unilaterally to a line drawn in its case twelve miles *interior* to the shore. That might be analogous to a statutory regulation of marriage choices or private sexual conduct, and no amount of juggling with definitions of domain boundaries could justify it.

Perhaps there is a strategy here for the tired liberal theorist who does not wish to quarrel over such trivial issues as seat belts, but does not want to abandon his basic principles either. But it is a strategy full of hazards and difficulties. Many writers have complained that Mill's self-and-other-regarding test is a difficult one to make precise and workable,[72] but its difficulties are minor compared to those involved in applying the criterion of "central," "pivotal," or "fecund" interests, or those "inseparable from the concept of ordered liberty," or those that express a person in "some essential and important way." As the experience of the Supreme Court has shown, it is difficult to apply a restricted concept of personal sovereignty in ways that do not seem arbitrary. (So, for example, our "privacy" permits viewing pornography in our own homes, but not homosexual relations between consenting adults in private.) The correlative of vagueness in a criterion is arbitrariness in its application.

Again, individual differences create great problems for the narrower boundary lines. Perhaps most motorcyclists who prefer not to wear helmets think of that preference simply as a matter of comfort and convenience. An imposed minor inconvenience is, as Gerald Dworkin put it, "a trivial interference with their freedom." There may be many others, however, for whom motorcycle expeditions are essential elements in a chosen life-style, and who view helmets as hated symbols of the nitpicking prudence they emphatically reject as they take to the open road, spirits soaring, their hair blowing in the wind. Can we justify permitting others their dangerous adventures in racing cars and on mountain slopes, yet deny the motorcyclist his romantic flair?

We shall return yet again to the vexatious question of mandatory safety regulations (Chap. 20, §8). Here it suffices to emphasize the point that if a philosopher is operating with a concept of *de jure* autonomy, and not mere *de facto* liberty or freedom, he may not compromise as Dworkin does, and balance "trivial interferences" against great increases in safety. There is no such thing as a "trivial interference" with personal sovereignty; nor is it simply another value to be weighed in a cost–benefit comparison. In this respect, if not others, a trivial interference with sovereignty is like a minor invasion of virginity: the logic of each concept is such that a value is respected in its entirety or not at all.

9. Alien dignity: some animadversions on Kantianism

My uncompromising appeal to personal autonomy in this chapter may suggest to many a Kantian stance in moral philosophy. The term "autonomy" is more firmly associated with the name of Immanuel Kant than that of any other philosopher. Kant, after all, gave great and repeated emphasis to the importance of treating people as ends in themselves and not as mere means, as persons rather than mere things, as rational beings, creatures with "dignity," and proper objects of "respect." Nevertheless the interpretation of *de jure* autonomy that I have advocated here is profoundly different from, and much more radical than, anything found in the Kantian writings, and I have no doubt that Kant would have rejected it.

Kant's notion of respect for persons is less pointed and personal, more abstract and (oddly) impersonal than the concept advanced here. We are enjoined by Kant to respect, not the deliberate choices of persons whatever they may be, but the "humanity" in each person; not the voluntariness of decisions as such, but their "rationality"; not a uniquely concrete being, but some abstraction within him; not a personal dignity, but the alien dignity of some extra-personal source. Kant's language implies that we must cherish and protect a person's choice, not because it is *his*, simply, but because of something within him, quite independent of his will, a kind of internal Vatican City not subject to his sovereign control.

The stark difference between Kantian "autonomy" and the personal sovereignty defended here emerges with special clarity in the specific moral judgments derived from each. Suicide is an especially revealing case in point. On the present conception, short of the garrison threshold and within the self-regarding domain, my life is mine, and I may do what I wish with it, even terminate it. Kant, on the other hand, treats suicide (and by implication voluntary euthanasia) as action unconditionally prohibited by the moral law, and beyond the pale of anyone's sovereign control. His arguments are not only unconvincing, but to anyone who thinks of personal sovereignty as rooted in common sense, they must appear forced and bizarre.

Among Kant's arguments are the following. "Suicide is contrary to the highest duty we have towards ourselves, for it annuls the condition of all other duties; it goes beyond the limits of the use of free will, for this use is possible only through the existence of the Subject."[73] In other words, if you are not alive then you have no free will. Since moral rules function to promote duty and freedom, there can be no moral rule permitting suicide. (This reminds one of Mill's argument against the alienation of freedom, that one can be free to do anything except be not free.)

A second argument is that "We shrink in horror from suicide because all nature seeks its own preservation; an injured tree, a living body, an animal does so; how then could man make of his freedom, which is the acme of life and constitutes its worth, a principle for his own destruction?"[74] Kant concludes that he who commits suicide therefore falls below nature, whereas the suicide himself might reply that, unlike mere animals, he can employ his autonomous free will to rise above nature. Surely the argument at this level is question-begging and inconclusive. A third argument may have a graver defect, depending on how it is interpreted. At first sight, at least, it appears to be a plain non sequitur: "Nothing more terrible [than suicide] can be imagined; for if man were on every occasion master of his own life, he would be master of the lives of others; and being ready to sacrifice his life at any and every time rather than be captured, he could perpetrate every conceivable crime and vice."[75] In other words, for one who is prepared to kill himself anyway, there can be no punishment terrible enough to deter him from other crimes he might commit first.[76] However this obscure argument is to be interpreted and evaluated (and its prospects are not good), it appears to plainly reject the notion of personal sovereignty.

Kant then makes his strongest appeal: to the "humanity" in one's person, that internal something which is the true object of the respect owed a person. The way Kant uses this notion, the reader must think of it as something other than his *self*. Kant does not respect *me*; he respects some alien presence in me that in some circumstances can be a burden, even an enemy. Consider this remarkable passage:

> Man can only dispose over things; beasts are things in this sense; but man is not a thing, not a beast. If he disposes over himself, he treats his value as that of a beast. He who so behaves, who has no respect for human nature and makes a thing of himself, becomes for everyone an Object of free will. We are free to treat him as a beast, as a thing, and to use him for our sport as we do a horse or a dog, for he is no longer a human being; he has made a thing of himself, and, having discarded his humanity, he cannot expect that others should respect humanity in him. Yet humanity is worthy of esteem . . .[77]

This passage shows how impersonal Kant's respect for persons is. When he respects a person, he respects him not as someone in rightful control of his own life, but rather as the locus or repository of abstract qualities which are the true objects of esteem, and which must be protected and preserved at all cost—even costs to *him*.

Kant's final arguments are religious, and these are the considerations to which he attaches the greatest importance. One's relationship to one's own life is now treated in a succession of metaphors. A man is a *trustee* (one who administers property for the benefit of another) for the life God has reposed in him (not an "owner" *simpliciter*, "master," or "sovereign"), and suicide is a "breach of holy trust."[78] Alternatively, a person's life is a military post, and the suicide "arrives in the other world as one who has deserted his post; he must be looked upon as a rebel against God,"[79] a soldier insubordinate to his commander. "Human beings are *sentinels* on earth and may not leave their posts until relieved by another beneficent hand."[80] Finally comes the metaphor, also employed by St. Thomas Aquinas,[81] that is most divergent from a conception of *de jure* autonomy as sovereignty: "God is our owner; we are His property; His providence works for our good. A *bondman* in the care of a beneficent master deserves punishment if he opposes his master's wishes."[82] I fail to see how the relation of chattel slave (property) to master (owner) generates a very exalted conception of human dignity. Indeed the "dignity" conferred in all three of Kant's religious metaphors is a borrowed dignity, a reflected glory, something not derived from the unique specificity of individual persons with interests, goals, and ideals peculiarly and centrally their own. Instead Kant thinks of a person as the treasure vault in which a creditor, commander, or owner has stored some precious metal for safekeeping.

Paul Ramsey, who endorses this kind of conception, puts it this way:

> One grasps the religious outlook upon the sanctity of human life only if he sees that this life is asserted to be *surrounded* by sanctity that need not be in a man, that the most dignity a man ever possesses is a dignity that is alien to him . . . A man's dignity is an overflow from God's dealings with him, and not primarily an anticipation of anything he will ever be by himself alone . . . The value of a human life is ultimately grounded in the value God is placing on it . . . His [a man's] dignity is "an alien dignity," an evaluation that is not of him but placed upon him by the divine decree.[83]

Whatever the merit of this conception, it seems clear to me not to be the only conception of human dignity compatible with "the religious outlook." I see no contradiction in holding that God created man, and conferred on each person a unique inherent value, a capacity for becoming something worthy of further respect by his own efforts, and a birthright of sovereign autonomy.

I find Kant's conception unconvincing for two basic reasons. First, it locates a person's dignity in abstract characteristics not peculiar to him, rather than, at least partly, in his own individuality. Moreover, I cannot see how it follows from the fact that all and only human beings have dignity that their dignity is derived entirely from those minimal traits that they share in common and that make them, by definition, human, or that "respect" is properly directed not at *them*, but at those traits in abstraction. Second, the human relationships of which Kant makes metaphorical use—trusteeship, military hierarchy, and chattel ownership, are not themselves persuasive models of "dignity" (to put the point mildly). If personal autonomy amounts to no more than that, it cannot be the same concept as that which we recognize and employ in everyday life. It certainly is not the concept to which appeal has been made in this chapter.[84]

20

Voluntariness and Assumptions of Risk

1. The soft paternalist strategy

The argument thus far has surely not proved that legal paternalism is morally untenable. All that can be claimed is that with a certain class of readers, at least, it has established a presumptive case against legal paternalism, deep grounds for suspicion of its moral credentials. Insofar as readers recognize in themselves the tendency to protest some actual or hypothetical interference in their affairs with such language as "That's *my* business, not yours," or "That's no concern of anyone else," and insofar as this language is accompanied by genuine feelings of indignation and the sense of usurped prerogatives, to that extent the reader embraces some notion, however vague, of personal autonomy. Insofar as legal paternalism draws domain boundaries very narrowly; insofar as it confuses one's right with one's good; insofar as it justifies prohibiting a person from voluntarily relinquishing future liberty or future autonomy, or justifies forcing a person to be free; just so far does it conflict with a plausible account of what personal autonomy is. And just so far must the reader who is disposed to embrace a plausible doctrine of personal autonomy (as a reconstruction of his own moral feelings) hold legal paternalism suspect.

Let us return then to the problem of reconciling our repugnance for legal paternalism with the seeming reasonableness of some apparently paternalistic regulations. If we can show that, first appearance to the contrary, the paternalistic regulations are not reasonable, or that the reasonable regulations are not really paternalistic, then the case against paternalism will no longer be merely "presumptive," but very close to being decisive. One way of account-

98

ing for the reasonableness of apparently paternalistic restrictions is to apply what we have called "the soft paternalistic strategy" (Chap. 17, §§3 and 6) to show that there is a rationale for protective interference that gives decisive significance, after all, to respect for *de jure* autonomy. Such an argument would show that the reasonableness of the restriction consists in the protection it provides the actor from dangerous choices that are not truly his own. This strategy makes critical use of the concept of a voluntary choice, which, as we shall see, is such a difficult notion that the case which rests upon it must be very complicated.

2. Some preliminary distinctions

The first step in the soft paternalist strategy, unsurprisingly, is to make some important preliminary distinctions.

Action of self vs. action of another. The first distinction is between the harms or likely harms that are produced directly by a person upon himself and those produced by the actions of another person to which the first party has *consented.* Committing suicide (if we consider the death so caused as a harm, that is, an invasion of the party's own self-interest) is an example of self-inflicted harm; arranging for a person to put one out of one's misery would be an example of "harm" inflicted by the action of another to which one has consented. This very basic distinction quickly suggests another, that between "consenting" in the sense of expressing one's willingness to do what the other suggests or requests, when the initiative and (usually) the more strongly desired gain is that of the other party, and "consenting" in the much stronger sense of initiating the action by making the request to the other party. Typically what is called "euthanasia" involves consent in the strong sense: a person who would kill himself if only he were able to (suppose for example that he is paralyzed from the neck down) urgently requests that another be an instrument of his will and do the job for him. On the other hand, if a terminally ill patient is approached by another person who requests that he submit to a surgical operation that would shorten his life only by a few days but which would enable the surgeon to transplant his organs promptly and save the lives of several children, he may agree out of moral scruple and with some reluctance to do what is proposed, in which case he has consented in the weak sense. In effect, he has agreed to become the "instrument" of the other party's will, rather than the other way around. The common denominator in the two types of consent is a genuine agreement, a deliberate choice, whoever the initiator, whatever the motive, wherever the expected major gain. Typically, commercial transactions involve strong consent on both sides. The seller wants very much to sell his product; *he* deliberately sets up shop; *he* deliberately advertises and solicits. The customer, on the other hand, needs the product; *he* sets out to look for it at favorable terms; *he* deliberately enters the shop. Either may be the first to propose the actual purchase, but considerable initiative has been exercised on both sides. The purchase may nevertheless turn out to be injurious to the interests of either party or both, in which case we would have to say that the "harm" was not directly self-inflicted, but only indirectly so, through the prior act of consenting (in at least the weak common denominator sense) to the directly harmful act of the other.

Directly self-inflicted harms are those that a person can produce himself by his own action, even though he may have to rely upon others who provide tools, weapons, or assistance. When the assistance is great enough the situation approaches the conceptual borderline between "aiding and abetting" and collaborative action. In the latter case the harm is both self and other-inflicted.

Even when a person acts entirely on his own so that the "harm" is wholly self-inflicted, something analogous to consent (here in the strong sense) may be involved. The notion of consent applies, strictly speaking, only to the actions of another person that affect oneself. For that reason, to speak of consent to one's own actions is to use a kind of metaphor, but one which is often quite apt. Indeed, to say that I consented to my own actions seems just a colorful way of saying that I acted voluntarily. My involuntary actions, after all, are from the moral point of view no different from the actions of someone else to which I have not had an opportunity to consent.

A person's directly self-affecting actions and the consented-to behavior of others that affects him are united and placed in the same moral category by the *Volenti non fit injuria* maxim to which we were introduced in Vol. 1, Chap. 3, §5. As we have seen, the *Volenti* maxim is most plausibly interpreted as applying not simply to harms in the sense of set-back interests but only to harms in the sense of personal wrongs or injustices. A person may indeed be harmed by what he consents to, in the sense that his interests may be set back, but he cannot be wronged. *Volenti* says, in effect, that if I cannot wrong myself by taking my own life quite voluntarily, then I am not wronged by another who kills me at my own request. From the moral point of view my consent to his action makes it as if it were by own. Neither will a consistent legal paternalism distinguish between the two kinds of cases. If it forbids voluntary self-mutilation, then equally will it forbid freely consented-to mutilation at the hands of another; if it disallows consent as a defense to homicide, equally will it prohibit voluntary suicide. And if the actor is aggrieved at the interference with his own purely self-regarding behavior, he will be equally aggrieved, in the same way and for the same reason, at restraints to the consented-to actions of another, for those constraints equally interfere with the implementation of his own will by rendering his consent ineffective. In the one case direct action is blocked; in the other, it is the act of consenting that is constrained. In the one case the agent is prevented from *doing* something; in the other he is prevented from *being done to* in the way he chooses. If the interference in either case is justified on paternalistic grounds, then his choices are blocked for what is thought to be his own good.

Direct and certain harm vs. the risk of harm. The second distinction cuts across the first. It is between cases of the direct production of harm to a person, when the harm is the certain upshot of his or another's action and its desired end, on the one hand, and cases of the direct creation of a risk of harm to oneself in the course of activities directed toward other ends. The person who knowingly swallows a lethal dose of arsenic will certainly die, and death will be imputed to him as his goal in acting. Another person is offended by the sight of his left hand, so he grasps an ax in his right hand and chops his left hand off. He does not thereby "endanger" his interest in the physical integrity of his limbs or "risk" the loss of his hand. He brings about the loss directly and deliberately. On the other hand, to smoke cigarettes or to drive at excessive speeds is not directly to harm oneself, but rather to increase beyond a normal level the probability that harm to oneself will result.

The distinction between direct harm and the risk of harm applies also to consented-to acts of others. I may consent to a dangerous operation that may cure my disability if successful, but will kill me if it fails, choosing this course in preference to an unacceptable *status quo* that neither kills nor cures. My act of consent does not kill me directly, but it does create a risk that I will die. Similarly, I may choose *not* to have my leg amputated when my surgeon informs me that the alternative is a high risk of spreading bone cancer and eventual death. In that case I directly assume a risk by *not* consenting to the actions of another. Both cases can be distinguished from the case of my consent to another's infliction of direct "harm" on me, where, for example, I hire a surgeon to amputate my left hand because I find it offensive, and I am unable or unwilling to saw it off myself. Here it would be as otiose to speak of the "risk" of losing a hand as it would be in the corresponding case of self-amputation.

The first two distinctions and the way they cut across one another can be rendered diagramatically (Diagram 20-1).

Reasonable vs. unreasonable risks. There is no form of activity (or inactivity either for that matter) that does not involve some risk. On some occasions we have a choice between more and less risky actions, and prudence dictates that we take the less dangerous course; but what is called "prudence" is not alway reasonable. Sometimes it is more reasonable to assume a great risk for a great

	One-Party Case: B Acts Himself	Two-Party Case: B Consents to, Or Requests A's Action
Directly Caused (Certain) Harm	1. E.g. suicide, "self-mayhem"	2. E.g. voluntary euthanasia, consent to "surgical mayhem"
Assumed Risk Of Harm	3. E.g. mountain climbing, motor racing, smoking, drug-taking, high-speed driving	4. E.g. dangerous therapeutic surgery, gambling (against another), usury

Diagram 20-1. Direct harms and assumed risks in one and two party cases.

gain than to play it safe and forfeit a unique opportunity. Thus, it is not necessarily more reasonable for a coronary patient to increase his life expectancy by living a life of quiet inactivity than to continue working hard at his career in the hope of achieving something important even at the risk of a sudden fatal heart attack at any moment. There is no simple mathematical formula to guide one in making such decisions or for judging them "reasonable" or "unreasonable." On the other hand, there are other decisions that are manifestly unreasonable. It is unreasonable to drive at sixty miles an hour through a twenty-mile-an-hour zone to arrive at a party on time, but it may be reasonable to drive fifty miles an hour to get a pregnant wife to the maternity ward. It is foolish to resist an armed robber in an effort to protect one's wallet, but it may be worth a desperate lunge to protect one's life, or the life of a loved one.

In all of these cases a number of distinct considerations are involved.[1] If there is time to deliberate one should consider: (1) the degree of probability that harm to oneself will result from a given course of action, (2) the seriousness of the harm being risked, i.e. "the value or importance of that which is exposed to the risk," (3) the degree of probability that the goal inclining one to shoulder the risk will in fact result from the course of action, (4) the value or importance of achieving that goal, that is, just how worthwhile it is to one (this is the intimately personal factor, requiring a decision about one's own preferences, that makes the reasonableness of a risk-assessment on the whole so difficult for the outsider to make), and (5) the necessity of the risk, that is, the existence or absence of alternative, less risky, means to the desired goal (Diagram 20-2).

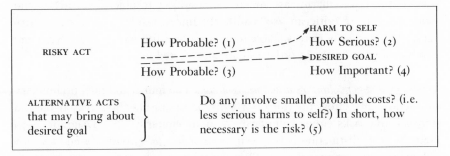

Diagram 20-2. Factors determing the reasonableness or unreasonableness of a risk to oneself.

Some judgments about the reasonableness of risk assumptions are quite uncontroversial. We can say, for example, that the greater are considerations (1), the probability of harm to self, and (2), the magnitude of the harm risked, the less reasonable the risk; and the greater considerations (3), the probability that the desired goal will result, (4), the importance of that goal to the actor, and (5), the necessity of the means, the more reasonable the risk. But in a given difficult case, even where questions of "probability" are meaningful and beyond dispute, and where all the relevant facts are known, the risk decision may defy objective assessment because of its component personal value judgments. Just how important is it *to me*, the actor must ask, that I climb to the top of Mount Everest? Is it worthwhile *to me* that I forego income from a job for two years in an effort to write a novel? These questions will be very difficult, perhaps impossible, for any outsider to answer on calculative or "rational" grounds. Indeed it is not clear that even the actor himself could "calculate" an answer to a question of comparative worthwhileness. In some cases the answer must simply be one of the "givens" in his deliberative problem.

In any event, it is a tenet of the soft paternalist view we are developing that if the state is to be given the right to prevent a person from risking harm to himself (and only himself), it must not be on the ground that the prohibited action is risky, or even that it is extremely risky, but rather on the ground that the risk is extreme and, in respect to its objectively assessable components, manifestly unreasonable to the point of suggesting impaired rationality. There are very good reasons sometimes for regarding even a person's judgment of personal worthwhileness (consideration 4) to be "manifestly unreasonable," but it remains to be seen whether (or when) that kind of unreasonableness can be sufficient grounds for interference. Judgments of probability, on the other hand, including judgments of the probability that the risk is "necessary" to achieve the desired goal, and judgments of the seriousness of the risked harm, are much more subject to objective criteria, and more often their criticism as "manifestly unreasonable" is beyond controversy. It is certainly unreasonable to cut off one's arm with a power saw, and risk bleeding to death, in order to cure an infected finger.

Voluntary and nonvoluntary assumptions of risk. The fourth and final preliminary distinction cuts across the third, for a person can assume both reasonable and unreasonable risks either voluntarily or nonvoluntarily. (See Diagram 20-3.) Actually, this distinction is between more or less *fully* voluntary and *not fully* voluntary assumptions of a risk. One can think of voluntariness as a matter of degree. At one end of a spectrum are the acts and choices that Aristotle called "deliberately chosen," and which I shall call for the moment (departing from Aristotle) *perfectly voluntary*. Only the actions of normal adult human beings in full control of their deliberative faculties can qualify for that description. Such persons assume a risk in a perfectly voluntary way if they shoulder it when fully informed of all relevant facts and contingencies, with their eyes wide open, so to speak, and in the absence of all coercive pressure. In the ideal case, there must be calmness and deliberateness (but see *infra*, §4, p. 117 for a qualification of this requirement), no distracting or unsettling emotions, no neurotic compulsion, no misunderstanding. To whatever extent there is compulsion, misinformation, clouded judgment (as for example from alcohol), or impaired reasoning, to that extent the choice falls short of perfect voluntariness. Most choices, of course, and perhaps even all choices, fall short of this ideal at least to some extent, and many choices must be made in circumstances which (as we shall see in §§4, 5) make it unreasonable to apply so stringent a concept of voluntariness for any practical purpose. We can nevertheless reserve the label *fully voluntary* for choices that come close to the "perfect" end of the spectrum, in contrast to those that fall substantially short of the ideal. The latter can be called relatively *nonvoluntary*.

At the very opposite end of the spectrum are those choices that even Aristotle agreed are not voluntary. We can call these, and only these, *involuntary* acts or choices. One's "choice" is completely involuntary either when it is no choice at all, properly speaking—when one lacks all muscular control, or when one is knocked down, or pushed, or sent reeling by a blow or an explosion—or when through ignorance one chooses something other than what one means to choose, for instance thinking arsenic powder is table salt, and thus choosing to sprinkle it on one's scrambled eggs. Most harmful choices, like most choices generally, fall somewhere in between the extremes of full voluntariness and complete involuntariness. It follows that we may formulate relatively strict (high) standards of voluntariness or relatively low standards of voluntariness in deciding, in a given context and for a given purpose, whether a dangerous choice is voluntary enough to be immune from interference. In some contexts we may even want to permit choices that are quite substantially *less* than "fully voluntary" to qualify as "voluntary enough." That is a theoretical option, at least, which is still open. Where on the spectrum the criterion of "sufficient voluntariness" should be marked is a problem to which we shall return in §§4 and 5.

The third and fourth distinctions, like the first and second, are represented in their relations to one another by a grid diagram (Diagram 20-3). No one would justify legal interference with voluntarily assumed reasonable risks, category (1). Neither is there controversy over category (4): hard and soft paternalists would agree that interference with unreasonably risky conduct, when the assumption of risk is substantially less than fully voluntary, may be justified, though perhaps the soft paternalist could settle for protective intervention and temporary detention, while the hard paternalist would be more likely to insist on coercion by prior prohibition backed by the threat of criminal punishment. Category (2), reasonable risks not voluntarily incurred, is also unproblematic, since all will agree that even substantially nonvoluntary choices, like the drunkard's choice of a ham sandwich at lunch, deserve protection unless there is some reason to judge them dangerous. Category (3), however, is the philosophically controversial one. Most of the conceptual subtleties that generate differences between hard and soft paternalists (less misleadingly called "paternalists" and "anti-paternalists," respectively) con-

	More or Less Fully Voluntary Assumptions of Risk to Oneself	Less Than Fully Voluntary Assumptions of Risk to Oneself
Reasonable Risk of Harm to Oneself	(1) E.g. most of the normally risky activities of life like driving a car or crossing a street.	(2) E.g. Those undangerous acts that are stumbled into unthinkingly while one is fatigued, distracted, or drunk, like shaking hands, ordering a sandwich, walking home.
Unreasonable Risk of Harm to Oneself	(3) E.g. cigarette smoking? (This is the controversial category. Are there any choices at all of this sort?)	(4) High speed automobile driving on an empty private road while drunk.

Diagram 20-3. Possible combinations of various degrees of voluntariness and reasonableness in risk assumptions.

cern the combination of risks that are at once *unreasonable and voluntarily assumed*. The hard paternalist is disposed to prohibit all and only unreasonable risk-taking, categories (3) and (4); the soft paternalist is disposed to prevent all and only dangerous nonvoluntary risk-taking, category (4) only. Therefore the hard paternalist would prohibit, and the soft paternalist would permit, voluntary unreasonable risk-taking—assuming that they can agree that there *are* any acts in this category.

3. Voluntariness, reasonableness and rationality

Can a person voluntarily assume a risk that is in fact unreasonable? The question is surrounded by bogs and snares. One possible source of disagreement is the confusion between *unreasonable* choices and *irrational* ones. If a person is severely retarded or deranged, or suffering from what lawyers call "insanity," then his "choices" (if the word applies at all) are likely to seem wildly irrational—patently inappropriate means to his own ends, invalid deductions from his own premises, gross departures from his own ideals, or actions based on grotesque delusions and factual distortions. Since the deranged or retarded person is incompetent in such ways, his irrational choices are not truly his—not "fully voluntary." "Unreasonable choices," however, are commonly made by fully competent persons in full command of their rational faculties. Part of the point of our calling such choices "unreasonable" is to suggest that they reflect judgments of comparative worthwhileness that *we* would not make were we in the chooser's position. Another part of the point is to hold the chooser responsible for the choices. If they are unwise choices, then he can be blamed for being unwise, but if they are irrational choices, then he is at least partially "exculpated," and there is no point in judging him "unwise." A person's true self is not represented by choices that are irrational. Thousands of eminently rational and responsible persons, however, judge that it is not worth the inconvenience to fasten their seat belts in automobiles, or that reducing their risk of getting lung cancer does not justify foregoing the pleasures of cigarette smoking, judgments that I, for one, with all due respect, find unreasonable. Perfectly rational persons can have unreasonable preferences as judged by other perfectly rational persons, just as perfectly rational men and women (for example, great philosophers) can hold "unreasonable beliefs" or doctrines as judged by other perfectly rational people. Particular unreasonableness, then, can hardly be strong evidence of general irrationality.

We apply the predicates "irrational" and "unreasonable" both in a general way to more or less enduring properties of persons, or as descriptions of specific choices and actions. Whether we are speaking of persons or actions, we sometimes mean by "irrational" no more than "extremely unreasonable" or perhaps "incomprehensibly unreasonable." But there is another usage in which "irrational" and "unreasonable" are defects that differ in kind, "unreasonable" standing for one end of the spectrum running from "sensible" and "wise" at one end to "foolish," "reckless," "short-sighted," or "perverse" at the other, and "irrational" referring to some gross cognitive incapacity that renders its possessor incompetent and his actions not subject to normal evaluations and judgments. (The actions of an insane person cannot be "wise," but neither can they be "foolish"; only competent people can act foolishly.) With unreasonableness, the concept as applied to specific acts is the fundamental and controlling one, and the notion applied to general properties of persons must be defined in terms of it. Thus, an unreasonable person is a person who is disposed to choose and act in unreasonable ways. Whereas with irrationality, the concept applied to persons is controlling, and the notion applied to specific acts is derivative, so that an irrational act is, by definition, an act of the sort an irrational (impaired, incompetent) person might do. In this sense, rational persons, on occasion, can choose or act irrationally, that is in a manner characteristic of irrational persons. If they are "temporarily insane," they are, of course, not responsible for their irrational behavior, but if they act irrationally while capable of doing otherwise, then their behavior may still be imputed to them, and they can be *judged* to be "willfully perverse," "wild," "unreasonable to the point of irrationality." The cognitive lapses are explained in these cases as the consequences of flawed character or temperament. The distinctions in this paragraph too can be expressed diagrammatically (Diagram 20-4).

Category (4) is the most interesting one for our purposes, for if unreasonable choices (counterproductive to the actor's *own* interests) may nevertheless be fully voluntary, the most likely candidates for that description are in this category. An unreasonable person characteristically departs from certain positive models of reasonableness which (unhappily for the terminology I proposed in Diagram 4) philosophers and economists tend to put in the language of "the perfectly rational person," or "practical rationality," or "economic rationality."[2] The rational person in this sense (I would still prefer the word "reasonable") is not merely *not* "irrational" in the sense of Diagram 4; rather he is a person with a definite positive description. He has a set of harmonious goals; he attaches weight to them carefully and ranks them so he will know how much to sacrifice of the lower to achieve the higher when he cannot get both; he carefully selects means that are likely to maximize the realization of his ends, avoiding those that have costs so high that they will be counterproductive; he avoids impulsive decisions, and whenever possible chooses after careful deliberation; he diversifies his investments to guard against unforeseen disaster; he balances his present desires against tomorrow's and next year's, his youth against his middle age and old age, and

	Irrational	Unreasonable
General Property of Persons	(1) Incompetence stemming from severe cognitive impairment.	(2) Defect of competent persons for which they are responsible, e.g. bad judgment, perversity, selfishness, recklessness, impulsiveness, etc. and which disposes them to chose and act unreasonably.
Specific Action or Choice	(3) The sort of behavior characteristic of irrational persons, done by rational people only while "temporarily insane" or because of extremely flawed character or temperament.	(4) Act or choice which is ill-designed to promote actor's goals, or promotes goals that do not integrate actor's network of goals. Based on factual or reasoning error, mistaken assessments of probability or alternative means, overevaluation of a particular goal, injudicious "balancing" decisions, etc.

Diagram 20-4. Irrationality and unreasonableness as applied to persons and acts.

treats all of his future selves equally, refusing to sacrifice one for another.[3] If such a person acts "unreasonably" on a given occasion, if for example he drinks to the point of a disabling hangover the next day, it is not because he doesn't care, or doesn't try. Very likely, it is because some distracting circumstances temporarily weakened his rational resolve, or because he made various miscalculations. He may have misread the probabilities, forgotten the alternative, misjudged the causal efficacy of his drinks or lost count of their number—simple intellectual errors. Surely his imprudent actions were not "deliberately chosen," and surely they don't accurately represent his settled values and preferences. They are not good examples then of "voluntary unreasonableness."

The generally unreasonable person, on the other hand (in the sense of Diagram 4) is disposed to depart from the model of economic rationality frequently, if not from calculative errors and traits like excitability, then from character defects like short-sighted self-indulgence. He may be unaware of his defect, refuse to acknowledge it, reject blame for it, and feel no regret after his follies. Such a person, I am inclined to say, acts both voluntarily and unreasonably. On the other hand, the morally defective unreasonable person may be similar to the model of rationality who suffers occasional lapses, in that he regrets his failings after they occur, and knows well their source. Such a person concedes his own dispositional unreasonableness and the frequent unreasonable acts to which it leads. He may suffer from the ill-named syndrome "weakness of will," a disposition to act in a way he knows at the time to be unreasonable, for example lighting another cigarette.[4] In a typical case, of this kind, it is not always possible to explain the "weak-willed" person's conduct as the result of compulsion, internal or external, or of some irresistibly powerful passion,[5] or even some especially enticing temptation. His unreasonableness is all the more troublesome (and puzzling to philosophers) for seeming fully voluntary. It would infringe his autonomy to coerce him into more reasonable self-regarding behavior, but he may nevertheless exercise his autonomy, if others agree to cooperate, by inviting such coercion in advance, in the manner of Odysseus at the mast.

A more interesting specimen still is the person whose deliberate departures from what others call "perfect (economic) rationality," are made by genuine preference, taste, or conviction. Imprudence may not pay off in the long run, and impulsive adventurers and gamblers may be losers in the end, but they do not always or necessarily have regrets. Hangovers are painful and set back one's efforts, but careful niggling prudence is dull and unappealing. Better the life of spontaneity, impulse, excitment, and risk, even if it be short, and even if the future self must bear the costs. We all know that there are people who have such attitudes and have them authentically. When they act in pursuit of these values they do not, of course, "deliberately choose" their actions; but they have long since "deliberately chosen" the way of life in which deliberate choices play no important role, or if even that is not true and their very life-plans are spontaneous and unexamined, their guiding policies do indeed reflect their characters in deep and important ways without being "deliberately chosen." Here we must make our first departure from the deliberative model of voluntariness. (And there will be more.)

To coerce the unapologetic romantic adventurer or gambler—the person with a genuine preference for the present to the future, for youth over old age—on the grounds that his preferences are not *voluntary* (truly and authentically his), then, is not possible. It would be even worse to coerce him into prudence while *admitting* that his reckless preferences are authentic, but on the quite distinct ground that voluntary or not, in departing from the philosopher-economist's model of "perfect rationality" they are unreasonable. (*We* don't think the goals he seeks are worth the risks he takes.) That is the path that denies his autonomy utterly. Richard Arneson is eloquent on this matter, condemning hard paternalism for failing "to safeguard adequately the right of persons to choose and pursue life plans that deviate from maximal rationality or that hamper future prospects of rational choice." And he gives examples of "deviations from maximal rationality" to add to our gallery of specimens—

> This failing is manifest when proposed paternalistic coercion would enhance someone's capacity for rationality by means of uprooting an irrational trait that is prominent in his self-conception or even in his ideal of himself. Consider the project of forcing adult education on a hillbilly who is suspicious of urban ways and identifies himself as a rural character. Somewhat similarly, the wild Heathcliff in *Wuthering Heights* would doubtless find his "ability to rationally consider and carry out his own decisions" considerably enhanced if psychotherapy coercively administered should extirpate his self-destructive passion for Catherine Earnshaw. Note that no taint of sympathy for rural parochialism or for grotesque romanticism need color the judgment that paternalism is unacceptable in such instances. Rather these examples recall to us the conviction that rationality in the sense of economic prudence, the efficient adaptation of means to ends, is a *value* which we have no more reason to impose on an adult against his will for his own good than we have reason to impose any other value on paternalistic grounds. A vivid reminder that rationality may sometimes be alien to some humans is the circumstance that persons sometimes self-consciously choose to nurture an irrational quirk at the center of their personalities. Perhaps it is appropriate to deplore such a choice but not to coerce it.[6]

What Arneson (and others) call the economic model of rationality is so fixed in our usage that even when we defend romantic departures from it, we refer to them, nevertheless, in a purely descriptive way as "unreasonable" or "less than rational" or even "irrational." This fixed conventional usage, unfortunately, lends itself to equivocation and question-begging. Normally, we *endorse* a line of conduct when we label it "reasonable" or "rational," and reject it when we charge that it is "unreasonable" or "not rational." It would be natural then for the impetuous romantic to defend his life style as "reasonable" or "rational" after all, but he cannot do this very well if these terms have been preempted for other uses. Now he must say, with Arneson, that it is not alien to his humanity "to nurture an irrational quirk." If that is what usage requires, very well. It serves our present purposes well, for the point to be emphasized here is that it is lack of voluntariness that justifies interference with a person's liberty for his own good, not lack of "rationality."

Nevertheless, it is possible to defend as "truly reasonable" or "not really contrary to reason," preferences that might otherwise be dismissed out of hand, as unworthy of either respect or protection. The important thing to note about "the economic model of rationality," even as presented by Rawls with subtlety and persuasive thoroughness, is that it purports to be no more than a *formal* conception. Numerous alternative and highly divergent lifeplans can satisfy it equally. The role of practical reason for Rawls is much the same as for Hume—to serve a persons's antecedently given wants, and select efficacious means to his antecedently given ends. Of course, ends themselves can be judged rational or irrational depending on how well they cohere with the antecedently given economy of ends which they are to join. "The aim of deliberation is to find that plan which best organizes our activities and influences the formation of our subsequent wants so that our aims and interests can be fruitfully combined into one scheme of conduct."[7] But coherence is not a sufficient test for wants; it cannot be true that each "rational" want or aim is adopted because of its unique capacity to cohere with all the rest. Our wants and values, our preferences and trade-off judgments of worthwhileness, must come, at least in part, from some other source. Many of the most basic of these will emerge as the natural expression of temperamental proclivities, acquired loyalties, and spontaneous tastes that must be taken as simply given. Some people quite naturally prefer adventure and risk to tranquility and security, spontaneity to deliberation, turbulent passions to safety. Instead of being ostracized as "not rational," these givens should become part of the test for the rationality of subsequent wants that must cohere with *them*.

Another snare in the approach to our problem is implicit in the discussion above. Some eccentrically imprudent behavior may not be "voluntarily unreasonable" not because, being unreasonable it cannot be voluntary, but rather because, dangerous though it may be, it is not truly unreasonable *in relation to the actor's own interests*. When we judge another's actions as "unreasonable," we are criticizing them, unfavorably evaluating them, rejecting them. Our judgment expresses our unwillingness to advise or encourage the actors to perform them,[8] on the ground that they are counterproductive means to the *actor's* goals. But when the actor assumes a risk that would in fact be unreasonable in relation to *our* goals, we have a tendency to project our goals (or the way we rank goals) onto him. From our point of view, what he chooses *is* unreasonable. His conduct would not be likely to promote his goals if his goals were like ours, and we are literally incapable of believing that another person's values (the degree of relative importance he attaches to his various ends) could be *so* different from our own. Of course, he might assume a risk that would be unreasonable if *we* assumed it only because his faculties of judgment were clouded or impaired, in which case his risk-assumption is less than fully voluntary. But if none of the voluntariness-reducing factors is present, his odd choice must be explained as due to his judgment that the goal he seeks is so important that it is worth the extreme risk he voluntarily takes. We may comprehend all this and still, understandably, label his conduct "unreasonable," but all we are doing is employing our own judgment of comparative worthwhileness in rejecting his. Conventional usage, embodying conventional judgments, may support us. Perhaps radical departures from prudence are "unreasonable" in some sense *by definition*. But "unreasonableness" so understood is not incompatible with voluntariness, and not a sufficient ground for coercive interference.

How can we summarize the complicated relations between voluntariness, on the one hand, and reasonableness and economic rationality on the other? "Rationality" in the sense of Diagram 4 merely rules out "irrationality" or incompetence, and the latter, except for borderline cases of extreme perversity, are of course not compatible with voluntariness. Rationality in the economist's sense, however, is more than a mere privative notion, meaningful only in ruling out its opposite.[9] It consists of definite rules for maximizing want-satisfaction over the course of a whole long life. The most apt opposite term for "rational" in this positive sense is "not rational," since "irrational" suggests wild and nonresponsible extremes. Actions which, in their self-regarding character, are not rational may also be called "unreasonable" by one who wishes to express disapproval of them while recognizing them as products of an intellectually unimpaired, hence responsible, agent. But this usage is dangerous insofar as it suggests that the "not rational" behavior is necessarily unworthy of respect, and that no case can possibly be made for it.

Voluntariness, though consistent with "not-rational actions," is ruled out by irrationality (derangement), since the severely impaired person we call "irrational" is presumed incapable of knowing sufficiently clearly what he is doing. On the other hand, perfectly competent persons sometimes act unreasonably even by their own standards, and when such behavior is simply the product of "calculative errors" and other mistaken or forgotten judgments, it is less than fully voluntary. There are various common examples, however, of behavior that is both fully voluntary and in some sense "unreasonable" or "not rational." Some of the actions deliberately chosen contrary to the actor's own standards out of "weakness of will" may be a case in point. Actions that stem from character defects unacknowledged by the actor are another. These we may wish to call "perverse," "wanton," "self-indulgent," "volatile," or "rash." When nevertheless we concede that they were done in character— "that is just what he *would* do," we say—we may have no reason to deny their voluntariness. Still another kind of case is that of the person who acts in character, but of whom it would be unfair or at least question-begging to apply one of the character-defect terms. Instead we have to say, in a more neutral way, that he is "adventurous," or "romantic," that he takes pride in an "irrational quirk" that is part of his self-image or self-ideal, etc. We might still wish to disapprove of him, and dissuade others from imitating him, toward which ends we may judge his self-regarding conduct as "not rational" or "unreasonable." Still, his conduct could satisfy the purely formal requirements of an economic model of rationality, and the actor's own values and ideals, provided that he holds no long term goals in a way that clashes with his dangerous life-style. Finally, whether we characterize his conduct as "rational" or not, since it represents him faithfully in an important way, expressing his settled values and preferences, it is surely voluntary. That is the important thing.

4. The elusive model of a "perfectly voluntary choice"

For the purposes of the soft paternalist strategy—the effort to find an autonomy-respecting rationale for reasonable, apparently paternalistic restrictions—how voluntary is voluntary enough? The question is more complicated than it may seem, and we shall be occupied with it through Chapter 27. We can make a start at it here by considering, and rejecting, standards of voluntariness that are too low, and others that are too high. In a way Aristotle gives us good examples of both (though of course that was not his intention). Let us consider here how Aristotle's definition of "voluntary action" provides us with standards that are too low, and his conception of "deliberate choice" with standards that are too high.

Voluntary actions, according to Aristotle, are those done (1) "not under compulsion" and (2) "not by reason of ignorance of the circumstances."[10] His notions of compulsion and knowledge are themselves so strict that it seems likely that he wishes to exclude from the category of voluntariness only cases like the examples already given of losing muscular control and being crucially misinformed. Everything that is not completely involuntary in the sense we have defined, then, is voluntary for Aristotle, and that includes all but the extreme lower end of the spectrum of voluntariness. Aristotle's concept of voluntariness is thus much more precise than modern ones, for example those used in modern legal systems, and also more rigorous, since it requires a great deal more to remove a person's actions from the realm of judgment. So for example, he insists that acts are voluntary even when done under coercion ("acts done from fear of greater evils . . . e.g. if a tyrant were to order one to do something base, having one's parents and children in his power, and if one did the action they were to be saved, but otherwise would be put to death"[11]), or from fear of natural forces (e.g. "the throwing of goods overboard in a storm"[12]). Moreover, he allows that infants, animals,[13] drunkards, and men in a towering rage[14] might yet act voluntarily if only they are undeceived about the crucial factual circumstances and not overwhelmed by external physical force.

We must remember that Aristotle's concern with voluntariness was not the same as ours. His purpose was to demarcate that class of "passions and actions," on which "praise and blame are bestowed," and he took the term "voluntary" to function primarily to refer to that class, while its logical contradictory "involuntary" serves mainly to identify those actions subject to neither praise nor blame, but instead to "pardon and sometimes also pity."

Even the sea captain, "forced" by an impending storm to jettison his cargo in order to save his ship, can be praised or blamed for his judgment or courage in the circumstances, whereas neither would apply if he himself were simply blown overboard by an irresistible gust of wind, for then the cause of his body's movement would not have been within him, and his course not chargeable in any degree to his own will. Aristotle was not concerned to determine when other parties might interfere rightly with a person's own liberty for his own good, or with other legal-political problems more characteristically the object of modern inquiry.

In any event, Aristotle's definition diverges from modern "common sense" in the following ways. First, it does not distinguish among persons in respect to their capacities, and thus lumps together as "voluntary" actors infants, mentally ill persons, mentally retarded persons, even animals, without distinction. Second, it includes as "voluntary," without qualification, acts done under influences that deprive the actor, at least temporarily, of full use of his reason—drug-induced illusions, drunkeness, blurred awareness, extreme fatigue, powerful moods, intense emotions—all conditions which lead observers to judge that the actor was "not really himself," or was "beside himself," or that he "didn't know what he was doing." Third, it includes as voluntary, acts done in general ignorance, not of factual circumstances, but of crucial consequences, particularly legal consequences of acts of consent. Fourth, it includes as voluntary, acts done without "fair opportunity" to do otherwise, acts emerging from threats, warnings, manipulative suggestion, or unequal bargaining leverage. All such acts are "voluntary" for Aristotle's purposes, and perhaps plausibly enough; but for our purposes, the construction of a credible soft paternalist theory, they are not nearly voluntary enough.

On the other hand, we cannot borrow Aristotle's concept of "deliberate choice" (as I did in my much criticized 1971 paper, "Legal Paternalism"[15]) because that would serve as so elevated a test of voluntariness that relatively few acts could satisfy it. In that case, interference with dangerous self-regarding behavior would very often be justified, and soft paternalism would differ little in its application from hard paternalism. Chosen actions, for Aristotle, are those that are decided upon by deliberation, and that is a process that requires time, information, a clear head, and highly developed rational faculties.[16] The soft paternalist, however, will condemn interference with some dangerous but self-regarding actions even though they are not preceded by deliberation, or are done under pressure of time, or in a state of excitement or depression, or are of dubious "rationality." The concept of deliberate choice then would not make a suitable criterion of voluntariness for his purposes, since it sets its standards of voluntariness too high and leaves them there inflexibly.

Even more extreme, perhaps, than Aristotelian "deliberate choice," is the elusive concept of a "perfectly voluntary choice" deficient in *none* of the ways that are *ever* taken into account for *any* moral or legal purpose in *any* context. All of the parts of this composite ideal have some relevance to some legal determination or another, but taken all together, they yield an unwieldy standard of dubious coherence. Diagram 20-5 lists the main elements of this impossibly high standard.

The reader will probably recognize each component of this complex as one which is sometimes relevant to a determination of voluntariness for some

A. THE CHOOSER IS "COMPETENT," i.e.
   Not an animal
   Not an infant
   Not insane (deluded, disoriented, irrational)
   Not severely retarded
   Not comatose
B. HE DOES NOT CHOOSE UNDER COERCION OR DURESS
   Not a forced choice of an evil less severe than the one threatened
   Not a forced choice of a lesser evil than one expected from a natural source
   Not a choice forced by a "coercive offer"
   Not a choice produced by "coercive pressure," e.g. from a hard bargainer in
   an unequal negotiating position
C. HE DOES NOT CHOOSE BECAUSE OF MORE SUBTLE
   MANIPULATION
   Not because of subliminal suggestion
   Not because of post-hypnotic suggestion
   Not because of "sleep-teaching," etc.
D. HE DOES NOT CHOOSE BECAUSE OF IGNORANCE
   OR MISTAKEN BELIEF
   Not because of ignorance (mistake) of factual circumstances
   Not because of ignorance of the likely consequences of the various
   alternatives open to him
E. HE DOES NOT CHOOSE IN CIRCUMSTANCES THAT ARE
   TEMPORARILY DISTORTING
   Not impetuously (on impulse)
   Not while fatigued
   Not while excessively nervous, agitated, or excited
   Not under the influence of a powerful passion, e.g. rage, hatred, lust, or a
   gripping mood, e.g. depression, mania
   Not under the influence of mind-numbing drugs, e.g. alcohol
   Not in pain, e.g. headache
   Not a neurotically compulsive or obsessive choice
   Not made under severe time pressures

Diagram 20-5. The model of a perfectly voluntary choice.

practical purpose, but will fail to think of many occasions in his own life when he made a choice that fully satisfied all of them. To require that a voluntary act, for any purpose, satisfy *all* of them *fully*, would be to apply an impossibly difficult ideal standard, one that would hardly ever be satisfied. Moreover, almost each element is subject, in special circumstances, to its own exceptions or qualifications, so few of them can be considered as necessary conditions even for a wholly voluntary act in those circumstances. For example, we distinguish for training purposes acts of dogs that are voluntary from those forced by the threat of punishment. By the standards applicable to dogs, not only are some canine acts more voluntary than others, but some are as perfectly voluntary as we could hope. A similar point can be made about small children whose "reflective faculties" are still largely undeveloped. Similarly, a retarded patient, despite his handicap, might exercise a perfectly voluntary preference for chocolate over vanilla ice cream. Perhaps only the comatose, among the incompetent, are utterly incapable of voluntary acts, but that is because they are incapable of action altogether.

Again, there are occasions on which life offers us only unhappy alternatives, and we must choose—voluntarily if possible—the lesser evil. Perhaps it cannot be said without fuller explanation that we chose an evil voluntarily when our choice was so limited in the first place, but we can choose more or less deliberately, more or less unneurotically, in a more or less well-informed state, and the choice we finally make *can* be as fully voluntary as was possible in the circumstances. Similarly, bargaining positions are rarely if ever exactly equal, yet voluntary agreements emerge often enough between unequals even given the background of uneven power and "coercive pressure." Then of course we must remember the distinction between agreements *in* unequal circumstances and agreements *from* (caused by) unequal circumstances. Aristotle distinguished similarly between choices in ignorance (but such that they would not change even if there were knowledge) and choices "by reason of ignorance." If we count the former as deficient in voluntariness, it is only because we do not know for sure whether the ignorance plays a determining role and we wish to be *sure* that the actor's choice is voluntary, not because we think it cannot be voluntary even in ignorance. Again, if we permit a false belief about the consequences of an action to count against its voluntariness, then all losing wagers, to take one humble example, are *ipso facto* nonvoluntary from the beginning, and no one can ever be said to gamble voluntarily until we learn that he has won.

We may have similar doubts about applying the nonimpetuousness standard, especially in cases where the deliberation that is its alternative is dauntingly complex, and the "gut feeling" strong. And in some cases the fatigue and nonagitation criteria may work against one another, so that a certain degree of tiredness may be necessary to take the edge off one's nervousness, leading to an optimally clear-headed state. Surely the total absence of nervousness in circumstances calling for alertness could be as bad as an excess. There are even more difficult problems in applying the "no passion standard." Relevant as it is in some circumstances, it is clearly not required in others. Are we to say for example, that a decision to cease benefitting gratuitously a person who has done us wrong cannot be voluntary if made in anger? Or that all acts of sexual intercourse entered into in sexual passion are *ipso facto* nonvoluntary (because of the passion)? Or that a decision to end one's own life can only be voluntary if made while one is not depressed? (See Chap. 27, §5.) Or that a neurotic person cannot marry or choose his profession voluntarily? Is the choice to take an aspirin less than voluntary if made by a person suffering from a headache? Are we to say that a jury's decision is made nonvoluntarily because a judge limits its deliberation period to seven days? What of the decisions of referee-panels at boxing matches, or at gymnastics and diving contests, which must be made in sixty seconds?

Obviously each of the criteria is properly used in *some* contexts, and for some purposes, but no one of them is used in *all* contexts for all purposes. (Even the "faithful expression" criterion, to which I have already had recourse [*supra*, p. 113] has its exceptions. Perhaps it is useful in most contexts to take the crux of voluntariness to be the faithful expression of the settled values and preferences of the actor, or an accurate representation of him in some centrally important way. What then are we to say of the person who voluntarily chooses, for some purpose of the moment, to act out of character?[17]) All of the components taken altogether may well define an ideal that has no application in the real world.

5. Variable standards for voluntariness: some rules of thumb

It may not always be possible, even in principle, to say of one act that it is more voluntary or closer to being voluntary than another, or that one has a certain quantifiable degree of voluntariness that places it at some arithmetically specifiable point in a ranking, so many units above or below the other. Still, we can conceive clearly of completely involuntary end points, and of some choices near the high end of a scale, and we can talk, with appropriate caution, of higher and lower standards of voluntariness, suggesting higher or lower cut-off points on a common scale. The discussion in section 4 suggests that we should treat voluntariness as a "variable concept," determined by higher and lower cut-off points depending on the nature of the circumstances, the interests at stake, and the moral or legal purpose to be served. In that case, we could expect higher standards in some circumstances and for some kinds of choice than for others. (See Diagram 20-6.) Confining our

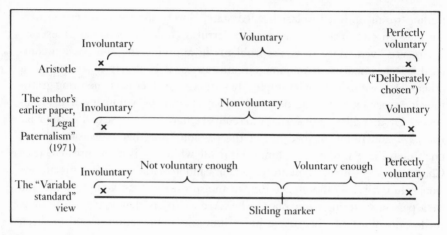

Diagram 20-6 Three ways of determining when conduct is "voluntary enough" to be immune from interference.

attention for the moment to one kind of political/legal purpose—that of determining when self-regarding dangerous choices are "voluntary enough" to be immune from restriction—we can begin to give substance to the variable conception of voluntariness by listing some rules of thumb suggested by common sense.

1. *The more risky the conduct the greater the degree of voluntariness required if the conduct is to be permitted.* It is not the aim of the soft paternalist to minimize nonvoluntary behavior as such. Persons may act as nonvoluntarily as is imaginable and as frequently as possible, so far as the soft paternalist is concerned, provided no harm is caused thereby. If A sees B about to put cherry jam on his toast under the impression that it is strawberry, he has neither the right nor the duty to intervene forcibly, though a timely warning would be nice. But if A sees B pouring arsenic on his eggs then he must intervene to determine whether B knows what he is doing. If B does know what he is doing, in the fullest sense, then further forcible prevention is not warranted. If A sees a very drunk B about to plunge into a safely shallow but icy pond, under the impression that it is a dangerously deep but comfortably warm pool, he might warn him that he might find the experience unpleasantly chilly, but that would hardly be a reason for physically preventing him. On the other hand, if the drunk is about to plunge into a dangerous stream at a point deep enough to drown in, then B has a duty to cross-examine him carefully to determine whether he fully comprehends the extent of the danger before permitting him to proceed. If B is only in danger of scratches, bruises, head colds, and the like, A might employ a much lower standard of voluntariness than if serious injury or death is risked; and if the probability

of serious injury is real but low (say 20%) the standards may be lower than if the probability were high (say 50%).

This may appear to be a compromise with hard paternalism and its commitment to harm prevention quite apart from voluntariness. But the soft paternalist's concern is not simply to prevent people from harming themselves, and not simply to prevent people from acting with low degrees of voluntariness. The defining purpose of the soft paternalist is to prevent people from suffering harm that they have not truly chosen to suffer or to risk suffering, and our first rule of thumb does not compromise *that* purpose.

The first rule of thumb entails that the voluntariness required for permissible self-endangering actions should be determined by standards whose stringency varies directly with the gravity of the risked harm[18] and with the probability of the risked harm occurring. What about the *reasonableness* of the risk? What further bearing, if any, should it have on the required degree of voluntariness? If the magnitude of the risk of harm to the actor, itself compounded out of the gravity of the harm risked and the probability of its occurring, is high, then we owe it to the actor to confirm that his assumption of the risk is voluntary by appropriately stringent standards. If we maintain that the risk is not only of high magnitude but also of dubious reasonableness, our grounds can only be that either (a) the goal for the sake of which the actor assumed the risk is not itself worth a risk of that magnitude, or (b) equally convenient and equally efficacious alternative means are available to the same goal that involve much less risk. But to jack up our standards of voluntariness because of (a) *would* be to compromise with the hard paternalist's policy of imposing his own judgments of worthwhileness on unwilling autonomous agents. What we would be doing, in effect, would be throwing into the equation for deciding voluntariness (and thus permissibility) our own judgments of worthwhileness instead of the actor's. That would be to give weight to unreasonableness as a factor in determining voluntariness—not so extreme a measure as that of the hard paternalist who keeps voluntariness and reasonableness separate and then gives decisive weight to unreasonableness, but a kind of compromise nonetheless.

On the other hand, if we learn (b) that less risky means are available and also that the actor does not know that they are available, then it follows that the actor's choice of the more dangerous course was by no means as voluntary as we first thought. If the magnitude of the danger in that course is very high, then his choice may not be voluntary enough until he learns of the alternative. Then if he is reasonable, he will probably change his mind, thank us for our help, and opt for the less risky alternative. If he sticks by his original choice, however, on the grounds (say) that there is some intrinsic appeal in that course of activity quite apart from its instrumentality, and though he cannot explain it further it is his considered preference, greater danger notwithstanding, then the soft paternalist must let him proceed. (The only exception to these conclusions acceptable to the soft paternalist is if the actor's judgments of worthwhileness and his preference for the unnecessarily perilous course seem so bizarre that they raise the suspicion of general irrationality, or insanity, which of course annuls voluntariness wherever there is any danger.)

2. *The more irrevocable the risked harm, the greater the degree of voluntariness required if it is to be permitted.* The reasoning behind this maxim is familiar enough. Many harmful decisions can be changed, cancelled, or compensated for, after the fact. Many harms can be repaired; illnesses can be cured; losses recouped; traps escaped. Once an irrevocable harm has occurred, however, it is too late to do anything about it. A mistake in judging the voluntariness of an irrevocably self-harmful act can never be corrected. So obviously, other things being equal, greater care is required in testing the voluntariness of such acts than in cases of comparably dangerous behavior when the risked harms can be repaired or undone. So much is elementary common sense.

As we have seen (Vol. 1, Chap. 1, §6), not all deaths are equally harmful to the one who dies, and some may not be very harmful at all. But all deaths are equally final and irrevocable. The voluntariness of decisions to terminate one's own life or to assume substantial risks of accidental death to oneself, therefore, must be determined, other things being equal, by stringent standards. The first and second rules of thumb, however, might in some cases work against one another, and where the death appears not harmful in itself, or not very harmful, the test of voluntariness may be pegged at a lower cut-off point than otherwise. Aged patients in terrible pain from incurable illnesses, in that case, might choose death voluntarily by standards a good deal lower than those applied to youthful depressed would-be suicides. But all deaths, it is worth repeating, are equally irrevocable, so the second rule of thumb would place a floor under our standards for testing the voluntariness of decisions to die or to assume serious risks of death. And if *all* we know, in a given case, is that the choice or risk is death, then until we know more, we must apply stringent standards of voluntariness.

Another example of a harmful choice which for all practical purposes may be irrevocable is the decision to begin taking an addicting drug. If the drug-taker has no idea that the drug is in fact addicting, or if he falsely believes that it will not be addicting in his case, then his decision falls well below the requisite level of voluntariness. In an important way he is like the person who knows that he is putting arsenic on his eggs, but believes that arsenic in such quantities is harmless or will be harmless in his case. There are further possibilities. He may know that the heroin he seeks is addicting, but falsely believe that it is addicting in a stable way, so that he can level off at a given dose and be happy with that relatively harmless amount for the rest of his (possibly shortened but otherwise normal) life. He believes, in short, that heroin is addicting in the manner of nicotine or caffeine, and that so long as he has the funds to satisfy his compulsive craving in a regular but moderate way, he is not running a serious risk. (For the sake of the example, assume that heroin is legal, so that there are no risks of the sort that stem from law enforcement.) Once more, we must judge that his choice is insufficiently voluntary, at least if we assume that heroin addiction is as it is commonly thought to be, unstable, that is, requires ever greater quantities to produce the same effect until the craved-for level itself is physically harmful or fatal. In that case the drug-taker does not really know the risks he is taking and his assumption of those risks cannot be voluntary until he finds out.

Suppose then that he does find out, and he still is willing to run the risk. He has enough money to keep him in supply for the forseeable future. Once he is hooked, he will not ever change his mind and try to become unhooked, and if he is eventually endangered by the prospect of overdoses, he will literally kill himself with pleasure, having led a brief but consistently, and maximally, pleasant life in the meantime. Such a choice comes much closer to being sufficiently well-informed for voluntariness, but it might yet fall short if the chooser's knowledge of the risk is only a dim cognitive awareness with no complementary emotional realization. He "knows" the risk, but he may not fully *understand* it and take it to heart. Perhaps it would help to talk to advanced addicts in their squalid hovels or to those in sanitoria who have attempted to go "cold turkey." In the end, of course, the drug-taker's resolution may not flag even after he has demonstrated a full and visceral appreciation, as well as a cognitive awareness, of the dangers. Then we must say that his self-destructive choice was voluntary by our appropriately elevated standards.

3. *In still other ways the standard of voluntariness must be tailored to various special circumstances.* The concept of voluntariness may have had its origin in common discourse and ordinary moral purposes, but it has found its main home in legal systems, where it has become ramified and reshaped into a technical term. It is used in all the major branches of the law as an either–or concept: any given testamentary will, or criminal confession, or contractual offer must in principle be capable of being judged voluntary or not voluntary without hedging or evasion, since legal judgments of validity, guilt, or liability hinge on voluntariness. Still, legal writers know that the forces and pressures, understandings and confusions, and other factors that determine voluntariness or involuntariness are themselves matters of degree, so that standards of voluntariness require that lines be drawn at points on scales, sometimes higher, sometimes lower, depending on the legal issue. "It was once said, for example, that circumstances that did not render a confession involuntary according to the Supreme Court would plainly have been sufficient to vitiate a will."[19] Simi-

larly, we can expect the point of legal voluntariness to vary depending on whether we are investigating a householder's consent to a policeman's warrantless search of his home, a defendant's agreement to a plea-bargaining proposal, a merchant's acceptance of proposed terms in a business transaction, an intervention in a causal sequence in a tort case, a plaintiff's assumption of risk, a patient's consent to surgery, a woman's consent to sexual advances in a rape trial, a plaintiff's conferral of a gratuitous benefit in a restitution case, and so on. Our present concern is more legislative than juridical, namely how the law should treat self-regarding harmful or dangerous actions and agreements, but this concern covers as many contexts and as diverse purposes as the corresponding juridical concern, and we should expect as great a variance in standards of voluntariness.

The main distinction that should be made under this head is between standards that are applied to a person's acts or choices against an unrestrictive or "normal" background, and those that are relativized to a specific actual background that may be in its very nature restrictive, for example, incarceration in a prison or confinement as a patient in a hospital. Suppose that a person who has already served nine years of a fifty-year prison term is given the option of having that term reduced to ten years if he agrees to become a subject for twelve months in a dangerous medical experiment. He agrees, though with some trepidation, to do so. Was his agreement voluntary? If we apply the standards of voluntariness appropriate to the unrestrictive or normal background, we must conclude that the prisoner did *not* voluntarily choose to be a subject in a dangerous experiment. He had little choice. Continued life in the hated prison environment was his alternative and that prospect exerted coercive pressure almost as great as a gunman's threat of death. On the other hand, if we take the prison situation as simply given, and apply our standards against that background, we may get quite the contrary result. Now our standards will apply to what was done in *those* circumstances, taking the person *talis qualis* (exactly as he is), not as he would be if his circumstances were normal and unrestrictive.

In those actual circumstances his decision *might* still have been less than voluntary. The prison might have put drugs in his food, threatened him with solitary confinement or beatings if he declined, hypnotized him and then "suggested" that he express his consent, or misrepresented the danger. Even judging him against *the normal prison background*, we would say in those cases that his consent was involuntary. But none of those things were done, so we can accept the consent as voluntary in its setting, even though when judged against the wider background of the normal world, its voluntariness was deficient. The choice of assumed backgrounds or "perspectives" is ours, to be determined by our purposes in undertaking the inquiry.

Contextual variations for ascriptions of voluntariness and the different perspectives from which they may be made will be a governing theme in Chapters 21 to 27, so we need not list examples here. A humble example we have already encountered will suffice. Where attention to detail and full understanding of the consequences is important for voluntariness, a severe headache may render one's consent less than wholly voluntary. But if a person must choose whether or not to take an aspirin, then standards of voluntariness may be applied to him *talis qualis*, headache and all, instead of from the perspective of a normal person in normal circumstances.

One purpose for ascribing voluntariness is to assist judgment (grading, blaming, giving credit, evaluating) of how a person performed in a certain set of unfavorable circumstances. To be sure, he was under coercive pressure from a gunman to do X, so we cannot attribute X to him as his own voluntary act just as if there had been no pressure at all. The coercion mitigates or exculpates, and judging from the normal unrestrictive perspective, we must find the person's action insufficiently voluntary to be blamed. But our purpose, like Aristotle's, may be to judge the person's performance, *talis qualis*, against the background of the circumstances that actually obtained (including the responsibility-cancelling coercive elements). Given that a gunman threatened to shoot him unless he did something dishonorable, how calm did he remain? How courageously did he act? With what wisdom or foolishness did he decide? Should he have given more consideration to resisting? Did he decide correctly? He may yet be responsible for his coerced behavior in these limited ways, that is subject to these evaluative judgments, even though he cannot be blamed for his action, which is involuntary from the normal perspectives presupposed by moral judgment.

On the other hand, the general purpose of inquiring into voluntariness may be to decide whether or not various kinds of moral/legal effect may attach to what a person did. Judged *talis qualis* the person may deserve credit for good judgment, coolness under fire, and courage, in a context that deprived his action of legal effect. The will that he signed at gunpoint may be invalid because it is involuntary from the normal perspective, but his act of signing it might not have been too short of voluntariness for him to be given credit for good judgment or perhaps blame for deficient courage. The latter evaluative judgments require voluntariness only as determined by standards tailored to the actual circumstances. Judgments of legal invalidity (or guiltlessness or immunity) normally require only involuntariness by untailored standards applied from a hypothetical normal perspective.

Another way of putting the same distinction is to speak of "relativity to the description of the act." Described as "signing that legal document," the act was involuntary. Described as "exercising the limited choice permitted by the gunman," the act was voluntary. How the person exercised his limited choice is something we may evaluate (as cool, sensible, unheroic); that *he signed the document* may not even be ascribed to him, for legal purposes, as his doing, and the legal effect is as if he had not signed at all.

6. The presumption of nonvoluntariness

In some circumstances there may seem to be another kind of reason for intervening in self-endangering conduct to determine whether it is "sufficiently voluntary," and perhaps also (though this is much less plausible) for applying relatively high standards of voluntariness to govern that determination. We may be obliged to intervene in this fashion when the act in question is of a type that is rarely chosen voluntarily, and relatively often chosen nonvoluntarily. This statistical information may rightly make us suspicious of the voluntariness in the case at hand, and lead us to check the actor's motives and situation very carefully before allowing him to proceed. The justification for our extra caution in these cases is not (necessarily) that the threatened harm is unusually grave, or that the assumed risk is unusually great, or that the harm would be relatively irrevocable, although when these factors are also present, there are even more reasons for great care and high standards. Our justification for extra caution in the present cases is simply our expectation based on experience that the act is not voluntary, and our need to make sure, therefore, that the present case is different in that respect from most others of its category. Our statistical information justifies the intervention itself in cases where there might not be sufficient ground otherwise, and it justifies somewhat greater skepticism and care in our subsequent inquiry, but it does not by itself justify the use of higher standards of voluntariness except insofar as these would be an expression of our greater resolution to avoid error. Perhaps we should say that the standards are determined only by the rules of thumb described in §5, but that in cases of the present kind they should be applied with all the greater care.

In the cases of "presumably nonvoluntary behavior," what we "presume" is either that the actor is ignorant or mistaken about what he is doing, or acting under some sort of compulsion, or suffering from some sort of incapacity, *and* that if that were not the case, he would choose not to do what he seems bent on doing now. In short, we think that his present choice is not his true choice, not the choice he really wants to make, and would make if given the chance. Mill would permit the state to protect a person from his own ignorance at least in circumstances that create a presumption that his uninformed or misinformed choice would not correspond to his eventual one.

> If either a public officer or anyone else saw a person attempting to cross a bridge which had been ascertained to be unsafe, and there were no time to warn him of his danger, they might seize him and turn him back, without any real infringement of his liberty; for liberty consists in doing what one desires, and he does not desire to fall into the river.[20]

Of course, for all the public officer may know, the person on the bridge does desire to fall into the river, or to take the risk of falling for other purposes. If the person is fully warned of the danger and wishes to proceed anyway, then, Mill argues, that is his business alone; but because most people do not wish to run such risks, there was a solid presumption, in advance of checking, that this person did not wish to run the risk either. Hence the officer was justified, Mill would argue, in his original interference.

On other occasions a person may need to be protected not from his ignorance but from some other condition that may render his informed choice substantially less than voluntary. He may be "a child, or delirious, or in some state of excitement or absorption incompatible with the full use of the reflecting faculty."[21] Mill would not permit any such person to cross an objectively unsafe bridge. On the other hand, there is no reason why a child, or an excited person, or a drunkard, or a mentally ill person should not be allowed to proceed on his way home across a perfectly safe thoroughfare. Even substantially nonvoluntary choices deserve protection unless there is good reason to judge them dangerous (Diagram 20-3, category 2).

Now it may be the case, for all we can know, that the behavior of a drunk or an emotionally upset person would be exactly the same even if he were sober and calm; but when the behavior seems patently self-damaging and is of a sort that most calm and normal persons would not engage in, then there are strong grounds, if only of a statistical sort, for inferring the opposite; and these grounds, on Mill's principle, would justify interference. It may be that there is no kind of action of which it can be said "no mentally competent adult in a calm, attentive mood, fully informed, etc., would ever choose (or consent to) that." Nevertheless, there are actions of a kind that create a powerful presumption that any given actor, if he were in his right mind, would not choose them. The point of calling this hypothesis a "presumption" is to require that it be overridden before legal permission be given to a person who has already been interfered with to go on as before. So, for example, if a policeman (or anyone else) sees John Doe about to chop off his hand with an ax, he is perfectly justified in using force to prevent him because of the presumption that no one would voluntarily choose to do such a thing. The presumption, however, should always be taken as rebuttable in principle. If there were an official tribunal to investigate such matters, it would require that once the presumption against voluntariness is established (perhaps by expert witnesses, perhaps from its own records), it must be overturned by evidence from some source or other, including the voluntary testimony of the petitioner, Doe himself. The "presumption" implies nothing about a "burden of proof." It would be a dubious compliment to Doe's autonomy to make him *prove* that he is calm, competent, and free, and still wishes to chop off his hand. The existence of the general statistical presumption requires only that an objective determination be made, either by the usual adversary procedures of law courts or, much more likely, by a collective investigation by the tribunal into the available facts. The greater the presumption to be overridden (assuming high risks, and grave or irrevocable harms), the more elaborate and fastidious should be the legal paraphernalia required, and though the actual standards of voluntariness need not be higher than in other cases, the standards of evidence should perhaps be more strict. (The law of wills might provide a partial model for this.) The point of the procedure would not be to evaluate the wisdom or worthiness of a person's choice, but rather to determine whether the choice really is his.

We are thus led to a liberal doctrine which, in its immediate effects, can be confused with paternalism, but which is essentially quite different from it, namely that the state has the right to prevent self-regarding harmful conduct when but only when it is substantially nonvoluntary, or when temporary intervention is necessary to establish whether it is voluntary or not. When there is a strong presumption that no normal person would—because few normal persons do—voluntarily choose or consent to the kind of conduct in question, that should be a proper ground for detaining the person until the voluntary character of his choice can be established.

Instantly, however, the point must be qualified. There are not many types of cases where statistics clearly support a presumption of nonvoluntariness. There may be some established psychiatric diagnostic categories of self-inflicted harm where the behavior is standardly taken to constitute a probable symptom of psychotic impairment. Mutilation of the genitals is one such category;[22] self-blinding is another. And mental hospitals are commonly familiar with patients who have inflicted stigmata on their own hands or bodies. Consider the unlikely case of a public official discovering a person mutilating himself in one of these "standard" ways, say in a public park, and interfering forcibly with him on the presumption that he is "not in his right mind." Surely we would not want a tribunal, the next morning, to require that he prove beyond a reasonable doubt, in some sort of adversary hearing, that he is not psychotic, before being allowed to proceed on his former path. Neither would we want a tribunal to decide the question of the detainee's liberty entirely on the basis of whether his act was wise or foolish, reasonable or unreasonable, by their standards. Reasonableness is one thing, and voluntariness is another. Yet one way of persuading a panel of the voluntariness of a presumptively nonvoluntary self-damaging act is to offer some reason for it, even a bad reason, so long as it is a relevant reason that renders the mysterious more intelligible. If the presumption of psychosis is correct, however, no such reason will be forthcoming.

Another category of presumptively nonvoluntary behavior is that in which Mill's unsafe bridge example falls. Here we need not have recourse to psychiatric data; mere common-sense expectations based on general experience will do. It is rare in the collective experience of the human race for people voluntarily to season their eggs with arsenic, or stroll across unsafe bridges, or swim in highly polluted waters. It is also rare, but by no means as rare, for people to do such things by mistake. Hence we are entitled to infer, in the absence of any other information, that a person intent on doing one of those things, is doing so by mistake. Indeed, we *owe* it to the person to make this assumption, while leaving open the possibility that in the case at hand it could be incorrect.

Having mentioned the psychiatric categories and typical mistakes of normal people, however, we quickly exhaust the kinds of cases that are clear. More interesting cases do not lend themselves to facile "presumptions." Consider deliberate suicide, for example. Acts of self-destruction are undertaken from such diverse motivations and for such a motley group of reasons, some reasonable some not, some rational some not, some normal some not, that if all we know about a person is that he intends to kill himself, we are probably not entitled to "presume" anything at all about the voluntariness of his choice.[23] In respect to suicide and other controversial self-regarding acts, there is commonly no reliable presumption at all of a statistical sort. Where interference, detention, and inquiry into voluntariness are justified, they are so because of the magnitude of the risks and the gravity or irrevocability of the harms, not because of the initial probability of nonvoluntariness.

If a person is capable of ending his life on his own, then the question of permissibility is effectively moot. No criminal prohibition can deter him, and the criminalization of suicide would probably harm innocent others more than him.[24] But where the would-be suicide requires assistance—weapons, drugs, or help in administering them—when he is too feeble to do it himself or is hospitalized or incarcerated, then the permissibility of assisting him becomes a critical issue, and determining the voluntariness of his request is the key question. (See *infra*, chap. 27).

7. Examples: dangerous drugs

Working out the details of the voluntariness standard will be undertaken in the following chapters, but some of the complexities, at least, can be illustrated by a consideration of some typical hard cases. Consider first of all the problem of harmful drugs. Suppose Richard Roe requests a prescription of drug X from Dr. Doe, and the following discussion ensues:

Dr. Doe: I cannot prescribe drug X to you because it will do you
             physical harm.   (1)
Mr. Roe: But you are mistaken. It will not cause me physical harm.

Under present law in a case like this, the state, of course, backs the doctor, and the medical researchers and laboratory experimenters employed by governmental regulatory agencies. Insofar as the question of "physical harm" is a purely empirical matter—a question of what effects on a person's bodily processes a given drug will produce—that is as it should be. The state is well advised to back its experimental scientists on matters within the scope of their technical expertise. (Indeed, it owes it to Mr. Roe to do so.) Of course, the term "harm" can always mask an evaluative element, which, being a matter of personal judgments of worthwhileness, may indeed be beyond the scope of external expertise. Virtually everyone may have a welfare interest in what medical scientists call "physical health," such that no ulterior interests can be advanced if it falls below a minimal par line. Mr. Roe may be one of the extremely rare exceptions. He may be a mystic whose drug-induced grand trances produce liver damage, and who thinks of "physical health" as a distraction, and not part of his personal interest at all. But the law must often be couched in general terms (see Vol. 1, Chap. 5, §2) that leave Mr. Roe no recourse but to conform, unless he could request a special administrative hearing from an equity board—an excellent idea where it is not too cumbersome and expensive. In any event, barring the remote possibility that Mr. Roe is so special a case, the example becomes one of a purely medical disagreement. As a general rule, if a layman disagrees with a physician on a question of medical fact, the layman may safely be presumed wrong. If nevertheless he chooses to act on his factually mistaken belief, his action will be substantially less than fully voluntary because of his mistake about what he is doing. That is to say the the action of *ingesting a substance that will in fact harm him* is not the action he voluntarily chooses to do. (Under another description, of course, his action is voluntary, namely *ingesting these particular pills*, but the fuller description is obviously the relevant one.) Hence the state intervenes to protect him not from his own free and informed choices, but from his factual ignorance.

Richard Arneson takes exception to this analysis, which, he says, "suggests that whenever a man acts on a mistaken judgment about the best means for achieving his goals, his act is to that extent nonvoluntary," and also that "whenever a man, even after deliberate reflection, temporarily misidentifies his most important values and acts out this mistake his action is to that extent nonvoluntary."[25] If my analysis indeed implies (and not merely "suggests" to a particular reader) these unwelcome consequences, then it clearly needs qualification. We can begin by noting the difference between factual mistakes, for example those about cause and effect, or means to ends, and mistakes in "identifying one's most important values." If someone makes mistakes of the latter kind, not because of coercion, distraction, incapacitation, or factual misinformation, but because of trouble making up his own mind, the mistakes are properly chargeable without qualification to him, as his own doing and his own responsibility. His "mistaken choice" is still *his* choice. To call it mistaken is simply to evaluate it as unwise or unreasonable, and Arneson and I agree that a person has a right to act in unreasonable self-regarding ways. But if, unknown to the person, someone has switched the labels on the arsenic and table salt containers, the mistake is a wholly factual one rendering his choice involuntary. That sort of mistake he does not have the right to make. Why should he ever want such a "right?"

Arneson's treatment of the arsenic–salt example is puzzling. He points out quite correctly that voluntariness-ascriptions are relative to act descriptions, so that the act in question can be described either as "putting what I believe to be salt on my food," or "putting what in fact is deadly poison on my food." I proposed calling the former a *thin* act-description and the latter a *thick* one. Actually they are "thick" and "thin" only relative to one another, since there is a kind of breadth spectrum permitting a whole range of act descriptions, some thicker than others. Examples of even thicker descriptions of the food-seasoning act than Arneson's would be "poisoning my liver" or "taking my life," and even thinner ones "shaking the bottle" and "raising and lowering my arm." Obviously, acts corresponding to the thinner descriptions tend to be voluntary, whereas those corresponding to thicker descriptions, incorporating consequences into the action itself that were not expected by the actor because of his mistaken factual beliefs, are a good deal less than voluntary. In the case at hand the acts as thickly described are completely involuntary. Arneson admits this, but insists that there is only one act, no matter how variously it is described, and for the purpose of deciding whether the actor should be at liberty to perform it, "some overall determination of the voluntary or nonvoluntary character of the act seems requisite,"[26] and that just because that act has one (or some) thick description(s) under which it is nonvoluntary, it does not follow that the "act *tout court*" is nonvoluntary. I cannot decipher what he means by an "act *tout court*," for it seems to me that there is one continuum of activity which we can slice up in as thin or thick parcels as we wish. Some of these relatively thick parcels contain thinner parts or phases—the simpler doings that produce the incorporated consequences. The important thing is that we know how to assess accurately the voluntariness of the segment we are describing, and how to use that assessment as a relevant reason for our own anticipatory or responsive reactions. In a way, Arneson's insistence on the unity of the act underlying its various descriptions works against his own purposes, for if he would permit interference with the action thickly described, because *it* is harmful and nonvoluntary, how can this possibly be done without interfering with the voluntary and intrinsically innocuous action it envelops as a part or phase of itself? The *only* way to prevent the person from poisoning his food (thick description) is to prevent him from pouring what he thinks is table salt on it (thin description).

Arneson concludes that my analysis commits me to "the distinctly un-Millian position that all acts involving mistakes are involuntary and as such fall beyond the protected scope of the anti-paternalism principle."[27] I might with as much (or as little) warrant ascribe to him the distinctly un-Millian position that *no* acts involving mistakes are involuntary, and thus properly subject to interference. It would be better, however, to admit that we both have a problem—the same problem—that of distinguishing between mistakes that diminish or cancel voluntariness and those that do not. On part of the solution, we both agree. People may voluntarily mistake their own values, and act, otherwise rationally, on bizarre and unreasonable judgments of worthwhileness. That reduces the area of our disagreement to the role of factual mistakes, and inevitably to Mill's unsafe bridge example. Arneson finds the example unproblematic for his own very hard anti-paternalism because the pedestrian approaching the bridge "lacks information he may be presumed to need, and cannot gain by himself." He adds that "there would be no grounds for even temporary interference if the bridge were plainly marked 'unsafe' in letters visible" to the approaching person. If the bridge is unmarked the pedestrian would have no way of knowing it is unsafe, and his mistaken factual belief then would not be one for which *he* would be responsible. Responsibility for mistakes seems to be the crux of the matter for Arneson, and indeed for Mill if Arneson is right about him: "Mill clearly believes that in the sphere of self-regarding action people have the right to make *their own mistakes* and suffer the consequences without interference by society" [emphasis added].[28]

The question then is when is a person's mistake "his own"? The answer seems clear enough in the arsenic–salt switch, when the diner, *ex hypothesi*, had no way of knowing that he was poisoning his own food. Despite the confusion in Arneson's discussion of this example, his own principle clearly leads him to approve of forcible preventive interference. One can of course imagine a Laurel and Hardy routine in which the diner believes mistakenly that the person warning him is only kidding, and refuses to accept his warning, frustrating the other party who *knows* that the "salt" is really deadly poison. The stubborn diner may willfully persist in his disbelief to a blamably unreasonable extent, so that any observer would hold him responsible, after a point, for his own error. Still, permitting him to suffer an immediate agonizing death which we know he neither wants nor chooses seems an excessive punishment for his stubborness and an odd way of showing respect for his autonomy. The point remains that the action interfered with, described in the relevantly "thick" way, is not only unreasonable; it is not the act the diner has voluntarily chosen. The parallel example in the bridge case would be that in which the policeman, to his amazement, sees the pedestrian read the sign and then start across the bridge anyway. He calls out a warning, on the chance that the pedestrian has not understood the printed sign (perhaps he can't read, or can't read English, or in some way has been deprived of the full use of his reasoning or perceiving faculties). Instead, the pedestrian tells him flatly that the warning is a plain lie (perhaps a capitalist plot), and that he will not be persuaded of the bridge's unsafe condition until it collapses under him and sends him to injury or death on the rocks below. He too is willful and perverse, not to mention a touch paranoid, but that is still another thing from voluntarily choosing to fall to the rocks and injure or kill himself. (It is important to reemphasize that the situation would be different if the desperate pedestrian were correctly apprised of the facts, and correctly assessed the risk, but was willing to run it anyway—voluntarily— for some further purpose of his own.)

Arneson's principle in the Roe–Doe case would imply only that Dr. Doe has a duty to warn Mr. Roe that the drugs will damage his health, and that if Roe willfully and unreasonably disagrees, and persists in his factual error, that is his problem only, and no further interference with his liberty is permissible. The example, however, seems on all fours with the table salt and unsafe bridge examples, and I see no reason to come to a different judgment here. My verdict assumes, however, that we *know* that the drug is unsafe, as the interveners in the other examples *knew* that the bridge was unsafe and that the "salt" was truly arsenic. But suppose that there is no *certain knowledge* of the harmfulness of Mr. Roe's drug, but that that judgment simply represents the most reliable "expert" opinion a governmental testing laboratory (itself inclined to "err on the safe side") has been able to deliver. Suppose further that Mr. Roe is really Dr. Roe, a distinguished biochemist, but a maverick often at odds with the majority of his colleagues. His own laboratory experiments, which he claims were more careful than the government's, show that the drug is not only harmless, but positively beneficial. Here again, we seem to have a case for special dispensation from an equity board. Dr. Roe, it would seem, does have a right, in the absence of sure knowledge, to "make his own mistake" about facts that are scientifically controversial, even when the controversy is entirely the result of his own work. But even Dr. Roe must be prevented from eating food we *know* has been poisoned, unless of course he voluntarily chooses suicide.

A final set of examples concludes our discussion of the role of factual error. Suppose an eccentric inventor takes an elevator up to the top of a tall building, and then having strapped cloth-wrapped iron "wings" to his arms, prepares to jump from the roof and "fly away." He does not think of himself as a dare-devil entertainer; he sincerely believes that his wings are safe and will work. He is not taking unreasonable risks voluntarily; rather his factual misassessment of the risk is a necessary condition for his willingness to assume it in the first place. As Aristotle put it, he acts not merely "in ignorance" but "by reason of ignorance." There is a thin description of his act, supposing no one prevents it, according to which it is voluntary. He jumped off the ledge voluntarily in that he was jumping *off* the ledge and not merely to another part of it. But he doesn't dive straight down voluntarily; he doesn't kill himself voluntarily; he doesn't die voluntarily. In these relevantly inclusive "thick" descriptions, what he does is nonvoluntary.

We can contrast that easy case with another genuinely difficult one. Another brilliant maverick scientist, Dr. Brink, has spent ten years in his laboratory fashioning a set of wings out of a new plastic material of his own invention, testing and redesigning them, and carrying on learned debates with other scientists, most of whom think that his claims are not supported by his data and that his experiments have subtle methodological defects. Now he is ready to put the major work of his career to the test and risk his own life in the process. The betting odds are long against him. Let us assume once more for the sake of the example that no one knows for sure the outcome. Here, too equity should recognize Dr. Brink's right to make his own scientific mistake and take the consequences.

In summary, Arneson would let factual mistake cancel voluntariness only when the person had no fair opportunity to avoid the mistake. Only then is his mistake truly "his own." But I have amended his criterion to permit even factual errors willfully persisted in against clear evidence to cancel voluntariness in cases in which there is an approximation to certain knowledge of the danger, while acknowledging that there are borderline cases in which there is only expert opinion without certain knowledge, and where the actor's purpose, in part, is to vindicate his own opinion. In some of these cases, equity (a "corrective of law")[29] would require recognition of the right to act on one's own sincere but factually mistaken beliefs.

Now for some easier examples, and judgments about them that will be, on the whole, more comforting to the resolute anti-paternalist. There are two more variations of the Dr. Doe–Mr. Roe dialogue. Suppose now that the exchange goes as follows:

Dr. Doe: I cannot prescribe drug X to you because it will do you physical harm.

Mr. Roe: That's just what I want. I want to harm myself.   (2)

In this case Roe is properly apprised of the facts. He suffers from no delusions or misconceptions. Yet his choice is so odd that there exists a reasonable presumption that he has been deprived somehow of the "full use of his reflective faculty." Note that it is not simply that we find his choice and its supporting explanation unreasonable and for that reason alone automatically label it "nonvoluntary." That would not follow, because an unreasonable

choice may yet be voluntary for all we know, so the unreasonableness of a
choice certainly doesn' prove its nonvoluntariness. But a choice may be so
extremely and unusually unreasonable that we might reasonably suspect that
it stems at least in part, not from odd values genuinely held, nor from simply
factual mistakes, but rather from deeper psychological impairment. If we are
to take extreme unreasonableness as the product of impairment, we must not
do so *a priori*, or by definition. We cannot render immune from counter-evi-
dence the judgment that no one in his right mind would choose such a thing.
If that judgment expresses a truth it is not an *a priori* one but rather one that
must be tested anew in each case by the application of independent, noncir-
cular criteria of mental illness or retardation. It would be circular to argue
that the choice *must* be a symptom of an illness, and that the illness in turn
renders the choice nonvoluntary. We must have *other* evidence of incapacitation to break the circle.[30] If no further evidence of derangement, illness,
severe depression, or unsettling excitation can be discovered, however, and if
there are no third-party interests, for example those of spouse or family, that
require protection, then our "voluntariness standard" would permit no further state constraint.

Now consider the third possibility:

Dr. Doe:	I cannot prescribe drug X to you because it is very likely to do you physical harm.
Mr. Roe:	I don't care if it causes me physical harm. I'll get a lot of pleasure first, so much pleasure in fact, that it is well worth running the risk of physical harm. If I must pay a price for my pleasure I am willing to do so.

(3)

It may be overly optimistic to describe this case as "easy," but I think it is
easier than cases (1) and (2). It is in fact the litmus test example for distinguishing the paternalist from the liberal. Roe's choice is not patently "irrational" on its face. He may have a well thought-out philosophical hedonism
as one of his profoundest convictions. He may have made a fundamental
decision of principle committing himself to the intensely pleasurable, even if
brief life. If no third-party interests are directly involved, and garrison thresh-
olds (see *supra*, Chap. 17, §5) have not been reached, the state can hardly be
permitted to declare his philosophical convictions unsound or "sick" and
prevent him from practicing them, without assuming powers that it will
inevitably misuse disastrously.

On the other hand, this case may be very little different from the preceding one, depending of course on what the exact facts are. If the drug is
known to give only an hour's mild euphoria and then cause an immediate
violently painful death, then the risks incurred appear so unreasonable as to
create a powerful presumption of irrationality and therefore of nonvoluntari-

ness. On the other hand, drug X may be harmful in the way nicotine is now known to be harmful; twenty or thirty years of heavy use may create a grave risk of lung cancer or heart disease. Using the drug for pleasure merely, when the risks are of this kind may be to run unreasonable risks, but that is not strong evidence of nonvoluntariness. Many perfectly normal rational persons voluntarily choose to run precisely these risks for whatever pleasure they find in smoking. The way for the state to assure itself that such practices are truly voluntary is continually to confront smokers with the ugly medical facts so that there is no escaping the knowledge of what the medical risks exactly are. Constant reminders of the hazards should be at every hand and with no softening of the gory details. The state might even be justified in using its taxing, regulatory, and persuasive powers to make smoking (and similar drug usage) more difficult or less attractive; but to prohibit it outright for everyone would be to tell the voluntary risk-taker that even his informed judgments of what is worthwhile are less reasonable than those of the state, and that therefore, he may not act on them. This is the purest hard paternalism, unmediated by the voluntariness standard. As a principle of public policy, it has an acrid moral flavor, and creates serious risks of governmental tyranny.

8. Examples: protective helmets

When Victor Vroom turned eighteen he purchased a second-hand motorcycle so that he could transport himself quickly and economically to his job. He did this despite the misgivings of his parents, who had read the chilling statistics—"In 1978, 166,000 Americans were admitted to hospitals for emergency treatment after motorcycle accidents; 4,700 of them died. Many others were crippled for life",[31] and heard the testimony of attending physicians— "Some of these kids look like ground hamburger when they're brought to us. They've been dragged along the ground for 40 feet with a 500-pound bike on top of them, or hurled through the air at 60 miles an hour before striking a tree. Anyone who rides a motorcycle is a potential human cannonball."[32] Victor was annoyed that state law required him to wear a hot and uncomfortable protective helmet while riding the motorcycle, on pain of a fifty-dollar fine. He also resented the special scrutiny policemen seemed to reserve for bikers; he knew there was no way he could flout that law without being caught.

One hot summer day, already late for work, Victor had to go out of his way to pick up his helmet, making him still later. He was tempted to leave the helmet and drive straight to work without it, but he did not wish to risk the fifty-dollar fine. For that reason only, he retrieved the helmet, and strapped it securely on his head as he began his fifteen-minute drive through

crowded city streets to his job. Half way through the trip, a confused motorist coming from the opposite direction made a sudden illegal left turn,
swerving right into his path. He could not avoid smashing into the side of the
automobile. The collision threw him high in the air over the top of the car,
and he landed on his head twenty feet away. He was rushed to the hospital
and treated for cuts and a minor concussion. Without the helmet, he was
told, he would have been killed or severely brain-damaged. Ever since the
accident Victor has worn his helmet faithfully, not only because the law
requires it, but because he wishes to be protected from other unforeseeable
accidents. But in the first instance, he would never have worn the helmet but
for fear of legal penalties.

Cyclists without helmets have not been as fortunate as Victor, and there is
strong reason to believe that safety helmets make all the difference. As one
judge in a 1971 case reported,

> Seventy-seven per cent of the motorcycle accident deaths studied by a California
> physician were caused by craniocerebral injury with no potentially fatal trauma
> to other parts of the body. A New York legislative report, citing the rapid
> increase in the number of motorcycle accidents, stated that 89.2% of these
> accidents resulted in injury or death and that almost all fatalities involved head
> injuries, most of which could have been avoided or ameliorated by the use of a
> proper helmet. An orthopedic surgeon testified in this case that he had cared for
> six persons injured in motorcycle crashes while wearing protective helmets.
> None had severe head injury.[33]

Similar statistical studies have led many state legislatures, beginning in 1966,
to pass statutes requiring that (in the words of the Michigan statute) "A
person operating or riding on a motorcycle or motor driven cycle shall wear a
crash helmet approved by the department of state police . . ."[34] Despite numerous constitutional challenges, at least four of which were successful[35]
when state courts decided that their state constitutions incorporated the doctrine of Mill's *On Liberty*, similar statutes are now law in a majority of
American states.

Compulsory helmet legislation then surely has a point, and because of that,
it is an embarrassment to the liberal and makes the strongest of the arguments for hard paternalism. John Kleinig notes that arguments attempting to
justify, on one ground or another, such statutes show "considerable coy-
ness," that the statutes "are clearly an embarrassment, and strenuous efforts
are usually made to justify them in non-paternalistic terms."[36] Gerald
Dworkin[37] shows how these life-saving statutes pose a kind of trilemma for
the liberal, who seems restricted to three possible responses: (1) He can argue
that helmetless motorcycle riding is typically (if not "necessarily") nonvoluntary by the appropriate standards; (2) He can argue that helmetless motorcycle riding, though typically voluntary (or voluntary enough) should be

banned, but on grounds other than hard paternalism, for example in terms of
the interests of third parties who are affected in ways they have a right to be
protected against; (3) He can argue that despite the self-harm prevented by
prohibitory legislation, the restrictive statutes are morally unjustified because
they infringe personal sovereignty, and that alternative noncoercive measures
should be adopted to increase safety. We have already dismissed (see Chap.
19, §8), albeit respectfully, a fourth alternative, namely to restrict the domain
boundaries of personal sovereignty to more fundamental interests or "significant projects" (Kleinig's phrase). A fifth possibility is to concede the game to
the hard paternalist, thereby giving him encouragement to use his principle
to justify criminal penalties for other forms of self-regarding risk-taking, from
cigarette smoking to surfing.[38]

The first alternative has little promise. It seems unlikely that we can justify
compulsory helmet legislation on soft paternalist grounds, given our earlier
analysis of voluntariness. The "typical" motorcyclist (if there is such a thing) is
not simply mistaken about the factual basis of the risks he takes. Although he
could no doubt profit from more detailed information about his vulnerabilities
and the available safety techniques, he does not ride his bike only because of
some grossly mistaken factual belief analogous to the belief that arsenic is table
salt or that iron is lighter than air. Few cyclists use their machines because
they are compelled to, or threatened, or coercively pressured, and there is no
evidence whatever linking the motorcycle preference to mental illness or other
incapacity. Perhaps there are many bikers, like Victor Vroom, who either
have a deficient understanding of the actual risks—underestimating their magnitude—or an insufficient emotional appreciation of their seriousness. Rather
than ascribing these shortcomings to the "typical motorcyclist," however, and
treating them as if they were necessarily linked to the very activity of motorcycling, we can take better advantage of the licensing requirements to assure that
every licensed cyclist has the requisite knowledge for voluntariness, even as
determined by an appropriately high standard. Applicants for licenses could
be required to take a state-administered course in safety, featuring training
films that graphically portray the dangers, including photographed collisions,
hospital scenes, interviews with doctors, and victims—ground hamburger
faces and all. Anatomy lessons too would be presented featuring the peculiar
vulnerabilities of the head, and the way helmets work, portraying experimental tests with dummy victims, and the like. Statistical documentation would be
presented of the relative risks of automobile driving, motorcycle driving with a
helmet, and motorcycle driving without a helmet. Then to make sure that
everyone was listening, simple written examinations would be administered.

After such a course of instruction there could be no plausibility in the
claim that the typical cyclist is insufficiently aware of the risks to choose
voluntarily to forego his helmet. Nevertheless, we could expect that a certain

small percentage would ride, either all or part of the time, without helmets. These people would fall into two categories, the romantic ideologues and the careless, and the latter would divide into two subclasses: those who understand the risks but judge them to be outweighed by the discomforts and inconveniences, and those "akratic" individuals who admit that they are unreasonable to ride unprotected, but just can't muster up the initiative, or go to the trouble, of wearing helmets. The person whose practice is an integral part of his adventurous life-style, deliberately adopted in part because of its symbolic reflection of his commitment to speed, excitement, even to danger, can hardly be said to have adopted it nonvoluntarily.

The incorrigibly careless person may seem more of a problem. He is unreasonable by the standards most of us use for judging the worthwhileness of risks, and his unreasonableness makes him seem strange to us. But if there are no other grounds whatever for judging him a victim of intellectual or emotional impairment, it only begs the question to assume that his odd preferences, in and by themselves, argue for nonvoluntariness. The point has to be made over and over again: one can be quite voluntarily unreasonable. Nobody is more so than the self-confessed akratic (weak-willed) person who can't bring himself to act according to his own sincere beliefs about what he ought to do. But lest we judge too hastily that his failures must be beyond his own control and therefore somewhat less than sufficiently voluntary, each of us should remember the many diverse occasions in our own lives when we quite voluntarily chose to do the convenient thing instead of something we knew at the time would be better to do, in situations where nothing prevented us from choosing the alternative except our own laziness, indifference, inertial habit, or short-term self-indulgence.[39]

C. Edwin Harris, Jr. applies an exalted standard of voluntariness to the nonideological bare-headed rider, from which he derives the judgment that his self-regarding character flaws render his behavior well short of "fully deliberate, responsible, or voluntary,"[40] His argument seems to be that if one acts irresponsibly enough, then one's action becomes not merely irresponsible (blamably unreasonable) but nonresponsible (one for which one is not wholly accountable), a claim that seems to me to be somewhat paradoxical. Mandatory helmet legislation, he claims, is justified "to protect people from their own foolhardiness, lack of sufficient forethought, and lack of discipline."[41] The hard paternalist would agree, but Harris purports to be arguing on autonomy-respecting soft paternalist grounds, so that agreement can give him no comfort. The soft paternalist, properly so-called, would argue that self-regarding irresponsibility, foolhardiness, and lack of forethought and self-discipline need be no more involuntary than any other of the character flaws for which people are blamed, and in the absence of independent corroborating evidence of cognitive or emotional impairment, their possessor has a right to act on his own unreasonable but genuine preferences and, if it comes to that, to pay the price.

If the soft paternalist, therefore, is to approve of mandatory helmet laws, it can only be on the second of the grounds distinguished by Gerald Dworkin— the perceived need to protect third parties or the public interest. One very direct appeal to the harm to others principle notes that motorcyclists are peculiarly liable to be struck in the face by stones propelled upward by their own wheels, or the tires of passing vehicles. Most of the laws requiring helmets specify that they include a face guard as well as such auxiliary safety features as reflectorized side panels and chin straps. Without face and head protection, flying stones may cause the cyclist to lose control of his vehicle with resultant injuries to *other* drivers or pedestrians.

Numerous writers have noticed how forced and contrived this argument seems when actually made in courts of law.[42] Some judges assume that a restrictive safety statute can be constitutional only if it bears some rational connection to the prevention of harm to persons other than the party restricted, and then grope in apparent desperation for possible harms of that sort. But there is no evidence that accidents of the envisaged kind occur with sufficient frequency to be statistically significant, a fact frequently pointed out by motorcycle associations.[43] The most successful of the legal rejoinders to this appeal to the interests of third parties is that made by (among many others) Judge A. C. Miller in *American Motorcyle Association v. Davids* in 1968. Judge Miller applies the principle (which we have already encountered in *Griswold v. Connecticut*, Chap. 19, §8) of the least restrictive alternative. He says of the "flying rock" rationale that —

> . . . such reasoning is obviously a strained effort to justify what is admittedly wholesome legislation. If the purpose truly were to deflect flying objects, rather than to reduce cranial injuries, a windshield requirement imposed on the manufacturer would bear a reasonable relationship to the objective and not vary from the norm of safety legislation customarily imposed on the manufacturer for the protection of the public rather than upon the individual.[44]

A rather more persuasive nonpaternalistic argument for mandatory helmet statutes appeals to the great public costs (in dollars and cents) of accidents. Salaries must be paid to policemen, paramedics, ambulance drivers, and nurses. Hospital rooms, operating rooms, physicians, medication, and medical machinery are very expensive. Many of these costs are paid from general tax revenues, others from higher insurance premiums. Indirect costs, like lost productivity and lost tax payments from injured workers, and welfare payments to their dependents, further raise the price. Mandatory helmet laws would reduce this great public expense and that is their true rationale—or so the liberal might argue.

Gerald Dworkin, however, has a paternalist rejoinder of some strength. If the reduction of publicly shared economic costs is the main part of our reason for passing compulsory helmet laws, then we can achieve that goal equally well without criminal prohibitions, simply by requiring the risk-takers to purchase extra medical insurance as a condition of their licensing.[45] Perhaps a supplementary scheme would be to require a contribution to a state-operated fund which would pay the full social costs of motorcycle accidents, just as users pay fees to get on bridges or turnpikes out of which maintenance costs are paid. The supplementary scheme would not be fair, however, to the prudent cyclists who drive cautiously and wear helmets, for they would pay the same fees as their more reckless colleagues whose more serious subsequent injuries are greater drains on the fund. The compulsory medical insurance system would be more equitable in that respect, by and large, since insurance companies could selectively raise the premiums of drivers who don't take elementary precautions. Perhaps the two plans could be combined into one which would require self-insurance not only for medical costs of accidents but for other costs (road maintenance, police time, etc.) as well. Compulsion would still be involved indirectly, but no longer through the mechanism of criminal statutes justified on paternalist grounds. Now punishment would be reserved as a backup threat against those who drive without a license and thus violate a quite unpaternalistic law.

These alternatives actually put the liberal in a better position and suggest ways out of his protective helmet quandary. Now he is tempted to take Dworkin's third option, and oppose mandatory helmet legislation on the ground that its need is obviated by improved licensing procedures, educational programs to ensure voluntariness in self-regarding risk-taking, and compulsory insurance to cover public costs. Now an "apparently reasonable paternalistic restriction" seems less reasonable to him. though no less paternalistic. But he is not out of the woods yet. There may still be other grounds for the helmet requirement that can justify it, though not on *obviously* paternalistic grounds. I refer to what Gerald Dworkin calls "psychic costs," and what Kleinig calls "the public charge argument." This is the consideration we have already encountered in our treatment of slavery contracts (Chap. 14, §5)—the ugly option we have of letting society's losers "sleep in the beds they have made themselves" or else undermine previous promises and threats at great public costs. *This* is the argument that justifies compulsory helmet laws if any argument does. The main question it raises is whether or not it is, at least in part, a paternalistic argument.

Suppose we install a system of compulsory insurance for motorcyclists which on the whole works well. Now we must consider the problem raised by the small but inevitable number of cheaters who intentionally fail to insure themselves and are not in a position to pay their own costs in case of an accident. Dworkin asks what we should do with such people, and comments:

> The libertarian [liberal] answer is that we announce ahead of time that such individuals will not be aided by us. But surely this imposes a psychic cost on us—that of ignoring or abandoning people in distress. There does seem to be an argument for interfering here because the rest of us do not want to be put in such a position.[46]

Dworkin's understated point is certainly correct. It is *unthinkable* that we leave the reckless, bareheaded, young motorcyclist to die in his own pool of blood because he has not contributed to the costs of his own care. One way to try to escape this dilemma is to pass helmet statutes with criminal sanctions. Another way is to adopt the humanitarian policy of rescue for those who are injured while violating the statute against driving without a license, and then prosecute them for violating *that* law (though punishment may seem somewhat redundant if the victim is permanently paralyzed in the hospital.) I see no clear advantage in the former method.

The argument from psychic costs, however, can apply altogether independently of the problem of economic costs and insurance schemes, and it is all the more forceful when it is more direct. If we permit a number of youths to be reckless with their own safety, the first dreadful consequence (cost) will be the damage to the unlucky victims themselves, quite apart from derivative costs, and the like. The resolute anti-paternalist stance that these victims of their own folly should be allowed to "pay the price" because "they asked for it" and knew what they were doing, sounds hard-edged and cruel after the fact of their injuries. When the damage is not too severe to be repaired, we might relent and bail them out of their difficulties, paying their costs out of simple humanity. In the case of irrevocable contracts, or hopeless gambling debts, or unwanted and unbreakable drug addictions, and other cases where a voluntary chooser was allowed to dig his own hole and then "got in too deep" to escape when he changed his mind (we have a hundred slang idioms for this situation), we are then entitled to resent being put in the cruel dilemma of allowing continued suffering or else paying an unfair cost to allay it. In that case we might seek protection *for ourselves* from such moral extortion by passing a law against the voluntary risk-taking of others that subjects us to it. That would be to create criminal laws which rest not on paternalistic grounds, but rather on the need to prevent harm (moral extortion) to others. But in the case of the motorcyclist with the smashed head, the harm is often irreversible, and the "psychic costs" already incurred irreparably. It is not that we can avoid the distress only at extortionate cost to our pocketbooks, as in the other examples; the point now is that we cannot avoid it at all. We suffer broken hearts as witnesses to, or participants in, violent accidents causing injuries aggravated by unprotected vulnerabilities; and our own liberal ideals seem to require us to shrug our shoulders and say "Well, he asked for it," or some such icy banality. Imagine the state of the motorist at fault in the Vroom collision if Victor Vroom had been killed or seriously brain-damaged. *He* needs protection too. And Victor's parents. And Victor's dependents. And attending medical workers. And traumatized witnesses. But *mainly* the other motorist.

That appeal to psychic costs to others is the strongest nonpaternalistic argument for an effectively deterrent statute. It is not a paternalistic rationale, but it is not as evasive as the other arguments that apply the (economic) harm-to-others principles, since it shares in the assumption of the paternalist that injury or death to the biker is the central point, not some relatively remote and indirect public harms that can be prevented in any case by insurance schemes and the like. It is not the derivative costs that ever suggested to a legislature that it should make helmets mandatory, but rather the direct and irreparable physical injury to the main actors in the drama.

Whether this employment of the harm and offense (psychic distress short of trauma) to others principles is sufficient to justify repressive statutes may be a close decision. Like every other legislative application of these principles it requires careful balancing. The interest of the biker in *not* wearing a helmet (mere convenience?, comfort?, a sense of freedom?, romantic symbolism?, adventurous life style?) must be weighed somehow against the interests and sensibilities of others, especially those others unfortunate enough to have been involved, with or without fault, in the accident. Gerald Dworkin is skeptical of the claim that the psychic costs can outweigh the biker's interests. "Others have to bear the knowledge that they have caused harm (perhaps death) to another," he writes, speaking of "hunters shot by other hunters because they do not wear brightly colored clothing." But he concludes that arguments of this kind when relevant, "do not seem strong enough to tip the scale by themsleves."[47] Dworkin is so convinced of the antecedent reasonableness of the coercive statutes, however, that he is prepared candidly to defend them on paternalist grounds, if other ways fail. I am less sure that the appeal to psychic costs won't suffice, but if it doesn't, I am so impressed, antecedently, with the claims of personal autonomy, that I would have no criminally sanctioned regulation at all, restricting the state to its still quite substantial role in educating, testing, licensing, taxing, and insuring autonomous bikers, all in the public interest.

A primary aim of this chapter has been to suggest a strategy for dealing with apparently reasonable paternalistic regulations from a liberal (anti-paternalistic) point of view, and to illustrate, in a highly tentative and programmatic way, how the strategy might be employed in respect to the regulation of drugs and motorcycle driving. No detailed analyses or specific recommendations of legislation could be attempted here without a long and digressive study of the nature and types of addiction, the extent of drug or helmet use measured against hypothetical "garrison-thresholds," the varieties of institutional controls, and other centrally relevant factual questions. But I have tried to identify and clarify some of the moral elements in argumentation over such matters. I have tried to show how outright prohibition of drug usage and helmetless riding can conflict with individual autonomy, and how the more egregious social harms of drug use and helmet neglect might be diminished, and autonomy protected too, through public efforts to ensure that decisions to use drugs and not to use helmets are both free and informed. In the final section I have tried to show how some apparently reasonable coercive rules might be supportable on nonpaternalistic grounds. Both arguments—that which casts doubt on the reasonableness of plainly paternalistic outright prohibitions and that which shows that certain reasonable prohibitions are not really paternalistic—rest heavily on the concept of voluntariness. All and only voluntary self-regarding actions, and consentings to agreements, are morally sheltered by one's personal autonomy. Often legitimate government intervention in dangerous situations is not intended to prevent harm so much as to guarantee voluntariness. It remains now to consider further whether the concept of voluntariness is sturdy enough to bear the argumentative weight that has been place upon it.

21

Failures of Voluntariness:
The Single-Party Case

1. Direct injury: suicide and self-mayhem as crimes

Should the law permit autonomous persons to act on their own in ways that
are harmful or unreasonably dangerous to themselves but not directly threatening to other persons? The most plausible liberal answer, that which employs the soft (anti)-paternalist strategy, answers boldly in the affirmative.
Entirely self-regarding and voluntary behavior is none of the criminal law's
business. But sometimes, perhaps more often than not, harmful or unreasonably risky behavior is a good deal less than voluntary, and the soft paternalist
would justify interference with it when, but only when, there is a well
founded suspicion that the actor's choice was not really his own. What this
part of the soft-paternalistic position implies about the proper role of the law
is also negative: the justified interferer should not himself incur either criminal or civil liability for his act. It is also consistent with soft paternalism, in
respect to the more serious and irrevocable self-harms, for example those
produced by suicide and self-mutilation, to empower some state agency to
investigate further the voluntariness of the choices of the frustrated actors, to
offer them counseling or therapy, even, in some cases, under conditions of
compulsory though nonpunitive confinement for carefully limited periods.
Our concern in this chapter is with the problem of determining voluntariness
in single-party cases. When is a harmful or dangerous choice "voluntary
enough" to preclude interference? Or, alternatively, when is it "nonvoluntary
enough" to warrant at least temporary interference?

The single-party cases are those in which a given actor chooses to act, on
his own, to produce the harm or risk of harm, as opposed to two-party

consensual cases in which the vulnerable party's only act is an act of consent to a second party's action that will harm or endanger him. Single-party cases can be divided into two broad classes, acts that inflict self-harms directly, and activities that essentially involve a high risk of harm. In the former rather sparse category are acts of (presumably harmful) self-destruction and self-mayhem; in the latter more populous category are dangerous but solitary sports, for example waterfall rafting or hang-gliding, or dangerously thrilling dare-devil feats like performing highwire acrobatics without a safety net, motorcycle leaping, or going over Niagra Falls in a barrel; using home-grown drugs in the privacy of one's home; and (more prosaically) driving with seatbelt unfastened or without a protective helmet. Even the risk-taking category is sparse compared to its counterpart in two-party cases, where dangerous activities of an endless variety involve the assistance of aiders, abettors, and provisioners, reciprocal agreements among buyers and sellers, or between competitors in contests, and other arrangements involving proposals and acceptances, requests and agreements. Drug use, for example, almost always involves collaboration or purchase, which is why we restrict our attention here to the less typical case of solitary use of "home-grown," and thus unpurchased, drugs. Dangerous gambling too, since it is always a form of contest *against* another willing party, must be excluded from the single-party case.

Self-mayhem and suicide could be discussed at length as prototypical single-party cases, but we will not consider them in detail here for two reasons. First, we have discussed elsewhere problems of interference with suicide attempts, tests of their voluntariness, and problems of second-party collaboration and exploitation.[1] Moreover, the first half of the soft paternalist's negative thesis, that forbidding the criminalization of the harmful acts themselves, seems almost moot, since both suicide and self-mutilation have characteristics that render them, for practical reasons, peculiarly unsuitable for direct prohibition by the criminal law, even if valid liberty-limiting principles permitted such prohibition. It would be foolish, for example, to reinstitute a crime of suicide, for the only sanctions with which the prohibition could be enforced would be likely to hurt innocent persons more than the deceased, who is largely beyond the range of punishment. Ignominious burial might yet invade one of his "surviving interests" (see Vol. 1, Chap. 2, §4), but this is no longer a plausible secular sanction, and its main alternative—confiscation of his worldly goods—would primarily harm his dependents, who may be entirely innocent of his crime. Those who fail in suicide attempts might be punished, of course, for *attempting* to commit a criminal act, as indeed they commonly were in England prior to 1921, and occasionally were until at least 1957.[2] If capital punishment is the most severe penalty in the state's arsenal, then it would be an unreliable deterrent to those who unequivocally desire to die. The more severe penalty of torturing to death is thought to be too barbarous for any crime, but if it is acceptable at all in principle, it would be reserved for the most atrocious crimes, which certainly do not include suicide. Such a savage penalty, it is true, might deter the irresolute, but it would goad the determined suicides to assure that they did not fail. Jail sentences on the traditional British model[3] would probably be the most cruel punishments of all for the failed suicides who are already so depressed that they cannot bear to continue living.

In any case, there is something moot in the philosophical debate over the propriety of suicide laws when a person with the resources and opportunities can kill himself if he is so determined, whatever the law says. "Ultimately," writes Glanville Williams, "society cannot stop a free man from committing suicide, nor should it try."[4] It is otherwise with less than free persons restricted to jail cells or hospital beds, or who are too feeble, or sick, or racked with pain, to escape their ordeals without the assistance of others. The twin problems of euthanasia and assisting another's suicide are about two-party cases, and as we shall see in Chapter 27, the moral legitimacy of criminal prohibitions in these cases is by no means moot.

The single-party crime of self-mayhem is also not suitable for extended discussion here, but for quite different reasons. Acts of self-mutilation can be sorted into three categories. In the first class are those done for fraudulent purposes, for example to cheat an insurance company or to escape conscription. These acts are parts of larger criminal strategems, and as such their prohibition is unproblematically justified by the harm to others principle. In the second class are those acts done by madmen who cannot be held responsible. (Mere "neurotics" do not scratch out their own eyes, or amputate their own limbs or sex organs.) In the third class are religious fanatics seeking purification or atonement by a traditional route of fleshly mortification, and whose legal punishment would seem not only cruelly inappropriate, but self-defeating as well, since incarceration itself might serve the same ends for them as mutilation. The two-party analogues are much more interesting and controversial, particularly in the most common type of consented-to mutilation by another, namely, the calculated and voluntary sale of a removed organ or bodily part to another. These cases are discussed in Chapter 31.

2. Circumstantial and personal coercion: analogies and differences

Both the single-party and the two-party acts, in their own ways, are subject to appraisal as voluntary or not. The object of judgment in the single-party case is the actor's choice to act as he did, or his action itself. In the two-party case, the object of judgment is the act of consent (either initiating or responsive) of one party to conduct of the other that will endanger him. In either case, then, it is *actions* that are relevantly voluntary or not, since choosing and performing are both forms of doing, just as are requesting, and expressing one's acquiescence or permission.[5] We might naturally expect the criteria of voluntary action to be independent of whether the action in question is solitary (choosing) or social (consenting), but remembering the point about contextual relativity among standards of voluntariness (Chap. 20, §§4, 5), we should be prepared for asymmetries.

When we turn our attention in Chapter 23 to the two-party cases, we will focus on that type of consent-vitiating factor called "coercion," which of course is always a relation between two persons or groups of persons—the coercer (A) and the coercee (B). But since our basic concern is with the degrees of voluntariness with which persons can be said to choose their own actions, our attention should be focused mainly on the coercee, and his plight often seems identical to that of a person in the one-party case who is forced by natural *circumstances* (not other persons)[6] to choose the lesser of two evils, much as he hates to do so.

It may not be immediately obvious but the distinctions between one and two-party cases, and personal versus "natural" (or "circumstantial") coercion cut across one another creating four categories, as illustrated in Diagram 21-1.

At first sight, the problem of evaluating voluntariness in cases (1) and (2), in which there is a personal coercer, seem perfectly parallel to those in (3) and (4), in which there is no "coercer," strictly speaking, at all, but only threatening circumstances. Suppose that a motor launch pulls up to B's boat and the pilot A, gun in hand, says to B: "Jettison your cargo or I will kill you." That of course would be for A to exert extreme coercive pressure on B. In the other (circumstantial) kind of one-party case, however, there is no coercer and hence no personal coercion, but the natural circumstances can impose the same degree of pressure on B's choice, compelling him just as effectively to jettison his cargo. In the latter version of the story (made famous by Aristotle[7]) a violent storm attacks the boat, presenting B with the choice: jettison the cargo or suffer the whole boat to be submerged and all its passengers drowned. In both the personal and the "natural" cases the option for B amounts to this: jettison your cargo or else die. The degree of voluntariness or involuntariness in the two cases seems precisely the same, and can be determined quite independently of any account of the motives, intentions, or other mental states of any coercer, or even (in the natural circumstances case) in the absence of any coercer altogether.

Harry Frankfurt makes quite the same point:

> Suppose first that a man comes to a fork in the road, that someone on a hillside adjoining the left-hand fork *threatens* to start an avalanche which will crush him if he goes that way, and that the man takes the fork to the right in order to

	Single Party Cases: Coerced Choice	Two-Party Cases: Coerced Consent
Personal Coercion	1. E.g. another person threatens: "Directly inflict this harm upon yourself (or assume this risk of harm to yourself) *or else* suffer this unacceptable consequence from me."	2. E.g. another person threatens: "Consent to (permit, acquiesce in, facilitate) my doing an act that will directly harm you (or create a risk of harm to you) *or else* suffer this unacceptable consequence from me."
"Natural" or "Circumstantial" Coercion	3. E.g. nature threatens: The storm is so severe that either I jettison the cargo or the ship will sink. The circumstances themselves "coerce" my choice. I jettison the cargo to avoid even worse consequences from nature.	4. E.g. nature threatens: The forest fire is approaching my land. Either I give permission to the fire department to start a reverse fire among my own timber or the original fire will burn my house down. The circumstances themselves "coerce" my assent. I grant permission in order to avoid even worse consequences from nature.

Diagram 21–1. Personal and circumstantial "coercion" in one- and two-party cases.

satisfy a commanding desire to preserve his own life. Next suppose that when the man comes to the fork, he finds no one issuing threats but instead notices that on account of the natural conditions of things he will be crushed by an avalanche if he takes the left hand fork, and that he is moved irresistibly by his desire to live to take the right fork.

There are interesting differences between these situations, to be sure, but there is no basis for regarding the man as acting more or less freely or of his own free will in the one case than in the other. Whether he is morally responsible for his decision or action in each case depends not on the source of the injury he is motivated to avoid, but on the way in which his desire to avoid it operates within him.[8]

The point that seems to emerge from these examples is this: *B* can be compelled to act in circumstances that give him "no choice about the matter" by forces of nature as well as by another person (*A*). Even in the personal coercion case, whether or not *A*'s action and/or proposal exerts coercive pressure upon *B* is not a function of *A*'s intentions, desires, or beliefs. Perhaps certain mental states must be present in *A* if *coercion* is to be attributed to him as his doing,[9] but in that case we can preserve our point by saying that what *A* did unknowingly, accidentally, unintentionally, excusably or justifiably had a coercive effect upon *B*, even though strictly speaking *A* did not coerce *B*. *A*'s circumstances and intentions are irrelevant to our main concern which is the degree of voluntariness of *B*'s choices in coercive circumstances, that is, in circumstances in which alternative choices are somehow rendered less "eligible" to him. Regardless of what we may wish to say about *A* or *his* degree of culpability, if any, our present question is about *B*—how voluntarily did *he* act?

Would that we could leave the distinction between factors bearing on assessments of *A* and factors bearing on the voluntariness of *B*'s response to *A* as is, and move on to the next question. Alas, the distinction seems tidy only because of the examples we have drawn on. Kent Greenawalt presents examples of personal and natural coercion from the two-party category which threaten to undermine our distinction altogether:

> If *B* is mortally ill, and *A* (a doctor) tells him he will die shortly if he does not have an operation that he has a 50% chance of surviving, *B*'s consent to the operation is "free." If on the other hand, *A* tells *B* he will shoot him unless *B* jumps from the third story, a jump *B* knows he has a 50% chance of surviving, we do not say that *B* has freely decided to jump. And our judgment would not be altered if we believed that *B*'s state of mind in respect to each choice was identical.[10] [Letter variables changed to preserve uniformity]

Greenawalt's conclusions from this example are the very opposite of the ones we have drawn from other examples, namely that "notions that consent is not voluntary go beyond the state of mind of the actor and the options available to him, and reflect judgments about comparative responsibility among interacting humans" or "some evaluative judgment about the behavior of others."[11]

In all of the examples we have considered—Aristotle's, Frankfurt's, and Greenawalt's—the chooser (or consenter) has a choice of the following form: Do *X* or else die. Only by doing *X* does *B* have a chance of surviving the storm, the avalanche, the disease, or the gunman's bullets. *B*'s options are closed in the same way in all the cases, that is, it has been made impossible for him both to survive *and* to avoid doing *X*, and since his desire to survive is presumed paramount, he must do *X*. Yet in one case only, the consent to surgery [and the structurally similar case (4) in Diagram 1, which I do not discuss further], we judge that his doing *X* (giving consent) is voluntary. What then distinguishes this case from the others?

Outside of the special legal context in which questions of consent to medical treatment are raised, I submit that nothing distinguishes this case from the others, and we would all see the point of the claim that the physician's warning (authoritative and credible as it was) gave *B* "no choice" but to submit to surgery. *B* had only the minimal freedom present in the other examples: he could have opted for death if he had chosen. Yet in this special legal context, that minimal freedom is deemed sufficient, for the legal purposes involved, to establish the effectiveness of his consent. Whatever it is that "forces" *B* to give his consent, it is not a coercive act or threat from the surgeon. Since the doctor is not the source of the compulsion himself, but only the messenger bringing the bad news, the courts permit the patient's consent (forced though it is by other factors) to confer a privilege on the physician to operate. That the physician gave a warning only, and not a threat to make things worse on his own, distinguishes this case from the other two-person examples in which direct threats of coercion are made by gunmen, and assimilates this case in priciple to those one-party cases where the "threats" of death come from nature itself. In those one-party cases, however, the actions forced on *B* by impersonal nature (jettisoning cargo, choosing a fork in the road) are not acts of *consenting* to further conduct by another party.

In a sense then the surgery example is a "three-party case," in which "nature" in the form of *B*'s disease is one of the parties. The disease is the source of coercive pressure on *B*, and *A*, the surgeon, is a "third party" who happens to be in a position to help. "Will you accept my help?," he asks in effect, and *B*, who is subject to no further coercive pressures or other voluntariness-defeating factors beyond those imposed in the first place by the disease, "freely" agrees. The "freedom" here refers to the absence of compulsion from any sources beyond what is "given" in the example, the lethal disease itself. To deny that *B*'s acceptance of medical assistance in his plight is voluntary would be like denying that a drowning swimmer's rescue was freely consented to, on the ground that the swimmer, after all, had no alternative to his rescue but death. To be sure the swimmer had "no choice" but to accept rescue, but that is hardly a reason for denying him the rescue he seeks!

In the surgery and drowning swimmer cases we accept the circumstances of the consenter *talis qualis* (exactly as we find them) and ask whether in those circumstances, or against that background, the consenter's choice is free, or whether some further factor has intervened to vitiate it. In all the gunman examples, on the other hand, we regard the gunman's conduct as an intervention on the stage rather than part of the stage-setting, and we ask whether his intrusive behavior, seen against the background of what is normally present, forced the consenter's choice. In other words, judgments of voluntariness for legal purposes tend to be made relative to a given context, and a coercive *threat* is always seen as an obtrusive intervention, rather than as an assumed background against which voluntariness-defeating factors can appear. So in the troublesome examples, consent can be interpreted as voluntary, given one kind of background, but nonvoluntary, given another. It all depends on what is taken as "given." Given the disease then, the diseased *B*'s response is free. He *finds* himself diseased; that condition is part of the "he" that must make the decision (freely or not) to suffer the surgery or accept his natural death. But in the gunman cases, we "subtract" the gunman's presence from the conditions that are "given." Given the normal conditions that would otherwise have obtained, the gunman's intervention is a factor that vitiates the consent subsequently given.

In the surgery case, *B* says in effect to *A*: "Given that I have a disease that is otherwise fatal, I consent to your surgery." In the gunman case, *B* says to *A*: "Of course, given that you have a gun at my back and have uttered a credible threat to kill me, I 'consent' to your taking my money (or to my jumping out the window, etc.). But why must all of that be 'given'? I did *not* consent to your pulling a gun on me and making the threat in the first place. The whole episode involving you was unconsented to, so the component part of that episode which you call my 'consent' was involuntary." To be sure one might say that *B* did not "consent" to the disease in the other case either, but the contraction of a disease is not the sort of thing to which it even makes sense to give or withhold consent. Nature does not literally make proposals or threats, and people do not literally consent or refuse in turn. Natural occurrences are simply given—and taken. On the other hand, given the illness, *B* did consent to the whole episode involving the doctor.

3. Classification of voluntariness-reducing factors

One of the conditions that tends to vitiate voluntariness in one-party cases, as well as consent in two-party transactions, is compulsion. This word covers a multitude of factors, as indicated in Diagram 21-2. Until Freud, the concept of compulsion was largely restricted to pressures that originated outside a person's body and exerted their force either literally against his body, as a push, shove, violent wind, explosion, or force of gravity would, or figuratively against his will, thus "forcing" him to move his own body in certain ways. The former category (A1) we can call "compulsion proper." When the compelling force works directly on one's body, bypassing one's will, it leaves one, in the strictest sense, *no choice*. One's body is moved from without, as any physical object might be; there is no action, no moving of his own body by the person himself, at all. And if there is no action, it follows *a fortiori* that there is no voluntary action.

The second category (A2) is that in which the person himself moves his own body; he *acts* under "pressure" from external dangers or threats, rather than out of natural preference. To say that he is compelled to do what he does is to speak with a certain useful inexactness, and to use a metaphor

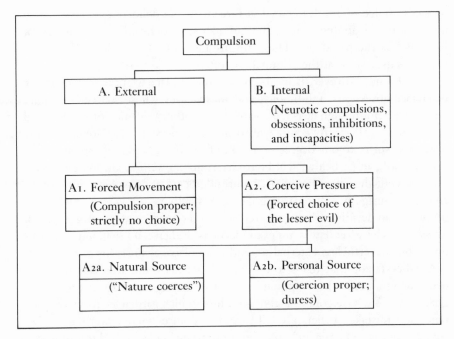

Diagram 21–2. Types of compulsion.

derived from the forced movement category. Strictly speaking, the person *does* "have a choice," but one of his alternatives is so unreasonable that it is as if "he has no choice" but to opt for the other one. His alternatives, through natural chance, or through the manipulations of another person, are arranged in such a way that all of them are undesired, and his only "freedom" is to choose the lesser of the evils, however distasteful it may be. This category (A2) is divided into two subcategories corresponding to the source of the coercive pressure. Category A2a consists of options that have been narrowed by nature, as in Frankfurt's example of the perceived imminence of a rock-slide along one of two paths open to a mountaineer. Other examples are given by our criminal law under the heading "the necessity justification." These include options narrowed not only by raw nature but by the complex of human needs and social circumstances—

> The policeman kills the kidnapper to save his innocent victim. The lost alpinist breaks into a mountain cabin to take refuge in a storm. The fire-fighters destroy property in order to confine the forest fire. The ambulance driver runs through a red light in order to rush a critically ill person to the hospital.[12]

In each case the actor confronts a dilemma of unsavory, even illegal alternatives, and is forced by the social and natural circumstances to choose the lesser evil. Category A2b, on the other hand, consists of cases in which a person's choice of the lesser evil is forced by the deliberate and calculated intervention of another party; the gunman who demands "your money or your life" is the paradigm. These are instances of coercion in the strict and narrow sense, or what the criminal law often calls "duress."[13]

Since Freud, however, it has become commonplace to speak of compulsive behavior, obsessions, inhibitions, and incapacities whose source is entirely within the actor though he is not aware of it, or otherwise unable to understand or eliminate it. Perfectly competent, responsible persons, who are in no sense deranged, suffer to one degree or another from these "internal compulsions," and our task, in §6 below, will be to determine how, if at all, these neurotic conditions of the actor should affect our judgments of the voluntariness of his choice to engage in self-regarding dangerous activity. Obviously part of the problem is in deciding whether to treat a person's neurosis as an integral part of his *self*, as a character flaw is, for example, or as an alien condition, internal to his mind, but nevertheless external to, and compulsive against, his self.[14]

Another factor that tends to diminish or defeat voluntariness is mistaken belief or ignorance. Its scope and diversity are suggested by the following Diagram 21–3. Category A1 contains the familiar garden varieties of ignorance and mistaken belief. We fail to know because "no one ever told us," or we have not read or remembered the appropriate books, or had the appropriate experiences. We have mistaken beliefs because someone or some book that we trusted misinformed us, or we have a distorted recollection of evidence, or we became confused in our inferences from what we do know. Category A2 corresponds to the personal coercion category in Diagram 2. In both cases another party deliberately manipulates our circumstances to get us

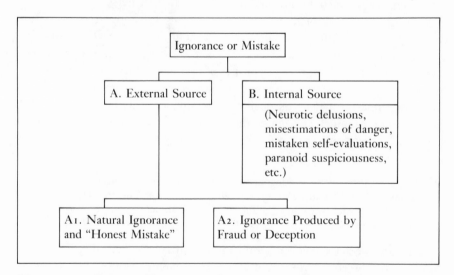

Diagram 21–3. Sources of ignorance and mistake.

to do something we would not otherwise choose to do, and does this with the calculated purpose of achieving some gain for himself, usually at our expense, Fraudulent deception can work as well as coercive force in getting someone to do what he is otherwise unwilling to do, and both tend to vitiate voluntariness in the single-party as well as in the two-party case. What remains to be seen is whether in certain contexts mistake induced by fraud has a more pronounced effect on judgments of voluntariness than mistakes from other sources. Finally, category B contains those mistakes and gaps in knowledge traceable to the tricks our own neurotic psyches play on us. Our ignorance is evidence-resistant and our persistence in error is as-if-willful, though we may be miserably unaware of how we trick ourselves. Part of the problem in evaluating the voluntariness of neurotic mistakes for certain practical purposes is to find a basis (if there is one) for treating them any differently from mistakes that are genuinely willful, or traceable to other character defects (credulity, greed, perversity, cowardice) whether neurotic or not.

4. External compulsion in risk-taking

Still other types of factors tend to vitiate consent, notably temporary lapses of capacity, for example in drunkenness, and seriously impaired or undeveloped capacity to the point of incompetence as in derangement (insanity), retardation, infancy, and the like. These factors when applied to the single-party dangerous risk cases that will now be before our minds, do not usually raise problems in as striking a way as they do in two-party consent cases, so we may postpone our discussion of them, with little loss, until Chapter 26. We are not tempted to permit drunks to cross unsafe bridges, much less go over Niagara Falls in a barrel; we have no reservations about forbidding five-year-olds from smoking cigarettes, much less home-grown marijuana; and no lover of freedom would permit a lunatic who is convinced he is Superman to jump off a skyscraper. What problems we have about the categories of infancy, insanity, and drunkenness, are those common to all the voluntariness-defeating factors, namely problems in classifying borderline cases, and tailoring standards to special contexts.

Compulsion and mistake are far more often problematically involved in the one-party risk-taking cases, though not every subcategory distinguished in our diagrams has a role to play. What we called "compulsion proper" or "forced movement" [Diagram 2, (A1)], in particular, raises few moral problems. If someone is headed toward the falls in his raft only because a powerful current is sweeping him along against his will, then obviously it is no wrongful invasion of his liberty to forcibly deflect his movement toward shore.

In this and the following section we can briefly run through the categories of compulsion and mistake that *do* raise conceptual or moral problems for us as we attempt to apply the "soft paternalist strategy" to the single-party risk-taking cases, especially to determinations of the degree of voluntariness that is "voluntary enough" to render the risky conduct of an autonomous actor immune from outside interference. We shall consider compulsions and mistakes with external origins first, and then turn to their neurotic counterparts in section 6.

Considering compulsion first, our question is whether an outsider (civilian or official) has a right to interfere with the self-regarding dangerous choices of another person on the ground (or well-founded suspicion) that his choice to run the risks is insufficiently voluntary because of coercive pressure either from natural circumstances or another person. Consider first the choices forced by natural circumstances. It is hard to imagine them in the home-grown marijuana case, or the dangerous sport and daredevil cases. It is virtually impossible to conceive of a person forced by natural circumstances to cultivate, harvest, dry, and smoke the leaves of marijuana plants in the privacy of his own home. It is almost equally difficult to imagine a person deciding to go water-skiing or hang-gliding because some complex of natural and social conditions made it the least of the evils he might choose at the time. There are, of course, risks that arise in the course of dangerous sports that have not been specifically addressed in advance by the sportsman and which he does not voluntarily assume, like being swept on one's raft by an unforseeable gale towards a waterfall; but as we have seen intervention in these cases is not interference with liberty, but highly welcome assistance to one who is in peril.

Sometimes natural disasters like storms, fires, and earthquakes so narrow a person's options that the least risky alternative open to him is itself so dangerous that it would seem reckless daredeviltry, or at least dangerous sport, if done in normal circumstances. Thus a mountaineer trapped in his cabin by a raging fire might choose his best chance of escape in making a dash for it on his skis down a precipitous slope through a portion of burning forest to safety. Here, of course, it would be absurd to interfere with him because of the presumption of nonvoluntariness due to coercive circumstances. The greater *this kind* of "coercion," the lower should be our standard of "voluntary enough." *Given* that the circumstances left the person no alternative to death but his dangerous activity, we cannot rightly interfere with him without causing his death. Interference could be justified at most for the sake of some safer third alternative unknown to the person, but then the nonvoluntariness that warrants interference was produced by ignorance, not natural coercion.

Coercive pressure from other persons is an even more unlikely cause of self-regarding risk-taking in the home-grown drugs, dangerous sports, and daredeviltry cases than is coercion from nature. Unlikely, but not impossible.

We can (just barely) imagine A, a very peculiar coercer, putting a gun to B's head (or to the head of Mrs. B or little Johnny or Mary B) and demanding that he cultivate and use his own marijuana, hang-glide, or go over a falls in a barrel. A may be a sadistic lunatic of a very mysterious sort, with no very coherent motivation, or he may be a wicked calculator implementing a very complicated scheme, but *his* purposes and mental states need not trouble us, since we are only concerned with our obligations to B in the circumstances. Just as in the circumstantial coercion cases discussed in the preceding paragraph, there are two possibilities. We can rightfully intervene to prevent B from taking the risks on the ground that his choice is "not voluntary enough," but only if our intervention takes the form of rescuing him from his coercer, A. This would be no more an invasion of liberty than rescue from drowning or burning would be. If we can somehow rescue the isolated mountaineer in the previous example by altering the naturally coercive circumstances in which he finds himself, perhaps by quenching the fire on an escape route that is more safely accessible, or by landing a helicopter to evacuate him, then we implement his free choices rather than interfere with his liberty. But what if he declines our help, having by now set his heart on the more exciting dangerous exploit he had already planned? In that case, provided he does not appear wild-eyed and hysterical, we must concede that his choice, while foolish, is nevertheless truly his, and he must be permitted to act on it, just as he would in the normal cases of dangerously exciting solitary sport. Ironically, his risky act is now clearly voluntary only because we intervened to change the coercive circumstances that had appeared to render his choice of that act considerably less than fully voluntary. It is as if, having been liberated from the gunman A, B calmly reconsiders and decides to do what A was trying to force him to do. Once again, that is his right, according to the liberal soft paternalist.

Suppose now that the parallel to the original mountaineer story holds in the personal coercion example. What if we are unable to interfere with B's coerced choice of the lesser evil except by bringing about, by our very intervention, the greater evil threatened by A (say the death of Mrs. B)? Then preventing B from acting on his coerced choice on the ground that it is not voluntary enough, would be like forcibly detaining the fire-threatened skier on the ground that *his* choice to flee is not voluntary enough. Thus, while the natural and personal coercion cases can require different assessments of voluntariness for some purposes (see *supra*, §2), they also present striking analogies in respect to the obligations they impose on intervening parties.

The more interesting cases of coercive pressure to assume self-regarding risks are also more familiar in our experience. These are cases in which the "coercion" is much more subtle than the gun-at-one's-head model, partly because the threats are mostly implicit, partly because the coercive circumstances include both circumstantial and deliberate personal components, partly because the unusual condition of the coercee is itself part of the coercive complex, and partly because something like "compulsion proper" is also involved, though short of necessitation. We need not invent bizarre hypothetical examples of this more subtle form of coerced risk-taking; the daily newspapers are full of them. For example, consider the law suits against the ABC television network for injuries incurred by dare-devil stuntmen while attempting dangerous feats for the titillation of millions of viewers of a weekly program called "That's Incredible." One dare-devil burned and mutilated his hands trying to walk through a tunnel of fire. Another crashed into a concrete wall in a failed attempt to leap over it on his motorcycle. A third, Steve Lewis, who became a successful plaintiff later, failed in an effort to leap over two cars as they passed a spot near him at one hundred miles an hour. He incurred serious injuries, including a mangled foot that had to be amputated. The outspoken television critic, Gary Deeb, explains how the accident happened:

> The taping took place last July [1980] in Arizona and appeared on the air six weeks later. That morning Lewis did a successful practice jump a few inches away from the cars involved. Later, however, when the cameras began to roll, he got cold feet, told the director he "didn't feel comfortable," and asked for a postponement of the jump.
>
> But the "Incredible" production crew pressured him to go through with it anyway. According to Lewis, the director screamed at him: "I want you to jump now! We have a plane to catch. It's getting dark . . . Wrap it up; wrap it up. Jump! Jump!"
>
> The ensuing leap ended in tragedy, and the production crew's "coercion" of Lewis turned out to be the foundation of his lawsuit.[15]

In what sense is this chilling tale an instance of a single-party case? Lewis had presumably made an agreement with the producers to perform his stunt for a certain payment. He consented to the terms of that agreement. That seems to place this hybrid case in the two-party consensual category. Nevertheless, the example shows more important affinities to simpler single-party cases. The genuine two-party consent cases are those in which one party, B, consents to the performance of an act by a second party A, which will harm or endanger B. In the paradigm single-party cases, B himself performs the action which is harmful or dangerous to himself, whether or not there is another party, A, somehow involved, for example as encourager, incitor, spectator, beneficiary, etc. In the "That's Incredible" case, the injurious act is performed by B himself, not by another party who has B's consent, and that act is itself something other than a mere expression of consent. That fact assimilates this case to the single-party category despite the fact that there was a contractual agreement with another party.

The question at issue for the soft paternalist is whether an intervening party might have rightly attempted to prevent the tragic act before it happened on the ground that in the circumstances its choice was "not voluntary enough." There is no direct question here for the criminal law. The soft paternalist could not advocate the prohibition of daredevil attempts on the grounds that they are universally and necessarily "not voluntary enough." The legal questions involving the third-party intervener are more indirect. If he does make an effort to prevent the jump, what are *his* subsequent civil and criminal liabilities?

I should think that the soft paternalist's answer would be as follows. If the intervention truly is justified, that is, if there was a well-grounded, good faith suspicion that the coercive climate would render the stuntman's jump not-voluntary-enough, and, further, if the intervention stopped short of unlawful force or violence, then the intervener should be free of criminal liability, and exempt also from civil liability to the producers to compensate them for losses caused by the delay or cancellation of the shooting. Somebody already legitimately on the scene, for example, might have stepped forward with a bull horn and countered the goading "screams" of the director with urgings that the stuntman stop and consider what he is doing, and warnings to the director of *his* possible civil liability in case of accident. He might do this in such a way that the filming would be impossible so long as he was in the center of things. But if the stuntman, after his reprieve and a careful reconsideration, agrees to try his jump then and there after all, then the intervener must take the stuntman's word for it that he is ready, appraise the risks as voluntarily (enough) assumed, and reluctantly withdraw.

Nobody put a literal or figurative gun to Lewis's head and threatened him with death or the like unless he jumped. How then could the civil jury decide that he acted under coercive pressure strong enough to vitiate the voluntariness of his choice? And why did Deeb, after his vivid account of the director's hectoring, nevertheless drape the word "coercion" in quotation marks? In the example, there is indeed neither compulsion proper nor coercion by explicit threat. Yet there are factors that can be called *compulsive pressure* short of necessitation and *coercive pressure* by means of implicit threats of consequences that are unwelcome though well short of being unacceptable. Then in addition, the stuntman's condition of fatigue and fright made him more susceptible to "pressure" than he would otherwise be, so that even though each factor in the total pressure taken by itself was reasonably resistible, the whole complex, acting on his weakened and distracted condition, might well have been unreasonably difficult for him to counteract.

The implicitly coercive threats were probably the least significant elements of pressure. Their explication here is perforce a matter of conjecture, but given the authority and influence of the production crew, Lewis might well have felt that his fee was in jeopardy, not to mention his reputation in the entertainment world. Clearly the prospect of general disappointment in him by important people and his likely loss of esteem both in their eyes and also with those who would subsequently hear of his hesitations, must have had some impact on his "choice" to jump. But the more important pressures may have bypassed his deliberative faculties and his will altogether, in the manner of compulsive forces that work directly on one's body. Peremptory shouts, screamed commands, urgent goadings, and noisy bluster may, in the right circumstances, function as verbal pushes and shoves. When the person made subject to them is already fatigued and in the grip of a difficult emotion, he may be so confused by them that he loses a grip on his previous resolution and is "moved" quite without thought or deliberation. They are angry, intimidating noises, which might make him "start" involuntarily, as if startled by a sudden explosion. The pressure is by no means comparable to the gravity that pulls one to earth after being pushed off a height, or a hurricane wind that blows a sailor overboard. The verbal shoves are not even comparable in strength to the energetic shoves of a large and powerful bully. They are more like physical shoves that one can easily resist being moved by if one is fresh and prepared for them with one's feet planted firmly on the ground. But even a weak shove, when one is distracted and off balance, may have the effect of a hurricane wind.

In other contexts mere resistible verbal pushes and shoves are quite insufficient to defeat voluntariness. When the purpose of the voluntariness determination, for example, is to establish responsibility for a very serious crime, it certainly won't get the accused off the hook (though it might get his incitor *on* the hook). But when the purpose is to determine the permissibility of preventive intervention in self-regarding dangerous conduct, or the civil liability of second parties for the self-inflicted harms of stuntmen, then ever so slight shoves, verbal or otherwise, may be enough.

Note the inverse relationship between establishing *excuses* for one's conduct when it is wrongfully harmful to another, and establishing nonresponsibility for self-endangering action for the purpose of authorizing outside interference. The more serious the harm caused or threatened to others by a person's wrongful acts, the *more* stringent the standards for determining the nonvoluntariness that can excuse it. In cases of extreme harm to others, his act must be very nearly totally involuntary for him to be excused. The more serious the risks to himself assumed by the actor, in the other context, the *less* stringent the standards for determining the nonvoluntariness that can warrant preventive interference for the actor's own sake (First Rule of Thumb, Chap. 20, §5). His act need not be close to the extreme of total involuntariness in order to be "involuntary enough" to warrant interference. The production crew did not make it *impossible* for Lewis to avoid the accident by postponing the jump. They did not "in effect leave him no choice." But they did make it unreasonably difficult for him in the circumstances to decline, and given how much was at stake for Lewis, they diminished his freedom just enough to become liable for the injuries caused by Lewis's less than fully voluntary choice.

5. Ignorance and mistake in risk-taking

Those mistaken beliefs and gaps in knowledge that stem from familiar and natural sources (here excluding for the moment deception from others) often bear heavily on our assessment of the voluntariness of risk-taking. For other moral, legal, and political purposes, it may also be highly relevant whether or not the ignorance is a product of the actor's own negligence. If we are investigating a person's possible criminal liability for unreasonable risks he caused to others, for example, it will not defeat the voluntariness required for liability to show that "he didn't know the gun was loaded," since that kind of ignorance is always presumed to be negligent. ("He should have known," we reply). But if a person playfully illustrates the game of Russian roulette with a fully loaded six-shooter, it utterly vitiates the voluntariness of his actions to show that he doesn't know the gun is loaded, and any better-informed spectator owes it to him to intervene forcibly for his sake.

Natural ignorance and mistaken belief, negligent or not, reduce the voluntariness of self-regarding dangerous conduct when the ignorance or mistake is relevant, and it is relevant when it is ignorance of the character or magnitude of the risks taken, or when it is ignorance about the availability of alternative courses. If the risk taken by a person is not in fact the risk he chooses to take, then he does not take *that* risk voluntarily. Similarly, if he is ignorant of the existence of alternative means to his end that are not as risky, then his choosing to take the risk, even while properly apprised of its character and magnitude, is less than fully voluntary. If the conduct chosen is *highly* risky, or if the risked harm is grave or irrevocable, then ignorance of alternatives may render it "not voluntary enough" to preclude temporary interference for the purpose of imparting the information that would restore its voluntariness.

It is worth emphasizing again, however, that eccentric, even "unreasonable" judgments of the relative worthwhileness of that which is risked and that which is gained do not count against voluntariness at all, provided that they in turn are not based on relevant and corrigible ignorance. The risk is often the price willingly or reluctantly paid for some good that is thought to be worth it, even when the price is more than others would be willing to pay, and even when it is in fact exorbitant. Just as there are basic individual differences among consumers in their attitudes toward spending, so there are natural temperamental differences among people in their judgments of the acceptability of risks. Some of those judgments may in some legitimate sense be "mis-taken," but even so, they might still be "voluntary enough" to be immune from interference. As we have seen (Chap. 20, §§3, 7, and 8), only when these judgments are so unreasonable as to raise the suspicion of impaired capacity, or lack of clear understanding (as opposed to mere true belief) of the relevant components of the risk, can interference be justified, but even then the harms risked must be very serious or probable, and the suspicions must be both well founded and treated as rebuttable presumptions.

How do these distinctions apply to this chapter's test cases? The person who chooses to grow and use his own marijuana, like the more common social smokers who buy the drug, deliberately assumes a risk to his health for the sake of the pleasures of smoking pot. What makes this case interesting is that in the present state of medical knowledge, no one knows exactly, or even approximately, what that risk is. There have been some experiments that suggest that various disorders are associated with the active ingredients in marijuana, and perhaps "it stands to reason" that a lifetime of inhaling smoke might damage the lungs. But hardly a soul is alive who has spent an actual lifetime of heavy pot-smoking. No one knows which frequency of usage is excessive, which moderate, which harmless. No one can cite statistical "probabilities" to the beginning user to apprise him of his chances. No one knows how the myriad of other variables in modes of usage, age, sex, general condition, and genetic disposition, affect the risks. In short, pot smoking is risk-taking under conditions of almost total ignorance. It is no doubt reason-able to suppose that some risk is involved—that heavy usage is more danger-ous *ceteris paribus* than no usage—but beyond that, accurate risk assessments are impossible.

Nevertheless, there is an important way in which the unavoidably ignorant person's decision to use this possibly dangerous drug, even to use it regu-larly, might still be voluntary. To be sure it cannot be both *perfectly* volun-tary and *that* ignorant, but we have already seen how useless the notion of perfect voluntariness is for moral purposes. It *can* be as voluntary as could be hoped for, given universal gaps in knowledge, by standards tailored to the actual circumstances that include that ignorance. If it is as voluntary as possible, given those background conditions, it may well be "voluntary enough."

The person who has all the relevant knowledge available about the risks of pot-smoking does shoulder the risk quite voluntarily, provided also that he has an accurate knowledge, at a higher level, of the scope and limits of his first-level knowledge. If he knows the little that current science can tell him, and knows how little that is; if he knows that conclusive evidence of the connection between nicotine and lung cancer did not accumulate until the first heavy-smoking generation had been at it for thirty years, and that there are as yet no comparable data about the effects of prolonged marijuana usage, but that such evidence could very well turn up; if he knows that there are already suspected links, based on inconclusive studies, between *some* amount of pot-usage and a variety of physical ailments, from loss of male hormone to diminished brain-function, and that the trend has been for the discovery of more and better confirmed connections of these kinds, then he has all the relevant information there is. If, given all that, he is still willing to take a chance, we have to admit that he knows what he is doing, and that his decision was not simply based on a mistake. It was made in ignorance, as Aristotle would say, but not "by reason of ignorance." Unavoidable ignorance is to some degree an element in all risk-taking, but to know which factors are unknown is itself to have knowledge of a relevant kind, contributing to responsible decision-making . All we need to assure ourselves of in assessing voluntariness is that the risk-taker knows exactly what the risk is that he is taking, and his ignorance is a vital component of that risk.

Similar points can be made about the dangerous sport and daredevil cases. Suppose the dangerous activity is to take place without the equivalent of a "safety net" on a frozen lake. The sportsman or daredevil might believe that the ice in a certain section of the lake is secure when it is in fact so, in which case he takes little risk (of drowning). If the probability of break-through at some weak point is only 1% and that is known to the sportsman, he does take *some* risk, but he takes it voluntarily. If he believes that the probability is 1% when in fact it is more like 99%, then he takes a big risk and takes it, in his ignorance, quite involuntarily. Suppose, however, that he simply does not know anything about the condition of the ice in that part of the lake. He does, of course, have general background knowledge. He knows that it is early April, a time when thaws begin, that the temperature has hovered near the freezing point for several days, that there is a *chance* that the ice is thin where he is going, but also a chance that it is not. But he does not know the depth of the water where he is headed or a dozen other relevant variables. He knows that he doesn't know these things and that they are important. Ice-boating would be fun in that part of the lake, so knowing the risk (including the part of the risk that consists of his own ignorance), he proceeds. This case differs from the home-grown pot case only in that the ignorance is personal and corrigible, rather than universal and for an extended time, incorrigible. Perhaps that difference makes it a close case, but on the whole one is inclined to say that since the sportsman understood exactly what risk he was taking, his taking of it was voluntary enough. That is to say that interference would be justified only by someone who knew more about the condition of the ice, for the purpose of apprising and warning the adventurous boatsman.

Suppose, on the other hand, that the sportsman is a skater, and as he approaches the shore he sees a sign posted by the Department of Recreational

Safety to the effect that skating is dangerous in this area whenever a red flag is flying, and there next to the sign flies the red flag. The intrepid sportsman, unfazed, continues toward the area anyway. Now a second party sees the impending folly, and rushes to intervene. At first his purpose is to warn. "Don't you see the flag? Don't you understand?" Upon being assured that the skater does indeed understand the meaning of the flag, but wishes to skate there anyway "because it is so pretty," the second party will suspect some sort of voluntariness-vitiating derangement. His next question naturally will be the rhetorical one: "Are you *crazy?*," and he will be justified in forcibly preventing the skater from moving on to the thin ice. If later, it should turn out that the skater, by independent tests, is not crazy after all, but merely foolish and eccentric (unlikely chance!), then his liberty must be restored.

What bearing, if any, does it have on judgments of voluntariness that the risk-taker's relevant ignorance or mistake was caused by the fraudulent misrepresentation of another person? For the most part, no bearing at all. A mistaken belief diminishes voluntariness for our present purposes (as opposed to the purpose, say, of determining criminal responsibility) whatever its cause. Perhaps ignorance caused by deliberate deception has a greater impact in the two-party case in which the voluntariness of one party's consent to the proposal of the deceiver is at issue (see Chap. 25, §6). In that case that fact the *A* lied to *B* may cancel the validity of *B*'s consent even if *B* was in fact undeceived when he consented, but this asymmetry with the single-party case may express a different purpose in looking at voluntariness—the desire to prevent *A*'s wrongful gain, instead of the desire to protect *B* from choices made by mistake. In general, the only relevance of fraud to determinations of voluntariness in the single-party case, is evidential. When we see *B* about to undertake some dangerous act, we may not know whether his relevant beliefs are true and whether he has the relevant knowledge with the appropriate understanding, so in our ignorance, we might hesitate to interfere. But if we do know that *A* lied to him about a relevant fact for some gain of his own, we have a much stronger presumption of nonvoluntariness-because-of-ignorance, strong enough to warrant interference at least for minatory and informative purposes.

6. Neurosis

We turn finally to compulsions, inhibitions, factual delusions and incapacities that have their origins, in some sense, "within" the agent. When these conditions manifest themselves in recognizably "neurotic" ways, psychologists do not hesitate to apply such terms as "compulsive" and "obsessive" to them. In fact, obsessive ideas, phobias (obsessive projected fears), and compulsive behavior are commonly found together, explained as parts of a complex neurotic syndrome. Even the obsessions themselves are "compulsive" in character: ". . .an obsession exists whenever a person cannot exclude thoughts from consciousness and, although he distinguishes them as unreasonable or without basis, is mastered by them."[16] The "force" of an obsession then is more like compulsion proper than coercion. More exactly, it exerts something like "compulsive force" even through it may not be literally irresistible. In that respect it is less like a hurricane that blows one over than like a powerful wind that can be kept out of one's house only by constantly leaning against the window shutters. The compulsive force is constant, and even though it is resistible, the measures required to withstand it might make unreasonable demands on one's vigilance and energy. Most of what is called "compulsive behavior," however, is not *felt* (by the actor) as compelled at all. His will is thoroughly implicated in his behavior; he makes no effort to resist felt pressures; he denies that he is acting unfreely. Yet his conduct reenforces his unhappiness, and troubles and perplexes both him and his acquaintances.

Theories of neurosis are as numerous as psychologists, so only a sketchy common-denominator account can be attempted here. The neurotic person, because of the way he is brought up, and in particular because of difficult personal relationships of various kinds, carries more than his share of a very painful and threatening *anxiety*. Perhaps the anxiety has been generated by a rage or hostility too strong to cope with, perhaps by the tension between instinctual impulses and repressive guilt, perhaps by both of these or various other causes (depending on the theorist). Psychologists don't always mean the same thing by "anxiety," but however that key notion is explained, it clearly is an unhappy state of mind. Karen Horney writes that "intense anxiety is one of the most tormenting affects we can have. Patients who have gone through an intense fit of anxiety will tell you that they would rather die than have a recurrence of that experience."[17] Yet that experience is always potentially present waiting to occur or recur, its presence sometimes only dimly perceived, its causes and objects unknown or misunderstood. Such a ravaging enemy within is a severe threat to the person as a biological organism, so efforts have to be made to defend against it. Paradoxically, a crucial element in the neurotic coping-strategy is to maintain one's ignorance of exactly what one is doing. From the biological point of view the neurosis functions "to maintain internal and external equilibria for the survival of the person."[18] From the psychological point of view, a neurosis is a huge trick played by the self on itself for its own self-protection.

The various defense mechanisms serve the neurotic person by protecting him from intolerable tension and anxiety. They have a large number of technical names—projection, inhibition, regression, displacement, phobia, and more, but what is interesting about them to the moral philosopher is that they are all either forms of compulsiveness (compulsive acting or compulsive inhibiting), mistake (delusive beliefs, paranoid suspicions, severe personal under- or over-assessment, etc.), or incapacity (e.g., inability to make decisions, to achieve up to capacity, to enjoy oneself). Compulsion, mistake, and incapacity, of course, are the chief categories of voluntariness-reducing factors.

Karen Horney writes that in our culture there are four chief ways in which the neurotic tries to escape his anxiety. (1) He can rechannel it toward substitute objects and then try to rationalize it, that is turn it into a "rational fear." Horney points out that extreme defensiveness usually indicates that the attitude defended has important functions for the individual; he *needs* it. She cites as an example the overprotective mother who can recite statistics about crimes and accidents suffered by children. This parent would maintain the neurotic attitude whatever the statistics showed, since it is a kind of "compromise solution" of her contest with a basic anxiety. (2) He can deny its existence by excluding it altogether from consciousness, so that all that appears of it are physical symptoms like shivering, sweating, choking, and excessive urinating. (3) He can "narcotize" it by any of a variety of techniques from alcohol and drug use to drowning it in work. The latter is a typical example of "compulsive behavior" when it is utterly undeviating and inflexible, and when intense uneasiness is felt on Sundays and holidays. Other commmonly used narcotizing techniques are compulsive masturbation or sex (where possible). (4) Through manipulation of his circumstances and responses he can avoid all situations likely to arouse anxiety. A common technique in this category is chronic procrastination. Another, usually more effective one, is a kind of self-deceiving "pretending," as when one declines an invitation on the ground that "I don't like parties anyway." In the more extreme cases the avoidance mechanisms operate automatically, in which case the neurotic inability to "do, feel, or think certain things" is called "inhibition"—the negative counterpart of obsession, and equally "compulsive."

What is meant by neurotic "compulsiveness"? Automatic obsessions and inhibitions are forms of compelled (or constrained) experience that, in the most extreme cases, irresistibly "force" one to do, feel, or think certain things, or prevent one from doing, feeling, or thinking other things. This is literal compulsion in the same sense as a locked door literally compels one to stay in a room, or a powerful push forces one to move. Sometimes the neurotic is at least dimly aware that these forces are working on him, but there is little he can do to counter them. Other times, as we have seen, his own will is involved in the compulsion without his awareness, and there is nothing he wants to do about it. The application of the term "compulsion" in the latter cases is problematic. Perhaps it is better to reserve the term "compulsive," as opposed to "compelled," for this sort of apparently voluntary behavior, to indicate that it shares characteristics with behavior that is literally compelled by forces from outside the (conscious) self, while leaving open the question of whether the determining causes really are "external" and over-powering. It is at least conceivable that a given instance of behavior could be compulsive though not compelled.

Compulsive behavior is that which emerges in the neurotic person as the solution to his underlying conflicts over guilt, anxiety, or hostility. The "solution" functions to protect him from something which he fears to so great an extent that he cannot even allow himself to be fully aware of it. If the solution performs its protective function adequately, the neurotic clings to it desperately, and will never simply be argued or persuaded out of it. Horney lists four general features by which a psychiatrist can recognize neurotic compulsiveness. The first is the contrast between what is felt as needed, and what is genuinely wanted, or between genuine interest in or enjoyment of work or play for its own inherent appeal, and pellmell pursuit of something to avoid the pain of not having it, even when it has no inherent appeal for its own sake. In the latter case there may even be "an utter disregard for himself, for his best interests," as when the neurotic continues to engage in the compulsive behavior not only in circumstances where it is inappropriate but in others where it patently endangers his material interests. Horney explains this unreasonableness, using the neurotic pursuit of glory as her example, as follows:

> When we call a drive compulsive we mean the opposite of spontaneous wishes or strivings. The latter are an expression of the real self; the former are determined by the inner necessities of the neurotic structure. The individual must abide by them regardless of his real wishes, feelings or interests lest he incur anxiety, feel torn by conflicts, be overwhelmed by guilt feelings, feel rejected by others, etc. In other words, the difference between spontaneous and compulsive is one between "I want" and "I must in order to avoid some danger." Although the individual may consciously feel his ambition or his standards of perfection to be what he *wants* to attain, he is actually driven to attain it. The need for glory has him in its clutches. Since he himself is unaware of the difference between wanting and being driven, we must establish criteria for a distinction between the two. The most decisive one is the fact that he is driven on the road to glory with an utter *disregard for himself, for his best interests.*[19]

The quotation raises several interesting conjectures. First, it is not clear why Horney does not think of the "neurotic structure" as part of the "real self." What the real self is, of course, is a deep philosophical question which neither she nor I could hope to enter. But if the neurotic structure is part of that self then it is a trait properly predicable of the person, like his bone structure and eye color, his talents and deficiencies, his character virtues and flaws—for better or worse part of the way he is. Since his conduct-generating mechanisms, in that case, are part of himself, the behavior they produce, while compulsive, is not compelled from without, but is at most "as if compelled."

His, after all, is a *compulsive self*, and compulsiveness on this hypothesis is a character flaw, no more vitiating in its effect on voluntariness and responsibility than greed, cruelty, recklessness, unreasonableness, or similar flaws. The second conjecture follows immediately upon the first. If Horney is right and the neurotic structure is best understood as external to the self, then it does compel (in something like the usual sense) the compulsiveness it produces, but more in the manner of two-party coercion than compulsion proper. The self, in this interpretation, puts a figurative loaded gun to itself and says not "Your money or your life," but "Use this compulsive defense mechanism or suffer your basic anxiety," where the only alternative to neurosis is as unthinkable as death in the gunman case. The neurotic self, moreover, forces itself not only into the required behavior patterns, but insists, as a condition of the deal, that the coerced self forget—or more accurately remain unaware of—the whole coercive transaction. Compulsive behavior then is "as if coerced" behavior.

The third interesting suggestion in the quotation is Horney's proposed criterion for distinguishing genuine wanting from compulsive needing. The behavior in question can be identified as compulsive if it is pursued ("fanatically" we might almost say) beyond the threshold of self-harm. I should think that this is only part of the test for *neurotic* compulsiveness and not by itself conclusive. But it does suggest that cigarette smoking, to mention one pattern or activity that many relatively non-neurotic people engage in, may well be compulsive in character, though perfectly voluntary. The habitual smoker may tell himself that he smokes because he "enjoys" it and it helps him "relax," when in fact what he enjoys is primarily relief from the pain of being without, and what relaxes him is cessation of the tension of deprivation. If he smokes even when it directly causes predominant pain (he has a chest cold and a raw sore throat) or harms his interests (he is a distance runner, actor, or opera singer) or threatens him with extinction (his family has a history of lung cancer), then the compulsiveness hypothesis has more plausibility than the enjoyment hypothesis, though *neurotic* compulsiveness, of course, is still another thing.

How do neurotically compulsive behavior patterns differ from merely powerful habits, given that the latter (especially in the form of addictions) can be equally compulsive? And what differences for our standards of voluntariness, if any, are posed by the two categories? Partly these are distinctions of degree. It is hard to break a twenty-year cigarette smoking habit, but virtually impossible, without considerable psychiatric assistance, to break out of a rigid neurotic life pattern. On the other hand, an addiction, which is an extremely powerful habit, having a biochemical base, may also be impossible to break (though easier to recognize) without professional help. Typically the neurotically compulsive life-style combines the power of the addiction with the self-deception and rationalization of some mere strong habits. ("I smoke because I love the taste.") Also, typically, it has its own characteristic auxiliary features (see below) and always its own distinctive etiology and mode of functioning. If one does not take the metaphor too seriously one can say that the genuinely compelled person is pushed from without; the neurotically compulsive person's self has become tangled in a powerful knot which he does not know how to untie, and which constrains him as effectively as an outside force; and the person in the grip of a compulsive habit is propelled forward by the force of his own inertial momentum, so strongly inclined in one direction that he cannot control his own trajectory. These are distinct images, and they accompany distinct concepts. But their different effects, if any, on our judgments of voluntariness are blurred. The person disposed by deeply rooted habit to act and feel in evil (greedy, selfish, cruel, deceptive, vindictive, petty, etc., etc.) ways, is our very model, according to Aristotle, of a genuinely wicked person, so that the more powerful the habit the more voluntary (in the modern sense), and hence the more blameworthy, the conduct. If we take neurotic compulsiveness to differ from merely bad habit in this respect, and actually to reduce the voluntariness (and incidentally the blameworthiness) of the behavior it generates, it must be because of some characteristic other than its compulsiveness as such, and it is not clear what that characteristic might be, unless it is the intense unhappiness which is an essential feature of the neurotic style of living,[20] there being no reason in principle why the merely habitual compulsive wrongdoer cannot derive great pleasure in "doing what comes naturally" to him. But the relevance of this acknowledged difference to judgments of voluntariness remains obscure.

The second identifying characteristic of neurotic compulsiveness (after "driving need"), according to Horney, is its indiscriminativeness. All of the drives that are compulsive cravings (love, power, glory, work) can of course be normal and noncompulsive in non-neurotic people. But the normal drive to be loved, for example, is not satisfiable by just anyone, but only by some. The corresponding neurotic craving requires satisfaction from *everyone*; it is utterly indiscriminate and insatiable. The neurotic is not interested in subject-matters or people for their own sakes. So whether or not the social situation calls for it, "he *must* be the center of attention, *must* be the most attractive, the most intelligent, the most original . . . He *must* come out victorious in any argument, regardless of where the truth is . . . His need for indiscriminate supremacy makes him indifferent to truth . . ."[21] The third feature of neurotically compulsive drives is their insatiability—"The relentless chase after more prestige, more money, more women, more victories and conquests keeps going, with hardly any satisfaction or respite."[22] Finally, the neurotic compulsive's response to frustration, both before and after the fact, is excessive, as "indicated by the terror of doom and disgrace that for many people is spelled in the idea of failure . . . entirely out of proportion to the actual importance of the occasion."[23]

Suppose now that our hypothetical self-regarding risk-taker—the home-grown pot smoker, the adventurous sportsman or the daredevil—is a certifiable (though not in fact certified) neurotic compulsive. How does this important new fact about his motivation affect our assessments, for practical purposes, of the voluntariness of his risk-taking? To begin with, risk-taking is a less typical form of neurotic compulsiveness than risk-avoiding. The neurotic, after all, is driven by fear, and is most clearly and commonly recognized by his excessive timidity, withdrawal, irrational avoidance conduct, or hysteria. But neurotic defense mechanisms are various, and also manifest themselves in other kinds of "excessive" life-styles—extreme competitiveness, glory seeking, and self-assertion, for example. Some of these self-defensive compensatory strategies can produce highly reckless life patterns too. For example, psychologists and psychiatrists speak of escapism in courted danger (this might apply to the home-grown pot smoker too, especially where marijuana use is illegal); of risks to self taken primarily to spite or threaten others; of neurotic glory-seeking ("I am uniquely best, most daring, most fearless, etc."); and of neurotic guilt and the need for self-punishment. Self-risks might compromise very neatly the neurotic need for punishment and the neurotic impulse to spite or threaten others, in this respect resembling a cross between direct self-harms (e.g. mutilation and suicide) and merely threatened self-harms that tease concerned second parties and keep them worried. Perhaps compulsive gambling, which has received much attention from psychologists, is a close two-party analogue to single-party daredeviltry in these motivational aspects.

The question whether the neurotic daredevil's unreasonably dangerous activities might yet, despite his compulsiveness, be voluntary or "voluntary enough" to exempt him from protective interference does not have great practical interest, despite its theoretical fascination. In practical life, for a number of reasons, we seem to have no choice but to answer it in the affirmative, despite our misgivings. Part of the problem is that we do not yet have reliable methods, at least without extensive and costly examinations, to identify severe neurosis with the confidence that would be required to justify interference with liberty. Secondly, the neurotic risk-taker himself will deny emphatically, and with perfect sincerity, that his risk-choices are not his own, and not made freely. He will make his case with cogency and conviction, for there need be no intellectual impairment in neurosis; his will may be wholly implicated in his choice; he may be unaware of compulsive pressure or of the inner clockwork that makes him tick. The extreme degree of danger in what he does, of course, is no proof of neurotic compulsiveness. Witness the famous flying Wallendas, a family of daredevil acrobats who merely conform to a family tradition of several generations when they fly through the air with the greatest of ease—with no safety net below. Finally the neurotic daredevil desperately needs his dangerous life-style; indeed if he is truly compulsive, nothing frightens him more than the prospect of being deprived of his life-endangering opportunities. Interference with him then will not be a "Minor incursion" but a major restriction of his liberty. The deprivation of what a person prizes or needs most, by the forceful intervention on paternalistic grounds by outsiders, is an ugly spectacle, earnestly to be avoided.

But the theoretical question remains, and its uncertainties rankle in the mind of the liberal philosopher. Supposing we did have some sort of quick litmus test of neurotic compulsiveness and that it was convincing even to the neurotic daredevil himself (if that is even possible). The neurotic still would be impervious to persuasion. "I am what I am," he might reply, "and I have a right to work out my own destiny—such as it is." Richard Arneson, for one, is quick to come to his aid, heaping scorn on the notion that mere neurosis could vitiate voluntariness when a person's basic life-style and highest values are involved, any more than any other "irrational quirk" at the center of his personality and vital to his own sense of identity. Indeed, the challenge for the person who would apply the high standard of voluntariness here is to distinguish neurotic daredevils from merely foolhardy, but non-neurotic daredevils, or in general to distinguish self-regarding character flaws rooted in a life-time of constantly reenforced habit, and the same character flaws when rooted in neurosis. Arneson, as usual, has a vivid example:

> The story is told of a famous rock climber who, arriving late one day at a climbing area he had not previously explored, proceeded to drink beer and eat ice cream at a local climbers' haunt until, inebriated and stuffed, he wandered off to the cliffs to try a hard climb by flashlight. No doubt this was a foolhardy act. But suppose the famous climber is notorious for his foolhardy character, so that if he falls from the cliffs a mourner could truly say at his funeral, "as he lived, so he died."[24]

It may of course be true that most *extreme* character flaws, whether self- or other-regarding, do have a neurotic base, even that the more extreme the flaw, the more likely that neurosis plays an important role in its explanation. Still, it is plausible to assume that some character flaws develop in the Aristotelian manner, through a whole lifetime of flawed choices and actions each of which in turn reenforces the ever more powerful habit of acting or feeling in the flawed fashion until it becomes a deeply rooted and scarcely eradicable disposition of character. The character which is flawed through deeply rooted habits may seem just as compulsive, by some tests, as the character flawed by a huge tangled neurotic knot of motives, so that the flawed acts produced in the two cases may be equally in character, and self-fulfilling. Aristotle's "thoroughly wicked man" (hardly the right term for Arneson's foolhardy rock-climber), gets pleasure, however, from his habitually flawed action, whereas the neurotic is incapable of more than momentary gratification, and remains plunged in misery, his character neurosis serving only to keep him afloat, while incidentally generating more anxiety through the very mechanisms designed to cope with anxiety. We can say then that both the habitually fool-hardy person and the neurotically compulsive foolhardy person freely act in character, but that the former's character produces its reckless conduct smoothly and naturally from "force of habit," whereas the latter's character produces it painfully from its own tortured conflicts and a desperate need to hold itself in equilibrium by a costly strategy of accommodation. Both characters are in their own ways "screwed up," but that need not affect our appraisals of the voluntariness of the attitudes and choices they produce, or even our judgments of the degree to which they *are* flawed. Perhaps the one clear difference in our responses is in the amount of sympathy we might have for the two. The neurotic suffers in his "wicked ways"; his own complicated "bad habits" are more like addictions, and unstable addictions at that. But the other party is merely doing what comes naturally, finding pleasure in the very exercise of his unreasonableness. It is harder to feel sorry for him.

All problems that require us to select appropriate standards for assessing voluntariness present us with the option of selecting wholly "untailored standards" applied against the background of normal conditions, or else standards tailored to some degree or other to the case at hand. How we make that decision is determined in large part by our purposes in making the voluntariness assessment. If our purpose is to determine whether a person had an excuse for harming or endangering others, then varying with the seriousness of the harm involved, we will select largely untailored standards. Given the circumstances normally present, we ask to what extent did intervening factors in this case diminish the actor's responsibility? If the actor's choice was impelled by a neurosis, we can take that fact to be an intervening factor, a significant deviation from normal conditions, reducing responsibility, in short a mitigation. We can argue that seriously neurotic behavior is not "voluntary enough" for the most severe penalties or the most vehement and unqualified blame, but quite voluntary enough for some lesser degree of responsibility and less severe sanction. The degree of the sanction increases, as it were, with the seriousness of the harm, and then is discounted by the degree of nonresponsibility for the harm. If, on the other hand, our purpose is to decide whether some person's impending dangerous but self-regarding conduct is voluntary enough to exempt him from protective interference, then we are likely to use standards tailored more closely to the special circumstances, and the existence of the actor's neurotic motives becomes part of the background against which we look for (other) voluntariness-diminishing factors, like factual ignorance and external coercion. (Interestingly enough, tailored standards work to the neurotic person's advantage in the prior restraint context and to his disadvantage in the *post facto* blame and punishment case, results we would probably welcome on independent moral grounds.)

In any event, if we do tailor the standards to the neurotic person's special features, we reject the bifurcation of the self proposed by various psychiatric writers to account for neurotic compulsiveness. We can accept the complicated causal account of the psychiatrists to explain how the neurotic person got that way and how his motives work, but given that the person has a compulsive character, no matter how he got that way, we accept him as he is, truly judge him to be the creator of his own tragic problems, tied in hopeless, self-restricting, misery-producing knots, neurotic *and* immoral or foolhardy, or whatever his distinctive character failing happens to be. He is in short *compulsive without being compelled* by forces external to himself. There is a rigid necessity in his conduct, but that is imposed on his actions not by a second party, but by the first party himself, quite without his own awareness.[25] Both in this and other contexts (see Chap. 19, §7 for a discussion of the "early" and "later" self bifurcation) there is a greater economy in the single person account than in the bifurcation hypothesis, and a greater all-around agreement with common sense. There may even be therapeutic advantages in the "compulsiveness without compulsion" approach, for the neurotic patient cannot achieve liberating self-understanding until he appreciates fully how his neurosis is a trick *he* played upon himself.[26]

22

Consent and its Counterfeits

1. The soft paternalist strategy for two-party cases

The dilemmas of legal paternalism arise in their most complicated forms in the two-party cases. When *B* requests that *A* do something for (or to) him that is either directly harmful or dangerous to *B*'s interests, or when the idea originates with *A* and he solicits and receives *B*'s permission to do that thing, then (in either case) *B* can be said to have "consented" to *A*'s action. If nevertheless the criminal law prohibits *A* from acting in such cases, it invades *B*'s liberty (by preventing him from getting what he wanted from *A*) or his autonomy (by depriving his voluntary consent of its effect). If the parties violate the law and it is *A* only whose act is deemed criminal, then of course *A* is treated even worse than *B*, for while both *A* and *B* are prevented from doing what they intended to do, it is only *A* who is punished (see Chap. 17, §2). Examples of two-party transactions that have been criminally prohibited include aiding and abetting a suicide, "mercy killing," agreed-upon surgical mutilation, duels, fist fights (in which both parties enthusiastically partici- pate), "statutory rape," gambling, drug sales, usury, bigamy, and prostitu- tion. Legislatures may enact such laws, of course, from motives that are at least partly moralistic as opposed to paternalistic, but typically the reason for disallowing *B*'s consent as a defense for *A*'s criminal conduct, is that *B*'s agreement must be overruled for his own good, which the state presumes to know better than he.

The soft paternalist strategy in the two-party cases is the same as in the single-party cases, namely to distinguish voluntary from nonvoluntary self-regarding actions and restrict the state's power to the regulation of the latter. In the two-party cases the acts whose voluntariness is at issue are *acts of consent*. As John Kleinig points out,[1] the word "consent" sometimes refers to a mental state rather than an act, in which case it means passive and unspoken acquiescence, but Kleinig rightly insists on the much greater social importance of consent in the sense of a public act, "in which a person explicitly facilitates the initiative of the other . . . a form of cooperation with the initiative of another whereby one shares responsibility for it."[2] *Acts* of consent are especially important when our attention centers on the criminal liability of the actor (*A*) in two-party cases, and the exculpatory effect of his reasons for action. He does not have any direct insight into *B*'s mental states, so the question of his responsibility must be settled by reference to the presence or absence of explicit authorization by *B*, not what *B*'s secret desires or hopes might have been. If *A* deliberately rapes *B*, it is no defense either in a court of law or in "the court of heaven" that *B* "secretly consented to what he did though she gave no sign." At most *B*'s inner states are relevant to the truth of moral and psychological judgments we might wish to make about *her*, but these are quite irrelevant to *A*'s responsibility for the violence he imposed on her without her indicated consent.

When the effects of *A*'s actions on *B*'s interests are not deep or difficult to reverse, *A* may feel morally justified in acting in a way that is moderately risky to *B* without *B*'s explicit permission, on the grounds that he had good evidence that *B* would be willing for him to do so, and would have explicitly signified his consent if *A* had only been in a position to ask for it. Even in that case however, *A* assumes a moral risk himself; if *B*'s interests, contrary to *A*'s expectations, are set back, then in virtue of the *Volenti* maxim, *A* has (with the best intentions) *wronged*, as well as harmed, *B*, and *B* has a grievance against him, and a claim for redress. That is because "consent" in the sense of mere psychological willingness or passive acquiescence is not *authorization*; it does not transfer responsibility for *A*'s act jointly to *B*. If the act in question is one which crosses the boundaries of *B*'s autonomy then it requires *B*'s permission if it is to avoid wronging *B* and thus falling within the range of the harm to others principle. If *A*, however, appeals in his justification to *B*'s "unvoiced authorization"—the explicit consent *B* would have expressed had there been opportunity to solicit it from her—then the appeal is indeed to consent in the appropriate sense (that of act rather than mere psychological state), but to the act of consent *A* presumes *B* was disposed to perform, not to an act she actually performed.

Dispositional consent then is not actual consent, and can only be presumed, not known. Where actual consent can be determined at little cost or delay, mere presumed dispositional consent will not be sufficient to transfer any responsibility to *B* for *A*'s act, or to deprive *B* of his rightful grievance after the fact. But where (1) the evidence of *B*'s disposition to consent is overwhelmingly strong (much more than a mere guess or a morally risky "presumption"), and (2) *A* has no opportunity to solicit it from *B* in the available time, and (3) the envisaged action of *A* is necessary not merely to secure a benefit for *B* but to avert a serious loss or harm, then the *Volenti* maxim can be stretched without strain to protect *A* from liability to *B* and to deprive *B* of any grievance against *A*. Thus if *A* sees a truck bearing down on *B*, who has his back turned to the danger, and there is no time even to shout a warning, he may with some violence push *B* out of the path of danger, even without *B*'s explicit authorization to do so. That is not because of some actual consent that existed unvoiced, but because of the reasonable expectation that normal authorization would have been forthcoming had there been an opportunity for it. There is a difference between inferred desire—a state of mind whose existence we infer from observed behavior or actuarial data—and dispositional consent—the act of authorization we assume would actually exist if only there were opportunity in the circumstances for it to be expressed. Inferred desire never satisfies the *Volenti* maxim; dispositional consent does bring *Volenti* into play, but only when the conditions mentioned above are satisfied. Since those conditions are vague, there will be many troublesome borderline cases.

In other examples, *B* does *act* to confer authorization upon *A* to proceed in an agreed upon way, but his "consent" is expressed (or otherwise indicated in conventionally understood ways) under such circumstances that it is not voluntary, or "not voluntary enough" to be valid. Invalid consent is signified consent that fails to have its normal effect of transferring responsibility. The soft-paternalist strategy requires us to give a fuller account of these nullifying circumstances, and also to specify the ways that failed consent affects the rights and duties of third parties—gratuitous interveners, legislators, and judges. When consent to a given kind of dangerous conduct is so rare and unlikely that it would hardly ever be given unless in ignorance, under coercive pressure, or because of impaired faculties, then a legislature might simply ban it on the basis of the harm to others principle, assuming for all practical purposes that consent to *that* kind of agreement never is voluntary enough. Such a rationale avoids (hard) paternalism and accords with the liberal's motivation.

For the possible rare cases in which the consent *is* voluntary enough, the soft-paternalist strategy can select among four alternatives: (1) it can reluctantly justify blanket prohibition *anyway* on the grounds that the few injustices resulting would be less than the injustice that would result from either blanket permission or case by case testing of voluntariness, not to mention the possibly heavy cost as well as fallibility of the latter (see Chap. 19, §6); (2) it can advocate blanket prohibition as in (1) but also call for the establishment of "equity boards" to hear appeals based on exceptional circumstances (see Chap. 20, §7); (3) it can establish tribunals to determine the voluntariness of specific agreements before granting licenses; or (4) it can give blanket permission but only after extensive education about the risks, administered by state or licensed private agencies, and perhaps counseling, qualifying examinations, or other such devices (see Chap. 20 §8). But given the costs and other practical difficulties of these alternatives, the state will often simply ban the agreements or activities in question, presuming nonvoluntariness conclusively. Thus, I have argued that dueling (Vol. 1, Chap. 6, §1 and *supra*, pp. 118–20), and contractual slavery (Chap. 14, §6) can plausibly be banned unconditionally on such grounds; and no doubt such reasons, plausibly applied or not, have been an important part of the actual legislative motivation for banning the sale of addicting drugs, and nullifying consent to surgical mutilation and usurious loans. The so-called soft-paternalistic strategy is simply the attempt to provide, when plausible, a nonpaternalistic rationale for such restrictive legislation, in fact a justification based on the harm to others principle as mediated by *Volenti*, and supplemented by empirical data bearing on the voluntariness of consent in the typical cases.

In respect to certain other kinds of self-regarding dangerous agreements, no across-the-board prohibition can be justified on liberal grounds. In these cases the "soft-paternalistic strategy" aims at designing exemptive rather than restrictive legislation to protect intervening third parties rather than threaten the primary bargaining parties. If C has good reason to think that B's consent to the dangerous or directly harmful conduct of A is "not voluntary enough" or that at least temporary intervention is necessary to determine whether or not it is voluntary, then, provided he acts reasonably, C should not himself be subject to civil or criminal liability. Thus, even though in theory liberal principles establish a right to euthanasia or to assistance in suicide, if C should see A about to shoot B, he ought to be entitled forcibly to restrain him without personal liability unless or until it can be established that B has consented, and consented "voluntarily enough." Since death is irrevocable, of course, what is "voluntary enough" must be determined by stringent standards, so that a mere reassuring word from the primary parties would not be enough to require C to withdraw. More formal and public procedures for determining voluntariness in cases like this would also be necessary to protect second parties like the merciful A, who otherwise would incur very grave personal risks.

Indeed it is the interests of second parties, their vulnerabilities as well as their opportunities for illegitimate gain, that make the two-party cases so much more complicated than the single-party cases. We must of course protect B from dangerous acts of A when B's "consent" to those acts was not voluntary enough to be valid. But if we impose subsequent liability on A even though *A* had no reason to know that coercive pressures or fraudulent misrepresentations were shaping *B*'s motives for agreeing, then our treatment of *A* is unfair to him, even though he *did* impose a risk on *B* without *B*'s *valid* consent. The coercion applied to *B*, for example, might have had its source, unknown to *A*, in a third party *C*, who threatened *B* with some dire consequence if he did not consent to an earlier proposal of *A*'s (see Chap. 23, §2). That threat reduces the voluntariness of *B*'s agreement with *A*, but we can not justly punish *A*, after the fact, if he had no way of knowing that *B*'s permission had been forced. In some rare instances the criminal law in English-speaking countries *has* imposed "strict liability" on hapless violators who had no way of knowing that the consent that warranted their actions was legally invalid. The permission of under-age females, for example, has not always defeated the charge of statutory rape, even when the man reasonably believed that his consenting partner was an older woman, and even when his mistake was caused by the girl's own misrepresentation.[3] But criminal rules of this kind have always been exceptional, and are now rarer than ever. When the liability imposed is to criminal punishment, strict liability is so unjust that it can hardly ever be justified.[4]

In Chapters 23 and 24, we shall consider one large category of voluntariness-reducing factors (considerations that reduce or nullify the voluntariness of acts of consent), namely *coercive pressure* on the consenter. Then in the following chapters the other main categories—ignorance or mistake, and impaired or undeveloped capacities—will be considered. But first we must give more attention to the concept of consent itself—what it is and what it is not.

2. The nature and effect of consent

When *A* acts so as to harm or endanger an interest of *B*'s, the consent which triggers the *Volenti* maxim and transfers to *B* part of the responsibility for *A*'s act is, as we have seen, an *act* of *B*'s, not merely a silent psychological state; and when there is no opportunity for active consent, *A* is entitled to infringe *B*'s autonomy to protect *B*'s interest, not in virtue of an inferred state of desire in *B*, but rather in virtue of a reasonable expectation that *B* is disposed to grant active consent in such circumstances, and thus would have done so had there been a chance. What kind of an act then is "active consent"? It is either a statement in language, or a communication by gesture or conduct understood by a symbolic convention to express consent. I have already spoken of consent as *authorization*, but now that point needs qualification. Whatever else consent may do, it transfers at least part of the responsibility for one person's act to the shoulders of the consenter. According to one very old conception of authorization, it is an agreement whereby the actor becomes the agent of the authorizer, who is then understood, by a kind of moral fiction, to be the "author" of his agent's acts (or of those acts specified in the authorization). "He that acteth for another," wrote Hobbes, "is said to bear his person, or act in his name."[5] In this way lawyers and others who might have B's power of attorney may sign B's name to checks and agreements, or buy and sell in B's name, and the consequences are charged to B as if these things were actually his own doing, and all because he "gave his authority" in advance for the arrangement. For the authorized actions of A, B bears full responsibility, and A himself bears none. (Nothing gets charged to *his* bank account.) Even if A has acted unwisely in B's name and is subject to blame or criticism from others, B can have no grievance since he voluntarily assumed the risk of unwise proxy actions in advance. *Volenti non fit injuria.*

But while some acts of consent fit the authorization model, by no means do they all. The mercy-killer, perhaps, who kills the paralyzed B at B's request, is only acting as the instrument of B's will, by which B in effect kills himself. He is B's agent, and "bears B's person." Others may blame or punish him for acting as he did, but surely B in virtue of his authorization could have no complaint; *his* rights have not been violated by A even if A was unjustified, all things considered, in acting as he did in B's name. The gambler A, however, when he bets a large sum against B and wins, does not "bear B's person" and act as B's "instrument" when he takes B's money. Neither does B's enemy in a grudge fight to which they both consented act as B's agent when he punches him in the face, though perhaps in a somewhat strained sense, B has "authorized" him to land the blow if he can, or permitted him to try to do so. B has consented to the risk of something happening that he does not want to happen and even tries to prevent.

Perhaps it would be less misleading in examples of this kind (and also prostitution, usury, and addictive drug purchases) to speak of the consent as a granting of *permission* rather than an authorization. In the grudge fight and gambling examples the mutual consent to the contest serves to split the responsibility for the consequences rather than to transfer it entirely to the shoulders of a single authorizer. The language of permission, however, might also have some tendency to mislead insofar as it seems to imply that the consenter has some authority over the other. Teachers give "permission" to students, employers to employees, parents to children, officers to enlisted men, but typically not *vice-versa*. There is, however, nothing necessary about the implication from permission to authority. Any act that crosses the boundaries of a sovereign person's zone of autonomy requires that person's "permission"; otherwise it is wrongful. In this sense all sovereign persons, like all sovereign nations, have "authority" over their own realms.

A vitally important point, to be developed in Chapter 31, is that B's consent to A's action, even though (in virtue of *Volenti*) it causes the forfeiture of his right after the fact to complain that A's act *wronged* him, does not automatically relieve *A* of all moral responsibility for subsequent harms he causes *B* by his permitted action. *B*'s consent may have been quite voluntary enough yet foolish, and as a result *A*'s permitted action may harm *B* while benefitting himself. In that case we might say that *A* is to blame for taking advantage of *B*'s foolishness, or for *exploiting* him. It is at least a somewhat disingenuous reply to this criticism for *A* to say "*B* brought it all upon himself; I was a mere passive instrument of his will," for in the permission as opposed to authorization examples, *A* might not have been an instrument of *B*'s will in any sense ("In bashing his nose in with my fist I was merely the instrument of his will" does not wash), and in the other cases, as Kleinig points out,[6] *A* actively chose or agreed to be the instrument of *B*'s purposes and cannot escape responsibility for his own choice. In virtue of *B*'s consent, *A* may escape responsibility *to him*; but he may yet be called to answer before his own conscience or to respond to the harsh judgments of third parties. Exploitation (in the sense to be explained in Chap. 32) of another's rashness or foolishness is often *wrong*, even when because of prior voluntary consent, it does not violate the other's right, wrong him, or treat him unjustly. In those instances it is wrong because deliberately setting back another's interest for the sake of one's own gain (when certain other conditions obtain) is something we ought not to do, even when the other can have no grievance against us.

When *B* approaches *A* and proposes the transaction that may eventually be harmful, his *offer* (if there is to be a service rendered or a price paid in exchange) or *request* (if he wishes a simple favor without reciprocation) is "consent in the strong sense." Of course such proposals are more than mere responsive grantings of "permission" ("consent in the weak sense") but they are never less than this. Strong consent ("please do") trivially implies weak consent ("you may"), although the opposite is not true. I may reluctantly agree to your proposal, thus giving you permission, without making any request of you that you do it, indeed while even preferring that you would not do what you propose.

Expressions of consent are similar to promises in some respects but quite different in others. Like promises, they are linguistic or symbolic performances that bring into existence new moral and legal relations. The point and effect of a promise is to create an obligation of the promisor to the promisee that would not otherwise exist. The promisor, in virtue of his voluntary performance of the requisite linguistic act (saying "I promise," or "I swear to . . . ," or "I will; you can count on it") places himself under an obligation to do or refrain from doing something in the future. In contrast, the point and effect of an expression of consent is not to create an obligation of the consenter; rather it is to grant a privilege to the consentee. Where formerly he had a duty to refrain from doing *X*, now he is at liberty to do *X* (at least until the consent is revoked). The immediate effect of promises is to create obligations in the speaker; the immediate effect of acts of consent is to cancel obligations in the one addressed.

The varieties of consenting situations distinguished by the patterns of moral-legal relations they create, can be represented hypothetically, using voluntary euthanasia as our example,* as follows:

1. *B's request to A:* "Will you please kill me and put me out of my misery?" This request implies a permission to do what is requested. Thus even an initiator (requester) grants consent in the weak sense (gives permission). *Moral-legal effect of B's request on A* (if the implied consent is thought of as voluntary and hence valid): It creates a privilege (liberty) to kill *B*, by cancelling the duty not to do so.

2. *A's request to B:* "May I kill you?" ("You are going to die in a couple of days anyway and I would like to transplant your organs right away into these critically injured accident victims. The need is urgent; they will soon die otherwise.") *B's response to A:* "Yes, you may." *Moral-legal effect of B's response on A* (again assuming it was voluntary enough to be valid consent): It creates a privilege (liberty) to kill *B* by cancelling the duty not to do so. Thus *B's* "consent in the weak sense" in this example has the same effect as his "consent in the strong sense" (initiating request) in example 1.

3. *A's offer to B:* "If you permit me to kill you, I will pay (I promise) $10,000 to your estate. May I do so on these terms?" *B's reply to A's offer:* "I accept your offer. You may kill me if you pay the offered sum to my estate." *Moral-legal effect of B's acceptance on A* (again assuming voluntariness): The effect is two-fold. (a) It creates a contractual right in *A* to kill *B*, cancelling his duty not to do so; (b) it imposes a duty on *A* to pay $10,000 to *B's* estate.

4. *B's offer to A:* "If you will kill me and put me out of my misery, I will pay you $10,000. Will you do so on these terms?" *A's reply to B's offer:* "I accept your offer. I will painlessly terminate your life (I promise) if you pay me $10,000." *Moral-legal effect of B's offer on A:* It expresses a conditional consent, and gives *A* the opportunity to convert it to actual consent. In itself it creates no new rights, liberties, or duties for *A*, but it does confer the power on him to create such new moral-legal relations himself simply by accepting. *Moral-legal effect of A's acceptance on B* (assuming voluntariness, etc.): It renders his conditional consent fully operative by accepting the stated condition. Thus it has a two-fold effect: (a) it creates a duty in *B* to pay *A* $10,000; (b) it confers a contractual right on *B* to be "euthanized" by *A* and imposes the correlative duty of performance on *A*.

---

*A more realistic treatment of this topic, not merely illustrating the logical consequences of consent, is given in Chapter 27.

Thus *offers* involve a complex interplay of acts of consent and promises, whereas *requests* involve only implied consent. The legal relations created at various stages of the contractual process include consent (explicit and implied, conditional and operative), legal powers, rights, and duties; whereas those created directly by simple requests and favors include only the consent implied in the request, and privilege (the revocable cancelling of duty). In no case should the act of consent itself be construed as a promise.[7]

3. When consent is problematic

Suppose that a criminal code based on somewhat more liberal principles than our own neither blanketly prohibits nor blanketly permits certain actions that tend to impose harms or risks on other parties, but hinges its permission on the prior consent of the endangered party, in some cases giving detailed specifications of the procedures to be used to determine that consent. In this imaginary code, if *A* kills *B*, that is the crime of homicide *unless* in the appropriate manner *B* had consented, in which case it is permissible euthanasia; if *A*, a surgeon, intentionally mutilates *B*'s body, that is the crime of mayhem *unless* he had *B*'s consent, in which case it is innocent surgery; if *A* attacks *B* with a sword, that is attempted murder or felonious assault *unless B* consented to a duel under the approved rules, in which case it is permitted; if *A* pummels *B* with his fists, that is criminal battery *unless* it occurred in a brawl which both voluntarily entered; if *A* injects medicine, drugs, or blood into *B*'s veins, that too is criminal battery *unless* done with *B*'s consent; if *A* has sexual intercourse with *B*, that is criminal rape *unless* he had *B*'s consent; if *A* takes *B*'s money after an unequal wager, or as excessive interest for a loan, or in exchange for telling *B*'s fortune, or for an addictive drug, then that is fraud, or extortion, or usury, or a crime of some other name, *unless B*'s consent to the risks was free and fully informed, in which case it is a legitimate business transaction. Now, let us suppose that unusual circumstances arise in which *A* has some strong reason to act in a way that *prima facie* violates *B*'s autonomy, or which would be criminal without *B*'s consent, yet there is no reasonable opportunity to determine in advance whether *B* does consent. In some of these cases inaction would seem to pose a threat to *B*'s interests. Normally we would say "That is for *B* to decide," but in the circumstances, *B* can have no opportunity to decide in time. How then should *A* proceed?

In response to this question philosophers have described various states of affairs that are said either to constitute "kinds of consent" or else be close enough to actual consent to have its usual moral or legal effect. None of them, I think, are actual acts of consenting at the time, which *ex hypothesi* are impossible in the circumstances, but some are plausible substitutes. Others on the list, however, are dangerous counterfeits of consent that cannot have the moral purchasing power of the real thing. Let us survey the proposals briefly.

Consent as inferred psychological state. I have already distinguished the silent desires, wishes, approvals, or tastes of a person, as inferred from his own past behavior or from actuarial tables, from his consent. *B* may in fact *like* some kind of activity which *A* can offer, approve of it, even to some degree desire it, yet for reasons of his own not consent to it. So these mental states, even when properly inferred, are not the same thing as consent. Yet in emergency circumstances, they may be the best guide we have to the actual consent *B* would express if he could.

Dispositional consent. When *B* is absent and incommunicado, or there is no time to communicate with him in the face of an imminent danger, or he is asleep, in a stupor, unconscious or comatose, and unless we act without his consent there is no averting the danger, the best substitute for his actual consent (which we cannot get) is his inferred disposition to express permission in circumstances like this. (See *supra*, §1.) Knowledge of his likes and desires, or other relevant states of mind may be the best evidence, inconclusive as it is, for this disposition. His own testimony, either in private conversations and letters or in public documents, is better evidence still. What we wish to know is: what would he say if we asked for his consent and he were in a position to grant or withhold it? If he has addressed that very question in the past, his own word is the best evidence of what he *would* say now. To be sure he may have changed his mind since he last spoke on the question, and if possible he should always be given a last chance to change his mind once more, but in our hypothetical circumstances that cannot be done, and his last word is still his best word.

Prior consent. If *B*, when he was forty, signed a "living will" (see Chap. 27, §6) consenting to be let die if he should *ever* be in certain desperate medical straits, and then, at the age of seventy, is in those very circumstances and no longer capable of signifyig his consent afresh, then provided the original consent was valid and he has had continuous opportunity over the intervening thirty years to modify or withdraw it, it is still operative. Similarly, if *B* is a Jehovah's Witness, and has signed a similar document, refusing *ever* to receive a blood transfusion even if his life depended on it, that consent not-to-be-saved continues to govern years later when the issue arises. In virtue of the extended temporal bounds of *de jure* sovereignty argued for in Chapter 19, §7, a competent autonomous person may consent for his future as well as his present self. Given satisfaction of certain stringent conditions, that consent stays alive. Proof that it was once validly granted is in that case not mere "evidence" of present "dispositioal consent"; it is a demonstration of actual consent still functioning.

Subsequent Consent. Suppose *A* violently forces his attentions on *B* without her consent, and she then prefers rape charges against him. But between the time of *A*'s indictment for the crime, and the scheduled date of his trial, he is visited constantly by *B* who gradually falls in love with him, and in the nick of time drops charges against him, leading to his release. "If I had known him then as well as I know him now," she says, "I would surely have consented." For practical reasons *A* cannot be convicted of rape without *B*'s testimony, but the question is, morally speaking, did he in fact rape her? Perhaps both *A* and *B* would be disposed to reply that her "subsequent consent" should be treated as retroactive, thus providing him with the same defense that her actual consent at the time would have provided.

A less paradoxical account of this bizarre adventure would avoid altogether the strange notion of consensual retroactivity. *A* did impose sexual intercourse on *B* without her consent; therefore he *was* a rapist without excuse. All *B*'s change of mind, months later, can do morally is to *forgive* him for his wrong, withdraw her grievance, and restore the moral equilibrium. Now *A* has no further duty of compensation to her, no further need for apology, contrition, atonement. But *B*'s forgiveness cannot change history, or magically recreate the past. Her forgiveness now has a point only because there *is* something to forgive, namely the rape that did take place in the past, present emotions notwithstanding.[8]

There is very little that can be done, despite the ingenious efforts of some philosophers,[9] to extract coherence from the strange notion of "subsequent consent." Most of the work assigned this concept can be handled adequately by the notion of dispositional consent. If a person is in no position to give his *voluntary* consent to our intervention in his behalf, we may have to guess (more typically, make confident inferences) what he would say *if* he were capable of voluntary choice. Then if our ascription of that disposition after the fact should turn out to be mistaken, we may still feel justified in intervening since we did the best we could, in good faith, to honor the other's autonomy. The "subsequent consent theory," on the contrary, holds that when we intervene we are "betting" our moral capital on the other's subsequent consent, and if it is not forthcoming, then it follows that we were not justified, and that we violated the other's right of autonomy. If we win the bet, on this view, that is only because, by an act of subsequent consent, the other "makes it true" that we acted with his actual consent at the earlier time.

"Betting on subsequent consent" is a paradoxical conception for most of the contexts in which a person lacks opportunity or capacity to consent voluntarily, but one can understand the temptation to apply it, as Gerald

Dworkin did somewhat tentatively,[10] to the case of small children whose liberty is interfered with without their consent only because they are not yet developed enough to consent voluntarily, and the intervention seems in their interest in the long run. In these cases parents cannot always infer the child's present dispositional consent, for the child may not yet have formed any firm disposition one way or the other. So the parent must decide in what he or she takes to be the child's best interests, and hope that when the child is a fully autonomous being, he will find that the earlier parental decision accords rather than conflicts with his subsequently evolved autonomy. What the parent "gambles" on is not that his present act will be "retroactively consented to" and thus justified, but rather that it will be retroactively welcomed, appreciated,[11] or at the very least forgiven. The parent does have an advantage in his "bet" against fate: the future autonomous self of his child will itself be influenced by the decisions made for him earlier. Those decisions have a better chance of according with the child's eventual autonomy for having been partial determinants of the preferences that will come to define that autonomy.[12]

Tacit consent. The notion of tacit consent has fallen out of favor in political theory since it was introduced by John Locke as part of his account of the basis of political obligation.[13] Objections to political consent theory, however, are only aimed at the uses to which Locke put the familiar concept of tacit consent, not to that concept itself. That one can consent to another's action without saying "I consent," or indeed without *saying* anything at all, is a perfectly coherent suggestion which finds a hundred corroborative examples in everyday experience. In one class of examples consent is expressed by an "act of omission," a deliberatre failure to express refusal when queried in a negative way. A. John Simmons gives a convincing ordinary example from this genre, which he reminds us is *not* "unexpressed consent deduced from conduct," but rather "consent expressed in a certain way—by silence."[14] He has us imagine a board meeting at which the chairman announces: "We will meet again next Thursday unless there are objections to that date. Does anyone have any objections?" There is silence for one full minute, at the conclusion of which the chairman notes that all have agree (consented) to his proposal.

In another class of examples, no explicit question is asked, and no explicit answer is given, yet we would surely say that consent was not merely inferred but actually expressed, and expressed not by "silence" but by symbolically appropriate conduct in the circumstances. For an example let us return to the impulsive lovers, *A* and *B*, in the preceding section, this time continuing the scenario beyond the point where forgiveness has been given and new love has begun. *A* and *B* have sexual relations in this new example without violence. As preliminary caresses are exchanged, *A* finds at each successive stage enthusiastic encouragement from *B*, who is all coos and smiles, though no words are exchanged, and no permission requested. After the fact he would be rightly astonished at the suggestion that he had acted without *B*'s consent. To fail to dissent when there is every opportunity to do so, while behaving in appropriately cooperative ways, is universally understood in such contexts to express consent. The consent is tacit as opposed to explicitly stated, but nevertheless directly received as opposed to merely presumed, guessed, or inferred, and quite actual as opposed to dispositional, hypothetical, or fictitious.

Hypothetical rational consent. The most commonly coined of the counterfeits of actual consent is that which Kleinig calls "hypothetical rational consent." This is the notion that we can ascribe to a person as his actual consent what a hypothetical, perfectly rational person *would* consent to in his circumstances. The assumption behind this attribution seems to be the claim, which we have repeatedly rejected, that only rational (ideally reasonable) action is voluntary. Sometimes there is a further metaphysical assumption that a person's "real will" is his "rational will," so that all we have to do to determine what a person actually chooses is to determine what it would be rational for a person in his shoes to choose, attribute that choice to him, and act accordingly, even if he should protest that his choice is something else. "I ought to know what my own choice is!", he might argue, but if we hold the notion of consent under discussion, we must respectfully dissent. If we are more "rational" then he, then what he chooses is what *we* say he chooses, not what his confused "empirical self" insists that he chooses.

    John Rawls is the contemporary philosopher who makes the greatest use of the idea of hypothetical rationality, indeed by deriving the basic principles of justice themselves from the presumed choices of hypothetical rational individuals wearing "veils of ignorance," convened to determine the principles that will govern the design of their social institutions. Rawls's discussion of paternalism,[15] however, is sketchy and does not give us clear warrant to attribute either the hypothetical-rational theory of consent or the "real will" theory to him. He does think it rational to have rules protecting people from their own possible irrationality, and as we have seen (Chap. 20, §3) if "irrationality" is interpreted in the strong sense of "derangement" or "incompetence," no one, not even the strongest liberal anti-paternalist, can disagree with him. But Rawls would also protect people from "irrational choices" in the somewhat weaker sense of choices at the expense of those "primary goods" which a person "presumably wants whatever else he wants,"[16] such as health, certain opportunities and power, income and wealth. Whether that kind of forcible protection is palatable depends upon whether one can *not* want a given primary good, or be willing to risk its loss for a nonprimary good, without being deranged or incompetent ("irrational" in the strong sense). Rawls's hypothetical "rational parties," he makes clear, would not make such choices, so those choices are clearly not "rational," in the sense he favors, when made by actual persons.

For the most part, Rawls's friendly remarks about paternalistic restrictions do seem to be made with the prospect of intellectual incompetence (derangement, retardation, immaturity) in mind, and thus do not seem to commit him to hard paternalism or to the real will theory in any objectionable sense. Thus he writes:

> In the original position the parties . . . will want to insure themselves against the possibility that their powers are undeveloped and they cannot rationally advance their interests, as in the case of children, or that through some misfortune or accident they are unable to make decisions for their good, as in the case of those seriously injured or mentally retarded.[17]

So far so good. Rationally incompetent persons must have proxy decisions made for them to safeguard their interests, and to many proposals by second parties they are incapable of granting (voluntary) consent, if only because they are incapable of fully understanding, in its most obvious ramifications, what is proposed. Those guardians who must grant or withhold consent in their behalf, must either appeal directly to what is in their interests, or decide hypothetically what they would choose if only they were minimally rational and in touch with their own wants.[18] The proxy-consenter then may very well simply represent the "hypothetically rational" version of the self he speaks for.

Unfortunately Rawls does not distinguish as we have (Chap. 20, §3) between irrationality in the strongest sense (incompetence) and irrationality in a weaker sense (chronic foolishness, unreasonableness, or imprudence). He continues:

> It is also rational for them [the parties in the original position] to protect themselves against their own irrational [subtle shift of sense] inclinations by consenting to a scheme of penalties that may give them a sufficient motive to avoid foolish actions and by accepting certain impositions designed to undo the unfortunate consequences of their imprudent behavior.[19]

In this passage Rawls has shifted from protection against one's own incompetence and helplessness to protection against one's "foolish actions" and "imprudent behavior." In both cases, he tells us, rational persons in an original position, choosing in ignorance of what their own traits and circumstances will be, will choose to be governed by restrictive rules imposing "rationality" on their future selves if their future selves should lack it. Since foolish and imprudent agreements can yet be voluntary, it follows that for those who would enter into them, the restrictive rules are (hard) paternalistic, unless it is assumed that their expressed consent is not real consent since it is not "rational." On the latter interpretation (which does not lead to hard paternalism), their true choices are those a proxy decision maker would make on their behalf of appealing directly, not to their wishes, but to what they would choose if they were more reasonable. For both deranged and merely imprudent persons "others are authorized to act in their behalf and to override their present wishes if necessary . . ."[20] This conclusion, to repeat, is a warrant for hard paternalism—the prohibition even of voluntary imprudence—unless it is conjoined with a hypothetical-rational theory of consent, in which case the paternalism is no longer "hard." But the price of that move is to permit the invalidation of actual consent whenever it should happen to be unreasonable. Individuals who think they are consenting to marriages that are in fact foolish marriages might learn to their amazement that they are not really consenting at all, and the state might thus refuse to grant legal recognition to their married status!

It is not clear, however, that Rawls holds the "hypothetical-rational consent" theory, so he may simply be a hard paternalist, on the grounds that it is rational for people to consent to hard paternalistic rules, whether they do or not. When he discusses the further question of how proxy decision makers should choose for "irrational" persons, he allows that they should be guided as far as possible "by the individual's own settled preferences and interests insofar as they are not irrational" (does he mean deranged, etc., or imprudent?), "or failing a knowledge of these, by the theory of primary goods . . . [trying] to get for him the things he presumably wants whatever else he wants."[21] These remarks, sketchy though they are, suggest that Rawls is not prepared to go to the extreme of the real-will theories and simply identify, in every case, what a person actually chooses with what he would choose if he were reasonable and prudent. But given the general drift of his theory, it is only Rawls's robust common sense that stops him short of the abyss.

4. Summary and transition

In the many situations if life in which we must risk invading another's autonomy in order to protect his on-balance interest, and there is no opportunity then and there to get his permission, we may have to settle for something less definitive than explicit consent. Philosophers have proposed at least six different kinds of surrogate-consent that may warrant rightful intervention in such circumstances. Two of these, *prior consent* and *tacit consent*, are forms of actual consent, fully operative and capable both of warranting the interference and activating the *Volenti* maxim in case things go wrong, thus immunizing the intervener from liability. A third, *dispositional consent*, is not actual consent, but under certain conditions it will have the same moral effect as actual consent. These conditions are: (1) there is very strong evidence (and even indirect statistical evidence may be very strong) of the other's disposition to consent in circumstances of that kind; (2) there is no opportunity in the available time to solicit consent directly; (3) the intervention reasonably appears necessary to prevent substantial loss or harm to the other party.

A fourth proposed consent-surrogate, an inferred psychological state (e.g. desire, preference, or liking) is neither actual nor dispositional consent, but it can be a relevant part of the evidential base for inferring dispositional consent, and morally significant for that reason. A fifth suggested substitute for explicit consent, *subsequent consent*, is actual consent that may or may not come, but even in the best case will come too late to be morally operative at the time the decision to intervene must be made. If it does come at a later time, it cannot have the effect of retroactively warranting the prior intervention. At the most it will express, after the fact, a forgiveness of the intervention (if it had been a wrongful infliction of harm), or signal the lack of a sense of grievance in the "consenter" for a harmless invasion of his sovereignty. The sixth proposed surrogate, *hypothetical-rational consent* is a complete counterfeit of actual consent. Its only moral relevance is as a guide to proxy decision-making on behalf of some intellectually incompetent persons. As a guide to the "real will" of absent competent persons it can be relevant only as part of the base for inferring the dispositional consent of people when they are known to be "reasonable" and prudent.[22] As a substitute for the explicit choices of competent persons who are "unreasonable," foolish, imprudent, or reckless with their own interests, it is a sham and an outrage.

The typical examples in this section have been cases of intervention in a person's (B's) affairs in which the only "second party" is the intervener (A) himself. A's problem is simply whether or not he has B's permission, at least constructively, to intervene. The same treatment of proposed consent-surrogates could apply to genuine two-party cases when the question of construing B's consent is not only a problem for A, who must decide whether he may act, but also for the third party C, who must decide whether A really does have B's voluntary consent to an agreement. When the perplexity results from the fact that B's explicit consent cannot be obtained because of his absence, or other temporary lack of capacity or opportunity, as assumed in this section, then A has warrant to assume agreement only if he has prior or tacit consent, or dispositional consent under the appropriate conditions, and C may constrain him only if he does not. If A elects to act only on the basis of improperly presumed dispositional consent, or one of the counterfeits of consent, then he has no right to act at all; and if his wrongful action threatens harm to B's interest, C may have the right to intervene to protect B, or it C is "the law," it may punish A after the fact.

The problems for *A* and *C* to be discussed from this point on, however, have a somewhat different form. From here on, we shall consider only genuine two-party cases in which *A* and *B* have come to some sort of agreement, and *A* clearly has *B*'s explicit consent or the tacit or prior equivalent. Nevertheless, that consent may fail of its normal effect because it is not valid consent, and *invalid consent* is no better than *no consent* at all. If a thief pulls a woman's handbag off her shoulder and flees, he takes her property *without her consent*, and thus wrongs her. If, on the other hand, he points a gun at her and warns that he will shoot if she does not hand over her purse, and she replies "no please don't shoot; here, take my purse and go away!", he takes her property with her explicit consent, but since her act of consent was not voluntary, it was *invalid consent*. What renders the consent involuntary and hence invalid in this example, as well as those to be considered throughout the next two chapters, is coercion, one of the standard voluntariness-reducing (or nullifying) conditions. A gun in one's face is a clear and simple thing to understand, but we shall soon see that the general concept of coercion is by no means simple, and its presence in some cases by no means clear.

23

Failures of Consent: Coercive Force

1. The spectrum of force

Acts of consent, like acts generally, are involuntary when the actor is *forced* to do what he does, whatever his own preferences in the matter. In the cases discussed in Chapter 22, the actor involuntarily suffers a wrong because his interests are invaded without his consent or with only a "counterfeit" of his consent. In the present chapter we shall consider cases in which the actor expressly gives his consent, but the consent lacks moral or legal effect (is "invalid") because it was forced rather than free.

There are many ways of "getting" a person to act as you want him to act, but only some of these can be described as "forcing him to act." Some of these various techniques (we shall postpone consideration of deception until Chaper 25) can be placed on a spectrum of force[1] running from compulsion proper, at one extreme, through compulsive pressure, coercion proper, and coercive pressure, to manipulation, persuasion, enticement, and simple requests at the other extreme. The line between forcing to act and merely getting to act is drawn somewhere in the manipulation or persuasion part of the scale, possibly moving within a narrow range as our purposes shift. Some manipulation and persuasion is forceful and some is not, so we shall not be concerned here with manipulation or persuasion as such, but rather with techniques of any kind only insofar as they are forceful. It is only techniques in the forcing part of the spectrum (wherever its boundary is drawn) that reduce or nullify the voluntariness of the induced response in the manner that presently concerns us.

Various ways of harming the other party without his consent are not on this scale at all, because they are ways of acting on him without his permission, for example burgling his house or snatching her purse, rather than ways of getting him or her to act, for example making her hand over her purse by threatening to shoot. Strictly speaking, as we shall see, compulsion does not belong on the scale either, and for the same reason. In the sense I shall assign the term, a person is not forced by compulsion to express his consent, or to *do* anything. Compulsion (See also Chap. 21, §§2 to 4), as well as burglary and theft, are ways in which things happen to a person, not ways in which he himself is impelled to act. Nevertheless the contrast with compulsion is a necessary part of our understanding of coercion, which does produce actions, including acts of consent, and it will be useful therefore to consider it first.[2]

Compulsion proper. A person is sent reeling or flying by a hurricane wind or an explosion, or he is pushed off a cliff and falls to his death on the rocks below, or a more powerful person compels him to drop a knife by pulling his fingers apart and forcing open his grip on it. In all these examples, either another person or an impersonal force makes one's body move directly, without the cooperation, grudging or approving, of one's own will. One does not *choose* or *decide* or *elect*, in these cases, to move one's own body; rather one's body is moved for one, and there is no role whatever for one's will, whether resistant or acquiescent. In other cases one is forced to do, or prevented from doing something by personal or impersonal forces working directly on the external world to destroy one's opportunities, and thus only indirectly restricting the movements of one's body. Turning a key in a lock may compel a person to remain within a room whatever he may wish, intend, prefer, or will. His mental states and acts are causally relevant only within narrow limits to the movements of his body. We can reserve the word "compulsion" for cases where options are closed, in the sense that some alternative, or all alternatives, to a given act are made impossible, whether the closing is brought about by natural, social, or internal causes, working either directly on one's body, or indirectly on external facilities. Thus a blizzard may compel me to miss an engagement that required air travel; a powerful gang may compel me to go to the destination they have chosen by dragging me by the feet; an obsession may prevent me from "tuning out" a troublesome thought or a repetitive tune.

Compulsive pressure. The same miscellany of forces that in other circumstances render alternatives impossible exert compulsive pressure, but when the pressures are resistible they do not necessitate movements or experiences; they simply render alternatives difficult, inconvenient, troublesome, or costly. In an analogy used earlier (Chap. 21, §6), a strong wind may not force my window shutters open but it may put such steady pressure on the shutters that I must constantly lean against them with all my weight to keep them closed. A snowstorm may not compel me to miss an appointment, but it may require me to leave inconveniently early, incur unreasonable expense, and assume dangerous risks if I am to make it. A bully may not compel me to go where he wishes, but he may force me into a fight which I win only after a prolonged struggle, in which case I may say that he subjected me to strong physical pressure to stay where I was, but that I escaped at some cost (injuries, anxieties, delays). I may not be compelled to experience obsessive thoughts all night only because I overcome the psychological "pressures" to do so by taking a powerful sleeping pill. In all these examples a person is subjected to compulsive pressures short of compulsion proper. Psychological pressures (commonly so-called) often become so great that a person's control cracks under their weight, and they bring about compulsion. Fear of one's own death, for example, may become paralyzing, and lead a person whose brakes have failed to drive his automobile into a group of children rather than swerve and go over the edge of a cliff (his only alternative). We may not think that he would have been justified in *choosing* the children's deaths as the lesser of the evils forced on him by circumstances, but if he acted from natural compulsion he may not have *chosen* at all. Indeed he may have been compelled to act contrary to his own conscious choice, in which case the law holds that he is excused, even though not justified, since he did not act, much less act voluntarily, at all.

Coercion proper. The distinction between compulsion and coercion cuts across the distinction among the various kinds of forces that can close our options, since it distinguishes two senses in which those options may be "closed." Whether the liberty-limiting factors be forces of nature, a person's own psychological condition (phobias, obsessions, "compulsions"), incidental consequences of human projects aimed at other goals (roads closed for repair, buildings condemned to demolition), or the deliberate intervention in our affairs by other persons, an option is closed by compulsion when one alternative has been made impossible. In contrast, coercion does not destroy the alternative, so much as destroy its appeal by increasing its cost. Our options in fact are being opened and closed, both in a strong and a weak sense, by natural forces or as incidental consequences of others' actions, millions of times every minute, usually to our ignorance or indifference. Whenever a person buys a reserved theatre ticket, I am *ipso facto* prevented from sitting in a given seat (*his* seat) during a given performance. For that matter, every time a group of persons occupies a park bench, I am prevented from sitting on that bench at that time. My option is not closed in the strong sense necessarily. The eliminated alternative has not been made *impossible*. I could buy the theatre ticket from its owner for a much higher price than he paid for it, or throw one of the bench-sitters off and take his place, but in each case that might be to incur unwelcome consequences, or to pay a price that would be unreasonable given my other interests. My options are closed in a weaker sense, namely that some alternative has been made not impossible but *unreasonable* for me, or (as some writers put it) *ineligible* for my choice.

The clearest examples of coercion resemble the theatre ticket example in that the option is closed in the weak sense: alternatives are made not impossible but too expensive to be eligible for choice. They also resemble the arm-twisting and push and pull examples of physical compulsion, however, in that they are deliberate forceful interference in the affairs of human beings by other human beings. What distinguishes the clearest cases of coercion is that they employ *threats*. Unlike cases of physical compulsion, the use of threats backed up by credible evidence of the power to enforce them applies "pressure" to a person's *will*; they are ways of making *him* choose to do what the coercer wishes. They force him to *act* and not merely to be moved or restricted in his bodily motions. In cases of coercion by threat, there is a sense in which the victim is left with a choice. He can comply, *or* he can suffer the probable consequences. But if the alternative to compliance is some unthinkable disaster—such as the death of a child—then one alternative choice is made so unreasonably costly that it is quite ineligible. In effect, as we say, it is no better than no choice at all. In intermediate cases, between the extremes of overwhelmingly coercive threats and mere attractive offers, the threat in effect puts a price tag on noncompliance and leaves it up to the threatened person to decide whether the price is worth paying. The metaphor of the price tag is especially useful since it reflects the fact that there are different degrees of *coercive pressure*, some greater than others, and the greater the coercion (the higher the cost) the less eligible is noncompliance, short of the limiting case of impossibility where coercion becomes compulsion proper.

It should be added as a corrective to the above that effective coercion does render certain *combinations* of alternatives strictly impossible, that even "closing options in the weak sense" closes *some* options tight. When the gunman effectively convinces you that you may keep either your money or your life, he shows you that one formerly open option is now thoroughly closed and hence "impossible" to choose, namely the option of keeping your money *and* your life. In general, effective coercion closes the option of noncompliance *and* avoidance of the threatened cost, while keeping open either without the other. You may choose X or you may choose Y, the coercer tells you, but you cannot choose the conjunction of X and Y. The coercer has closed the conjunctive option by forcibly manipulating your alternatives. His own forcible intervention by means of a weapon in the crude cases, or more sophisticated determinants in other cases, has changed the alternatives among which you must choose, and eliminated some of them altogether.

Coercive pressure. Just as compulsive force can fail in a given case to compel, and thus remain simply resistible pressure, so coercive impositions may fail in given cases to coerce since the "cost" of the threatened alternative is judged worth paying in preference to compliance with the demands of the coercer. Coercive pressure can fail to coerce, just as compulsive pressure can fail to compel. Ineffective coercion can fail for reasons of various distinct kinds. The threat may not be credible, or it may not in fact be believed; it may become a "called bluff" because the coercer in fact lacked the power he claimed to have; or it may be no bluff, so that when challenged it leads to costly consequences for the coercee that he would not have elected had he found the threat credible. I propose, however, to reserve the term "coercive pressure" for a different kind of case. The threat is real, credible, and in fact believed, but nevertheless it constitutes for the coercee a cost that he is willing to pay in preference to submitting to the alternative. Since he thinks of it as a real cost, one that he doesn't *want* to pay, it puts (in an obviously metaphorical sense) "pressure" on him, but since he prefers paying it to relinquishing another good, it is *mere* pressure, and not yet effective coercion. One advantage of the pricing analogy is that it gives some sense to judgments of comparative "pressure". Threat X exerts more coercive pressure than threat Y on B in circumstances C just in case B is more willing to accept Y as an alternative to some other good than he is to accept X, and to say that he is more willing to accept Y than X implies that there is some possible good that he would relinquish in preference to incurring X but would not relinquish in preference to incurring Y. The greater the perceived cost to one's interests, in short, the greater the coercive pressure on one's choice.

We can think of natural events like rockslides and hurricanes as also posing "threats" (Chap. 21, §2), though natural threats are often less precise and harder in general to gauge than explicitly voiced personal ones. When a hiker chooses one fork in a mountain trail rather than the other because of the perceived likelihood (a "threat") of a rockslide on the other fork, he deliberately makes a choice to minimize his risks. He judges the impact on his life and limb of the "threatened" rock slide to be too great a price to pay for what would otherwise be his preferred route, so he opts for the lesser evil under "pressure." Even though there is no personal coercer in this example, the determinative pressure, operating on the hiker's choice, is more like coercive pressure than compulsive pressure, and had better be classified as such. On the other hand, if the hiker opts for the dangerous path, and is knocked down a hill by a falling boulder, or forced to turn back by an uncrossable fissure in his path, then his movements are determined by natural compulsion, that is, irresistible compulsive force that bypasses his "choice" altogether.

Hard cases to classify. Suppose that John Grunt and Joe Groan have an arm wrestling match to determine who can force the other's arm to the table, as they push with all their strength, their hands locked in a grip, their elbows serving as fulcrums. If Grunt finds, to his dismay, that the sheer force of Groan's exerted pressure is moving his own arm inexorably downward and that he lacks the strength to force it back, then clearly his arm is forced down by compulsion. If he is able to hold but not improve his starting position, thereby producing a stalemate, then he has resisted compulsive pressure. Suppose however that he is just barely able to hold his own but at the cost of great pain. Finally he *decides* that the pain is intolerable and *chooses* to end it by ceasing his resistance. About this case we must make a surprising judgment. Groan's physical pressure on Grunt is both compulsive (but resistibly so) and coercive in its effect, and the deliberate choice to succumb to compulsive pressure on the grounds that continued resistance is possible only at too great a cost is to give in to *coercion* by choosing the lesser evil. The threat in this case is a tacit one. Groan does not have to say to Grunt: "Either cease resisting or I will continue to cause you this pain," since that option is clearly understood from the context, and the present experience of pain make the threat of its continuance all the more credible.

Similarly, if a group of soldiers bind a prisoner, attach a rope to his bonds, and then pull him along the street to his (their) destination, they have applied irresistible compulsive pressure to his body, leaving him no choice whatever but to move in the direction his captors choose. But if they move him instead by forcing him to walk, jabbing him from behind with bayonets whenever he falters, the compulsive pressure of their jabs has a coercive effect on his will. He could refuse to budge, and choose thereby to suffer painful bleeding wounds, torn flesh and punctured organs, loss of blood, even death, as a price worth paying for his noncompliance. But he prefers to walk instead, understanding each jab to be both an infliction of pain and a tacit threat to inflict more unless he complies. The case therefore is properly described as one of coercion.

In many cases it will be nearly impossible to distinguish a coerced decision made under severe duress (a coerced choice to succumb to compulsive pressure), on the one hand, from being forced without any act of choice by suddenly irresistible, psychologically compulsive force to give in, on the other. One's resistance might suddenly collapse as a direct causal consequence of the pain or suffering itself, and one's sudden inability to endure it any further in that case might be a product of the automatic responses of the nervous system independent of one's conscious control. There could, in some very traumatic circumstances, be a wholly psychological paralysis, also independent of the will, a sudden massive failure of courage or nerve. Since no conscious decision has been made to succumb in these cases, they are strictly speaking cases of compulsion rather than coercion. Such cases must surely be rare, however, and often impossible to verify even when they do occur, since there are few behavioral differences between sudden automatic capitulation and sudden choice to capitulate. When the pressure has been produced by another person whose *intent* was coercive, no practical consequence hinges on the precise mechanism by which the desired response was produced. An expression of consent, for example, will be involuntary and hence invalid, in either case. Acts of consent, however, are hardly ever produced by deliberate compulsion alone. The usual way of *forcing* a person to consent is by means of a threat conjoined with evidence of its credibility. One highly credible kind of "evidence" is compulsive pressure with the tacit threat of its continuance, but it is by no means the only kind. A prominently displayed gun will do as well, quite without compulsion.

2. Second party coercion; intent and control

We must now focus our sights more narrowly on coerced acts of consent by returning to our old friends A and B and considering only those transactions between them in which B's consent is involuntary because of coercion, and in which A's subsequent action therefore wrongs B, making A properly subject to criminal liability. The coercion that forces B's consent to A can stem from any of three sources—from A, from C (a third party), or from "natural circumstances." Two important matters hinge on whether or not B's consent is free (unforced): (1) A's criminal liability, and (2) the privilege of some third party (call him D) to intervene to protect B from A's invalidly warranted dangerous conduct. If the coercion stems from A himself, if A, for example, deliberately threatens B with harm in order to acquire B's consent to conduct that will injure or endanger him, then A may properly be subject to criminal liability. His conduct will be of a sort that falls under the harm to others principle and may therefore legitimately be prohibited by the criminal law, and A does not have B's valid consent, so he does not have *that* defense (though he may have other excuses) in a court of law. If the coercion, on the other hand, stemmed from the earlier threats of some third party, C, which were unknown to A, then as we saw earlier (Chap. 22, §1) A cannot be fairly punished for what he believed in all innocent good faith he had B's voluntary consent to do. B may then be harmed (in the purely interest-invading sense) by A, but not wronged by A. To be sure, B has also been wronged, but by C, not A. In all but extraordinary cases it would be unfair to punish A at all for his role in producing the harm to B, but not unfair to punish C for the whole wrongful harm of which A's conduct was an innocent but direct contributor, and his own conduct a wrongful but indirect contributor. If, on the other hand, A knew in advance the C had threatened B and that B's consent would not otherwise have been forthcoming, and he quite intentionally takes advantage of that situation to act just as if B's consent were voluntary, then it will be difficult for him to escape responsibility for the ensuing harm, and all the more so if he were actually a party to the coercion, having planned the whole episode with C, his partner. In the latter case, it is clearly irrelevant to the question of A's culpability whether it was C or he who actually uttered the threats to B.

Finally, if the "threat" to B comes from nature (say, a sickness) rather than from A or any other person, then in all probability we would take that threat simply to be one of the background conditions against which B's consent is expressed rather than an intervening force rendering his decision involuntary (see Chap. 21, §2). Jeffrie G. Murphy points out that the "mere grimness of all alternatives" to the action consented to, is often

> nothing more than the 'legitimate inequalities of fortune' which all of us must inevitably confront—i.e. a sad fact about the human condition rather than any unjust disadvantage brought on by the wrongful actions of others against us. And it is by no means obvious that any agreement which one is prompted to make by the inequalities of fortune is invalid . . . If it is, then the law of contracts—indeed the whole of capitalism—is in serious moral trouble indeed.[3]

Murphy's general observation reflects common sense, but it is subject to two caveats. First, what appears to be merely bad luck, an unforeseeable natural occurence forcing us to act in unhappy ways we would not otherwise have chosen, in fact is often a natural occurence for which human beings share a large part of the responsibility. The cancer that is caused by a chemical company's reckless disposal of wastes it *not* just the luck of the draw—"a legitimate inequality of fortune." If chemical wastes threaten the residents of a community with injury and disease, and destroy the resale value of their land and homes, and the responsible company steps in and offers homeowners a paltry sum for their property on a "take it or leave it" basis, then the less than willing consent of the frightened owners to the terms is not *merely* the product of "threats from nature," not merely the effect of "circumstantial coercion." In this case, A, the chemical company, has itself produced the conditions that exert coercive pressure on B, the homeowner, thus rendering his consent less than voluntary. On the other hand, if one contracts a lethal disease as a genuinely unforeseeable stroke of ill fortune, then the hard choices it causes one to make may nevertheless be *"voluntary in the circumstances."* B, the unlucky victim of the disease, may (in Murphy's example) be "driven to ask a friend [A] for a loan by the threat of financial disaster (brought on, we may imagine, by heavy medical expenses) . . . ."

His unfortunate position does not invalidate his "promise to repay the loan at a reasonable rate of interest,"[4] even though his consent to the loaner's terms was his only alternative to intolerable circumstances.

The second caveat is that even where the consent of the unlucky person (B) is voluntary given the circumstances, there may be other grounds for prohibiting A from taking advantage of it. If A's terms are hard for B, and because of circumstantial coercion, B has no real choice but to accept them, thus producing great profit for A, it may well be the right of the state to interfere, not on the ground that B's consent was coerced by A, or by any other person, but rather on the quite distinct ground that the agreement is unfair to B even though B's consent was voluntary, and that A's profit was parasitical, exploitative, or otherwise "unconscionable." (This argument goes well beyond the harm to others principle as mediated by *Volenti*, however. See Chap. 31.) Consider the chemical waste example again, and suppose that the chemical company responsible for B's plight is now a third party, C, not directly involved in the transaction, and the A is an opportunistic real estate and salvage operator who can make "quick bucks" by offering minimal terms to the desperate homeowners. Presumably *he* did not coerce B's consent (the possibility of "coercive offers," however, will be considered in Chap. 24); and while he may know of C's role in the "circumstantial coercion" of B, he had no part in the process himself and is in no sense a partner of C's. If blamed for his heartless opportunism, he may reply in his defense that he did not wrong B since he had B's consent, which given the background conditions over which neither he nor B had any control, was given voluntarily. A disgusted observer might nevertheless condemn A unconscionable exploitation (if not coercion) of the bad luck of another person.

Our primary concern here, however, is not with exploitation, as such, whether it makes a good thing for the exploiter of a coercive situation produced by a third party or by "the legitimate inequalities of fortune." Rather we must focus now on the central cases in which consent is a product of coercion employed by the second party to the agreement, A himself, or a third party in cahoots with A. Since the consent, in these cases, is forced by coercion, it is not voluntary, hence not valid, hence lacking in its usual legal effect of exoneration, while having the effect of exempting third-party protective interveners from liability when they act reasonably. If the agreements are of a kind presumptively harmful or dangerous to B, then the behavior of A's that they purport to authorize may be criminally prohibited by a legislature employing the harm to others principle, and A may be convicted of some such crime as homicide, mayhem, battery, rape, usury, or bigamy, depending on the nature of the harm.

We can now consider a schematic analysis of direct coercion of one party (B) by a second party (A) when it is strong enough to nullify the "consent" of the first party. *A* coerces *B* into agreeing to his harmful or dangerous treatment of *B* in these cases when:

1. *A* demands that *B* consent to it;
2. *A* makes a threat to *B* (or in some cases a "coercive offer") that he (*A*) will cause or fail to prevent some consequences that *B* finds unwelcome unless *B* complies with the demand;
3. *A* gives *B* some evidence of the credibility of the threat, usually a demonstration of his power as well as his willingness to carry it out; and
4. unless he is bluffing, *A* has actively intervened in *B*'s option-network to acquire control of the relevant option-switches; in particular he can close tight the conjunctive option that consists of *B*'s noncompliance with the demand *and B*'s avoidance of the threatened unwelcome consequences; and
5. *B* understands the proposal and is frightened by it, and at least partly to avoid an unwelcome projected consequence, complies with *A*'s demand.

Condition (4) in the above analysis has an anomalous status. We could delete the phrase "unless he is bluffing," thus making actual control part of our definition of "coercion." Then coercion proper could be usefully contrasted with pseudo-coercive bluffs. The problem with that procedure is that it ignores the fact that mere bluffs can be coercive too. Perhaps the wisest course is to distinguish coercion proper (which is no bluff), pseudo-coercive bluff (which is no coercion), and coercive bluffs which, like toy guns in bank robberies, can nullify the voluntariness of consent as effectively as coercion proper.

Other conditions could no doubt be added to the list. We might wish to require that the credibility of *B*'s threat and the "unwelcomeness" of the threatened consequences be determined by objective rather than subjective standards (see *infra* §5) so that any reasonable person in *B*'s circumstances would believe the threat, or attach significant probability to it, or at least take it seriously, and also find the threatened consequences unwelcome. Perhaps we might require further that *A*'s behavior have the serious intention of forcing *B*'s compliance, and that *B* should comply because of it. But our concern here is not to put *A* on trial, or to determine in the abstract the conditions of his culpability, so we can safely avoid these further complications.[5] Our interest here is sharply focused on what it means to call *B*'s consent voluntary, and with the legal consequences, for *B*'s interest, of the judgment that his consent, being forced, was not "voluntary enough." Even if coercion is determined by subjective standards tailored to *B*'s actual beliefs and values, then if his transfer of money to *A*, for example, was coerced according to those standards, it cannot be regarded as a *gift*, even if, determining *A*'s coercive behavior by objective standards, and requiring actual coercive intention, we cannot convict *A* of larceny. (See *infra* §5.) It is conceivable, in some cases, that justice calls for the acquittal of *A* but also requires the restitution of *B*'s loss. In those cases we may say that A did not voluntarily coerce B, but that because of the unintended effect of his actions on B, B did not voluntarily consent either.

3. Differential coercive pressure: how coercive is coercive enough?

Coercive pressure sometimes forces consent and sometimes does not. In any event, it is subject to degrees and comparative judgments of more and less. It is not *literally* "pressure" at all, unlike compulsive physical force and its closer psychological analogues, but is "pressure" or "force" only by virtue of a somewhat strained but still useful metaphor. Coercive pressure exerts "force on the will" only by virtue of the coercee's desires which it threatens to turn against one another by rendering their joint satisfaction impossible. It thereby requires the coercee to make a choice between unwanted exclusive alternatives, which in turn, requires that he rank his desires in order of preference. Each envisaged outcome will be unwelcome, but he must select the one that is less unwelcome than the others. Even "evils" can be ranked in an order of preference. So in order to choose the lesser evil, the coercee B must be prepared to make his own judgment of comparative worth, and he may make that judgment perfectly rationally yet opt for an outcome other than that which equally rational persons with different preferences would have chosen in his position. In a certain sense, then, it is B's own subjective characteristics, values and preferences peculiar to him, that determine how coercive the pressure is. The degree of pressure is a function of how much he wants X, or fears Y, and how he ranks his preferences.

Imagine ten different coercive demands that A might make of B in as many different hypothetical scenarios:

1. Betray your fellow soldiers by handing over secret military plans to me (the enemy).
2. Assassinate my rival for the Mafia leadership.
3. Let me kill you and transplant your organs, while they are still fresh, to others.
4. Sign over to me all your worldly goods.
5. Let me sleep with you (that is, have sexual relations).
6. Make me a "gift" of $10,000.
7. Make me a "gift" of $100.
8. Let me amputate your leg to arrest the possible spread of bone cancer.
9. Agree to be a posthumous organ donor.
10. Pour me a cup of coffee.

The nature of the coercer's demand is not the only variable in the situation that can generate scenarios. Imagine the following ordering of alternative threats for backing up demands. "Accede to my demand," says A, or else—

1. I will detonate a nuclear bomb over your city.
2. I will torture and kill your spouse and children.
3. I will kill you.
4. I will burn down your house.
5. I will break your legs.
6. I will smash your windows.
7. I will soap your windows.
8. I will tell all your friends what a mean person you are.
9. I will withhold my friendship from you.
10. I will be momentarily annoyed.

Let us assume that all the threats in the second list are credible, that (for simplification) they are not bluffs, and that the demands in the first list are all unwelcome to *B*, yet within his power to satisfy. Assume finally that *B*'s judgments of comparative worth (evil) lead him to rank the demands in just the way indicated in our first list, and to place the threats in exactly the same order of unwelcomeness indicated in our second list. I take it that these orderings are intuitively plausible, that is, not "irrational" at face value, although equally reasonable persons, or persons in different life situations, might differ here and there over particular rankings in the lists. There are then one hundred scenarios in which *B* must choose whether to comply with the demand or pay the threatened price. (That is, for each of the ten demands there are ten possible coercive threats.) Our hierarchy permits us to place the one hundred scenarios on a scale of "coercive pressure," having used *B*'s own subjective preferences, and not necessarily our own or those of a hypothetical "reasonable person" to generate the scale.

At the top of the scale of "differential pressure" is the coercive proposal— "Pour me a cup of coffee" (number 10 on the demand list) "or else I will detonate a nuclear bomb over your city" (number 1 on the threat list). At the other extreme, at the bottom of the scale, is the coercive proposal—"Betray your fellow soldiers" (number 1 on the demand list) "or else I will be momentarily annoyed" (number 10 on the threat list). If *B* is faced inescapably with the option in the first example, he will decide that the coercive pressure is far too great to resist, and his compliance with the demand will be an instance of a coerced choice for which he (probably) bears no responsibility. If *B* "succumbs" to the trivial coercive pressure in the second example, we have reason to suspect that his choice was not really coerced at all by so trivial a coercive pressure and should therefore be treated as voluntary—certainly as "voluntary enough" for the purpose of assigning moral responsibility to *B* for it. Neither of these easy examples, of course, involves a demand for an act of *consent*, but leaving the threat the same in each instance, we can substitute a consent-demand and produce equally easy cases. Suppose *A* says "consent to my using your organs for transplant after you die (presumably many years from now)" (number 9 on the demand list) "or else I will detonate a nuclear bomb over your city now" (number 1 on the threat list). Then B's consent can plausibly be treated as having been forced by immense coercive pressure and very likely insufficiently voluntary (being very involuntary indeed) to be valid, and at no subsequent time will A or anyone else be at liberty to transplant B's organ on its warrant. On the other hand, if A says "Consent to my killing you and using your organs" (number 3 on the demand list) "or else I will be momentarily annoyed" (number 10 on the threat list), and B complies, we doubt that B's consent was actually coerced by such meagre pressure and suspect instead that his consent was quite genuine.

The strongest coercive pressure, then, is that of the proposal that combines the lowest ranked demand and the highest ranked threat, while the weakest coercive pressure is that of the proposal with the highest ranked demand and lowest ranked threat. Then as we go up the ranks of the demands and down the ranks of the threats the coercive pressure diminishes, and as we go (from the opposite direction) down the ranks of the demands and up the ranks of the threats, the coercive pressure increases. When we get to the middle region of the scale of pressure, where the posed choices are between demands and threats of roughly equal ranking (demand number 1 or threat number 1, demand number 5 or threat number 5, demand number 10 or threat number 10, etc.), then it can become very difficult for the coercee to decide whether to comply or not, and the differential coercive pressure is right at the threshold of coercion proper. It does not overtax our imaginations to think of reasonable individuals who would find it terribly difficult to choose between betraying soldiers thus causing their certain annihilation or having an atomic bomb exploded over a city, between consenting to sexual relations with an odious stranger or having one's legs broken, or even between getting someone a cup of coffee or having him momentarily annoyed.

We must, of course, avoid the mistake of taking our arbitrary number assignments too seriously. It is a simple-minded error to infer that "because we can assign numbers to different degrees of a quality, e.g. degrees of "unwelcomeness", the different degrees always bear to each other the same ratio as do the numbers we have assigned them."[6] From the fact that a given situation can be placed in a ranking order with other situations in respect to its possession of some characteristic or other, and that numbers can be used to indicate the place each situation occupies in that ranking order, it does not follow that the numbers stand for some measurable magnitude possessed in greater degree by some of the ranked entities than others in direct proportion to the arithmetical relations between the numbers themselves. It B ranks one of A's threats fifth on a list and another tenth, it is not correct to say that the former is exactly twice as unwelcome as the latter. The mistake is in suppos-

ing that because one projected outcome is higher up in the scale of unwelcomeness than the other, it contains more of something called "unwelcomeness," and that "it contains a unit amount of it a certain number of times."[7]

Nevertheless, I propose to use numbers in this inappropriate way, as an
illustrative device, fully mindful of the mistake that comes from treating
nonadditive qualities (like places in a ranking order) as if they were additive.
Let us suppose for a moment then that A's demands and threats cannot only
be ranked but that in virtue of some objectively measureable characteristic
which we can call their "cost," they can be assigned numbers which can then
be manipulated to yield resultant sums called "coercive pressure". Suppose
that we attach cost indicators to A's demands as follows, using the dollar sign
not to stand for actual U.S. currency, but for a fictional "as if currency."
The number 1 demand (betraying comrades) has a $10 cost to B, the number
2 demand (assassinating the rival) has a $9 cost to B, the number 3 demand
(consenting to death) has an $8 cost to B, and so on, down to the number 10
demand (pouring a cup of coffee) which has a tag of $1. Of course it is absurd
to suppose that B would be so peculiar as to think of the bother of pouring a
cup of coffee as exactly one tenth as great a cost as betraying his comrades, so
that it would be a matter of indifference to him whether he betrayed his
comrades or poured coffee ten consecutive times! But for the purpose of our
illustration, let us suspend disbelief, or else imagine that there is some possible set of demands other than that in our example for which this price tag
model is more convincing.

Now suppose that we attach price tags in a similar way to A's threats. The
number 1 threat (the nuclear bomb explosion) has a $10 cost to B (if we were
playing this game more realistically, we might attach an astronomical number, even an infinite one), the number 2 threat (the torture of his family) a $9
cost to B (more realistically, another only slightly smaller astronomical cost),
the number 3 threat (B's own death) an $8 cost (realistically, in the trillions),
and so on, down to the number 10 threat in order of severity (momentary
displeasure of the threatener) which has a cost of $1.

On these simplified (and simple-minded) assumptions, we can generate a
scale of "differential coercive pressure" for the one hundred hypothetical
scenarios. The greater the difference between the "cost" of the threat and the
"cost" of the demand, the greater the coercive pressure. The most coercive
proposal would be that forcing a choice between a $10 threat (the number 1
ranked threat in our artificial example) and a $1 demand (the number 10
ranked demand). The second most coercive proposal would be a tie between
the $10 threat and the $2 demand, and the $9 threat and the $1 demand.
Toward the middle of the coerciveness scale we would find the $6 threat
disjoined with the $5 demand, which still yields a positive balance of coercive
pressure, and all of the other combinations in which the threat is $1 more

costly than the demand. Then there would be the fifty–fifty cases in which the coercive pressure is right at the threshold of sufficiency, followed by the close cases yielding a negative balance, for example the $6 threat and the $7 demand, and finally the "easy" cases of only minor coerciveness, for example, the $2 threat and the $6 demand.

Differential coercive pressure is great enough to become coercion proper at just the point where the costs of the threatened consequences exceed the costs of complying with the demand. (See §4, however, for a qualification of this point.) If in fact the balance of costs is negative—the demand exceeding the threat—then the coercive pressure is not great enough to force the consent. Even in these cases, however, the fact that coercive pressure was applied at all, may have moral—and should have legal—relevance in a number of ways. The very making of a threat to harm may in some circumstances be a crime; the carrying out of the threat in a fruitless effort to force the demand will be a crime; an unsuccessful bluffing threat could be an attempted crime ("Sleep with me or I will shoot you in the leg," said by a bluffer with a toy pistol, may be attempted rape.) And the law will allow coercive pressure as such, in some circumstances, to be great enough to invalidate consent, even when in fact it was not great enough to coerce. Courts have no way of knowing the exact price tags that individuals place on various unwelcome alternatives, and when consent was made under coercive pressure plausibly deemed sufficient in a standard case to force consent, it will be presumed to have been sufficient in the case at hand. Readiness to make that presumption means that some "victims" of harmful two-party transactions may have genuinely consented "voluntarily," though under coercive pressure short of coercion proper, and yet their partner will be deprived of consent as a defense because the court allowed the threat itself to invalidate the consent. But if the courts use objective standards that really do reflect the price tags placed on options by most people, then it follows that in most cases justice will be done. And in the few cases where a threatener actually does receive genuine consent, despite having attempted to coerce it with a threat, he cannot complain of injustice either, since he was prepared to act whether the consent was genuine or not, and for that intention he is answerable.

4. Other measures of coercive pressure

The conception of coercive pressure sketched in the preceding section is not the only one available to us, and in fact it may be less useful than some of its alternatives for our study of the factors that reduce the voluntariness of expressions of consent to dangerous or harmful proposals. I have labelled that conception *differential coercive pressure* since it measure the *difference* between the costs of the threat and the cost of the demand that is presented as the sole alternative to the threat. What it measures then is how much more unwelcome to the coercee the threat is than the demand, or (put roughly) "how much choice" he had in the circumstances to reject the demand. It may sometimes be relevant to our moral purposes to know what the differential pressure was before making certain judgments about the coercee, but there are other moral purposes that are less well served by this information, and in fact the differential measure of coercive pressure for some purposes may lead us to make judgments in particular cases that are highly counter-intuitive.

Suppose that the powerful villain *A* makes the following coercive proposal to *B*, a woman in his power: "Sleep with me or I'll break both your legs." Suppose further that *B* is utterly repelled by the demand, putting a price tag of 9 on it, but even more terrified by the threat, to which she attaches a price tag of 10. Since the cost of the threat is even greater than that of the demand, she very reluctantly succumbs to the coercive pressure. Now consider a second example involving the same persons. *A* says to *B:* "Get me a cup of coffee or I'll break both your legs." Fetching a cup of coffee is a mere minor inconvenience to *B* with a price tag only of 1, but getting her legs broken is as terrifying as in the first example and has the same high cost, namely 10. *Of course B* gets *A* the cup of coffee, acting involuntarily under extreme coercive pressure.

The differential coercive pressure in the first example is 10 minus 9, or 1, whereas the differential coercive pressure in the second example is 10 minus 1, or 9. If this is our only conception of coercive pressure, this result will strike many as starkly in conflict with common sense. It seems incredible that there was not only more, but immensely more, coercion in the coffee case than in the sexual imposition case, or that the woman in the first example had "more of a choice," or acted "more voluntarily" than the same woman in the second example, It might seem then that it is not *differential* coercive pressure that reduces voluntariness but coercive pressure in some other sense, or as determined by some other measure.

One ready alternative is to identify coercive pressure in the relevant sense as that constituted by the degree of unwelcomeness of the threat alone. We can distinguish this second conception of coercive pressure by labelling it *coercive force*. Since the cost of the threatened alternative is the same in our two examples (10), we can say that the same amount of coercive force was exerted in both, and that therefore the degree of coercive pressure, in the appropriate sense, was the same in both. But this result will make us uneasy in some cases too. Is it really true that the coercive pressure on *B* in the sexual imposition example, where she is put under enormous stress and strain, and "squeezed" hard from two sides, is exactly equal to the coercive pressure in the coffee example, where her choice is extremely easy, where the strong pressure comes from one side only, and her psychological strain and prospective loss are much less? Suppose the threat in the first example was to break only one of her legs, at a subjective cost of $9\frac{1}{2}$, and we compare that proposal to the second example as unchanged. Now there is slightly greater coercive force exerted in support of the coffee demand than in support of the sexual demand. Does it follow that B in the second example is under greater coercive pressure than in the revised first example? She *is* under greater differential pressure, and subject to greater coercive force, but are these accurate conceptions of the sort of coercive pressure that reduces voluntariness? I think that thoughtful people would balk at the judgment that B succumbed to A's sexual demands more voluntarily (because under less pressure) than she succumbed to his coffee demand.

Let me now distinguish a third conception of coercive pressure, which we can call *total coercive burden*. We measure this magnitude not by subtracting the cost of the demand from that of the threat, but rather by adding the two together to yield a sum. Thus the total coercive burden in the original sexual imposition example is determined by adding the cost of the demand (9) to the cost of the threat (10), a total of 19. This result compares more realistically to the burden in the coffee example, which is 10 plus 1, a total of 11. If this is the proper conception of the coercive pressure that reduces voluntariness, we must say that neither the action of "consenting" to sex in the first example nor that of fetching the coffee in the second example was very voluntary, indeed that neither is voluntary enough to be valid for various moral and legal purposes; still the coffee-fetcher acted less involuntarily (because under a smaller coercive burden) than the sex-succumber. I think this judgment comes closer to common sense than those that are derived from the first two conceptions of coercive pressure.

A fourth and final conception of coercive pressure is that of *the coercive minimum*, which consists simply of the cost of the best available option. In the sexual imposition case, insofar as the coercion truly is effective, blocking off all options except that of the demand and the threatened alternative, those two remaining options have costs of 10 and 9. The least cost the unfortunate coercee can get away with is 9, and that is the coercive minimum; whereas in the coffee-fetching example, the cost of the best available option is only 1. It follows that the voluntariness-reducing coercive pressure in the sexual example is immensely greater than in the coffee-fetching example, even though the coercive force was the same in the two cases. That result too may make us squirm a bit, but it finds support in the common-sense observation that the woman in the second example, given her subjective preference scale, was presumably *less unwilling*, right from the start, to fetch the coffee than she was to go to bed with B, so that her doing so in the face of great coercive force was less involuntary.

The advantage of the coercive burden criterion over the coercive minimum criterion is that it does justice *both* to the degree of force exerted and to the degree of unwillingness initially presumed, rather than to either one without the other. Consider a pair of examples in which the total coercive burden and the coercive minimum are more divergent. In our earlier example, 1, the total burden was 19 and the coercive minimum 9. In example 2, the burden was 11 and the minimum 1. So the difference in coercive pressure between the two examples is the same (8) whether we use the total burden conception or the coercive minimum conception. But now we can consider example 3, in which the total burden is 15 and the coercive minimum is 1, and example 4, in which the total burden is 15 and the coercive minimum is (say) 7. Suppose that in the new example 3, *A* threatens to torture *B*'s child (cost: 14) unless she pours him a cup of coffee (cost: 1), and in the new example 4, *A* threatens a different *B* that he will steal her purse with $1,000 in it (cost: 8) unless she sleeps with him (cost to this *B:* 7). Now the differences in coercive burdens and coercive minimums for the four examples can be tabulated (Diagram 23-1).

The difference in degrees of coercion between examples 1 and 2 comes out to be the same whether we use the total burden or the coercive minimum tests. By either criterion there is more coercive pressure in example 1 by 8 units (19 to 11, or 9 to 1). Example 1 is also more coercive than example 3 by either test, but it is only slightly more coercive by the total burden test (19 to 15) but immensely more coercive by the minimum standard (9 to 1). There are greater divergences still in some of the other comparisons. Example 3 (torture child or fetch coffee) is more coercive than example 2 (break legs or fetch coffee) by the total burden criterion, but exactly the same by the coercive minimum criterion. Example 4 (lose money or submit sexually) is much more coercive than example 3 (torture child or fetch coffee) by the coercive minimum criterion but exactly the same by the total burden criterion. These results are charted in Diagram 23-2.

The two criteria diverge most emphatically in the comparisons between examples 2 and 3 and examples 3 and 4. Which proposal generates the

	Total Coercive Burden	Coercive Minimum
Example 1.	19	9
Example 2.	11	1
Example 3.	15	1
Example 4.	15	7

Diagram 23–1. Alternative tests of coercive pressure.

Examples Compared	Total Coercive Burden	Coercive Minimum
1 vs 2	1 (19 to 11)	1 (9 to 1)
1 vs 3	1 (19 to 15)	1 (9 to 1)
1 vs 4	1 (19 to 15)	1 (9 to 7)
2 vs 3	3 (15 to 11)	Even (1 to 1)
2 vs 4	4 (15 to 11)	4 (7 to 1)
3 vs 4	even (15 to 15)	4 (7 to 1)

Diagram 23–2. Divergent results of tests of coercive pressure.

greater coercive pressure: (2) Fetch me coffee or I'll break your legs, or (3) Fetch me coffee or I'll torture your child? Again, where is the greater voluntariness-reducing pressure: in (3) Fetch me coffee or I'll break your legs, or (4) sleep with me or else lose $1,000? If we use the coercive minimum test then the pressure in the two coffee-fetching cases is exactly the same, even though the coercive force of the threat is much greater in the one case than the other. And if we use the coercive minimum test, the coercive pressure to succumb to sex is much greater than that to fetch coffee, even though the coffee demand is enforced by a much more severe threat (to torture a child) than the sex demand (to take money) (Diagram 23-3).

I, for one, do not have any clear "intuitions" to use in settling the matter, and this leads me to believe that quite distinct senses of "voluntariness" must underlie the problem. In the sense of voluntariness that is determined by degree of subjective willingness, the coercive minimum (cost of the best option) as such is a voluntariness-reducing factor: the higher the minimum the greater the voluntariness-reducing coercive pressure. Clearly, the woman in example 4 sleeps with her coercer much less willingly than her counterpart in example 3 fetches coffee for hers. Minor coercive force, a mere cost of 2, would have been sufficient pressure to bring about the coffee fetching. The actual threat to torture a child was an unnecessary coercive surplus, not needed to affect the coercee's motivation, which was sufficiently swayed by the small cost of the demand, and a small show of force. In the sex example, every last bit of the threatened cost was necessary to force acquiescence, because of the high degree of unwillingness to do what was demanded. That initial unwillingness alone determines how voluntary or involuntary the coerced choice is, and how much force was required to coerce it.

Subjective unwillingness, however, is not the only thing we can mean by involuntariness. (See Chap. 24, §8.) The dictionary tells us that "voluntary" sometimes means "willingly" and sometimes "unforced," among other things, and both of these "states" occur to different degrees. Normally, when we are

	Burden	Minimum
Example 2. Fetch coffee (cost: 1) or have legs broken (cost: 10)	11	1
versus		
Example 3. Fetch coffee (cost: 1) or have child tortured (cost: 14)	15	1
Example 3. Fetch coffee (cost: 1) or have child tortured (cost: 14)	15	1
versus		
Example 4. Sexual submission (cost: 7) or have money taken (cost: 8)	15	7

Diagram 23–3. Divergence of the "total burden" and "coercive minimum" tests of coercive pressure.

forced to do something we do it "against our will"; we struggle, resist, seek alternatives, or succumb under protest. What tends to cause confusion, however, is the fact that people sometimes act quite *willingly* under force. Suppose that Mother Theresa is told "Give me your money or I will blow your brains out," by an armed street urchin just as she was about to offer him all her money anyway out of Christian charity. She hands over her money quite willingly, even eagerly, though of course she has no choice. The demand in this example had no real cost to be the coercee. In that respect the example differs only slightly from the coffee-fetching examples in which the demand has only a minor cost, and the unwillingness was real but relatively slight. Mother Theresa's act is "involuntary" in the sense that it was done *under coercion*, but not in the sense that it was done *from coercion*.

If we are concerned in our role as moralists to determine the degree to which the coercee acted from coercion (unwillingly) it will often be sufficient to know the subjective price tag of the demand and the fact that the coercive force of the threat in fact surpassed that threshold. It is not necessary to know the extent of the coercive surplus—the degree to which coercive force exceeded what was necessary—in order to gauge the degree of actual unwillingness, that is, the degree to which the actor chose "from coercion." If, on the other hand, we are concerned as jurists to learn the extent to which the coercee acted "under coercion," either as part of an inquiry into the seriousness of the coercer's culpability or the harmfulness of his threatening behavior, or as part of an inquiry into the degree of psychological force exerted against the coercee, or how free he was to do otherwise, then we shall want to consider the whole coercive burden under which he acted.

It remains to explain why differential coercive pressure, the concept explicated in §3, will not be a relevant measure of voluntariness for some purposes, though it may be useful for others. Let us return to example 1, in which A threatens to break B's legs (cost: 10) unless she agrees to sleep with him (cost: 9). The coercee acts under an enormous amount of coercive pressure in this example, and consequently with very little voluntariness. But the differential pressure, consisting of the difference in the costs of the two options, is very slight indeed, only 1. What this shows is that the pressure to do X rather than Y (the only options available) is relatively small. Thus, if the charge leveled at B is that she should have chosen Y instead of X, then it is relevant to point out that the pressure to do *the one instead of the other* was slight, and that her choice of *the one instead of the other* was not all that involuntary. But differential coercive pressure only measures, if you will, differential responsibility, that is responsibility for choosing X instead of Y where it is given that these are the only alternatives, and a judgment of voluntariness is to be made by means of standards tailored, *talis qualis*, to these circumstances. The differential standard does not measure the much greater pressure to do X instead of what the coercee genuinely prefers, namely neither X nor Y, but rather a state in which no costs are incurred. B's preference was to go her own way minding her own affairs, neither submitting to sex with an abusive stranger, nor having her legs broken. The pressure against *that* alternative was overwhelming, and her responsibility for not exercising it was nil.

The inadequacy of the differential conception of coercive pressure for some of our larger purposes in determining voluntariness is best illustrated by the case in which the differential pressure is negative. Suppose A demands that B do something with a subjective cost of 10 and threatens that if she does not comply, he will do something that in fact has a subjective cost of "only" 9. The threat in this case will not be severe enough to force compliance with the demand, since B will choose the lesser evil which is noncompliance. That result led us in §3 to claim that the coercion fails in this example, which in an obvious sense is true. The coercer A fails to get what he wants. But it is worse than misleading to draw from this the conclusion that B suffered no coercion or that she was free altogether of coercive pressure. If she now must pay the price of the coercer's threatened alternative, that payment is a consequence of the immense coercive pressure imposed upon her, to which the demand and the threat both contributed, and she will rightly claim that she was forced to suffer that loss against her will, entirely involuntarily. Even in this case, however, the differential conception can have some utility. If the differential pressure to comply with the demand was negative 1, then the differential pressure to suffer the threatened alternative (instead of complying) was "only" positive 1. And if we think that there was an objectively determined moral obligation to choose the demand-option instead of that threat-option because it is objectively the lesser of the two evils to all concerned, then we might judge the differential pressure to be insufficient to defeat the differential responsibility (blame) for the choice. Coercive pressure there was, we might concede, but it was insufficient to reduce the voluntariness of *B*'s wrongful choice to the point of nonresponsibility. This point makes a natural transition to the next topic.

5. Subjective and objective standards

Up to this point we have only used subjective standards (sometimes called "internal standards"), tailored to *B*'s actual preferences, to determine whether the coercive pressure exerted on her by *A*'s threat is sufficient to force her choice, and thus count as coercion proper in those simplified circumstances in which the threat need not be discounted for credibility. We have assumed, all along, that *B*'s choice under pressure will not be literally compelled by psychological pressures such as immobilizing fear, and that it is not temporarily distorted by such factors as weakness of will, neurosis, or anomie. The coercee, we have assumed, has a choice, despite the pressure to which she is subjected, and exercises it by choosing the lesser of the evils left open to her as determined by *her own* standards of judgment. If the choice is between an unwelcome consequence threatened by *A* or compliance with *A*'s demand for consent, and *B* chooses compliance as the lesser evil, the consent is then properly characterized as coerced (forced) rather than free.

But now we must complicate our account. In many contexts the law will apply objective (sometimes called "external") standards to *B*'s choice, being less interested in *B*'s judgments of comparative evil than in the judgments it deems reasonable to make, those that would be made by an ideally reasonable person in *B*'s situation. (Actually there are two kinds of "objective" standards sometimes used by courts: appeal to the judgments or characteristics of *most* people or the *average* person, on the one hand, and appeal to an ideal *reasonable* person, on the other.) When only *A* and *B* have interests directly involved in the transaction between them, and the law's sole (proper) concern is to protect *B* from a harmful or dangerous agreement to which she has not voluntarily consented, then it is sufficient that *B*'s choice was not actually produced by effective coercion as determined by her own standards of preference, to qualify the consent as free, and (barring the presence of other voluntariness-nullifying factors like ignorance or impaired faculties) as valid. However, when *B*'s choice is other-regarding, and the interests of various third parties, or the public in general, may be affected, then the law may judge the voluntariness of *B*'s actions by rather more demanding standards. That is especially true when what is at issue is whether *B* has a defense to a criminal charge. If she agreed to provide military secrets to the enemy A rather than endure further torture, there is probably no doubt that her choice was the product of coercion proper, as we have thus far analyzed it. The cost of her continued suffering, according to *her* preferences, was greater even than the cost of betraying her comrades, so she paid the lesser price. Given that thousands of innocent human lives were thereby sacrificed and the entire national interest endangered, the law might hold that by the judgments of a hypothetical "reasonable person," the price-tag on betrayal was higher than that on continued torture, and by those governing standards, B's conduct, though done under extreme coercive pressure, was *not* coerced. A somewhat less paradoxical-sounding way of putting the same judgment, and the way I prefer, is to say that though B's action was actually coerced (by her own subjective standards), and was not done *very* voluntarily, nevertheless given the interests at stake it was "voluntary enough" for B to be held responsible for it.

Restricting our attention, however, to wholly self-regarding situations, and the problem of protecting B's choice about matters that directly concern only her own interest, I find no reason to apply any price tags to B's options but those that B applies herself. If B accedes to A's unwelcome proposal only because the cost she attaches to A's threatened harm is even greater than the large cost of A's demand itself, then her consent has been coerced no matter how eccentric her judgments of comparative evil may be, even if those judgments are unreasonable or perverse. And since that consent was coerced, it must be counted as insufficiently voluntary to be valid, hence probably insufficient to provide A with a criminal defense.

Once more, however, we must complicate our account, this time to accommodate the case of an "eccentric" B who is abnormally vulnerable to threats of a certain kind, so that proposals that would be coercive by his subjective standards would not be coercive to most people or to an ideally reasonable person. Consider A's effort to exploit B's eccentricity in a hypothetical case which directly involves only the interests of A and B themselves, leaving third parties and the general public largely unaffected. B is an extremely neurotic person who cannot bear to be patted on the back. A, who is larger and stronger than B, knowing of this peculiar sensitivity, demands that B sign over to him most of his worldly goods or else A will pat him on the back. Filled with genuine horror by A's threat, B complies with the demand. C witnesses the whole episode and reports it to the police, resulting in charges of criminal extortion lodged against A who pleads in his own defense that B freely consented to his "request" for his goods, and that his so-called "threat" was mere playfulness. Given the account of voluntariness developed in these chapters, it would be an entirely intelligible result if the courts were to acquit A of the criminal charge, but find for the plaintiff B in his subsequent civil suit for full restitution. *B*'s consent was voluntary enough to provide *A* with a defense to a criminal charge, since the coercive pressure applied was not coercive enough (by objective standards) for criminal liability, but the consent was not voluntary enough (this time measured by *B*'s own subjective standards) to render the transfer a legal *gift*.

The back-patting case is a fanciful example of an eccentric cost ordering that leads to "consent" to an action by another party which causes harm directly to the consenter himself. There is a similar construal of the rationale for using objective standards for criminal liability in other-regarding cases where the consenter "agreed," under pressure, to do something harmful to third parties or the general public, and the question is whether the coercive pressure nullified the voluntariness of his harmful act, providing him with an exculpatory excuse. Consider the following exchange between evil *A* and an "eccentric cost-ranker," *B*, who is in his power:

A: I have just taken $100 from you. I will keep it unless you betray military secrets to me.

B: Your threat to me, given my eccentric cost-ordering, is more costly than the demand, so I accede to the demand under coercion.

Given that *B* is telling the truth, that he is genuinely "eccentric" in the extraordinarily high value he attaches to money, but that he also attaches the very high value that we expect of him to faithfulness and to national security, his agreement *is* effectively coerced. On these unlikely facts, he is an honorable, trustworthy, and patriotic man to an admirably high degree, but he just happens to react to the loss of even trivial sums of money the way others respond to physical torture. Of course in a real case no one would believe this description, but *if* it were true then *B* would be genuinely coerced, according to his own subjective preferences, into a harmful action. Even accepting this description, however, we would judge that his conduct was not coerced by objective standards, for a reasonable person in his circumstances (even the average person in his circumstances) would have preferred losing $100 to betraying his country. Using objective standards then, we would rightly judge that *B*'s action was voluntary enough for him to be criminally liable for it. What he is actually punished for, if it comes to that, is having the kind of character that is defined by his "cost-orderings." Those preferences themselves are the grounds of his culpability, and he will be sentenced to imprisonment or worse, in effect, for being the kind of person who has that kind of preference hierarchy, even though, given that he *is* that kind of person, he was in an intelligible sense, *coerced*. If there is a sense in which one cannot act otherwise when one acts in response to coercion, then in that sense, the Kantian dictum that "ought implies can" fails in this case.

6. Moralistic theories of coercion

In what sense is coercion a "mere psychological concept"? Insofar as our analysis is entirely in terms of the coercee's own subjective preferences and desires, themselves analyzable in terms of psychological states and dispositions, coercion seems to be a psychological concept. But the preferences themselves produce judgments of comparative worth or "unwelcomeness," which can be assessed objectively as reasonable or unreasonable, correct or incorrect. When these judgments are made in self-justification they have the appearance of moral judgments, and in the case of our hypothetical B and those of us who resemble him, the findings of unwelcomeness may give due weight to considerations of humanity and justice. Indeed, the betrayal, annihilation, bombing, and torturing of *others* bore the highest price-tags in B's scale of unwelcomeness, partly, no doubt, in virtue of B's altruistic sentiments, partly in virtue of his allegiance to certain moral principles. Moreover, as we have seen, third parties may use moralistic (objective) standards of reasonableness to guide their determinations, in given cases, of whether the coercive pressure imposed by A on B was coercive enough to nullify the voluntariness of B's choice, for some moral or legal purpose. In the example of the betrayed military secrets, a purely psychological account of the concept of coercion would lead us to say that the pressure was great enough (given B's preferences) to be coercion proper but that coercion proper, in the circumstances, was not sufficient to nullify voluntariness. Alternatively, introducing the objective standards into the analysis of coercion itself, we might say that the coercive pressure did not, in the circumstances amount to (exculpating) coercion, since B's preference-rankings which made the coercive effect possible were themselves morally defective. On balance, I think the former account may be the plainer of the two, and the least likely to mislead, although from the moral point of view they both lead to the same result: B's betrayal of the soldiers was voluntary enough for his conviction, even though, on the preferred account, it was produced by coercion. (In the alternative account, the coercive pressure did not amount to coercion proper, because of B's morally defective preferences, and for *that* reason, it did not nullify voluntariness.)

Even if coercion then is understood in the sense explained as a "psychological concept," it is related, both internally and externally, to moral and other evaluative considerations in a fashion that is so intimate, that it may be pointless to take very seriously the distinction between moral and psychological as applied to analyses of coercion. And even if our analysis is psychological in the sense explained, we need not be led by it to confuse coercive and psychologically *compulsive* pressure. When there is coercive pressure the coercee always has a choice, and even coercion proper "forces" (without necessitating) a choice which the coercee would not avoid without changing his values and revising his preferences, but which can nevertheless be subject to moral criticism as stemming from mistaken values or distorted preferences. In contrast, when one's psyche "cracks" or "breaks" under compulsive pressure, one is subject at most to the criticism that one is weak, but if the subject did everything he could to resist before being overwhelmed by sensations, emotions, or shock beyond the control of his will, he can hardly be subject to moral criticism for his behavior. Coercion then, even though it is a "psychological" notion, is of far greater moral interest than psychological compulsion.

The distinction between psychological and moralistic theories of coercion is raised (though not in those terms) by J. G. Murphy whose own analysis is "moralistic" in a sense stronger then any we have considered. His analysis makes coercion out to be an essentially moral concept in the sense that (in the words of David Zimmerman) "its conditions of application contain an ineliminable reference to moral rightness or wrongness."[8] Murphy assumes yet another context for judgments of voluntariness. He is not concerned, as we are, with the problem of soft paternalism—justifying protective interference with the harmful agreements coerced parties sometimes make with their coercers—nor is he primarily concerned with judgments of moral or criminal responsibility made about the conduct of individuals that is wrong or harmful to others. Rather his interest, in the article in question, is directed at the ancient problem of political *obligation*, and particularly at efforts like those of John Locke to ground political obligation in the voluntary consent of citizens to the authority of their rulers. Consent in these theories explains the continuing obligation of B to A when B has accepted A's authority over him. If that consent is not given freely, of course, it is not valid, and thus fails to support a continuing obligation of obedience. David Hume had argued that in modern nations that consent is not freely given since citizens have no real choice but to continue living in the land of their birth. Since obligation is accepted then only as the lesser of the evils in a forced choice, its acceptance is forced by coercion, and cannot be morally valid.[9]

Murphy begins his criticism of Hume by presenting a straightforwardly moralistic *definition* of coercion, extracted from one paradigm instance, the gunman model: "In the paradigm duress situation (*Gunman:* 'Give me your money or I will blow your brains out'), an agreement or promise or act of consent is extracted from a person B because another person A threatens to do to B *that which A has no right to do*."[10] Murphy thus restricts coercion to the acts of persons, and more narrowly to acts which consist of making threats, and more narrowly still to acts which are wrongful—threatening to do what the coercer has no right to do. He goes on to make it clear that even when the threat is to do something that the coercer does have a right to do, the threat to do it is coercive if it is a threat that he has no right, in the circumstances, to make. Moreover, the whole proposal might be coercive even if the threat component, considered by itself, is not wrongful, provided the demand component, considered by itself, is wrongful. The boss who tells his secretary, "Sleep with me or you're fired," does make a coercive proposal, because he has no right to demand that from her, but if he says, "Come to work on time or you're fired," his statement is not coercive.[11] This analysis does justice then not only to the paradigm gunman case, but to a wider range of examples as well. There are various other examples of coercion, however, that do not appear to fit the pattern very well.

Consider first, examples of threats that are *prima facie* no less coercive for threatening to do what the coercer has a perfect right to do if he chooses. These are examples of threats with morally permissible *content*, apart from the question of whether the coercer has a moral right to perform the act of making the threat. A teacher warns a child not to repeat his bad conduct "or else I will tell your mother"; a judge warns the parolee that if he is convicted again, "I will impose the maximum sentence on you, without mercy"; a creditor threatens his debtor to sue if he does not pay up immediately. In all these cases credible threats are made, coercive pressure is applied, and what is threatened is something the coercer has a right to do if he chooses. Whether the coercer had the moral right to perform the act that consisted of making the threat then and there, depends of course on the circumstances, but there must surely be *some* circumstances in which such threats are justified. The policeman's act of threatening the holed-up fugitive whose building is surrounded by armed police, "Come out with your hands up or we will open fire," utters a coercive threat to do what he has a right to do, and in the appropriate circumstances the act of making such a threat would be morally permissible.[12] And the state's threat in general to inflict "sanctions" on those who violate criminal laws is commonly called "legal coercion" by persons who do not wish to deny the propriety or the deterrent effect of legal punishment.

A weaker version than Murphy's of a moralistic account of coercion would survive these counterexamples, namely a theory that concedes as a conceptual point that coercion can employ threats to do what the coercer has a right to do anyway (though this is not typical), and also concedes as a moral point that the making of coercive threats is often justified on balance, but insists that coercion is *prima facie* wrong because it restricts another person's liberty, so that it always needs justification as a kind of necessary evil. Even criminal statutes, since they make coercive threats, stand as a class in need of moral justification according to most philosophers who have taken "the problem of punishment" seriously. But classifying coercion as *prima facie* wrong is to make a moral judgment about the practice of coercion, not to offer a moralistic analysis of the concept of coercion. And in any case the justification that coercion is said always to need is often enough forthcoming.

7. Coercive proposals: offers and threats

The most obvious cases of coercion, as we have seen, involve the making of threats, but are there some coercive proposals (to use a generic term) that coerce by means of attractive offers rather than unwelcome threats? Learned writers disagree over this question,[13] so we must approach it with caution. The controversy has tended to rest on the interpretation of certain (by now) standard examples of purportedly coercive offers. Those who reject the examples either admit that they are coercive but deny that they are offers, or else admit that they are offers but deny that they are coercive. Resolution of the issue, then, requires both examining the distinction between offers and threats (this section) and further refining the distinction between coercive and noncoercive proposals (Chap. 24).

There is a familiar polarity in the distinction between offers and threats that masks its underlying complexity. An offer, we might well expect, is a proposal to confer a good, or a benefit, or at least something welcomed or desired, whereas a threat is a proposal to inflict an evil, a harm, or at least something unwelcome or unwanted. Actually, coercion relates directly to our desires and preferences rather than our interests or needs. Although there is great overlap between what most people want and what they think is good for them (what they need, or what is in their interest), it is also true, however uncommon, that people on some occasions desire things other than their own good, even things that are personally harmful. Offers and threats then had better be analyzed in terms of desires and preferences, rather than interests. An offer is a proposal to contribute to a person something he wants or finds welcome, something he would prefer having to not having.[14] A threat, on the other hand, is a proposal to inflict on a person[15] something he wants not to have, whose existence he finds unwelcome, something he would prefer not having to having. A logically possible third category consisting of proposals greeted with perfect indifference we shall simply not be concerned with, as we confine our attention here to *preference-affecting proposals*, the genus of which offers and threats are the two species.

Threats and offers, however, are more than simple "proposals"; they always involve a *reciprocation condition*, the "demand" in the case of threats, and the "request" in the case of offers, or more generally, the *quid pro quo*—"what is in it for the proposer"—language that covers both threats and offers. One kind of preference-affecting proposal then is a demand backed up by a threat; the other is a request backed up by an inducement (offer). The relation between demand and threat and between request and offer expressed by the ambiguous phrase "backed up" is that of conditionality, which in turn can be necessary condition, sufficient condition, or both. We can think of the preference-affecting proposals as typically biconditionals; the action that A requests or demands from B is said or implied to be both a sufficient and a necessary condition of A's reciprocation. "I will do X to (or for) you *if and only if* you will do Y for me." Thus two conditionals are asserted—

1. If you do Y, then I will do X, and
2. If you do not do Y, then I will not do X.

A's offer of \$1,000 for B's car thus translates—

1. If you give me your car, I will give you \$1,000, and
2. If you do not give me your car, I will not give you \$1,000.

   In other cases the proposal is more complex, involving the conjunction of biconditional proposals. We can call these "double biconditionals." Robert Nozick provides an example: "If you go to the movies, I'll give you \$10,000; it you don't go, I'll kill you."[16] This translates as—

1. If you go to the movies, I will give you \$10,000, and
2. If you do not go to the movies, I will not give you \$10,000, and
3. If you go to the movies, I will not kill you, and
4. If you do not go to the movies, I will kill you.

Double biconditional proposals of this complex sort are always mixtures of inducements (e.g. promises of benefit) and intimidation (e.g. threats of harm). They are at once, therefore, offers and threats.

   Our problem is that at first sight even many of the simpler biconditionals, insofar as they are *bi*conditional, seem also to have both threatening and nonthreatening components. Even the clearest example of a threat, insofar as it is biconditional, seems less than pure: A makes a threat to B by proposing to harm him if and only if B fails to satisfy some condition. Thus "Give me your money or else I will shoot you" translates—

1. If you don't give me your money, I will shoot you (threat), and
2. If you do give me your money, I will not shoot you (non-threat).

The corresponding clear example of an offer is also less than pure: A makes an offer to B by proposing to benefit him if and only if B will satisfy some specified condition. Thus "Clean up your room," (said by a parent to a child), "and I will give you \$5," translates—

1. If you clean up your room, I will give you \$5 (offer) and
2. If you do not clean up your room, I will not give you \$5 (non-offer).

Tentatively, then, we can say that insofar as a biconditional preference-affecting proposal consists of one statement that is a threat, and one that is neither threat nor offer (as in the gunman example), then it is a threat overall, and insofar as a biconditional preference-affecting proposal consists of one statement that is an offer, and one that is neither an offer nor a threat (like the room-cleaning example), then it counts as an offer overall. But now we must inquire whether genuinely mixed cases (other than the double biconditionals) are possible, and if so, how they are to be classified.

Consider first other threats to kill that are more puzzling than the standard gunman example. Suppose a Hobbesian conqueror says to a captured enemy soldier after a war of conquest: "I will spare your life and give you your freedom if you swear your lifetime allegiance to me as your sovereign." Put biconditionally, this proposal translates—

1. If you do not promise to obey me, I will kill you (threat), and
2. If you do promise to obey me, I will not kill you (non-threat).

At first sight (1) is a threat, a conditional proposal of an unwelcome result, and equally clearly (2) is not a threat. So far the resemblance to the gunman case holds. But could (2) in the circumstances be not simply a non-threat but also a positive *offer*? If so, we seem to have a genuinely mixed case. Given certain assumptions about "the normal course of events" (the assumptions Hobbes in fact made and defended),[17] that interpretation is at first sight plausible. On these assumptions the proposal amounts to saying something of the form—"if you do not do *X*, then I will do *what would be done anyway in the normally expected and* (as Hobbes believed) *morally permitted course of events,* namely kill you, but if you do *X* I will depart from the norm and permit you to live—a benefit you could neither have anticipated nor demanded." In that case (2) is an offer of something welcome that would not otherwise, in the normal course of events, be possible. But if the Hobbesian interpretation makes (2) into an offer, by the same token it renders (1) into a non-threat, since the unwelcome result projected by (1) is what the soldier had coming anyway. To "threaten" a person who is about to die with death is about as pointless as inviting an already seated person to sit down.

Similar interpretations can be given of a governor's proposal to a prisoner on death row that his sentence be commuted if and only if he agrees to be a subject in a medical experiment. This translates as—

1. If you do not agree to be an experimental subject, I will have you executed, and
2. If you do agree, I will commute your sentence.

The very reasons we might give for classifying (2) as an offer also require that (1) not be classified as a threat. If these illustrations are typical, then apparent examples of single biconditional preference-affecting proposals that are mixed cases of threat and offer do not stand up to examination.

We get the same result by trying to reinterpret apparent examples of pure offers conjoined with mere non-offers, like that of the child's room-cleaning.

Suppose the parent had *promised* the child $5, and the child had relied on the promise, expected the money, and very much coveted it. Then (2)—"if you do not clean up your room, I will not give your $5 (after all)"—is more than a mere non-offer; it becomes a positive threat. But by the same token (1)—"if you clean up your room I will give you $5"—is no longer a genuine offer since the welcome consequence it projects is simply what the child had coming anyway, in the normal, indeed the morally required, course of events. We can conclude then that a biconditional preference-affecting proposal is a threat overall when one of its component conditionals is a pure threat on its own, linking an unwelcome consequence to a demand, and the other component conditional is neither a threat nor an offer. Similarly, such a proposal is an offer overall when one of its component conditionals is a pure offer on its own, linking a preferred consequence to a request, and the other component conditional is neither an offer nor a threat. A proposal one half of which is a threat and the other half "no offer–no threat" is a whole threat on balance, whereas one consisting of one half offer and the other half "no threat–no offer" is a whole offer on balance. There appears to be no genuinely mixed third category.

8. Norms of expectability

There are still a large number of component conditionals, however, whose classification as offer or threat remains uncertain and controversial. The reason for this has to do with the variety of ways in which we can interpret "the normal course of events." Both threats and offers, in their own quite opposite ways, are projected departures from the normal, and yet what is normal can be determined by various alternative standards, some tailored closely to the actual circumstances that obtained, others more hypothetical; some moral, some nonmoral. (Other writers speak equivalently of measuring deviations from alternative "benchmarks" or "baselines.") Threats are projected consequences which are unwelcome compared to the consequences that would have resulted "otherwise," or "in the normal course of events," or "what might normally have been expected," whereas offers are projected consequences which are welcome when seen against that same background or measured from that same baseline. What generates controversy and confusion is that there are as many as four different interpretations of the normalcy standard.[18] We can use (1) the *"talis qualis* test" and compare the proposer's projected consequence to a norm consisting of the exact circumstances that obtained with the projected act substracted, or (2) a richer hypothetical test (or "statistical standard"), comparing the projected consequence to a statistically normal set of circumstances with the entire episode subtracted, or (3) a moral test, comparing the projected consequence to a morally proper or morally required state of affairs, or finally (4) the more complex "Zimmer-man test," suggested in a recent article by David Zimmerman.[19] Examples below will illustrate the four interpretations, their strengths or weaknesses.

1. (From R. Nozick[20]) *B*'s boat has capsized and he has been swimming for hours near the center of a large and seldom frequented lake. He is nearing exhaustion when *A*'s boat approaches. *A* says to *B:* "You may climb into my boat and avoid drowning if and only if you promise now to pay me $10,000 within three days." Rendered biconditionally—

1. If you promise to pay $10,000 within three days, I will rescue you, and
2. If you do not promise to pay $10,000 within three days, I will not rescue you.

At first thought, most of us would be inclined to characterize (2) as a threat and (1) a "no threat–no offer," but whether or not this judgment is correct depends on the background or baseline of normal expectability we measure the projected consequence (drowning) against. Suppose we ask whether *B* would be worse off (in terms of his own preferences) if the projected conse-quence (drowning) occured than he would be in the normal course of events that could have been expected had *A* never even chanced upon the scene. In that hypothetical event, *B* would almost certainly have drowned, so the projected consequence would *not* make him worse off than he would other-wise be; hence it would not be a more unwelcome consequence, and hence (2) is not a threat. The result of this hypothetical test is so counter-intuitive, however, that we should consider revising the tentative criterion that yielded it.

A second interpretation (number 1 on page 219) of "what could normally be expected" is tailored more closely to the actual circumstances that prevailed. It interprets normal expectability as the conditions that would obtain in the exact same circumstances without the projected consequence (non-rescue). On this leaner hypothetical test we are to ask whether *A*'s omitting to rescue *B* makes *B*'s condition worse than it would have been "otherwise," that is if *A* would not omit to rescue him. It is *not* true that *B* would be equally bad off in either case, for in the "otherwise case" he would be alive, and in the case projected in *A*'s proposal he would be dead. So *A*'s proposal is a threat after all.

Let us call the lean interpretation of the "otherwise condition" the *talis qualis* test, from the Latin phrase, often used in the law, for "exactly as it is." In applying the "otherwise test" *talis qualis* we take the actual circumstances exactly as they are and ask what would happen *in those circumstances* but for *A*'s projected action. The alternative way of interpreting the counter-factual test, the way that yielded a counter-intuitive result in this case, makes it much more hypothetical. Instead of asking what consequences could be ex-pected "otherwise" in the exact circumstances that in fact obtained (subtracting only A's projected conduct toward B), it has us ask what consequences might have been expected "otherwise" in quite different hypothetical circumstances, say in the hypothetical case in which "A had not chanced upon the scene at all." (On this isolated lake not to encounter anyone would have been normal, or "what could have been expected.") In other words, on the more hypothetical test, we are to project a normal course of events subtracting the whole episode involving A. The test that is more closely linked to the actual circumstances takes those circumstances as given and has us consider a normal course of events subtracting only A's projected conduct toward B, given that A is on the scene and would normally remain on the scene whether he acts in his projected way toward B or "otherwise." The latter test seems to yield the preferred result in this case, that A did threaten not to rescue B.

A third test also yields the preferred result in this case. Given that A encountered the drowning B, what further conduct would be *morally expected* (i.e. required) of A? Clearly a rescue, with no conditions, and "no questions asked." Compared with *that* interpretation of what would happen "otherwise, in the normal course of events," the projected consequence of A's proposal in the actual case (drowning) is clearly to make B worse off, and is therefore unwelcome. The proposal, therefore, is a threat.

2. (Also from Nozick[21]) B is a slave of A's. Normally A beats B every morning (a way of starting the day with healthy exercise and discharge of aggression). Today, however, A makes the following proposal to B: "I will not beat you this morning if you do X (some moderately disagreeable task, but preferable to a beating)." His intentions are captured in the following biconditional:

1. If you do X, I will not beat you, and
2. If you do not do X, then I will beat you (as usual).

Not beating B is the alternative A favors since he hopes to get B to do X; that was the whole purpose of his making the proposal in the first place. Beating B then is the projected consequence of that alternative which is unfavored by A. We can refer to it as the PCUA (projected consequence of the unfavored alternative). Now we ask, as in the other examples, whether (2), the conditional containing the PCUA, states a threat, and that of course depends on whether from B's standpoint the PCUA is less welcome than what would happen otherwise. The two non-moral ways of interpreting the "otherwise" test yield different results. The leaner hypothetical (*talis qualis*) test asks an easy question: would the beating-as-usual make B worse off (and therefore be less welcome to B) than he would be were A not to inflict it in this case (everything else the same)? The answer clearly is affirmative. Keep everything the same but subtract the projected beating-as-usual, and the result in

that "normal course of events" would be beneficial, hence presumably welcome, and *A*'s PCUA would also be unwelcome to *B*. Thus (2) is a threat.

The richer hypothetical test, on the other hand, yields the opposite result.
It might ask whether the PCUA, the beating-as-usual, would be more unwelcome than that which would occur in the hypothetical circumstances in
which this morning proceeds in the usual way, which of course includes a
beating, so the answer clearly is negative. Since the PCUA would not make
B worse off than he would be "otherwise" (intepreting "otherwise" in this
way), (2) is not a threat. In this example, common sense seems to agree with
the richer hypothetical test. When *A* says to *B*, "Do as I say or I will treat
you as I usually do," he is not making a threat to *B*. In fact conditional (1),
since it projects the prospect of a welcome departure from the usual routine,
is a pure offer. That too seems to accord with common sense, since what *A*
holds out to *B* must seem, from *B*'s standpoint, a carrot, not a (new) stick.

The test of moral expectability in this example yields a result that corresponds with the *talis qualis* test. It was Nozick who first gave emphasis to the
distinction between the normally expected course of events (interpreted in
the richer hypothetical way) and the morally expected (required) course of
events, and he used the slave example to show how the statistical (richly
hypothetical) and moral standards can diverge. Beating the slave, as we have
seen, would not make him worse off than he would be in the statistically
normal and expected course of events (in which he is beaten anyway), so the
master's proposal is not a threat but an offer. On the other hand, in the
morally required course of events the slave would not be routinely beaten.
Hence this PCUA is a departure from *that* norm which would make the slave
worse off than he would be "otherwise," that is *if the moral norm were followed*.
Thus the proposal *does* contain a threat. If we were justified in attributing to
common sense the "offer" verdict, then the moral criterion applied to this
example is counterintuitive.

3. (From Daniel Lyons[22]) A lecherous banker (*A*) says to the impoverished
maiden (*B*) who owes him mortgage payments: "Sleep with me or I will
foreclose the mortgage and turn you out into the streets." Expressed biconditionally, the full proposal is as follows:

1. If you sleep with me, I will not foreclose.
2. If you do not sleep with me, I will foreclose.

Under normal circumstances this might appear, at first sight, to be a threat
designed to force the maiden to do what she might find utterly repugnant.
But that judgment could be too hasty. Once more the two non-moral tests of
expectability yield divergent verdicts. The PCUA is foreclosure of the mortgage which we can imagine will make *B* substantially worse off than she

would be (a) "otherwise" (if only that consequence were subtracted from the circumstances that actually obtained *talis qualis*), but *not* worse off than she would be (b) in the hypothetical "circumstances that might normally have been expected" from which the whole episode, or some larger stretch of it, is subtracted. (Hypothetical (b) might plausibly refer to the circumstances in which the woman's mortgage is unpaid and the bank's usual procedures are followed with no salacious proposition ever made by anyone. Imagine for example that the unscrupulous lecher is not on the scene at all, or that he doesn't even exist, and that a more usual or "expectable" sort of banker is handling the case.)

Thus the banker's proposal is a threat if we use the *talis qualis* test, but not if we use the richer hypothetical test. By the latter test we can judge that the banker is offering the woman a "benefit," that is, an exemption from the harm that would normally be expected to follow from default of payment, much like an offer of clemency to a prisoner on condition that he "volunteers" to be the subject in a medical experiment. This is the result, I think , that accords best with common sense. (This may be a case, however, where we shall want to say that a mere offer can be coercive. But more about that in Chap. 24.)

The moral criterion applied to this case also supports the common sense judgment. In the morally required course of events, *B* would not suffer the attentions, much less the proposals, of any lecherous bankers. Being unable to make her mortgage payments, she would suffer foreclosure straightaway. That hypothetical consequence would be no worse, in fact exactly the same as the PCUA. Since the PCUA would not be more unwelcome than the consequence expectable in the morally normal course of events, the conditional statement of which it is a part is not a threat. Conditional statement (1), on the other hand, projects a consequence (the PCFA—not foreclosing) that is more welcome than what would otherwise happen in the morally required course of events. It therefore is an offer.

The three criteria of normal expectability applied so far to our test examples do not yield any clear or satisfactory result. The pre-analytic common-sense judgment in example (1) (the drowning swimmer) is that the proposal is a threat, the verdict reached by the *talis qualis* and moral criteria, but not by the statistical standard. The common-sense judgment in example (2) (the slave case) is that the proposal is an offer, a verdict supported this time by the richer hypothetical test but *not* by the other two. In the third example (the lecherous banker), common sense seems to characterize the proposal as an offer, a verdict supported by the richer hypothetical and moral criteria, but not by the *talis qualis* test. These divergences are so striking that they suggest that none of these three criteria are correct, and that when one of them is right in a given case, it is so accidentally, rather than necessarily.

For that reason, it is with hope that we turn to the criterion proposed recently by David Zimmerman.

On Zimmerman's view, the relevant object of the addressee's preference is the "move into the proposal situation," not simply the projected consequences of the proposals themselves. A proposal to B is an offer, he writes, "only if B prefers moving from the 'pre-proposal situation' to the 'proposal situation'; it is a threat if B strongly prefers not making this move."[23] The standard gunman example shows the plausibility of the Zimmerman test. "Not being suicidally inclined, the highwayman's victim . . . does have an overriding desire to hand over his money once he is in the threat situation. What he does not want to face is a disjunctive choice between his money and his life at all."[24] So far so good, but if I understand the Zimmerman criterion correctly it does less well on the drowning swimmer example since it implies that the proposal is an offer, because B in this case would prefer having a choice—any choice—to being alone and exhausted with no alternative to drowning. That is the result we have (with some diffidence) found opposed to common sense. If it is a mistake, it is one the Zimmerman criterion shares with the statistical test. But the Zimmerman test does better in the other two examples. "The slave does in fact prefer to move from the pre-proposal situation in which he is beaten every day to the proposal situation in which he is spared the customary beating for performing the disagreeable task, so let us concede . . . that the slave-owner is making a genuine offer."[25] That judgment seems to accord with common sense since one cannot "threaten" someone with a consequence that was bound to occur anyway. Similarly, the impoverished woman, whatever her final decision, would prefer being in the proposal situation (though perhaps not by much) to her prior position of complete hopelessness. She is unlike the gunman's victim who possessed his money and his life *both* in the pre-proposal situation. She possesses her honor but no claim to her property in the pre-proposal situation; she can maintain that *status quo ante* or else have her property but not her honor in the subsequent proposal situation. The additional option, however exercised, must make the proposal *situation* not unwelcome.

In our three examples then, both the Zimmerman criterion and the richly hypothetical test seem correct two times out of three, faltering only on the drowning swimmer case. That suggests that there may be something strange in that example rather than something deficient in the two criteria. The example is difficult because it falls within the range of vagueness of both of the criteria that have trouble with it. The example is useful because it enables us to discover vagueness in the criteria that we might not expect otherwise.

Upon closer examination the statistical criterion is not just *one* "richly

	Paradigm Gunman Case	Nozick Boat Case	Nozick Slave Case	Lyons Lecherous Banker Case
Common Sense Judgment	Threat	Threat	Offer	Offer
Statistical Test (Richly Hypothetical)	Threat	Offer	Offer	Offer
Talis Qualis Test	Threat	Threat	Threat	Threat
Moral Propriety Test	Threat	Threat	Threat	Offer
Zimmerman Test	Threat	Offer	Offer	Offer

The Statistical Test: Would the PCUA make B worse off than he would be in the statistical course of events? If so, a threat; if not, an offer.

The Talis Qualis Test: Would the PCUA make B worse off than he would be otherwise, everything else being the same? If so, a threat; if not, an offer.

The Moral Propriety Test: Would the PCUA make B worse off than he would be in the morally required (proper) course of events? If so, a threat; if not, an offer.

The Zimmerman Test: Would B prefer moving from the pre-proposal situation into the proposal situation? If so, an offer; if not, a threat.

Diagram 23–4. Tests for distinguishing threats from offers.

hypothetical test," but a whole range of richer hypothetical tests. In the drowning swimmer case, for example, we can compare A's PCUA:

1. what would happen if the circumstances were the same but the proposal were not made at all (the *talis qualis* test), or (more hypothetically)
2. what would happen if A's boat had not appeared on the scene at all (the statistical probability was that no further opportunity for rescue would have occurred)

Or, comparisons could be made to the results of certain generalizations not tailored specifically to the circumstances of this case:

3. what generally happens when one is afloat without support in the middle of this lake, or
4. what generally happens when one is afloat in the middle of (any) lake (or any large lake, or any remote lake, etc.), or
5. what generally happens when a drowning swimmer encounters a boat

whose occupants have the ability to rescue him (what the swimmer has an "epistemic right" to expect), or

6. what generally happens when a drowning swimmer encounters a boat whose occupants have the ability to rescue him *and* everyone involved does what is morally right (what the swimmer has a moral right to expect)

We have been assuming that the relevant statistical test is number (2), and that the judgment yielded by that test is that the proposal of the boatman is an offer. If that assumption were correct, then we would be tempted to find support in the *talis qualis* test (number 1) for the common-sense judgment that the proposal is a *threat not to rescue*, or in the moral criterion, number (6). Both of these, however, yield counter-intuitive results in other hypothetical examples. The test that now seems clearly to be presupposed by the common-sense judgment of threat, however, is number (5)—an appeal to what generally happens in cases similar to this one in all relevant details. And that is an appeal to what the person addressed by the proposal has a right to expect based on his experience and general practice. If the general practice were like that in the Hobbesian conquest, and rescuers assumed the same privileges as Hobbesian conquerors, to murder, ravage, pillage, or loot, then the swimmer, expecting the worst, could be grateful for the boatsman's *offer* to spare him. But given the practices that prevail in our community, the PCUA in the boatsman's proposal would be a shockingly unwelcome deviation from the normal expectation, so that the disappointed swimmer would rightly take it as a *threat to let him drown.*[26]

The appropriate statistical test in this case yields the same result as the moral criterion, number (6), but that is simply a coincidence. It just happens that the general practice rightly expected by the swimmer in our example is the morally required practice. If the facts were otherwise, and boatsmen on large bodies of water were generally (and correctly) expected to be pirates, then the general practice and the morally required practice would not coincide, and when A proposes to exempt B from his "inevitable" though "immoral" fate, he is like the Hobbesian conqueror offering reprieve. Application of the appropriate statistical test would produce the judgement that A makes an offer, whereas the moral criterion would yield the judgment that the proposal is a threat.

The drowning swimmer example also brings out the vagueness of the Zimmerman criterion. What exactly are the boundaries between the "pre-proposal" and "proposal" situations? Suppose we ask Zimmerman's question to B at the moment A's boat comes into view in the distance. Does B prefer at that moment to go into the proposal situation or does he prefer to see the boat turn and vanish? Clearly from *this* position in the pre-proposal situation B has a strong preference to enter the proposal situation; thus on Zimmerman's test,

A's proposal is an offer, a result that conflicts with common sense. On the other hand, the Zimmerman question could be posed at a different point in the pre-proposal situation. Suppose that at the very moment the boat hauls within shouting range of *B*, and just before *A* begins to speak, when *A*'s capacity and opportunity to rescue *B* are manifest, at just that moment the question is posed to *B*. Does he prefer to go into the proposal situation, and thus have a new complication introduced into his affairs at just the point when optimistic expectations have returned, or does he prefer to remain in non-proposal situation in which the expected events naturally take their course? Clearly he prefers not to enter any proposal situation when his alternative in the pre-proposal situation is expected to be unconditionally advantageous. In that case, on that interpretation of the Zimmerman test, the proposal is a threat, and common sense is vindicated. The Zimmerman test, so interpreted, however, seems to presuppose the appropriately formulated statistical test, since it includes *B*'s normal expectations as part of the characterization of the preproposal situation. For that reason, the Zimmerman test is an application of, and not a genuine alternative to, the statistical test.

In summary, the genus of which threats and offers are the two exclusive and exhaustive species is the single biconditional preference-affecting proposal made by *A* to *B*. The proposal is made by *A* to induce or force *B* to do something *A* wants. That part of the proposal which puts a condition on *B*'s doing the thing *A* wants ("If you do *X* then I will do *Y*"), projects a consequence of *A*'s favored alternative (a PCFA). If *B* judges that PCFA to be a welcome deviation from what he could normally expect, then that part of the proposal is an *offer*, and the other part of the proposal, which states the consequence of *B*'s noncompliance, is a "no threat–no offer". That part of a proposal which puts a condition on doing the thing *A* does not want ("If you do not do *X* then I will not do *Y*") projects a consequence of *A*'s unfavored alternative (a PCUA). If *B* judges that PCUA to be an unwelcome deviation from what he could normally expect, then that part of the proposal is a *threat*, and the other part of the proposal, which states the consequences of *B*'s compliance, is a "no threat–no offer."

The crucially vague part of the definition is the phrase "what he could normally expect." We have seen that there are numerous ways of interpreting normal expectability. The *talis qualis* test sometimes yields results that accord with common sense, but more often does not. In the distinctively difficult problem cases like the three examples we considered, it will always yield the judgment that the proposal is a threat. The moral criterion will accord more often with our pre-analytic judgments, but it fails where prevailing and expectable practice is immoral. Where it works, its success derives from the coincidence of prevailing practice with the morally required course of events. The correct criterion of normal expectation is a statistical test, more richly hypothetical than the *talis qualis* test, and independent of the moral standards employed in the moral requiredness test. Very often the appropriate hypothetical test will apply a statistical generalization, as in our boat example, about general practice in situations of the kind in question, from which is then derived the reasonable expectation that we can attribute to B as his pre-supposed baseline in the proposal situation.

We have seen that all credible threats enforcing unwelcome demands are coercive, but do all "coercive proposals" contain threats? That depends on whether offers can themselves, in some contexts, be coercive, a question to which we turn in the next chapter.

24

Failures of Consent:
Coercive Offers

1. Coercive and noncoercive offers

We have now looked at four *prima facie* examples of coercive offers: the governor's offer to commute the prisoner's death sentence if he will "volunteer" for a dangerous medical experiment, the Hobbesian conqueror's offer not to kill the captured prisoner on condition that he swear his fealty, Nozick's slave who is offered respite from his daily beating if he performs some unpleasant task, and Lyons's offer from the lecherous banker to the woman in default of her mortgage payments. The examples, we have now decided, are definitely offers because the projected consequence of that alternative of *B*'s which is favored by *A* (the PCFA) is from *B*'s standpoint a welcome departure from what *B*, on the basis of relevant statistical generalizations, could have expected in the normal course of events. They appear at first sight also to be coercive, since they seem likely to be effective in forcing *B* to opt for the alternative that *A* wants him/her to select. But for the moment we shall leave that question open and consider one final dramatic example.

Suppose opportunistic *A* holds out to unfortunate *B* the prospect of rescue or cure—but for a price. *B* is in an otherwise hopeless condition from which *A* can rescue her if she gives him what he wants. He will pay for the expensive surgery that alone can save her child's life provided that she becomes for a period his mistress. *A* thus uses his superior advantages to manipulate *B*'s options so that she has no more choice than she would have if a gunman pointed his pistol at her healthy child's head, and threatened to shoot unless she agreed to become *his* mistress. The difference between the two cases, of course, is that the lecherous millionaire makes no unlawful *threat*. If B declines his proposal her child will die, but that will no more be A's doing that it would be the doing of any other person who was rich enough to pay but in fact did not; whereas if B declines the gunman's proposal in the other example, the gunman will commit murder. That is the difference between the two cases that has led many writers to refer to proposals like that of the lecherous millionaire as "coercive offers." They appear to be coercive in that they rearrange a person's options in such a way that he "has no choice" but to comply or else suffer an unacceptable consequence. They are offers because the proposer does not threaten any harm beyond what would happen anyway without his gratuitous intervention.

The gunman's coercive threat would invalidate the woman's "consent" to his intimacies, thus at once depriving him of a defense to criminal rape charges and exempting a third party from liability for a forceful intervention. The millionaire's "coercive offer," on the other hand, would not invalidate the unfortunate woman's consent to *his* advances; he could use that consent as a defense; and he would be subject to no rightful interference from third parties. Yet, from the woman's standpoint, the millionaire's terms were as irresistible as the gunman's would have been and every bit as repugnant. In either case the option seen from her point of view is: "Sleep with me or your child dies."

The case against characterizing the millionaire's offer as *coercive* is simple enough. It is misleading, some have claimed, to label as "coercion" a proposal whose effect is to create a net *increase* in a person's open options, giving him or her a choice not previously possible. Surely the woman in our example has one new alternative after receiving the proposal that she did not have before, so in a sense her *freedom on balance* has been increased. Since coercion is understood, at least before analysis, as something that *decreases* freedom, offers like those in our examples cannot be coercive, according to this argument.

Our fruitful railroad metaphor (see Vol. I, Chap. 5, §7) can be used once again to illustrate the effect on B's freedom of A's putative "coercive offer" (Diagram 24-1). The railroad maze indicates how, with respect to her child, B has no eligible choice but to suffer its death. Positioned as she is on the track network, the only track open to her is one that leads to a dead end. The switch on the main line is locked shut to entry, as is the switch on a branch to the left. Diagram 24-2 shows how A's offer enlarges her freedom. In making his offer, the millionaire A has built a new section of track—the line in the lower right corner that leads directly to Y with a short connecting link to X. In so doing he has enlarged B's range of choices: she can go everywhere she could go in Diagram 24-1, with none of the old options closed, but now in addition she can do one new thing she could not do in Diagram 24-1, namely avoid X (at the cost of proceeding to Y instead). Since she can do everything in Diagram 24-2 that she could do in Diagram 24-1, but not vice versa, she is clearly freer on balance after the offer than before.

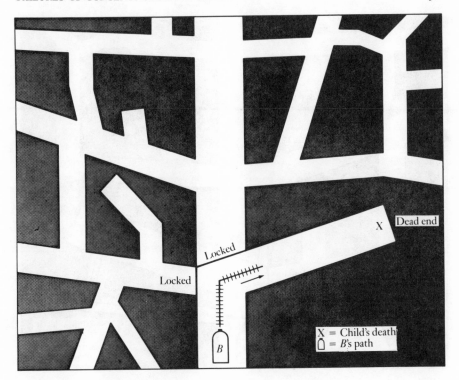

Diagram 24-1. Before A's offer.

And yet the fact remains: A has forced B to go to Y, not by compelling or necessitating that choice, but rather in the manner more characteristic of coercion—by rendering the only alternatives to the PCFA too costly to be eligibile for B's choice. We seem to have a genuine conceptual dilemma here. How can we resolve the paradox? One way (among others) is to attempt to have it both ways after all, and suggest that an offer can be coercive (in respect to a particular consequence), yet freedom-enhancing on balance too. This compatibilist solution may resolve the conceptual muddle but it very quickly introduces another puzzle: what effect does the coerciveness of a freedom-enhancing offer have on the voluntariness of the consent it produces? Under what conditions, if any, is such consent invalid for a given legal purpose (in particular for the purpose of implementing the soft-paternalist strategy)?

A second possible resolution of the paradox of coercive offers is to rely heavily on the distinction between coercion, understood as necessarily *restricting* freedom, and the *exploitation* inherent in our putative "coercive offers," which on this view need not be coercive at all. We can call this second approach to the riddle, the "Zimmerman solution," since David Zimmerman is the recent writer who has given it clearest expression.[1] The Zimmerman solu-

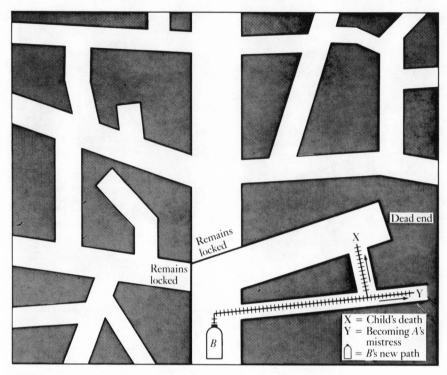

Diagram 24-2. After *A*'s "coercive offer."

tion raises its own puzzles: what effect does the exploitativeness of a noncoercive offer have on the voluntariness of the consent it produces? Under what conditions, if any, is such consent invalid for a given legal purpose (in particular for the purpose of implementing the soft-paternalist strategy) even though it is in this view uncoerced, hence free?

Consider first what can be said for the compatibilist solution. The proposal of the lecherous millionaire is an offer because it does not threaten harm beyond what would be expected anyway. Moreover, his offer appears to come very close to satisfying our preliminary definition of second-party coercion (*supra*, Chap. 23, §2). *B* complies with *A*'s "demand" in order to avoid the PCUA, having accepted credible evidence from *A* of his ability and willingness to allow the PCUA to occur. There is some question whether *A* has "actively intervened in *B*'s option network" (condition 4 of the definition). The interventions of coercive *threateners* like the paradigm gunman are typically much more active and manipulative. We shall return to this point in §4, but it suffices now to remind the reader of the manner in which the lecherous millionaire did intervene. He did not himself produce the child's possibly fatal ailment, nor did he cause the price of the remedial surgery to be so high. But he did alter B's options in a sufficiently manipulative way to warrant our use of the metaphor of new track construction. His role was not entirely passive. It cannot be far off the mark then to call his proposal both an offer and coercive.

Finally, it must be conceded that this offer (and others relevantly similar to it) enlarges B's freedom by opening an otherwise closed option. Hence, it is a *freedom-enhancing coercive offer*. Why should that description be paradoxical? It is a coherent description simply because it is a fact that one person can effectively force another person to do what he wants by manipulating his options in such a way as to render alternative choices ineligible and, in so doing, quite incidentally enlarge his freedom in general. This fact of life seems paradoxical only when there is uncritical acceptance of the dogma that coercion *must* have the immediate effect of restricting freedom on balance. A's purpose is to force B to do what A wants, so when thought of as an instrument for achieving A's goals, his offer is an exercise of coercion. From B's standpoint, as we have seen, her only choice is a coerced one—sleep with me or your child dies—so there is a real point in characterizing A's offer as coercive. She must now do as he wishes. Yet there is also a point in B's welcoming an option she did not have before. Hence from B's standpoint, the description "freedom-enhancing coercive offer" is entirely felicitious in having this double point, and it is a small price to pay for this felicity to jettison the dogma that enlarged freedom and specific coercion cannot coexist.

2. *Noncoercive enticements*

The major apparent difficulty for the compatibilist solution is that it must now explain how effective offers can ever be *noncoercive*. What reason is there for calling the lecherous millionaire's offer (or the Hobbesian conqueror's, the governor's, the slave-master's, etc.) coercive, but not (say) the job offer of one company to an employee of another? Suppose A in Houston offers B in New York a job at $2,000 more than his present salary. B is attracted to the higher salary, the greater challenge of the work, and the better prospects of promotion, but he prefers the retirement plan of his present employer, and is reluctant to leave his friends and relatives in New York. A increases the offer by another $1,000, and that makes the difference. His offer is one that B "can no longer resist." He accepts it because the greater salary and other benefits of the Houston job now seem to outweigh in his deliberations the disadvantages of leaving the New York job. But he has been lured by inducements, not frightened by dangers, pulled rather than pushed. His was a choice of the greater good, not the lesser evil.[2] If ever there was an example of a noncoercive offer it is this one.

Yet couldn't one argue in the manner of the compatibilist that B was coerced in this case too? How does this example differ from that of the lecherous millionaire? Both offers were biconditionals of the form—

1. If you do X, I will do Y, and
2. If you do not do X, I will not do Y.

In both cases, B does X because the advantages of getting Y seem to outweigh the disadvantages of doing X. The difference seems to be partly one of degree. The impecunious mother in the one examle ranks getting Y (saving her child) so high in her scale of preferences that hardly any cost is too high. Not getting Y is to her an unthinkable disaster. The New York employee in the other example also values Y ($3,000 more a year) highly, but it is by no means near the top of his scale of values. Not getting Y would not be a source of deep disappointment, much less as unthinkable disaster. He can live happily without Y if necessary, as indeed he has in the past.

Let us attach make-believe number values to the preferences in the two cases. For the impecunious mother, Y (saving the child's life) is valued at 10,000,000 (gain). On the other hand, the price tag of doing X (becoming A's mistress), while high in itself, is quite low compared to the value of Y, say 10,000 (cost). Her only choice, after A's manipulations, is between Y (worth 10,000,000) and not-X (worth 10,000). Clearly her desires are overwhelmingly on the side of X, and she "has no other choice." The "differential coercive pressure" of the offer is ten million minus ten thousand, or 9,990,000. For the New York employee on the other hand, the choices are closer to being even, and the decision harder. It is as if the price tag on X (giving up his New York job) is 4,500 and the value tag on Y (taking the Houston job) is 5,000. The "differential coercive pressure" of the offer then is a mere 500, such a pittance that we don't count it as "coercive" at all.

There is, however, a more important point to be made. The impecunious mother must choose among evils, and one evil is much worse than the other. The New York employee, on the other hand, chooses among goods, or at least non-evils. If we change the examples so that he is miserably unhappy in his New York job and the Houston offer is the only one he can get, then his situation begins to resemble thaty of the impecunious mother, except that the projected consequence of his offered alternative (the Houston job) is still a positive good and not merely a lesser evil. If we change the example yet again so that his New York job is so odious that it is intolerable, no welfare payments are available to him, and the Houston job, his sole alternative, is itself distasteful and unrewarding though by far the lesser of the evils, then the offer has crossed the threshold of coerciveness. What distinguishes coercive from noncoercive offers then is not only (1) the degree of "differential coercive pressure," that is, the gap between the value tag of what is offered and the price tag of what is required, but also (2) that at least one of the exclusive alternatives is thought to be in itself a very great evil, and not merely a lesser good. It is possible therefore to explain how the great run of offers are noncoercive (and freedom-enhancing) while holding, nevertheless, that there can be some unusual offers that are coercive (and freedom-enhancing). The latter are those that offer a prospect that is not simply much preferred, but one which is an exclusive alternative to an intolerable evil.

The coerciveness of a proposal is thus a function of two variables, (1) the *polarity* (that is the recipient's assessment as "good" or "evil") of the projected consequences of the posed alternatives, and (2) the *proximity* of the alternative projections on the recipient's scale of preferences, how "close" and therefore difficult the choice, or "distant" and therefore unavoidable the choice. Offers are classifiable as coercive in their effect only when they satisfy a requirement of appropriate polarity; typically they force a choice between evils, and perhaps sometimes (although this is doubtful) they may force a choice between an evil and a good. Given satisfaction of the appropriate polarity requirement, the degree of coerciveness then varies with the proximity of the alternative projections: the more distant the more coercive. Choices made under great coercive pressure are in a sense "easier" than those made under less coercive pressure, since the chooser has "less choice" when the gap between his options is great.

It is important to understand that choices that fail to satisfy the polarity requirement, even when they seem to leave the chooser "no choice" because the alternatives are distant on his preference scale, are nevertheless not coercive. I refer to proposals that are (1) clearly offers, (2) force a choice between a desirable *status quo* (a "good") and an even more desirable alternative (a "greater good"), and (3) exert great "coercive pressure" (actually "attractive pressure") in the sense that what is offered is thought by the recipient to be *vastly* more desirable than its quite satisfactory alternative, that is, its value-tag (say 1,000,000) is much greater than the price-tag of losing the lesser good (say 10,000). Because of (3) some people speak loosely of such offers as "coercive," but much more accurate words would be "inducing," "enticing," "alluring," "immensely attractive," "tempting," "seductive," etc. VanDeVeer gives an example and gets the point exactly right. He refers to: ". . . cases of extremely enticing or seductive offers which we are tempted to describe as cases of 'offers one can't refuse', or 'compelling', or 'coercive offers'. For example, it may be difficult for an outstanding college athlete to turn down a several-million-dollar offer to play a professional sport in order to complete his degree. Here we have a noncoercive, enticing offer."[3]

Diagram 24-3 then lists all the possible types of offers generated by our distinctions in which there is forced choice between exclusive alternatives, and classifies them in terms of degrees of coerciveness, if any.

Illustrative pairs of examples follow, with negative numbers attached to

Forced Choices			
	Between Evils	Between an Evil and a Good	Between Goods
Distant ("Easy" Choices)	1. Coercive offers of high differential coercive pressure	3. Impure coercive offers with high coercive pressure	5. Extremely enticing offers, but wholly noncoercive
Close (Difficult Choices)	2. Coercive offers of lower differential coercive pressure	4.Impure coercive offers with low coercive pressure	6. Moderately enticing but noncoercive offers

Diagram 24-3. Effects of variations in proximity and polarity among choices stemming from offers.

alternatives to indicate subjective costs on a scale from −1 to −20. Degrees of "coercive pressure," as determined by each of the four methods distinguished in Chapter 23, are expressed in positive numbers.

1. Forced but "easy" choice (virtually "no choice") between evils
    a. Sleep with me (−10) or I will let your sick child die (−15).
    This translates:
        i. If you sleep with me (−10), I will pay for the surgery that alone can save your child's life.
        ii. If you do not sleep with me, your child will die (−15).
    b. Take the offered Houston job which sounds bad (−10), or continue in the New York job which is intolerable (−15).
    This translates:
        i. If you take the job I offer you in Houston (−10) then you will escape the intolerable unhappiness of your present job in New York.
        ii. If you do not take the job I offer you in Houston, then you will continue to be intolerably unhappy at your job in New York (−15).

Coercive pressure
Differential coercive pressure: 5
Coercive force: 15
Total coercive burden: 25
Coercive minimum: 10 (Cost of the best alternative)

2. Forced and close choice between evils
    a. Sleep with me (−10) or you will get into deep financial trouble (since I won't pay your debts) (−12).

This translates:

i. If you sleep with me (-10) then I will pay your debts which alone can prevent deep financial trouble for you. (The maiden is chaste and/or the speaker is repulsive.)

ii. If you do not sleep with me, then you will be in deep financial trouble (-12).

b. Take the offered Houston job which sounds bad (-10) or continue in the New York job which is even worse (-12).

This translates:

i. If you take the job I offer you in Houston (-10) then you will escape slightly greater unhappiness in your job in New York.

ii. If you do not take the job I offer you in Houston, then you will continue to be unhappy in your job in New York (-12).

Coercive pressure:
Differential coercive pressure: 2
Coercive force: 12
Total coercive burden: 22
Coercive minimum: 10

The second set of examples, like the first, satisfy the polarity rquirement in that they are both forced choices between evils. Moreover, the second set of examples, insofar as they more fully satisfy the proximity standard, are less coercive than the first, at least in the sense that they exhibit less differential coercive pressure. Given the numbers we have assigned, the second examples are also less coercive in respect to coercive force (12 to 15) and total coercive burden (22 to 25) and no more coercive in respect to the coercive minimum (10 to 10).

It should be emphasized here, in connection with offers, as it was in Chapter 23 §4 in connection with threats, that differential coercive pressure measures only the pressue on the chooser to opt one way *rather than the other* among artificially limited options. It is often a misleading and distorting measure of how coercive the proposal is, how much coercion the coercee struggles under on the whole, how coerced his response is as measured against a normal baseline, how coerced it is for the purposes of assessing its voluntariness, and so on. For these latter purposes, total coercive burden (consisting both of compliance costs and threat costs) and coercive minimum (the costs of the best alternative, which is usually the cost of what is proposed or demanded) are the more accurate gauges. Alan Fuchs shows how misleading it can be to use the differential test when other measures are more appropriate.

Consider the following. The impecunious mother . . . goes into a posh men's club to beg for the funds for her child's operation. The first millionaire she encounters, M1, is the knave [who appears in this chapter's examples]. He offers the money on the condition that B (what a lovely name!) become his mistress. Their conversation is overheard, however, by several other millionaires. M2, a slightly more compassionate and somewhat less lecherous blackguard, proposes: "Come to my room and strip for me. I promise not to touch you and will give you the money for your child's operation." [Lower compliance cost, lower total coercive burden, lower coercive minimum.] But just as B is about to give in to this demand or request—it is so much better then M1's—M3 interjects: "Lovely maiden, they are exploiting your tragic situation. I will give you the money if you but give me a kiss, though I realize that you would not ordinarily want to embrace such an old and uncommonly ugly man." "You dirty old men," M4 cries out. "I will help this poor child if she but pours me a snifter of brandy from this decanter. She so reminds me of my daughter, whom I haven't seen in years, that it would be worth it to me to give her the money if she would only tarry a while and serve me a postprandial libation."[4]

Fuchs then points out that even though the coercive pressure as measured by the differential test becomes progressively greater in these examples so that M4's offer is the most coercive of all by that test, in fact the total amount of coercion in the situation becomes less with each example, and "B's acceptance of M4's offer is hardly coerced at all, and for most purposes it would be considered as almost voluntary".[5] That is correct, I believe, because B's coercive burden decreases, and the extent of her loss on the best alternative open to her in M4's offer is very small (a minor boring inconvenience). Nevertheless, as the cost gap between alternatives in a forced choice becomes greater, it becomes harder and harder to resist the proposal, and at some point no reasonable person could be expected to do so. (Fuchs proposes calling this form of influence "rational pressure" rather than "coercive pressure".) If there should happen to be something fishy or suspect about the accepted proposal, so that the coercee is required to answer for her own conduct in accepting and acting on it, then she would presumably defend herself by pointing out that she had only two alternatives, and she chose as she did because the cost gap between them was very great. Her subsequent action may not have been very involuntary in the sense of "unwilling," since she paid a small cost for it, but the cost of the sole alternative was so great that she had "no choice" but to do the fishy thing she did. If the question is why she did that fishy thing rather than the only other thing open to her, then the greater the cost gap between the two, the greater the coerciveness she can cite in her own defense. Her *action* as such may not have been very involuntary, but her choice of that action rather than the other may have been rendered virtually unavoidable by the differential coercive pressure.

The third and fourth sets of examples below are of mixed polarity, involving a forced choice between an evil and a good. As we shall see, this feature of the examples complicates our arithmetic in such a way that we must be reluctant to call these examples "coercive offers" at all. Perhaps they are best characterized as "impure coercive offers," since they contain an element of enticement as well as an element of coercion. When the enticing option has no cost but only attractive benefit, I will use a positive number for its "price-tag".

3. Forced but "easy" choice between an evil and a good
    a. Sleep with me (said to a woman who is favorably disposed, in small degree, to do so in any case) (+1), or I will let your sick child die (−15).
    This translates:
        i. If you sleep with me (+1), I will pay for the surgery that alone can save your child's life.
        ii. If you do not sleep with me, your child will die (−15).
    b. Take the offered Houston job which sounds not bad (+1) or continue in the New York job, which is intolerable (−15).
    This translates:
        i. If you take the job I offer you in Houston (+1), then you will escape the intolerable unhappiness of your present job in New York.
        ii. If you do not take the job I offer you in Houston, then you will continue to be intolerably unhappy at your job in New York (−15).

Coercive pressure:
Differential coercive pressure: 15 plus 1 = 16
Coercive force: 15
Total coercive burden: 15 minus 1 = 14
Coercive minimum: −1
(The "cost of the best alternative" is no cost at all, but but a positive benefit.)

4. Forced and close choice between a (not very) evil and a (not very) good
    a. Sleep with me (said to a woman who is moderately predisposed in any case) (+1), or you will be in minor financial difficulty (since I will not pay your $200 debt) (−2).
    This translates:
        i. If you sleep with me (+1) then I will pay your minor debt.
        ii. If you do not sleep with me then you will be in minor financial difficulty (−2).
    b. Take the offered Houston job, which sounds moderately good on the whole (+1) or continue in the New York job in which you are on the whole quite unhappy, although tolerably so (−2).
    This translates:

  i. If you take the job I offer you in Houston (+1) then you will escape the moderate unhappiness of your job in New York

  ii. If you do not take the job I offer you in Houston, then you will continue to be mildly unhappy in your job in New York (−2).

Coercive pressure:
Differential coercive pressure: 2 plus 1 = 3
Coercive force: 2
Total coercive burden: 2 minus 1 = 1
Coercive minimum: −1
(The "cost" of the best alternative is no cost at all but a positive benefit.)

  The third and fourth sets of examples, being of mixed polarity in that they are forced choices between an evil and a good, are only impurely coercive. By the measures of differential coercive pressure, and coercive force, given our number assignments, the third set of examples is even more coercive than the second. By the measure of differential coercive pressure (only) the third set is even more coercive than the first, and by the measure of coercive force, equally coercive as the first. The fourth set of examples, however, is not *very* coercive by any measure. It is important to note that by the sometimes vitally relevant standard of the coercive minimum, *none* of these examples of mixed polarity is coercive at all. That is because the "cost" of the best alternative in all these cases is a "negative cost," that is a positive benefit. The proposal in these examples, though it imposes a forced choice on the chooser, puts her in a position to lose if she chooses one way, but to gain if she chooses another. Unlike more standard cases of coercion, it is not true that the best she can do in any event is suffer some loss. On the other hand, the push of one alternative combined with the pull of the other creates a differential pressure which, in "easy choices" like those in the third set, can indeed "force" her to do as the proposer wants. Since one of her options is seen by her as a benefit, however, she is best described as acting *under* coercion but not *because* of coercion. The coercive force of the unattractive option is redundant in his case; she may well act willingly just as the proposer wishes her to act anyway.

  The fifth and sixth sets of examples, however, are in no sense, and by no measure, coercive. Given that they involve forced choices between perceived goods, all of the "price-tags" must be assigned negative numbers and the resultant units of coercive pressure, by all four measures, will be represented by negative numbers. Negative coercive pressure, of course, is no coercive pressure at all, but rather something that might be caled "allurement" or "attractiveness."

5. Forced but "easy" choice between goods

    a. Be my mistress and collect $100,000 (net +10) or remain in the *status quo* in which you have a satisfactory alternation of lovers, you are not troubled by moral misgivings, and you have an adequate but modest income (+3).

This translates:

    i. If you become my mistress on these terms (+10), I will provide you with a more comfortable and remunerative life than your present one.

    ii. If you do not become my mistress, then you will remain in your adequate but modest circumstances (+3).

    b. Take the offered Houston job which involves a much higher salary, and more pleasant and secure work (+10), or remain in your New York job which is satisfactory, comfortable, and pays moderately well (+3).

This translates:

    i. If you take the job I offer you in Houston (+10), then your salary and working conditions will be considerably better than at your present job.

    ii. If you do not take this job I offer you in Houston, then you will remain in your adequate and moderately well paying New York job (+3).

Coercive pressure: Not applicable, since by all four measures, the "coercion" would be expressed in negative numbers. The "alluring pressure" (pull), however, is expressible in positive numbers.
Differential "alluring pressure": 7
"Alluring force": 10
Total "attraction load": 13
"Beneficial minimum" (benefit of the worst alternative): 3

6. Forced and close choice between goods

    a. Marry me with my slightly superior prospects and attractiveness (+5) or marry George who also plans to propose (+4).

This translates:

    i. If you marry me (+5) I will provide you with more benefits than you would enjoy otherwise.

    ii. If you do not marry me, then you will enjoy almost but not quite as beneficial a marriage with George (+4).

    b. Take the offered Houston job with its slightly superior benefits (+5) or continue in your almost as good job in New York (+4).

This translates:

     i. If you take the job I offer you in Houston (+5) it will provide you with more job benefits than you would enjoy otherwise.

     ii. If you do not take the job I offer you in Houston, then you will enjoy almost but not quite as beneficial a job in New York (+4).

Coercive pressure: Not applicable since it would be expressed in negative numbers. The "alluring pressure" (pull), however, is expressible in positive numbers.
Differential "alluring pressure": 1
"Alluring force": 5
Total "attraction load": 9
Beneficial minimum (benefit of the worst alternative): 4

    The fifth set of examples exhibits greater alluring pressure for the superior option than the sixth set does by all the measures except that of "beneficial minimum." The worst the forced chooser can do in the sixth set (4) is better than in the fifth set (3). But by all the other measures, and especially that of "differential alluring pressure," the fifth set of examples shows an offer of greater alluring pressure. In neither set of examples is there the slightest trace of *coercive* pressure. No matter how the forced chooser chooses, he cannot lose.

    The compatibilist view next must explain what bearing, if any, the coerciveness of an otherwise freedom-enhancing offer has on the consent which it produces. In the examples of harmful or dangerous activities of *A* toward *B*, which on liberal grounds would be permitted if and only if *B* has voluntarily consented, the voluntariness of *B*'s consent seems not sufficiently reduced by *A*'s coercive offer to be invalidated. The lecherous millionaire could hardly be convicted of rape. Since a lecherous gunman who forces his will on *B* by threatening to kill her child *would* (or should) be criminally liable for rape (among other things) it seems that it makes a great deal of difference whether coercive effects on *B* are produced by freedom-restricting threats or freedom-enhancing offers.

3. Coercion and exploitation: the Zimmerman solution

That is not to say, of course, that the lecherous millionaire is immune from moral judgment, or that we must praise him as a benefactor. He has shamelessly taken advantage of the impecunious mother, ruthlessly *exploiting* her vulnerability. The Zimmerman solution to the coercive offer problem makes a special point of distinguishing exploitation from coercion, and arguing that some exploitation can be noncoercive. *A*'s offer to *B* is coercive, according to Zimmerman, "only if *B* would prefer to move from the normally expected preproposal situation to the proposal situation" [that much makes the proposal an *offer*], *"but he would strongly prefer even more to move from the actual pre-proposal situation to some alternative pre-proposal situation."*[6] The impecunious mother, for example, welcomes the lecherous millionaire's proposal, but would much have preferred finding the requisite funds for the surgery without having to consider indecent proposals (the preferred alternative pre-proposal situation). Zimmerman then adds what he calls "feasibility" and "nonprevention" conditions to what can count as an "alternative preproposal situation," the gist of which is that *A*, the proposer, must not have intervened himself to prevent an otherwise feasible, much preferred, pre-proposal situation from existing. If he has so intervened, then his offer is not merely exploitative, but coercive as well.

Thus Zimmerman would hold that the lecherous millionaire, if he is merely an opportunist who makes the most for himself of *B*'s troubles, having had no role himself in creating those troubles, is merely an exploiter, not a coercer (although noncoercive exploitation is bad enough—see Chaps. 31, 32). But if he had himself injected the child with organ-impairing microbes and/or exerted pressure on the only available surgeons to keep their prices high, then his proposal, while still an offer and still freedom-enhancing in the artificial circumstances *A* has created, and still shamefully exploitative, would also be genuinely coercive.

Zimmerman provides his own examples to illustrate the distinction between exploitative offers that are, and those which are not, on this theory, coercive.

> *A* kidnaps *B*, brings him to the island where *A*'s factory is located, and abandons him on the beach. All the jobs in *A*'s factory are considerably worse than those available to *B* on the mainland. The next day *A* approaches *B* with the proposal "Take one of the jobs in my factory and I won't let you starve."[7]

This is a genuine example, on Zimmerman's view, of a coercive offer. The Hobbesian conqueror and slave-owner examples would presumably also be coercive offers, but the lecherous millionaire example would not, since it fits more closely Zimmerman's contrasting example of a merely exploitative but noncoercive offer:

> *C* also owns a factory (the only other one) on the island, in which the jobs are just as bad. Seeing *B*'s plight, he beats *A* to the scene and makes the same kind of proposal . . . I would claim that only *A* makes a coercive offer. The intuitive idea underlying coercion is that *the person who does the coercing undermines, or limits the freedom* of the person who is coerced, so coercing goes beyond exploiting, however objectionable the latter may be.[8]

In effect, Zimmerman attempts to bolster the doctrine that coercion *must* restrict freedom (the doctrine rejected in the the compatibilist solution) by separating in the hard cases the act that restricts the victim's freedom from the act of making the coercive offer. The compatibilist, however, can point out that the offer appears equally as coercive to B (its recipient) in the case where A (the offerer) merely takes advantage of restrictive circumstances as it does in the case where A himself had earlier created the restrictive circumstances. "Work or starve" and "Sleep with me or your baby dies" are as coercive in the one case as in the other. From B's point of view he has "no choice" but to comply no matter how he got into the mess in which the offer is made. The *effect* of the offer is coercive in either case and the intent of the offer is coercive in either case. To be sure, it was necessary in order for the coercion to be effective that B's freedom be diminished earlier by the events that created his vulnerability, but once he is in the vulnerable circumstances, C's offer, contrary to Zimmerman, has all the appearance of being coercive.

However, Zimmerman does have an important point. In the case where A created the circumstances of vulnerability in order later to exploit them with a coercive offer, he has doubly wronged B, first by undermining his freedom, and then by taking advantage of him. In the other case, the coercive offer does not itself undermine freedom but opportunistically takes advantage of the circumstances that made coercion possible. The whole wrong in that case is the making of the offer. But whether there was a single or a double wrong done the victim, in either case, the offer itself *in the circumstances in which it was made* was plainly coercive.

Zimmerman's distinction also has important practical consequences for our judgments of voluntariness. When A deliberately creates the circumstances of vulnerability which he later exploits with a coercive offer, his coercion virtually always reduces the voluntariness of B's consent sufficiently to render it invalid. But when A merely exploits circumstances that he finds ready-made, then frequently, though not always, B's consent, so produced, remains valid. Zimmerman himself does not acknowledge this difference, but that may be because he is misled by his unrepresentative selection of examples. He writes that—

> If A throws B into the water and then offers to save B (where he can do so at relatively little cost to himself) only if B promises to give him his life savings afterwards, the offer is coercive and the promise void. If A just happens upon the scene, sees B drowning, and offers to rescue him on exactly the same terms, B's promise is probably just as void, morally speaking anyway, since A's offer is so grossly exploitive.[9]

I think this example is misleading in two ways. In the first place, it is not a clear example of an *offer* at all. By the test of statistical normalcy endorsed in Chapter 23, §8, it appears to be a coercive threat. Furthermore, if as was claimed in Vol. I, Chapter 4, A has a moral duty to rescue B (unlike, say, the lecherous millionaire who has no duty to save the desperate woman's child in our paradigm example of a coercive offer), then A's exploitative proposal in Zimmerman's example is a threat by the moral expectability standard as well. Secondly, it does not seem to be a necessary truth that exploitation as such invalidates consent, as numerous other examples show. A "just happens on the scene" in the lecherous millionaire case, and also in Zimmerman's own example of the opportunistic factory owner, yet in neither case would B's consent be invalid on the grounds that A's exploitative offer gave him no eligible choice. Very likely the gubernatorial commutation example is another case in point. The criminal created his own vulnerability by committing a capital crime, but once he is in precarious circumstances, the state takes advantage of him in order to achieve a public benefit. His consent is not properly invalidated despite the gross (and coercive) exploitation.

It is important in treating these subtle issues to specify exactly what is being consented to by B, a specific proposal or a whole episode of which the proposal is only the climactic event. It is absurd to ascribe to B voluntary consent to a whole episode that consists (1) of his liberty being undermined by A's deliberately forcing him into vulnerable circumstances and (2) his being offered rescue from those circumstances in a highly exploitative offer from A that he cannot reasonably refuse. If the question before us is whether B's consent to (2) serves as a defense for A against charges of having wronged B by producing the whole episode, the answer is clearly negative. Given that B was in the unhappy circumstances anyway, then against that background his consent to the coercive offer is voluntary, but he has not consented to being placed in those circumstances, so there is no valid consent to the whole episode produced by A to force his choice. If the question is whether a third party is exempt from liability for his forceful interference with A's plans, then the answer, despite the consent extracted from B by A, is affirmative, though the third party could not have forcefully restrained A if A were a mere exploiter who "happened to chance on the scene."

A further comment is in order about Zimmerman's examples. B's coerced consent to A's exploitative offer could hardly serve as a defense to A for a whole episode in which A's manipulative role was itself criminal, like kidnapping in one example and throwing a person in the water in the other. In fact, most of the examples in which A deliberately creates the circumstances which he later exploits with a coercive offer involve the commission not merely of a separate wrong but also an independent crime, that is a crime other than extortion.

4. Coercion and exploitation: summary and conclusion

There are some examples of preference-affecting proposals that are at once offers and coercive. The Hobbesian conqueror case and Nozick's slavemaster case are unusual but relatively clear examples. Both satisfy the definition of offers given in Chapter 23, §§7, 8, and they are coercive since they offer an unappealing consequence as the sole alternative to a much greater evil (as judged by the recipient of the offer). The lecherous milionaire's offer to the impecunious mother is typical of a wider class of less clear, more controversial cases. These examples differ from the clear cases in that A has not himself deliberately created the circumstances of B's vulnerability which are exploited by his offer to B.

There are three possible responses to these various examples of exploitative offers. Some writers deny that *any* of them are coercive, properly speaking, since they have the effect of enlarging rather than closing B's options, and (they assume) coercion cannot be freedom-enhancing. In reply to this, the position I have called "compatibilist" holds that *all* of the examples in question are coercive offers even though they are freedom-enhancing, since they are coercive both in intent and in their effect on B: they force B to do what A wants him to do by creating a solitary and unappealing alternative to a course that B finds intolerably evil. A third position is that of David Zimmerman who classifies as coercive offers only those proposals made by A when A himself has deliberately created the circumstances in which B is trapped, and then exploits the very vulnerability he has created by offering B an alternative fate preferred by B only as the lesser evil. Thus Zimmerman would classify the Hobbesian conqueror and the Nozick slavemaster examples as coercive offers, but the lecherous millionaire and (probably) the gubernatorial commutation cases as exploitative but not coercive, since A turns to his own advantage precarious circumstances of B's that are not of A's own making.

I have argued in favor of the compatibilist position and against Zimmerman on the purely conceptual question of whether A's offer to B can be called "coercive" (as well as "exploitative") when the circumstances A exploits to force B to do as A wants are not of A's own deliberate making. But the purely conceptual question is inherently murky (given the vagueness of ordinary language) and not theoretically important (given our primary purpose of determining which kinds of influences may render B's consent ro A invalid for the purposes of the soft-paternalist strategy). On the important question, I have concluded that coercive offers made in circumstances deliberately created by the offerer for the purposes of exploitation do normally invalidate consent, whereas coercive offers made by a party who had no role in creating the circumstances of vulnerability (those called merely exploitative by Zimmerman) very often do not invalidate consent. The former are simply the climactic events in whole episodes created to undermine B's freedom, whereas the latter enlarge B's freedom *in the circumstances*, so that his consent *given those circumstances* may be voluntary enough to be valid (for some purposes).

Assuming that we have achieved some clarity in our examination of the effects on consent of these distinct modes of influence, does it matter whether they are both called "coercive" or only one is called "coercive" and the other "merely exploitative"? Let us retrace our steps. Any analysis of the prototypical coercive transaction between A and B (e.g. the gunman example) will list conditions of three kinds. It will specify those that define (1) *coercive effect* on B's choice, (2) *coercive intent* in A's mind, and (3) the characteristic or necessary *coercive mechanism* employed to achieve the intended effect. All along, our main interest has been in (1), since we are concerned less with judging A than with protecting B. When we move from the paradigmatic cases of coercion to the problematic "coercive offer" cases, we find that two sets of defining conditions are clearly satisfied, but the third only partially satisfied at most. In the lecherous millionaire example there is surely coercive intent, since A's purpose in making his proposal is to force B to do his bidding. Equally surely there is coercive effect, since B is left with a forced choice between evils, one of which is extreme and intolerable to her, and therefore "ineligible," while the other, that favored by A, is highly repugnant but the lesser of the evils has to choose between.

What is not as clear is whether the mechanism used by A to achieve his intended effect on B is of the proper sort to be called "coercive." In the paradigm cases the coercive method involves active manipulation by A to close B's options, thus creating the very circumstances that A intends to exploit to make his subsequent offer effectively coercive. In the borderline cases we can also ascribe some "manipulation" to A, but no active intervention in B's affairs to close B's options and thus *create* the exploitable circumstances. In these cases, A is an opportunist, not an arranger, so very likely his manipulations are not active enough to satisfy the initial defining conditions of "coercive mechanism."

So now the question becomes this: is coercive technique (mechanism) essential to the classification of a proposal as coercive when the offer's intention and (especially) its effect are so manifestly coercive, or is it nonessential and merely generally characteristic of the offers we call coercive? I know no way of settling this question, considered as *merely* a conceptual question, except by looking at the common usage of the term "coercion", and that seems very unpromising given that "coercion" is not a term of well settled ordinary parlance, and even in its technical use it seems vague.

Adherents of the Zimmerman position might well propose a different test. However else coercion is defined, they might insist, whatever conditions are specified and however these conditions are weighted in importance, the definition must preserve the supposed truth of the proposition that coercion vitiates consent. If we accept this proposal, then we might say of borderline cases that if they do not invalidate consent (by reducing voluntariness) then they are not instances of coercion. That strategy would appear to vindicate Zimmerman after all, since as we have seen, the exploitative offers he refuses to call "coercive" very often do not invalidate consent. The adherent of the compatibilist account of coercive offers, however, need not accept in advance that coercion necessarily and always invalidates consent. That proposition must be tested against our intuition in great varieties of cases in great varieties of types of context. What must be accepted in advance is a somewhat different proposition, namely that coercion as such always *reduces* the degree of voluntariness, but whether it must always reduce the voluntariness of consent to the point of invalidity is much more controversial. It may be, for example, that only coercive *threats*, as opposed to coercive offers, or only *freedom-restricting*, as opposed to freedom-enlarging, coercion can be counted on to invalidate consent utterly. In that case a freedom-enhancing offer could still be called "coercive" (in virtue of its intention and effect) even though it does not totally defeat the voluntariness of the consent it produces.

The important thing for our purposes, however, is to determine what sorts of influence do invalidate consent, not deciding what word to apply to those influences. About this substantive question there is more agreement. Active coercion which both creates and exploits a situation of vulnerability always reduces voluntariness, typically to the point where consent is invalid, whereas offers that exploit a condition already made also reduce voluntariness, but usually *not* to the point where consent is invalid. In the latter cases, the opportunistically discovered circumstances of the vulnerable party become part of the stage-setting against which the offer occurs, and not themselves interventions against a more normal background. Given that those circumstances are already in place, the exploitative offerer enlarges the vulnerable party's opportunities even as he makes him an unappealing or repellant "offer that he cannot resist." As for the less important conceptual-verbal question, it is better to stipulate than to dogmatize. I will call both threats and offers "coercive" when they are coercive in *effect* since it is their effect on the recipient's choice that is the critical factor in evaluating his consent. I am therefore committed to the view that not all coercion invalidates consent, though it all reduces the voluntariness of expressions of consent.

Like Zimmerman, we too shall have occasion (Chap. 31) to speak of "noncoercive exploitation," because we shall discover then that there are exploitative offers whose acceptance can be fully voluntary, neither coerced, deceived, nor the product of impairment, and we shall want to decide whether the criminal law has any legitimate concern with such agreements *simply* because they are exploitative. When coercive offers exploit a ready made condition of vulnerability in order to achieve their coercive effect, then they too are in the class of voluntarily—or voluntarily enough—consented-to exploitation, and we shall want to consider them along with the other varieties in this category, including genuinely noncoercive exploitation. Our question then shall be: Is there a reason for punishing A for exploiting B even when A, without using coercion, has won *B*'s voluntary consent to the treatment that is in fact exploitative? Is the prevention of exploitation as such an independent ground for criminal prohibitions? An affirmative answer would endorse either legal paternalism or a form of legal moralism.

5. Unequal bargaining positions: unconscionability

The more familiar examples, actual and hypothetical, of proposals that satisfy our definition of coercive-exploitative offers are commerical exchanges. Most of these come from the law of contracts, but they are not misleading models for agreements which have caught the attention of legislators of criminal statutes, so it might be instructive for us to consider them here. In these examples, *A* and *B* are independent negotiators, each trying to strike a bargain with the other that will help his own interests, but they are very unevenly matched in bargaining strength. Either *A* has superior power and *B* greater vulnerability, or *A* has control of that on which *B* depends, or *A* has a monopoly of that which *B* needs. In general, *B* needs *A* more than *A* needs B.

There is no necessity that unequal initial bargaining conditions will yield exploitative or coercive agreements. The more powerful party need not choose to take advantage of the reluctant but helpless weaker party. The inequality of the initial bargaining position is not in itself a voluntariness-reducing factor, since the strong and weak party *can* make a perfectly voluntary agreement. Nevertheless the temptation to exploit is always present when the positions are unequal, and in some cases the strong party following his own self-interest, with no coercive intent, will make an offer that is coercive in effect because of the weak party's one-sided dependence. *A* may not *want* to exploit *B*. When he says "take it or leave it," his statement may express genuine indifference. He has many other options open, but he finds *B* with most of *his* options already closed. *A* can consider a proposal and "take it or leave it;" *B* can only take it.

Even when there is both coercive intent in *A* and coercive effect on *B*, the offer will not properly be called "exploitative" unless its terms are either harsh in their costs to *B*, or uneven or disproportionate in their gains for *A*, or both. When they are exploitative in this sense, and also coercive in intent and effect, they are what the law of contracts calls "unconscionable." They need not be coercive in the stronger Murphy-Zimmerman sense to be unconscionable. It is sufficient that *A* finds *B* already vulnerable. He has him "over a barrel" and can get him to pay almost any price for that which *A* has to offer him.

Various writers have claimed that certain institutional arrangements essentially involve exploitative agreements coercively extracted from weaker parties. Medical experiments on prisoners in exchange for reduced terms of imprisonment,[10] plea-bargaining agreements,[11] payments to blood-donors,[12] employment contracts under "pure capitalism,"[13] the "voluntary army,"[14] and Medicaid's disallowance of abortion expenses[15] are most commonly cited as examples. But these are complex and controversial. Our hypothetical stories of the leacherous millionaire and the gubernatorial commutation have an artifical and useful simplicity. To these we may add a more explicitly commerical example from J. G. Murphy:

> Suppose I own the only water well within a two hundred mile radius of desert. A man, nearly dead from thirst, drags himself to my well and begs for water. Realizing (a) that the well is lawfully owned by me and that I am entitled to all its water, and (b) that the thirsty man's predicament is no fault of mine . . . I say "I will sell you a glass of water only if you sign over to me all your worldly goods."[16]

Murphy's example, like many real cases from the law of commercial transactions, involves the transfer and consumption of the coercively offered, desperately desired object, before the contracted price is fully paid. Hence the consumer can break his promise and defend himself in court against a breach of contract suit. These cases are, in that practical respect, unlike our earlier examples where the price is paid first (sexual favors, submission to a medical experiment), so that any subsequent legal action, based on the claimed invalidity of consent, would be *via* the law of torts or the criminal law. Murphy rightly comments on his example that the consent extracted by the well owner was not valid, even though on Murphy's view (as on Zimmerman's) it was not coerced. Its invalidity, according to Murphy, derives entirely from the fact that the consenter's "desperate vulnerability was so shamefully and unjustly exploited."[17]

The proper way of interpreting these terms of moral condemnation, Murphy suggests, can be found in the "emerging doctrine of unconscionability" in the law of contracts. As Murphy interprets this doctrine, it implies that "there are respects in which inequality can produce an unfair agreement for reasons which have little or nothing to do with duress,"[18] and that it is this "unfairness," not coercion, that can invalidate the agreement so produced. Most courts and legal commentators, however, have preferred to label as coercive *tout court* any agreement whose intent on one side and effect on the other were coercive. Unconscionable contracts, including what are often called "contracts of adhesion," are simply one subclass of contracts consented to under duress, the duress in these cases not stemming from threats of force or violence, but from the inequality of the bargaining position itself, and the advantage taken of that inequality by one of the parties. A "contract of adhesion" is one whose terms are printed in a uniform way on a standardized form throughout an industry, one that typically contains "risk-exclusion or limitation provisions for the benefit of the large firm with immensely greater bargaining power than the consumer with whom it deals."[19] The consumer cannot seek a better deal with a rival giant firm because there too he will confront the same standardized contract, and will be told that the printed provisions are unalterable and non-negotiable, "take it or leave it." (In most cases the exploitation is even worse, since the contract will contain in its fine print obscurely worded "oppressive provisions" of which the purchaser may not even be aware.)

In the classic case of *Henningsen v. Bloomfield Motors, Inc.*[20] a buyer contracted to buy a new automobile from a Chrysler dealer. The contract contained a warranty binding Chrysler to replace defectively manufactured parts at its own expense, but in its fine print there was a disclaimer of any *further* express or implied warranty. Henningsen, whose wife had been injured while driving a defective automobile shortly after its purchase from Bloomfield Motors, claimed that Chrysler should be liable for medical and other expenses of persons injured in a crash caused by defective parts, despite the apparent contractual limitation of liability to simple replacement of the parts. The dealer replied that Henningsen has signed the contract and was bound by its terms. The Supreme Court of New Jersey found for the purchaser, commenting sympathetically about his plight:

> The gross inequality of bargaining position occupied by the consumer in the automobile industry is thus apparent. There is no competition among the car makers in the area of express warranty. Where can the buyer go to negotiate for better protection?[21]

The Court rightly implies that Henningsen's options have been restricted in the manner of all coercively extracted agreements. He may take the car on the manufacturer's terms, take a car from a different manufacturer on precisely the same terms,[22] or go without a car. That forced option in turn is coercive, according to our previous analysis, because it offers a lesser evil (a car without protection from accidents caused by defective workmanship) as the sole alternative to an extreme evil (no car at all). To be sure there was no literal gun at Henningsen's head when he signed the contract, and the "greater evil" posed as his alternative was not as unthinkable as having one's brains blown out, but "the difference," writes one commentator, "is only one of degree if the same individual is compelled to sign the typical standardized form contract to purchase an automobile where the only 'alternative' is walking."[23]

It seems clear from the legal doctrine as so far developed that a contract is "unconscionable," hence invalid, when and only when:

1. it is either *coercive* or *deceptive*, coercive because the weaker party has no reasonable alternative to the terms offered by the stronger party and is

thus forced to choose what to him appears the lesser evil, *or* deceptive because the weaker party never even becomes aware of the terms he agrees to since they are buried in fine print, or else he fails to understand them because they are obscured by incomprehensible legal jargon; *and*

2. the terms are *harsh* to the weaker party because of provisions that "shock the conscience" or "wreak with oppression" and "unfair surprise"[24] (in a narrower usage this alone is the element called "unconscionable"); *and*

3. the terms are *unequal* involving disproportionate benefit, or "excessive profit" to the stronger party.

An agreement is unconscionable if it is, in Zimmerman's phrase, "grossly exploitative," that is when *A* takes advantage of *B*'s vulnerability by making an offer that is either coercive or deceptive (or both), and is excessively profitable to the stronger party, as determined by governing standards of fairness. Finally, when these conditions of unconscionability are satisfied, the consent of the weaker party is invalid, and if he has not already discharged his side of the agreement, he may breach the contract with impunity. If the agreement requires the weaker party to perform first (as in the lecherous millionaire example) she will have no remedy in the law of contracts, though the "unconscionable agreement" could, under some conceivable arrangements, invalidate her consent for the purposes of the criminal law or the law of torts.

A good example of the coerciveness of unconscionable contracts is the famous case of *United States v. Bethlehem Steel Corporation*[25] in which the unlikely "weaker party" was the United States government. In this case, left over from World War I, the United States sued to revoke the contract under which Bethlehem made extraordinary profits with no risk to itself for building the ships that were desperately needed for the war effort. The United States Supreme Court upheld the contract, but in his dissenting opinion Justice Frankfurter argued that the company had grossly exploited the dependence of the government on it, by "compelling" the government to agree to excessive and unconscionable profits. The company, he claimed, had the government right where it wanted it, helplessly dependent on the company for its unique shipbuilding expertise and terribly rushed by the exigencies of the war. The government bargainers deeply resented the company's "attitude of commerical greed but little diluted with patriotic feeling," but they were "faced with the alternative of either agreeing to Bethlehem's terms or taking possession of its shipyards and having the Government itself construct the vessels . . . the Government representatives felt that the latter course could not have accomplished the shipbuilding program with the speed which was essential."[26] The "unconscionable terms of the contract," he concluded, "were forced on the Government by the dire necessities of national self-preservation."[27]

That the terms were excessively costly to the government and inordinately profitable to the company were beyond dispute. There was also no evidence of fraud or fine print foolery. The sole contested issue was whether in the circumstances of inequality that prevailed the agreement was coercive-in-effect on the government. Frankfurter left no doubt about his view on that question. That the government representatives entered into the contracts "with their eyes wide open" does not imply, he argued, that they were not acting under coercion. The authority of Holmes himself is then invoked: "It is always for the interest of a party under duress to choose the lesser of two evils. But the fact that a choice was made according to interest does not exclude duress. It is the characteristic of duress properly so called."[28] Rescission of unconscionable contracts, Frankfurter argues further, is a legal policy centuries older than the current use of the word "unconscionable." "The rule of chancery is well established. When a person is encumbered with debts, and that fact is known to a person with whom he contracts, who avails himself of it to exact an unconscionable bargain, equity will relieve upon account of the *advantage and hardship*."[29] In other words, there can be no enforcement of contracts that are both coercive in effect and harsh for the weaker party, in a word—"unconscionable."

A consistent position about the case of the lecherous millionaire now suggests itself. If B contracts to become A's (permanent) mistress in exchange for his underwriting the surgery that will save her child's life, and then after the surgery she reneges, she will not be liable for breach of contract, because her promise was coerced by A's offer. Because the contract was unconscionable,[30] the voluntariness of her consent was reduced accordingly, and the element in the unconscionability that reduced the voluntariness was its coercive character. For the purpose of contract-enforcement the consent was no longer sufficiently voluntary to be valid, and the contract is thus rescinded. But for the purpose of establishing A's criminal liability (for example for rape), B's consent is not sufficiently nonvoluntary to be invalid.

On the other hand, if B agrees to sleep with A for a few nights until the day of the operation, and she fulfills her part of the bargain before A fulfills his part, there is no breach, and the only questions that remain are whether she deserves compensation for the "pain and suffering" caused her by A's intimacies (assuming there was no other compensable harm)—which is extremely implausible given her great gain on balance—and whether her consent to A was sufficiently nonvoluntary to be invalid as a defense for A to criminal charges. Again, the answer seems to be that even though her consent was sufficiently nonvoluntary to have nullified a contract if the issue had arisen, it was more than voluntary enough to provide a valid defense to A against tort actions and criminal prosecutions. How then can we account for this relativity?

6. Coercion, voluntariness, and validity

What emerges from this discussion is that the three independent concepts, coercion, voluntariness, and validity of consent, are not only each difficult on their own accounts, but they also stand in complex and subtly shifting relations to one another. Coercion *does* tend to reduce voluntariness; it is a "voluntariness-reducing factor." But coercion and voluntariness are both in various ways matters of degree, and coercion is sometimes not sufficiently strong to vitiate voluntariness altogether. Unlike literal compulsion, coercion is not always a "voluntariness-defeating factor." Voluntariness, in turn, being also a matter of degree, is sometimes reduced to the point where it is insufficient for the validity of consent. When that is so, the act of consent is so deficient in voluntariness that it lacks legal or moral effect—it is invalid, null and void, no better than no expression of assent at all. Validity is an all or nothing term; it does not admit of degree. How coercive then must *A*'s proposal be in order to reduce the voluntariness of *B*'s act of consent to the point where it is invalid? That is where contextual relativity comes in. The point of "insufficient voluntariness" will vary depending on the nature of that to which consent is expressed, and the legal or moral purpose for which consent is considered.

Variations in the modes and degrees of coercive effect. Coercive effects on choice are produced both by threats and offers. There is no difference in the degree of coercion exerted on *B* by the lecherous millionaire *A*'s offer and a parallel threat we can imagine delivered by a criminal, *C*, who has the child imprisoned somewhere and threatens to have him killed unless *B* sleeps with *C*. In either case the effect of the proposal is to force *B* to choose between sleeping with the proposer and losing her child. Coercive effect does genuinely vary in degree, however, with the degree of "coercive pressure." If our ultimate concern is to decide whether the pressured chooser's consent was valid when what he consented to was morally fishy somehow, the relevant measure of the pressure may be the difference between the "cost" of the chosen alternative and the "cost" of the sole permitted alternative. If that difference was not great, then the "differential coercive pressure" was not great, and consequently the choice of the lesser subjective evil *instead of the slightly greater subjective evil* was not as greatly reduced in voluntariness as it might have been, and for some purposes the consent that issued from the pressure may yet be valid. On the other hand, if we wish to gauge the coercive pressure forcing the victim to choose a lesser evil in a forced choice between evils *instead of a normal course in which there is no need to choose either of the evils*, then the coercive pressure as appropriately understood might be the cost of the "threatened" or sole permitted alternative, or the cost of compliance with the demand, or the sum of the two ("total coercive burden"), or the cost of the best option (that of the demand, if the coercion is effective), which, even when heavy, is the least cost the coercee can incur.

A third distinction among coercive proposals distinguishes those whose projected consequences are appraised by means of the recipient's own standards of relative undesirability, and those judged according to "objective" or "external" standards, the rankings of most people, or of some ideal person. When objective standards are used, actual choices and acts of consent may be deemed more voluntary than they would be according to the "subjective standards" of unwelcomeness used by the recipient of the proposal himself. We have seen that this variation is important in permitting us to require greater coercion and greater involuntariness to exonerate wrongdoers when their acts are other-regarding or social in effect than we use in deciding whether to prevent autonomous choosers from consenting to actions that are primarily self-regarding in their harmful or dangerous effects.

We have also seen that coercive proposals can be distinguished in respect to whether they are freedom-enhancing or freedom-restricting on balance (the latter being the effect of all threats and some offers, namely those in which the proposer himself has closed the receipient's options) and that a freedom-enhancing coercive offer, while also diminishing the voluntariness of the consent it produces, does not often reduce it to the point of invalidity. Finally, we have seen that some coercive offers are harsh and unequal, a good deal more *exploitative* than others that may be almost equally coercive but less "unconscionable." The isolatable factors of harshness and inequality may render coerced consent invalid for some legal purposes (particularly in the law of contracts) where similarly coercive agreements without such harsh terms may have been hardly more voluntary and yet would have been legally valid.[31]

Variations in the modes and degrees of voluntariness as affected by coercion. If we consider voluntariness only as affected by coercion then it seems possible to construct a metric scale in which degrees of voluntariness are correlated with degrees of coercive pressure as determined by the "price-tags" of the projected alternatives in the coercive proposal. But of course coercion is only one kind of voluntariness-reducing factor among others, and if our talk about comparative degrees is to make any sense at all it must be restricted to contexts where fraud, mistake, ignorance, and the various relevant sorts of impairment are simply not present. In those contexts we may conceive of a scale of voluntariness running from perfect involuntariness at one extreme to approximately full voluntariness at the other. Absolute involuntariness would attach only to those bodily movements which are produced by compulsion (see Chap. 23, §1), without the help of any proposal at all, whereas the acceptance of a proposal would be fully voluntary in just those cases where both compulsion and coercion are totally lacking. These cases will include responses to conditional proposals whose posed alternatives both have positive value-tags rather than negative "price-tags." Thus pure enticements are entirely noncoercive. A professor at Northern Idaho State may find himself forced to choose between offers from Harvard and Yale, both of which are vastly more attractive than his baseline situation in which, let us imagine, he is unhappy. He may have a very hard choice between these almost equally good altelrnatives but the fact that he will be forced to relinguish the lesser good when both goods are so very appealing does not count against the voluntariness of his choice. It is true also that similarly disjoined lesser enticements may produce as fully voluntary choices as the greater enticements, provided that the forced choice does not require the chooser to pay any "price" beyond relinquishing the lesser good.[32] Sometimes, however, enticements do seem to carry their costs. The student athlete who is enticed by a million dollar offer to abandon his education for a career in professional sports may choose *because* of the great gain and *despite* the loss of another real gain, simply because he weighs the one gain greater than the loss of the other. However, the offer is not for this reason properly characterized as "coercive." Below these cases of nearly equally attractive enticements on the scale of voluntariness will be cases of minor coercive pressure, greater coercive pressure, extreme coercive pressure, and finally at the limit of the scale, pure compulsion.

The ambiguities of the words "voluntary" and "involuntary" introduce further complications into our account of the connections between voluntariness and coercion. The dictionary tells us that "voluntary" sometimes means "unforced" and sometimes "willingly." Among its antonyms are not only "involuntarily" and "forced," but also "unwillingly" and even "reluctantly." What tends to cause confusion, as we saw in the example of the forced robbery of a willing contributor (Chap. 23, §4), is the fact that people sometimes act quite willingly under force, thus "voluntarily" in one sense but not in another. This ambiguity infects much of our discourse, as a few other examples will show.

John Doe is a patriot. He pays his taxes willingly because he thinks they are just and that it is his duty to pay them. Does he then pay them *voluntarily?* One might reply that nobody pays taxes voluntarily in this country since we have a system of compulsory taxation. We all pay under penalty of law, that is to say under legal coercion. So in one sense Doe pays voluntarily (willingly), in another not voluntarily (under coercion).

Richard Roe is even more of a patriot than Doe. He not only pays his taxes willingly; he makes an additional payment as a gift. When asked by the tax collector, "Do you make this contribution to the government as an advance tax payment?," he replies, "No, I make it as a voluntary contribution above and beyond my compulsory tax payments (not under coercion), and above and beyond my moral and legal duty (gratuitously)." Roe's payment then is voluntary in the sense that Doe's is too, but also voluntary in the sense in which Doe's is not.

Marvin Moe is asked whether he left his job voluntarily or whether he was fired. The question puzzles him. "I was of course *reluctant* to become unemployed; I need the money. But in the end I was *willing* to risk it. I was absolutely miserable in the job, and was prepared to take almost any job in preference to it, even a very bad job, or no job at all, as a lesser evil. So I made up my mind to quit, and quit I did." "Oh, so you left voluntarily?" Moe is asked. "Well they made things so miserable for me I *had* to quit; but I wasn't fired. I could have stayed on had I chosen." Moe resigned *reluctantly* (not "voluntarily"), but *willingly* (that is "voluntarily"), and under coercive pressure (the implicit threat of continued unhappy circumstances), but he was not *compelled* to leave (firing is a kind of "legal compulsion"). How do we add all of this up?

A reporter asks a group of American expatriates in Brazil during the period when there was no extradition treaty between the United States and Brazil, "Did you leave your homeland voluntariy?" One person replies that he was deported (legally "kicked out"). Deportation, like firing, is a kind of legal compulsion. So the first expatriate had no choice; he was forced out. But suppose he hated America, and left willingly, even eagerly? A second emigrant replies that he escaped from an American prison and fled to Brazil. His only choice was between prison in the United States and freedom in Brazil. He left regretfully, even reluctantly, and very definitely *under* coercion (the threat of re-imprisonment) and *because of* coercion. A third says that he fled when a warrant was issued for his arrest. He could have stayed and fought in court but he would probably have lost, so he fled in terror of imprisonment. A fourth reports that he wanted to stay but he couldn't find work. He left reluctantly, even unwillingly, because of coercive pressure, having been forced to choose between unemployment in America and work in Brazil. A fifth had a terrible job in the United States and was offered a better one in Brazil which he didn't like either but accepted as the lesser evil. A sixth left despite his deep love for his native country because he had been denied legal custody of the child he loved even more. He fled with the child. A seventh left to escape onerous alimony payments to his former wife. Only the deportee had no choice in a literal sense. The others exercised choice under one or another degree of coercive pressure, some leaving under pressure but willingly, most leaving under pressure and *because* of that pressure.

If we consider only the more or less objective fact of coercive pressure in these examples, we can appraise the degree of voluntariness or involuntariness in every case, and even attempt comparative evaluations and rankings. If we consider the subjective factor of degree of *willingness* (protest, reluctance, regret, acquiescence, agreeableness, eagerness, zeal), we shall be closer to the truth about motivation, but objective assessments of voluntariness will become inexact, uncertain and (if both standards are used) incommensurable. For moral purposes we should always use the subjective "willingness" standard, and judge voluntariness by reference to the actual motivation of the person whose choices are at issue. That is the approach that is most respectful of autonomy and individuality, judging each individual as he is, not as the actuarial tables say he probably is. That is surely the approach that would be taken in the Court of Heaven where all the facts are known. In human legislatures and courts of law, however, a person's degree of willingness while under coercion is often permanently shrouded in obscurity, and legislatures are forced for practical reasons to formulate rules based on the presumptive preferences of standard persons, thus discouraging subsequent judicial inquiry into actual preferences of real individuals.

Where the law *can* take "willingness" of consent into account without arbitrariness and uncertainty, however, it *should* do so, and thereby measure the voluntariness of particular responses and consentings on the subjective scale. If Mother Theresa (recall the example in Chap. 23, §4) tells the court that she *wanted* the urchin to have her money, then respect for *her* autonomy requires that the urchin be allowed to keep the money as a gift, rather than return it as ill-gotten loot. Her consent to his having it, even though originally expressed under coercion, can nevertheless be independently verified as genuine. If the criminal has killed her, however, and fled with her money, the law would have no choice, without her testimony, but to presume unwillingness on her part, and infer that what is done under coercion is done because of coercion. The gunman (or gun-urchin) would be held criminally liable in either case, not necessarily for wrongfully coming into possession of the property of another (for in the one case the money is legally a gift), but for making illegal threats, restricting another's liberty, and subjecting the other to coercion. Such behavior in itself is both harmful to the interests of the coercees and full of social danger, since its tendency in the preponderance of cases is to produce either the harm it demands or the greater harm it threatens, so that no penal code based on the harm principle can tolerate it.

It is natural enough that the vountariness of consent be determined by the subjective willingness standard whenever that is feasible, since the presence and degree of coercive pressure, for many legal purposes, is itself determined by reference to the actual preference orderings of individual subjects. When A forces B to choose either X or Y, we determine whether that is coercion by inquiring (among other things) whether B himself finds X or Y or both to be evils he would prefer not to suffer. If we have direct access to B's testimony we do not need to learn whether most people regard X and Y or both as evils. We can of course be highly confident in advance that any given person will regard the loss of his own life as an evil, and the loss of his property as an evil too, though a lesser one. We can also assume that a threatener shares the same statistical presumption, so that even when the presumption does not hold, coercive *intention* can be ascribed confidently to him.

When we do have independent access to an individual's preferences, however, we pay due regard not only to the person's autonomy but also to his status as *responsible* agent when we use his own values in assessing the voluntariness of his actions and consentings. If B, an employee in A's firm, covets and prays for the opportunity to take over the Ajax account, and then is told one day by the boss that either he accept the assignment to the Ajax account or be fired, his eager and grateful acceptance loses no voluntariness for having been made under coercion. If B later complains that the threat of a sacking forced him against his will to consent to what turned out to be harmful to his career, his argument of course is a disingenuous attempt to evade responsibility.

Most preference-affecting proposals that disjoin a severe evil with the single alternative course preferred by the coercer are highly coercive. In most cases the severe evil is chosen in order to tip the coercee's motivational scales toward what he regards as another evil, since the assumption is reasonable that a person will agree to an evil only to avoid a greater one. But it is possible for a coercer to miscalculate and threaten an evil far greater than is necessary. If the alternative to that intolerable evil is actually welcomed by the coercee anyway as a good (as in our Ajax example), then the proposal, while still a threat, is in its effect not coercive at all. There is in that case, of course, considerable "differential coercive pressure," but the choice is "easy" not because the coercive threat is so overwhelming, but rather because the coercive demand is so undemanding. If a gunman who wishes to give money to B (whom he wrongly supposes reluctant to accept it), says: "Take this money or I'll blow your brains out!" (or more realistically, "Take this money or I'll kill your child who is in my custody"), then he creates a redundant intimidation—what might even be called a "noncoercive threat"—a proposal that is coercive in intention and technique but not in effect—to a willing "victim" whose acceptance of his terms is entirely voluntary, and who may not evade responsibility for his avarice later by pleading coercion.

The use of subjective standards would incline courts in a definite direction in a class of cases that recently bedeviled them, namely the "voluntary" participation of prisoners in biomedical and behavioral research performed on them. These actual cases are a good deal less dramatic than our earlier hypothetical examples of coercive offers to hapless prisoners on death row,

for they do not involve offers to withdraw an intolerable penalty in exchange
for the assumption of risks that most persons would avoid if possible. "Those
who are opposed to prison research point out that prisons are inherently
coercive and restrictive environments. Those who see no intrinsic harm (including many of the potential research subjects themselves) claim that depriving prisoners of the right to participate in research is a further affront to their
autonomy and, most important, prevents them from taking advantage of one
of the rare opportunities to relieve the boredom of prison life and earn a little
money."[33] Among those who would restrict the experiments on grounds that
the coercive environment of prisons makes the voluntariness of consent suspect was the Federal Drug Administration which in May, 1980, banned
research "not related to the health or well-being of the subjects or to conditions affecting prisoners as a class." Then in 1981 four prisoners in a Michigan State Prison, including one Fante, joined the Upjohn pharmaceutical
company in a suit to prevent implementation of the F.D.A. rule, arguing
that they freely agreed to be part of the experiment, voluntarily and without
coercion, and that the effect of the new government rules was arbitrarily to
cancel their "right to participate as research subjects."[34] That suit apparently
forced the F.D.A. to rewrite the rules, but in October, 1981, the results
were not yet clear. If our analysis is correct, however, the offers of researchers under liberalized but protective rules would not necessarily be
coercive, for instead of forcing a choice between evils, or between a moderate
good an intolerable evil, they offer a positive inducement (measured against
the baseline of normal prison routine) to choose to submit to a carefully
regulated risk (a relatively minor evil).

Still, the tendency worldwide is to prohibit or severely restrict experiments on prisoners.[35] How can that be explained, given that the opportunity
offered prisoners to participate *can* be such as to make voluntary consent
possible? Three reasons suggest themselves. The first is that while there is no
necessity that subtle coercive pressures from prison authorities be used to
force the *apparently* "voluntary" consent of prisoners, nevertheless wherever
there is such great disparity in the power of the parties, the opportunity and
indeed, temptation, to coercion is always present. A mere frown from a
prison guard can be interpreted, and sometimes correctly so, as a tacit threat
to inflict harsh treatment later. A restrictive rule would prevent such abuses.
The point is not that disparities in power are inherently coercive, but rather
that if they are great enough they make abuses likely. A second reason for
prohibition is that it appears morally repugnant to many, and contrary to the
dignity of human beings, that researchers should use humans, even volunteers, as if they were laboratory animals. This Kantian sentiment is quite
consistent with the admission that prisoner consent *can* be voluntary. Finally
one might find prison experiments repugnant on a related but independent

ground. Research on prisoners, especially when conducted by commercial companies, is a way of benefitting the researchers who take advantage of the vulnerable position of weaker parties. One could acknowledge that prisoner consent is often voluntary but condemn the practice anyway on the ground that it is (noncoercive) *exploitation* (see Chaps. 31, 32). The objection in that case is not that the researchers *wrong* the voluntary consenters (that judgment is ruled out by the *Volenti* maxim) but that they make a unjust gain for themselves.

Contextual variations in standards of voluntariness required for validity. The third concept in our trio, consensual validity, differs from the other two in that it is not subject to gradations of degree. Validity and invalidity, like guilt and innocence, liability and no liability, are all-or-nothing concepts. Moreover, the validity of an expression of assent cannot simply be read off the facts or derived from an analysis of the concepts of voluntariness and coercion. How much voluntariness is required for a valid (legally effective) act of consent is at least partly a matter of policy, to be decided by reference to a rule itself justified by the usual legislative reasons of utility and social justice. These rules will specify standards of voluntariness whose stringency varies with the nature of the context (implied warranties in automobile purchases, voluntary research in prisons, plea bargaining before trials) and the particular legal outcome at issue (contractual obligation, criminal liability, assumptions of personal risk). By and large, as we have seen, the degree of voluntariness required for a valid contract will be more than that required for a second party's criminal defense. (The desperate mother's consent to the lecherous millionaire's proposal to become his mistress was not voluntary enough to bind her to it after the millionaire performed his side of the bargain, but it was voluntary enough to provide an exculpatory defense for him to a criminal charge.) Similarly, the amount of nonvoluntariness in the conduct of a primary party that is sufficient to exonerate him from a charge of wrongdoing will vary with the amount of social harm threatened or produced. The more harmful to others the act in question is, the greater the amount of coercion-involuntariness required to excuse it. In the more serious cases, as we have seen, wrongdoers are held to objective standards of voluntariness. They are guilty even though their wrongful choice was coerced, provided that a morally exemplary person in their circumstances would not have succumbed to the same coercive pressure. The more serious the social harm that could have been foreseen, the more stringent the objective standard, and the more heroic the hypothetical exemplar.

The most troublesome of the variations are those stemming from the relativity of selected baselines available for measuring voluntariness. As we have seen (Chap. 20, §§4,5), we can measure the voluntariness of an act *talis qualis* in the circumstances in which it occurs, or we can consider those circumstances themselves to be deviant, and judge the act instead against a hypothetical normal background. Which approach we adopt will be determined both by policy considerations and considerations of fairness. Prison environments are restrictive in their very nature, so if we judge the voluntariness of a prisoner's consent to a coercive offer against the normal background of "the man on the street," it will seem quite nonvoluntary indeed. Still, judged against the baseline of the prisoner's actual circumstances, it may be a reasonable choice, even the product of an inducement, and quite voluntary in the circumstances. If we assume both that it is essential to the public interest that the prisoners be so confined, and also that it was not unfair to this particular prisoner that he is confined, then there is no point in judging his choice by the hypothetical standard. His acceptance of the proposal might be highly voluntary *in the circumstances*, and the circumstances themselves, though freedom-restricting, might be unmodifiable and just. In that case his consent is voluntary enough to be valid. On the other hand, the coercive offer made to the slave in Nozick's example will produce a consent that is voluntary relative to the circumstances of his slavery, but insofar as those circumstances themselves are unjustified, one might assess his assent against a different background, and derive the judgment that it is invalid for such larger legal purposes as getting the criminal slave-owner off the hook, or defeating the slave's suit for compensation. Henningsen's consent to Bloomfield Motor's contractual terms was "voluntary in the circumstances" when assessed against the background of prevailing commerical practice, but that practice itself was both modifiable and unfair (indeed "unconscionable"), so the appropriate norm to apply is the hypothetical one in which warranties are themselves negotiable. Against that hypothetical background, Henningsen's actual circumstances are coercive, and his consent was by no means "voluntary enough" to be valid.

7. Applications to criminal law problems

The soft paternalist, being highly respectful of personal autonomy, holds that a third party is justified in interfering forcibly on *B*'s behalf with actions of *A* if and only if those actions are harmful or dangerous to *B*, and either *B* has not consented to them, or his consent was not sufficiently voluntary to be valid. Similarly, the state is morally entitled to protect *B* from *A*'s actions by threatening *A* with criminal liability when and only when *A*'s action is harmful or dangerous to *B*, and *B* has not consented in a manner sufficiently voluntary to be valid. One of the factors that tends to reduce the voluntariness of any expressed assent is coercion. When some one other than *A* has coercively pressured *B* into consenting to *A*'s harmful proposal, *A* can be held responsible for harming *B* only if he was somehow party to the coercion. When A himself has coerced B into cnsenting, then B's expression of consent (when it is not "voluntary enough") will fail to provide A with a valid defense to criminal charges.

When B himself, for his own reasons, without coercion from any other party, requests that A act in the manner harmful or dangerous to B's interest, then provided his request was not produced by A's trickery, or A's taking advantage of B's intellectual impairment, B's "consent" is entirely voluntary. He, after all, was the initiator of the agreement to which A consents, rather than the other way round. Similarly, if A requests B's consent by appealing to such motives as benevolence, pity, friendship or the like, or if he bolsters B's incentive with positive inducements, or alluring prospects of gain, once more B's consent will be voluntary. Even if A happens upon B in a condition of vulnerability and asks his consent to the terms of an exploitative "coercive offer," B's acceptance, while short of perfect voluntariness, will usually be voluntary enough to relieve A or *criminal* responsibility. But if A forcibly intervenes in B's affairs to create the conditions of vulnerability and then deliberately exploits those conditions with a coercive offer, B's consent so extracted will usually not be voluntary enough to provide A with a defense, and *a fortiori* consent produced by a credible *threat* of harm will have no legal force in any court, civil or criminal.

These summary results allow us to sort out the traditional crimes affected by coerced consent from those for which the whole topic is moot or irrelevant. In general, the problem of coerced consent is likely to arise in crimes that consist essentially of actions by A pursuant to a *quid pro quo* agreement between A and B, proposed initially by A, and dangerous or patently harmful to B. The issue of coercion is not likely to arise in crimes consisting of A's favors or gratuitous services to B, originally requested by B despite their *prima facie* harmful or dangerous character. Thus the issue arises in the "crimes" of usury and bigamy, but not in the crimes of euthanasia-homicide or assisted suicide. The request of an aged, suffering, terminally ill person for a merciful death at the hands of his or her spouse cannot be treated as an instance of consent coerced by the other party, even if it should be judged less than fully voluntary by other criteria. A rapid survey of "relevant crimes" follows.

Usury. The taking of interest for loans was traditionally condemned as sinful and unnatural by the Church, but since it was essential to the emerging system of capitalism it came in modern times to be tolerated. The charging of "excessive, exorbitant, and usurious rates of interest,"[36] however, has often been forbidden by regulatory statutes, as it is to this day. Usury, defined as charging in excess of the legal rate for the use of money, has not been a crime in the English common law, though it was an ecclesiastical offense from the thir-

teenth century on, and was subsequently prohibited by various criminal statutes until "all existing laws against usury" [i.e., penal statutes] were repealed
in 1854.[37] One can understand why highly exploitative money lending was
traditionally execrated. In times of economic hardship the loaner has the borrower over the barrel. He has what the other desperately needs and he will
charge him every last penny for it that his market advantage can exact. The
borrower can find no more reasonable terms elsewhere; he must "take it or
leave it."[38] His option is between an intolerable evil like imminent starvation
and a barely lesser evil, the onerous costs that threaten his future solvency.

Usurious agreements, then, when they impose hard terms on the weaker
party, are indeed *coercive* in the manner of all "unconscionable contracts." In
our analysis, their coercive character reduces the voluntariness of the consent
of the weaker party whose position is very much like that imposed by the
well owner on the man dying of thirst in Murphy's example, or that of the
impecunious mother in the lecherous millionaire example. An even closer
analogy is that to another class of devious commercial practices, those called
"forestalling, ingrossing, and regrating" in the old English statutes forbidding
them, or "hoarding and profiteering" in current language. "The forestaller
intercepted goods on their way to market and bought them up so as to be
able to command what price he chose when he got to the market. The
ingrosser or regrator—for the two words had much the same meaning—was a
person who, having bought goods wholesale sold them again wholesale,"[39]
that is, having bought up large quantities of some commodity, controlled the
supply in a given market for the purpose of raising the price. The difference
between these unfair and extortionate business practices and usurious agreements, however, is that in the former cases the bargaining parties perform
their respective sides of the agreement more or less simultaneously—they
exchange money for goods—whereas in usurious money-lending, the more
powerful party performs first, trusting the other to repay on agreed terms at
a later time.

The state, it seems to me, can protect the weak party (the borrower)
without threatening the strong party (the lender) with criminal punishment.
In fact that is the way modern states (in non-Moslem countries) regulate the
moneylending industry. The state sets maximum rates of interest with an eye
both to promoting economic efficiency and protecting the relatively helpless
from exploitation. If a borrower nonetheless is "forced" in coercive circumstances to consent to higher than legal rates, his promise to repay *at those rates*
is unenforcable. That provision of his contract is invalid. If he then repays at
the permissible rate only, his creditor cannot win a breach of contract suit
later in an effort to collect the surplus. Given that usurious contracts are
invalid, moneylenders have no incentive to offer them, and the practice is
then effectively discouraged without resorting to the criminal law.

To be sure, mobsters might nevertheless have their own incentives for making illegal loans. They might warn their borrowers that failure to repay at the agreed upon illegal rate will lead to dire consequences, not from the law, but from criminal "enforcers" who have their own methods. Money-lenders of that stripe are indeed in the "business of extortion," and their readiness to use illegal means of enforcing agreements is itself punishable as a more familiar kind of crime. But where such means of enforcement are neither used nor threatened, there need be no resort to the criminal law to protect borrowers from unconscionable contracts.[40] There is no rationale provided by liberal principles for making usury as such a crime.

Bigamy. Even on the assumption that monogamous marriage is a uniquely valuable social institution worth upholding and protecting by public policy, I see no very persuasive reason for making bigamy[41] a crime, and surely no reason at all for making it a serious felony. A bigamous marriage is legally no marriage at all. Blackstone wrote in 1755 that "such second marriage, living the former husband or wife, is simply void, and a mere nullity, by the ecclesiastical law of England. And yet [he adds] the legislature has thought it just to make it a felony, by reason of its being so great a violation of the public economy and decency of a well-ordered state."[42] One would think, contrary to Blackstone, that nullification of second marriage contracts as contrary to public policy would be quite sufficient to protect the personal and public interests involved without the help of the criminal sanction (just as in the case of usurious contracts), but this has been a very uncommon opinion in discussions of the topic. Lord Devlin chides H.L.A. Hart for what he takes to be Hart's inability to construct a rationale for criminalization on wholly liberal grounds, and Hart in his turn argues that the public harm principle and the offense principle are quite capable of generating a plausible rationale for the crime of bigamy.[43] The view I propose differs from both of these. I agree with Devlin that there are no convincing liberal reasons for the crime, but contrary to both Hart and Devlin, I suggest that there should be no such crime at all—the proper liberal position.

Some bigamous marriages, of course, are contracted fraudulently. A man[44] may deceive his second "wife" by keeping secret his marriage to a first, or he may deceive the first by concealing his pseudo-marriage with the second. In both cases at least one of the women is likely to be harmed. The new wife in particular is vulnerable. She may make critical life decisions, financial invest-ments, and personal commitments in the good faith expectation that she has one legal status when in fact, because of fraud, she has another. The harm to the first wife is less clear. She is being "cheated," without question, but when one subtracts the wrong caused her by the adultery from the wrong caused her by the bigamy, the residue is barely discernible. Criminal statutes against adultery as such have long since been discredited; in most places they have been repealed, and where they are still on the books they have fallen into desuetude. There is a vanishingly weak case then, based on the need to protect the *first wife* from harm, for criminalizing even fraudulent bigamy. The second "wife," on the other hand, when her lover's prior marriage is concealed from her, is the victim of a swindle from which she will typically suffer both direct and indirect harms. *Fraudulent* bigamy might then plausibly be made a crime to protect her, although a legislature should be made cautious by consideration of the many civil remedies that may already be available to her.

There is a much weaker case for punishing bigamy when it is not based on deception of one of the "wives." Who needs the protection of the criminal law in this kind of case? The first wife has the option of suing for divorce on the grounds (if grounds are needed) of adultery. She has been wronged by her husband's infidelity, but that wrong in normal circumstances is not aggravated by his mock wedding ceremony with the new woman and the legally invalid marriage contract it produces. That "contract" is a worthless piece of paper in the eye of the law, with no legal significance whatever. If the first wife is not deceived, she has the power to assure that legal agencies are not deceived either, so that there will not be the public harm that consists in the confusing of the public records, or the misrepresentation of illegitimate children as legitimate.[45] If nevertheless, the public records do get distorted, the only plausible criminal offense, given the rarity and triviality of the harm, would be a very minor misdemeanor. The second "wife" is even less in need of the protection of the criminal law when she goes through a wedding ceremony with a man she knows is already married. If there is any crime in such an action she is a party to it rather than its victim.

Strangely enough, the *Model Penal Code* not only makes bigamy a crime whether or not deception is involved, it actually makes the more open variety in which both spouses voluntarily participate without deception (which it calls "polygamy") the more serious crime: "A person is guilty of polygamy, *a felony of the third degree*, if he marries or cohabits with more than one spouse at a time in purported exercise of the right of plural marriage." The wife (or wives) too would be guilty of the same serious crime. The *Code's* distinction between the misdemeanor of bigamy and the felony it calls polygamy seems to imply the principle that a trivial crime becomes a serious one when it is openly committed or publicly flaunted by the perpetrators in what they claim to be an exercise of their rights. An obvious target of the proposed polygamy statute are Mormons and others who claim a religious right to multiple spouses. It is difficult to see why the state in normal times should be so frightened of such groups. To be sure the voluntariness of the consent of

the added spouses might be suspect, but that would be a ground for nullifying their matrimonial contracts rather than punishing the contractors. One
suspects that the ultimate target of the statute is the practice, even when
wholly voluntary, of open cohabitation between or among people of the
opposite sex who are not legally married.[46] When that cohabitation assumes
an air of purported legitimacy, which then goes unchallenged, the state may
fear that by its own tolerance it promotes the appearance of respectability
and weakens moral restraints. Severe criminal prohibition then is necessary
to protect "public morals," a purpose legitimized not by the harm principle
so much as by the principle of legal moralism.

Extortion. Blackstone, reporting the common law, defined extortion as a
crime against public justice committed by public officials, consisting in "an
officer's unlawfully taking, by color of his office, from any man, any money
or thing of value, that is not due to him, or is more than is due, or before it is
due."[47] When a public official like a toll collector, revenue agent, or policeman demands a payment, for example a "tip" beyond what is due him, he
uses the power of his office at least implicitly to make a threat, and exploits
the fear he thereby induces in the citizen to gain at his expense. Such a
wrongful use of the coercive power of political authority is a way of taking
money or property by coercion. Soon the word "extortion" came to stand for
all unlawful obtaining of money from another by means of a threatened
harm. To extort, according to *Black's Law Dictionary*, is "to exact something
wrongfully by threats or putting in fear." In twentieth-century language any
person can be an extorter, not only public officers. In modern penal codes
"extortion" seems to be the name given to any crime that consists of taking
another's property by coercive threat, unless that crime already happens to
have another more specialized name like "armed robbery" or "blackmail."
    Terminological confusion is so great that the authors of the *Model Penal
Code* proposed an extensive revision of usage. Section 223.1 establishes a
"consolidation of theft offenses": "Conduct denominated 'theft' in this Article
constitutes a single offense embracing the separate offenses heretofore known
as larceny, embezzlement, false pretense, extortion, blackmail, fraudulent
conversion, receiving stolen property, and the like." The *Code* then distinguishes "Theft by Unlawful Taking or Disposition" (Section 223.2), "Theft
by Deception" (Section 223.3), and "Theft by Extortion" (Section 223.4),
among other categories.[48] "Theft by Extortion" is then defined as obtaining
the property of another by threatening to act in any one of several damaging
ways, including the threat to inflict bodily injury, to make accusation of
criminal offense, to expose secrets tending to subject one to hatred or contempt, to take or withhold action as an official (what Blackstone called taking
"under color of one's office"), to bring about or continue a strike or boycott,[49]

to testify or withhold testimony with respect to another's legal claim or defense, and (the usual catch-all) to "inflict any other harm which would not benefit the actor." The common theme unifying these diverse wrongs under the rubric of extortion is that they all involve one person taking advantage of his greater power, another's dependence on him, or a vulnerability either chanced upon or deliberately created, to coerce the other to hand over his property to him. ("Property" must be construed very broadly if we are also to include the body of the woman who consents to the lecherous millionaire's demands.)

Extortion differs from some other forms of theft such as burglary (unlawful taking) in that the extorter takes by getting the other to give. He forces the other to agree to his terms by manipulating his options and leaving him no reasonable choice. It differs from theft by deception (e.g. taking under false pretenses) by utilizing threats rather than false pretenses, but it resembles that category in that it extracts an agreement from the victim, under circumstances that render the assent invalid as a defense. The victim no more parts with his money voluntarily under threat than he does to the burglar who takes it without benefit even of extracted "consent." Extortion then is an unproblematic model of wrongful harm imposed upon another by coercing his agreement. There is no question that it should be criminal under liberal principles, whether it be a crafty "protection racket" or an unsubtle highway robbery.

25

Failures of Consent: Defective Belief

1. Division of categories

Coercive force is by no means the only kind of factor that can reduce or vitiate the voluntariness of consent. Deficient or mistaken information is another. When B honestly believes that he is consenting to one proposal (P_1) from A when in fact (A later claims) he is consenting to another (P_2), then he has not voluntarily consented to P_2. At the most we can say that he assented to P_2 "by mistake" or "through a misunderstanding." Even when A and B have the same understanding of the proposal to which B appears to have consented, B might have been ignorant of, or mistaken about, certain facts which, if known at the time of the agreement, would have led him not to consent. Those facts may or may not have been known to A, who may or may not have had a "duty of disclosure" to B. Again, A may have disclosed the relevant facts but inadvertently misrepresented them. In at least some of these cases, B's consent will be considerably less than fully voluntary. Finally, B may have agreed to A's proposal only because he was tricked or deceived, either by A himself or by some third party. In this fraudulent category, typically, B's ignorance is not so much the product of simple nondisclosure as of deliberate misrepresentation, either about the proposal itself, about relevant background facts, or future occurrences.

The diverse situations in which the voluntariness of consent is called in question because of the consenter's defective beliefs, then, can be represented by Diagrams 25-1 through 25-4. Diagram 25-1 shows that a person's consent may be nonvoluntary because of defective beliefs in any of three different categories, and that his ignorance or mistake may either be the consequence

	As to What Is Being Agreed to	As to Background Facts	As to Future Occurrences
Ignorance or Mistake			
Deception			

Diagram 25-1. Causes and subjects of defective beliefs.

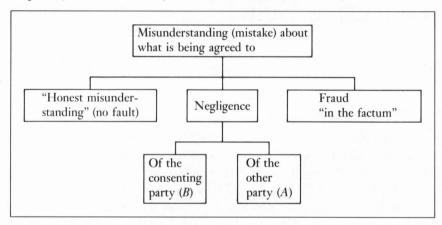

Diagram 25-2. Defective beliefs about the agreement itself.

of another's fraud, or the product of causes of another kind. Diagrams 25-2 through 4 divide more finely in overlapping ways. Diagram 25-2 distinguishes the possible causes of divergent understanding about what is agreed to. Diagram 25-3 distinguishes the causes of the main categories of consenter's mistake or ignorance about collateral facts—beliefs that might lead him to consent involuntarily to an agreement. Finally, Diagram 25-4 focuses exclusively upon agreements invalidated by *fraud* and classifies them by the source and subject of the deception. Hardly a category in these four diagrams is without its own philosophical perplexities. The charts themselves help only to provide a guide to our tour through the labyrinth.

2. Misunderstanding over what is being agreed to

There are cases in which the proposer and the consenter do not have the same interpretations of their agreement and the confusion is not clearly any-

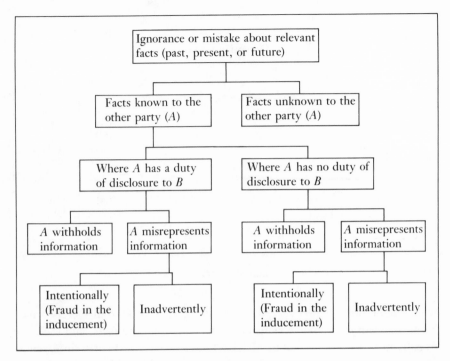

Diagram 25-3. Defective beliefs about collateral facts.

one's fault. *A* may have proposed in slurred speech, or with a heavy accent, or his written request for consent may have been in obscure handwriting, or there may have been a subtle unnoticed ambiguity in his terms, or perhaps *B*, a foreigner, does not speak the language in which the agreement is made very well. Perhaps papers have been inadvertently switched and myopic *B* has signed an agreement other than the one he intended to sign. Such mistakes may occur even after scrupulous efforts of both parties to achieve genuine agreement. In these cases of "honest misunderstanding" when *A*, acting with what he reasonably but incorrectly believes to be *B*'s consent, harms or endangers *B* in a way prohibited by the criminal law in the absence of consent, what judgments are entailed by liberal principles?

First of all, a third party who is aware of the misunderstanding should be entitled to interfere with *A* to protect *B* without himself incurring liability. If it is feasible, of course, the third-party intervenor should interfere nonforcibly, or even by utilizing the legal machinery of the courts or the police, and such machinery should be available to him. By hypothesis, *A* is as innocent of fault as *B*, and he may himself stand to suffer losses if he is prevented from acting in reliance on *B*'s presumed consent. This fact can so complicate the issue that a well-meaning intervenor may seem to be wrong

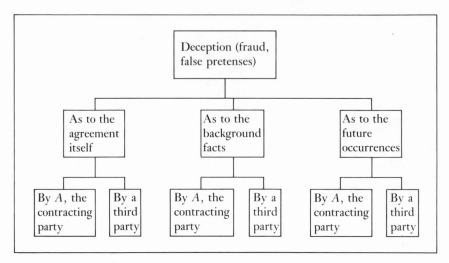

Diagram 25-4. Defective beliefs induced by fraud.

whatever he does. Moreover, intervention might save *B* from merely trivial harms or from *prima facie* serious ones, depending on the facts, and the same hypothetical variations apply to *A*. The hapless third-party intervenor, forced to decide the issue under pressure, must be held to a standard of reasonableness in the circumstances, but no higher standard than that. He may use force it it seems necessary to prevent proportionately serious harm, but not otherwise. And he may not intervene at all if there is time for the police or even the courts to make the difficult and responsible decisions for him. One principle clearly applies, however. If *B* has not voluntarily (knowingly) consented to *A*'s dangerous conduct, then for *A* to engage in that conduct is to invade *B*'s autonomy, and this is true even though *A*, acting in good faith, is without fault.

A's innocence, however, should shield him from criminal liability. After all, if the misunderstanding was an honest, genuinely faultless one, then *A*'s action is itself substantially less than voluntary. He violates *B*'s autonomy but does so by mistake. He honestly and plausibly thought he had *B*'s consent, but in fact he did not. But mutual faultlessness is the exceptional case. In most instances one party or the other bears a heavier initial duty to ensure that there has been no misunderstanding, and the party with the greater duty of care is the party who is negligent if that duty is not discharged. In general, the party with the lesser vulnerability to harm is the party with the greater duty to prevent misunderstanding by taking steps to "make sure," and the greater the possible harm the greater that duty of care. If Doctor *A*, seeking organs for transplant, thinks he hears patient *B* say "You may kill me," when in fact *B* has said "You may bill me," he will have no defense to homicide even in an ideally liberal legal system if he shoots B then and there, without taking any further steps to corroborate voluntariness. His mistake may have been an "honest" one, but that hardly excuses him for his failure to avoid it. Indeed, totally faultless misunderstandings in criminal cases will be so rare, when one takes into account the duty to make sure, that for all practical purposes we can presume the harm-causer to be guilty until he proves that he had taken all reasonable precautions against consent-by-mistake, and that the misunderstanding occurred *anyway*.

In some relatively rare cases, the party who "consents by mistake" may have been in a uniquely favored position to be aware of potential sources of misunderstanding. Perhaps he knows that his understanding of English, or his hearing or eyesight, is weak, and that his contracting partner had no reason even to suspect such handicaps. In that case, the consenter himself had the heavier duty to avoid a type of misunderstanding the danger of which only he could have suspected. If B is negligent in this fashion, and his negligence is the cause of his assenting to a proposal of A's that he had not intended to accept, A may plausibly claim after the fact that B's consent to the proposal *he* (A) thought he was making should be treated as "voluntary enough" in the circumstances to be valid. If A is right about this, then we have an exception to a maxim that may have seemed self-evident, that—"For a person to have voluntarily consented to P he must have believed that he was consenting to P." Now, in sympathetic response to A's claim, we may wish to amend the maxim by adding the clause—"or he ought to have known that that was what he was doing," to cover the case of the grossly negligent consenter.

Most of these complex uncertainties could be avoided, however, by rules requiring formal public consenting procedures, witnesses, notaries, questionnaires, "cooling off periods," and the like, before the expression of assent becomes legally valid consent.

The remaining category of misunderstanding about what is agreed to consists of cases in which A tricks B into formally consenting to one agreement under the impression that he is consenting to another. This kind of case is philosophically interesting mainly because of the contrast between "fraud in the *factum*" and "fraud in the inducement," and we will consider it in detail in section 7, below.

3. Ignorance or mistake about background facts

When B consents to A's proposal even though it may be dangerous to his interests to do so, he acts because certain beliefs about the matter of the proposal mesh with his desires in such a way as to constitute reasons in favor of accepting it. That subclass of B's total set of beliefs about the world that

are germane as reasons for or against the proposal we can call the "inducement" for the proposal. If some of these beliefs were to change, then the case
for the proposal would be weakened or strenthened accordingly. Other beliefs are so critical to B's motivation that were they to change, B would no
longer choose to consent. For example, if B agrees to trade his horse for A's
cow for purposes of cattle breeding only, and then learn that the cow is
barren (changed background belief) he will withdraw his consent. If the
transaction has already taken place when B learns the truth, he may argue
that his consent was not voluntary because of the falsity of the belief that led
him to grant it in the first place.¹ Mistaken inducement beliefs clearly are
among the factors generally thought to diminish the voluntariness of consent
to ordinary contractual exchanges, though (as we shall see) they are not
allowed to play so important a role when A's criminal liability is at issue, and
even in the law of contracts their presence is not by itself decisive.

The key issue in the law of contracts is the scope of the seller's duty to
disclose the facts that are likely to be critically germane to the buyer's
decision.² If the seller failed to discharge his duty to disclose, then insofar as
the undisclosed facts undermined an assumption that was a critical (necessary) part of the buyer's inducement, the buyer's consent to the transaction
was involuntary (as in the barren cow example). The situation is more complex when the wrongfully hidden information does not strike at a belief that
is *necessary* to the buyer's consent but is nevertheless one that he takes to be a
part of the case for consenting. Perhaps he would still be willing but somewhat more reluctant to agree, or perhaps now he will still buy but only for a
lower price. Depending on how vital a role the belief in question plays in the
buyer's motivation, its falsity will diminish to a proportional degree the
voluntariness of his consent. In still another way, then, voluntariness is
subject to degrees. But when the owner has no duty of disclosure, his concealment of relevant information from the buyer will not affect the voluntariness of the buyer's consent for legal purposes, or, in any event, it will not
void that consent, since the agreement will be held to be "voluntary enough"
to be valid. In that case, let the buyer beware!

A duty of disclosure, if imposed by a vague rule, could be onerous for the
seller. How can he know exactly what facts will be critical for every possible
buyer, given the large range of personal differences? What can protect him
from the whims of the occasional unpredictable eccentric? Once again the
law must create order and predictability by using some notion of a "standard
individual." A seller cannot be expected to anticipate the motives of every
possible purchaser, but he can be expected to know the concerns that are
common to most people—for example a preference for noncorroded pipes,
nonleaky roofs, and the absence of termites—and the law can even help him
here by explicitly listing some of the more important standard interests and

requiring explicit reports in respect to them. In such a way public rules take both the arbitrariness and the vulnerability out of voluntary transactions both for buyer and seller. When a buyer has special interests not mentioned in the rules and not easily anticipated by the seller, the burden is on him to make inquiries, and on the seller to answer fully as well as truthfully.

The standard person will not only have certain concerns—for example learning whether the pipes in the house he is considering buying are made of copper or iron—he also will have certain "deep background beliefs," for example that in this locality there are several nights each winter in which the temperature falls below the freezing point, or still deeper background beliefs, such as that water freezes at $32°$ F. If the buyer in question should lack these standard background beliefs, the seller cannot be blamed for not disclosing them to him, although, of course, if the buyer inquires even about such general questions as these, the seller has a duty to answer truthfully. The information the seller should be required to disclose on his own initiative, however, consists primarily of data about the particular object (e.g. house, land, car) he is selling, not about matters of standard knowledge or belief.

What hinges on the satisfactory performance of the various duties relating to disclosure, of course, is whether the bargainers' agreement is legally valid, and whether their contract is to be enforced or rescinded. Criminal liability is quite another matter. If, despite a clear duty of disclosure, the seller conceals vital information, then the buyer, when he learns later of the sad truth, may have the contract of sale abrogated, and the court will "release the parties from further obligation to each other and restore [them] to the positions they would have occupied if the contract had never been made."[3] For a large number of reasons criminal liability is not imposed in such cases. In addition to the standing case against using criminal sanctions, based on collateral social costs, a chief reason against them in these cases is that they are not necessary to protect buyers from inadequate or misleading information about the items they buy. The "weapon" of contractual rescission should be sufficient to keep sellers alert to the duties of their role, since there is no gain for them if a court later orders that arrangements on which they have come to rely be undone. Moreover, in these nondisclosure cases, if they are handled outside the criminal law, there is no need to make difficult determinations of the seller's "mental states" during the negotiations. If all that rides on the court's decision is the validity of a contract, the court need not determine whether the nondisclosure was intentional or merely negligent since the contract will be rescinded in either case.

Fraud, on the other hand, is a more proper subject for criminal investigation, for when it is at issue, what must be established is that the seller deliberately lied to the buyer, misrepresenting some fact he knew to be a vital part of the buyer's inducement, to the buyer's great disadvantage. Fraud is at once more difficult to protect against (a simple "explicit inquiry" will not help), a more serious moral offense, and a wrong more likely to be repeated, more likely to be seriously harmful, and less likely to be repaired by merely civil remedies. Usually the fraudulent deceiver's intentions are to gain at the other party's expense simply by tricking him into the agreement, and then fleeing with his loot. By the time the fraud is discovered and the contract rescinded, the damage has been done, and it cannot be undone by rescission merely. Contractual revocation as such, therefore, holds no terrors for the defrauder.

The line between deliberate misrepresentation (fraud) and intentional nondisclosure, however, is often hard to draw, as Anthony Kronman points out:

> . . . many will be tempted to acknowledge explicit misrepresentation as. . . illegitimate. . . but insist that the line be drawn there—limiting the conditions necessary for voluntary exchange to two (absence of physical coercion and fraud). Suppose however that the seller makes no threats and tells no lies, but does say things that, although true, are meant to encourage me to draw a false conclusion about the condition of the house and to inspect the premises less carefully than I might otherwise. (The seller tells me, for example, that the house has been inspected by an exterminator from the Acme Termite Company every six months for the last ten years, which is true, but neglects to inform me that during his last visit the exterminator dicovered a termite infestation which the seller has failed to cure.) By telling me only certain things about the house, and not others, the seller intends to throw me off the track and thereby take advantage of my ignorance and naivete. The same is true if he tells me nothing at all, but simply fails to reveal a defect he knows I am unaware of—a case of pure nondisclosure.[4]

There are those who think that ignorant and naive buyers "have only themselves to blame" if they are taken in by such ruses, and that instead of burdening the seller with strict duties of disclosure the state should expect the buyer to protect himself by having experts inspect the object for sale, requiring specific sellers' warranties, and so on. According to this "ethic of caveat emptor," the state should encourage private resourcefulness by imposing no duties of disclosure on the sellers. But as Kronman points out, the same reasoning taken to an extreme would require buyers to protect themselves against the risk that they "will be forced to sign a contract at gunpoint by hiring a bodyguard to accompany [them] wherever [they] go,"[5] and to protect themselves from explicit misrepresentation by requesting sellers to take lie detector tests. Whether to protect "consentors" by imposing legal duties on "proposers" is of course a policy question, and the differences among the alternatives to having rules against coercion, misrepresentation, and nondisclosure differ only in degree, but it is reasonably clear that in all these cases the alternative to protective rules would be general distrust, cumbersome procedures, accidents, misunderstandings, and widespread insecurity. There may be a point, as we shall see, to caveat emptor, but that maxim is misapplied when extended to basic information about products for sale in ordinary commercial exchanges. Freedom requires that society leave a place for contests of wit and skill, even extremely risky ones, but to convert all the routine transactions of economic life into such embroilments would be a burdensome complication that few if any would find in their interest to accept.[6]

4. Mistaken expectation of future occurrences

Many voluntary exchanges are consented to because one or both of the parties has as a key part of his inducement the belief that some event will occur in the future that will render the present transaction advantageous. Since nobody *knows* the future in the way one knows the characteristics of objects in his present attention, the language of "disclosure" and "nondisclosure" seems inappropriate. A person is not said to "disclose information" when he expresses his opinion about the future course of gold prices, changes in the pattern of economic development, or the amount of precipitation that will fall on crops in some future time. People whose decisions to buy or sell are based on beliefs of this uncertain kind are often called "speculators." However, what is "speculative opinion" when expressed by one person may well be "disclosed information" when expressed by another who is more privy to secret decisions already made. B may guess that the legislature will decide to build a highway in a given location, but A, who is himself a legislator on the crucial committee and who has polled his colleagues, may know already what decision the legislature will make.

How voluntary is a person's consent to a proposal when the key belief in his inducement is both speculative and false? Suppose B buys from A because he expects the price to go up so that he can resell at a profit, but in fact the price goes down and he must resell at a loss. Was B's consent to A's offer to sell voluntary in the first place? Clearly the answer must be affirmative, else we would have to characterize all losing gamblers as victims of larceny! The gamblers may be involuntary (i.e. unwilling) *losers*, but they are quite voluntary *risk-takers*. The way, therefore, to characterize their actions in the respect in which they *are* voluntary is as "assumptions of risk." (See §5 below.) A "competitive gamble" or "bet" can be defined as a voluntary agreement between two parties, both of whom have as a key part of their inducement a belief about some future occurrence, when one party's belief contradicts the other's. Part of the agreement to which each bettor freely consents is an understanding of how the risks are assigned— each agrees to forfeit the right to complain of unfairness if his predictions turn out to be false. Clearly not all contractual risk-assumptions are competitive in the present sense. B's contract with A may be risky to B because of independent future contingencies and yet offer no prospect of correlative gain to *A*. When *B*, a New Yorker, moves to California and buys *A*'s home on the San Andreas fault, *B* assumes a risk but *A* can anticipate no corresponding gain because (let us suppose) he must move to Illinois in any case, and no gain will come to him in Chicago if *B*'s home is destroyed by an earthquake in California.

The voluntariness of the assumption of risk is reduced, however, to the extent that the speculator does not really know the risk he is taking, or does not understand how and why it is a risk, or does not fully appreciate the seriousness of the risk he may, in some merely intellectual way, "understand." If *C* tells *B* falsely that he *knows* (having just been told by his congressman) that the express highway will not be built at the location of *A*'s store, *B* may buy *A*'s store without any sense that he is taking risk, and then suffer a grave loss, to his surprise and disappointment. Unless *A* releases him subsequently, however, his less-than-fully-voluntary consent will be "voluntary enough" for a valid and irrevocable contract. (That is partly because our law conceives of much private commerical enterprise as inherently competitive activity in which rival vendors match their wits, and partly because *A* too may have innocent interests to be protected, since *he* did consent to the deal voluntarily and in good faith, and might suffer losses from its revocation.)

Sometimes the institutional setting and the momentous issue at stake require that consent be "informed." Since no one, *ex hypothesi*, is "informed" about the uncertain future, it might seem that this condition is never satisfied in the case of consent to risk. If, however, one is accurately informed that there *is* a risk, and accurately apprised of its magnitude (insofar as that is possible), and if one has all the information bearing on the risk that is available, little as it may be, then his act of risk-taking is as informed as it can be in the circumstances, and that may render his consent "voluntary enough" to be valid. "The requirement that consent be informed," writes Dan Brock, "requires that no relevant information be deliberately withheld from the one who consents, but not that consent under uncertainty cannot be informed."[7] One of the elements of adequate information is knowledge of the extent to which one's other information is incomplete. (See Chap. 21 §5.) If a physician tells his patient everything known about the possibly dangerous effects of a recommended therapeutic drug except that long-range effects on the kidneys have not been studied yet and are not known, then to that extent the patient's assumption of risk is not informed, and may even be insufficiently voluntary to be valid.

Because of the impossibility of foreknowledge, and our necessary dependence on predictions that are highly fallible even when "fully informed," almost all the voluntary agreements that people enter into involve some significant risk. To take a job in California is to become subject to increased risk of an earthquake; to live in a big city is to become more vulnerable to street crime; to work in certain industries increases one's statistical chances of cancer. Indeed, who knows what special risks (unrevealed in the actuarial tables) attach to every particular job, every place of residence, every potential marriage partner, every way of life? When one of these unanticipated risks materializes, one "loses one's stake," even when the risk was uncompetitive and there was no "player" on the other side of the table to take one's loss as his gain. But if the unfortunate loss were automatically taken to invalidate the prior consent, then all distinction between unfortunate loser and aggrieved victim would be obliterated, every loser would have a *personal* grievance, and all harms made possible by interpersonal agreements would be wrongs. If agreements entered into only because of false expectations of future occurrences by one of the parties are thought to be null and void *ab initio*, then those of us who think that we are now legally married may turn out to be mistaken, the contractual obligations of others toward us may be baseless, and even the consensual defense to criminal liability in many cases may turn out to have been without merit all along. Such costs are obviously much too great to pay for so stringent a standard of voluntary consent. All that we can demand in an uncertain world is that no information bearing on risks be deliberately withheld or concealed from us when we consider entering into agreements with others.

In some contexts even that may be more than we can "demand." Where contractors are thought to be playing a competitive game one against the other, contractual negotiations are thought to be "battles of wits" in which the parties try to exploit their superior judgments, superior skill, superior knowledge, or superior strength to achieve gains at their rivals' expense, and all assume the risk of losing. The problem for legal policy raised by this conception is to determine the boundaries of the area, if any, in which this conception applies, and to distinguish legitimate from illegitimate modes of advantage-taking even within that area. Obviously, superior physical strength and superior weaponry cannot be used to force another into an agreement in any area of our common life (except perhaps in "love and war"), and the same is true of mendacity and the cruder forms of deception. On the other side, the transactional advantages of superior wealth have only been limited, not destroyed, by such rules as the doctrine of "unconscionability" in contract law (see Chap. 24, §5), and statutes forbidding usury. Kronman shrewdly observes that money is but one kind of advantage among others, in principle no different from superior knowledge or shrewdness. Wealth in the broadest sense, he suggests, includes not only money but also things like "information, intelligence, and physical strength." Moreover, he adds,

> . . . it is wrong to think of money—wealth in the narrow sense—as anything other than a transactional advantage . . . [giving] its possessor a leg up in the exchange process. Money enables an individual to acquire other transactional

advantages (for example, superior information) to withstand pressures that might otherwise force him to make agreements on less favorable terms, to outbid competitors, etc,; other things being equal, the more money an individual has, the better he is likely to do in his transactions with other persons. In fact, money not only gives its possessor a transactional advantage: unlike intelligence or physical strength, it gives him nothing else. A sailor stranded alone on a desert island may benefit from his physical and mental abilities; unless he has someone to transact with, however, the money in his pocket does him no good at all.[8]

For these reasons, Kronman concludes that it is wise to treat all forms of advantage-taking as on a par, subject to one kind of policy for all, and derived ultimately from a single principle of justice. "No one should be allowed to exploit his financial resources in transactions with others to any greater extent than he should be allowed to exploit his superior intelligence, strength, or *information*."[9] And to how great an extent is that? The question cannot be pursued further here, since our main concern is to explore the many-faced concept of voluntariness, not to sketch a complete theory of distributive justice. We can only note in passing that part of the question does call for an analysis of the concept of voluntariness and part is a question of economic justice. We can say in answer to the conceptual query that insofar as one contracting party withholds relevant information (i.e. information that would be part of the other's inducement) from the other party, even when that information is only partial evidence for a fallible prediction, the second party's consent is less than fully voluntary. Whether it is sufficiently less than fully voluntary to be invalid depends on (a) how much less than fully voluntary it is, its degree being a function of, *inter alia*, the importance of the party's uninformed expectation to his total inducement; (b) the area of social life in which the proposed agreement lies (is it a marriage?, a medical experiment?, an employment contract?, a commerical exchange?, a "business deal"?); (c) how much like a competitive "game" that area is rightly thought to be; (d) the utilitarian (e.g. economic) effects of the rule we adopt on social practice generally; (e) the principles of justice we use in determining and appraising answers to (c) and (d). It is wiser to think of these various questions as having bearing on our adoption of a rule for determining the validity of consent than on our analysis of voluntariness. The question here as elsewhere is: How voluntary must an agreement be to be "voluntary enough" for validity?

5. Limits to the assumption of risk

Surely there are some areas of social life for which the competitive game model is wholly out of place. One of these is the realm of friendly neighborliness in which invitations to enter private places are tendered to friends and acquaintances, salespeople and solicitors, even strangers on unknown business, in that spirit of amiable trustingness so essential to tolerable community life. "May I enter?" asks the one; "Come right in" says the other; or "Won't you stay for dinner?" asks the one, and "I'd be delighted" replies the other. Legally speaking, the relation called "invitation" has been created. The "invitee" may have initiated it by requesting permission to enter, or the idea may have originated with the host and only been responded to by the invitee. In either case the host's affirmative words to the other party confer on him the legal status of "invitee" and are said to express the inviter's *consent* to his entry. Any number of things may follow the entry of the invitee. Which of them has the inviter consented to by virtue of his original invitation? One never knows, of course, exactly what an invitee might do, any more than one knows (for sure) any other proposition about the future. It is even possible that the invitee might be the cause or occasion of some harm to the inviter. Has the inviter by the mere fact of his invitation assumed the risk of unexpected harms? Some perhaps, but surely not others. The invitee might inadvertently spill his coffee on the rug or pass on his infectious cold germs. These things happen, and are not all that surprising or remarkable. But if the guest flies into a rage and intentionally smashes all the host's crockery, he cannot claim afterward that he had the host's implied consent to do just that in virtue of the original invitation.

The scope of the inviter's consent has recently been treated in a surprisingly wrongheaded way by the American courts in cases where the invitee is a secret police agent. The case of *United States v. Arthur Baldwin*[10] is an illustrative horror story. The facts of the case are summarized here by that tireless chronicler of the law journals, Ferdinand Schoeman,[11] who describes the relentless efforts of the Memphis, Tennessee, police department to close down a legally operating topless bar by finding some reason to arrest its owner, Arthur Baldwin:

> Not having any basis for suspicion of illegal behavior on Baldwin's part, the police sent in an undercover agent whose task was to insinuate himself into Baldwin's life and see what he could come up with as a basis for criminal prosecution. The police agent ended up working in Baldwin's bar, serving as Baldwin's chauffeur, looking after Baldwin's child, and living in Baldwin's house for six months. During this period the police undercover agent noticed some white powder out on the top of Baldwin's dresser. The agent took some of the powder, had it analyzed, and on the basis of this analysis had Baldwin arrested for possession with intent to use and distribute cocaine. Baldwin was convicted and though he repeatedly appealed, his conviction stands. Also standing is the declaration of the legitimacy of the police practice.[12]

Baldwin's conviction was upheld despite the Fourth Amendment's ban on illegal seizures, despite the deception used to gain entry, despite the lack of grounds for suspicion of any specific crime, and despite a search of six months' duration. Among the arguments employed in this and similar cases upholding the constitutionality of this police technique, two are of special interest here. One claims that the householder voluntarily consented ("in effect") to the search, and the other that he assumed the risk of police detection by his act of inviting the agent in.

Baldwin's home would never have been entered by the secret agent, his premises never searched, his intimate life never revealed, nor his privacy ever invaded, had he not "voluntarily" invited in the person who in fact was a police agent. So the first argument goes. But Baldwin did not know that he was a police agent, goes the rejoinder, so he did not voluntarily consent to the *entry of a police agent*—the relevantly full description of the event in question. All the more so, it is false that he voluntarily consented to having his conversations revealed or his premises searched. In every other branch of the law the misinformation induced by deception undercuts the voluntariness of consent; why is this apparently arbitrary exception permitted? The answer to this question leads into the assumption of risk rationale. "The Fourth Amendment," said Judge Boyce Martin in rejecting Baldwin's appeal, "does not protect wrongdoers from misplaced confidence in their associates,"[13] and in an earlier case, Supreme Court Justice Stewart tried to explain why: "Neither this Court nor any member of it has ever expressed the view that the Fourth Amendment protects a wrongdoer's misplaced belief that a person to whom he voluntarily confides his wrongdoing will not reveal it . . . In the words of the dissenting opinion in *Lopez*, 'The risk of being overheard by an eavesdropper or betrayed by an informer or deceived as to the identity of one with whom one deals is probably inherent in the conditions of human society. It is the kind of risk we assume whenever we speak.' "[14] There no doubt is a sense in which this is true, but whether it was true in Baldwin's case depends on what *kind* of risk exactly it was that he assumed in inviting his friend to be his house guest. He might well complain that he voluntarily assumed only the normal risks "inherent in the conditions of human society," not the added risks of an elaborate hoax, carefully designed and executed by an agency of the state, to penetrate the usual barriers of one's privacy.

Schoeman paraphrases the Stewart argument so as to highlight its character as a *non sequitur:* "If it is legitimate for A to reveal x to B, and if on learning of x, B could then legitimately tell x to the police, then it is all right for the police to trick A into revealing x to the police directly."[15] Schoeman's view apparently is that fraudulent deception as such makes a difference—the important difference—to voluntariness, so that when B agrees to A's proposal, his agreement, while perhaps less than fully voluntary, is nevertheless nowhere near as nonvoluntary as it would be if, everything else being the same, his false belief was caused by A's deliberate misrepresentation, or A's elaborate scheme of deception. If a good friend unpredictably betrays your confidence (on this view), that is simply your bad luck. There is always some risk of that sort of thing, and in this case you assumed that risk unwisely. But if you are set up by the police as Baldwin was then you cannot blame yourself for what happened, because your choice had no role in the matter; you did not assume *that* risk.

Schoeman's opponents might reply that if the courts have ruled that a secret agent may legitimately gain entry into a private house by misrepresenting his identity, then it follows that a householder *does* assume a risk, however tiny, that any stranger he invites in is a police agent. The question then is: *ought* it to be the case that the risks are assigned in this way? For the courts to defend their answer to *that* question of judicial policy by citing the false analogy with more familiar cases of assumption of risk is to evade the responsibility of giving a justification of the appropriate kind—one in terms of the social values (crime detection, on the one hand, personal intimacy, privacy, trust on the other) at stake.

One might take exception, however, to Schoeman's *general* assumption that fraud as such, rather than the simple misinformation which is one of its elements, is an independent voluntariness-reducing factor. On an alternative account of the matter, the nonvoluntariness is a function only of the degree and motivational importance of the mistaken belief, no matter how that belief was caused. On this second view, the cases might nevertheless be treated differently by the law, even though the degree of nonvoluntariness in each is the same, for the law can then claim that where there is not only misbelief but fraud, then the agreement is not *voluntary enough* to be valid even though its voluntariness would have been sufficient had the misbelief had some other, nonfraudulent, source. In other words, the courts should use a higher standard of validity, that is, require more voluntariness, where fraud is involved.

Suppose that B's nephew from Seattle, A, whom he has not seen for years, and whom he does not know well, comes to his house for a visit. After an extended stay of six months or so, A finds suspicious white powder in a kitchen cupboard, and reluctantly reports it to the police. Did B "assume the risk" that this might happen when he voluntarily invited his sister's son into his home? Clearly he did not voluntarily invite into his house a person-who-would-report-him-to-the-police. Under that description his consent to A's visit was not voluntary; but the question is whether that description is the correct one for our purposes. In the contrasting case, we can ask whether Baldwin voluntarily invited into his house a police-undercover-agent-who-would-seek-to-find-anything-criminal. Again the answer seems to be "under that description, no." The examples seem *prima facie* to be on a par, in which case we should judge them equally nonvoluntary, one no more than the other. They do differ significantly, of course, in that the false belief about future occurrences that renders the second case equally as nonvoluntary as the first was itself caused by a deliberate conspiratorial plan, fraudulent intent, and conscious misrepresentation. On the view we are considering, the law should introduce a higher standard of validity because of the deception, and rule that *B*'s "consent" to the police search was insufficiently voluntary to be valid, even though the equally nonvoluntary consent to the risk of the nephew's action in the other case was quite voluntary enough to be valid.

There is a disanalogy, however, between the two examples that complicates the question, and renders the examples less than suitable illustrations of the second account of the matter. The mistaken belief (or ignorance) in the *Baldwin* case is about the *identity* of the invitee, not (only) about his future conduct, as in case of the nephew. It may therefore vitiate the voluntariness of the *factum* of the agreement, that is, "what it was that was agreed to" when the invitation was proferred. Baldwin was inviting in one sort of person (a secret agent) when he believed he was inviting in another sort (an employee and friend). His mistake concerns the present identity of the other party, not background facts or future occurrences. This distinction is difficult to draw in some cases, but it must be made if we are to avoid the slippery slope that renders involuntary all agreements that rest on mistaken expectations of the future.

Suppose that Betty marries John voluntarily. She is not incompetent to to decide; she is not coerced into it; she does not marry him under the mistaken impression that he is Bill when he is actually John in disguise. However, she does marry him precisely because of certain expectations she has about their future together. She believes, falsely as it turns out, that they will be prosperous, raise a large family in a comfortable home, and be happy with one another through a long shared life. Two years later John shows alcoholic tendencies she had not suspected. Three years later he is fired from his job. Four years later, a physician diagnoses him as sterile and incurably impotent. Five years later, John dies of cancer. Did Betty voluntarily marry a man-who-would-be-alchoholic?, impotent?, sterile?, unemployed?, dead within five years? Surely not. Yet unless her consent to marry John was voluntary enough to be valid, her marriage was null and void from the beginning—an absurd consequence given the facts of the case. We cannot let ignorance of future occurrences automatically reduce voluntariness without opening Pandora's Box, for there are always countless descriptions under which any voluntary act seems involuntary.

Perhaps some, but only some, of these descriptions ought to count against voluntariness because of tacit advance understandings about "assumption of risk." For example, if John marries in good-faith ignorance that he will become impotent and/or sterile (say, through an accident) hours after the

ceremony, perhaps even the Catholic Church will declare the marriage annulled. On the other hand, much of the traditional wedding ceremony is
designed to rule explicitly in advance that each partner hereby *assumes the risk*
of unforeseeable unhappy future occurrences involving the other: their promises hold "for better for worse, for richer for poorer, in sickness and in
health . . ."

What makes practices like that of the police in the *Baldwin* case controversial is that there has been neither clear tacit understanding of the limits of an
inviter's risk-assumption, nor explicit assignments of risks (on the wedding
model) to him. The question then is what understanding we *ought* to have of
the *proper* limits of an inviter's risk-assumptions, and that is not a conceptual
question so much as a policy issue for courts and legislatures, requiring them
to pass moral judgment on the practice of police deception to gain entry into
private homes. Our law is clear that householders do not "consent" to entries
by stealth into their homes or to entries by force. The status of entry by
deception is therefore a curious anomaly. It seems especially unjustifiable
given the nature of the values involved. When secret agents are permitted to
exploit the natural trust of persons in the absence of any evidence of wrongdoing, and then win their friendship, even their intimacy, through an extended campaign of ingratiation, all for the purposes of a "fishing expedition," the values of trust, friendship, and intimacy themselves are tarnished
and threatened.[16] Schoeman makes the point with vivid succinctness:

> We would never tolerate a sham marriage or engagement whose whole point is
> to gain incriminating evidence. Nor would we tolerate a policeman disguising
> himself as a priest to gather incriminating evidence in confessionals. So too
> should it be with intimate relationships in general.[17]

Police prying is one risk that penitents, spouses, good friends and neighbors
never voluntarily assume.

6. Fraud: false pretense and false promise

Not even in the business world—that one area of social life where the "battle
of wits" competitive-game model is most persuasive, and people match the
shrewdness of their judgments and the cleverness of their stratagems for
getting the better of one another—not even here do rivals voluntarily assume
the risk that the other party to an agreement is an outright liar, getting the
better of one by plain deceit. Indeed, the idea of fraud (the legal term for
"intentional deception resulting in injury to another"[18]) first entered the
criminal law as a kind of commerical crime, or crime against property—a
form of theft by deceit.

In the English system the protection of property by means of the criminal law began with the prohibition of theft by force or violence, when the transfer of property is rendered involuntary by compulsive violence or coercion. That early crime bore the name of *robbery*. Protection of property soon expanded to include the prohibition of seizures of property without the owner's consent, even if no force was used. Then the crime that included both robbery and theft by stealth was called *larceny*. The courts then expanded the idea of larceny to include wrongful appropriation of goods by persons who already had the goods in their possession by the consent of the rightful owners—the germ of the later crimes, created by statute, of *embezzlement* and *breach of trust*.[19] The common law was very slow to recognize thefts by fraud as punishable crimes. The misdemeanor called *cheating* was primarily a merchant's offense, typically consisting of using false weights or measures, and thus overcharging for transferred commodities. "One may suspect," write Kadish and Paulsen,"that this was an outgrowth of guild regulation of unfair competition as much as a protection of the buying public."[20] However, the cheating that consisted of one person swindling a specific victim (as opposed to the general consuming public) was viewed with a more tolerant eye: "a mere lie for the purpose of deceiving another in a business transaction did not become criminal until the Statute of . . . 1757 created the misdemeanor of obtaining property by false pretenses."[21]

Why was the law so slow to criminalize injurious misrepresentations? Kadish and Paulsen attribute the reluctance to the influence of "the ethic of *Caveat emptor*" which was given its "classic justification" by Chief Justice Holt in a 1703 case: "We are not to indict one for making a fool of another."[22] A whole complex of ancient attitudes towards dupery, including several that still survive, are expressed in Holt's opinion. One is the attitude that led to the contributory negligence rule in the common law of torts: if an accident victim's own negligence, no matter how slight compared to that of a second party, was a causal factor without which the accident would not have occurred, then he is not entitled to a penny of compensation from the second party for his injuries even though the second party luckily was unscathed. Similarly, a dupe is himself negligent, according to the prevailing assumption, for having assumed risks on the word of a liar, so he cannot complain afterwards of being badly used. "He has no one to blame but himself," we say, even though the other was at fault too. When we believe that ordinary prudence would have sufficed to protect one party from the mendacity of another, we sometimes opine that "anyone that gullible *deserves* to be swindled." The model for this situation in our own time is the motorist who leaves his key in the ignition of his unlocked car in a crime-ridden neighborhood and then expects sympathy from us when his car is predictably stolen. "He asked for it," we say, adding righteously, "Maybe this will teach him a lesson." People should be responsible, it is sometimes said, for their own folly. Often when we think of the realm of economic transfers as a contest of wits, it seems natural to judge that stupidity ought not to be rewarded or encouraged, as if gullibility were a moral flaw deserving of punishment. This attitude in turn is often linked with a "Social Darwinist" conception that swindlers, like predatory animals, only prey on the (mentally) weak, thus strengthening the herd as a whole. Sometimes, of course, gullibility, while not itself a moral flaw, is the consequence of character flaws worse than carelessness and stupidity. People often fall victim to "con artists" because their natural caution is overwhelmed by cupidity and greed.

The extreme view of Judge Holt, however, that unscrupulously clever people have a right to take advantage of fools could not survive that simpler time when it was supposed that only fools were vulnerable to swindlers. When changing times made even sensible, prudent people vulnerable, then fear of deceivers made everyone more sympathetic to "fools." As a principle of criminal law, the *Caveat emptor* rule was in time consumed by its own exceptions and qualifications. First, commerical "cheats" were made criminally liable (though only for misdemeanors) for false weights and measures. That sort of trickery was more difficult to detect even by the person of "ordinary prudence"; it threatened the public as a whole, rather than selected dupes; and to be always on guard against it was a terrible bother. When businesses combined into ever larger associations, their power over individual consumers increased proportionately so that misrepresentations were much more difficult to detect, and *everyone* could be cast in the role of Judge Holt's "fools." And then in the increasingly urban society, the old distinction between neighbors and "strangers" broke down, so that it became more difficult to restrict one's economic transactions to trusted associates with familiar faces. Strangers, no longer subject to traditional suspicions, perfected elaborate strategems for defrauding their clients—false tokens, counterfeit money, forged letters, false pretenses of myriad kinds. Statutes were passed creating the new crime of "larceny by trick" (as opposed to the narrower "common-law larceny"), and finally in our own time, criminal codes have consolidated the various crimes of theft to include fraudulent techiques with the other means of acquiring a person's property without his voluntary consent. Theft by fraud is now on the same footing as theft by force and theft by stealth, and it is now (at last) universally recognized that taking another's property with his fraudulently induced "consent" is no different in principle from taking it when there is no expression of consent at all.

The great variety of criminal frauds can be divided into two large classes— acquiring property by false pretenses and the special case where the false pretenses are false promises. The common-law crimes of larceny were expanded in the latter half of the eighteenth century to create the crime that came to be known as "larceny by trick," which in turn gradually converged with the expanded false-pretense statute[23] so that all intentional misrepresentations of fact for the purpose of taking another's property and converting it to one's own uses became criminal, regardless of the techniques of deception. And the techniques are legion. They are available to sellers who can deliberately misrepresent their goods to purchasers, or to purchasers who deliberately misrepresent their credit to sellers; to borrowers who can misrepresent their purposes or their capacity to repay, or to loaners who misrepresent the terms of the loan; to challengers to wagers as well as to acceptors; in short to anyone who obtains the property of others by means of false representations.

The plainest technique is the baldfaced lie, but there are equally effective, more subtle means of misleading too. The *Model Penal Code* in its definition of the comprehensive fraud offense that it calls "Theft by Deception" uses neither the term "lie" nor the phrase "false pretenses," but it enumerates the relevant forms of deception as follows in Section 223.3:

1. *General.* A person is guilty of theft if he obtains property of another by
   means of deception. A person deceives if he purposely:
       a. *Creates or reinforces an impression* which is false and which he does not
       believe to be true; or
       b. *prevents another from acquiring information* which the actor knows
       would influence the other party in the transaction; or
       c. *fails to disclose* a lien, adverse claim, or other legal impediment to the
       enjoyment of property being sold or otherwise transferred or encumbered, regardless of the legal validity of the impediment and regardless
       of any official record disclosing its existence;
       d. *fails to correct a false impression* which he knows to be influencing
       another to whom he stands in a relationship of special trust and
       confidence.[24]

All of the modes of deceiving enumerated above involve contributing somehow to the other party's false belief about some matter of fact that is central to his inducement. The belief may "relate to value, law, opinion, intention, or other state of mind."[25] One would expect, therefore, that the making of a *false promise* would be an especially clear and egregious way of causing a relevant false belief, as when a scoundrel obtains another's money by promising to repay, and then absconds with it. Yet the question of whether false promises are to be treated as a form of false pretense for the purposes of the criminal law (in particular for interpreting "false-pretenses" statutes) is one of the most controversial issues in the history of the law of criminal fraud. There has never been unanimity among the various Anglo-American jurisdictions on this question, but until the middle of this century the majority view was that expressed in the influential commentary of Francis Wharton that "the false pretense, to be within the statute, must relate to a state of things averred to be at the time existing, and not to a state of things thereafter to exist."[26] On the other side, a minority of states, even in Wharton's time, held that false promises are a species of false pretenses, so that when a person obtains property from another on the basis of a promise he has no intention of keeping at the time he makes it, and, having thus deceived the other, he converts the money to his own purposes, he has violated the statute against obtaining goods by false pretenses. Since the case of *People v. Ashley*[27] in 1954, more and more states have departed from the former majority view, and they have been reenforced by the recommendations of the *Model Penal Code*.

The issue does not go to a deep philosophical level, centering as it does primarily on the question of whether juries can be trusted to decide whether a broken promise was made with or without an intention of being kept. When a borrower takes money from a loaner on the basis of a promise to repay and then stumbles into unforeseen misfortunes so that he is unable to repay, the loaner may seek various remedies from the civil law, but the unfortunate debtor has committed no crime. Similarly, when the debtor renounces his debt because he disagrees with his creditor about the terms of the original agreement, the creditor can sue for repayment, but again no crime has been committed. In order for the defaulting party to be guilty of theft by deceit, the jury would have to find that he had no intention in the first place of keeping his promise, that the promise was made simply as part of a fraudulent scheme to deprive the victim of his property. The danger, of course, is that "ordinary commerical defaults might be subject to vindictive prosecutions and innocents who have met with commerical misfortune may be convicted of crime."[28]

In the early nineteenth century, still under the influence of "the ethic of *Caveat emptor*," some courts refused to convict a defendant who had defrauded by means of a false promise because the pretense "was merely a promise of future conduct, and common prudence and caution would have prevented any injury from arising from it."[29] In short, the trusting victim of the most blatant form of fraud has nobody to blame but himself, even though his deceiver has exploited what would normally be thought to be a social virtue like friendliness, trust, or neighborliness. The nineteenth century, however, was also the time of reaction against the abominations of the debtors' prisons, and the danger of jailing innocents for their bad luck was thought by many to be much graver than the danger of leaving other innocents unprotected against fraud. That the danger of "convicting the innocents who have met with commerical misfortune" is by no means a negligible one even in our time is eloquently argued by Justice Schauer in his dissenting opinion in *People v. Ashley:*

With the rule that the majority opinion now enunciates, no man, no matter how innocent his intention, can sign a promise to pay in the future, or to perform an act at a future date, without subjecting himself to the risk that at some later date others, in the light of differing perspectives, philosophies, and subsequent events, may conclude that after all, the accused *should* have known that at the future date he could not perform as he promised—and if he, as a "reasonable man" from the point of view of the creditor, district attorney and a grand or trial jury—*should* have known, then it may be inferred, he did know. And if it can be inferred that he knew, then this court, and other appellate courts will be bound to affirm a conviction.

The danger that juries *might* reason in this way canot be denied, but the hypothetical reasoning described by Justice Schauer could hardly establish guilt beyond a *reasonable doubt*. Indeed it might even be a useful paradigm for the instruction of juries in criminal cases how *not* to reach their verdicts. At the very most the inference from what a reasonable person should know to what the defendant did know might have evidential relevance in a civil action for deceit, where what is at issue is compensation rather than punishment, and the standard of evidence is correspondingly lower.

It is interesting to note that the sophistical reasoning by the jury that Justice Schauer feared has its analogue in an argument *favoring* the defendant. One might argue equally well (or equally badly) on the other side that when a person falls victim to a promise made without intention to perform, he might have protected himself from injury by common prudence and caution, and since a "reasonable man" would have so protected himself, and the "victim"—himself apparently a reasonable person—did not protect himself, he must have been willing to consent to the agreement even without the promise, so that he voluntarily assumed the risk of nonrepayment, and no wrong was done him! That is what comes of over-reliance on hypothetical intentions uncritically "presumed."

The traditional view that excludes false promises from the scope of false pretenses overestimates the special difficulties of determinations by juries of defendants' mental states in false promise cases. In fact, the retrospective determination of a promisor's intention is no harder a task in false pretense cases than it is anywhere else in the criminal law where "specific intent" is an element of the crime to be proved.[30] In particular, lying promises are on quite the same footing in this respect as lying assertions. To show that a deceiver lied to his victim about some matter of fact, one must not only establish that what he asserted was false, but also that he did not himself believe that it was true, just as to show that a person made a lying promise one must establish not only that he did not do what he promised, but also that he never *intended* to. Moreover, both the lying promise and the lying assertion must be made with the *intention* of deceiving the person addressed. Both intentions and beliefs are "mental states," equally inaccessible directly to others, yet equally subject to indirect evidence of their existence. In short, "The problem of proving intent when the false pretense is a false promise is no more difficult than when the false pretense is a misrepresentation of existing fact . . ."[31]

The crime of acquiring property by false pretenses then can be committed by means of a false promise when the promise is made with no intention of being kept and for the specific purpose of deceiving the other party and inducing him to give up his property, and in fact it has that result. If the promise is genuine and the false promisor later decides to break the promise, then his crime (if he has committed one) may be embezzlement, or if the promise was broken because the promisor lacked the means of keeping it, there may be no criminal liability but only liability for breach of promise, restitution, or the like. When the promise was fraudulent from the beginning, the promisee can be said to have transferred his property "voluntarily" to the deceiver (thus describing his action very narrowly) or to have consented to the other's proposed terms, but he did *not* "voluntarily" assume the risk that the other party would default. When the default occurs, therefore, he has been wronged as well as harmed.

7. Fraud in the factum versus fraud in the inducement

Of all the many distinctions legal writers make among the various modes of fraud, perhaps the most interesting one to philosophers is that between deception as to what is consented to and deception about collateral matters for the purpose of inducing the victim to consent. Rollin M. Perkins explains the distinction as follows:

> The general rule is that if deception causes a misunderstanding as to the fact itself (fraud in the *factum*) there is no legally recognized consent because what happened is not that for which consent was given; whereas consent induced by fraud is as effective as any other consent, so far as direct and immediate legal consequences are concerned.[32]

So, for example, it is *fraud in the inducement* if A proposes to sell to B stock in a nonexistent company, and B signs over to him a promissory note for $1,000 in exchange for a worthless stock certificate. The fraud is in the inducement since B "knew he was signing and delivering a note and intended to do so. It is in fact and in law his note and the direct and immediate consequences are the same as if no fraud had been perpetrated."[33] Thus, if A cashes the note before B can repudiate it, then it belongs to C, the new holder, as his property, and is no longer B's. On the other hand, if A takes advantage of B's bad eyesight to induce him to sign a note for $1,000 under the false representation that it is only a receipt for a package (having slyly interchanged the papers), then that is fraud in the *factum* since *B* did not consent to sign a note but rather to do something altogether different, namely sign a receipt. His signature on the note is no more valid than if it had been forged, and he may recover his money even from a subsequent "holder in due course."

What difference does it make whether a victim is wronged by a fraud in the *factum* or a fraud in the inducement, it the result is the same, namely that his rights are invaded? In respect to some crimes the difference is slight, requiring only terminological adjustments in the way the crime is character-ized, but in respect to other crimes, there may be liability for one kind of fraud but not the other, or the penalties for one kind of fraud may be much more severe than for the other. The problem for the philosopher is to explain these variations. The distinction rests on an apparent contrast between *no consent* at all to what is done by the deceiver (fraud in the *factum*) and *consent* that is less than voluntary because of defective belief induced by deception (fraud in the inducement), so the philosopher's concern is in large part with the question of when, if ever, nonvoluntary consent should be treated differ-ently from no consent.

The criminal law has had various options in classifying crimes consisting of procuring another's signature (to a note, a deed, a contract, a will, or some other legal document) by fraud, but there rarely have been any problems of substance left over after the terminological questions have been solved. The most common consideration of the problem has been in connection with the attempt to distinguish the crime of *forgery* from the crime of taking property under false pretenses. When the fraud is in the inducement merely, the victim does intentionally sign the document, and if that which he knowingly signed is a note, it will be negotiable unless repudiated in time. It is therefore not merely a matter of wrongful possession but wrongful transfer of title to prop-erty. There is no "false writing" on the document (one of the elements of the traditional crime of forgery), and as Perkins notes, the fraud is "squarely within a clause commonly found in the statute on false pretenses."[34] When, on the other hand, the signature is produced by fraud in the *factum*, for example by substituting papers by sleight of hand, then in the absence of the signer's negligence, his signature is in no sense valid, and if the paper signed was a note, it will not transfer ownership to a future holder in due course. Since the crime of forgery is defined in such a way that the "false writing" on the document need not be made with the forger's own hand, there is a case for classifying fraudulently procuring another's signature, where the fraud is in the *factum*, as forgery, rather than false pretenses, and that was once the prevailing practice. But now the tendency understandably has been to mini-mize the distinction between the two kinds of fraud in signature-procuring cases, and to classify them both as false pretenses. This is "reasonably accept-able," says Perkins, "since the moral turpitude is the same in both; it is simpler to treat them alike in the forgery cases; and there is no prejudice to the wrongdoer since the result tends to operate in his favor rather than otherwise."[35] Nothing of importance hinges on how we classify in these cases, since both kinds of fraud will be grounds for criminal liability however we name them, and the degree of punishment will vary with other factors unaffected by our classification of the type of fraud.[36]

It is another story when the crime is rape. It is not widely realized that rape can be committed by fraud as well as by violence or coercion. Sometimes the fraud by which a victim is led to engage in sexual intercourse is in the *factum* and sometimes in the inducement, but unlike the forgery cases, much more hinges on the kind of fraud used than mere terminological or classificatory questions. For sexual relations induced by fraud in the *factum* the perpetrator will be held criminally liable for rape and punished severely, whereas if the fraud is in the inducement merely, he may not be criminally liable at all, despite the use of false pretenses in obtaining consent, or he will be punished for a lesser crime, or to a lesser degree. Any woman, then, is protected by the criminal law from the imposition of sexual relations without her consent, but, in general, women are not equally protected when their expression of consent is involuntary by virtue of a mistaken motivating belief produced by deception. This apparent anomaly requires some explanation.

First, however, we should consider the standard examples of fraudulent sexual relations of each type. Again, Perkins is invaluable. Here is his account first of *fraud in the inducement*:

> In several cases a doctor or pretended doctor has had sexual intercourse with a female patient under the fraudulent pretense of medical treatment. In some of these cases the doctor has not hesitated to make it clear that he intended to have sexual intercourse with the patient, his fraud being in the deceitful suggestion that this was necessary to cure some malady, which was fraud in the inducement since the patient knew exactly what was to be done and was deceived only in regard to a collateral matter—the reason why it was to be done. And here as usual the direct and immediate consequence of consent obtained by fraud in the inducement is the same as consent given in the absence of fraud, and since the patient consented to the intercourse it was not rape so long as she was over the statutory age.[37]

In part, Perkins' conclusion rests simply on terminological grounds. Rape has always been defined as a kind of criminal imposition *without consent*, never as intercourse without *informed consent*, or *voluntary consent*. And it should be added that doctors who deceive their patients in the way described above may be subject to the discipline of the medical profession, for example to suspension of license, or to civil liability for malpractice or tortious battery, for example, or even to some criminal charge less severe than rape. But tradition precludes charges of rape when consent has been expressed, even when that consent was fraudulently procured.[38] The question then remains: why does not fraud in the inducement utterly *vitiate* consent to sexual intercourse as it does to transfer of property in "theft by deceit" cases? Why should fraudulently produced consent have any different status from no consent at all? This is the question to which we shall return.

Physicians have also been the culprits in cases of sexual intercourse with patients produced by fraud in the *factum*. Perkins continues,

> In these cases the woman did not realize what was happening but supposed it was merely a vaginal examination or surgical operation. 'The evidence in this case, if the prosecuting witness is to be believed, is to the effect that she supposed the doctor was examining her physically with his fingers' (*State v. Ely,* 114 Wash. 185, 192, 194 N.W. 988, 881, 1921). In another case the patient had believed 'that what was taking place was a surgical operation and nothing else,' believing that penetration was being affected with the hand or with an instrument' (*The Queen v. Flattery,* 2 Q.B.D. 410, 413, 1877). Again: 'The evidence wholly fails to show that Rebecca ever consented to, or even had knowledge of, the act of sexual intercourse, until after it was fully accomplished' (*Pomeroy v. State,* 94 Ind. 96, 100, 1883). In such cases the unlawful intercourse is rape for the very sufficient reason that it was without the woman's consent. 'She consented to one thing, he did another materially different . . .'(*Per* Mellor, J. in *Flattery* at 414.)[39]

An intermediate sort of case in which the fraud is harder to classify is that in which a man enters a woman's bed in the dark of night posing as her husband, and she consents because of the belief, natural enough in the circumstances, that he *is* her husband. Since she does consent to sexual intercourse with this man, some courts hold that there is no rape. Other courts argue in the fashion preferred by Perkins that the fraud is in the *factum* since the woman's consent was to intercourse *with her husband,* "while what is actually perpetrated on her is an act of adultery."[40] Under *that* description the act is one to which she did not consent. Her participation in the act, on this theory, is analogous to signing the wrong paper in dim light when two pages have been switched by a guileful deceiver.

This suggestion of Perkins' is plausible, but there is danger in packing too much into the description of what was consented to, since it could undermine altogether the distinction between fraud in the *factum* and fraud in the inducement. The consent to intercourse with a physician when fraudulently induced by medical misrepresentations, for example, could be reclassified as fraud in the *factum* and therefore rape after all, since the woman could always argue that though she consented to sexual intercourse, she was not consenting to what in fact was done, but rather to an *act of therapy* that was not in fact administered. All conceptual boundary lines are hard to draw, and that between the two kinds of fraud is no exception, but as Perkins points out, the disagreement over the "deception in the dark" case is not over the principle that rape cannot be committed with a consenting partner, but rather over its application to a borderline case where the description of the consent is in doubt. The question of principle then still awaits our attention, and it has both a conceptual and a moral aspect. When sexual relations are at issue, why should fraudulent inducement fail to vitiate consent utterly? And why, if at all, is rape by fraud in the *factum* morally more serious than sexual relations consented to only because of fraud in the inducement?

We can begin by somewhat narrowing the question. Sometimes fraudulent inducement does not significantly reduce the voluntariness of consent, at least for the purposes of the criminal law, whereas sometimes it apparently does. Our main distinction then is not between sexual acquiescence caused by fraud in the *factum* and the same caused by fraud in the inducement, but rather between those cases of fraud in the inducement that reduce the voluntariness of consent substantially and those that do not. Fraud in the *factum* should not be the focus of our inquiry since the conduct it produces is *wholly involuntary* by any reasonable standard, and does not vary in degree. There may well be a spectrum of voluntariness, however, corresponding to variations in the fraudulently produced inducement to consent, just as there seems to be a spectrum of voluntariness corresponding to degrees of coercive pressure (see Chap. 23, §§3, 4).

Speaking of fraudulently induced consent to sexual intercourse, Perkins writes: "It is quite obvious by way of analogy that obtaining sexual intercourse with a prostitute by giving her counterfeit money does not constitute the crime of rape."[41] The point is a good one but the presumed illegality of prostitution adds an unnecessary complication. Moreover, the prostitute, even if not herself working illegally, is a businesswoman selling her services. If she is defrauded of her payment she is a victim of an offense against property, presumably theft of services effected by means of false pretenses. The harm suffered by the women in Perkins' medical example is rather more difficult to characterize, but it is certainly not a harm to the property interest, or a "theft of services," and whatever its proper characterization, it is surely not the sort of harm that can be suffered by a prostitute.

A better example would be that of a doctor (say) obtaining sexual intercourse with a patient by promising a large cash payment and then paying in counterfeit money, or not paying at all. This would be a case of fraud in the inducement, but it would not reduce the voluntariness of the consent sufficiently to support a rape prosecution, or even a charge of "theft of services." The fact that a woman is willing to have sex for money implies that the sexual episode in itself is not a clear harm to her when she is not paid. In fact it is plausible to say that the woman in this case consented to the intercourse, and consented to the terms offered by the doctor, but did not voluntarily assume the risk of his default of payment. If the payment had been forthcoming then her consent to the whole episode would have been highly voluntary.

There does seem to be a contrast, however, between the woman cheated out of the payment that had induced her to consent and the patient induced to submit to sexual intercourse with her doctor because of the belief he fraudulently induced in her that such "treatment" was the indicated therapy for her illness. Most of the cases in the criminal record of this sort of fraud date back to the final decades of the nineteenth century when respectable women could be seriously harmed (in a proper sense of the word) by unwarranted loss of virginity, and were at the same time often remarkably benighted, hence gullible, about the facts of reproductive biology. It is almost impossible to imagine similar frauds occurring today, except—and here is the late twentieth century analogue—in the offices of psychiatrists. Few persons are so ignorant these days as to believe, even on the immense authority of a doctor, that sexual intercourse (with him) will cure or prevent cancer, but even the sophisticated (especially when desperately neurotic) will accept a similar opinion on the authority of their psychoanalyst.[42] And the desperately neurotic are especially vulnerable to pain and injury.)

It is likely, however, that if an occasional non-neurotic but uneducated person faithfully "obeys the instuctions" of her gynecologist, submitting on his recommendation to what otherwise would fill her with abhorrence, she would find few persons in these enlightened days to give her sympathy. Again the old attitudes of *Caveat emptor* would surface. "If she is that stupid, she deserves what she gets" are words that would come easily to many lips. And indeed her own negligence, or what would be judged as negligence by her self-righteous associates, would have been a contributing factor to her harm. (She could at least have sought a second opinion.) But negligent or not, stupid or not, she could have been severely harmed by her experience, and subject to the pains of depression, shame, loss of self-esteem, and tortured conscience, if not pregnancy and more obvious harms. To her, unlike the woman cheated out of her cash payment, the very fact of illicit sexual intercourse may have been a traumatic harm in itself, and if we assume that she did, in her ignorance, genuinely believe and trust her doctor, it seems uncompassionate at the very least to withhold legal remedies from her, or to deprive others like her of legal protection against similar exploitation. After all, people do not forfeit their rights simply by being ignorant or naively trusting, and even stupid people—*especially* stupid people—can be taken advantage of and harmed.

Fraud in the inducement does not vitiate the consent that is required by the crime of rape, which is one of the most severely punished crimes in our penal codes. It can reduce the voluntariness of consent, however, to the point that it is invalid as as defense to tortious battery, or to malpractice suits, or to professional discipline. It would reduce the voluntariness of consent to the point where it is invalid as a defense to the criminal charge of taking property under false pretenses if only the interest harmed were a property interest. But given that in the sexual cases no property is wrongfully taken, and no "services" wrongly unpaid, the typical false pretense statute does not apply to them. That the offense is neither rape nor theft, however, does not imply that it cannot be another crime, and in fact, it has always been possible to prosecute some sexual misconduct as criminal assault and battery, again taking the voluntariness of certain types of fraudulently induced consent to be insufficient to constitute valid defenses.

The *Model Penal Code* recommends that legislatures create a separate, specifically sexual offense distinct from rape because consent *is* sometimes expressed though fraudulently procured, and distinct from battery because the characteristic harms are different, battery often leading to physical injury. The crime is called "Gross Sexual Imposition" in the model code and is defined broadly enough to include submission produced by coercive threats less severe than those required by rape (the threats in rape are defined as "force or threat of imminent death, serious bodily injury, extreme pain or kidnapping"), exploitation of the incompetent, and fraud in the *factum*.[43] Crimes of fraudulent inducement are not mentioned at all in this section, suggesting that the drafters of the code thought of them as exclusively crimes against property, or forms of theft. The specifically sexual offenses defined in the section entitled "Rape and Related Offenses" (gross sexual imposition is the only "related offense") are all graded as felonies, though of different degrees of seriousness. Aggravated rape is a felony of the first degree (most serious). It consists of rape in which the actor inflicts serious bodily injury, and his victim was not a "voluntary social companion" of the actor at the time, and had not previously permitted him sexual liberties. Ordinary rape is a felony of the second degree of seriousness. It consists of compelling a victim by force or by threat of the most serious harm including imminent death, or having sexual intercourse with her knowing that he has impaired her power to control her conduct by administering drugs for that purpose, or when she is unconscious, or less than ten years old. Gross sexual imposition is a felony of the third degree, seriously punishable but less grave than rape. It consists, as we have seen, of coercion to sexual intercourse by threats less severe than those in rape but which nevertheless would "prevent resistance by a woman of ordinary resolution," or by deliberate exploitation of an insane or retarded person, or by that one (why only one?) species of fraud in the *factum* that consists of deceiving the victim into believing that the actor is her husband.

One can quibble with various parts of the code's definitions, but by and large, I think, they correspond to the graded judgments that most people would make about "rape and related offenses." They do, however, downgrade rape by fraud, not mentioning fraud in the inducement at all, mentioning only one form of fraud in the *factum* and ranking its gravity well below that of forceful or violent rape. We might well ask then, once more, why is rape, especially in its aggravated form, more serious than rape by fraud; why is sexual imposition by fraud in the *factum* more grave than imposition by fraud in the inducement, and the latter not even serious enough to be a crime at all?

The answers will not be simple. It is not possible to find a single key to these moral gradations in the notion that they correspond to varying degrees of voluntariness in submitting to the same harm, namely the harm of unwanted sexual intercourse as such. Violent rape, for example, does not differ from the related offenses in simply employing a different, more effectively voluntariness-reducing *means* to produce one and the same harm as the others. Rather, rape, as the code defines it, is a violent imposition of one person's will on another's, which is not just an alternative means to the same harm as the others, but *an important part of the harm itself*. The rapist manifests his willingness to go to all lengths, to kill, to inflict injury, to cause pain; he evokes terror by his violence or his ominous menace; resistance threatens to lead to a physical overwhelming and complete violation of the person. It is not simply that overpowering another's will is somehow more voluntariness-reducing than merely tricking it, for that is not true. Rather, the force or threat of violence is itself an integral part of the total harm produced. Compulsion is not necessarily more destructive of voluntariness than deception is, but it is normally more harmful in itself. Those who consent to impositions under its influence have not given a prior consent to being made subject to *it*, as a separable harm, in the first place.

Sexual participation produced by fraud in the *factum* is equally as involuntary as that produced by coercive violent rape. Indeed it is often more so, since—like conduct produced by overwhelming compulsion—it is totally involuntary, not involving the will whatever; whereas rape by coercive threat, where the threats are severe enough to be effective yet not near the end of the spectrum of coercive pressure, though substantially nonvoluntary, is not totally involuntary. In some cases, as we have seen, sexual participation produced by fraud in the *factum* not only fails to implicate the victim's will to any degree whatever, but it may not even be a part of her knowledge for hours or days, falling outside the range of her awareness. It follows that the difference in moral gravity between rape and fraudulent sexual imposition is not always a function of differences in the degree of voluntariness of the victim's assent. The difference, as we have seen, is in the degree of harm imposed on the equally unwilling victims.

There is an analogy to this point in the law of theft. When a thief knocks down him victim and violently wrenches away her purse by force, or when he forces her to hand it over by placing a knife at her throat or a gun in her ribs, or by threatening to kill her child who is in his possession, he inflicts a harm on her property interest, but the total harm inflicted includes that and more—trauma, terror, anxiety, dread, violent imposition of an alien will. On the other hand, a burglar commits theft by stealth, and his victim may not even know he has been harmed for days afterward. Here the whole harm is the economic loss. (The analogy in the second example is to the doctor who "enters" the patient while pretending merely to examine her.) A third way of producing the same economic harm may be to enter the victim's house under false pretenses, posing for example as an exterminator, and then while unobserved taking away the silverware. (This example is more or less analogous to imitating the husband in the dark in the sexual examples.) Again the whole harm is the economic loss. Theft by force or threat is the more serious crime, not because its victim is involved less voluntarily, but because it inflicts a harm and a danger well beyond the economic harm it shares with the other forms of theft.

If there is a disanalogy between the property examples and the sexual ones, it is probably that the common-denominator harm in the sexual examples is a smaller proportion of the whole harm of rape than the loss of money is to the whole harm of violent theft. If that is true it is because (1) in grand larceny, at least, the loss of money is typically more harmful to the victim than unwanted sexual intercourse as such is in the sexual examples, and (2) the combination of physical violence and unbridled wantoness in rape typically inflicts a far greater violation of the person than the more businesslike ruthlessness in forceful theft.

We come now to fraud in the inducement, the topic unmentioned in the *Model Penal Code* discussion of sexual crimes. In what relevant ways does fruad in the inducement differ from violent force, and fraud in the *factum*, when we consider crimes of sexual imposition? Here there may well be differences in the degrees of voluntariness with which the victim participates in the crime, though the spectrum of voluntariness is not correlated in a straightforward and unequivocal way with degrees of harm or degrees of moral gravity. Fraud in the inducement is a form of manipulation in which some traits of the victim are used—turned against her—by the deceiver. It is not misleading to say that even her will is to some extent involved, as well as her general desires (with new mistaken beliefs subsumed under them), and such traits as credulity, naiveté, cupidity, or trustfulness. No doubt some rough scale of voluntariness can be contrived that would order the degrees of voluntariness in correspondence to various features of the content of the false promises and lying inducements that motivated her. No doubt in some cases her participation would turn out to be only slightly less than fully voluntary (in which case she was not gravely wronged), while in other cases it was substantially less than voluntary, just as in some of the less egregious instances of rape by coercive threat. But all of this is beside the point if our aim is to explain the traditional gradations of sexual offenses, and in particular the traditional reluctance, shared by the drafters of the *Model Penal Code*, to consider sexual imposition by fraudulent inducement to be a crime at all.

The correct explanation has already been adumbrated. The sorts of fraudulent inducements that would tend to reduce voluntariness most markedly, it is commonly supposed, create at the same time a presumption that the sexual relations that result are *not very harmful*, if harmful at all. It is implausible, for example, to think that a woman who consents because of a false promise of a cash gift has suffered a grievous harm consistenting in "unwanted sexual intercourse as such." Indeed her consent to the terms that later proved fraudulent indicates that at most the sexual intercourse was an "evil" or a "cost" to her for which a certain modest amount of cash was considered adequate compensation, so it could not have been thought to be a very great evil in itself. In terms of the victim's psychological state, the primary "harm" suffered was disappointment or resentment at the loss of an anticipated benefit, more a matter for contract than criminal law. And at the time the "harm" was inflicted she had no way of knowing whether her own participation was genuinely voluntary (some genuinely voluntary behavior can be unhappy, reluctant, halfhearted) or nonvoluntary because deceived. Her mental state at the time would have been the same in any case, and not unhappy or traumatic enough to be a harm in itself.

It is otherwise, however, with our hypothetical trusting soul who submits to her doctor on his undoubted testimony that he is administering the indicated therapy for her condition. Whether the doctor lies or not, her participation may seem to her at the time a terrible evil, a jolting trauma, and an enormous "cost" that she pays (she thinks voluntarily) but with sorrowful regret. She is like the patient who consents to an amputation on the assurance of her physician that she has gangrene and that death is likely otherwise, only to discover too late that she has been told a lie, and thus deprived of her arm. If legislatures choose to follow the *Model Penal Code* and withhold from persons like her the protection of the criminal law, it can only be because people with her vulnerabilities have become exceedingly rare, or for other practical reasons, like the difficultly of finding evidence of the vulnerability even where it does exist. But there is no reason in principle why sex by fraudulent inducement in cases *where it is plausibly harmful* (as in our example) could not legitimately be made a crime.

8. False belief and degrees of voluntariness

Differences in degree of harm, therefore, and not differences in the degree of voluntariness with which the victim submits to the harm, are the major part of the explanation for the *Model Penal Code* gradations. Still, a conceptual question remains. The voluntariness of actions, including acts of consent, does seem to vary under different kinds of fraud, and this must be explained, quite independently of the question of the gravity of the risked harm. We have already seen that mistaken belief induced by fraud in the *factum* renders consent as totally involuntary as bodily movements compelled by hurricanes or earthquakes. The victim consents to one thing, and the perpetrator does another quite different thing to which he has not consented. Fraud in the *factum* then anchors one end of our voluntariness scale. We have also seen (§3) that beliefs produced by fraud in the inducement can be ranked roughly according to their degree of centrality in the victim's set of inducing beliefs ("inducement set"). Is the mistaken belief the whole of the person's reason for consenting, or a sufficient condition in the circumstances for consenting, or a critical element in a more complicated sufficient condition? Is it a necessary but insufficient condition for his consenting, perhaps by being an essential element in a complex of beliefs itself sufficient? Or is it merely a considera-tion with a certain amount of motivational weight on the side of consenting? Does it have a great deal or only a little bit of motivational weight? Perhaps "Consenting will earn you thousands of dollars" is a heavily motivating be-lief, whereas "Consenting would have pleased your dear departed mother, bless her soul" adds only a little bit of further inducement.

There is a more interesting, and perhaps more useful way of ranking the false beliefs that might be created and exploited by a deceiver. We can begin by distinguishing four categories of fraudulently produced beliefs within which rank orderings are possible;

1. Bluffing threats (extortionate fraud)
2. Bluffing warnings
3. False promises
4. Other false pretenses

Bluffing threats. Suppose A demands that B consent to A taking B's money, and informs B that if he does not consent, then A will shoot him, while all along, unknown to B, A's gun is a toy, and A has no intention of harming him in any case. This false threat differs from a false promise in that what is "guaranteed" is that the person addressed will be harmed if he does not act in the directed way, whereas the promise "guarantees" that the person ad-dressed will be benefitted if he does act in the directed way. The falseness of the threat, however, is adventitious; it neither adds nor subtracts from the voluntariness of the response it forces if it is credible and in fact believed. It is pointless therefore to attach any significance to the fact that it is fraudulent as well as extortionate, except perhaps from the perspective of the actor rather than the victim, for the falseness of the threat is evidence of lack of intent to impose the threatened harm, and that might be mitigation. On the other hand, the falseness of a promise is the whole point in an account of how the promise reduces the voluntariness of the person who consents because of it. The very same promise, if it had been sincere, would not have reduced the voluntariness of the procured consent one iota. Threats, of course, do reduce or defeat voluntariness, whether they are sincere or not, but we have already discussed them and the ways they can be rank-ordered in terms of their effects on voluntariness, in Chapters 23 and 24, on coercion.

Bluffing warnings. When the physician in his examining room lies to his trusting patient, and gets her to believe she has an illness that can be cured only by sexual intercourse, he implicitly *warns* her of the dire consequences, not of his making, of her refusal. His deceptive technique, then, differs from that of the bluffing threatener only in that the unwelcome consequences he mentions are said to be caused by factors independent of his own will, and to be inevitable if steps are not taken to avoid them. The fraud consists in his deliberately making this warning when he knows it is false. Then he proceeds to make an "offer" to help which, given the direness of his false warning, has coercive force on his believing victim's will. This technique, therefore, combines fraud and coercion in such a way that the coercive pressure that reduces the voluntariness of the victim's consent would not exist but for her fraudulently induced false belief. The more dire the warning, of course, the more coercive its effect, and the less voluntary the consent it procures. If we use objective standards of voluntariness and require also that the warning be at least minimally credible, then the voluntariness of the procured consent might also vary with the degree of credibility. If the physician backs his bluffing warning with forged articles allegedly from medical journals, and other rigged evidence, his warning then would be more credible, and the procured consent correspondingly less voluntary. In whatever way we handle the credibility problem, however, we can say that in the case of bluffing warnings, *the worse the harm* (or better, *the more unwelcome the consequences*) *warned of, the more involuntary the consent procured*, on analogy with the scales of coerciveness sketched in Chapter 23. Here too the scale involved should be a subjective one, as determined by the victim's own scale of unwelcomeness.

False promises. These, being future oriented, affect the voluntariness of the promisee's consent in still another way. Like threats, they purport to be guarantees of the promisor's future performance, but they also release the promisee from responsibility if the promise is defaulted. The risk that the promisor will not perform as promised is not assumed by the promisee. Let us return to the overworked lecherous millionaire of Chapter 24. We saw there that his offer to save the sick child of the impoverished woman, while coercive in its effects on her choice, nevertheless enhanced her freedom by enlarging her options, so that her consent to his terms was voluntary enough to preclude criminal liability for him and cancel the right of third parties forcefully to interfere with the compact. But now let us add the element of fraud, and suppose that the millionaire's promise was a lie, and he uses it only to procure her consent to his uses, and then defaults on his part of the bargain. His promise was binding even though he was lying when he made it. His victim, therefore, did not voluntarily assume the risk of his default when she voluntarily consented to his terms. Her consent even to her part of those terms is vitiated by his lie, and all the more does he lack her consent to the whole complex episode which he so carefully staged. I see no reason *in principle* then why he should not be liable to charges of rape—or at least "gross sexual imposition"—in an ideal liberal criminal code.

A scale of degrees of voluntariness is also presupposed in the false promise category. The more coercive the promised offer the less voluntary its acceptance if the promise should turn out to have been a lie all along. If the millionaire had promised only to pay a year's tuition for the woman's child as his part of the bargain, his lie would render her consent to his proposition less than fully voluntary, but less nonvoluntary than in the life-saving example. That is because the postponement of the child's education would be less of an evil on her scale of unwelcomeness, and the offer, therefore, (whether a lie or not), proportionately less coercive. If the lying promise was to set up the woman and her healthy child in a luxury apartment (an improvement over her present quite adequate facilities), then her consent, while still less than voluntary, would be much closer to the voluntary end of the scale than in the earlier examples, since the offer (lie or not) is no longer coercive, holding forth an attractive prospect merely, rather than the elimination of an intolerable evil. Surely now her consent is no longer sufficiently nonvoluntary to deprive him of a defense to criminal charges for having lured her to bed.

Other false pretenses. This fourth category is a miscellaneous one. Hardly any imaginative example is too bizarre to be included in it, for the simple reason that beliefs of an endless variety are capable of becoming part of the inducement sets of different people. Still, fraudulent inducements can be rank-ordered in terms of their effects of voluntariness. Those which are coercive in their pressure on choice, for example, are the most destructive of voluntariness, much more so than beliefs to the effect that the solicited consent would lead to some *benefit* for the consenter, no matter how great. Thus when the doctor tells the gullible patient that her otherwise fatal cancer can be cured only by sexual intercourse as soon as possible, his fraudulent inducement has a coercive effect on her will since she believes that her consent to intercourse is her only alternative to an intolerable evil. But if he says, equally impressively and speaking *qua* physician, "Come sleep with me; it will be very good for your complexion," he holds forth merely a benefit, and perhaps a minor one at that, given her own standards of preference. If, having already performed as "prescribed," she learns of the fraud, she can complain that it reduces (in retrospect) the voluntariness of her consent, but unlike the earlier example, it does not utterly vitiate that consent, since her false inducement belief exerted no coercive pressure on her choice.

For a second example, consider a false pretense, not about a future occurrence, or a causal connection between a present event and a foreseen result, but rather a deception about a present fact, in this case, a person's identity. Suppose *B* is an enthusiastic fan of the rock star Johnny Limbo. She has heard all his records but has never seen his photograph. Upon learning of this, the villainous *A* proclaims that *he* is Johnny Limbo and invites her to come to bed with him. The ruse works, let us suppose, and now the question is how nonvoluntary was her consent for such purposes as determining his criminal liability. If we consider this deception to be fraud in the inducement, then the voluntariness of her consent is reduced but to nowhere near the extreme of total involuntariness, for its inducement was an envisaged good, not the avoidance of a dreaded evil. Hence it had no coercive force. Her consent was still voluntary enough to serve as a defense for him to criminal charges.

On the other hand, if we consider the deception in this example to be fraud in the *factum*, on the analogy with the case of the nocturnal *poseur* mistaken in the dark by his willing victim for her husband, then the consent is totally involuntary and utterly vitiated. Indeed on that analogy the rock-star-imitator would be as guilty of rape, under the traditional statutes, as the husband-imitator. The issue reduces to that of deciding on relevant act-descriptions for the conduct consented to, and the conduct that actually took place, in the two examples. Perkins says of the imitated husband example that the woman consented to an act of marital intercourse, not to the act of "adulterous intercourse" that in fact took place, and that for that reason the fraud was in the *factum*. The fan of the rock star cannot make a distinction between act-descriptions of the same categorial kind. She cannot claim that she was tricked into adultery. The wife in the other case can be presumed to suffer a greater "harm," or at least more severe psychological trauma on discovering her mistake, whereas the rock fan's distress will consist mainly in disappointment at not having been with her idol after all. The distinction between the two reactions thus seems to have a structural similarity to that between harm and mere nonbenefit, or more generally, between suffering an evil and missing a good. Whether or not this is an accurate account of psychological reactions in "standard cases," it is probably part of the actual reason for classifying the fraud in the fake husband example as in the *factum*, and in the fake rock star example as in the inducement. The remainder of the case is provided by the legal policy of giving greater protection to married people from unwanted adulterous intercourse than to unmarried people from intercourse by mistaken identity. In virtue of that policy the marital status of the actors, and not merely their identity, is considered an essential part of the act-description in the fake husband example, whereas in the fake rock star example, adultery is not involved, and mistake as to the identity of the partner is treated in the same way as any other mistaken factual belief, not as an essential part of the description of the act consented to.

9. Informed consent in medicine

Physicians and medical researchers must often consider whether to adopt risky therapeutic measures or to test them on human subjects who may or may not themselves stand to receive the benefits or suffer the costs. It is widely agreed that such therapeutic or experimental risks can rightly be imposed on people only with their consent, so the question naturally arises in medical contexts how voluntary that consent must be to be valid. This is not typically an issue for criminal law except in those cases when the consent condition is egregiously or maliciously violated, so there is little point in a detailed discussion here. It will be useful, however, to consider some of the problems for medical ethics and for civil law insofar as they bear on our attempt to analyze the concept of voluntary consent generally.

Consent to medical treatment,[44] of course, cannot be voluntary if it is coerced or if it is expressed by a person whose rational faculties are undeveloped, severely impaired, or destroyed. The most frequently discussed voluntariness-reducing factor in medical contexts, however, is neither of these but rather a factor in the general category of defective belief, namely inadequate information. Consent to medical treatment (whether by a patient-subject or a proxy) may be insufficiently voluntary to be valid if inadequately informed. Following Louis Katzner,[45] we can call this requirement for validity "the information condition," and restrict our attention here to it. A duty of disclosure is imposed on the physician by the information condition, and one much discussed problem is how to formulate the appropriate standards of disclosure for the various medical contexts in which voluntary consent is sought. How full and detailed must the disclosure be? In particular, does the standard of disclosure ever permit intentional nondisclosure? Other problems concern the effect on voluntariness of the patient-subject's defective comprehension of the disclosed information, the permissibility of voluntary waivers of the information condition by the patient-subject, and the problem of mistaken beliefs in which the patient-subject stubbornly persists. These are the questions we shall now address.[46]

Standards of disclosure. Out and out paternalistic standards have now fallen out of favor in the American law. Formerly, the law was content simply to apply the standard of what is customary in the local medical community, and what was customary was the view that doctors were obliged to disclose risks only to the extent that candor seemed in the patient's best interests as determined by the expert judgment of the physician.[47] What is coming to replace this older standard is the standard of "what the reasonable patient or exper-imental subject would want to know." Where this standard is in effect, the patient-subject's consent is valid only if he has been told all the facts that a hypothetical reasonable person in his situation could be presumed to need to make his own decision. That certainly is an improvement from the point of view of anyone who seriously respects personal autonomy, but it may not be enough to protect each and every patient or subject. Perhaps the only infor-mation the physician should be required to disclose on his own initiative is information he could presume any reasonable patient would want (or need) to know, but the given patient in the bed may want to know that and more. In that case, the burden switches to the patient to ask for the further data, and the autonomy-respecting physician will be obliged in response to divulge the information if he has it, or to honestly acknowledge his ignorance if he does not. As we have seen (Chap. 20, §3), even unreasonable persons can act voluntarily; it can also be the case that a given person can act voluntarily *only* if he acts unreasonably (by our standards.) To choose voluntarily, he may require information that more reasonable persons would deem irrelevant.

The reasonable person standard does define the physician-researcher's duty to the patient-subject in the first instance, however, so it is important to have a clear notion of what the reasonable person would want to know before making his decision. "The subjects need not be told everything," notes Louis Katzner, "but they do have to be told the *important* things"[48]—the general features of what is to be done, the likely costs (in pain and discomfort) and benefits (to the patient or to others), the risks to the patient's life or general health, the chances for success, the costs of *not* proceeding in the way in question, and the extent of the investigator's uncertainty in estimating any of the other factors. If these matters are disclosed to the actual patient, the information he receives thereby will probably include everything he wants to know and more, in which case he can discard the "more" if he wishes. But if there is some further information of concern to him, which seems irrelevant to the physician using the "reasonable person" standard, then he has a right to ask for, and receive *it* too, provided, of course, that the information is reasonably accessible to the physician. Then, at that point, as fully informed as he can be about everything that a reasonable patient would want to know, and possessed of additional information, which he idiosyncratically required, he must decide whether to assume the risks for the sake of the possible benefits. That decision must be entirely his.

The idiosyncratic considerations of a given patient might well seem and really be associated with deliberations that are "unreasonable" or "nonrational." The patient may be neurotic and be impelled by beliefs that are not related to his decisions. These actually motivating beliefs may include, in Katzner's examples, "such things as the individual's feelings toward the investigator (Does the subject like the investigator? Does he or she want to please the investigator?) and feelings toward himself or herself (Is the subject looking for an escape from marital problems? Is the subject feeling guilty about his or her parents' death?)."[49] In deciding because of such factors as these (or if we may so speak, on the basis of such bad "reasons" as these), the patient-subject is deciding foolishly or neurotically, but the foolish or neurotic decision may yet be *his* fully informed decision. (He is simply a foolish or neurotic person.) It the decision-maker is not rationally impaired to the point of incompetence, there is no reason why his or her foolish or neurotic decision cannot be a sufficiently voluntary one. (See Chap. 20, §§2–5, and Chap. 21, §6.) If he is an autonomous being, he has the right to decide foolishly in self-regarding matters.

At this point, we can re-introduce the notion of an "inducement set." This phrase refers to all the true propositions which, if a given subject believed them, would be part of his inducement for or against a given act or decision. If a belief is part of a subject's inducement set in respect to action X, then it will incline him to some degree either to perform or refrain from X. If X is giving his consent to surgery, then his belief that he has only a fifty-fifty chance of surviving the operation is part of his inducement (presumably a negative part), and the belief that a successful operation will relieve his ailment once and for all is a positive part of his inducement. His beliefs that Lisbon is in Portugal and that $2 + 3 = 5$ are not in his inducement set at all. The information condition is satisfied then to the extent that propositions known or easily learnable by the physician-researcher that are also part of the patient-subject's inducement set are disclosed to, and apprehended by, the patient-subject. Further, when the investigator simply doesn't know the truth value of a proposition which if true would be part of the patient's inducement set, that ignorance must also be divulged. An ideal "fully informed" consent, then, would be one in which every proposition in the patient-subject's inducement set has been disclosed to him unless its truth is unknown, in which case *that* has been revealed to him too.

Intentional nondisclosure. Suppose that *B* is an apparently competent adult whom Dr. *A* wishes to treat with a drug injection, but Dr. *A* has learned that *B* would literally rather die than have a hypodermic needle enter his flesh. Should Dr. *A* then trick *B* into receiving the shot or let him die? This is indeed a hard case for the uncompromising defender of human autonomy, whose only plausible argument is that *B*'s preference (based only on his admittedly neurotic fear of the needle, not on religious or other conviction) is so unreasonable as to be presumed the effect of voluntariness-defeating impairment. Bearing this troublesome model in mind, then, consider the case in which the sole ground of *B*'s refusal to consent to treatment would be a proposition in his inducement set that has not yet been disclosed to him, namely that the lifesaving serum the doctors wish to inject in him contains live cancer cells. *B* in this example has a nonrational fear of anything labeled "cancer" which is so strong that if he acquires the belief that the cells are in the serum he will withhold his consent to the treatment. Would Dr. *A* be justified in withholding this one item of information from him?

Katzner wisely distinguishes between the therapeutic and experimental contexts before giving his verdict. If *B* is a voluntary subject is a research experiment devoting his services as a gift so that others might one day benefit from greater medical knowledge, then of course the critical information may not be intentionally concealed from him. If he is a patient himself, however, and his own life is at stake, the problem is more difficult. If, in this example, Dr. *A* deliberately fails to disclose an item that is a negative part of the patient's inducement set, he has invaded that patient's autonomy. There are hypothetical circumstances invented by ingenious philosophers which are so desperate that almost anything in those circumstances can be morally justified, but nevertheless, deliberate invasions of personal sovereignty put an enormous burden on the would-be justifier. Of course, if *B* is so demented or hysterical that his refusal to consent would not count as voluntary, then therapeutic treatment against his will may not in fact invade his autonomy, but there is no way of confirming such impairment without raising the question of the proposed injection with the patient and attempting to reason with him about it. That in turn makes the trickiness required for nondisclosure almost impossible. Even an outright lie about the contents of the injection will be hard to tell convincingly after a candid reasoning session with the patient, so that recourse to an injection by stealth or force might then seem necessary, in which case there is less than "involuntary consent," in fact no consent at all. On balance, full disclosure is the better policy, though it can be very dangerous to the unreasonable patient.

An equal and opposite problem arises in the wholly experimental context when a voluntary subject *agrees* to a somewhat risky treatment on "nonrational grounds," say a stubborn conviction in the face of all evidence that the live cancer cells will increase his sexual powers or his longevity.

Defective comprehension. To know bare facts and to fully comprehend their significance are two quite different things. Information without understanding is not a firm ground for voluntary decision-making. In most contexts physicians or researchers can do more than simply "disclose" facts; they can try to interpret them, tie them together, and explain their significance. They can ask repeatedly "Do you understand?," "Can I make it clearer?," and offer to explain. They can delay treatment when feasible until they are satisfied that the responses of the patient-subject are more than mere parrotings expressing trust but no understanding.

The only philosophical—as opposed to practical—issue raised by this procedure is whether it is possible even in theory for a layperson in the role of patient or experimental subject to acquire from such a process the full comprehension required by voluntariness, especially when great risks are involved. There seems to be a dilemma for the physician-researcher: if he provides enough education to the patient-subject to assure adequate comprehension, he may have to pursue the illusory ideal of "total disclosure," explaining everything down to the finest detail, describing contingency-options that he himself can hardly anticipate, filling in the background in biochemistry, immunology, molecular biology, and so on. But if he fails to do that, then the patient-subject's consent will be in large degree based on faith, rather than understanding, and the comprehension required by voluntariness will be at best suspect. Therefore (it is said to follow), informed consent in medical contexts is often, or even usually, impossible.

The best reply to this argument is that which reaffirms the importance of our distinction betwen the *voluntariness* of consent, itself a matter of degree measured on various sliding scales from total involuntariness to the ideal "full voluntariness," and the *validity* of consent when it is "voluntary enough" for a given moral or legal purpose. Employing similar distinctions, Beauchamp and Childress give what seems to me to be the proper reply to the argument:

> So long as one clings to the ideal of complete disclosure of all possibly relevant knowledge . . . claims about the limited capacity of subjects will be given credence. But if this ideal standard is replaced . . . there should be no longer any temptation to succumb to this pessimism. From the fact that we are never *fully* voluntary, *fully* informed, or *fully* autonomous persons, it does not follow that we are never *adequately* informed, free, and autonomous . . . A different lesson is to be learned: because comprehension is both limited and difficult, we should strive harder in biomedical and educational contexts to foster information and to avoid undue influence. Apprehending one's medical situation is not substantially different from apprehending one's financial situation when consulting with a C.P.A., or one's legal situation when consulting with a lawyer, or even one's marital situation when consulting with a marriage counselor. The shades of understanding are manifold, but various degrees of apprehension may nonetheless be adequate for an informed judgment.[50]

Doctors and lawyers, we must note, are experts whom we hire to do services for us that we cannot perform as well for ourselves. If we could understand as much as they do about our medical or legal plight and the available remedies, perhaps we would dispense with them. But in hiring them in the first place (when we have any choice in the matter) we consent to their independently exercising their own judgment, at least within certain limits. But rarely if ever will a prudent person give them *carte blanche* discretion to do what they will, without further consultation or approval. After all, they are professionals whom we retain to represent our interests, and in the end, we presume, we are the authorities about what those interests are. If the question before them concerns the choice of effective means to our ends (when our ends are clearly known, not merely presumed), then we happily consent to their own independent judgment whatever it might be. If the question calls for a choice among risks, however, it may require that the principal rather than his agent, with all the "important information" at his disposal, make his own evaluation and authorize the expert to attempt to put it into effect.

Voluntary waivers. Suppose that a competent adult patient (or voluntary ex- perimental subject) deliberately adopts the policy of blind trust, and author- izes in advance whatever measures the physician-researcher chooses to adopt in his case. In particular, the trusting patient elects to *waive the information condition* altogether. He is willing to consent to treatment, but only on the condition that he *not* be informed about the harrowing and distressing de- tails. He just wishes to remain tranquil and trusting, undisturbed by the anxieties inevitably produced by conscious absorption in his problems and the techniques of their resolution. In short, he "refuses to accept as much information as the reasonable person would [want] . . ."[51] Again, the re- specter of personal autonomy is faced with a dilemma. On the one hand, if he grants his approval to the use of force or stealth to make patient-subjects receive the information against their will, then he has invaded their auton- omy without their consent. Similarly, if he refuses to give any treatment until they consent in a fully informed way, despite their wishes to the contrary, he either sets back their interests (or withholds help) without their consent, or coerces them by threat of such withheld assistance into accepting his conditions. On the other hand, if he honors the patients' request to withhold information about his proposed treatment, then their consent to that treatment, since it fails to satisfy the information condition, may seem insufficiently valid to be voluntary. It seems that the patient will be wronged whatever the doctor does.

The respecter of autonomy need not despair. He should consider that a *waiver of a right*, like the *expression of consent* to a proposal, is a linguistic performance with normative consequences, an act that can itself be voluntary or involuntary. In order to be voluntary enough to be valid, a waiver of the right to be informed as a condition of consent to medical treatment must *itself* be informed, uncoerced, and unimpaired. What information then is relevant to the voluntariness of a waiver of the right to be informed before consenting to treatment? When we get this far removed from the primary treatment, we can require that the would-be waiver be told virtually everything that is "important" or "relevant" to his choice. That is because the relevant data will be highly abstract, and easily summarized. "Before you sign this waiver," the autonomous but timid patient should be told, "you must realize that your treatment *might* involve risks, dangers, and problematic decisions that you will not be told about, and that even when there are questions about what weight to assign to potential risks and benefits, you will not be consulted, so that your doctor's values and preferences might be substituted for your own."[52] If a competent patient comprehends a warning of his kind, he knows what a "reasonable person who prefers ignorant tranquillity to informed anxiety" needs to know in order to decide whether to waive his right to further information, and his subsequent waiver, if free of coercive pressure, will be voluntary enough to be valid. If he has an idiosyncratic desire for further information of a special, perhaps "irrelevant" or "nonrational" kind, before signing the waiver, he should be encouraged to ask for it too before signing. Such procedures are fully compatible, it seems to me, with respect for the autonomy of the patient with unusual preferences, and has many fewer problems than the alternative approach which coercively imposes un- wanted information on the patient for what the imposer believes to be "his own good."

When the doctor later, acting as a proxy, asumes a risk for his trusting patient, can we say that the patient himself has consented when in fact he knows nothing of it? If he voluntarily signed the information waiver, in effect he assumed the risk of the risk-occurring-without-his-foreknowledge, from which it follows, I think, that he consented, however indirectly, to the doctor's treatment. Because his waiver was valid, his consent to the risky treatment was sufficiently voluntary to be valid, even though he was una- ware at the time even that it was happening.

We cannot conceive in a similar way of a demented person waiving the requirement that he be sane in order for his consent to be valid, or an infant waiving the maturity requirement, or a drunk the sobriety require- ment. The waivability of the information condition thus distinguishes it from the category of voluntariness-reducing factors involving rational im- pairment. (Surprisingly, however, there are parallels in the category of coercive force. When one acts under coercion but not because of coercion, and thus willingly does what one would be forced to do in any case, one can waive the coercion requirement after the fact, so to speak, and revalidate one's consent. That would be to relieve another party of responsibility for wronging one except, as we have seen (Chap. 24 §6), for the detachable wrong of imposing coercion itself.) The case under discussion is not that of an ignorant person waiving the information condition so much as that of a person sufficiently informed to waive the information condition, and effectively doing just that.

Stubborn persistence in error. A competent patient's mistaken beliefs can cause more serious problems even than simple ignorance can, especially when those beliefs are adamantly maintained in the teeth of contrary evidence and testimony. I exclude from this category deranged beliefs ("I am Napoleon"), psychotic delusions, paranoid fears, and the like, for these present no problem for our application of the voluntariness tests. Rather, I refer to the sort of belief we have already considered in our discussion of intentional nondisclosure, for example, that injections of live cancer cells are always unreasonably dangerous or fatal. Experience shows that this is the kind of belief that can be maintained unreasonably (or because of "nonrational factors") even by competent, generally rational persons. In our earlier discussion, we considered briefly whether a physician and/or researcher could intentionally conceal the fact that there are live cancer cells in an injection from the patient who is already known to be unreasonable on the subject. Now, however, we must inquire whether the doctor or researcher can impose the treatment after the fact of disclosure when deception is no longer possible. At that point can he inject the serum without the patient's consent, on the grounds that otherwise great harm or even death will ensue, and that the patient's *refusal* to grant consent, being "misinformed," was not voluntary enough to have effect? An equal and opposite problem arises in the wholly experimental context when a voluntary subject *agrees* to a somewhat risky treatment on "nonrational grounds," a stubborn conviction in the face of all evidence that the live cancer cells (say) will increase his sexual powers or his longevity.

   It is unlikely that we can formulate a satisfactory general answer to questions of this kind that would apply equally to treatments of high and low risk, in research experiments and therapeutic treatments, to consentings and refusals to consent. The distinctions between therapeutic and experimental contexts, and between granting and withholding consent, generate four distinct kinds of cases, as indicated in Diagram 25-5, and variations in degree of danger suggest still further complications. In all four cases the mistaken belief definitely *reduces* the voluntariness of the response. Such reduction of voluntariness is always a consequence of falsity in an inducement belief. If we assume further (as we shall for simplicity) that the belief in question

	Treatment	Patient's or Subject's Response	Reason for Response
1	To some degree risky experimental	Wants to consent	Because of false belief stubbornly persisted in
2	To some degree risky experimental	Refuses to consent	Because of false belief stubbornly persisted in
3	To some degree risky therapeutic	Wants to consent	Because of false belief stubbornly persisted in
4	To some degree risky therapeutic	Refuses to consent	Because of false belief stubbornly persisted in

Diagram 25-5. False belief and medical treatment.

occupies a central position in the person's inducement set, that it is (let us say) both necessary and sufficient for the person's response, then the reduction of voluntariness is substantial. So, at least, we would judge if we knew that the false belief in question would quickly change in the face of disconfirming evidence, like the tea drinker's belief that he has put sugar in his cup when in fact he has put arsenic. When the mistaken belief is stubbornly persisted in, however, it may be because of a "voluntary character trait" like credulity or suspiciousness, trust or distrust of authority, timidity or boldness, fanaticism or perversity. If we think of this trait as central to the person's identity, essential to "the way he is," then we might not downgrade quite so substantially the voluntariness of the response it produces, for better or worse.

Finally let us suppose, for simplicity's sake, that the degree of risk is high, and equally so, in the four cases. Now we can ask in each case whether the response is voluntary enough to be valid. We shall discover, I suspect, that we have here four cases in which the degree of voluntariness is the same (low), but that contextual variations among them require that different standards of validity be applied.

Case 1: The subject wishes to consent to dangerous experimental treatment because and only because he falsely and stubbornly believes it will increase his sexual potency. His consent is not *very* voluntary, but if the risk were low, if for example he had nothing to lose but the time he contributed to the experiment, then his consent would be voluntary enough to be valid anyway. The experimenter can judge that if the subject is stubborn in his nonrational beliefs, that is his problem, and no business of the researcher. But if the risk is high (as we have assumed), that is another matter. (See Rule of Thumb number 1, Chap. 20, §5.) The stubborn volunteer can no more be permitted to risk his life substantially nonvoluntarily than the tea drinker to drink his arsenic by mistake. If the researcher permitted the stubborn volunteer to assume his risk by mistake, he would be failing to save him from a danger that he did not really choose. That is no way to respect his autonomy. Moreover, the researcher's gain at the "volunteer's" expense would be gross *exploitation* of the subject's imprudent character, a blamably unfair gain at his expense, even if not a wrongful harm imposed upon him. (See Vol. IV, Chap. 31, §6.)

Case 2. The subject refuses to consent to dangerous experimental treatment because of his stubborn and nonrational belief that the live cancer cells he is to receive are necessarily fatal, or (to preserve symmetry) that they will cause sexual impotence no matter how the experiment turns out in other respects. Here the subject's refusal to consent is substantially less than fully voluntary but is nevertheless quite voluntary enough to have effect as a refusal, that is to nullify the researcher's right to impose the unwanted treatment on him. That is because the *nonparticipation* in the experiment to which the person commits himself by his refusal is itself not dangerous—no more "risky" than the normal everyday life that is the person's baseline for risk comparisons. Interfering with his choice in this case would not be to "save" him from anything, but rather to force him to make a kind of charitable contribution, against his will and at his risk, to the experiment.

Case 3: The patient wants to consent to the therapy that is recommended by his physician although the doctor warns that it could have dangerous side effects and might not work in his case. Dangerous as it is, the doctor argues, it is the least risky of the alternatives, including no treatment at all. The patient agrees, not for the doctor's reasons, but because and only because of his own stubborn erroneous belief that the chemicals in the proposed treatment will increase his sexual potency. Because of this false belief and its central place in the patient's inducement, we must downgrade the voluntariness of his consent, but probably not to the point of invalidating it. Starting the proposed treatment is risky, but less risky than withholding it would be. In the circumstances then, the treatment is relatively low-risk and thus calls for lower standards of consensual validity than more dangerous and less necessary conduct would.

Still, the doctor might understandably feel some uneasiness at starting treatment he knows the patient would not consent to if he knew the truth, and the truth abut an entirely "irrelevant" matter at that! If the patient were disabused of his false belief, he would not consent, and his refusal, while highly dangerous to him, would no longer be based on false belief; hence it would no longer be "substantially nonvoluntary." Thus there would no longer be an autonomy-respecting rationale for imposing treatment. The doctor thus knows, in the case at hand, that he is able to pursue his therapeutic goals only by taking advantage of the patient's perverse ignorance. The patient's defective belief is put to use for his own good, after every effort has been made to change it to a belief that would make the beneficial treatment impossible! Thus autonomy has been given its due, and by a lucky twist of fate, the patient's own good is promoted too.

Case 4: The patient refuses to consent to therapeutic treatment that is probably necessary to save him from irreparable injury or death. The treatment itself has its dangers, but forgoing the treatment is by far the more risky course. Moreover, the patient refuses because and only because of his stubborn erroneous belief that the chemicals employed in the therapy would cause sexual impotence. Now the question is whether the refusal, based solidly on a mistaken belief the doctor has tried his best to change, is voluntary enough to be effective as a bar to the proposed therapy. Given that the relative dangers of forgoing therapy are extreme, the standards for the validity of a refusal must be correspondingly high. The voluntariness of the refusal in this case is so low because of the mistaken belief that it cannot possibly satisfy the appropriate standards of validity. To take the other course would be to permit the patient to harm himself by a refusal he would not make if he knew the truth. Intervening to force the patient to have the treatment is like preventing the tea drinker from tasting his poisoned tea when he sincerely insists that the arsenic he put in it is sugar. In neither case is there a desire to die; hence in neither case is there invasion of autonomy.

In Chapter 27 the terms of the problem change as we consider the voluntariness of consensual transactions with patients who *want* to die.

26

Failures of Consent: Incapacity

1. Forms of moral and legal incapacity

A third category of voluntariness-reducing factors is far more miscellaneous even than the categories of force and defective belief. Even when there is no external compeller, coercer, or deceiver, a person may be incapable of validly consenting to a specific agreement because of various internal deficiencies of his own. If he is so impaired or undeveloped cognitively that he doesn't really know what he is doing, or so impaired or undeveloped volitionally that he cannot help what he is doing, then no matter what expression of assent he may appear to give, it will lack the effect of genuine consent.

From the theoretical point of view, incapacity appears to be less fundamental a category than force and defective belief. Instead of being a third independent type of voluntariness-reducing factor, incapacity is derivative from the other two. If we ask *which type* of incapacities tend to defeat voluntariness, the answer is—the volitional and cognitive ones; and if we ask how incapable a person must be to lack the power of valid consent, the answer is—incapable of fully understanding the agreement in question, or incapable of choosing otherwise. Ultimately the grounds for dismissing an expression of assent as insufficiently voluntary to be valid reduce, as Aristotle claimed, to two: "He couldn't help it" and "He didn't really know (or understand) what he was doing." The forms of impairment that may bring into operation these basic types of voluntariness-reducers are not still additional voluntariness-reducers; rather they are ways in which Aristotle's two basic types of failing may be produced. They are also independently evidential—conditions we are entitled to take as evidence of the presence of more basic voluntariness-reducing factors. If we know, for example, that an alleged consenter was only two days old at the time, or that he was an adult who was in a drunken stupor or a psychotic rage at the time, then we have strong reason to suspect that the expressed "consent" was less than fully voluntary.

Another equally plausible way of relating the three categories is to make a broader, more general concept of incapacity basic, and then distinguish among the *sources* of incapacity. Thus *B* may have been incapable (in the broader sense) of consenting to the transfer of his funds to *A* because

1. *A* had a gun in his back, or because *A* twisted his arm (both *force*), *or*,
2. because *A* lied to him about what he was signing, or about some matter in his inducement (both *fraud*), or because *A* deliberately or negligently failed to inform him of some critical fact (another way of producing defective belief) *or*,
3. because *B* was only two days old, or dead drunk, or in a psychotic rage (all cases of undeveloped or impaired faculties).

In either classificatory scheme two important distinctions must be recognized and preserved. Voluntariness-reducing incapacity may be either volitional or cognitive, and it may be the product either of external factors or "internal" disabilities, that is, undeveloped or impaired faculties.

It may seem to oversimplify matters to restrict the relevant types of disability to Aristotle's two, and as we shall see, in order to make the restriction work, we shall have to interpret the notions of "volitional" and "cognitive" in a very broad and flexible way. We shall have to say that a person suffers from a volitional incapacity not only when he literally "can't help it" or acts clearly "against his will" (as in irrational compulsion), but also when he cannot form a preference at all because of a kind of affective dullness or incorrigible indifference, a breakdown or distortion of volition generally, even when there is no cognitive impairment. He may not be "forced" to act against his will, but rather be incapable of having a will in respect to some option, even though he adequately realizes his situation. His will, in short, may not be frustrated so much as paralyzed or unformed. Similarly, we shall have to say that a person suffers from a cognitive incapacity not only in those clear cases when he assents through mistaken belief or because he is prevented by some psychological block from acquiring certain information, but also when his undeveloped or impaired condition makes it impossible for him to form the relevant beliefs at all, or to avoid mistaken beliefs, or to attend carefully to the beliefs he already has, or to fully comprehend their significance. Cognitive disabilities (in the appropriately extended sense) include not only inabilities to make correct inferences, but also failures of attention and memory, failures to understand communications, and even failures to *care* about a belief's grounding and implications, leading in turn to a failure to grasp its full import, or adequately to appreciate its full significance.

I shall use the term "incapacity" as it is sometimes used in the law, as a generic term for those inabilities, whether cognitive or volitional, that are consequences of undeveloped or impaired faculties. As here used, therefore, the term is not so generic as to include the multiform varieties of externally imposed force and fraud discussed in Chapters 23 through 25. The voluntariness-reducing incapacities can be divided in respect to their durability into two major classes, those thought to be permanent impairments and those deemed merely temporary, and a third overlapping category for alternating or recurring impairments.

Permanent impairment. A patient not yet legally dead who is in a deep and irreversible coma is obviously capable of doing nothing at all except simply surviving, and even that achievement may require the help of respirators and constant medical supervision. Quite clearly he cannot understand a proposition put to him by a questioner, much less form and express his voluntary consent to it. Our legal system creates a special status for such a person which he shares with less drastically impaired people who are severely retarded, deranged, or incurably psychotic. I refer to the legal status called "incompetence." When a person is officially declared incompetent he is deemed incapable of managing his own affairs, and a legal guardian will be appointed by the court to perform this function for him until that time, if ever, when a court is satisfied that the relevant capacity has been recovered. In the meantime the incompetent individual is stripped of most of his legal powers and many of his legal liabilities. He or she is "legally incompetent" (lacks the legal power) to enter into contracts with others, to consent to sexual relations, or to dispose of property except through the proxy representation of a guardian. He may lack certain "liberties" as well, the right to vote, to drink, to drive. Even legal vulnerabilities are stripped from him—he may be "incompetent to stand trial," or lack the legal status even to commit a crime (whatever he does). If he has money in the bank (under the control of his guardian), however, he may maintain the capacity to be a defendant in a civil suit, fully accountable for his torts.

Even permanent and serious impairments, of course, are matters of degree. Most incompetents are capable in fact (and even legally capable) of consenting to some things but not to others. Hence we must distinguish, for conceptual purposes, those (like the irreversibly comatose) who are incapable of granting or withholding their consent to *anything* from those (like the moderately retarded) who are incapable of granting or withholding their consent to some, many, or most things. This is a distinction that cuts across that between the permanently and temporarily impaired. A brain-damaged retarded person may be capable of consent to some but not all offers even though his impairment is permanent, and a newborn infant may be incapable of consenting (on its own) to anything, though its "impaired condition" is (assuming it will grow up) only temporary.

There is a sense of "competent," as we have seen,[1] which is simply "capable of performing a task," and another sense, the technical legal one, which is "possessed of all the normal legal powers, liberties, and liabilities of citizenship." Those of us who are *capable* ("competent" in the first sense) of governing our own affairs are also judged *competent* (in the legal sense) to vote, enter contracts, buy, sell, consent, refuse to consent, commit crimes, stand trial, etc. But even those who are declared legally incompetent and thus in need of guardians, unless their incapacities are near-total, will maintain *some* legal powers corresponding to what capacities they do have. Thus, "An individual declared incompetent to attend to his daily affairs may nevertheless be competent to make a will."[2] That is because legal competence to make a will requires only certain minimal capacities that even generally incapable, legally incompetent people might still possess—understanding the extent of one's property, identifying "the natural objects of one's bounty" (family members), and understanding what wills are.[3] Both *de facto* incapacity and legal incompetence then can be partial and relative to specific tasks, or total and absolute, as in the case of the irreversibly comatose. But the terminological situation is complicated further, as we have seen, by the fact that "incompetence" in the law is also the name of a general legal status for those whose *de facto* incapacities are extreme enough to require guardianship and deprivation of most (but not necessarily all) the normal legal powers and liabilities[4] of citizenship.

An interesting subcase of permanent extreme impairment, distinct from the deep unconsciousness which is coma, is near-total motor paralysis without loss of awareness and understanding. The dreadfully unfortunate person whose heart beats on its own, but whose breathing is done by a respirator, who can move hardly any of his voluntary muscles, but who yet maintains his capacity to hear and understand (and perhaps feel pain), is still capable of choosing to grant or refuse consent to proposals put to him; but short of a system of eyeblinks perhaps, he may have no way of expressing his consent, and no way in any event of initiating proposals of his own. If he wishes his life-sustaining treatment discontinued, he may have no way of communicating his choice whose voluntariness is clear and beyond suspicion, even though that choice in fact is voluntary through and through.

That form of mental retardation, usually the result of brain damage, which renders a grown person into a "small child grown large," barely able to speak a language, and unable to manage his personal hygiene, much less do sums, form abstract concepts, and the like, at the same time deprives him of the competence to consent in a comprehending and morally effective way to all but the most transparent proposals. His condition in this respect, however, must be contrasted with that of his "retarded" counterparts at the other end of the scale who may be only slightly below average in intellectual skills and quite capable of doing without guardians, though perhaps not capable of doing well.

Derangement is a disorder of a much more radical kind than mere retardation. I refer to the person whose whole range of cognitive, affective, sensory, and volitional capacities are disturbed and thrown into confusion. Such a person is subject to frequent or constant delusions or hallucinations, and he is permanently disoriented in respect to space, time, or personal identity. The utterly deranged person will be judged insane even by the strictest legal standards. It is hard to conceive of him consenting—say to the sale of some of his property—if he sincerely believes that he is Napoleon, or a boiled egg, or an omnipotent God. The question of whether the lunatic is (also) retarded is both otiose and impossible to settle. It is like asking whether the physically paralyzed person also is awkward. Even if the deranged person would be unintelligent if he were not deranged (and how would one ever know that?) it would be extremely implausible to *attribute* the derangement to a prior retardation merely. No degree of unintelligence is sufficient in itself to convince a person that he is God.

Other forms of permanent psychosis may render a person incompetent to consent even in the absence of cognitive impairment or derangement. For example, a person in severe chronic depression may simply not *care* about anything enough for the question of consent even to arise. Compared to his constant and pervasive despair, no options may have any vitality whatever. He may be genuinely indifferent to all of them and literally incapable of forming preferences for anything but surcease of suffering through sleep or death. Similarly, the unhappy psychotic who is subject to constant fits of manic rage may be more inclined to attack the messenger who brings an offer than rationally to deliberate over its terms and "voluntarily" accept or reject them.

Permanent or chronic conditions of alternating capacity and incapacity. The distinction between permanent and temporary impairments is somewhat ragged at the edges, making it difficult in borderline cases to tell where one class blends into the other. Not only is it vague, however; there is also, in many cases, an "on again, off again" pattern of alternation between capacity and impairment. It is especially difficult to separate the sheep from the goats when the two are constantly turning into one another! Most of the refractory problems of assessing the voluntariness of assent, insofar as they involve impairment, are in this category. As we shall see, many cases of consenting to (or calling for) one's own death (our primary example in Chap. 27) involve persons whose impaired states come and go in alternating fashion. Even short of the dramatic choice of death, however, there are many familiar cases of alternating capacity and impairment. It is hard to imagine an epileptic voluntarily consenting to a business deal while he is in the throes of a seizure, but five minutes later he may be as capable as anyone else of consenting to an agreement. Lunatics may have relatively lucid as well as deranged intervals. Gloomy souls may alternate periods of intense depression with intervals of genuine cheerfulness. And drug addicts may be perfectly calm and rational immediately after their "fixes," though lost in a euphoric glow shortly after, and then tormented to distraction when the effect wears off, and they crave their next dose.

Temporary impairment. There are other kinds of incapacity that "come and go," but unlike those we have already considered, there is no reason that these need ever come back, because they are not elements of larger chronic patterns. Immaturity, for example, in its very nature, is subject to "cure" by the passage of time. Infancy becomes juvenility which brings much more developed faculties and capacities. Juvenility in turn blends imperceptibly into adolescence and then adulthood when the cognitive and volitional capacities are thought to be fully operative and already tested by practice and experience.

Drugged states short of addiction also fall into this category. When the normal person gets drunk, for example, he is (temporarily) in no condition to enter into a serious agreement with another party, but a few days later he may be as sober as ever. For certain purposes he was not a responsible or competent agent while drunk, but there is nothing permanent or even necessarily recurrent about his incompetence. In a similar way, a debilitating but curable illness may leave a person incompetent while in high fever, pain, or extreme debility, to consent to certain kinds of agreement—who would want his feverish or delerious self to be the spokesman for his deep and abiding wishes?—but with the passage of time competence returns, perhaps never to depart again in quite the same fashion.

A final class of temporary impairments are the moods, emotions, passions and pains whose demands on our attention can be so peremptory in their several ways that we are, while under their influence, utterly distracted from whatever business may be at hand. (We have already included depression among these moods, but some elevated mood states, especially those that combine euphoria and high agitation, also belong on this list.) Careful deliberation is difficult at best under such circumstances, and expressions of consent may distort rather than represent the abiding desires of the normal self who will soon return.

These then are the standard "forms of moral and legal incapacity"—coma, motor paralysis, severe retardation, derangement, psychosis; recurrent seizures, depressions, manias, and rages; addiction; infancy and immaturity; intoxication and other nonaddictive drugged states; fever, nausea, pain, and extreme debility or fatigue; gripping moods and distracting emotions. These states all tend to diminish the voluntariness of agreements made under their influence, but they differ from one another in the degree of their effect on a given agreement, and in the kinds of disagreement they can invalidate for a given purpose. Just these conditions and not others (like citric acid content in the blood) are taken to be standard forms of moral-legal incapacity, because experience has shown that these conditions generally impair the ability to reason, plan, deliberate, comprehend, be aware of our deeper desires, form preferences, attend, and care. Hence their presence in a given case can be taken as *evidence* of such impairments. These conditions, however, are best understood not as voluntariness-diminishing factors in themselves so much as evidential signs of the impairments that reduce or defeat altogether the voluntariness of a choice.

2. Incompetent status

Quite clearly those persons who, because of coma, severe retardation, derangement or other psychosis, are utterly incapable either of comprehension or deliberate volition, are for that reason incapable of consenting on their own to most or all of the important proposals that may affect their interests, or of preparing such proposals themselves. If they are nevertheless to be parties to agreements, consent must be expressed in their names by guardians or other proxy representatives. The guardian in that case may construe his own role in either of two distinct ways. He can think of himself as the representative of the incompetent party's *interests*, and consent when but only when the agreement serves those interests; or he can think of himself as the spokesman for the other party's *presumptive will*, and consent or not as he supposes the other party would choose were he not incompetent. In the language now used by the courts, the "proxy decision-maker" might use either a "best interest standard" to promote the incompetent's welfare, or he might use a "substituted judgment standard" to determine what the incompetent's own choice would be if he were capable of having and expressing one.

Two celebrated legal cases in recent years have dramatized the problem of proxy consent. One of these, *In Re Quinlan*,[5] involved a young patient, Karen Ann Quinlan, who was irreversibly comatose; the other, *Superintendent of Belchertown State School v. Saikewicz*,[6] involved and elderly patient, Joseph Saikewicz, who was severely retarded. At issue in the Quinlan case was whether the court should permit the pulmonary respirators to be disconnected from a patient whose cognitive brain centers had been irretrievably destroyed, thus endangering the "biological life" of her body. (The respirators were finally ordered disconnected, but Quinlan's body lived on without them, although she never recovered consciousness.) The New Jersey Supreme Court ruled that evidence of Karen Ann Quinlan's own preferences in the matter (if any) would be relevant, since the substituted judgment standard was to be used if possible to establish the comatose patient's own "consent" or "refusal to consent" to the discontinuance of vital support for her unconscious body. The patient's preferences had never been expressed with clear explicitness, and no hypothetical directives from Miss Quinlan in written form could be found. Quinlan's parents introduced "vague anecdotal testimony" that their daughter had spoken of her preference for death in hypothetical circumstances like those that later obtained, but the court ruled that the testimony lacked probative weight. In the end, the respirators were ordered disconnected not on the ground that that is what Miss Quinlan had or would have chosen, but rather on the ground that "most reasonable people would not want to be maintained in her condition."[7] It is not clear whether the court appealed to "most reasonable people" in an effort to support a statistical inference of what Quinlan's actual preference was or would have been, or whether it was an abandonment of the substituted judgment standard altogether for a standard of reasonableness. The latter interpretation (which is that of Allen Buchanan[8]) implies that the court gave up, for lack of evidence, its effort to consent vicariously for the comatose patient, and appealed directly to what is reasonable (according to "most people"), whatever Miss Quinlan's views might have been.

Joseph Saikewicz, unlike Karen Quinlan, never had been competent. He was born brain-damaged and achieved a mental age only of about one year and an estimated I.Q. of 10. He had spent all of his sixty-seven years in state institutions where, despite his full growth, he had to be cared for as if he were an infant child. In his sixty-eighth year he was diagnosed as suffering from a fatal form of leukemia. The estimate of consulting specialists was that if he submitted to a regimen of painful and debilitating chemotherapy his life might be extended for as much as a year, but Mr. Saikewicz would have to consent to the treatment, or waive the treatment, if he preferred an earlier less difficult death. But Saikewicz had no way even of understanding his options, being incapable of forming, much less employing, the concepts of life, death, health, sickness, treatment, and chemotherapy. Still, the court ruled that consent or its refusal must be decided by proxy for Saikewicz according to the standard of substituted judgment.

That assignment in the Saikewicz case was hopeless. In Quinlan's case, the court could at least raise the question of what the patient would have decided had she not *become* incompetent. There was a prior competent period to look back to and seek evidence about. But in Saikewicz's case the only similar question was how he would have decided were he not (all his life) incompetent, a question whose answer can be known only to God, and for which there is no conceivable evidence for any human surmise (except the dubious statistical appeal to what is preferred by "most normal people").

The only way a proxy decision-maker can claim to be speaking for the incompetent party he represents is for him to discover strong evidence of what we have called (Chap. 22, §3) "dispositional consent"—the inferred disposition to express or refuse permission in circumstances like those now present. Sometimes it is possible to find such evidence in the remembered opinions, statements, conversations, or letters of the party before he became incompetent. That process of evidence gathering is altogether different from inferring a person's actual psychological state at the time, or reading his prior expressed consent to just this contingency (as in a living will), or apprehending another's tacit consent, or reconstructing the choice of a hypothetical "rational consenter." When the party is incompetent and there is no living will expressing his prior consent, we can only guess from what is generally known about his prior competent self what he would have decided if he had not become incompetent. Sometimes, of course, there is direct evidence, and sometimes even indirect statistical evidence, when overwhelming, will do. We can infer with confidence from the premise "Almost *all* normal persons would prefer being pushed rudely out of the way of a truck to being run over" the conclusion that John Doe, if only he were in a condition to decide, would also have that preference. But it is a shakier matter when the appeal is to a mere majority, and value differences sharply divide that majority from a dissenting minority. We cannot attach probative weight to the inference from the premise "Fifty-two percent in a recent Gallup Poll preferred dying painlessly in the natural course of events to prolonging their lives one year through painful chemotherapy" to the conclusion "John Doe, if only he were in a condition to decide, would also have that preference."

When it is not feasible to infer dispositional consent either because no evidence is available (as in *Quinlan*) or because no evidence is possible (as in *Saikewicz*), soft paternalism permits recourse to the best-interest standard. One can intervene forcibly in another's affairs without invading his autonomy, provided one does not harm the other's interests thereby, and one does not override his voluntary choices. When the other party is incapable of voluntary choice one way or the other, than benevolent interference may properly be described as subjecting him to treatment without his consent, but that is quite another thing than forcing benevolent treatment over his voluntary refusal to consent. Benevolent interference in such situations is analogous to depositing money in a comatose person's bank account—of course "without his consent." Perhaps the closest political analogy is that in which one sovereign nation sends an unsolicited relief expedition to a foreign country whose government has fallen and where anarchy, plague, and famine reign. This is charity "without consent," but not exactly an invasion of national sovereignty.[9]

3. Immaturity

Under our law infants may own property in the sense that wealth can be held in trust for them, in funds administered by guardians, until they are of sufficient age to decide how to use them themselves. Since three-year-olds usually have a sufficient understanding of language to express or refuse to express agreement to proposals put to them by adults, it would be possible in theory for the law to permit salesmen to approach property-owning three-year-olds directly, offer to sell them (say) real estate in exchange for their whole fortunes, and then pocket the cash when the child "voluntarily" consents to the deal. Such consent, of course, cannot be valid, because a three-year-old can have only a dim concept of what money and real property are. He quite literally would not know what he was doing. A ten-year-old might have a better idea of what is going on, but he could not have the experience to tell a prudent exchange from a reckless one. A fifteen-year-old could have a good deal of economic sophistication, but his "consent" would be suspect on the grounds that he cannot yet have a full visceral appreciation of the significance of an irrevocable transaction for his future interests over the course of a lifetime. He approaches closely, but has not yet reached, the age of discretion at which his agreements to proposals can have full legal effect.

Similarly, a six-year-old could in theory be given the option of undertaking the normal twelve-year course of elementary and secondary school education or else spending that period of his life playing or being apprenticed to some trade. He may, in some minimal cognitive sense, understand what the alternatives are, but he could hardly appreciate the full costs, paid over a whole lifetime, of forfeiting an education. He can be told that he would never be able to be an engineer, computer analyst, or research physicist, and in some sense he may "understand" what this means, but he cannot know in relevant detail what these lost careers are, why they would be lost, or whether their loss would ever actually matter to him; and just as importantly, he cannot bring himself really to *care* now, since the immediate future stands so large in the view of a child that he cannot see beyond it to a less real distant time.

About such matters then as the management of property and the submission to elementary and secondary schooling, decisions must be made for the child by parents and other guardians (including the state, which, according to the doctrine of *parens patriae*, has a "sovereign power of guardianship" over minors and the responsibility of protecting them from abuse even from their own parents). How should the proxy decision-maker make vicarious choices when the incompetent party is a small child? In almost all the important cases, when the options have serious ramifications for the child's subsequent life, the correct policy is to avoid making any decision at all. In that way the guardian keeps the child's central options open until the child reaches an age of adequate capacity and can make the choices himself. When "no decision" itself will have the effect of closing the child's future options, then the guardian's proxy decision should be for the course that keeps as many life-options as possible open for the adult the child will one day become. *That* is the liberal rationale behind compulsory education to a certain age: it leaves all of a child's occupational alternatives open so that the matured informed student can later select his future path himself.[10] Quinlan's and Saikewicz's decisions could not be deferred until they recovered the competence to make the choice themselves. Fortunately, the problem with infantile and juvenile incompetents is much easier than that.

Childhood, of course, is not all of a piece. There is no sharp line between the capacities of childhood and adulthood; they are only useful abstractions from a continuous development every phase of which differs only in degree from that preceding it. Many or most of the capacities presupposed by legal rights and powers are present by the time a child is ten or twelve. Any "mere child" beyond the stage of infancy is only a child in some respects, and already an adult in others. Such boundary lines as the eighteenth or twenty-first birthday are simply approximations (plausible guesses) for the point where *all* the person's decision-making capacities are fully matured. Needless to say, just before that point *almost all* will already be matured or very nearly so. And as the child gradually acquires all the relevant capacities, he should ideally come into possession, as he goes along, of all the corresponding legal liberties, rights, powers, and liabilities.

Yet the law cannot do without rigid lines dividing "standard persons," who because of their age are presumed to have sufficient capacity to play some given legal role, from those below that age who are not. That is because direct tests of capacity in particular cases without recourse to such rules would be cumbersome to administer, or unreliable, or both. Age qualifications have varied with numerous factors—the type of proposal to which consent is required (medical treatment, marriage, sexual relations, contraceptive purchases, property sales and purchases); the type of legal relation to be created (duty, liberty, liability, immunity, power); the branch of the law involved (criminal law, torts, contracts); the status to be created (voter, driver, drinker, conscript).

The legal counterpart to the ordinary concept of adulthood (the time when capacity has ripened to the point of *full* qualification for *all* rights, duties, liabilities, and powers of citizenship) is the concept of *majority*. Traditionally the "age of majority" in common law countries has been twenty-one. That is the age "when a person is legally capable of being responsible for *all* his activities, e.g. he can no longer rescind a contract on the grounds of being a minor."[11] Steven Gifis adds to this that in most American states the age of majority "is rapidly becoming eighteen, due at least in part to the enactment in 1972 of the Twenty-Sixth Amendment to the United States Constitution allowing those eighteen years of age to vote in federal elections."[12] A resultant anomaly is that full citizens who have reached the new "age of majority" may not yet have qualified, by reason of age, for at least one other kind of right shared by other citizens, namely the right to purchase and use alcoholic beverages, which in many states is reserved for those who are nineteen, twenty, or twenty-one. (See Vol. I, Chap. 5, §5) This may be due partly to an inevitable confusion among laws (as for example when the age of legal marriage is lower than the age of consent to sexual relations), and partly to the perception that drinking in a motorized age requires capacities of judgment and control that mature even more slowly, on the whole, than those required for voting in elections. The main factor, however, is neither of these, but rather the extent to which drinking and driving are other-regarding activities. A single incompetent drinker behind the wheel of a car can do more harm to others than a single incompetent voter in the voting booth. Even if the incompetent teenage drinker is unrepresentative of his age group in this respect, the others are made to wait for their rights until many of those like him, as indicated by the statistical tables, catch up with the majority. When an activity is not socially dangerous, legal rights or powers to engage in it are withheld only until that age when the *typical* person has the capacity; but when the activity is socially dangerous, qualification is often delayed until an age (never beyond the traditional twenty-one) when the percentage of those with the requisite capacities is as high as it is ever likely to become.

The age of twenty-one is also the traditional point, in the law of contracts, when the full and unqualified power of exchanging contractual commitments is acquired. Before that age children may enter into contracts and receive consideration in exchange for their promises to perform in an agreed-upon way in the future, but such promises cannot be enforced against a child if he chooses to plead infancy as a defense to a breach of contract suit.[13] Interestingly, these nonenforceable juvenile pseudo-contracts were said in common law not to be *void* but only *voidable*. They are not void *ab initio* for at least two reasons. First, if the other elements of a valid contract are present, the child can usually enforce them against the other party. (This gives the child the best of both worlds: contractual rights without contractual duties.) Second, under the common law the child, upon reaching the age of twenty-one, has the power to fully validate the previously voidable contracts he made during childhood. "A new promise by him to perform in accordance with his previously made agreement is binding without any new consideration."[14] This is so because of the child's formerly unenforcable promise made in the past and the consideration that was *then* given for it. In short, even the voidable promise of a child has a kind of dormant legal existence until he reaches majority when it can be, as it were, retroactively ratified, or revitalized.

In the criminal law, age qualifications are of two kinds: those specifying the minimum age at which a person can be criminally responsible and those (of more interest to this work) specifying minimum ages of valid consent as a defense to various crimes. The traditional common law treatment of the age of criminal responsibility (or "the capacity for guilt") is more complicated than a modern reader might expect. It divided children (or "infants" as the law has usually referred to minors) into three classes. Those below the age of seven cannot be indicted or punished for any offense, whatever they do, because of the unrebuttable presumption that they are *doli incapax* (incapable of guilt). Those who are fourteen and over are as qualified for indictment, guilt, and punishment as adults. Those between seven and fourteen are subject to no conclusive presumptions. Rather they are presumed, like the younger children, to be incapable of the guilt requisite for criminal liability, but that presumption is rebuttable. So much is clear. What is hazy is the nature of the case that can succeed in overcoming the presumption of criminal incapacity for this middle group. A typical statement of the nature of rebutting evidence is that of Judge Southard in an 1818 case: "If the intelligence to apprehend the consequences of acts; to reason upon duty; to distinguish between right and wrong; if the consciousness of guilt and innocence be clearly manifested, then this capacity is shewn."[15] But moral education for most children begins shortly after the acquisition of language, and as early as the age of four or five, surely, the child knows that violence against others, taking without permission, and lying are wrong (or at least forbidden by accepted authorities), and manifestations of guilt and remorse are common. If the emphasis, however, is heavily placed on the capacity to "*reason* upon duty," then perhaps a rationale for excluding the sub-sevens can be elaborated. The case would have to be made with care, however, if we are not to relieve most adults (save only moral philosophers) of the capacity for criminal guilt.

In a leading case with a vintage as recent as 1938,[16] Justice Barnhill of the North Carolina Supreme Court, in summarizing the law pertaining to the criminal capacity of infants, endorsed a view that rests heavily on the "knowledge of good and evil" test, better known from its use in the application of the insanity defense. The presumption of incapacity as it applies to a child in the seven to fourteen age group can be rebutted, he writes (quoting earlier authority) "if it appears to the court and jury that he is capable of discerning between good and evil, and in such cases he may be punished."[17] The quoted authority then leaves no doubt about precisely which cases these are:

> The cases in which such presumption may be rebutted and the accused punished when under fourteen years of age are such as an aggravated battery, as in maim, or the use of a deadly weapon, or in numbers amounting to riot, or a brutal passion such as unbridled lust, as in an attempt to commit rape, and the like. In such cases if the defendant be found *doli capax*, public justice demands that the majesty of the law be vindicated and the offender punished publicly, although he be under fourteen years of age, for *malice and wickedness supply the want of age.*[18]

The judge seems to be saying that if the crime is shocking enough, then it matters not that the perpetrator's actions were, in virtue of his age, substantially less than voluntary, for the shocking aspects of his conduct can "supply the want of age." In fact, however, we should expect no clear correlation between the seriousness of the crime and the degree of responsibility of the juvenile actor for it. A ten-year-old who attacks his mother with a carving knife might, for all the dreadful seriousness of his wrong, fall short of being *doli capax*, whereas a 13-year-old can be as morally guilty as an adult in stealing a pack of cigarettes from a supermarket. Voluntariness should not be confused with harmfulness, shockingness, or the other elements of wickedness. No matter how shocking the deed, guilt is automatically reduced according to the degree to which the offender "couldn't help it" or "didn't know (*really*) what he was doing." If we forget this distinction, we are likely to argue in effect that if people are sufficiently outraged at a defendant for the harm he caused, then it doesn't matter that he is only a child. We might as well maintain that outrageousness can "supply the want" of sanity, or the want of freedom, or the want of knowledge—other conditions of responsibility.

Much more could be said about conditions for the criminal responsibility of children, but our main concern here is not with children as perpetrators but with children as victims. At what age may a child's consent to another party's conduct provide the latter with a defense to criminal liability? The crimes for which consent is a defense in our criminal law for the most part fall into two categories: rape and other sexual offenses, and larceny and other crimes against property. It is the former category that has provided almost all the critical discussion of the validity of consent by minors to conduct of others that would otherwise be criminal. So concentrated is the literature of juvenile consent upon sex crimes, in fact, that the phrase "age of consent" (unless specified further) has virtually come to mean "age at which consent to sexual intercourse can be legally effective."

The common law defined "rape" as "unlawful sexual intercourse with a

female person without her consent." Note that the unconsenting female person could be of any age. A distinct felony, often called "carnal knowledge of
a child," was usually defined as "unlawful sexual intercourse with a *willing*
female child under the age of consent." Over the last two centuries the
common law has been revised in numerous places by statutes declaring that
carnal knowledge of a child, with or without her "willingness," is also rape.
(Hence the common but unofficial term "statutory rape.") These statutes, in
effect, specify that below a certain age a female child is legally incapable of
consenting to intercourse no matter how "willing" she may be. Hence her
expressions of willingness are not to count as legally valid consent. In the
United States, the age varies from state to state, and runs the whole range
from ten to twenty-one, with sixteen being the most common. Some states
now apply the "age of consent" to boys as well as girls, and like the Revised
Code of the state of Washington, include within the offense of carnal
knowledge of a child "the act of a woman who has sexual intercourse with a
boy below that age."[19]

Washington is also representative of those states that employ a sliding scale
of penalties for sexual offenses committed against minors, depending on the
age of the child. When the child is under ten, the punishment is life imprisonment, when the child is from ten to fourteen, the punishment is imprisonment up to 20 years; when the child is from fifteen to seventeen, the offender
may be imprisoned for no more than 15 years. The rationale of this schedule
of penalties is obscure to me, but it seems more likely to be based on
assumed differences in the amount of harm done the victim[20] than on degrees
of voluntariness in his or her consent. If the latter, however, then the implicit
rationale for the scale is novel indeed. Elsewhere in the law the distinction
between valid and invalid consent is an all-or-nothing one. Expressions of
assent may vary in degree of voluntariness, but short of that degree required
for validity, a miss is as good as a mile. In this case, if the interpretation we
are considering is correct, no degree of voluntariness short of validity will be
legally effective in respect to exculpation, but there are legal effects on degree
of punishability created by, and corresponding to, the varying degrees of
voluntariness of the willing juvenile. This must be one of the rare places in
the law where voluntariness that is insufficient to make consent valid nevertheless has other legal effects, in this case mitigating ones.

When a person of either sex commits "an act of indecent familiarity" with
another person (short of intercourse) without the latter's consent, he or she
has commited both criminal and civil battery upon the other, and as Perkins
puts it, "if the act is committed upon one who is incapable of giving consent
by reason of immaturity . . . , it is without consent so far as the law is
concerned . . . "[21] (Perkins completes the sentence by adding, confusingly,
"even if consented to in fact," when a more perspicuous phrase would be

"even if the minor expressed his or her willingness.") A standard example follows.

> It is a battery, for example, for a man to take indecent liberties with a five-year-old girl [or boy, for that matter], because she has no understanding of the nature of the act and is legally incapable of consenting thereto. The sound view, although authority to the contrary can be found,[22] is that a girl under "the age of consent" is just as incapable of giving a legally recognized consent to an indecent fondling of her person as she is of giving such consent to the act of intercourse itself, and hence her consent to such indecent liberties is no defense.[23]

Again, it would be less confusing if "expression of willingness" in the last sentence replaced "consent". Consent *is* a defense to rape and it *should be* to "battery," at least to that kind of battery that consists of indecent fondling. The point is that an infant is legally incapable of giving consent, *not* that consent, were it possible, would not be a defense. To deny exculpating effect to *B*'s fully voluntary hence valid consent to *A*'s conduct is not only unjust to *A*; it is also an objectionably paternalistic interference with the autonomy of *B*—even if *B* is a child. Insofar as children are (or would be) capable of consenting voluntarily, it is indefensible paternalism to prevent them from doing so.

Now the interesting question arises whether a five-year-old is capable of giving valid consent to *anything*, and if so, why not to sexual fondling? Clearly there are things a child can consent to. He or she can give a coaxing adult a hug or a kiss on the cheek, or refuse to do so, and while the law might be indifferent to the matter, it would nonetheless be a kind of moral wrong to force even such harmless gestures on an unwilling child (that is, "without his consent"). Similarly an adult or another child might ask "May I have one of your candies?," and the child addressed might either consent or refuse to consent to his taking one. Sexual fondling is presumably different from these simpler examples for being potentially more harmful in its subtle effects, and since these effects are unknown to the child or not understood by him, he cannot therefore consent to them. This rationale does not confuse harmfulness and voluntariness. The point is not simply that the child runs risks in submitting to the adult fondler, but rather that these are risks the child cannot possibly anticipate, understand, or appreciate. But then how well do we adults understand them? Presumably they include the risk of encouraging the adult fondler to more extreme gestures still, the risk of incurring deep and costly emotions before the psyche is sturdy enough to bear them, or the risk of developing habits of mind toward sexual conduct that will serve the child ill as he grows older, or of suffering guilt, anxiety, shame, or remorse in ways that also carry their own heavy psychic costs. This *form* of argument is quite satisfactory, but it does have empiricial presuppositions that have been little investigated and are suspiciously convenient for us to believe. It may be that the generating motive of our refusal to permit juvenile consent to indecent advances is based less on this straightforward rationale than on a blend of deep-seated pre-rational repugnance, on the one hand, and an understandable aversion to adult *exploitation* of children (even if it should be harmless and validly consented to—see Chap. 31), on the other.

Two final points about the effects of immaturity on voluntariness should be made before we leave the subject. The first concerns the faculties and powers whose insufficient development can reduce voluntariness of responses to the various kinds of agreements minors might wish to enter. Sometimes the incapacity for valid consent is a consequence of *subtle forms of incapacity* that persist into the later years of minority (and in fact, alas, often well beyond). The law typically pegs the age of consent at its highest point for agreements like the "marriage contract" that require these subtler capacities. Fitness for marriage is not simply the product of some ability or skill that can be acquired with training or from books. Rather, time must be allowed for natural changes through growth and experience that cannot in most cases be artificially hurried.

The second point is that we can expect variations in the stringency of our standards of voluntariness, and in the minimum age at which voluntary consent is deemed possible, with the degree of revocability of what is undertaken. This point is simply an application of the "rule of thumb" elaborated in Chapter 20, §5 that "The more irrevocable the risked harm, the greater the degree of voluntariness required if it is to be permitted." This rule no doubt has been a factor in the rise in the minimum age for marriage in modern times, but it is losing its force with the rise in the divorce rate and concomitant decline in the conception of marriage as irrevocable.

4. Intoxication

Persons can be prevented from reasoning up to their usual standard for fixed periods of time as a consequence of causes as diverse as intoxicating drugs and private emotions. These causes impair either by incapacitating or distracting, or both. Alcohol can obscure vision, impair coordination, or weaken reasoning power (incapacitation); sadness, mania, or anger can so thoroughly possess one's attention and energy that one cannot bring one's full power to bear on a problem for decision (distraction), or distort one's judgment.

The generic appellation for drugged states in the criminal law has traditionally been "intoxication." Under this heading, rules have evolved for the disposition of problems caused by ordinary drunkenness (primarily) but also for the comparable altered mental states produced by other drugs. In the criminal law, statutes have commonly made public drunkenness a crime in itself, but the more interesting rules about intoxication are those that specify its relevance or lack thereof as an excuse, mitigation, or even aggravation when a quite distinct and more serious crime is committed under its influence—in short the effects of intoxication on criminal capacity. The criminal law is also concerned with the effects of intoxication on the voluntariness of expressions of assent to what would be criminal without consent. Other branches of the law too must concern themselves with the effects of intoxication on voluntary consent to proposals of many sorts, some of which can be dangerous or directly harmful to the consenter. It will be instructive to note how the standards of voluntariness differ, and with what factors they vary, in these different contexts.

Like the other forms of intoxication, drunkenness can be either voluntary or involuntary. The criminal law treats it as involuntary when either the drunkard did not know and had no reason to know that the substance he consumed, in the quantities in which he consumed it, was intoxicating, or else he was compelled by brute force or coercive threat to consume it. In either of these cases, the defendant has a complete defense to the charge of public drunkenness. (On the other hand his drunkenness will be deemed voluntary and classified as "reckless overindulgence" if it comes about simply because the drinker misjudges his own capacity.) There are crimes for which even involuntary intoxication is no excuse unless evidence is produced to show that it is so extreme as to amount to a kind of insanity.[24] I refer especially to laws prohibiting the performance of certain activities, for example driving a car, while under the influence of drugs. Short of intoxicated madness, a drunk person is presumed to be capable of knowing that he is drunk and still aware of the prohibition against driving. Hence if he is charged with drunken driving, the court can concede that his drunkenness was involuntary, while insisting that nevertheless his decision to drive while in that state was "voluntary enough."

The law's skeptical attitude toward voluntary intoxication as an excuse is as old as Aristotle,[25] and as plain as common sense. Drunkenness is an excuse for committing what would otherwise be a serious crime only when its influence deprived the actor of the capacity to know what he was doing or that it was wrong (prohibited). When the actor, however, consumes his liquor or takes his drug on his own without voluntariness-defeating mistake or compulsion, then he is fully responsible for putting himself into the state that deprived him of his capacity of self-government. Most drunkenness is to be treated as an "artificial, voluntarily contracted madness."[26] One cannot voluntarily create one's subsequent involuntariness and then claim it as an excuse for the most heinous crimes! When one drinks to the point of "temporary frenzy"[27] one assumes oneself the risk of the consequences. As for the foreseeable effects of alcohol or other drugs well short of frenzied madness, like calming one's nervousness, the point applies all the more strongly to them. "One who drinks to nerve himself for the commission of a crime already decided upon is already guilty of that crime."[28]

Sir Edward Coke went so far as to treat voluntary drunkenness as an *aggravation* of the offense[29] (not a mere failed mitigation), and Blackstone speaks with favor of the law of Pittacus in ancient Greece " 'that he who committed a crime when drunk should receive a double punishment',[30] one for the crime itself and the other for the inebrity which prompted him to commit it."[31] Despite the sympathy of leading writers with the attitudes underlying the Coke-Blackstone claim that drunkenness makes things all the worse, it has never been true that drunkenness is an automatic aggravation in the common law. What would ordinarily be manslaughter is not made into murder by the fact of the killer's drunkenness.[32] Morally speaking, allowing oneself to become intoxicated is a kind of negligence or recklessness in itself, and it can "aggravate" into criminal status otherwise innocent behavior like driving an automobile, as well as increasing the guilt for reckless driving, which is made to appear all the more reckless for being drunken too. But that is a relatively unusual treatment of drunkenness in our criminal statutes, not, as Coke and Blackstone would have it, the rule.

On the other side, there is no tendency in the criminal law to treat voluntary intoxication as an automatic excuse either. Whether, morally speaking, intoxication mitigates guilt depends on a multiplicity of factors too complex to examine here, one of which is the truth of a counterfactual conditional statement about the offender: Would he have performed the same act even while sober? Or did he have a disposition to perform acts of this kind in similar circumstances, from time to time, whether sober or drunk? If the answer is affirmative, then the judgment on a drunken killer by one court is quite understandable: "A drunken malice is as dangerous and may be as wicked as a sober malice."[33] But when the answer is negative then the malice in a homicide may not be "aforethought" as is usually required by murder, and we can sympathize with Rollin Perkins who writes: "He who, while unduly excited by liquor, has committed a prohibited deed he would never have thought of doing while sober, is not in the same scale of culpability, even if the intoxication was voluntary, as another who has done the same thing without such excitement, or who made the decision first and drank to nerve himself for the perpetration."[34] The scale of culpability of which Perkins speaks must be culpable negligence or recklessness rather than the guilt characteristic of deliberate or even impulsively intentional killings. The voluntary drinker who without prior conscious design is maddened by his intoxication, and thus acts entirely out of character, is guilty of lack of due care for the safety of others, or of conscious disregard of the unjustified danger he creates for others. He may not have known that he was making himself *non compos mentis*, but he ought to have known that he *might* be doing so. Hence he assumes the risk of the harm that results through his culpable negligence. That is guilt enough, but guilt of a different order from that of a drunk who is only acting in character when he kills, and whose drunkenness merely serves to actualize his latent tendencies more readily.

Voluntary intoxication sometimes plays a quite different role in determinations of voluntariness for purposes other than establishing criminal capacity. When B, in his drunken stupor, expresses his assent to conduct of A's that is dangerous or directly harmful to B, his expressed willingness cannot function as voluntary consent licensing A's subsequent conduct toward B and conferring immunity on A to criminal responsibility for it. If B is so drunk that he literally does not know what he is doing, or is incapable of appreciating or even caring about the risk, his consent is plainly invalidated by voluntariness-defeating factors in the defective belief category. Even if his drunkenness is not that severe, but nonetheless effective in blurring his perception, distracting his attention, and distorting his judgment ("clouding his head" as we say), or perhaps only effective in weakening the restraints on his natural recklessness, his expression of assent is still not voluntary enough to be valid, if only in virtue of the first rule of thumb (Chap. 20, §5) that "The more risky the conduct the greater the degree of voluntariness required if the conduct is to be permitted."

The more important point for our present purposes, however, is that B's assent has no greater approximation to sufficient voluntariness for being produced by drunkenness that was itself voluntarily produced. A cannot be allowed to plead after the fact that though B didn't know what he was doing when he permitted A's harmful conduct, A cannot be held responsible for the harm since B brought it on himself by creating his own vulnerability. In this important respect, standards for determining the voluntariness of consent in the criminal law, as in ordinary morality, must differ from the standards used to determine criminal capacity. If both A and B are very drunk in the present example, and after securing B's "permission", A injures him, then A is responsible for his wrongdoing (it was "voluntary enough") even though at the time he didn't quite know what he was doing, because getting drunk in the first place was his own voluntary doing. But B, whose drunkenness was equally voluntary, cannot validly consent. In his case it is irrelevant that he brought on his intoxication himself. Once again we see how standards of voluntariness vary with context and purpose.

For the most part our present criminal codes decree that an intoxicated person's agreement to the injurious conduct of another that would be criminal without his consent is insufficiently voluntary to exculpate the other, even when the intoxication itself was voluntary. Uniformity is lacking, however, because of difficult problems of interpretation raised by differing sorts of harm and (especially) by differing forms of alcoholic incapacity. The authors of the *Model Penal Code* themselves fell into factions while debating the effects of various psychological incapacities on consent to sexual relations. One would think that if a temporarily insane female cannot validly consent, and if Blackstone was right in interpreting extreme drunkenness as "voluntarily contracted madness," then the extremely drunk female cannot validly consent either. But the situation is not that simple, especially when the drunken incapacity is less severe. The final draft of the code obviously produces a vaguely worded compromise on the question. One of the ways in which a male can commit the crime of "gross sexual imposition" on a female not his wife is to have sexual intercourse with her when "he knows that she suffers from a mental disease or defect which renders her incapable of appraising the nature of her conduct,"[35] and therefore incapable, presumably, of validly consenting to it. The Institute Reporter, in his comment on the wording of this section, says that it

> is a much-narrowed version of a provision which evoked considerable resistance at the 1955 meeting, and which the Reporters [authors] agreed to reconsider. The earlier version would have made it a felony for a man to have intercourse with a woman if he knew that she submitted because of "substantially complete incapacity to appraise or control" her conduct because of mental illness, intoxication, etc. There was a somewhat complicated clause designed to exclude situations where intercourse occurred following joint indulgence in drugs or liquor. The revised draft limits criminality to situations of known mental disease or defect so serious as to render the woman "incapable of appraising her own conduct." Conditions affecting only the woman's capacity to "control" herself sexually will not involve criminal liability. Also, by specifying that the woman must lack capacity to appraise "the nature" of her conduct, we make it clear that we are not talking about appraisals involving value judgments or consideration of remote consequences of the immediate acts. The typical case that remains within the revised clause would be the case of intercourse with a woman known to the defendant to be manifestly and seriously deranged.[36]

My initial preferences are for the earlier version of this provision, but I can sympathize with the severe problems of drafting that it involved. A fully adequate rule, I should think, would accomplish the following objectives:

1. It would impose liability when the assent comes from a woman who is "out of her mind" at the time, whether the condition be permanent, chronic, or only temporary, and whether it is produced by mental illness or defect, or intoxication, and whether the intoxication was itself voluntary or involuntary. (*Certainly* there should be liability when it is involuntary!)
2. It would not impose liability when the effect of the woman's drunkenness was only to release her from her normal inhibitions and thus render her willing or eager to engage in sex with the defendant, in the absence of substantial cognitive or volitional impairment. It would be folly for the

law to attempt to eliminate the vague term "substantial" for anything
more precise, but it should be understood that forgetting or rejecting one's
own moral convictions is not strong evidence of "substantial cognitive
impairment." Where there *is* "substantial impairment," even short of utter
madness, there should be liability.

3. It would invoke a more stringent standard than (1), allowing liability for
assented-to impositions where the woman's intoxicated state is less severe
than temporary madness or derangement, if the defendant knew that
sexual intercourse would be especially dangerous or harmful to the
woman in the circumstances because of her age, inexperience, medical
condition, or psychological vulnerability. In the absence of these special
dangers, the only "harm" produced by the imposition is a contact that
would be offensive and unwanted by the woman were she sober. Objective (3), in effect, applies Rule of Thumb 1 of Chap. 20, §5.

Another place in our current criminal codes where the question can arise
whether *B*'s willingness, expressed while drunk, can relieve *A* of liability is in
the statutes on crimes against property—larceny for example. The question,
in effect, is whether the transfer of *B*'s property to *A* counts as a freely made
gift when *B*'s agreement to the transfer was influenced by liquor or drugs, or
whether it is a taking and keeping without consent, and thus a kind of *theft*
by *A*. In order for it to be theft, *A* must not have taken the property under
the "honest claim of right to it," since that would be to punish him for an
honest mistake about the effectiveness of *B*'s agreement, or about other matters. And *A* must have intended to keep the property or quickly dispose of it
by sale before the recovered *B* could demand restitution; otherwise the matter might better be settled civilly than criminally, with *B* suing for recovery
of his property. But given satisfaction of the usual "mental conditions" for
criminal liability, we can ask whether *B*'s assent, given while drunk, will
count as valid consent and thus provide *A* with a defense to the charge of
theft.

Here, I think, a factor hithero unmentioned, enters the situation. One
would expect some relevance to be attached to the matter of *initiative*. Who
initiated the process that led to the transfer? One can imagine that bar-room
drinker *B*, besotted with drink, his hand clutching a clip of $100 bills,
imposes himself on a reluctant fellow patron *A*, hugs him, pats him on the
back, avows his eternal affection and esteem for him (perhaps he knows him
but little or even not at all), and then thrusts the money into astonished *A*'s
hand, declaring it a "gift." His avarice now aroused, *A* takes the money,
lavishly thanks a beaming *B*, and disappears into the night with no intention
of ever seeing *B* again, much less of returning the money. Perhaps we should
say in this case that the loss serves *B* right. He assumed the risk of such harm

when he voluntarily chose to drink to excess, and he is little more wronged by it than by the hangover he will have the next morning—another harm he might have anticipated.[37]

But we can also imagine a different scenario. In this version of the story, *B* is noisily drinking to excess in the same public cocktail lounge. He gets friendlier and friendlier the more he drinks, but other patrons rebuff his approaches, leaving him feeling thoroughly unloved. The shrewd and opportunistic *A* decides to take advantage of *B*'s condition of vulnerability. After carefully observing *B*'s behavior from a distance, he decides upon a strategy. He approaches *B*, introduces himself (though perhaps they are distant acquaintances or old friends), and much to *B*'s delight heaps flattery on him as they drink together. Then at just the right moment, and in just the right tone of excited jocularity, *A* himself proposes to *B* that *B* make a gift to him of the $2,000 watch *B* is wearing. *B* instantly agrees, though he would never have thought of such an idea himself, drunk or sober, and hands over the watch to *A*, who expresses his gratitude lavishly, then promptly vanishes into the night, as before.

Shall we say now (i) that for the purposes of criminal liability *B*'s agreement was insufficiently voluntary to be valid, even though it is voluntary or involuntary to precisely the same degree, no more no less, than in the first version of the story? (After all in the two versions of the story *B* is equally drunk.) Or perhaps we should say (ii) that voluntariness being the same in the two stories, its legal effect should be the same too, and since its effect was to relieve *A* of liability in the first story, it should do so in the second as well. Or perhaps we should say that (iii) since the assent is drunken in both stories, it should be treated as invalid in both stories too, but that the more manipulative and exploitative *A* in the second story should be punished more severely for his greater initiative. The only interpretation we must reject out of hand is a fourth one to the effect that the consent in both stories is valid, but that the recipient of the "gift" should be held liable anyway even though, in virtue of *Volenti*, he did nothing to harm (wrong) the other. That would be to tumble into hard paternalism or moralism—traps we are endeavoring to avoid.

The correct interpretation otherwise is not clear, but I look with most favor on the first one, since it seems to fit best the apparent intuition that the more manipulative involvement of *A* in the second story justifies harsher treatment, and there is no paradox, once we have adjusted to the variable-standard theory of voluntariness defended here, in the idea that two equally nonvoluntary expressions of consent can have different legal effects in different contexts—in this case depending on whether or not another party initiated the proposal.

At one end of the spectrum of contextual variation is the use made, under

---

Case 1. The Initiative Is the Drunkard's. (B's)
Case 2. The Initiative Is the Recipient's. (A's)

Alternative Judgments of the Two Cases:

i. In Case 2, *B*'s agreement was insufficiently voluntary to be valid even though it is voluntary or involuntary to precisely the same degree as in Case 1 where *B*'s consent *is* valid. Initiative is what makes the difference.
   or
ii. Voluntariness being the same in the two stories, its legal effect should be the same (valid) too. Since its effect was to relieve *A* of criminal liability in the first story, it should do so in the second as well.
   or
iii. Since the assent is drunken in both stories, it should be treated as invalid in both stories too, but the more manipulative and exploitative *A* in the second story should be punished more severely for his greater initiative.
   or
iv. The consent in both stories is valid, but the recipient of the "gift" should be held liable anyway even though by virtue of *Volenti non fit injuria*, he did nothing to wrong the other. (Legal paternalism or legal moralism)

Diagram 26-1. The two cases of drunken "gifts."

recently passed statutes in several states, of drunkometer tests. Normally, if a thoroughly drunk person is presented with a difficult option requiring his careful consideration and likely to bear very heavily on his interests over an extended period, his intoxicated decision would be so far from being voluntary that it would be unfair to hold him to it. Rather we would insist that he be given the opportunity of rethinking the matter after he sobers up. All the more would we discount his drunken choice if we learned that it was made under coercive pressure. Nevertheless, in some American states, a thoroughly drunk motorist is deemed legally competent to grant or withhold his consent (the choice is entirely for him to make if he can) to a drunkometer test. If he consents, then (given the assumption that he *is* "thoroughly drunk") his blood will be shown to have more than the permissible maximum of alcohol, and the test result will be incriminating evidence of drunken driving, a crime punished by a jail sentence and loss of license. On the other hand, if he refuses to consent to the test, he automatically loses his driver's license (typically) for six months for "voluntarily" withholding his permission. Given that he *is* drunk, neither his consent nor his refusal could be considered very voluntary, but since the main point of the procedure is to determine *whether* he is drunk, and to protect others from him if he is, it is no affront to justice to treat his "choice" as *voluntary enough* for these purposes. His choice would be more voluntary twenty-fours hours later, but by then the condition we wished to measure will be gone irretreivably, and our test will have no point.

The alternatives to the present system are (1) to let the drunken motorist refuse to take the test and turn him loose to endanger others, (2) to try him for a serious criminal offense when the only evidence of his guilt is highly impressionistic, hence subject to "reasonable doubts," or (3) to permit the police to use brute force, or the threat thereof, to force suspected drunken drivers to take the drunkometer test. The third alternative might also be a way of treating quite nonvoluntary behavior as "voluntary enough" for certain purposes, but there are differences. First of all, brute force, whether compulsively employed or coercively threatened, renders an act just about as nonvoluntary as it possibly can be, and an act that is *totally involuntary* cannot be "voluntary enough" for *any* purpose. Secondly, the present system cannot easily degenerate into a system of unrestrained police violence—an ever present danger of the third alternative.[38]

5. Illness, pain, and distracting emotion

The drunkometer test example has many parallels in situations where a voluntariness-reducing impairment is produced by illness, pain, or emotion, and yet there is no possibility of postponing the choice to a more propitious time. Before considering these parallels, let us briefly reconsider how the capacity to choose is diminished by sickness, suffering, and strong feelings. Typically these conditions interfere with voluntary choice less by directly impairing cognitive-perceptive faculties (in the manner of intoxication) than by distracting attention. Persons do not *usually* experience hallucinations, delusions, or loss of logical acumen when they suffer from ordinary fever or debility, generalized physical malaise, pain, depression, anxiety, or bad temper, but they are less able to bring their unimpaired deliberative faculties to bear on the matter at hand when their energies are monopolized by these states, and their attention diverted. It is as if a crucial life decision had to be made with brass band blaring or bass drum beating loudly in the the background. Often there is no "turning down the internal volume" short of using sedative drugs which then come themselves to dominate the subject's mental states and render him less capable than ever of deliberation. The distracting states, unsedated, can be so peremptory that they prevent the suffering decision-maker from looking at factors he might otherwise want to consider carefully, for example, events in a future beyond the scope of his present pain, or effects on persons other than himself, or the dictates of his ideals or scruples.

Yet there are occasions when a decision rendered substantially less than ideally voluntary by such distractions must be respected as the most reliable available spokesman for the unhappy person, hence voluntary enough, in these special circumstances, to have full valid effect. The "special circumstances" have at least three identifying characteristics. The first, of course, is unfeasible postponability. Secondly, the factors from which attention is naturally diverted by the distracting state are not centrally relevant to the problem of the choice. Recall our earlier example (Chap. 20, §4) of the choice of a person with a headache to take two aspirin. A severe headache can be as fatal to careful thought as a bass drum at full volume, but if the sufferer's strongest interest is to cease the clamor or stop the pain, his attention is not distracted from *that* relevant factor; rather the pain "concentrates his mind marvelously" on the business at hand. In the example there are no risks to his future interests created by the aspirin, no involvement of other parties, no bearing on scruples or ideals. He would, of course, be distracted from considering such factors if they were involved, but, in the example, they are not. It would be different were the headache sufferer allergic to aspirin, so that he had to decide carefully whether it would be worthwhile to dull his present pain at the cost of expected side effects or the risk of future harms, even fatal ones. In that quite different example, the present pain incapacitates the sufferer for disinterested balancing of all the important factors bearing on his decision, so that he might deliberate and decide differently from the way he would were his mind clear. Many variations can be spun on the headache-aspirin example to make it exceedingly difficult, but in its initial simple form, it seems a clear instance of a decision rendered less than fully voluntary by normally distracting pain, but which is nonetheless voluntary enough in the circumstances because the factors cheated of their due consideration are not centrally involved in the first place.

Thirdly, the situation that produced the need for decision is a causal consequence of the very factor that makes clearheadedness difficult, and is linked inseparably to it. We cannot postpone the decision until clearheadedness returns because then (just as in the drunkometer example) there will no longer be any occasion for choice and the matter will be moot. We cannot tell the patient with the headache—"Wait until the pain goes away; then you will be clearheaded enough to choose voluntarily to take two aspirin." Nor can we prevent a person from turning down the volume on his stereo on the grounds that it is making such a racket that the person cannot think clearly enough to decide whether or not to turn it down! To generalize the point: sometimes the unique time for a decision is the present, so that a person must decide now or not at all. That is because, in the cases we are considering, the option before him is whether or not to do something (measure the alcohol, palliate the pain, turn down the volume) about the very factor that makes clearheaded deliberation impossible. In these cases, a choice whose voluntariness is diminished may be better than no choice at all. It may well be "voluntary enough," and a better guide to a person's abiding will and governing values than any choice a proxy decision-maker is likely to make.

There is another explanation of how causal linkage renders a decision uniquely timed and nonpostponable. If the decision is linked to the factor that makes clearheaded thought about it impossible, then postponing the decision is in effect to make the decision once and for all, and to make it negatively. In our example the pain-wracked deliberator's choice-option is: should I take two aspirin now to muffle *this pain that I feel now* or wait until the pain is gone and *then* think about it clearheadedly? If he opts for postponement, he has in effect decided *not* to buffer this pain here and now, thus making this decision negatively. But if his condition at the time of choice rendered voluntary decision impossible, his negative choice is just as nonvoluntary as a positive one would have been. The question is: which of two equally distracted choices should be recognized as the chooser's own when there is no possibility of avoiding them both until a later time? Since one choice would be just as nonvoluntary as the other, the one which reflects his felt preference at the time should govern.

Not all cases of decisions made in distracted states fit the above model. In the non-fitting examples, either (1) there is no causal linkage between the matter of the decision and the factor causing the distraction, or (2) either for that or still other reasons, the decision can be postponed, or (3) the factors from which the chooser's attention is distracted *are* centrally important to his decision. In these cases, the chooser's decision, even though entirely self-regarding, may *not* be voluntary enough to prevent justified interference from others.

If our headache sufferer must decide whether or not to accept a proposal of marriage, she might well request of her suitor that he come back later when she can attend to what she is doing, or if she accepts while in the grip of her pain, she might later demur, explaining that her earlier apparent consent (or refusal) had been overly influenced by her headache, and as such was not voluntary enough to be in any sense binding. This example clearly differs in all three relevant ways from the aspirin example. First, the decision-maker was not deliberating about whether or not to get rid of the pain, but rather about an entirely independent matter, whether to agree to marry her suitor. Hence, the condition of linkage is not satisfied. Second, the decision is clearly postponable. Third, though her mind is marvelously concentrated on her pain and the need to get rid of it, as in the aspirin example, it is by that token *not* concentrated on the prospect of a lifetime wed to her suitor—where it should be. In fact, she cannot think about that without the pain getting worse. So, because of (1) the failure of linkage between the matter of deliberation and the distracting factor, (2) the feasibility of postponement, and (3) the irrelevance of the forced focus of attention—not to mention the momentousness of the decision—the headachy assent falls short of sufficient voluntariness for a valid promise.

Similarly, a depressed person, even while in the grip of his depression, may consent voluntarily enough to a doctor's offer of anti-depressant pills, but he probably cannot voluntarily choose, while in the grip of severe clinical depression, to give away all his wealth, or to have his house burned to the ground. The linkage condition is not satisfied in the latter example; the decision is not uniquely tied to the present, and can be postponed; and the factors from which the chooser's attention is naturally distracted by his depression are those he would normally (while undepressed) find at least relevant and worthy of serious consideration.

Once more, a person in the grip of a pathologically obsessive, raging resentment against another may be influenced to choose some malicious (though legal) business strategem that will hurt both his enemy and himself, a choice he would not make in his normal state. It is hard to say whether the linkage condition is met by this example, since the decision might be characterized as a choice to "do something" about the distracting condition, namely to satisfy the resentment and thus quiet it down. But there is hope in this example that calm will return before irrevocable harm is done, so that even though the resentment persists, the decision to do or not to "do something about it" can be made in a calmer moment when the obsessiveness has receded. And there is no reason in this example why the decision cannot be postponed until then.

27

The Choice of Death

1. Voluntary euthanasia

The most important example of the influence of distraction or impairment on the voluntariness of consent is also the most difficult. I refer to the deliberate choice of one's own death made by a person who is incapable of killing, or unwilling to kill, himself. Single-party acts of suicide pose less complicated problems for the criminal law, and we have forborne discussing them in detail, because the impossibility of deterring free and resolute persons intent on their own death, and the inevitable costs to the innocent in trying to do so, render the question of criminalization "moot" (Chap. 21, §1). If those who choose to die and cannot kill themselves are to get what they wish, they must do so by "consenting" to their own killings at the hands of second parties. In all but extremely rare cases, the proposal of the killing is initiated by the would-be "victim" himself; he "consents" only in the sense that he makes the *request* that the other kill him, and typically the request is made in the most importunate entreaties. There is no reason in principle why a person cannot consent voluntarily to a proposal that he be killed that originates with the other party, but in fact there is often a suspicion of nonvoluntariness in such cases that is difficult to rebut, especially when the other party stands to gain from what he proposes, and there is the suspicion of subtle psychological manipulation.[1]

The persons who are strictly incapable of killing themselves, and therefore the most likely to request euthanasia, are found most commonly in sick beds, and under supervision, either at home, in nursing homes, or hospitals, or else in prisons and other institutions where liberty and privacy are restricted.

Occasionally we hear of a convicted murderer who pleads in court for his own capital punishment, or who instructs his attorney not to appeal a death sentence, and occasionally we read of persons who request to die for altruistic reasons, to relieve the burden on their children or to make their organs available for transplant, but far and away the most common occasion for euthanasia is an injury or illness whose consequences are so severe that they make the patient's continued existence seem intolerable to him. Not infrequently a person is charged with the "mercy killing" of his or her pain-racked and incurably diseased spouse, and charged with criminal homicide, but the issue of euthanasia most commonly arises in hospitals when patients, or their next of kin, request that life-saving treatment be withheld or terminated. Other patients would request the positive termination of their lives, say by painlessly lethal injections, but in the present state of the law that request would be hopeless, since only failures to save (passive euthanasia), not positive killings (active euthanasia), are ever permitted. Nevertheless, here we are concerned with what the law ought to be, and with the application of the soft-paternalist strategy that would permit active euthanasia when, but only when, the patient's consent (request) is voluntary enough to be valid.

The voluntariness of the death request is not the only issue in the euthanasia debate, but there is no doubt that it is a central issue, and for the soft paternalist very nearly the only issue of any difficulty. Writers frequently distinguish "voluntary" from "involuntary" and "nonvoluntary" euthanasia. A killing qualifies as voluntary euthanasia when it is validly consented to by the subject; it is involuntary when imposed on the subject against his will or without his consent even though he was capable of consenting; it is nonvoluntary when consent is missing because the subject, being only an infant, or comatose, or insane, is incapable of giving his voluntary consent. What the word "euthanasia" adds to the simpler term "killing," in all three of these categories, I presume, is the suggestion of the killer's humanitarian motivation. The death, as Philippa Foot puts it, must be thought of, as "for the sake of the one who is to die."[2]

So far as I know, no one since the fall of the Nazi regime in Germany has advocated involuntary euthanasia. Even the Nazis themselves equivocated on the term "euthanasia" to conceal their true motivation which was in no sense "humanitarian" or "for the sake of the one who is to die." The Nazis were not paternalistic killers except in some of their transparent propaganda, and in their choice of the cosmetic term "euthanasia" for the barbarous killings. In their primary justificatory arguments they killed misfits, retarded people, psychotics, epileptics, and other handicapped persons because they were "useless" and "a burden on society."[3] Even among respectable paternalistic social philosophers of this day, no one defends a paternalism that is so "hard" as to justify involuntary euthanasia for the victim's own good.[4] Nonvoluntary euthanasia finds more numerous advocates, especially when the "victim" is to be a newborn infant suffering from an incurable genetic disorder or painful disease thought to make its expected brief life "not worth living,"[5] or an irreversibly comatose person, or a terminal patient so maddened with pain that he cannot "voluntarily" consent to die. For beings who cannot make choices of their own, proxy-decisions must be made for them, and these cannot always employ a "substituted judgment criterion" (or "dispositional consent test") in a nonarbitrary way, especially when the represented party is a newborn infant. In these cases soft paternalists might agree with the hard paternalists and opt for a scheme which permits proxies to appeal to the incompetent party's "own good" rather than his voluntary choice. Since, by hypothesis, the being in question can make no choice of his own, benevolent intervention by another can hardly be an invasion of his autonomy.

It seems evident to the soft paternalist, however, that when a person *is* capable of making his own voluntary choices in self-regarding affairs, those choices should govern, even in—perhaps especially in—matters of life and death. But even those not opposed to voluntary euthanasia often argue against its legalization, not in virtue of its own intrinsic moral demerits, but because they fear that legislators and jurists may step on to the "slippery slope" that leads from voluntary to nonvoluntary to involuntary euthanasia, with the dreaded Nazi horror at the end of the slide.[6] The slippery slope argument against legalized voluntary euthanasia has two forms, one logical, the other empirical (see Vol. 2, Chap. 9, §7). The former is an instance of the *reductio ad absurdum* technique. The proposition at issue is shown to logically entail other propositions which are either "absurd" or else antecedently unacceptable to the person who advocates the initial proposition. This *reductio* argument, in all the forms in which it has been leveled against legalized voluntary euthanasia, is a dismal failure. If one explicitly restricts one's advocacy to *voluntary* euthanasia, then one can hardly be vulnerable to the charge that one's advocated position logically entails involuntary euthanasia or the Nazi programs of non-euthanasian murders. In its empirical (and more plausible) form, the slippery slope charge is part of a "falling dominoes" argument. To be sure, voluntary euthanasia does not *logically entail* involuntary euthanasia, but rather the dominoes are so arranged that once a particular legislature legalizes voluntary euthanasia, then inevitably political pressures will mount for the legalization of nonvoluntary euthanasia, which will in due time be legalized, softening up public opinion for involuntary euthanasia, encouraging politicians to move in that direction, and so on. Whether the argument is a good one depends on how the dominoes are in fact placed, and that is a complicated empirical question about which no one can pronounce with dogmatic confidence. But if there is a powerful independent moral case for the legalization of voluntary euthanasia, one would think that the burden would be on its opponents to show that the dominoes are lined up in order, and that the fall of those that are likely to topple would be a bad thing. We are concerned in this book only with the moral case that might be made for the legalization of *voluntary* euthanasia considered in its own terms, a case that is often tacitly conceded by those who rest their whole argument against it on the empirical slippery slope claim or other practical difficulties.

A final way of arguing against the legalization of voluntary euthanasia on practical grounds is the most interesting for our present purposes, since it focuses on the question of voluntariness. Death is thought by many people to be the most extreme harm anyone can suffer, and while the petitioner for euthanasia will certainly not share that assessment, he cannot deny that, harmful or not, death is utterly irrevocable. Hence, by the second Rule of Thumb (Chap. 20, §5), a very high degree of voluntariness is required of consent to one's own death, if it is to be acceptably valid. Surely this appropriately exacting standard cannot be satisfied by people in drunken fits, or in manic-depressive episodes, or by small children. At the very least we should require the drunk to sober up, the clinical depressive to come out of his gloom, and the small child to grow into his maturity. Newborn infants and incorrigible incompetents whose lives are, or are likely to become, miseries to themselves, cannot decide voluntarily enough either; and the decision must be made for them "nonvoluntarily" by proxies—a dangerous thing to permit if active euthanasia is at issue, since it is difficult to be sure that the proxy decision-maker is not being swayed mainly by the prospect that the incompetent's continued existence would be a misery to *others* so that his killing would not be, in a proper sense, euthanasia at all.

But proxy decision-making for the incompetent is not our problem here. We are concerned with the question of whether the criminal law, following liberal principles, might permit the euthanasia, passive or active, of competent adults who request it, and our hardest cases in theory are the most common ones in practice, namely requests from "patients" who are suffering from impairing and/or distracting illness, pain, or depression. The request for death made by suffering competent persons raises conceptual problems about voluntariness in their most poignant and perplexing form. The remainder of this chapter will be devoted to the question of how the request for death made by an acutely suffering or depressed person can be voluntary enough for an enlightened criminal law to recognize it as ground for a kind of justified homicide.

2. Rachels' modest proposal

In his essay on euthanasia,[7] James Rachels makes a very simple and radical suggestion of a way to legalize active euthanasia. Instead of proposing to a legislature that it draw up a complex statute granting authority to some "citizen committee" to give or withhold approval to active euthanasia (or "mercy killings" as Rachels alternatively calls them), with elaborate safeguards against abuses, specified time periods, procedures for investigations and testimony, diverse assignments of responsibility, and other complications, Rachels proposes only a simple statute binding on criminal courts, declaring that "a plea of mercy killing be acceptable as a defense against a charge of murder in much the same way that a plea of self-defense is acceptable as a defense."[8] When a mercy-killer is tried for murder, under Rachels' proposed new statute, the burden would be on the prosecution to prove the defining elements of the crime, that the accused did in fact kill the deceased and that he or she did so intentionally. The defense could concede all that, but plead "mercy-killing" as a justification. At that point, the burden of proof would switch from prosecution to defense, just as it does when the plea is self-defense. Now the defense must prove (a) that the diseased was suffering from a painful terminal illness and (b) that he or she "while competent requested death."

> In practice this would mean that anyone contemplating mercy killing would have to be very sure that there are independent witnesses to testify concerning the patient's condition and desire to die; for otherwise, one might not be able to make out a defense in a court of law—if it should come to that—and would be legally liable for murder. However, if this proposal were adopted, it would *not* mean that every time active euthanasia was performed a court trial would follow. In clear cases of self-defense, prosecutors simply do not bring charges, since it would be a pointless waste of time.[9]

This "modest proposal" definitely has the merit of simplicity, but it may be too simple to cover all the complexities thrown up by real cases. To begin with, Rachels' statute would benefit people struggling with painful death in a family setting at home, but would offer little help to the dying sufferers who live alone, or who have no loyal spouse, parent, or friend willing to perform this last great service for them at some risk to themselves. Perhaps most of the people who would wish to use the Rachels defense are confined, under close supervision, in hospitals or nursing homes. Who should be *their* voluntary executioners? Their doctors? That is hardly feasible since the doctors who specialize in diseases of the most dangerous kind, or in the treatment of aged patients, would be called on over and over again to perform this service, in theory subjecting themselves to the risk of criminal prosecution each time. It is not very likely that doctors and nurses could purchase "criminal liability insurance" on the model of malpractice insurance, and few would find it any consolation if they could. It would be an enormous emotional burden for a doctor or nurse to bear in any case, even without serious risk of imprisonment or harassing trials. And then Rachels' system would provide no safe-guard against the misuse of the doctor's awesome responsibility, killing those who are not really ready, or refusing to kill those who are. The possibilities for mistake and abuse would be so great, and the interest of the prosecutor so intent and constant, that the hospital might as well provide space for a prosecutor's office, so that a criminal investigator could be ready and on hand as mercy killings occur.

Very likely, medical personnel would choose to have nothing to do with such a scheme, short of better defined rules and guaranteed immunities. That would leave the mercy killing of hospital-confined patients, in Rachels' proposal, up to the initiative of private friends or relations of the suffering patient. But that too would have unacceptable consequences for the hospitals, which could not tolerate many killers like Robert Weskin whose "mother was dying of leukemia in a Chicago hospital, in terrible pain [when] Weskin took a gun into the hospital and shot her three times. He made no attempt to hide what he had done, saying 'She's out of her misery now. I shot her.' "[10] Hospitals and lethal gunfire simply don't mix—a point that hardly needs belaboring. But how else is the would-be mercy-killer to proceed? Is he to walk into the ward and politely ask the nurse for permission to poison his mother (on his own responsibility of course)? And what are the rights and duties of third parties? May they intervene to prevent the killing? May they use force? If they do use force, may the mercy-killer forcefully oppose them? These problems do not normally arise in the privacy of the home. Rachels' plan, at best, would need supplementary legislation for the hospital context.

No doubt part of the hospital problem could be solved if the patient were still sufficiently competent to request to be sent home, and to hire a lawyer to see to it that this is done, if necessary through a writ of *habeus corpus*, or its equivalent. The hospital would be understandably reluctant to release a patient under such circumstances without legally certified evidence of the voluntariness of the *release-request*. (The voluntariness of the subsequent request for active euthanasia would be somebody else's problem.) If a judicial officer were then required to judge the legitimacy of the release-request, there would be new bureaucratic complications introduced into the hospital setting at the most inopportune times, and with painful delays and intrusions into the patient's privacy. By the time we get to this stage, " . . . the legal machinery is . . . so formal and so tedious as to offer the patient far too little solace."[11] For the dying hospital patient this is the best that Rachels' proposal can promise him. At its worst the plan offers him nothing, for it will not help if the time has passed when he can competently consent to his release, or if there is no "home" for him to go to in any case, or no loyal friend or spouse to honor his ultimate request when he gets there.

For the better-placed dying person, Rachels' plan may be an improvement on the present system (or non-system) which relies on juries to misapply the law or falsify the facts in order to avoid harsh injustice to humane persons who have been driven by their conscience and sympathy to break a rigid law that should not have applied to them in the first place. But even for the family mercy-killer at home, Rachels' proposal runs into difficulties. Rachels claims, plausibly enough, that the effect of his proposal "would be to sanction officially what . . . juries already do,"[12] but it does so at a still unacceptable level of risk. The risks are of two kinds: to the genuine mercy-killer who could be punished for murder if anything goes wrong at his trial, and to the victim, if his "mercy-killer" has manipulated him into expressing his grudging or unwilling "consent," or taken advantage of his pain-induced weakness of mind, or otherwise abused him or deceived the witnesses to his consent. The more abuses there are of the latter kind (and there are bound to be more under Rachels' rule), the more skeptical courts and juries are likely to become, and that in turn increases the risks to the genuine mercy-killer who may find an aggressive prosecutor to challenge his evidence of the victim's consent, confuse his witness's testimony, and convince an unfriendly jury of his guilt. Surely the prudent mercy-killer would want to get some authority's approval first, but under the Rachels system (as under the present one) he has no place to turn. He must shoulder a grave personal risk or watch helplessly as his loved one continues to suffer unbearably.

Then again, the Rachels plan requires that the defense prove not only that the deceased "while competent" requested death, but also that he was suffering from a "painful terminal illness" at that time. That means that an earlier conditional consent will not do. That is, it will not be acceptable as a legal defense that the deceased once requested that *if* or *when* his pain became intolerable, then he should be delivered from it. Rather the reliable witnesses have to be rounded up and ready to observe the formal request after the pain has already become severe, and this may create practical difficulties for the humane killer, since there may be little time between the advent of the severe pain and the disappearance of "competence." The suffering may threaten to continue indefinitely after competence has gone, giving the humane comforter no alternative to permitting it to continue or making himself subject to a murder charge. Another danger is that if the dying person wishes to hold on to life until the point when the pain is intolerable, there may be only a brief interval when his final request can be valid (and validly witnessed), and deciding to wait for that may be, in effect, to decide that the request be made "only if the victim is both sane and crazed by pain."[13] And yet one cannot have one's witnesses hear the voluntary request days or weeks before the actual killing; they must be ready to hear it at the very last moment, lest the victim has changed his mind between the early request and the killing. In short, it may not be easy for the humane killer to arrange for "independent witnesses" to be present at just the right moment.

By restricting his remedy to terminal patients in severe pain, Rachels has also denied legal deliverance to those who would end their lives, if only they could, for reasons other than to escape present pain, and wish to die long before they are, in any proper medical sense, terminal. Some such people would commit suicide if they were able, but cannot because they are paralyzed, or closely supervised, or both. If these people are as capable as the suffering terminal patients of making voluntary requests, and as likely to convince humane and decent second parties to honor those requests, then by the liberal principles elaborated in Chapters 17 through 20, it would be an unwarranted invasion of their autonomy to deny those requests when they are primarily self-regarding. To the liberal, it is only the voluntariness of the death request (given its self-regarding character) that counts; pain and suffering and the shortness of the life remaining are not necessary for its legitimate fulfillment.

3. Whose life is it anyway?

Moralists can be content to discover what it is that makes a choice voluntary to a given degree, but legal philosophers must press on to the further question of how we can know when voluntariness (as understood by the moralist) is present. Perhaps a given choice is indeed voluntary enough to have legal effect, even though it exhibits none of the identifying marks of sufficient voluntariness and thus must be treated by the law as invalid. This no doubt is true when whole categories of death requests are rejected *a priori* on grounds of suspect voluntariness, even though it is likely that some of them are in fact voluntary enough. It is simply that we cannot know with sufficient certainty how to identify these individual cases, given the strong presumption of nonvoluntariness for acts in their category. And when irrevocable death is involved, it is better to err on the safe side.

One such category of death-requests are those made by prisoners in jails and penitentiaries. It stands to reason that occasionally a person who has been convicted of serious crimes and sentenced to incarceration for a large part or all of his natural life, who is loathed and mistreated by his guards, and distrusted and abused by his fellow prisoners, might genuinely prefer to die, and would kill himself if only he could find the means to do so cleanly. Can we be certain that a formal death request from such a person must have been coerced, ill-informed, or the product of impairment or distraction? Surely not; but prisons are highly coercive institutions, seething with barely contained violence, and founded on mutual distrust. Penal authorities always have an incentive to get rid of trouble-makers if they can. The suspicion of manipulation or intimidation would always be present, no matter how authentic the request might seem, and furthermore, once euthanasia of prisoners were approved in principle, the incentive for foul play would be all the greater. It is quite understandable why self-destruction in prisons should be prohibited absolutely.[14]

The more likely place to look then for verifiably voluntary death requests from persons who are *not* in severe pain and *not* suffering from terminal illnesses is in the hospitals that sustain quadriplegics and others suffering from permanent and near totally disabling physical "handicaps." The best example for our purposes is a fictitious but highly believable one. On March 12, 1972, Granada TV in Great Britain produced an hour-long drama by Brian Clark called *Whose Life Is It Anyway?*[15] The television play was taped, replayed, and widely distributed. It was adapted for the stage and produced in London in 1978 and in New York a year later. In 1982 it was made into a motion picture and widely seen. The story is about Ken Harrison, a young man of great wit and charm who is a sculptor who loves his work, a creative and sensual man in his late twenties. His spine has been ruptured in an automobile accident, and in the first scene he learns from Dr. Emerson that his paralysis from the neck down is incurable, and that he must remain hospitalized for the rest of his life. He has suspected that fearful fact for most of the six months that have elapsed since the accident. He has deliberated calmly and continuously over that period, and decided finally that he prefers to die now rather than live out his remaining four or five decades in a hospital. Since he is physically incapable of killing himself, and active euthanasia is forbidden by law, the only way he can satisfy his desire is to be released from the hospital and sent home where, without his sustaining treatments, he is sure to die within a week.[16]

Dr. Emerson, speaking for the hospital, will not permit it. It is his duty as a doctor, he says, to preserve life. Besides, Mr. Harrison is suffering from depression and is therefore "incapable of making a rational decision about life and death." Mr. Harrison, unimpressed by this argument, consults his solicitor who then petitions a court on his behalf for a writ of *habeus corpus*, alleging that his client has been deprived of liberty without proper cause. The writ is issued; the hospital accepts the challenge of showing that the detention is proper; and a judicial hearing is hastily arranged to be held in the petitioner's hospital room with a presiding judge, Mr. Harrison and his counsel, a "friendly" outside psychiatrist, Dr. Emerson, *his* counsel, and the hospital staff psychiatrist all in attendance.

The hearing is brief, the testimony terse but trenchant, the relevant philosophical arguments on both sides given their due. Dr. Emerson testifies about Harrison's physical injuries and the projected course of treatment. "It is common in these cases," he adds, "that depression and the tendency to make wrong decisions goes on for months, even years" (p. 132). But under cross-examination he admits that there are no objective tests or measurements that can be used to distinguish between a medical syndrome and a "sane, even justified, depression," and that he must rely simply on his "thirty years of experience as a physician dealing with both types" (p. 133). Dr. Barr, the consulting psychiatrist selected by Harrison's lawyer, testifies in rebuttal. He does not dispute that Harrison is depressed but judges that his attitude is not simply an expression of clinical depression; rather ". . . he is reacting in a perfectly rational way to a very bad situation" (p. 135). He too concedes that since the patient's physical condition masks the usual symptoms of clinical depression, there is no objective way of telling which sort of depression he has, save "by experience," and "by discovering when I talk to him that he has a remarkably incisive mind and is perfectly capable of understanding his position and of deciding what to do about it" (p. 136). Then comes the question with the dramatically surprising but philosophically stimulating answer: "One last thing, Doctor, do you think Mr. Harrison has made the right decision? The psychiatrist answers without hesitation: "No, I thought he made the wrong decision."

Harrison himself is not called upon to testify, but he agrees to a brief interrogation by the judge who then concludes that he is satisfied that "Mr. Harrison is a brave and cool man who is in complete control of his mental faculties, and I shall therefore make an order for him to be set free" (p. 144). Harrison's only remaining life prospect now is "to get a room some place" and begin the gradual and inevitably messy dying process. One would think that by this point, when he has won every other victory, a painless lethal injection would be a humane favor, a decent thing to do, but of course that is impossible under the prevailing law. (At this juncture Rachels' modest proposal looks very good indeed; under its terms a mercy-killing physician in these circumstances would surely escape prosecution.) Instead, Dr. Emerson offers the most that his conscience and the criminal law will permit, a room in the hospital with cessation of treatment and even feeding stopped if the patient wishes—a kind of supervised passive euthanasia. "You'll be unconscious in three days, dead in six at most" (p. 146). Dr. Emerson wants to be as kind as he can, but he also wants witnesses at hand in case the patient undergoes a last minute change of mind. And so the story ends with mutual respect between the antagonists, and British decency all around, but no ground given in the moral and philosophical debate.

This fictional tale serves as a much better test for the soft paternalist's position and its attendant theory of personal autonomy than do the more common cases of aged patients with painful terminal diseases, because it isolates the factor of voluntary choice and focuses our attention on it. (It also raises the question sharply which we shall consider in the next section whether a choice to die made by a person in severe depression can ever be voluntary enough to be valid.) Its moral (if one can be attributed to it) is that respect for personal autonomy alone justifies our non-interference with a competent person's primarily self-regarding choice of death, quite independently of further humanitarian considerations. Mr. Harrison is not a terminal patient. He can expect to live on for another forty years or more if he stays in a hospital. (He becomes "terminal" only after the judge's release order). No rule is applied which limits the recognition of voluntariness to choices of death by persons whose whole reason is the desire to escape pain and who will die soon in any case. Whatever Mr. Harrison's reasons are, they are good enough, provided only they are *his* reasons. The soft paternalist, if he can be convinced that the choice is voluntary enough by reasonable tests, is firmly committed to a policy of non-interference with its implementation, for the life at stake is Mr. Harrison's life not ours. The person in sovereign control over it is precisely he.

In his final exchange with the judge, Harrison cites as the chief reason for his choice (and of course in his view the ground of its reasonableness or correctness) his desire for *dignity*. He is eloquent about the indignity of being forced to live in total dependence on others for even the basic primitive functions. In response to the judge, he then concedes that "many people with appalling physical handicaps have overcome them and lived essentially creative, dignified lives" (p. 142), but the point, he insists, is that "the dignity begins with their choice." It would be an indignity to force the others to die against their will, but an equal indignity to force him to remain alive, as a kind of "medical achievement," against his will. Human dignity is not possible without the acknowledgement of personal sovereignty.

4. Understandable depression

Early in the first act of *Whose Life Is It Anyway?* occurs one of the most moving episodes. Dr. Emerson imposes a large injection of tranquilizer on Mr. Harrison against his will. The paralyzed patient, helpless to resist, sputters in indignation. The doctor, called upon to justify his overruling of the patient's will, does so tersely: "You're very depressed." "Does that surprise you?," asks the patient. "Of course not," comes the reply "it's perfectly natural. Your body received massive injuries; it takes time to come to any acceptance of the new situation. Now, I shan't be a minute." "Don't stick that fucking thing in me!" (pp. 43–44) shrieks the patient to no avail, and the forceful invasion of his bodily autonomy that follows is a dramatically shocking event, akin to watching a rape on the stage.

The implicit justifying argument of Dr. Emerson is that the patient was too depressed for his refusal of the tranquilizer to be voluntary (or voluntary enough to be valid). Mr. Harrison's reply (as he puts it later in the play) to the physician's diagnosis of "acute depression" is to concede the point, and then add "Is that surprising? I am almost totally paralyzed. I'd be insane if I *weren't* depressed" (p. 138). Some depression then is *understandable*, even proper, rational, and justifiable, a state of mind any normal person would experience if he were to suffer certain losses. "Depression" is also the name of a clinical syndrome marked by "affective disorders," involving "an accentuation in the intensity or duration of otherwise normal emotions."[17] Psychologists have not agreed on any simple criterion for distinguishing accentuated affective states that are "clinical" from those that are less extreme or less debillitating conditions, but they often speak of a plurality of symptoms, at least some of which are present in clinical depression, in addition to the depressed or "disphoric" mood (sadness, gloominess) that is common to both the clinical and nonclinical species. These symptoms include anhedonia (inability to find pleasure in previous sources like food, sex, hobbies, sports, music, friends), appetite loss, sleep disturbances, fatigue and lethargy, or restless agitation, "slowed thinking," lowered self-esteem, pessimism, bodily complaints, thoughts of death.[18] If clinical depression is determined by the presence of one or more of such symptoms in high degree, quite independently of their cause or occasion, then it cannot be sharply contrasted with that "understandable depression" which is a "perfectly rational reaction to a very bad situation." In the ordinary layman's sense, depression is simply despondency, whatever its attendant characteristics. That depression may be a realistic or understandable reaction to loss, yet *also* be accompanied by some of the "symptoms" (e.g., anhedonia, loss of appetite, insomnia) that mark it as "clinical." And even if understandable depression is also clinical depression, it need not involve any distortion of cognitive function. To be sure, *some* clinical depressives are also "psychotic" (i.e., crazy), but most are not. Indeed, psychosis is not even essential to clinical depression when it is not occasioned by objective loss or understandable cause, and "fewer than 15% of depressed patients are psychotic in a strict sense."[19]

The physicians and psychologists in *Whose Life Is It Anyway?* also distinguish between "endogenous" and "reactive" depression, and speak as if this were the same distinction as that between "clinical" and "nonclinical" depression, but this is a confusion. The distinction between "endogenous" and "reactive," introduced by R. D. Gillespie in an influential article in 1929,[20] has in recent years fallen into disuse.[21] In severe cases, "Gillespie noted the apparent nonresponsiveness of the patient's symptoms to the environment once the depressive episode had begun. He therefore regarded severe depressive conditions as 'driven from within,' autonomous and unreactive to the immediate environment, and thus endogenous".[22] Clinical depression, it would seem, is a genus of which "endogenous" and "reactive" depression

are species. (It is a mistake then simply to identify "clinical" and "endogenous.") The distinction between endogenous and reactive is intended to
correspond to two separate modes of etiology (roughly internal and external). Endogenous depression may be caused by subtle biochemical imbal-
ances, injury to the central nervous system, physical disease, or deep psychological disorders. Reactive depression, on the other hand, is occasioned
by precipitating events in the patient's experience of the world, though it
may be excessive or disproportionate to its occasion and/or disabling in its
effect. If endogenous and reactive depressions can both be clinical, what
can we mean by "nonclinical depression"? The latter term must refer to
those moods of sadness, whatever their occasion or cause, that lack the
accompanying symptoms that constitute the clinical syndrome, or if some
of those symptoms are present, they are less severe or less durable. The
clinical–nonclinical dichotomy, in short, is a way of classifying accompanying characteristics or symptoms; the endogenous–reactive dichotomy is a
way of classifying causes; and the two distinctions cut across one another.
Furthermore, the distinction between realistic-rational-understandable reactions and unrealistic-excessive-disproportionate reactions cuts across the distinction between clinical and nonclinical depression. These distinctions,
rough as they are, are charted in Diagram 27-1.

   Mr. Harrison's extended depressive episode was a major one, with many of
the physical symptoms of the clinical syndrome present in severe degree
(though we are not told this explicitly). Some of these symptoms may be
masked by his physical paralysis, so that we cannot tell, for example,
whether his appetite loss and disordered sleep are direct consequences of the
paralysis or would be present anyway as a consequence of his depression. It
is safe to assume, in any case, that Mr. Harrison's condition is properly
classified as clinical depression of the kind that does not involve psychosis or
chronicity.[23] We are also to assume from the drama that his clinical depression is "reactive" in origin, a response to his perceived loss and disappointment (though it is possible, I suppose, that his "biological condition"—the
paralysis—itself is a direct causal contributor, in which case the depression
is partly endogenous too). The preponderance of the evidence in the play
favors placing Mr. Harrison's reactive clinical depression in the "realistic" or
"understandable" subcategory. What is at issue in the play then is whether
Harrison's depression, so categorized, is consistent with rational self-assess-
ment and voluntary choice. If his depression were a realistic-disphoric reaction of the *nonclinical* kind, there would be less of a problem, for there would
be no symptoms (or fewer symptoms) that could plausibly be suspected of
interfering with clear perception and sound judgment. The same would probably be true if the depression were a minor episode on the clinical side of
the chart. The problem would be equally easy if it were a major episode of

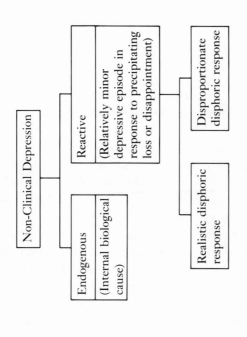

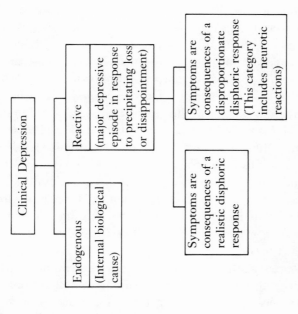

Diagram 27-1. Varieties of depression.

the clinical sort but with psychotic symptoms—congnitive dysfunction—as well as disordered sleep, loss of appetite, and the like. In that case, it would be clear that Harrison's affliction is a voluntariness-defeating impairment. But the case before us poses a more difficult problem. The patient has a major clinical depression, but with no sign of any cognitive dysfunction. How does this category of depression affect the voluntariness of his life and death choices?

Severe depression, whatever its cause, can *distract* the suffering person, and deflect his attention from the problem at hand. In an example of a choice-option quite different from Harrison's, a person grieving over his recently incurred bodily paralysis, or the death of a spouse, may not have the patience to attend to the details of some complex business transaction while he grieves; he may not even be able to bring himself to care about the details. This description obviously does not apply to Harrison and his problem. Moreover, in normal cases, when the depressive episode does not produce cognitive derangement, the griever's judgment insofar as it can be freed from distraction is not radically distorted by his pain; he has no tendency to make some spectacularly irrational gesture, to give his wealth away, burn his house down, or allow himself to be grossly cheated.

There must be more to say, however, about the bearing of depression on voluntariness than this account of "the normal case." In extreme cases, reactive clinical depression *can* distort as well as distract. A merely psychological pain can, in effect, be maddening. "Can be" is the key term. It *can be* maddening, but it *need not be* so. And the way to tell whether a reactive depression is distorting judgment is to interview the person directly and subject his reasoning processes to independent tests. Is he fully aware of his situation? Does he reason coherently? Does he manifest a sense of relevance? Is he consecutive and consistent? Just such tests were applied to the deeply depressed Mr. Harrison, and he passed with flying colors. These tests, moreover, showed that after six months of deliberation, Harrison's judgment was neither distorted nor distracted from the matter at hand. Indeed, he was not only fully attentive to his plight; his attention was marvelously concentrated on it. He was in fact incapable of concentrating long on anything else. Reactive depression is indeed distracting, but sometimes it distracts only from matters that are irrelevant to the question at issue, and focuses the mind on the problem at hand.

Mistaken inferences from depression to some specific incompetence are often profoundly unfair to the depressed person. Characteristically they deprive him, *a priori* as it were, of any opportunity to make a case for himself. Argumentatively, he is trapped in a destructive dilemma that defeats him from the start, leaving him no conceivable ground on which to stand. Mr. Harrison, at one point in the play (p. 97), complains that one of the justifications for refusing his request to die is a version of Catch-22. The term "Catch-22" comes from Joseph Heller's 1961 anti-military novel of that name,[24] in which it is used characteristically for a certain kind of military rule that places a petitioning soldier in an inescapable dilemma, in effect barring approval of his petition *a priori* in language that falsely suggests that there are conditions under which the request could be granted, when in fact those "conditions" are contradictory. One example: an Air Force man can be grounded if he has become crazy, but to be relieved of combat duty on this ground, one must make a formal request. Any combat pilot who does not request relief on this ground must be presumed crazy (and therefore qualified for relief), and for those who do request release, there is a catch—Catch-22— "Anyone who wants to get out of combat duty isn't really crazy."[25] So the rule (or policy) says that in order to qualify, you must both apply and not apply—a logical impossibility. You are damned if you do, and damned if you don't; that is the dilemma.

The term "dilemma," of course, is the technical name for a certain deductively valid argument form.[26] If the Air Force's only aim, in Heller's literary fantasy, was to *demonstrate* (and thereby justify) that one cannot get out of combat by reason of insanity, then it has committed no intellectual error. But instead, it held out hope by formulating an enabling-rule purporting to specify how one may be relieved of duty by reason of insanity, and then specified logically impossible conditions! As an argument for a conclusion, a dilemma is rigorous and valid; as an enabling-rule it is absurdly defective, failing altogether to achieve the presumed aim of such a rule. Moreover, as a purported rule, it is a cruel tease, offering with one hand, and taking away with the other. If a new university were to announce that students can qualify for admission by proving that they are neither male nor female, neither living nor dead, it would commit no merely logical error, but then neither would it accept any students.

Actually, there are as many as four Catch-22 arguments in *Whose Life Is It Anyway?* that beg the question against Mr. Harrison and make it *a priori* impossible for him to prove the voluntariness of his request. Consider Catch-22, number 1. This version focuses on suicide, a passive version of which is essentially that for which Harrison requests permission. Dr. Emerson and the friendly psychiatrist agree that the crucial question is whether or not Harrison's acknowledged clinical depression is the sort that impairs judgment. Dr. Emerson finds the answer self-evident. "You haven't understood," he says to Dr. Travers with ill-concealed impatience. "He's *suicidal.* He's determined to kill himself." The assumption apparently is that if a depressed person requests to die that *proves* that his depression impairs judgment, and his request therefore is insufficiently voluntary to be granted. This argument suggests that only persons who are happy are capable of voluntarily choosing suicide, and of course they are precisely the ones who won't apply. Thus if you are unhappy you *cannot* voluntarily choose suicide, and if you are happy you *will not* commit suicide. The conclusion: no suicide. Yet the context of discussion presupposes that the issue is initially an open question to be settled by discussion and evidence. Catch-22 rules out all evidence *a priori*. The assumption that no choice of suicide can be voluntary is the very question at issue in the case at hand, not one presumed to be settled in advance.

The second Catch-22 argument follows closely on the first, and is also concerned with the voluntariness of death requests. Another party takes up the argument against Dr. Emerson, one of his subordinate physicians, Dr. Scott, who reminds him that "It's *his* [Harrison's] life." Emerson replies "But my responsibility." "Only if he is is incapable of making his own decision," rejoins Dr. Scott. "But he isn't capable," insists Emerson—"I refuse to believe that a man with a mind as quick as his, a man with enormous mental resources, would calmly choose suicide." Scott replies: "But he has done just that." "And therefore," interjects Emerson, "I say he is unbalanced" (pp. 91–92). Again the case is begged against the petitioner. His request cannot possibly be voluntary, not because it fails to satisfy independent formal tests of voluntariness, but entirely because of what it is a request *for*. The whole point of the hearing is to determine whether this death request is voluntary. To judge in that context that no death request, simply as such, *could be* valid is to apply a circular test. This approach is very much like that of a college which, when interviewing applicants for admission, rules out all those who apply on the ground that anybody who could apply for admission here *must* be "unbalanced."

Catch-22 number 3 is a closely related corollary of the preceding. The hospital staff psychiatrist, Dr. Travers, warns Harrison: "But your obvious intelligence weakens your case. I'm not saying that you would find life easy, but you do have resources that an unintelligent person doesn't have." This is the observation that prompts Harrison's remark about Catch-22: "If you're clever and sane enough to put up an invincible case for suicide, it demonstrates that you ought not to die" (p. 97). The characterization of this requirement as "Catch-22" is perfectly apt. The authorities meet to hear the petitioner's case. They invite him to present his arguments for their granting his request. It is understood that if his arguments are weak, they will turn him down. Better then that the arguments should be cogent, except for Catch-22, which declares that if the arguments are convincing then the request cannot be granted, for in that case the petitioner's obvious intellectual resources undermine the case for his death. However he argues, he cannot win. Why then have the hearing at all?

The final Catch-22 argument is put forward half-heartedly by the sympathetic Dr. Scott, when she senses Harrison's excitement at the approach of his life-or-death judicial hearing, and his zest for the debate. "I think you are enjoying all this," she says. "I suppose I am in a way," he replies, "for the first time in six months I feel like a human being again" (p. 108). This exchange underlines the paradox: Harrison is never so alive as when he is staging and winning his fight for death. But to make too much of the point is once again to put the petitioner in the position of Catch-22. If he enjoys getting what he wants (permission to die), then he is not depressed and has less reason to die, but if he is not pleased at his victory then he must not really have wanted to die after all, and that casts doubt on the authenticity of his prior desire. Either he is pleased or he is not pleased. Therefore, he must not be permitted to die. That is a purely *a priori* abstract argument that spares everyone the effort of examining *evidence* for and against voluntariness in the case at hand. It could have been formulated in advance of the hearing and saved everyone the trouble of having a proceeding of inquiry in the first place. Harrison himself turns the dilemma on its ear.[27] "I know I'm enjoying the fight," he concedes, but "I had to be sure that I wanted to win, really get what I'm fighting for, and not just doing it to convince myself I'm still alive" (p. 109). The pleasure he experiences, in short, proves to him (as it could to the others) that his desire to die is strong, constant, and genuine. How else can he account for the unalloyed pleasure he feels in the fight and the prospect of victory? He derives pleasure from the fight, which would not be the case were he is fighting *simply* to get the pleasure.

Before leaving *Whose Life Is It Anyway?*, we should pay some heed to Dr. Barr's surprising admission that Harrison's decision to die, while carefully reasoned and voluntary, is nevertheless in his opinion the wrong decision. He might very well have put the point in the language I have suggested (Chap. 20, §3) by saying that the decision is unreasonable (not one Dr. Barr would have made in the circumstances) but not irrational, and hence not involuntary. Why should a person be permitted to implement a "wrong" or "unreasonable" decision to die? The only answer possible is simply that it is *his* decision and *his* life, and that the choice falls within the domain of *his* morally inviolate personal sovereignty. But why does Dr. Barr think that the decision was the wrong one to make? In the play, the question is left for our conjecture, but we may surmise that Dr. Barr's reason is his anticipation that in the course of time, if only Harrison would wait more patiently, his mind would change, and he would be happy that he had not chosen death earlier. Harrison himself admits that possibility in an earlier discussion with the sympathetic Dr. Scott (pp. 68–69):

H: I grant you, I may become lethargic and quiescent. Happy when a nurse comes to put in a new catheter, or give me an enema, or to turn me over. These could become the high spots of my day. I might even learn

to do wonderful things like turn the pages of a book with some miracle
of modern science, or to type letters with flicking my eyelids. And you
would look at me and say: "Wasn't it worth waiting?" and I would say:
"Yes," and be proud of my achievements. Really proud. I grant you all
that, but it doesn't alter the validity of my present position.

S: But if you became happy?

H: But I don't want to become happy by becoming the computer section of
a complex machine. And morally you must accept my decision.

Exactly so. Harrison's situation is similar to that of the nineteenth century
Russian landowner discussed earlier (Chap. 19, §7). In order to become
reconciled at a later date to his condition (a sculptor without the use of his
hands, a sensualist without the use of his genitalia, a living tribute to the
ingenuity of modern technology), he will have to become a very different
person with very different values, and the person he is now, applying the
values that he has now, prefers not to become that repugnant future person.
The future self does not yet exist; the sovereign chooser is the clearheaded
and determined present self. Whatever the hypothetical future self would
say, it is only the actual present self who has the right to decide. The choice
is squarely within the temporal boundaries of his sovereign domain.

5. Alternating moods

Few actual patients are as constant in their feelings as the fictitious Mr.
Harrison. Much depression comes and goes, or mixes and alternates clinical
and nonclinical, endogenous and reactive, realistic and unrealistic features.
The resultant inconstancy in the patient's choices creates especially sensitive
problems for those who wish to respect his autonomy. Robert D. Bastron,
M.D., of the University of Arizona, contributes the following case from his
own clinical experience:

> A 59-year-old male farmer was kicked in the back of the neck by a cow. He
> was found approximately 10 hours later and admitted to a hospital with diag-
> noses of exposure and a fractured neck with a spinal cord injury. He was fully
> conscious but unable to move his arms or legs and could not cough or take a
> deep breath. He was transferred to intensive care.
>   Within a few hours edema of the spinal cord made ventilatory support neces-
> sary. The patient required ventilatory support for two weeks and then did well
> without the respirator. He gradually regained the ability to shrug his shoulders
> and to weakly flex his arms. He was transferred to an intermediate care area
> after eight weeks in intensive care.
>   Ten days later he was readmitted to intensive care for ventilatory support and
> treatment of pneumonia caused by inhaling food and stomach contents. He was
> weaned off the respirator after four weeks, and six weeks later was transferred to
> an intermediate care area.

This cycle was repeated two more times consuming a total of six months hospitalization and approximately $375,000—the limit of his hospitalization insurance. Further care would require selling stocks valued at $100,000 and then the family farm. The patient, his wife, and three sons declared that no ventilatory support should be instituted. This desire of the patient was documented by physicians, nurses, a social worker and a member of the Hospital Pastoral Service.

Three weeks later the patient again inhaled food and developed aspiration pneumonia and pulmonary insufficiency. He was readmitted to intensive care for treatment but refused mechanical ventilatory support. In spite of oxygen therapy and nursing care his pulmonary status deteriorated and he became hypoxic. Because of the lack of oxygen supply, his mental status deteriorated and he became progressively agitated and disoriented. He *then* requested mechanical ventilatory support but his sons insisted the patient's previous wish, stated when he was rational, be honored and that no support be provided although death would then be inevitable.

The unusual feature of this case is that it requires us to judge the voluntariness of a *life-request*, unlike the major run of cases in which the voluntariness of a *death-request* is at issue. (Put alternatively, there is a request for, rather than a refusal of, life-saving treatment.) There appears to be an "asymmetry" (as Ronald Milo puts it[28]) in our normal response to the two kinds of requests. When a temporarily impaired patient withdraws his earlier instruction to maintain his life-support and, in his impaired condition, requests death, we are prone to discount the request as insufficiently voluntary in the circumstances. But if the sequence is reversed, and the temporarily impaired patient withdraws his earlier death-request, we are prone to honor his later request, impaired or not.

The problems raised by Dr. Bastron's case have troubled not only attending physicians who are permitted by the silence of the law to decide on their own whether to withhold life-saving treatment, but also legislators struggling with the wording of proposed statutes that would empower patients to make "living wills." The first such bill to be passed by a state legislature, the California Natural Death Act of 1976 (to be discussed in more detail in §6 below), recognizes that "adult persons have the fundamental right to control the decision relating to the rendering of their own medical care, including the decision to have life-sustaining procedures withheld or withdrawn in instances of a terminal condition." It then specified, with almost excessive caution, the strict conditions that must be satisfied before a patient's directive to withhold or withdraw sustenance can have legal effect—special witnessing requirements, proof of terminal condition, time requirements, etc. In addition we can presume that the usual common-law conditions of voluntariness would be observed. The directive would presumably be invalid if signed in ignorance or by mistake, or under coercion (or even neurotic compulsion) or by an incompetent (infantile, insane, or retarded) person, or even by a person whose choice is made in circumstances that are temporarily distorting—while he is fatigued, excessively agitated, under the influence of raging passion or extreme depression, or a mind-numbing drug, or the like. On the other hand (and this is another example of the "asymmetry" of which Milo speaks), *no* such tests of voluntariness whatever are required if the patient should subsequently change his mind: "A directive may be revoked at any time by the declarant, *without regard to his mental state or competency* . . . by written revocation . . . [or] a verbal expression." Thus a decision by the physician to reconnect the respirator in the case we are considering would be made mandatory by laws that follow the California model.

It is clear why the standards of voluntariness used in judging requests that treatment be commenced and those used in judging requests that treatment be withheld or withdrawn should differ when the requester's life hangs in the balance. (What is unclear is whether they should differ so radically as they do in the California statute.) Of all the harms persons may incur, death is commonly thought the most severe, and in cases of the sort we are considering, its occurrence, if treatment is withheld, has been deemed certain. If we think of risk as compounded out of the degree of harm and the probability of its occurring, the gravity of the risk incurred by the patient's instruction to withhold treatment is as great as it can be. That is why the tests of the genuineness of the patient's choice are so stringent. Moreover, as we have seen, death (unlike most but not all other harms) is irrevocable; once it occurs it is too late to reconsider. That is why we give the benefit of the doubt to the patient's choice to revoke an earlier decision even when we think that the choice to revoke is substantially less than fully voluntary. As long as there is a chance that he might truly desire the restoration of treatment, even in the face of genuine doubts that it is his "true self" speaking, we must act on that chance. If we are mistaken, we can always act differently the next time; if we overrule the request now there will be no next time. Finally, it would be an odious spectacle, utterly demoralizing to involved parties and witnesses, for a patient to cry out that he wants to live and for his doctors to refuse to save him.

The correct choice in Dr. Bastron's example, then, is to provide the ventilatory support requested by the patient even though he is agitated and disoriented. But what if the established cycle then continues as the family's resources dwindle? What should the doctors do the next time? Or the time after that? What should a "natural death statute" say about that contingency? Suppose that the patient, whenever calm and out of immediate danger, emphatically and convincingly repeats his original request and supports it with undeniably rational argument, but whenever faced with the immediate prospect of death as he drifts into a state of hypoxic disorientation, cries out in panic for the respirator? The California approach would have us continue the harmful round of "rational give–irrational take back" indefinitely. And each time the patient recovered he would (let us suppose) be more and more disappointed that his deeply desired choice, his constant preference but for moments of hypoxic disorientation, had been overruled. This hypothetical example, I think, shows that one can err on the side of caution as well as recklessness, even when the stakes are life or death.

The California statute goes too far then in requiring revocation "without regard to mental state or competency." But in rewriting this section of the statute I would try not to state necessary conditions for valid revocation with great precision. I would not require that it be less than the third or fifth or eighth time (or any other set number) that rational consent had been withdrawn under hypoxia. The discretionary judgment of the decision-maker cannot be totally dispensed with. But an adequately drafted section would allow for those special circumstances in which a predictable cycle has been established. When the patient himself has become aware of his cyclic alternations and—to the satisfaction of qualified witnesses employing strict standards—he takes them fully into account in requesting that his next hypoxic request for revocation be ignored, then his settled preference, now manifest, should be honored. In that case he would be like the person who requests that his spouse wake him at 5:00 the next morning without fail so that he can perform some important errand—"and do not take no for an answer from my disoriented, half-asleep, future self," he may add. When the time arrives, the spouse may honor the protestations of the sleepy self on the bed, thus ignoring the earlier instructions, but if it is the second, or fifth, or eighth time this cycle has been repeated, and each time the earlier request is made with increased self-understanding and confidence, there can be diminishingly little justification for overruling it.

Unfortunately, there are cycles and cycles, and formulating a legislative rule in advance to cover all of them may seem a hopeless task. Consider some of the variations. Suppose first that hypoxia and physiologically based disorientation are not involved, but that in other ways the facts resemble Dr. Bastron's case. The patient, in his calm and lucid moments, before adequate witnesses, registers his considered request to be let die should his survival once more depend on mechanical ventilatory support, and as before he shows rational understanding of his plight and perfect sincerity and conviction. But in this version of the story, when the time for decision arrives, he gets extremely fearful and in an agitation of terror, screams that he doesn't really want to die. Suppose the whole explanation of his panic is sudden fear of immediate death with no help from hypoxia, or the like. Then suppose that the same scenario is repeated six, eight, or ten times, as his condition worsens and the funds waste away. Should we say that the rational instructions to withhold treatment given during the calm stages of the cycle are the voluntary ones truly representative of the patient's basic convictions, and dismiss the withdrawals as less than voluntary products of excitement and hysterical fear? Or should we take the true preferences of the patient to be those he falls back on, time and again, during the "moment of truth" when the chips are down? Or perhaps all we are entitled to say is that these cyclic variations show that the patient himself is profoundly ambivalent, and that both of his inconsistent attitudes are truly representative of him?

Consider a second variation. Imagine now that the patient suffers from daily alternation of contentment (or resignation) and deep depression. Predictably, every morning he is depressed, and every afternoon he is calm and collected. Predictably too, every morning he requests that he be allowed to die, and every afternoon he revokes the request. He may have a terminal illness in its last stages, or only a very serious and incurable one requiring permanent hospitalization. (If the latter, he or she is excluded from coverage by California's Natural Death Act and similar statutes.) In either case, we can suppose that the patient is kept alive by some drug or mechanical apparatus from which he could be separated. The alternation of mood is a consequence either of his own peculiar psychological cycles, or of the disease itself, or of the life-extending drug, or some combination of these causes impossible to separate out. (Does it matter which?) In any case, he is clear-headed and rational in the afternoons, and while in that condition always prefers to live on to the end. That hypothetical case may seem easier than the others, at least for practical policy if not for reconstructing consistent rationales. But we can spin more puzzling variations on its themes. Consider a third case, for example, which is the same as the second, except that the patient always requests to be allowed to die in the afternoon when he is calm and collected and without a trace of depression, and always changes his mind the next morning when he is depressed, and weeping bitter tears over his own lack of courage.

Finally, to add still another puzzling twist, suppose that the patient is kept on a steady diet of some pain-killing drug which as a side effect induces euphoric mental states. When the drug begins to wear off, the euphoria disappears, and for an hour or so he is in a calm rational state, undistracted by pain or pleasure. In that state, he regularly requests that his life support system be discontinued. When the euphoria takes over again, however, he always revokes the earlier request. Should drug-induced euphoria have any more weight in our assessments of voluntariness than drug-induced depression?

I will tax the reader's patience no longer with such riddles. There is nothing in our elaborate theory of voluntariness, as so far developed, that would enable us to solve them, though I do not despair that the requisite further details could in principle be provided. What deserves discussion here, instead, is the view that all these puzzlements can be obviated by a rule that permits all responsible adults who have settled preferences and convictions about such matters to register them, while they are still young and healthy and in full command of their capacities, on a legally effective document which could then be filed away, like a will, or perhaps entered in a central computer bank where it could be made instantly accessible to hospital or judicial authorities at a future date. The document, in this respect also like a will, would be amendable or revocable at any future time in which the signer is still of sound mind. It could list all the puzzling contingencies caused by the various kinds of possible disablements and diseases, patterns of depression, alternations of mood, etc., and decide in advance what must be done in each of the foreseeable contingencies. In that way the fully competent autonomous person could determine for himself, while he is able, what life and death decisions are to be made for him when he is no longer able to make them himself. The document would be a kind of "last will and testament," except that it would determine the disposition not of the testator's estate, but of the last days of his life. For that reason it has come to be called a "living will."

6. Living wills and their problems

Proposals to give legal effect to living wills and similar directives have been introduced regularly in American states since 1906 when the Ohio legislature voted down a bill for the legalization of voluntary euthanasia for "certain incurable sufferers" by a vote of 79 to 19.[29] Similar bill were introduced, with no more success, in legislatures in Nebraska (1937), Connecticut (1951 and 1959), Florida (1968, 1970, 1971, 1972, 1973), Idaho (1969), Wisconsin (1971), Delaware (1973), Montana (1973), Oregon (1973), Washington (1973), California (1974), Maryland (1974), and Massachusetts (1974). In Great Britain, euthanasia bills were debated in the House of Lords (1936, 1950, and 1969) and in the House of Commons (1970). For the most part, these defeated bills of legislation authorized acceptance of petitions made by competent patients who are already suffering from diseases or injuries that are irremediable, terminal, and intensely painful, rather than directives made in advance by healthy competent persons. Either no distinction was made between active and passive euthanasia, or the definition of euthanasia clearly included taking active steps to end the suffering patient's life. Thus the Connecticut bill authorized only witnessed written petitions by terminal patients for euthanasia, which it defined as "termination of human life by painless means for the purpose of ending severe physical suffering." Such patients, it decreed, could have euthanasia "administered," and the administration of euthanasia is spoken of as "anticipating death." The British Voluntary Euthanasia Bill of 1969 also provided for what it called "the administration of euthanasia to persons who request it who are suffering from an irremediable condition," meaning by "euthanasia," "the painless inducement of death." Unlike most of the earlier American bills, however, it also enabled "persons to request in advance the administration of euthanasia in the event of their suffering from such a condition at a future date"—the living will, properly speaking. The more recent trend in voluntary euthanasia legislation has been to emphasize the advance directive rather than the last minute "petition," and to restrict euthanasia quite explicitly to passive "letting die," ruling out active "administration" of life-terminating drugs.

The 1969 British proposal for a legally effective living will makes an interesting comparison with the standard American form for a nonbinding living will circulated by Concern For Dying (the former Euthanasia Educational Council). In their respective ways, each requests active hastening of death in certain circumstances, but the emphasis in both (but particularly in the American) is on not taking positive steps to prolong life after a specified point. The British Form of Declaration Under the Voluntary Euthanasia Act (had that ill-fated legislation succeeded) would have been as follows:

I declare that I subscribe to the code set out under the following articles:

A.   If I should at any time suffer from a serious physical illness or impairment reasonably thought in my case to be incurable and expected to cause me severe distress or render me incapable of rational existence, I request the administration of euthanasia at a time or in circumstances to be indicated or specified by me, or if it is apparent that I have become incapable of giving directions, at the discretion of the physician in charge of my case.

B.   In the event of my suffering from any of the conditions specified above, I request that no active steps should be taken, and in particular that no resuscitatory techniques should be used, to prolong my life or restore me to consciousness.

C.   The declaration is to remain in force unless I revoke it, which I may do at any time, and any request I may make concerning action to be taken or withheld in connection with this declaration will be made without further formalities . . .

The less legalistic American form treads somewhat more gingerly:

. . . If the time comes when I can no longer take part in decisions for my own future, let this statement stand as an expression of my wishes and directions, while I am still of sound mind.

If at such time the situation should arise in which there is no reasonable expectation of my recovery from extreme physical or mental disability, I direct that I be allowed to die and not be kept alive by medication, artificial means or

"heroic measures." I do, however, ask that medication be mercifully administered to me to alleviate suffering even though this may shorten my remaining
life . . .

In both cases it is requested that a person no longer capable of sufficiently
voluntary choice be represented by the testament of his earlier self, made
while he was still of sound mind. By the summer of 1984, twenty-three
states had passed legislation, giving legal effect to living wills of one sort or
another, most of them resembling the earlier American models, and all of
them applying to "passive euthanasia" only.

In 1958, well before the passage of the first passive euthanasia bill, the
eminent legal commentator, Yale Kamisar, published his influential "Objections" to voluntary euthanasia legislation generally,[30] apparently aiming at
both the active and the passive kinds. How reliable, he asked, is the witnessed, signed and sealed request of a healthy young (or middle-aged) person, re-endorsed regularly over a period of years, as a guide to his presumed
will at a later time when he is racked with the pain and hopelessness of an
incurable disease? How can one know in advance what the conditions one
dreads are truly like?

> Can such a consent be deemed an informed one? Is this much different from
> holding a man to a prior statement of intent that if such and such an employ-
> ment opportunity would present itself he would accept it, or if such and such a
> young woman were to come along he would marry her? Need one marshal
> authority for the proposition that many an "iffy" inclination is disregarded when
> the actual facts are at hand?[31]

At first reading it may be difficult to appreciate the force of these remarks of
Kamisar's, since they seem to support the patient's right to revoke his earlier
request and not "hold him to it" if he should change his mind, provisions that
are never denied by living will advocates. (Indeed the British form quoted
above gives great emphasis to the right to revoke at any time.) What worries
Kamisar, however, is that the patient may no longer be in a condition to give
clear expression to his wishes, and will be held to the relatively uninformed
request of his earlier self despite his actual will. Even if he is no longer
capable of having an "actual will," the circumstances may be so different
from those earlier envisaged that we might presume a dispositional preference for revoking, and attribute it back to the earlier controlling self. Yet the
binding earlier directive may preclude our intervention.

Suppose that ten years or more have passed since the living will was
signed, and now the signer is hospitalized in an advanced stage of an illness
that has deprived him of the power to communicate a clear and reasoned
choice. Can we terminate, or fail to prolong, his life without his current
consent, when he has had no opportunity to reconsider and revoke if he

chooses? Even if he would wish to revoke the earlier agreement, given that he
is suffering and depressed, and often fatigued and confused, the voluntariness of his new choice might be suspect, and he may lack the power to
communicate it clearly in any case. Again, we might suppose that the patient
falls into an alternation of depression and calm, renouncing and reaffirming
on alternate days the earlier agreement. Can we be sufficiently confident that
the earlier self, acting on the basis only of a partial anticipation of the
eventual situation, would not himself have chosen to revoke had he been able
to foresee precisely these circumstances in every relevant detail?

Kamisar also worries about subtly coercive pressures on the dying patient's
choice, and motivating factors that may mask, whatever the patient says, his
true preference to go on living. Some persons may choose to die, and then
die as they have chosen, in a truly voluntary way, but given the inevitable
pressures, and the difficulty of discerning true preference, many others may
only *seem* to be electing their preferred choices.

> Will we not sweep up, in the process, some who are not really tired of life, but
> think others are tired of them; some who do not really want to die, but who feel
> they should not live on, because to do so when there looms the legal alternative
> of euthanasia is to do a selfish or a cowardly act? Will not some feel an obligation
> to have themselves "eliminated" in order that funds allocated for their terminal
> care might be better used by their families, or financial worries aside, in order to
> relieve their families of the emotional strain involved?[32]

Clearly Kamisar's bias, and that of most legislatures who have considered the
matter, is to err on what they take to be the safe side, if error there must
inevitably be. Just as some criminologists have argued that it is better that a
hundred guilty persons go free than that one innocent person be punished,
the cautious Kamisar might well judge it better that a hundred patients be
denied the death they voluntarily choose than that one patient be denied the
extra life he truly prefers. The living-will advocate will reject this comparative judgment and urge those who make it to become better acquainted with
the problems, sufferings, and indignities of helpless terminal patients. Only
then will they come to appreciate that wrongfully prolonged life can be as
tragic an error as wrongfully terminated life. In life's unhappier end games,
there can be no "safe side" to err on.

In 1976, cautious California legislators, impressed by the demands of their
constituents for action, but determined to include safeguards against mistakes
and abuses of the kind feared by Kamisar, passed the first American "right to
die" bill, and in the process probably erred in the opposite direction. The
Natural Death Act, as it is called, is so narrow in its grudging permissions
that it may actually make it harder rather than easier on balance for patients
in California to arrange in advance for the hastening of their deaths should
they become incompetent. To begin with, it explicitly reaffirms the prohibi-

tion of active euthanasia. It restricts passive euthanasia to patients who have been certified as "terminal." It explicitly excludes pregnant women from the class of persons who "have the right to die without prolongation of life by medical means." It permits revocation at any time "without regard to the patient's competence" at the time. A terminally ill person must wait two weeks after receiving a diagnosis of a terminal condition to sign a directive for the first time. Forgery of a directive or concealment of a revocation which results in a hastened death are treated as felonious homicide, but destroying the directive without the patient's consent is only a misdemeanor, and failure of a physician to follow a directive is no crime at all, but only "unprofessional conduct." Wrongful prolongation of life, obviously, is seen as a morally trifling matter compared to wrongful shortening of life, even among suffering terminal patients.

The most limiting restrictions in the act, however, are the ones defining the "life-sustaining procedures" that may be withheld, and the state of the patient required if they are to be withheld or withdrawn. Only "mechanical or other artificial means to sustain, restore, or supplant a vital function" may be withheld or withdrawn and only when "death is imminent *whether or not life-sustaining procedures are utilized.*" The Directive to Physicians, which functions as a living will under the terms of the Act, concludes that only such "artificial" procedures should be withheld or withdrawn, and only in such dire circumstances, so that "I be permitted to die naturally." Hence the name of the law—The Natural Death Act.[33]

Karen Lebacqz points out some of the consequences:

> Had Karen Ann Quinlan signed the "directive to physicians" . . . , it would have made no difference to her treatment. In her case, death was *not imminent* "whether or not" life-sustaining procedures were used. The "directive" would not have been applicable. Similarly, the signing of a "directive" would not have prevented the involuntary treatment of a young burn victim in Texas whose treatment required no "artificial" or "mechanical" means, but only the "natural"—and excruciatingly painful—application of wet compresses to his gaping sores.[34]

It is impossible for me to discern any moral relevance of the distinction between "artificial" and "natural" procedures to the question of whether a dying life should be prolonged. And the withholding or discontinuing of life-sustaining procedures only at the point when they are bound to fail in any case is hardly much of a favor to the patient who had earlier expressed his preference for hastened death. Those other patients who had never signed a directive to their physician in the first place are liable, in effect, to have their dying process extended to the last possible moment, after pointless and painful resuscitations. Lebacqz concludes that patients in these neglected categories have their moral right to die abrogated, and that on the whole, this law makes it harder to die. The Director of the State Department of Health apparently agreed, since he is said to have recommended that the governor veto the bill, "judging that the existing ambiguity was better than the anticipated hardening of medical hearts."[35]

7. Durable power of attorney

It bears repeated emphasis that competent persons, under our traditional laws, do not need additional protection of their autonomous right to refuse medical treatment. Any physician who imposes medical treatment on a competent patient despite the latter's explicit refusal has committed a "battery" upon him. Court cases abound in which there are official judicial pronouncements of this common-law doctrine. Lebacqz quotes a relatively recent example: "Anglo-American law starts with a premise of thoroughgoing self-determination. It follows that each . . .[person] is considered to be master of his own body, and he may, if he be of sound mind, expressly prohibit the performance of lifesaving surgery or other medical treatment."[36] But in the trying final days of one's life, one may be so weakened or distracted that one cannot make one's lifelong abiding will effective. A person's genuine reasoned preferences, developed over a lifetime in accordance with his settled values, may be overriden because he can no longer convincingly communicate them. It is to prevent this injustice that legal validation of living wills has been sought.

Most of us will remain fully competent until the end, and most deaths, for the competent and incompetent alike, involve no moral complications, no occasion for hard decisions. We die sudden violent deaths or quick and unanticipated peaceful deaths. In neither case does the question of euthanasia arise. But for an increasing number of sick or elderly persons, improved medical technology creates difficult options they had not previously considered. Not only are there new possibilities of hastening death or prolonging life, where such questions are relevant, but also the possibility of undergoing more exotic therapies—organ transplants, radical surgery, experimental drugs, and the like. Whatever the patient's values, he will have to choose among risks. He will need to process large quantities of medical information and come to as accurate as possible an appreciation of the dangers, both in consenting and refusing (Chap. 25, §8). It is impossible for a mere written document, composed decades earlier, and automatically re-endorsed at intervals thereafter, to anticipate all the problems and provide clear and unambiguous directions. If all the physician has to guide him is an earlier written directive, he may find no true guidance at all, but at most what Kamisar dismissed as "iffy inclination."

Until recently, the only alternative to written prior directives as a way of

implementing a person's will after he has lost the capacity to do so himself
has been the proxy decision-maker—the physician in charge, or the court-
appointed guardian. But in recent years a movement has developed to replace
or (better) supplement the written directive not with just *any* proxy, but with
an agent selected by the person himself while still of sound mind. This seems
to offer a person the combined best features of the living will and the proxy
decision-maker, without some of the disadvantages. He will have at least an
indirect say about how he is later to be treated, in virtue of his prior discussions with his agent. (The agent, most likely, will be a spouse, adult off-
spring, or close friend.) He will be able to select as his eventual spokesman
someone whose knowledge of his values and loyalty to his wishes he can
confidently trust. This arrangement will take both moral and legal pressure
off the physician and avoid the time-consuming, cumbersome, and costly
procedures associated with court-appointed guardianship.

Under the common law, a person can always grant another his "power of
attorney" either for some limited purpose or for general purposes, so that the
appointed person may act in the first party's name with full legal effect.
There have been some understood limits to what the appointed representative may do in the principal party's name. He cannot, for example, perform a
contracted personal service in the name of the other. An artist who contracts
to paint a customer's portrait cannot delegate the task to one of his assistants
to perform in the contractor's name. Moreover, under various statutes one
cannot have power of attorney for another to cast a vote in an election or be
his stand-in in a wedding ceremony. For the most part, however, a person
may grant power of attorney to another to do any lawful act that he may do
himself. Under the common law of agency, the power of attorneyship can be
revoked at any time by a simple declaration of the principal. But the common-law power also terminates automatically when either the principal or
the agent dies or *becomes incompetent*. It is the latter provision, of course, that
makes common law agency an unsuitable device for the protection of a
person's right of self-determination after he has lost the capacity to make
medical decisions for himself.

Beginning with Virginia in 1950, more than thirty American states have
revised the common law of agency to permit the power of attorney to survive
the competence of the principal to oversee his own personal or property
interests. For the most part, the motivation of the legislatures was to assist
elderly persons to look after their business and property affairs, but in most
cases the wording of the statutes seems to leave open the possibility of a
"durable power of attorney" to make "personal" as well as business decisions,
including decisions to accept or refuse medical treatment. So construed,
durable power of attorney could be an effective device for protecting individual self-determination that also avoids some of the difficulties Kamisar finds

in living wills. Written directive, composed in necessarily general terms, could then serve as back-up support for the incompetent patient's agent should his decisions be challenged as plainly contrary to the principal's stated preferences, or drastically opposed to his indicated values. The living will would express mainly general principles, placing limits on the agent's discretion and providing at least general guidance to a physician should there be no immediate access to the appointed agent, or a designated substitute. The combined system would not only protect elderly and dying patients from the indignities and suffering of a death that would soon occur anyway, but also others who for religious or other personal reasons choose to forego or discontinue treatment that could sustain their lives for many years (as in cases of comatose Jehovah's Witnesses whose families refuse blood transfusions for them).

No agent or directive, of course, can impose a duty on third parties to administer *active* euthanasia, but there is in principle no *legal* difficulty, at least, to their conferring the liberty *cum* immunity to do so if the third party is willing. If the criminal law continues to forbid voluntary active euthanasia absolutely, the justification can only be in terms of "pragmatic" policy considerations, such as the need to provide safeguards against mistake and abuse. The reasons endorsed by liberal liberty-limiting principles would not otherwise support criminalization, since harm (in the sense that includes "wrong") is not done to the patient who has voluntarily consented to his own painless death. If the only adequate safeguard against the inadvertent or contrived deaths of nonconsenting patients is an absolute prohibition, then and *only then* can a consistent liberal approve of the continued ban on active euthanasia.

Notes

17. Legal Paternalism

1. John Stuart Mill, *On Liberty* (Indianapolis and New York: Bobbs-Merrill, 1956), p. 13.

2. This is largely a consequence of H. L. A. Hart's usage in *Law, Liberty, and Morality* (Stanford, California: Stanford University Press, 1963), pp. 30–34, 38. Hart's opponent, Patrick Devlin, adopted Hart's usage while rejecting, of course, his substantive position. See Devlin's *The Enforcement of Morals* (London: Oxford University Press, 1965), pp. 132–36. The full "debate" between Hart and Devlin was so widely read, and taken up by so many other writers on both sides, that their common usage of the phrase "legal paternalism" became standard.

3. " . . .paternalism—the protection of people against themselves—is a perfectly coherent policy. Indeed, it seems strange in the mid-twentieth century to insist upon this, for the wane of laissez faire since Mill's day is one of the common-places of social history, and instances of paternalism now abound in our law, criminal and civil . . ." *op. cit.*, pp. 31–32. ". . . Mill carried his protests against paternalism to lengths that may now appear to us as fantastic." p. 32

4. John Kleinig warns that the pejorative impact of the word "paternalism" can be overstressed. "Paternalism," he suggests, is more like the word "killing" than the word "murder." Murder is always wrong, and always a crime, "by definition," whereas there is only a standing presumption against "killing" that can be over-ridden in some cases. The controversial question about paternalism, according to Kleinig, is when, if ever, the presumption against it can be overridden. See his *Paternalism* (Totowa, New Jersey: Rowman & Allanheld, 1983), chap. 1.

5. Perhaps this should be called "mentorism" rather than "paternalism" since it recalls procedures characteristic of grammar school classrooms.

6. For authoritative accounts of this doctrine, its origin, history, and present uses, consult the following articles: Stuart J. Baskin, "State Intrusion into Family Affairs: Justifications and Limitations," 26 *Stanford Law Review* 1383 (1974); Neil

Howard Cogan, "Juvenile Law, Before and After the Entrance of 'Parens Patriae'," 22 *South Carolina Law Review* 147 (1970); Joel S. Moskowitz, "Parental Rights and State Education," 50 *Washington Law Review* 623 (1975); and "Notes and Comments: Civil Restraint, Mental Illness, and the Right to Treatment," 77 *Yale Law Journal* 87 (1967).

7. Consider for example the case of Mrs. Lake as described in Alan M. Dershowitz's "Psychiatry in the Legal Process: A Knife That Cuts Both Ways," 4 *Trial* 29 (1968): "Mrs. Lake, a 62-year-old woman, suffers from arteriosclerosis which causes periods of confusion interspersed with periods of relative rationality. One day she was found wandering around downtown Washington looking confused but bothering no one, whereupon she was committed to a mental hospital. She petitioned for release and at her trial testified, during a period of apparent rationality, that she was aware of her problem, that she knew that her periods of confusion endangered her health and even her life, but that she had experienced the mental hospital and preferred to assume the risk of living—and perhaps dying—outside its walls. Her petition was denied, and despite continued litigation, she is still involuntarily confined in the closed ward of the mental hospital."

Dershowitz goes on to comment, "Compare Mrs. Lake's decision to one made by Supreme Court Justice Jackson who, at the same age of 62, suffered a severe heart attack while serving on the Supreme Court. As Solicitor General Sobaloff recalled in his memorial tribute, Jackson's 'doctors gave him the choice between years of comparative inactivity or a continuation of his normal activity at the risk of death at any time.' Characteristically, he chose the second alternative, and suffered a fatal heart attack shortly thereafter. No court interfered with his risky decision. A similar decision, though in a lighter vein, is described in a limerick entitled "The Lament of a Coronary Patient":

My doctor has made a prognosis
That intercourse fosters thrombosis
But I'd rather expire
Fulfilling desire
Than abstain, and develop neurosis.

Few courts, I suspect, would interfere with that decision. Why then do courts respond so differently to what appear to be essentially similar decisions by Mrs. Lake, Justice Jackson, and the coronary patient? Because these similarities are obscured by the medical model imposed upon Mrs. Lake's case, but not upon the other two. Most courts would distinguish the cases by simply saying that Mrs. Lake is mentally ill, while Jackson and the coronary patient are not, without pausing to ask whether there is anything about her "mental illness" which makes her case functionally different from the others."

8. Note on "Civil Restraint, Mental Illness, and the Right to Treatment", 77 *Yale Law Journal* 87 (1967).

9. Confusion and misunderstanding often stem from this double function of "ism" words, so that it sometimes seems useful to separate the functions by assigning them to separate words. Dictionaries used to distinguish rather sharply, for example, the senses of "egoism" and "egotism." The former is the name of a *theory* that human conduct is or ought to be ultimately selfish. The latter is the name of the *practice* of acting from motives of the sort the egoistic theory ascribes or recommends. Most egoistic philosophers are not apparent egotists,

whereas some of those who reject the egoistic theory, no doubt, are egotists, in practice.

10. Bernard Gert and Charles M. Culver, "Paternalistic Behavior," *Philosophy and Public Affairs*, vol. 6, no. 1 (Fall, 1976), pp. 45–57.

11. *Ibid.*, p. 46.

12. I used the label "Extreme Paternalism" in my *Social Philosophy* (Englewood Cliffs, New Jersey: Prentice-Hall, 1973), p. 33.

13. Michael Bayles distinguishes between "preservative paternalism" (our "paternalism proper," or "harm-preventing paternalism") and "promotive paternalism" (our "extreme paternalism" or "benefit-promoting paternalism"). See his important work, *Principles of Legislation* (Detroit: Wayne State University Press, 1978), p. 120.

14. Gerald Dworkin, "Paternalism," in *Morality and the Law*, ed. Richard A. Wasserstrom (Belmont, California: Wadsworth, 1971), pp. 110–111.

15. *Ibid.*, p. 111. I have two further quibbles with the quoted part of Dworkin's definition. First, *both* classes of persons have their "freedom restricted," so Dworkin should have said what he meant, namely, *the class of persons made criminally punishable* by the restrictions. Second, in the examples he gives (suicides, seat belts, blood transfusions) it is clear that Dworkin has in mind "harm-preventing," not "benefit-promoting" paternalism. Hence instead of "whose benefit is intended to be promoted" he should have said what he meant, namely, *the class of persons whose harm is intended to be prevented*.

16. In my article "Legal Paternalism," *Canadian Journal of Philosophy*, vol. I, no. 1 (1971), I made the same distinction using the terms "strong" and "weak" paternalism. That terminology is still commonly used, and is perfectly interchangeable with "hard" and "soft." My impression, however, is that the latter is now more common, and I will adopt it here.

17. Tom L. Beauchamp, "Paternalism and Bio-Behavioral Control," *The Monist*, vol. 60, no. 1 (1976), p. 67.

18. *Loc. cit.*

19. Gerald Dworkin, *op. cit.* (see note 14), p. 108.

20. James Fitzjames Stephen, *Liberty, Equality, Fraternity* (London: 1837), p. 163.

21. "Sentences of twenty, thirty, forty years—even life imprisonment—have been imposed for the possession or sale of marijuana"—Arthur D. Hellman, *Laws Against Marijuana: The Price We Pay* (Urbana, Illinois: University of Illinois Press, 1975), pp. 297–98. Hellman cites numerous horrible examples.

22. Gerald Dworkin, *op. cit.* (see note 14), p. 109.

23. In his "Paternalism: Second Thoughts," in *Paternalism*, ed. Rolf Sartorius (Minneapolis: University of Minnesota Press, 1982), Dworkin seems to change his mind. He discusses there very briefly the problem of the coercive provision of public goods, and uses fluoridation of the water supply, rather than social security, as his example: "Suppose we do have a good argument that most people in a community would consent to a certain practice but that a minority would not. The best solution would be to exempt the minority, but considerations of administrative and economic efficiency may make this very expensive. It is both more effective and cheaper to put fluoride in the community water supply than to distribute fluoride pills to those who want them or to supply nonfluoridated water to those who do not want fluoride . . . Here I am inclined to think that some balancing of interests is appropriate. Knowing that we will be in the minor-

ity on some issues, and in the majority on others, it is reasonable to not demand unanimity on certain issues.

The relevant features are that the majority interest at stake be important (such as health), the imposition on the minority minor (they have to buy their own water), the administrative and economic costs of not imposing on the minority very high.

On this analysis the restriction on the minority is not motivated by paternalistic considerations but in the interest of a majority who wish to promote their own welfare. Hence these are not paternalistic decisions . . ."

24. Gerald Dworkin, "Paternalism," *op. cit.* (see note 14), p. 109.
25. Richard J. Arneson, "Mill versus Paternalism," *Ethics*, vol. 90, no. 4 (July, 1980), pp. 471–72.
26. *Ibid.*, p. 471.
27. The examples were offered as alleged instances of "*prima facie* justified paternalism" by John Hodson in his earlier article, "The Principle of Paternalism," *American Philosophical Quarterly*, vol. 14 (1977), p. 62. Arneson's discussion is on p. 471 of "Mill versus Paternalism," *op. cit.*
28. Gerald Dworkin is very good on this subject. See his "Paternalism," *op. cit.* (note 14), p. 110.
29. In fact there is often a social *benefit* in self-harming behavior, at least as measured in wholly economic terms. Richard A. Ahearn made the point vividly in a tongue-in-cheek letter to the editor of *The New York Times* (October 23, 1979). "Recent news stories told us that:

> Thirty-three percent of all Americans smoke. An actuarial study by State Mutual Assurance Company concluded that a healthy, non-smoking 32 year old man can expect to live 7.3 years longer than a healthy, smoking 32 year-old man.

If we assume that smoking is only half as hazardous at other ages and to women, we need merely multiply 220 million by one-third by 7.3 by one-half to come up with the number of years that smoking is taking from the ends of the lives of Americans who are living now: 267.6 million.

During most of these lost years, say 80% of them, the victims could have drawn Social Security and other government benefits. If we can estimate Social Security, Medicaid, and possibly food stamps and related costs at a conservative $5,000 per year per person, we come up with a 1979 figure of $1.07 trillion. That amount, so vast that it is hard to comprehend, is the money smokers are saving nonsmoking taxpayers.

The dissembling miscreants at the Tobacco Institute should use this argument in their lobbying for government subsidies, advertising media access, etc. It's the only case that can be made for smoking."

Of course, Ahearn doesn't mention economic costs on the other side—increased insurance rates, higher hospital costs, premature loss of productivity, etc. But his accounting of savings is impressive anyway.

30. For an expansion of this point see chap. 19, §3, "Personal Sovereignty and Domain Boundaries."
31. Robert Harris, "Private Consensual Adult Behavior: The Requirement of Harm to Others in the Enforcement of Morality," *U.C.L.A. Law Review*, vol. 14 (1967), p. 585n.

32. Beauchamp, *op. cit.* (see note 17), p. 78. Beauchamp in the last quoted sentence may be underestimating the resources of legislative draftsmanship. It may be possible (at least in principle) to outlaw unreasonably dangerous behavior undertaken for self-regarding reasons (e.g., to experience thrills, set records, conquer mountains, win prizes) while permitting it when undertaken for public-spirited, altruistic, or conscientious reasons. Courts have been required to make equally difficult discriminations among motives in other areas (e.g., determining when motives are "sincere," "spiteful," "malicious," etc.).

33. Moreover, there are examples of private paternalistic behavior, quite outside the context of legal coercion, that would strike almost everybody, including most liberals, as justified. Gert and Culver's examples (see note 10) of white lies told to deathbed patients are cases in point. The liberal must explain why these instances of deception by private individuals do not objectionably invade autonomy, whereas instances of *coercion* by the *state* do.

34. John Stuart Mill's rhetoric against paternalism expresses this absolutistic attitude. He is especially fond of such political metaphors (which we will examine in Chap. 19) as independence, legitimate rule, dominion, and sovereignty. In affairs that affect only (or primarily) his own interests, the individual is morally independent, the only legitimate ruler of himself. He has absolute dominion in that self-regarding sphere, and has "sovereignty over himself."

18. Autonomy

1. The *Oxford English Dictionary* lists three senses of "autonomy." The first and oldest is political; the other two are biological and social. The first is: "Of a state, institution, etc.: The right of self-government, of making its own laws and administering its own affairs." The earliest cited use of the word in English is in this sense (1623). Plato, when he refers to "the ruling part of the soul" in the *Republic* quite self-consciously creates a political metaphor. C. S. Lewis writes that the Greek *eleutheria* and the Latin *liberas*, which are usually translated as "freedom," were used in ancient times "chiefly, if not entirely, in reference to the freedom of a state. The contrast implied is sometimes between autonomy and subjection to a foreign power; sometimes between the freedom of [within] a republic and the rule of a despot." If Lewis is right, one of the oldest senses of "free," if not the original one, is "autonomous" as applied to a state, a sense which still survives. See his *Studies in Words* (Cambridge: Cambridge University Press, 1961), pp. 124–25.

2. The word "free" is more complicated, but it too has an ambiguity similar to that of "autonomous" and "independent," especially when applied to nations and states. When colonies achieve independence of an imperial power they are said to have won their freedom, though their citizens may not be any freer as individuals. When we speak of people as (generally) free or unfree, we can mean either that they are generally capable of acting or omitting to act as they please (the "optionality" discussed in vol. 1, chap. 5, §7), or that they are independent, "sovereign" beings, persons in actual and/or rightful control of their own choices. See the essay "The Idea of a Free Man" in my book *Rights, Justice, and the Bounds of Liberty* (Princeton, New Jersey: Princeton University Press, 1980), pp. 3–29.

3. See Hans Kelsen, *General Theory of Law and State*, translated by Anders Wedberg (Cambridge, Massachusetts: Harvard University Press, 1945), pp. 90–92.

4. *Ibid.*, p. 91.
5. Daniel Wikler, "Paternalism and the Mildly Retarded," *Philosophy and Public Affairs*, vol. 8 (1979), pp. 377–392.
6. Dan Brock, "Paternalism and Promoting the Good," in *Paternalism*, ed. Rolf Sartorius (Minneapolis: University of Minnesota Press, 1983), p. 241.
7. Wikler, *op. cit*, p. 384. Emphasis added.
8. The point applies to higher animals too. Could a cow, for example, if given the choice of living on a ranch in Texas or Nebraska, decide *at all*, much less "wisely" or "foolishly"? There is a kind of minimal compliment in being called "foolish."
9. But see, *inter alia*, Timothy Duggan and Bernard Gert, "Voluntary Abilities," *American Philosophical Quarterly*, vol. 13 (1979); Harry Frankfurt, "Freedom of the Will and the Concept of a Person," *Journal of Philosophy*, vol. 68 (1971); Jonathan Glover, *Responsibility* (London: Routledge & Kegan Paul, 1970), chaps. 3–7; and Hans Kelsen, *General Theory of Law and State* (Cambridge, Massachusetts: Harvard University Press, 1945), part one, chaps. VII–IX.
10. This is a truth that the ancient Greeks, in their diverse ways, struggled to come to terms with. See Martha Nussbaum's engrossing account in *The Fragility of Goodness: Luck and Rational Self-sufficiency in Greek Ethical Thought* (Cambridge: Cambridge University Press, 1986).
11. Perhaps the most famous portrait in world literature of this sort of inauthenticity is Tolstoy's account of Stepan Arkadyevitch near the beginning of *Anna Karenina*, trans. Constance Garnett (New York: Dodd, Mead & Co., 1966), part one, chap. 3, pp. 7ff. "Stepan Arkadyevitch took in and read a liberal paper, not an extreme one, but one advocating the views held by the majority. And in spite of the fact that science, art, and politics had no special interest for him, he firmly held those views on all these subjects which were held by the majority and by his paper, and he only changed them when the majority changed them—or more strictly speaking, he did not change them but they imperceptibly changed of themselves within him.

 Stepan Arkadyevitch had not chosen his political opinions or his views; these . . . opinions and views had come to him of themselves, just as he did not choose the shapes of his hat and coat. And for him, living in a certain society— owing to the need, ordinarily developed at years of discretion, for some degree of mental activity—to have views was just as indispensable as to have a hat . . ."— This passage is also quoted by Gerald Dworkin in his "Moral Autonomy" in *Morals, Science, and Sociality*, ed. H. Tristram Englehard, Jr., and Daniel Callahan (New York: Hastings Center, 1978), p. 160. Dworkin is probably our most sensitive writer about autonomy, and I am indebted to him at numerous places.
12. David Riesman, *et al.*, *The Lonely Crowd* (New Haven: Yale University Press, 1950). Abridged paperbound ed. (1961), p. 15.
13. *Ibid.*, p. 31.
14. Gerald Dworkin makes this point vividly both in his "Moral Autonomy" (note 11, *supra*) and in his article "Autonomy and Behavior Control," *Hastings Center Report*, vol. 6 (February, 1976). In the latter he writes (p. 24): "We all know that persons have a history. They develop socially and psychologically in a given environment with a given set of biological endowments. They mature slowly and are heavily influenced by their parents, siblings, peers, and culture. What sense does it make to speak of their convictions, motivations, principles, and so forth as

"self-selected" [self-created]? This presupposes a notion of the self as isolated from the influences just enumerated, and, what is almost as foolish, that the self which chooses does so arbitrarily. For to the extent that the self uses canons of reason, principles of induction, judgments of probability, etc., these also have either been acquired from others or, what is no better from the standpoint of this position, are innate. We can no more choose *ab initio* than we can jump out of our skins. To insist on this position is to make autonomy impossible."

15. Aristotle, *Nicomachean Ethics*, Book III, chap. 5. "The man then must be a perfect fool who is unaware that people's characters take their bias from the steady direction of their activities. If a man, well aware of what he is doing, behaves in such a way that he is bound to become unjust, we can only say that he is voluntarily unjust." In such a way do people "choose their own characters," and make themselves what they are.

16. Jean-Paul Sartre, "Existentialism is a Humanism" in *Existentialism* (New York: Philosophical Library, 1947), p. 18. "Man is nothing else but what he makes of himself."

17. G. Dworkin, "Autonomy and Behavior Control," *op. cit.*, p. 25. (See note 11.)

18. Immanuel Kant, *Fundamental Principles of the Metaphysic of Morals*, trans. H. J. Paton, in *The Categorical Imperative* (London: Hutchinson's University Library, 1947), p. 180.

19. As Paton puts it, *loc. cit.*, "We make the law which we obey. The will is not merely subject to the law: it is so subject that it must also be regarded as making the law, and as subject to the law *only* because it makes the law." Emphasis added.

20. Immanuel Kant, *Fundamental Principles of the Metaphysic of Morals*, trans. Thomas K. Abbott (Indianapolis: Bobbs-Merrill, 1949), p. 49.

21. Robert Paul Wolff, *In Defense of Anarchism* (New York: Harper & Row, 1979), p. 14.

22. John Rawls, *A Theory of Justice* (Cambridge, Massachusetts: Harvard University Press, 1971), p. 516. Rawls's later discussion of autonomy in his John Dewey Lectures is no longer subject to these objections. There he clearly distinguishes between "rational autonomy," a mere "device of representation" used to characterize the abstract individuals in the original position, and "full autonomy," a moral ideal which applies to "free and equal" moral agents in the real world. The latter corresponds closely to the conception of autonomy developed in this work. See John Rawls, "Kantian Construction in Moral Theory: Rational and Full Autonomy," *Journal of Philosophy* 77 (1980), 515–35.

23. Gerald Dworkin, "Moral Autonomy," *op. cit.* (see note 11), p. 158. One of Dworkin's more forceful arguments is from the social character of moral principles: "What my duties are as a parent, how close a relative must be to be owed respect, what duties of aid are owed to another, how one expresses regret or respect, are to some extent relative to the understandings of a given society. In addition moral rules often function to provide solutions to a coordination problem—a situation in which what one agent wishes to do depends upon his expectations of what other agents will do—agents whose choices are in turn dependent on what the first agent will do. Such conventions depend upon the mutual convergence of patterns of behavior . . . all of these preclude individual invention." *Ibid.*, p. 159.

24. Gerald Dworkin calls this "substantive" as opposed to "procedural" independence. Autonomy, as he and I both see it, more strongly requires the latter than the former.

382   NOTES

25. Dworkin cites a famous example: "There is something admirable about the person who acts on principle, even if his principles are awful. But there is something
to be said for Huck Finn, who 'knowing' that slavery was right, and believing
that he was morally damned if he helped Jim to escape, was willing to sacrifice
his integrity in favor of his humanitarian impulses." "Moral Autonomy," *op. cit.*
(see note 11), p. 163.

26. As I put it elsewhere: "There are necessarily two aspects of autonomous self-government. The governing self must be neither a colony of some external self, or
'foreign power,' nor powerless to enforce its directives to its own interior subjects. If we appropriate William James's usage (modified for our own purposes)
and call the 'inner core self' the I, and the rest of the comprehensive self over
which it rules its Me, then we can put the dual aspect of personal autonomy
felicitously: *I am autonomous if I rule me, and no one else rules I.*" *Rights, Justice, and
the Bounds of Liberty, op. cit.* (see note 2), pp. 20–21. The reference to William
James is to his *Principles of Psychology* (New York: Henry Holt and Co., 1890), vol.
I, chap. X.

27. Plato, *The Republic*, Books II–IV. The clearest modern statement of a similar
"parapolitical conception of the self" may be that of Joseph Butler in his *Five
Sermons Preached at the Rolls Chapel, and A Dissertation Upon the Nature of Virtue*,
published in one volume (Indianapolis: Bobbs-Merrill, 1950). The sermons were
originally published in 1726.

28. Butler, *Ibid.*, preface, p. 11.

29. David Hume, *A Treatise of Human Nature* (London, 1739), Book II, Part III,
Chapter III. "Reason is, and ought only to be the slave of the passions, and can
never pretend to any other office than to serve and obey them."

30. Emile Durkheim, *Suicide*, trans. John A. Spaulding and George Simpson (New
York: Free Press, 1951), pp. 241–276.

31. Ralph Waldo Emerson, "Self-Reliance," *Essays, First Series* (Boston, 1841).

32. *Ibid.* The quoted passage consists of the final two sentences of the essay.

33. See my "Causing Voluntary Actions" in *Doing and Deserving* (Princeton, New
Jersey: Princeton University Press, 1970), pp. 152–186.

34. Richard J. Arneson, "Mill versus Paternalism," *Ethics*, vol. 90, no. 4 (1980), p.
475.

35. For a detailed account of the variety of responsibility judgments, see my *Doing
and Deserving, op. cit.* (see note 33), pp. 119–251.

36. See my discussion of responsibility as "representational attributability" in *Doing
and Deserving*, pp. 250–251.

37. *Shorter Oxford English Dictionary*, 3rd ed. (Oxford: Clarendon Press, 1933), p. 497.

38. Bernard Crick, "Sovereignty," *International Encyclopedia of the Social Sciences* (New
York: Free Press, 1968), vol. 15, p. 77.

39. S. I. Benn and R. S. Peters, *Social Principles and the Democratic State* (London:
George Allen & Unwin, Ltd., 1959), p. 247. They write there:

> "The nation" is a relatively modern conception, just as nationalism is a
> modern political ideal. In the Middle Ages, men did not think of themselves
> as Englishmen, Frenchmen, or Germans, but as vassals of their overlord,
> subjects of their king, and ultimately members of a universal order of Chris-
> tendom. Gradually the monarchs of Western Europe strengthened them-
> selves against the Emperor and the Pope on the one side and their barons on
> the other, each building up an increasingly centralized structure of political

authority, and becoming a more important focus for loyalty than any competitor. At this stage the idea of nationality [nationhood] was co-terminous with political allegiance.

40. "A nation's history is a sort of myth, holding up heroes for reverence and imitation, and thus setting standards and ideals." *Ibid*, p. 251.

41. *Ibid.*, p. 251.

42. I discuss this sense of "person" under the rubric "normative personhood" and contrast it with "descriptive" or "commonsense personhood" in my "Abortion," in *Matters of Life and Death*, ed. Tom Regan (New York: Random House, 1978), p. 186ff. and in my *Rights, Justice, and the Bounds of Liberty*, *op. cit.* (see note 2), pp. 191–193.

43. Cf. Ralph Barton Perry, *Realms of Value* (Cambridge, Massachusetts: Harvard University Press, 1954), pp. 62–63. We are persons (in the nonjuridical sense), according to Perry, to the extent that our interests are integrated: "That which makes a man a person is the integration of his interests, both time-wise and space-wise. The person can look ahead, and plan accordingly; he can launch upon trains of purposive activities; he can relate his past to his future fortunes, and the distant to the near; he can keep his bearings; he can manage the household of his diverse interests; he can put first things first; he can hold in mind the wood, despite the trees; and all this he can do because of his cognitive capacities . . . A man is a person insofar as there is a central clearinghouse where his interests . . . take account of one another, and are allowed to proceed only when the demands of other interests are consulted, and are wholly or partially met." Note how similar things might be said about the extent to which a group of persons is "a people," or a "community," or a "nation."

44. It has been pointed out to me by Alan Fuchs that the way nation-states actually behave towards one another today shows that the stringent traditional conception of political soverignty has been much weakened, or at best only honored in the breach. Governments now openly acknowledge that they send "spy-satellites" over one another's territories, and one of the worst-kept secrets in the world is that governments monitor other nations' radio and telephone signals, plant listening devices in foreign embassies, and support similar clandestine activities. The counterpart of spying in the personal realm would be an outrageous violation of privacy, and hence of personal autonomy.

19. Personal Sovereignty and its boundaries

1. In this connection see David Loth and Morris L. Ernst, *How High Is Up?* (Indianapolis: Bobbs-Merrill, 1964), chap. 1.

2. John Stuart Mill, *On Liberty*, chap. IV, para. 10.

3. Joel Feinberg, *Social Philosophy* (Englewood Cliffs, New Jersey: Prentice-Hall, 1973), pp. 31–32.

4. Much of this paragraph and parts of the succeeding paragraphs are drawn from my essay "The Child's Right to an Open Future" in *Children's Rights*, ed. Hugh LaFollette (Totowa, New Jersey: Rowman & Littlefield, 1980). That essay discusses paternalism specifically in the context of child-raising and in particular the demands imposed on others by the personal autonomy (even) of children. I treat the concept of self-fulfillment in much more detail in my article "Absurd Self-ful-

fillment" in *Time and Cause, Essays Presented to Richard Taylor*, ed. Peter van Inwagen (Dordrecht, The Netherlands: Reidel, 1980), pp. 255–281.

5. This is the famous "moral muscles argument," developed in the first eight paragraphs of chapter III of *On Liberty*. In effect the argument proceeds as follows.

   (i) (The explicit departure from hedonism): The highest good for man is neither enjoyment nor passive contentment, but rather a dynamic process of growth and self-realization, in which uniquely human faculties—perception, judgment, discriminative feeling, powerful human emotion, mental activity, and moral preference—are progressively perfected.
   (ii) These powers, like the muscular powers, are improved only by being used (exercised).
   (iii) Exercise of the moral muscles requires constant choice-making, which in turn requires freedom to make even foolish (self-regarding) choices, freedom not only from legal coercion but also from the tyranny of custom.
   (iv) Therefore interference with free choice hampers the development of distinctive human propensities in whose fulfillment consists a person's good.

6. This is a quite distinct argument from the "moral muscles argument." It is found in several places in *On Liberty*. Sometimes the emphasis is on the actual likelihood of error when an outsider presumes to know a person's interests better then he (chap. IV, para. 13: "The strongest of all the arguments against the interference of the public with purely personal conduct is that when it does interfere, the odds are that it interferes wrongly [mistakenly] and in the wrong place," *et seq.*). In other places the emphasis is on the advantages of the individual over others in knowing his own interest (chap. IV, para. 4: ". . . with respect to his own feelings and circumstances the most ordinary man or woman has means of knowledge immeasurably surpassing those that can be possessed by anyone else.")

7. J. S. Mill, *On Liberty*, chap. V, para. 11. One would think that if Mill is a consistent utilitarian, then promotion of human well-being and the prevention of harm are primary in his system, so that even so basic a right as that of self-determination must be derived in this way from its conducibility to them. It is now widely acknowledged, however, that Mill's fidelity to utilitarianism, despite his protestations to the contrary, wavers in *On Liberty*, and he is often inclined to appeal to an underivative personal autonomy and other natural rights. See especially C. L. Ten, *Mill On Liberty* (Oxford: Clarendon Press, 1980) for convincing documentations of Mill's departures in *On Liberty* from a consistent utilitarianism.

8. This third interpretation of autonomy rights is defended in my essay "Legal Paternalism," *Canadian Journal of Philosophy*, vol. I (1971), and also in my "Freedom and Behavior Control" in the *Encyclopedia of Bioethics*, Warren T. Reich, ed. (New York: Free Press, 1978).

9. See, for example, Jonathan Glover, *Causing Death and Saving Lives* (New York: Penguin Books, 1977), pp. 74–85, and John Kleinig, *Paternalism* (Totowa, New Jersey: Rowman & Allenheld, 1984).

10. The most convincing interpretation of Mill as a consistent anti-paternalist is that of Richard J. Arneson. See his "Mill versus Paternalism," *Ethics*, vol. 90, no. 4 (July, 1980), pp. 471–72. The most powerful case I know for (ii) in the text—the defense of paternalism in cases when a person's right to choose conflicts with his own good—is Dan Brock, "Paternalism and Promoting the Good," in *Paternalism*, Rolf Sartorius, ed. (Minneapolis: University of Minnesota Press, 1983), pp. 237–60.

11. *Supra*, Chap. 17, p. 26.

12. *Loc. cit.*

13. Isaiah Berlin has argued persuasively that not every kind of inability is an unfreedom. See his classic essay, "Two Concepts of Liberty," in *Four Essays on Liberty* (London: Oxford University Press, 1969), pp. 118–172. Berlin is not alone in arguing that "Mere incapacity to attain a goal is not lack of political freedom" (p. 122). He quotes the eighteenth-century writer Helvetius, for example, as saying: "The free man is the man who is not in irons, not imprisoned in a jail, not terrorized like a slave by the fear of punishment . . . it is not lack of freedom not to fly like an eagle or swim like a whale" (*loc. cit.*).

14. *Ibid.*, pp. 122–131. See also my *Social Philosophy* (Englewood Cliffs, New Jersey: 1973), pp. 8–9.

15. Arthur Schopenhauer, *Essay on the Freedom of the Will*, trans. Konstantin Kolenda (New York: The Liberal Arts Press, 1960), p. 19.

16. For an ingenious elaboration of this "second level" account of freedom to will, see Harry G. Frankfurt, "Freedom of the Will and the Concept of a Person," *The Journal of Philosophy*, vol. 68 (1971), pp. 5–20.

17. Impaired psychological capacities are not the only cause of closed choice-options. When persons undertake moral commitments they may be "morally bound" not to choose in the way they would (otherwise) prefer to. A person with powerful scruples may find that he "cannot bring himself" to act in the way he intensely wants to act. It is not plausible to treat integrity as "an impaired psychological capacity," but the honorable person, nevertheless, has fewer open choice-options than the dishonorable person. One can, therefore, have too much of a good thing called "free will."

18. One of the sources of the value of freedom, as we have seen, (chap. 18, §3) is as a necessary condition for, and useful means toward, *de facto* self-government. The *de facto* autonomous person needs luck to achieve autonomy as an actual condition. If his health is ruined, his finances destroyed, or his political liberty crushed through no doings of his own, then no matter how developed his capacities and virtues, he will no longer have the opportunity for self-government. The political prisoner locked in a tiny cell may preserve his integrity intact, but he lacks the liberty required for *de facto* self-government. But above the essential minimum, many persons have governed themselves quite thoroughly, chugging back and forth to their heart's content on a limited stretch of track, unimpeded in fact in the execution of all their decisions.

19. The following four paragraphs are taken from my article "Freedom and Behavior Control," *Encyclopedia of Bioethics* (New York: Free Press, 1978) and are reprinted here with the kind permission of the publishers.

20. See my essay "The Child's Right to an Open Future," *op. cit.* (see note 4), pp. 124–153.

21. J. S. Mill, *On Liberty*, chap. V, para. 10.

22. Jean Jacques Rousseau, *The Social Contract*, Book I, chap. VII, and the criticism in Isaiah Berlin's "Two Concepts of Liberty," *op. cit.* (see note 13), pp. 131–134, 147–148, *et passim*.

23. Hardly any actual instances of slavery, at least in historical times, have been quite this extreme, but this description will serve well as an hypothetical example—all the better for being so extreme.

24. John Stuart Mill, *On Liberty*, chap. V, para. 10.

25. John D. Hodson, "Mill, Paternalism, and Slavery," *Analysis*, vol. 41, (January, 1981), p. 61.
26. *Ibid.*, p. 62.
27. J. S. Mill, *On Liberty*, chap. V, para. 11. The remainder of this paragraph is devoted to the problem of irrevocable contracts in general, and argues that "there are perhaps no contracts . . . except those that relate to money" that should preclude possibility of retraction. He explicitly advocates no-fault divorce (as it has since come to be called) in this passage.
28. *On Liberty*, chap. I, para. 11, ". . . I forego any advantage which could be derived to my argument from the idea of natural right as a thing independent of utility."
29. *Ibid.*, chap. I, para. 9.
30. Perhaps the leading example is John Kleinig in his important new book *Patenalism* (Totowa, New Jersey: Rowman & Allanheld, 1984). Gerald Dworkin gives a favorable nod to the principle that "Paternalism is justified only to preserve a wider range of freedom for the individual in question." See his "Paternalism" in Richard Wasserstrom, ed., *Morality and the Law* (Belmont, California: Wadsworth, 1971), p. 118. I think the principle Dworkin probably prefers is that paternalism is justified only to prevent a drastic and (perhaps) irrevocable diminution of freedom. See also Donald Regan, "Paternalism, Freedom, Identity, and Commitment," in *Paternalism*, ed. Rolf Sartorius (Minneapolis: University of Minnesota Press, 1983).
31. Arneson, *op. cit.* (see note 10), p. 474.
32. *Loc. cit.*
33. Mill, *op. cit.*, chap. IV, final paragraph.
34. Arneson, *op. cit.* (see note 10), p. 476.
35. It follows, as Robert Schopp has pointed out to me, that liberal principles cannot justify "chattel slavery" in the strict and literal sense according to which human slaves become in every moral and legal respect exactly like cattle. Because human negotiators cannot agree to alienate their *personhood* they cannot by simple contractual agreement make themselves immune from general criminal statutes that protect the rights of others. That fact places severe limits on what sorts of slavery contracts can conceivably be recognized and enforced by law. For another discussion of this point and related matters, see Arthur Kuflik, "The Inalienability of Autonomy," *Philosophy and Public Affairs*, 13 (1984), 271–98.
36. I am indebted to Joan Callahan for persuading me to make this correction of my earlier emphasis on costs.
37. Arneson, *op. cit.* (see note 10), p. 472.
38. Homer, *The Odyssey*, Book XII, 36–58, 144–200. In the verse translation of Richard Lattimore (New York: Harper & Row, 1965), the passages are on pp. 186–190.
39. For the best statement of such an argument, see Donald Regan, *op. cit.* (see note 30).
40. *Ibid.*, p. 125.
41. See Ronald Bailey, "Facing Death, A New Life Perhaps Too Late," *Life*, vol. 53 (July 27, 1962), pp. 28–29, reprinted in *Philosophy and the Human Condition*, ed. W. Blackstone, T. Beauchamp, and J. Feinberg (Englewood Cliffs, New Jersey: Prentice-Hall, 1980).
42. In *Philosophy and Personal Relations*, ed. Alan Montefiore (Montreal: McGill-Queen's University Press, 1973), pp. 137–169.

43. *Ibid.*, p. 145.
44. Arneson, *op. cit.* (see note 10), p. 475.
45. It is too late for Mrs. Boris to refuse to make a promise or to argue that her husband put her in an unreasonable position when he extracted the promise in the first place. For the sake of the example, let us suppose that young Mrs. Boris shared her husband's strong socialist convictions and willingly played her role in supporting them. It is morally irrelevant whether the old Mrs. Boris has changed her political beliefs.
46. See my "Supererogation and Rules" in *Doing and Deserving* (Princeton, New Jersey: Princeton University Press, 1970), pp. 4–9.
47. The territorial metaphor is spelled out quite explicitly by Milton R. Konvitz, who writes of constitutional privacy: "Its essence is the claim that there is a sphere of space that has not been dedicated to public use or control. It is a kind of space that a man may carry with him, into his bedroom or into the street. Even when public, it is a part of the inner man; it is part of his 'property' . . . ," "Privacy and the Law: A Philosophical Prelude," *Law and Contemporary Problems*, vol. 31 (1966), pp. 279–80. Thomas Emerson takes the idea of a privileged zone further: "It [the right to privacy] seeks to assure the individual a zone in which to be an individual, not a member of the community. In that zone he can think his own thoughts, have his own secrets, live his own life, reveal only what he wants to the outside world. The right of privacy, in short, establishes an area excluded from the collective life, not governed by the rules of collective living." *The System of Freedom of Expression* (New York: Random House Vintage Books, 1970), p. 545.
48. *Griswold v. Connecticut*, 381 U.S. 479 (1965).
49. *Ibid.* at 482.
50. *Ibid.* at 485.
51. *Ibid.* [quoting *NAACP v. Alabama*, 37 U.S. 288, 307 (1964)].
52. *Ibid.*
53. *Ibid.*
54. *Ibid.* at 498 (Goldberg, J. concurring) [quoting *NAACP v. Alabama.* 377 U.S. 388, 307 (1964)].
55. 405 U.S. 438 (1972). In *Eisenstadt*, the Supreme Court invalidated a Massachusetts statute that prohibited distributing contraceptives to unmarried persons. The Court held that the statute's separate treatment of married and unmarried persons violated the equal protection clause.
56. 388 U.S. 1 (1967). The State of Virginia had banned interracial marriages by statute. Mildred Jeter, a black woman, and Richard Loving, a white man, were married in the District of Columbia and then moved to Virginia. The Supreme Court reversed their convictions pursuant to this statute on the basis of both the equal protection clause and the due process clause of the fourteenth amendment. The Court concluded that the fourteenth amendment requires that the freedom of choice to marry not be restricted by invidious racial discrimination.
57. 394 U.S. 557 (1969). Mr. Stanley was indicted and convicted for possessing obscene films, which were confiscated from his bedroom pursuant to a search warrant for bookmaking activity. He argued that the Georgia obscenity statute, insofar as it punished mere private possession of obscene matter, violated the first amendment. The Supreme Court agreed with Stanley and reversed his conviction. The Court recognized as a fundamental right the right to be free from unwarranted intrusion into one's privacy.

58. 431 U.S. 494 (1977). In *Moore*, a city zoning ordinance specified the categories of relatives that could live together. The ordinance made it a crime for a grandchild to live with his grandparent. A grandmother, Mrs. Moore, was convicted of a violation when she failed to remove her grandson from her home. The Supreme Court reversed, holding the ordinance violated the due process clause of the fourteenth amendment. The governmental interests advanced and the extent to which they were served by the ordinance were insufficient to uphold the ordinance.

59. 410 U.S. 113 (1973). *Roe* was a class action brought by a pregnant woman to challenge the Texas abortion laws, which allowed abortion only to save the mother's life. The Supreme Court held that the statute violated the fourteenth amendment's due process clause because it was an invasion of privacy (which includes the right to terminate pregnancy).

60. Of course, if the fetus is a person with its own right to life, then the decision to terminate pregnancy is *not* a wholly self-regarding one, hence not within the zone of the pregnant woman's sovereignty. The crucial issue in the abortion controversy is not a legal one, or even a primarily moral one, but a metaphysical (or conceptual) issue, the status of the fetus.

61. Thomas C. Grey, *The Legal Enforcement of Morality* (New York: Random House, 1983), p. 8.

62. *Loc. cit.*

63. *Griswold*, 381 U.S. at 498.

64. *Ibid.*

65. 367 U.S. 497 (1961).

66. *Ibid.* at 545 (Harlan, J., dissenting).

67. *Ibid.* at 552 (Harlan, J., dissenting).

68. *Ibid.* at 553 (Harlan, J., dissenting).

69. *Paris Adult Theatre I v. Slaton*, 413 U.S. 49, 65 (1973) [quoting *Palko v. Connecticut*, 302 U.S. 319, 325 (1937)]. The State of Georgia sued for a civil injunction to stop the showing of two allegedly obscene films. The Georgia Supreme Court found that the films were obscene and therefore fell outside the protection of the first amendment. Georgia's civil standards, however, did not conform to the Supreme Court's obscenity test established in *Miller v. California*, 413 U.S. 15 (1973). The Supreme Court remanded the case for proceedings consistent with *Miller*.

70. *Ibid.* at 66. ·

71. Gerald Dworkin, "Paternalism: Some Second Thoughts," in *Paternalism*, ed. Rolf Sartorius (Minneapolis: University of Minnesota Press, 1983), p. 110.

72. For thorough discussions of these charges, and interpretations or reinterpretations of Mill's self-and-other-regarding distinction, see J. C. Rees, "A Re-reading of Mill On Liberty," *Political Studies*, vol. 8 (1960), pp. 113–29, and C. L. Ten, *Mill On Liberty* (Oxford: Clarendon Press, 1980), pp. 10–41.

73. Immanuel Kant, *Lectures on Ethics*, trans. Louis Infield (New York: Harper & Row, 1963), p. 149. All of the quotations from Kant that follow are from this book, which Lewis Beck describes in his foreword (p. xii) as "our most valuable source of information about the development of Kant's ethical views."

74. *Ibid.*, pp. 150–51.

75. *Ibid.*, p. 151.

76. Compare *Ibid.*, p. 153: "Let us imagine a state in which men held as a general opinion that they were entitled to commit suicide, and that there was even merit

and honor in so doing. How dreadful everyone would find them. For he who does not respect his life even in principle cannot be restrained from the most dreadful vices; he recks neither kings nor torments." Kant does not distinguish (as he should) between respecting one's life and respecting *oneself*.

77. *Ibid.*, p. 151.
78. *Loc. cit.*
79. *Ibid.*, pp. 153–54.
80. *Ibid.*, p. 154.
81. St. Thomas Aquinas, *Summa Theologica*, vol. II, part II, question 64, A5, "Whether it is Lawful to Kill Oneself?"
82. Kant, *op. cit.*, p. 154. Emphasis added.
83. Paul Ramsay, "The Morality of Abortion," in *Life or Death: Ethics and Options*, ed. Daniel H. Labby (Seattle: University of Washington Press, 1968), pp. 71, 72, 73–74.
84. Note how the Kantian and the partisan of personal sovereignty would diverge over voluntary euthanasia. If a long-suffering dear one, not in a position to take his own life, requested the partisan of sovereignty to help him die "while I still have my dignity," the partisan of sovereignty would reply (circumstances permitting): "I hate to do it, but out of my respect for you and your right to govern your own life and death, I shall. It is, after all, *your* life." The Kantian, on the other hand, would reply: "Much as I hate to see you suffer, I must decline to implement your choice, and I decline out of respect not for you but for the human life within you." The former response, it seems clear to me, pays more respect to the person than the latter, and particularly to his *autonomy*.

20. *Voluntariness and Assumptions of Risk*

1. The distinctions in this paragraph are taken from Henry T. Terry, "Negligence," *Harvard Law Review*, vol. 29 (1915).
2. The best statement of this model is probably that in John Rawls, *A Theory of Justice* (Cambridge, Massachusetts: Harvard University Press, 1971), pp. 407–424. This discussion is strongly recommended.
3. Cf. Rawls, *Ibid.*, p. 420: "We are to see our life as one whole, the activities of one rational subject spread out in time. Mere temporal position, or distance from the present, is not a reason for favoring one moment over another. Future aims may not be discounted solely in virtue of being future, although we may of course ascribe less weight to them if there are reasons for thinking that, given their relation to other things, their fulfillment is less probable. The intrinsic importance that we assign to different parts of our life should be the same at every moment of time."
4. See Michael Bratman, "Practical Reasoning and Weakness of Will," *Nous*, vol. 13 (1979): Donald Davidson, "How is Weakness of the Will Possible?" in Joel Feinberg, ed., *Moral Concepts* (Oxford: Oxford University Press, 1969): and Ronald D. Milo, "Wickedness," *American Philosophical Quarterly*, vol. 18 (1982).
5. Compare J. L. Austin, "A Plea for Excuses," in his *Philosophical Papers* (Oxford: Oxford University Press, 1961), p. 146: "I am very partial to ice cream, and a bombe is served divided into segments corresponding one to one with persons at High Table: I am tempted to help myself to two segments and do, thus succumbing to temptation and even conceivably (but why necessarily?) going against my

principles. But do I lose control of myself? Do I raven, do I snatch the morsels from the dish and wolf them down, impervious to the consternation of my colleagues? Not a bit of it. We often succumb to temptation with calm and even with finesse."

6. Richard J. Arneson, "Mill versus Paternalism," *Ethics*, vol. 90 (1980), p. 474.
7. Rawls, *op. cit.* (see note 2), pp. 410–411.
8. Cf. Richard B. Brandt, "The Concept of Rational Action," *Social Theory and Practice*, vol. 9, nos. 2–3 (1983), pp. 143–64.
9. For a perceptive discussion of "privative" and "positive" concepts, see G. H. von Wright, *The Varieties of Goodness* (New York: The Humanities Press, 1963), pp. 54–56 *et passim*.
10. Aristotle, *Nicomachean Ethics*, trans. W.D. Ross (London: Oxford University Press, 1925), III, 1, 110a.
11. *Ibid.*, 1110^a, 3–7.
12. *Ibid.*, 1110^a, 8–10.
13. *Ibid.*, 1111^a, " . . . acts done by reason of anger or appetite are not rightly called involuntary. For in the first place, on that showing none of the other animals will act voluntarily, nor will children . . . "
14. *Ibid.*, 1111^b, "Again, what is the difference in respect of involuntariness between errors committed upon calculation and those committed in anger? Both are to be avoided, but the irrational passions are thought not less human than reason is, and therefore also the actions which proceed from anger or appetite are the man's actions. It would be odd, then, to treat them as involuntary."
15. *Canadian Journal of Philosophy*, I (1971), 105–24.
16. *Ibid.*, III, §2, 111^b, 1, " . . . both children and the lower animals share in voluntary action, but not in choice, and acts done on the spur of the moment we describe as voluntary, but not as chosen . . . acts due to anger are thought to be less than any others objects of choice."
17. Cf. W. Somerset Maughan, *The Summing Up* (New York: Mentor Books, 1946), p. 35. "I have at times fallen victim to a snare to which the writer is peculiarly liable, the desire to carry out in one's own life certain actions which I made the characters of my invention do. I have attempted things that were foreign to my nature and obstinately persevered in them because in my vanity I would not confess my self beaten . . . "
18. Similar rules are familiar in the quite different moral-legal context in which voluntariness is to be determined after the fact for the purpose of establishing moral or criminal responsibility for an action that was harmful to *others*. Hart and Honoré comment: "This is indeed a point at which the concept of a fully voluntary action incorporates judgments of value. A man who hands over his purse to a highwayman to save his life, and one who hands over strategic plans to the enemy to save his, are treated differently because the value of the interest sacrificed is different." H. L. A. Hart and A. M. Honoré, *Causation in the Law* (Oxford: The Clarendon Press, 1959), p. 147. The Hart-Honoré examples differ from one another in two ways. In the highwayman example the determination of voluntariness or involuntariness is needed to decide whether the transfer of the purse was a gift or the effect of a crime; what hinges on it is whether someone, other than the person whose choice is at issue, committed a crime. The threatened consequences to the chooser are much more harmful than those of the alternative allowed him, so the cut-off point where involuntariness begins is low

on the scale. In the wartime example, the issue is criminal responsibility for the chooser himself, and while the harm threatened to him was equally great, the harm to others resulting from the alternative allowed him was catastrophic, so the cut-off point at which involuntariness begins is much higher. Another way to put this: the standards of voluntariness in the wartime case are much stricter than in the highwayman case.

19. Kent Greenawalt, "Voluntary Undertakings," an unpublished grant application, 1981, p. 7.

20. John Stuart Mill, *On Liberty* (1859), chap. V, para. 5.

21. *Loc. cit.*

22. Albert Fish, the infamous cannibalistic child-killer, whose criminal career extended through the twenties and thirties, "had eaten his own excrement. He had put cotton, saturated with alcohol, up his rectum and had set fire to it. X-rays showed twenty nine needles inserted in his body between the scrotum and the anus. 'If only pain were not so painful!' he exclaimed, when he spoke of his attempts to insert needles into the scrotum and beneath his nails." Curtis Bok, *Star Wormwood* (New York: Alfred A. Knopf, 1959), p. 127.

23. Even less then are we entitled to say *a priori* that the person *must* be out of his mind, irrational, grossly ill-informed, or otherwise not choosing voluntarily. We are not entitled to presume conclusively (making the presumption immune from rebuttal) of *any* kind of behavior that it is nonvoluntary, especially that "no one in his right mind" could *ever* voluntarily choose it. The contrary opinion is muddled and lamentably common both in legal and psychiatric circles. Consider, for example, a legal brief submitted to the Utah Board of Pardons in the case of Gary Gilmore, the convicted murderer who waived his right to appeal his death sentence: "a criminal defendant such as Gilmore, who declines to pursue legal proceedings which could save his life is, in fact, choosing to commit suicide, and the overwhelming majority of psychiatric opinion regards the impulse to suicide as a form of mental illness." Quoted by Norman Mailer, *"The Executioner's Song* (New York: Warner Books paperback, 1979), p. 685.

24. Suicide was a crime under the common law but subsequent statutes have removed it from the criminal category in Great Britain and in most American states, though aiding and abetting, counseling, and procuring suicide are still criminal in most jurisdictions and "active euthanasia" is in all. The practical effects of the prohibition of suicide as such in the past were (1) ecclesiastical forfeitures, (2) official dishonoring of the corpse, (3) forfeiture of the property of the suicide, (4) the voiding of life-insurance policies, (5) punishment by imprisonment for unsuccessful attempts at suicide, (6) punishment for incitement and conspiracy to commit suicide, (7) conviction of murder for deaths to others accidentally caused while attempting suicide, and (8) imposition on all citizens of a "duty to interpose" to prevent another's suicide. (Glanville Williams comments on (8): "It is a freak result of present legal principles that there is a duty to save a would-be suicide from drowning, when there would be no such duty if he did not wish to die"!) See Glanville Williams, *The Sanctity of Life and the Criminal Law* (New York: Alfred A. Knopf, 1957), chap. 7. The quotation is on p. 287.

25. Arneson, *op. cit.* (see note 6), p. 484, commenting on Joel Feinberg, "Legal Paternalism," *Canadian Journal of Philosophy*, 1 (1970).

26. *Loc. cit.*

27. *Ibid.*, p. 485.

28. *Loc. cit.*

29. Aristotle defined "equity" as "a correction of law where it is defective owing to its generality." *Nicomachean Ethics, op. cit.* (see note 10), Book V, section 10.

30. An example of a circular argument:

    A: Roe's choice of *X* is clearly non-voluntary.

    B: It doesn't seem so to me. Why do you think so?

    A: Because his mental illness must have produced it.

    B: But what makes you think he has a mental illness?

    A: Because no one in his right mind could choose *X*.

    B: So you argue that the choice is evidence of the illness, and the illness in turn makes the choice involuntary. But the choice, while odd, seems possibly voluntary to me. So I wonder, what reason other than the choice itself (which is the very point at issue), is there for believing Roe has a mental illness?

    A: I have no other evidence, and none is required.

31. W. Gifford-Jones, "Don't Become the Shot Heard Round the Block" (syndicated medicine column), *Arizona Daily Star*, January 12, 1981.

32. *Loc. cit.*

33. *State v. Eitel*, Fla., 227 So. 2d 489 (1971). This and similar testimony suggests that there is little factual basis for Gerald Dworkin's surmise that "on purely economic grounds it is quite likely that the effect of motorcycle helmets is to cause badly injured persons to survive (requiring care) who otherwise might have died from head injuries." "Paternalism: Some Second Thoughts," in *Paternalism*, ed. Rolf Sartorius (Minneapolis: University of Minnesota Press, 1982).

34. This statute was invalidated in the 1968 case of *American Motorcycle Association v. Davids*, Mich. 158 N.W. 2d 72.

35. *People v. Fries*, 42 Ill. 2d 446, 450, 250 N.E. 2d 149, 151 (1969), *State v. Betts*, 21 Ohio Misc. 175, 184, 252 N.E. 2d 866, 872 (1969), *Everhardt v. City of New Orleans*, 208 So. 2d 423, 426 (La. App.), *rev'd* 253 La. 285, 217 S. 2d 400 (1968), *appeal dismissed and cert. denied* 395 U.S. 212 (1969), and *American Motorcycle Association v. Davids, op. cit.* Judge Miller in the latter case quotes Mill with approval: " . . . the individual is not accountable to society for his actions insofar as these concern the interests of no person but himself."

36. John Kleinig, *Paternalism* (Totowa, New Jersey: Rowman & Allanheld, 1984), p. 82.

37. Gerald Dworkin, "Paternalism: Some Second Thoughts," in *Paternalism*, ed. Rolf Sartorius (Minneapolis: University of Minnesota Press, 1982).

38. *The Journal of the American Medical Association* has published a table of risks in various everyday activities which shows that motorcycling is the most dangerous (1 chance in 50 of eventual serious injury or death). The comparable risk in smoking 20 cigarettes a day is 1 in 200; drinking one bottle of wine per day, 1 in 13,300; power boating, 1 in 5,900. Compare various "involuntary risks": Being struck by an automobile, 1 in 20,000; injury from an earthquake (in California) 1 in 588,000; injury from a falling aircraft, 1 in 10,000,000. See "Life in America: Dangerous, but we must risk it," by Ronald Kotulak, *Chicago Tribune*, Sunday, September 14, 1980.

39. "Does it never happen," asks Donald Davidson, *op. cit.* (see note 4), p. 100, "that I have an unclouded, unwavering judgment that my action is not for the best, all

NOTES 393

things considered, and yet where the action I do perform has no hint of compulsion or of the compulsive? There is no proving such actions exist; but it seems to me absolutely certain that they do."

40. C. Edwin Harris, Jr., "Paternalism and the Enforcement of Morality," *Southwestern Journal of Philosophy*, VIII (Summer, 1977), p. 88.
41. *Loc. cit.*
42. See Kleinig, *op. cit.* (see note 35), "Note", *Michigan Law Review*, vol. LXVII (1968), 372, and Kenneth M. Royalty, "Motorcycle Helmets and the Constitutionality of Self-protective Legislation," *Ohio State Law Journal*, vol. XXX, 3 (1968), pp. 371–393.
43. Kenneth M. Royalty, *op. cit.* (see note 41), p. 367.
44. *A.M.A. v. Davids, op. cit.* (see note 34), p. 75.
45. Cf. G. Dworkin, *op. cit.* (see note 37), p. 8.
46. *Ibid.*, p. 9.
47. *Loc. cit.*

21. Failures of Voluntariness: The Single-Party Case

1. Suicide attempts are discussed in chap. 20, §§3, 5, 6. Tests of voluntariness for self-destructive acts are discussed in chap. 19, §§6, 7 and in Chap. 20, §§3–6 *et passim*. Second-party collaboration is discussed in chap. 27, §§1–3. Exploitation of a person who requests mutilating surgery is discussed in chap. 31, §3.
2. The latter date is the time of the publication of Glanville Williams' *The Sanctity of Life and the Criminal Law* (New York: Alfred A. Knopf, 1957). The book lists examples of punishments for attempted suicide under statutes still in force at the time on pp. 280–281. In 1955 there were 5,220 attempted (but failed) suicides known to the police in Great Britain of which only 43 were punished. "It would be interesting to know," writes Williams, "on what principle a small minority were selected for incarceration in prison. Can it be that there was no other principle than the idiosyncracy of the judge or magistrate?" (p. 281).
3. *Ibid.*, p. 278, "Before the First World War, imprisonment was quite a regular punishment for attempted suicide, and for a second or subsequent attempt it might be as long as six months. This was sometimes rationalized as a measure 'in the interests of defendant's health' . . . "
4. *Ibid.*, p. 293.
5. That consent is always itself an *act* is convincingly argued by John Kleinig in his "The Ethics of Consent," *Canadian Journal of Philosophy*, vol. 11 (1981).
6. Coercion *can* be involved in the one-party case too. Suppose *A* demands that *B* commit suicide within 72 hours, and threatens some unacceptable harm to *B*'s family, or reputation, or country, if he does not. If *B* then kills himself because of the threat, his act is a "one-party case," since he inflicts the harm on himself by direct action of his own, and not by consenting to another's direct infliction of the harm. His is an act of unassisted suicide, not of "consenting to homicide." Yet the act, because of coercion from another person, may be considerably less than voluntary.
7. Aristotle, *Nicomachean Ethics* Book III, §1. See the discussion *supra*, chap. 15, §4, *et passim*.
8. Harry Frankfurt, "Coercion and Moral Responsibility" in Ted Honderich, ed., *Essays on Freedom of Action* (London: Routledge & Kegan Paul, 1973), p. 83.

9. Cf. Robert Nozick, "Coercion," in *Philosophy, Politics, and Society*, Fourth Series, ed. Peter Laslett, W.G. Runciman, and Quentin Skinner (Oxford: Basil Blackwell, 1972). See especially p. 102, conditions (1) (that the coercer *knows* he is making a threat) and (3) (he makes the threat in order to get the coercee [not] to do something, intending that the coercee realize that he is being threatened).

10. Kent Greenawalt, "Voluntary Undertakings," unpublished grant application (1981), p. 21.

11. *Ibid.*, p. 23.

12. Herbert L. Packer, *The Limits of the Criminal Sanction* (Stanford, California: Stanford University Press, 1968), p. 114. See also the *Model Penal Code* (Philadelphia: American Law Institute, 1962), §3.02.

13. *Model Penal Code*, §2.09. The *Code* treats what it calls "the generalized defense of necessity" as a justification; whereas duress is treated as an excuse. The justification defense requires the defendant to show, *inter alia*, that the evil he tried to avoid is greater than the evil he reluctantly chose to produce; the duress defense, available only in the case where there is a human being threatening harm, in effect argues that whether or not the choice was the lesser evil (and hence justified), the general frailty of human nature makes it unreasonable to expect that the actor could have done differently even if he had sincerely wanted and tried to. Hyman Gross offers a plausible rationale for the distinction in his *A Theory of Criminal Justice* (New York: Oxford University Press, 1979), pp. 290–291. It seems unlikely, however, that the distinction between choices forced by human threats and choices forced by natural circumstances maps neatly on to the distinction between excuse ("he could not help it") and justification ("he chose the most reasonable alternative"). Herbert Packer, *op. cit.* (see note 12), p. 117, gives a hypothetical example where the mapping fails, and a choice forced by circumstances functions as an excuse: "A man driving down a narrow, winding mountain road comes upon a disabled car completely blocking the road. In it are five people. He steps on the brake which, to his horror, does not hold. His possible choices are either to run off the road, thereby surely killing himself, or to plough into the disabled car, with a substantial likelihood of killing its occupants. He chooses the latter course, and all five occupants of the car are killed in the ensuing crash . . . Clearly, he made the 'wrong' choice . . . he chose to sacrifice five to save one. Yet no honest judge or juror could say that confronted with the same dilemma he would have done otherwise." On the other hand if a military prisoner succumbs to the demonstrably credible threat of continued torture (duress) and betrays an entire army, his behavior is so patently unjustified that it cannot even be excused. That is an example of a choice forced by coercers that does not excuse. Again the M.P.C. mapping fails.

14. For illuminating discussions of the relation of freedom to the conceived dimensions of the "person" or "self," see John Hospers, "Free Will and Psychoanalysis," in Joel Feinberg, ed., *Reason and Responsibility*, 5th ed. (Belmont, California: Wadsworth, 1981), pp. 352–361; Harry Frankfurt, "Freedom of the Will and the Concept of a Person" in Joel Feinberg, ed., *Reason and Responsibility, op. cit.*, pp. 388–396; Frithjof Bergman, *On Being Free* (Notre Dame, Indiana: University of Notre Dame Press, 1977), pp. 15–40; and John Wilson, *Reason and Morals* (Cambridge: Cambridge University Press, 1961), pp. 57–71.

15. Gary Deeb, syndicated column, "Injured stunt man's lawsuit costs 'Incredible' $180,000," *Arizona Daily Star*, July 14, 1981. Copyright *Chicago Sun Times*, 1981.

16. Henry W. Brosin, "Obsessive-Compulsive Disorders," *Encyclopedia of the Social Sciences*, vol. 11 (New York: The Free Press, 1968), p. 241. See also "Notes Upon a Case of Obsessional Neurosis," *The Standard Edition of the Complete Psychological Works of Sigmund Freud*, vol. X (London, 1953).

17. Karen Horney, *The Neurotic Personality of Our Time* (London: Routledge & Kegan Paul, 1937), p. 46.

18. Brosin, *op. cit.* (see note 16), p. 243.

19. Karen Horney, *Neurosis and Human Growth* (New York: W. W. Norton, 1950), p. 29.

20. See Samuel I. Greenberg, *Neurosis is a Painful Style of Living* (New York: North American Library, 1971).

21. Horney, *op. cit.*, p. 30.

22. *Loc. cit.*

23. *Ibid.*, p. 31.

24. Richard J. Arneson, "Mill versus Paternalism," *Ethics*, vol. 9 (1980), p. 488.

25. Nevertheless there may be some intuitive "level" at which the person *knows*, however dimly and inarticulately, what he is doing.

26. See William Glasser, *Reality Therapy* (New York: Harper & Row, 1965). R. D. Laing, if I understand him correctly, would characterize the self-deceived neurotic's choice, in some circumstances, as not only voluntary, but even reasonable, since it does work as a solution to his basic problem, protecting him, even at great cost, from intolerable stress, all imposed in the first place by an unreasonable social world. See *The Divided Self* (London: Tavistock, 1960).

22. *Consent and Its Counterfeits*

1. John Kleinig, "The Ethics of Consent," *Canadian Journal of Philosophy*, supp. vol. VIII (1982), pp. 93–96.

2. *Ibid.*, p. 93. Kleinig also draws the corollary from his main point, that active consent need not be whole-hearted or unreserved. It can still be valid consent though given reluctantly, grudgingly, thoughtlessly, or with feelings of guilt. One can even actively consent to that of which one morally disapproves, as in Kleinig's example of parents' reluctant consent to their child's marriage despite their quite explicit disapproval of it.

3. The standard textbook example case is *Regina v. Prince* 2 C.C.R. 154 (1875). The crime was not called "statutory rape" but "unlawfully taking an unmarried girl, being under the age of sixteen years, out of the possession and against the will of her father."

4. See my *Doing and Deserving* (Princeton, New Jersey: Princeton University Press, 1970), pp. 110–113, 222–225.

5. Thomas Hobbes, *Leviathan*, Michael Oakshott (Oxford: Basil Blackwell, 1946), part I, chap. 15, p. 105.

6. Kleinig, *op. cit.* (see note 1), pp. 96–98.

7. As it is by A. Weale, "Consent," *Political Studies*. XXVI, 1 (March, 1977), pp. 65–77. Weale and the "many others" who "see consent as a . . . kind of passive promising" are persuasively criticized by Kleinig, *op. cit.* (see note 1) p. 114.

8. I agree emphatically, in this paragraph, with the view I have since found in an article by Donald VanDeVeer, "Paternalism and Subsequent Consent," *Canadian Journal of Philosophy*, vol. 9 (December, 1979), esp. pp. 638–639.

9. Most notably Gerald Dworkin, "Paternalism," in *Morality and the Law*, ed. Richard Wasserstrom (Belmont, California: Wadsworth Publishing Co., 1971), and Rosemary Carter, "Justifying Paternalism," *Canadian Journal of Philosophy*, vol. 7 (1977).

10. Gerald Dworkin, *Ibid.*, p. 119.

11. Dworkin himself in some passages seems to prefer this less paradoxical way of putting his point. Consider: "Parental paternalism may be thought of as a wager by the parent on the child's subsequent recognition of the wisdom of the restrictions" (p. 119). There is nothing in that sentence implying a power of retroactive alienation of one's right, and other such absurdities.

12. This point is developed in my "The Child's Right to an Open Future," in *Whose Child?, Children's Rights, Parental Authority, and State Power*, ed. William Aiken and Hugh LaFollette (Totowa, New Jersey: Rowman and Littlefield, 1980), pp. 140–151.

13. John Locke, *Second Treatise of Government*, first published in 1689. For a persuasive account of the inadequacies in Locke's political and argumentative uses of the concept of tacit consent, see A. John Simmons, *Moral Principles and Political Obligations* (Princeton, New Jersey: Princeton University Press, 1979), pp. 75–100. See also my "Civil Disobedience in the Modern World," *Humanities in Society*, vol. 2 (1979).

14. A. John Simmons, "Tacit Consent and Political Obligation," *Philosophy and Public Affairs*, vol. 5 (1976), p. 279. The example is also found in Simmons' book, *op. cit.* (see note 13), pp. 79–80.

15. John Rawls, *A Theory of Justice* (Cambridge, Massachusetts: Harvard University Press, 1971), pp. 248–250.

16. *Ibid*, p. 249.

17. *Ibid.*, pp. 248–249.

18. For a penetrating discussion of the problems of proxy-decision–making for incompetent patients in hospitals, see Allen Buchanan, "The Limits of Proxy Decision Making," in *Paternalism*, ed. Rolf Sartorius (Minneapolis: University of Minnesota Press, 1982).

19. Rawls, *op. cit.* (see note 15), p. 249.

20. *Loc. cit.*

21. *Loc. cit.*

22. Such an argument might run as follows: (1) More often then not *B* chooses the reasonable and prudent alternative in circumstances like the present. (2) Therefore, he probably would decide reasonably and prudently in the present circumstances if he had the opportunity. (3) A hypothetical reasonable person in these circumstances would grant his consent to *A*'s proposed action. (4) Therefore, *B* would consent to *A*'s action if he had the opportunity to do so.

23. Failures of Consent: Coercive Force

1. I am using the word "force" in this expression in much the same sense as that the law assigns to the word "duress"—a generic term including both compulsion, constraint, and coercion by threat. I include any of the techniques by which one person can "force" another to do, forebear, or experience something. My usage is even broader than that, however, since it includes "pressures" short of necessity and forces with impersonal origins. Our focus in this chapter, of course, is not on

excusing conditions in criminal or civil law (where the concept of duress is at home) but on the conditions that reduce or nullify the voluntariness of one party's consent to the harmful or dangerous behavior of another, and which thus defeat the other party's defense to criminal charges and confer the privilege to interfere on third parties. For purposes of comparison, *Webster's* 2d ed. definition of "duress" is as follows: "*Law.* Compulsion or constraint by which a person is illegally forced to do or forebear some act. This may be actual imprisonment or physical violence to the person, or by such violence threatened (specif. called *duress per minas*). The violence or threats must be such as to inspire a person of ordinary firmness with fear of serious injury to the person (loss of liberty or of life or limb), reputation, or fortune. Such violence or threats exercised upon the wife, husband, ascendants, or descendants of a person may constitute duress of him."

2. Both "compulsion" and "coercion" (but especially the latter) are somewhat abstract terms, vague around the edges, and the products in large part of the work of theorists with various axes to grind. I cannot claim for my definitions any perfect fidelity to ordinary usage. At most, I can claim only a rough correspondence to a distinction commonly made in this or similar language by philosophers, and even in respect to it I have no doubt taken certain liberties. However uncertain may be linguistic usage, the conceptual distinction I express in these terms is, I think, clear and useful.

3. Jeffrie G. Murphy, "Consent, Coercion, and Hard Choices," *Virginia Law Review, vol. 67 (1981), p. 82. Murphy borrows the felicitious phrase "legitimate inequalities of fortune" from Justice Pitney in Coppage v. Kansas 236 U.S. 1, 17 (1914).*

4. *Ibid.*, p. 83.

5. Robert Nozick, in his ingeniously complicated analysis of coercion, seems more concerned with the conditions for properly *charging A* with an act of coercion than with the conditions for applying a voluntariness-nullifying condition to *B's* consent. Hence, he is careful to include many conditions bearing on the coercer *A*'s state of mind that we have excluded from our account which is from the perspective of the coercee, *B*. See Nozick's article "Coercion" in *Philosophy, Science, and Method, Essays in Honor of Ernest Nagel*, ed. Sidney Morgenbesser, Patrick Suppes, and Morton White (New York: St. Martins Press, 1969), pp. 440–72.

6. Morris R. Cohen and Ernest Nagel, *An Introduction to Logic and Scientific Method* (New York: Harcourt, Brace & Co., 1934) p. 294.

7. *Ibid.*, p. 296.

8. David Zimmerman, "Coercive Wage Offers," *Philosophy and Public Affairs*, vol. 10 (1981), p. 122.

9. David Hume, "Of the Original Contract," in *Essays* (Oxford: Oxford University Press, 1963), p. 462.

10. Murphy, *op. cit.* (see note 3), p. 81. Italics added, letter variables altered to preserve uniformity.

11. J. G. Murphy, "Blackmail: A Preliminary Inquiry," *The Monist* 63, no. 2 (1980), p. 158.

12. Furthermore, as Murphy himself points out in an ingenious observation, we are sometimes morally justified in making a threat that we would not be justified in carrying out. "It is wrong to kill somebody in order to prevent him from stealing my color television set; it does not follow from this, however, that it is wrong to threaten to kill him unless he abandons his attempt to take the television set from my living room." Murphy then goes on to qualify his analysis of the concept of

coercion: "The very making of the threat must itself be wrong" if the threat is to be understood as coercive. But I have anticipated this move in the text. See Murphy, *op. cit.* (see note 3), p. 81.

13. Among the leading contributions by philosophers to the discussion are Robert Nozick's "Coercion" in *Philosophy, Science, and Method*, ed. Sidney Morgenbesser, Patrick Suppes, and Morton White (New York: St. Martins, 1969); Harry G. Frankfurt's "Coercion and Moral Responsibility," in *Essays on Freedom of Action*, ed. Ted Honderich (London: Routledge and Kegan Paul, 1973); Virginia Held's "Coercion and Coercive Offers," in *Coercion: Nomos XV*, ed. J. Roland Pennock and John W. Chapman (Chicago: Aldine-Atherton, 1972); Michael D. Bayles' "Coercive Offers and Public Benefits," *The Personalist*, vol. LV (1974); Daniel Lyons' "Welcome Threats and Coercive Offers," *Philosophy*, vol. L (1975); Vinit Haksar's "Coercive Offers (Rawls and Gandhi)," *Political Theory*, vol. IV (1976); Donald VanDeVeer's "Coercion, Seduction, and Rights," *The Personalist*, vol. LVIII (1977); Theodore Benditt's "Threats and Offers," *The Personalist*, vol. LVIII (1977); and David Zimmerman's "Coercive Wage Offers," *Philosophy and Public Affairs*, vol. 10 (1981).

14. The proposal need not be to contribute anything *directly* to the person addressed. It can be to contribute to third parties, or even to "contribute" to no one at all but simply to do something, constructive or destructive, that the addressee wants done, thus "contributing" to the addressee only indirectly, that is contributing only desire-fulfillment to *him*.

15. The proposal need not be to inflict anything directly on the addressee but desire-frustration, which of course can be painfully disappointing even when it does not directly harm him.

16. Nozick, *op. cit.* (see note 13) p. 449.

17. Thomas Hobbes, *Leviathan* (1651), Chap. 20, "Of Dominion Paternal and Despotical."

18. The central importance of standards of normalcy to the analysis of threats and offers was first made clear in the article by Nozick, *op. cit.* (see note 13). That article will be treated for many more years as the *locus classicus* for this whole subject.

19. Zimmerman, *op. cit.* (see note 13).

20. Nozick, *op. cit.* (see note 13), p. 449.

21. *Ibid.*, p. 450.

22. Daniel Lyons, *op. cit.* (see note 13), p. 430.

23. Zimmerman, *op. cit.* (see note 13), p. 129.

24. *Ibid.*, p. 128.

25. *Ibid.*, pp. 131–132.

26. The fact that there are often several hypothetical tests that we might use, employing various statistical generalizations of plausible relevance to the case at hand (e.g., the drowning swimmer case), suggests that there might be some relativity in the judgments we make of preference-affecting proposals. Perhaps in difficult cases there is no uniquely correct answer to the question of whether the proposal is an offer or a threat, and instead we should say "relative to generalization G_1 is a threat, but relative to generalization G_2, which may also be relevant, it is an offer." If such relativity is sometimes involved, that might explain why the "common-sense judgment" to which we appeal in testing proposed baselines might itself be unclear or controversial.

24. Failures of Consent: Coercive Offers

1. David Zimmerman, "Coercive Wage Offers," *Philosophy & Public Affairs* 10 (Spring 1981), part II.
2. I prefer the language of "goods" and "evils" to "harms" and "benefits" since it is sufficiently generic to include preferences that are not in fact beneficial or even believed to be so, but are *wanted* or *preferred, graded high,* or *found welcome* for some other reason. In short, I shall continue to treat coercion and liberty as related to wants and preferences rather than interests.
3. Donald VanDeVeer, "Coercion, Seduction, and Rights," *The Personalist* LVIII (1977).
4. Alan Fuchs, unpublished note written in connection with the N.E.H. Summer Seminar for College Teachers, Tucson, Arizona, 1984.
5. *Ibid.*
6. Zimmerman, *op. cit.* (see note 1), p. 132.
7. *Ibid.*, p. 133.
8. *Ibid.*, pp. 133, 134.
9. *Ibid.*, pp. 134, 135.
10. See "Anatomy of a Regulation: The Continuing Case of Research on Prisoners," *The Hastings Center Report*, vol. II, no. 5 (October, 1981), pp. 2–3.
11. See Alan Wertheimer, "Freedom, Morality, Plea Bargaining, and the Supreme Court," *Philosophy & Public Affairs* 8 (Spring, 1979), pp. 203–34.
12. See Richard Titmuss, *The Gift Relationship: From Human Blood to Social Policy* (London and New York: Pantheon Books, 1971).
13. See Allen Buchanan, "Exploitation, Alienation, and Injustice," *Canadian Journal of Philosophy* 9 (1979).
14. See Jules L. Coleman, "Liberalism, Unfair Advantage, and the Volunteer Armed Forces," in Robert K. Fullinwinder, ed., *Conscripts and Volunteers* (Totowa, N.J.: Rowman and Allenheld, 1983).
15. See the dissenting opinions of Justices Brennan, Blackman, Marshall, and Stevens in *Harris v. McRae* 448 U.S. 297 (1980).
16. Jeffrie G. Murphy, "Consent, Coercion, and Hard Choices," *Virginia Law Review* 67 (1981), pp. 88–89.
17. *Loc. cit.*
18. *Ibid.*, p. 90.
19. John Edward Murray, Jr., *Murray on Contracts* (Indianapolis and New York: Bobbs-Merrill, 1974), p. 737.
20. *Henningsen v. Bloomfield Motors, Inc.*, 32 N.J. 358, 161A, (2a) 69 (1960).
21. *Ibid.*, p. 84.
22. In the supposedly competitive automobile industry, all the companies printed contract forms with "the uniform warranty of the Automobile Manufacturers Association to which all major automobile manufacturers belonged . . . " *ibid.*, p. 69.
23. J. G. Murphy, *op. cit.* (footnote 47), p. 740.
24. *Ibid.*, p. 764. Quoted by Murray (see note 19) from the *Uniform Consumer Credit Code*, §2–302, comment 1.
25. *United States v. Bethlehem Steel Corporation*, 315 U.S. 289 (1942).
26. *Ibid.*, p. 325.
27. *Loc. cit.*

28. Quoted at *ibid.*, pp. 326–27 from Justice O.W. Holmes, Jr., in *Union Pacific R. Co. v. Public Service Commission*, 248 U.S. 67, (1970).

29. Quoted at *ibid.*, pp. 328–29 from *Administrators of Hough v. Hunt*, 2 Ohio 495, 502 (1826). Frankfurter finds the same "historic principles of duress" in recent cases "where a customer of a gas or electric company pays charges which he asserts he is not obligated to pay, rather than have his service disconnected. Payments made in such circumstances are regarded as coerced." (p. 329).

30. The bare bones of the hypothetical example do not clearly indicate whether the agreement is "unconscionable." In order to settle that question we have to know whether *B* was really "over the barrel," whether she had *any* bargaining power, whether she could have "shopped around" for better terms, whether carnal relations with *A* as such really were a "harsh cost" for her, given her values and attitudes, etc. The example is more difficult than the legal cases of unconscionability because the transaction is not the usual kind of commercial exchange, and it is hard to speak with any precision of "excessive costs" or "inordinate profits." In terms of literal profit made, the weaker party in this example was the greater gainer.

31. Suppose that the well-owner in Murphy's example had charged the man "nearly dead from thirst" $10 for a glass of water instead of demanding "all his worldly goods." The desperate man's consent to the exorbitant price in this new version of the tale is hardly more voluntary than his consent to the extortionate demand in the original version. The alternative projections in the new version are more "distant" than in the original, that is the choice between "no water" and "no $10" appears easier than the choice between "no water" and (say) "no $100,000," which are much more closely ranked evils. But if the dying man attaches an infinite value, or at least an "astronomical value" to staying alive, he may have very little more choice in the original version than in the new one. The coercive pressure measured by the difference between "one hundred trillion" and "ten" is insignificantly greater than the coercive pressure measured by the difference between "one hundred trillion" and "one hundred thousand."

32. When forced to choose between two good things that are closely matched one can always have some regrets that one cannot have one's cake and eat it too. This reluctance does not count against voluntariness in any morally interesting sense, though it does show that one's choice was not as *wholehearted* as it might have been. A perfectly voluntary but not perfectly wholehearted choice is one made *for* certain good reasons and ("reluctantly") *despite* good reasons on the other side.

33. *Hastings Center Report, op. cit.* (see note 10), p. 2.

34. *Ibid.*, p. 3.

35. "Meanwhile, research in prisons is hard to find these days. Some states have banned it in their prison systems, and the pharmaceutical companies appear to be wary. In 1975 the President's Commission found that sixteen drug companies used at least 3,600 prisoners in research. Now only two—Upjohn and Hoffman-La Roche—are interested in continuing research. The United States, it appears, is slowly joining the rest of the world; no other country surveyed by the National Commission permits research to be conducted in prisons." *Loc. cit.*

36. *Commonwealth v. Donaghue*, 250 KY. 343, 63 S.W. (2d) 3 (1933). The language quoted is from an indictment for "conspiracy," alleging that the defendants, among other things, "loaned hundreds of . . . persons from $5 to $50 at from 240 to 360 percent per annum." The judgment of the appellate court upholding the

indictment characterized the indicted conduct as "a nefarious plan for the habitual exaction of gross usury, that is, in essence the operation of a business of extortion . . . systematic preying upon poor persons . . . taking an unconscionable advantage of their needy conditions . . . oppressing them . . . "

37. James Fitzjames Stephen, *A History of the Criminal Law of England,* vol. III (London, 1883), pp. 196–99.

38. Not only poor people have been taken advantage of by unscrupulous moneylenders. Profligate youths and high living nobles who had "only themselves to blame," were also prime marks. Stephen, who rejects criminalization on Benthamite grounds, nevertheless finds much to sympathize with in the "sentiment" on which criminalization rests: "It seems to me that the trade of the scoundrels who live by pandering to the folly and vice of the young, and driving with ignorant people in difficulties bargains so hard that no one in their senses would enter into them if they understood their provisions, might be stopped with no great difficulty and without interfering with anything which could by courtesy be called a real commercial operation." *Op. cit.* (see note 37), p. 196. What Stephen calls pandering is a form of exploitation which might nevertheless be accepted with sufficient voluntariness to be permitted by a penal code based on wholly liberal principles. The emphasis on "ignorant people" not "in their senses," however, suggests that Stephen's main target is *fraud,* a factor that vitiates voluntariness altogether.

39. *Ibid.,* p. 199. See also Sir Edward Coke, *Third Institutes.*

40. In the case of *Commonwealth v. Donoghue* (see note 36), Justice Clay in his persuasive dissenting opinion, clearly makes the distinction between usury *per se* and illegal means of enforcement:

> At common law, as adopted in Kentucky, it was not a crime to charge usury, and it has never been made so by statute. Therefore, it was essential to a good indictment to allege that the defendants charged usury by criminal or unlawful means . . . It was not alleged that the defendants . . . resorted to force, threats, intimidation, or fraud . . .

41. Bigamy is the state of a man who has *two* wives or a woman who has *two* husbands living at the same time. In ordinary language the word "polygamy" is commonly used for having a *plurality* (greater than two) of wives or husbands at the same time, but "the name 'bigamy' has been more frequently given to it in legal proceedings." *Black's Legal Dictionary* explains why:

> The use of the word 'bigamy' to describe this offense is well established by long usage, although often criticized as a corruption of the true meaning of the word. 'Polygamy' is suggested as the correct term, instead of 'bigamy' to designate the offense of having a plurality of wives or husbands at the same time, and has been adopted for that purpose by the Massachusetts statutes. But as the substance of the offense is marrying a second time, while having a lawful husband or wife living, without regard to the number of marriages that may have taken place, 'bigamy' seems not an inappropriate term.

An earlier reason for avoiding the term "bigamy" is no longer relevant since the canon law is no longer a part of the law of the state. The ecclesiastical offense of bigamy had a different definition still, namely marrying two wives or husbands successively (after the death of the first), or marrying a widow or widower.

The *Model Penal Code* distinguishes two separate crimes called "bigamy" and "polygamy," respectively, and its definitions differ in another way from traditional ones. The misdemeanor of "bigamy" consists in a married person's contracting or purporting to contract another marriage. The felony of "polygamy" consists in "marrying or cohabiting with more than one spouse at a time *in purported exercise of the right of plural marriage . . .* " Righteously flaunting one's illicit relationships, according to the Code, is apparently a morally aggravating circumstance, more punishable than its clandestine and deceptive counterpart. See *Model Penal Code* (1980), Vol. 2, §230.1, p. 370.

42. William Blackstone, *Commentaries on the Laws of England*, Book Four, chap. 13, §2.
43. See H. L. A. Hart, *Law, Liberty, and Morality* (Stanford, Ca.: Stanford University Press, 1963), pp. 38–43, and Patrick Devlin, *The Enforcement of Morals* (London: Oxford University Press, 1965), p. 138.
44. For expository convenience I shall refer throughout this discussion to male bigamists and pluralities of wives, but everything I say applies also, *mutatis mutandis*, to female bigamists and pluralities of husbands.
45. See Hart, *op. cit.* (see note 43), p. 40.
46. That is the motive behind those few "cohabitation" or "fornication" statutes that still survive. Cf. Section 11-8 of the Illinois Criminal Code of 1961: "Any person who cohabits or has sexual intercourse with another not his spouse commits fornication if the behavior is *open and notorious . . .* " "Go ahead and commit sexual improprieties on the sly," the law seems to say, "but we are prepared to punish you severely if you set a bad example for others or argue for the legitimacy of your conduct."
47. Blackstone, *op. cit.* (see note 42), Chap. 10, §21.
48. There are five others: "Theft of Property Lost, Mislaid, or Delivered by Mistake," "Receiving Stolen Property," "Theft of Services," "Theft by Failure to Make Required Dispositions of Funds Received," and "Unauthorized Use of Automobiles and Other Vehicles."
49. Unless "the property is not demanded or received for the benefit of the group in whose interest the actor purports to act."

25. Failures of Consent: Defective Belief

1. In his useful article, "Contract Law and Distributive Justice," *Yale Law Journal* 89, (January, 1980), Anthony T. Kronman cites the case of *Sherwood v. Walker*, 66 Mich. 568, 33 N.W. 919 (1887) in which the sale of a cow was rescinded by the court when the animal, "assumed by both parties to be barren, later proved otherwise."
2. See Kronman, *ibid.*, and also his "Mistake, Disclosing Information, and the Law of Contracts," *Journal of Legal Studies* 7 (1978). There are also controversial issues over the scope of the *buyer's* duty to disclose information about the seller's property to the *seller*. See note 6 *infra*.
3. Steven H. Gifis, *Law Dictionary* (Woodbury, N.Y.: Barron's Educational Series, Inc., 1975), p. 178.
4. Kronman, *op. cit.* (see note 1), p. 482.
5. *Loc. cit.*
6. It would also have high economic costs that would be against everyone's interests, as a larger percentage of society's energies and resources went into nonproductive

uses associated with improving security against force, misrepresentation, and deceptive nondisclosure.

Kronman argues that the case for required disclosure is overcome when the rule would have the opposite effect and deter *productive* uses of social resources. In that event, the consequence of a rule requiring the proposer to reveal his superior information to the consenter would be, in the long run, to neither party's advantage—"Suppose that B owns a piece of property that unbeknownst to B, contains a rich mineral deposit of some sort. A, a trained geologist, inspects the property (from the air, let us assume), discovers the deposit, and without disclosing what he knows, offers to buy the land from B at a price well below its true value. B agrees, and then later attempts to rescind the contract"—because of the nondisclosure. In fact, our law does not impose duties of disclosure in cases like this, and Kronman, who approves of that policy, attempts to provide it with its rationale. A has invested effort and money in his search, he points out, and if he is prevented from exploiting his informational advantage over B, both he and others will be discouraged from making similar efforts in the future, leading to less geological information and less efficient allocation of land ("the allocation of individual parcels to their best [most productive] use"). That consequence, Kronman concludes, would be in neither A's interest nor B's, since A loses his large profit, and B has to pay higher prices for oil and aluminum "because the incentive necessary to determine which pieces of land contain those resources in the first place will have been ruined" (p.489). Kronman is here applying what he calls "the principle of Paretianism" to the question of which informational advantages should be permitted in contractual negotiations. Only those that "work to the benefit of all concerned" (p. 488) should be permitted.

In the example under discussion, however, Kronman would have been better advised to wrap his intuitions in a weaker principle, perhaps invoking some conception of "the public interest" weaker than that which entails benefitting *everyone's* interest. The rule permitting nondisclosure in cases of deliberate search for mineral wealth does not benefit B if it means that he must forfeit a one million dollar windfall and settle (say) for a fifty thousand dollar sale, even though a result of the rule is that his gasoline and aluminum product purchases will be a few dollars less expensive in the future. As a result of his windfall he would have been able to afford the higher prices which he would share with all other consumers. The rule will benefit B only if its absence means not only higher prices, but no windfall sale to A either—the outcome Kronman presumably has in mind.

7. Dan Brock, "Moral Prohibitions and Consent", in *Action and Responsibility*, ed. Myles Brand and Michael Bradie (Bowling Green State University, 1980), p. 113.
8. Kronman, *op. cit.* (see note 1), pp. 496–97.
9. *Ibid.*, p. 497. Emphasis added.
10. *United States v. Baldwin*, 6th Cir., 621F.2d 251 (1980).
11. Ferdinand Schoeman, "Privacy and Police Undercover Work," *Moral Issues in Police Work*, ed. Frederick Elliston and Michael Feldberg (Totowa, N.J.: Roman and Allanheld, 1985), pp. 147–62. See also Nat Hentoff, "A Live-In Cop Who Loved to Clean House," *Village Voice*, March 25–31, 1981, and "If the Brethren Fail Us, No Home Will be Safe," *Village Voice*, April 1–7, 1981.
12. Schoeman, *op. cit.* (see note 11), p. 147.
13. *United States v. Baldwin*, *op. cit.* (see note 10), pp. 252–53.

14. *Hoffa v. United States*, 385 U.S. 283, 302, 303 (1966), as quoted by Schoeman, *op. cit.* (see note 10), p. 148.
15. Schoeman, *Ibid.*, p. 151. He adds that "such logic has been precluded explicitly [in other areas], in the case of electronic surveillance, in the case of attorney client privilege, in the case of spousal confidential communication privilege, in the case of confession obtained through deception after the indictment of the suspect."
16. The value on the other side—efficient detection of crime—seems no more involved in the defense of entry by fraudulent deception than it would be in the defense of entry by stealth (breaking in, or bugging, or using electronic tracking devices) or force ("open up or we'll blast our way in"), and yet the courts scrupulously guard householders from the latter but not so zealously from the former. This is so, Schoeman remarks, "even though the damage which results from deception may be greater than that which results from the other forms of search and surveillance." The "damage" Schoeman has in mind, he tells us, "is to public confidence in trust-relationships." (p. 160).
17. Schoeman, *loc. cit.*
18. "It usually consists of a misrepresentation, concealment, or nondisclosure of a material fact, or at least misleading conduct, devices, or contrivance. It embraces all the multifarious means which human ingenuity can devise to get an advantage over another. It includes all surprise, trick, cunning, dissembling, and unfair ways by which another is cheated." S.H. Gifis, *op. cit.* (see note 3), p. 86.
19. Kadish and Paulsen explain the initial reluctance to think of embezzlement as a form of theft on a level with robbery and larceny:

> Our criminal law reached larceny first and embezzlement later because of real distinctions between stranger theft and the peculations of a trusted agent. If the move to punish embezzlement was a natural one, it was nevertheless a momentous step when the exceptional liability of servants for stealing from their masters was generalized into fraudulent conversion by anyone who had goods of another in his possession. The ordinary trespass-thief was a stranger, an intruder with no semblance of right even to touch the object. He was easily recognized by the very taking, surreptitious or forceful, and so set apart from the law-abiding community. No bond of association in joint endeavor linked criminal and victim. In contrast, the embezzler stands always in a lawful as well as an unlawful relation to the victim and the property. He is respectable; we tend to identify with him rather than with the bank or insurance company from which he embezzles. The line between lawful and unlawful activity is for the embezzler a question of the scope of his authority, which may be ill-defined.

S.H. Kadish and M.G. Paulsen, *Criminal Law and its Processes*, 3rd ed. (Boston and Toronto: Little Brown, 1975), pp. 633–34.
20. *Ibid.*, p. 633.
21. *Loc. cit.*, "Even this statute was not at first believed to make mere misrepresentation criminal. It was thought to require some more elaborate swindling strategem, just as the French law to this day requires." The false-pretenses statutes of most American states, incidentally, are directly traceable to this English antecedent.
22. *R. v. Jones*, 91 Eng. Rep. 330 (1703). See Kadish and Paulsen (see note 19), p. 662.

23. Kadish and Paulsen, *op. cit.* (see note 19), p. 664. The two categories apparently diverged again, however, creating considerable terminological confusion. In 1953, just before the *Model Penal Code* redefinitions, an authoritative article explained the distinction as follows:

> the offenses are . . . aimed at quite different acquisitive techniques. False pretenses is theft by deceit. The misappropriation it punishes must be effected by communication to the owner. Larceny by trick is theft by stealth. It punishes misappropriation effected by unauthorized disposition of the owner's property. The former focuses on defendant's behavior while face to face with the owner: did it amount to a false pretense? The focus of the latter is upon defendant's behavior behind the owner's back: did it amount to an unauthorized appropriation?
>
> One cause of confusion of the offenses is that larceny by trick requires some deceit in addition to the unauthorized disposition of property which is its gravamen. It is thus thought of as a type of theft by fraud. However, the requirement of deceit in larceny by trick stems from its history rather than its function and plays a minor role . . .

Pearce, "Theft by False Promises," *University of Pennsylvania Law Review* (1953), p. 953. Note that another way of putting the distinction is that in larceny by trick one fraudulently acquires possession of another's property, whereas in obtaining property by false pretenses one fraudulently acquires both possession and title (ownership).

24. American Law Institute, *Model Penal Code*, Tentative Draft No. 2 (Philadelphia, 1954). It is interesting that the M.P.C. makes a nod to the competitive game model of commerce in its part (4) of this section, entitled *Puffing Expected:* "Exaggerated commendation of wares in communications addressed to the public or to a class or group shall not be deemed deceptive if: (a) it would be unlikely to mislead the ordinary person of the class or group addressed; and (b) there is no deception other than as to the actor's belief in the commendation; and (c) the actor was not in a position of special trust and confidence in relation to the misled party. Commendation of wares 'includes representation that the price asked is low.' *Caveat emptor* and tough luck to fools!

25. *Ibid.*, (2).

26. Francis Wharton, *American Criminal Law*, 1st ed. (Boston, 1846), p. 542.

27. *People v. Ashley*, Supreme Court of California 1954 (42 Cal. 2d 246, p. 2d 271).

28. *Ibid.*

29. *Rex v. Goodhall*, Russ. & Ry. 461 (1821), as quoted by Justice Traynor in his majority opinion in *People v. Ashley*, *op. cit.* (see note 27).

30. See H. L. A. Hart, "Intention and Punishment," and "Legal Responsibility and Excuses," in his *Punishment and Responsibility* (New York and Oxford: Oxford University Press, 1968), for discussions of what can count as evidence for mental states such as belief and intention.

31. Justice Traynor in *People v. Ashley*, *op. cit.* (see note 27).

32. Rollin M. Perkins, *Perkins on Criminal Law* (Brooklyn, N.Y.: The Foundation Press, 1957), p. 856.

33. *Loc. cit.*

34. Perkins, *op. cit.*, p. 299.

35. *Ibid.*, pp. 300–301.

36. The essential arbitrariness of the differing classifications in the past is well illustrated by three of the many fraud in the *factum* cases cited by Perkins, p. 300. On
the one hand, in *State v. Shurtliff*, 18 Me. 368 (1841), "Following an agreement for
the sale of one acre of a farm, the grantee prepared a deed which correctly
described the area agreed upon. After the grantor read the deed, the grantee
substituted another which conveyed the grantor's entire farm and which the
grantor signed supposing it was the paper he had read. This [fraud in the *factum*]
was held to be forgery. On the other hand, in *Commonwealth v. Sankey* 22 Pa. 390
(1853), "*D* wrote a note for $141.26, payable to himself and fraudulently read it
to another as a note for $41.26, and procured him to sign it as maker. This was
held not to be forgery," and in *Johnson v. State*, 87 Miss. 502, 39 So. 692 (1905),
"An illiterate was persuaded to sign a deed under the false representation that it
was a pension paper. It was held that this was not forgery but was expressly
included under the statute on false pretenses."
37. Perkins, *op. cit.* (see note 32), p. 857.
38. See, *inter alia, Don Moran v. People*, 25 Mich. 356 (1872), cited by Perkins, p. 857,
note 16: "In reversing a conviction of rape because of an instruction that: 'If the
woman ultimately consented to such intercourse, such consent . . . being obtained
through . . . fraud . . . then the offense is rape,' the court said: 'We are satisfied
that it is never proper or safe to instruct the jury in any case that the crime of rape
may be committed with the consent of the woman, however obtained . . . '."
39. *Loc. cit.*
40. *Ibid.*, p. 858. "Her innocence seems never to have been questioned in such a case
and the reason she is not guilty of adultery is because she did not consent to
adulterous intercourse."
41. *Ibid.*, p. 457.
42. See the following articles, among many others: S. H. Kardener, "Sex and the
Physician-Patient Relationship," *American Journal of Psychiatry* 131 (1974): 1134–
36; Armand M. Nicholi, Jr., "The Therapist-Patient Relationship" in *The Harvard Guide to Modern Psychiatry* (Cambridge, Mass.: Harvard University Press,
1978), pp. 17–21; and Searles, H.F., "Oedipal Love in the Countertransference,"
International Journal of Psychoanalysis 40 (1959): 180–90.
43. The definition occurs in Section (2) of Article 213, "Sexual Offenses" of the
Proposed Official Draft of May 4, 1962, as follows:

   2. *Gross Sexual Imposition.* A male who has sexual intercourse with a female not
   his wife commits a felony of the third degree if:
   a. he compels her to submit by any threat that would prevent resistance by a
   woman of ordinary resolution; or
   b. he knows that she suffers from a mental disease or defect which renders her
   incapable of appraising the nature of her conduct; or
   c. he knows that she is unaware that a sexual act is being committed upon her
   or that she submits because she falsely supposes that he is her husband.

44. I shall use the phrase "medical treatment" henceforth as a generic expression to
cover both therapy and experiment.
45. Louis I. Katzner, "The Ethics of Human Experimentation: The Information
Condition," in *Medical Responsibility, Paternalism, Informed Consent, and Euthanasia*,
ed. Wade L. Robison and Michael S. Pritchard (Clifton, N.J.: The Humana
Press, 1979), pp. 43–56.

46. I borrow this division of questions from Tom L. Beauchamp and James F. Childress. See their very useful primer, *Principles of Biomedical Ethics* (New York: Oxford University Press, 1979), esp. pp. 70–80.

47. Beauchamp and Childress cite "Note: Informed Consent and the Dying Patient," *The Yale Law Journal* 83 (1974) and *Canterbury v. Spence*, U.S. Court of Appeals, District of Columbia (1972), 464 Federal Reporter, 2d series, 772.

48. Katzner, *op. cit.* (see note 45), p. 46.

49. *Ibid.*, p. 49.

50. Beauchamp and Childress, *op. cit.* (see note 46), p. 78.

51. *Loc. cit.* Beauchamp and Childress cite studies that "claim to show that over 60% of patients want to know virtually nothing about procedures or the risks of the procedures . . . and other studies [which] "indicate that only about 12% of patients use the information provided in reaching their decisions." The cited studies are: Ralph J. Alfidi, "Controversy, Alternatives, and Decisions in Complying with the Legal Doctrine of Informed Consent," *Radiology* 114 (January, 1975), and Ruth R. Faden, "Disclosure and Informed Consent: Does It Matter How We Tell It?" *Health Education Monographs*, vol. 5 (1977), pp. 198–215.

52. In a sense the patient must already have had this "information," else he would have had no motive for waiving his right to still more information.

26. Failures of Consent: Incapacity

1. *Supra*, Chap. 18, §2.

2. Steven H. Gifis, *Law Dictionary* (Woodbury, N.Y.: Barron's Educational Series, Inc., 1975), p. 38.

3. *Loc. cit.*

4. There is no *necessity* that a person judged legally incompetent must be so deficient in capacity as to be incapable of criminal guilt. He will be found competent to stand trial if "he has sufficient present ability to consult with his lawyer with a reasonable degree of rational understanding and . . . has a rational as well as factual understanding of the proceedings against him." Quoted by Gifis from 362 U.S. 402. Three sets of incapacities may be distinguished: (1) the incapacity to manage one's affairs generally, (2) the incapacity to understand what is involved in making a will, and (3) the incapacity to understand the criminal proceedings against oneself. People who have the first set of incapacities are declared "legally incompetent." Nevertheless, *some* of the persons with this legal status do not lack the capacity to understand the elements involved in making wills. It is not inconceivable, I should think, that some of these would also be capable of understanding what a criminal prohibition is (at the time when they violate one), and what a particular criminal proceeding is (at the time when they are brought to trial). But of course we would expect their numbers to be relatively small.

5. *In Re Quinlan*, 70 N.J. 10 (1976).

6. *Superintendent of Belchertown State School v. Saikewicz*, Mass. 370 N.E. 2d 417 (1977).

7. *In Re Quinlan*, *op. cit.* (see note 5), p. 647. See the criticism in Allen Buchanan, "The Limits of Proxy Decision Making," in *Paternalism*, ed. Rolf Sartorius (Minneapolis: University of Minnesota Press, 1983), pp. 153–70.

8. *Ibid.*, p. 157.

9. The disanalogy in the political example, of course, is that civil unrest, famine,

and plague can rarely be known to be "permanent and irrevocable," or "fatal" to the state (as opposed to much of its population).

10. I discuss this point in much greater detail in my article "The Child's Right to an Open Future," in *Whose Child? Children's Rights, Parental Authority, and State Power*, ed. William Aiken and Hugh LaFollette (Totowa, N.J.: Rowman and Littlefield, 1980).

11. Gifis, *op. cit.* (see note 2), p. 122 (emphasis added).

12. *Loc. cit.*

13. "As long as such an agreement is wholly executory [not fully accomplished but still contingent upon the performance of some act in the future] on both sides, the infant is under no enforceable duty whatever. When sued for an alleged breach, all the infant has to do is plead his infancy as a defense . . . [but] if the infant had received a part performance and still retains it at the time of suit, it will be necessary for him to give it up; its continued retention by him after his becoming of age soon operates as a ratification." Arthur Linton Corbin, *Corbin on Contracts* (St. Paul, Minnesota: West Publishing Co., 1952), pp. 10–11.

14. *Ibid.*, p. 318.

15. *State v. Aaron*, 4 N.J.L. 231, 245-246 (1818).

16. *State v. Smith*, 213 N.C. 299, 195 S.E. 819 (1938).

17. *State v. Yeargan*, 117 N.C. 706.

18. *Loc. cit.*

19. Rollin M. Perkins, *Perkins on Criminal Law* (Brooklyn, N.Y.: The Foundation Press, Inc., 1957), p. 111.

20. Why are legislators more confident that the amount of harm done a willing child by sexual intercourse with an older person is invariably far greater in earlier childhood than in later childhood? The explanation remains obscure, but part of it no doubt is in the amount of natural repugnance we feel in contemplating such matches, and part in the anachronism that loss of virginity as such is the main element of the harm and that it is more likely to be involved and somehow is more harmful the earlier it happens. Perkins quotes a 1935 Florida opinion (*Deas v. State*, 119 Fla. 839, 161 So. 729) that suggests such an interpretation of legislative intentions: "The statute denouncing as a felony carnal intercourse with any previously chaste unmarried person under the age of 18 years was designed to protect youths of both sexes from the initial violation of their chastity, rather than consequences of their subsequent voluntary indulgence in sexual intercourse."

21. Perkins, *op. cit.* (see note 18), p. 83.

22. *Regina v. Martin*, 2 Moody 123, 169 Eng. Rep. 49 (1840).

23. Perkins, *op. cit.* (see note 18). Bracketed words added.

24. In *People v. Penman*, 271 Ill. 82, 110 N.E. 894 (1915), a "friend" gave the defendant two cocaine pills as a practical joke, identifying them as "breath perfumers." Penman later "committed homicide, the evidence indicating that he had done so while completely out of his mind as a result of the drug unwittingly taken" (Perkins, p. 784). In *Burrows v. State*, 38 Ariz. 99, 297, p. 1029 (1931), the 18-year-old defendant, while driving across the desert with an older man who had been drinking heavily, was asked by the man "to have a drink, which he refused because he had never tasted liquor and did not wish to do so. Thereupon the man became abusive and insisted with great vehemence . . . and [the boy] fearing that he might be put out of the car and left penniless on the desert, did drink several bottles of beer and later, after further vehement insistence, some

whiskey, as a result of which he went completely out of his head and killed the man without knowing what he was doing" (Perkins, p. 785). The jury was instructed to decide whether on these facts the boy had been compelled to drink against his will, with the assumption that the involuntariness of his intoxication, the latter amounting to madness, would totally excuse.

25. Aristotle, *Nicomachean Ethics*, Book Three, chap. 5 *et passim*.

26. Sir William Blackstone, *Commentaries on the Laws of England*, Robert Malcolm Kerr adaptation, Book 4, p. 25.

27. *Loc. cit.*

28. Perkins, *op. cit.* (see note 18), p. 789.

29. Sir Edward Coke, *Institutes*, vol. I, p. 247.

30. Samuel von Pufendorf, *Of the Law of Nature and Nations* (London, 1710), Book 8, chap. 3, quoted in Blackstone (see note 31).

31. Blackstone, *op. cit.* (see note 25), p. 24.

32. In fact, the direction of relevance runs in the opposite direction. What would "ordinarily" be murder might be reduced to manslaughter in a given instance because the killer, being drunk and "out of his mind," did not satisfy all the elements of *mens rea* that may define the crime of murder (e.g. a specific intent of a certain description). In that sense, voluntary intoxication may be a "mitigating factor," but it could be misleading to call it an "excuse." It is certainly not an excuse for the doing of the *actus reus*, that part of the definition of the crime referring to behavior (e.g. killing someone). It simply means that the intoxicated criminal must be charged with a crime of a different name and definition, usually one that is punished less severely (e.g. manslaughter). Nor is it an excuse in the sense of a bar to *all* criminal liability.

33. *Nichols v. State*, 8 Ohio St. 438 (1858).

34. Perkins, *op. cit.* (see note 18), p. 794.

35. American Law Institute, *Model Penal Code*, Tentative Draft No. 2 (Philadelphia, 1954), Article 213, section 2(c), p. 143.

36. *Ibid.*, p. 144.

37. Note that a similar scenario could be composed for the "gross sexual imposition" case, when the drunken woman herself takes the initiative, propositioning the defendant.

38. If the suspected drunken driver has "passed out," and while in custody has gone into a deep sleep, then the police might test his breath without waking him, a procedure that would not require "brute force." In that case the suspect would not be acting "totally involuntarily", if only because he would not be acting at all. But still it is not possible for his consent to be "voluntary enough" if there was no consent to begin with, even though the police testing was not done *against* the suspect's will, but only *without* an expression, one way or the other, of that will. A more candid rule would permit the breath testing in these cases even without voluntary consent. Such a rule on its face would not be unjust, but it might encourage abuses, if police could get away with treating protesting suspects as if they were unconscious suspects, and then falsifying the record.

27. The Choice of Death

1. The possibility of such manipulation is not altogether missing even in the standard case of requested euthanasia. See Yale Kamisar, "Euthanasia Legislation:

Some Non-Religious Objections," *Minnesota Law Review* 4 (1958), and Philippa Foot, "Euthanasia," *Philosophy and Public Affairs* 6 (1977).

2. Foot, *ibid.*, p. 87.
3. *Ibid.*, p. 86.
4. Jonathan Glover manages to present ingenious hypothetical examples of individual paternalistic killings that might be justified on utilitarian moral grounds even though punishable, perhaps, on public policy grounds. See the examples on pp. 40 and 73 of his *Causing Death and Saving Lives* (Harmondsworth, Middlesex: Penguin Books, 1977). Glover's example in fact does not involve the criminal law at all, and presents instead a problem for the individual moral choice:

> Suppose I am in prison, and have an incurable disease from which I shall very soon die. The man who shares my cell is bound to stay in prison for the rest of his life, as society thinks he is too dangerous to be let out. He has no friends, and all his relations are dead. I have a poison that I could put in his food without him knowing it and that would kill him without being detectable. Everyone else would think he died from natural causes . . .
>
> . . . His life in prison is not a happy one, and I have every reason to think that over the years it will get worse. In my view, he will most of the time have a quality of life some way below the point at which life is worth living. I tell him this, and offer to kill him. He, irrationally as I think, says that he wants to go on living. I know that he would be too cowardly to kill himself even if eventually he came to want to die, so my offer is probably his last chance of death. I believe that in the future his backward-looking preference for having been killed will be stronger than his present preference for going on living . . .
>
> . . . at least in principle, it is possible for a . . . utilitarian to be committed to a "paternalist" policy of killing someone *in what are taken to be his own interests, but against his expressed wishes* . . .

5. For a discussion of the meaning of this phrase and its possible uses in the civil law, see Joel Feinberg, "Wrongful Conception and the Right Not to be Harmed," *Harvard Journal of Law and Public Policy* 8 (1985): 59–77.
6. Kamisar (*op. cit.*, see note 1), who has argued most effectively against the legalization of voluntary euthanasia, concedes that there is often a genuine moral right to euthanasia, but argues against creating a legal right anyway, even in those cases, partly because he doubts whether consent can ever be, or be known to be, voluntary enough for legal purposes, and partly because he thinks that the "law in action" will act as a corrective to the "law on the books" (through prosecutorial discretion, jury nullification, clemency, and the like). He is opposed to tampering with the law on the books, however, because he thinks the dominoes are in place for various serious abuses. Foot (*op. cit.*, see note 1) comes to a similar position. In striking contrast, Antony Flew, in his classic article defending the legalization of voluntary euthanasia, comes to the very opposite conclusions. He admits that there might not (always) be a moral right to euthanasia, but argues for a legal right anyway even in those cases where there is no moral right. The moral right is suspect, I suppose, when one's death is likely to be harmful to others, or appears cowardly or perverse. But Flew employs exclusively liberal liberty-limiting principles and firmly rejects legal moralism, arguing that one should have a legal right to do even what is immoral, if one's action is a primarily self-regarding

exercise of one's personal sovereignty. See his "The Principle of Euthanasia" in *Euthanasia and the Right to Death*, ed. A. B. Downing (London: Peter Owen, Ltd., 1969).

7. James Rachels, "Euthanasia," in *Matters of Life and Death*, ed. Tom Regan (New York: Random House, 1978), esp. pp. 61–63.

8. *Ibid.*, p. 62.

9. *Loc. cit.*

10. *Ibid.*, p. 52. Rachels adds that Weskin "was indicted for murder and legally it was an open and shut case. But the jury refused to convict him".

11. Kamisar, *op. cit.* (see note 1), p. 979.

12. Rachels, *op. cit.* (see note 7), p. 63.

13. A Frohman, M.D., "Vexing Problems in Forensic Medicine: A Physician's View," *New York University Law Review* 31 (1956): 1222.

14. The "voluntary euthanasia" of prisoners waiting in Death Row for their executions raises further philosophical questions of great interest and subtlety. If these doomed prisoners had the option of dying privately and painlessly in their sleep from a pill served with their last suppers, or from a painless lethal injection, then they would be able, in effect, to "cheat the executioner" and avoid their punishment, since their sentence is not to death *simpliciter* but to death in the electric chair, or before the firing squad, or on the gallows—death with the reprobative symbolism essential to punishment. (See my *Doing and Deserving*, Princeton, N.J.: Princeton University Press, 1970, chap. 5.) I think a case can be made for giving doomed killers this option, though I cannot make it here. Our present interest is in the conceptual question: could the doomed convict's death request in these circumstances be voluntary enough to be valid? Taking the circumstances simply as given *talis qualis*, I think the answer is yes.

15. The stage version is now available in paperback: *Whose Life Is It Anyway? A Play by Brian Clark* (New York: Avon Books, 1978).

16. Harrison's solicitor tells him: "I am informed that without a catheter the toxic substance will build up in your bloodstream and you will be poisoned by your own blood." *Ibid.*, p. 115.

17. Gerald L. Klerman, "Affective Disorders," *The Harvard Guide to Modern Psychiatry* (Cambridge, Mass., and London: Harvard University Press, 1978), chap. 13, p. 255.

18. *Ibid.*, pp. 255–58.

19. *Ibid.*, p. 262.

20. R. D. Gillespie, "The Clinical Differentiation of Types of Depression," *Guy's Hosp. Rep.* 79 (1929): 306–44.

21. There are at least two reasons for this change. Klerman gives the first: "In clinical practice, the endogenous–reactive dichotomy as a diagnostic tool arranges patients along a continuum rather than establishing clearly defined groups; most patients appear to lie at midpoints on the continuum, few at the extremes." *Op. cit.* (see note 17). The second reason is a related one. Robert Schopp, whose help I have found invaluable, finds the distinction conceptually questionable in any case. In correspondence he writes: "If S responds to stressful life situation X with Y degree of depression, and Y is more severe than the average person would experience, is this depression reactive or endogenous?" Clearly such a response is at least "reactive," but the explanation of its excessive degree may require reference to an inner biological condition. "Since individuals vary widely in response

412 NOTES

to depressing stimuli, does this support the conclusion that all responses are in some sense endogenous?"

22. Klerman, *op. cit.* (see note 17), p. 262.

23. Early in this century, the term "psychotic" came to indicate the disturbance of higher-level mental functions—memory, language, orientation, perception, and thinking. Freud and other psychoanalysts believed that psychoses involved the 'loss of reality testing' . . . the classic meaning of the term 'psychotic' emphasized loss of reality testing or impairment of 'higher' mental functioning, manifested by delusions, hallucinations, confusion, and impaired memory . . . " Klerman, *ibid.*, p. 265. The distinction between "acute" and "chronic" is applied with difficulty to depression. Writers speak commonly of "depressive episodes." Some of these, those which are relatively brief and nonrecurrent, are "acute episodes." Chronic depression, on the other hand, manifests a standing disposition, whose episodes are marked by relatively long duration or frequent recurrence.

24. Joseph Heller, *Catch-22* (New York: Dell Publishing Co., 1961).

25. *Ibid.*, p. 47.

26. One form of the dilemma is an argument of the form: If p then q; if not p then q; either p or not p; therefore q. If the premises of an argument of this form are true then, clearly, the conclusion must be true.

27. For a very clear discussion of how dilemmas can be rebutted by means of counter-dilemmas, see Irving M. Copi, *Introduction to Logic* (New York: Macmillan, 1953), pp. 214–16.

28. In an unpublished commentary on this case.

29. My source for this information as well as other accounts below of unsuccessful euthanasia legislation is O. Ruth Russell, *Freedom to Die: Moral and Legal Aspects of Euthanasia* (New York: Human Sciences Press, 1975), Appendix, pp. 286–97 and 334–35.

30. Yale Kamisar, "Euthanasia Legislation: Some Non-Religious Objections," *Minnesota Law Review* 4 (1958).

31. *Ibid.*, p. 989.

32. *Ibid.*, p. 990.

33. At the time of writing, twenty-two other states have passed some sort of living will statutes. The remaining states, at least for the time being, apparently rest content with the ambiguity of extralegal practices, despite their greater uncertainty, but because of their greater flexibility.

34. Karen Lebacqz, "On 'Natural Death'," *The Hastings Center Report*, 7 (1977): 14.

35. Michael Garland, "Politics, Legislation, and Natural Death; The Right to Die in California," *The Hastings Center Report* 6 (1976):6.

36. Justice Schroeder in *Natanson v. Kline*, (1960). Quoted by Lebacqz, *op. cit.* (see note 34).

Index

413